AMERICA'S
TEST KITCHEN

PRAISE FOR AMERICA'S TEST KITCHEN TITLES

"A terrifically accessible and useful guide to grilling in all its forms that sets a new bar for its competitors on the bookshelf. . . . The book is packed with practical advice, simple tips, and approachable recipes."
PUBLISHERS WEEKLY (STARRED REVIEW) ON *MASTER OF THE GRILL*

Selected as one of the Amazon Best Books of 2015 in the Cookbooks and Food Writing category
AMAZON ON *THE COMPLETE VEGETARIAN COOKBOOK*

"A beautifully illustrated, 318-page culinary compendium showcasing an impressive variety and diversity of authentic Mexican cuisine."
MIDWEST BOOK REVIEW ON *THE BEST MEXICAN RECIPES*

"The editors at America's Test Kitchen, known for their meticulous recipe testing and development, are back at it again. This time, they've trained their laser-eyed focus on reduced-sugar baking. . . . Cooks with a powerful sweet tooth should scoop up this well-researched recipe book for healthier takes on classic sweet treats."
BOOKLIST ON *NATURALLY SWEET*

"An exceptional resource for novice canners, though preserving veterans will find plenty here to love as well."
LIBRARY JOURNAL (STARRED REVIEW) ON *FOOLPROOF PRESERVING*

"The sum total of exhaustive experimentation . . . anyone interested in gluten-free cookery simply shouldn't be without it."
NIGELLA LAWSON ON *THE HOW CAN IT BE GLUTEN-FREE COOKBOOK*

"The 21st-century *Fannie Farmer Cookbook* or *The Joy of Cooking*. If you had to have one cookbook and that's all you could have, this one would do it."
CBS SAN FRANCISCO ON *THE NEW FAMILY COOKBOOK*

"This title would serve as an excellent gift for college students, young professionals, newlyweds, and anyone who's learning to cook."
LIBRARY JOURNAL ON *100 RECIPES*

"The perfect kitchen home companion. . . . The practical side of things is very much on display . . . cook-friendly and kitchen-oriented, illuminating the process of preparing food instead of mystifying it."
THE WALL STREET JOURNAL ON *THE COOK'S ILLUSTRATED COOKBOOK*

"A one-volume kitchen seminar, addressing in one smart chapter after another the sometimes surprising whys behind a cook's best practices. . . . You get the myth, the theory, the science, and the proof, all rigorously interrogated as only America's Test Kitchen can do."
NPR ON *THE SCIENCE OF GOOD COOKING*

"Some 2,500 photos walk readers through 600 painstakingly tested recipes, leaving little room for error."
ASSOCIATED PRESS ON *THE AMERICA'S TEST KITCHEN COOKING SCHOOL COOKBOOK*

"The go-to gift book for newlyweds, small families, or empty nesters."
ORLANDO SENTINEL ON *THE COMPLETE COOKING FOR TWO COOKBOOK*

"This book upgrades slow cooking for discriminating, 21st-century palates—that is indeed revolutionary."
THE DALLAS MORNING NEWS ON *SLOW COOKER REVOLUTION*

"This book is a comprehensive, no-nonsense guide . . . a well-thought-out, clearly explained primer for every aspect of home baking."
THE WALL STREET JOURNAL ON *THE COOK'S ILLUSTRATED BAKING BOOK*

"This encyclopedia of meat cookery would feel completely overwhelming if it weren't so meticulously organized and artfully designed. This is *Cook's Illustrated* at its finest."
THE KITCHN ON *THE COOK'S ILLUSTRATED MEAT BOOK*

"Buy this gem for the foodie in your family, and spend the extra money to get yourself a copy too."
THE MISSOURIAN ON *THE BEST OF AMERICA'S TEST KITCHEN 2015*

THE COMPLETE
MEDITERRANEAN
COOKBOOK

500 VIBRANT, KITCHEN-TESTED RECIPES
FOR LIVING AND EATING WELL EVERY DAY

THE EDITORS AT
AMERICA'S TEST KITCHEN

Library of Congress Cataloging-in-Publication Data
Names: America's Test Kitchen (Firm)
Title: The complete Mediterranean cookbook : 500 vibrant,
    kitchen-tested recipes for living and eating well every day /
    the editors at America's Test Kitchen.
Description: Brookline, MA : America's Test Kitchen, [2017] |
    Includes index.
Identifiers: LCCN 2016037753 | ISBN 9781940352640
Subjects: LCSH: Cooking, Mediterranean. | LCGFT: Cookbooks.
Classification: LCC TX725.M35 C56 2017 | DDC 641.59/1822--dc23
LC record available at https://lccn.loc.gov/2016037753

AMERICA'S TEST KITCHEN
21 Drydock Avenue, Boston, MA 02210

Manufactured in Canada
20 19 18 17

Distributed by Penguin Random House Publisher Services
Tel: 800-733-3000

Pictured on front cover: Grilled Swordfish Skewers
with Tomato-Scallion Caponata (page 262)
Pictured on back cover: Turkish Pide with Eggplant and
Tomatoes (page 357), Egyptian Barley Salad (page 123), Baked
Stuffed Mackerel with Red Pepper and Preserved Lemon
(page 251), Spicy Roasted Carrots with Cilantro (page 206),
Roasted Pears with Dried Apricots and Pistachios (page 372)

EDITORIAL DIRECTOR, BOOKS: Elizabeth Carduff

EXECUTIVE FOOD EDITORS: Suzannah McFerran and
    Dan Zuccarello

SENIOR EDITORS: Debra Hudak and Anne Wolf

ASSOCIATE EDITORS: Leah Colins, Melissa Herrick,
    Lawman Johnson, Nicole Konstantinakos, and
    Russell Selander

TEST COOKS: Kathryn Callahan, Tim Chin, Afton Cyrus,
    Joseph Gitter, and Katherine Perry

ASSISTANT EDITOR: Samantha Ronan

EDITORIAL ASSISTANT: Alyssa Langer

ART DIRECTOR, BOOKS: Carole Goodman

PRODUCTION DESIGNER: Reinaldo Cruz

GRAPHIC DESIGNERS: Katie Barranger and Matthew Warnick

PHOTOGRAPHY DIRECTOR: Julie Cote

SENIOR STAFF PHOTOGRAPHER: Daniel J. van Ackere

STAFF PHOTOGRAPHER: Steve Klise

ASSISTANT PHOTOGRAPHY PRODUCER: Mary Ball

ADDITIONAL PHOTOGRAPHY: Carl Tremblay

FOOD STYLING: Catrine Kelty, Marie Piraino, Maeve Sheridan,
    Elle Simone Scott, and Sally Staub

PHOTOSHOOT KITCHEN TEAM:

    SENIOR EDITOR: Chris O'Connor

    TEST COOKS: Daniel Cellucci and Matthew Fairman

    ASSISTANT TEST COOKS: Allison Berkey and Mady Nichas

PRODUCTION DIRECTOR: Guy Rochford

SENIOR PRODUCTION MANAGER: Jessica Lindheimer Quirk

PRODUCTION MANAGER: Christine Walsh

IMAGING MANAGER: Lauren Robbins

PRODUCTION AND IMAGING SPECIALISTS: Heather Dube,
    Sean MacDonald, Dennis Noble, and Jessica Voas

COPYEDITOR: Barbara Wood

PROOFREADER: Pat Jalbert-Levine

INDEXER: Elizabeth Parson

CHIEF CREATIVE OFFICER: Jack Bishop

EXECUTIVE EDITORIAL DIRECTORS: Julia Collin Davison and
Bridget Lancaster

Contents

Welcome to America's Test Kitchen

This book has been tested, written, and edited by the folks at America's Test Kitchen, where curious cooks become confident cooks. Located in Boston's Seaport District in the historic Innovation and Design Building, it features 15,000 square feet of kitchen space including multiple photography and video studios. It is the home of *Cook's Illustrated* magazine and *Cook's Country* magazine and is the workday destination for more than 60 test cooks, editors, and cookware specialists. Our mission is to empower and inspire confidence, community, and creativity in the kitchen.

We start the process of testing a recipe with a complete lack of preconceptions, which means that we accept no claim, no technique, and no recipe at face value. We simply assemble as many variations as possible, test a half-dozen of the most promising, and taste the results blind. We then construct our own recipe and continue to test it, varying ingredients, techniques, and cooking times until we reach a consensus. As we like to say in the test kitchen, "We make the mistakes so you don't have to." The result, we hope, is the best version of a particular recipe, but we realize that only you can be the final judge of our success (or failure). We use the same rigorous approach when we test equipment and taste ingredients.

All of this would not be possible without a belief that good cooking, much like good music, is based on a foundation of objective technique. Some people like spicy foods and others don't, but there is a right way to sauté, there is a best way to cook a pot roast, and there are measurable scientific principles involved in producing perfectly beaten, stable egg whites. Our ultimate goal is to investigate the fundamental principles of cooking to give you the techniques, tools, and ingredients you need to become a better cook. It is as simple as that.

To see what goes on behind the scenes at America's Test Kitchen, check out our social media channels for kitchen snapshots, exclusive content, video tips, and much more. You can watch us work (in our actual test kitchen) by tuning in to *America's Test Kitchen* or *Cook's Country* on public television or on our websites. Download our award-winning podcast *Proof*, which goes beyond recipes to solve food mysteries (AmericasTestKitchen.com/proof), or listen to test kitchen experts on public radio (SplendidTable.org) to hear insights that illuminate the truth about real home cooking. Want to hone your cooking skills or finally learn how to bake—with an America's Test Kitchen test cook? Enroll in one of our online cooking classes. And you can engage the next generation of home cooks with kid-tested recipes from America's Test Kitchen Kids.

Our community of home recipe testers provides valuable feedback on recipes under development by ensuring that they are foolproof. You can help us investigate the how and why behind successful recipes from your home kitchen. (Sign up at AmericasTestKitchen.com/recipe_testing.)

However you choose to visit us, we welcome you into our kitchen, where you can stand by our side as we test our way to the best recipes in America.

f facebook.com/AmericasTestKitchen
twitter.com/TestKitchen
youtube.com/AmericasTestKitchen
instagram.com/TestKitchen
pinterest.com/TestKitchen

AmericasTestKitchen.com
CooksIllustrated.com
CooksCountry.com
OnlineCookingSchool.com
AmericasTestKitchen.com/kids

Introduction

Photos (clockwise from top left): Whole Roasted Snapper with Citrus Vinaigrette (page 260); Barley with Roasted Carrots, Snow Peas, and Lemon-Yogurt Sauce (page 120); Orange Polenta Cake (page 385); Shaved Mushroom and Celery Salad (page 90)

THE MEDITERRANEAN DIET

The Mediterranean Sea is surrounded by an extraordinarily diverse group of countries: Italy, France, and Spain to the north, Greece, Turkey, Israel, Lebanon, and Syria to the east, and to the south, the North African countries of Egypt, Tunisia, Morocco, Algeria, and Libya. This means that there isn't a single "diet" that encompasses the entire Mediterranean region—the spice-laden dishes of Morocco bear little resemblance to the lemon- and caper-laced cuisine of southern Italy. Rather, the Mediterranean diet is about what these cuisines have in common: a daily emphasis on vegetables and fruits, beans and lentils, whole grains, more seafood than meat and poultry, and heart-healthy olive oil. This is the essence of the Mediterranean way of eating and was our overriding principle when deciding what to include in this book.

The Mediterranean Diet Pyramid

For guidelines we consulted the Mediterranean Diet Pyramid. The Pyramid was originally developed in the 1990s as part of a collaboration between the Harvard School of Public Health and Oldways, a nonprofit organization whose mission is to inspire good health through cultural food traditions. The Pyramid was based on the outcome of the famous Seven Countries Study, which was begun in the late 1950s by an American physiologist named Ancel Keys. He found that the people of Crete tended to have lower incidences of coronary heart disease than participants in other countries, a fact that he attributed to their traditional diet, which was low in saturated fat and heavily reliant on vegetables, grains, and legumes. The Pyramid paved the way for the diet's popularity here in the United States, and it is a useful tool for anyone who is interested in eating this way. We wanted our recipes to follow the Pyramid and reflect the major tenets of the diet.

How did we do it? First, in the relative importance we've placed on each chapter. The most common elements of Mediterranean meals—fruits, vegetables, grains (mostly whole), olive oil, beans, legumes, nuts, seeds, herbs, and spices—form the base of the Mediterranean Diet Pyramid, so one of the biggest chapters is devoted entirely to vegetables, another sizable chapter to grains, and still another to legumes. Moving up the Pyramid, fish and seafood are prominent elements that are consumed often, at least two times per week, so that chapter also contains a huge selection of recipes. Further up are poultry, eggs, cheese, and yogurt, which are consumed in moderate amounts, daily to weekly, and at the top of the Pyramid are meats and sweets, which are consumed in relatively small quantities and least often. To reflect this, we've combined poultry and meat recipes into a single, moderately sized chapter. There is also a chapter for sweets, but you won't find chocolaty confections or towering cakes in it. In fact, you won't even find butter, which we've opted to leave out of the book altogether since it is high in saturated fat. What you will find are fresh fruit desserts and more modest treats, like Greek Sesame-Honey Bars (page 377) and White Wine–Poached Pears (page 373).

The Pyramid is also reflected in the dishes themselves. Small amounts of cheese and meat are often used as seasonings instead of main ingredients. Dishes aren't drowned in sauce but instead drizzled with extra-virgin olive oil or a yogurt- or tahini-based sauce to add flavor and richness. While many American dinner plates are centered around meat or chicken, Mediterranean meals are designed differently. Rather than being the centerpiece, meat is eaten in smaller quantities (in this book, a serving of fish, poultry, or meat is usually 4 to 6 ounces) with the intention that it will be paired with a few other—usually plant-based—dishes of equal portions, like fresh salads, vegetable and bean dishes, and whole grains. We've created some sample menus (see page 6) to help you start thinking about how to put together a Mediterranean meal.

Finally, we went to great lengths to make sure the recipes in this book were healthy. Since the original Seven Countries Study, countless studies have proven that the benefits of the Mediterranean diet go far beyond cardiovascular health—and, unlike most trendy diets, the health effects have been studied over the long term. You can hardly read the news without coming across an article detailing the findings of yet another study on the benefits of the Mediterranean diet. With its high amounts of vegetables and olive oil, which contains heart-healthy monounsaturated fats, the diet has been said to promote healthy blood sugar levels, improve cognitive function, and even prevent diseases like Alzheimer's and certain types of cancer. And while the Mediterranean diet isn't low in fat, some studies have found that people who eat this way do tend to weigh less and have improved body mass index, lower cholesterol, and lower blood pressure. Other studies indicate that adhering to a Mediterranean diet results in better overall health, both physical and mental.

Putting the Pyramid into Practice

So, with the help of the experts at Oldways, we established guidelines for ourselves limiting the amount of unhealthy saturated fats, salt, and calories. We focused on the interesting flavors of the ingredients and how to bring out their best qualities by using lots of herbs and spices and utilizing cooking techniques meant to do the same, like roasting, braising, and grilling. And we put nutritional information for every recipe in the back of the book.

But the real heart of the book is the food. No diet, no matter how healthy, is sustainable unless the food is satisfying and, dare we say, a bit exciting. Anyone who has been to the Mediterranean knows this food is both, and we wanted our recipes to reflect that. What makes our book different is that we've designed the recipes with the home cook in mind. Our recipes are authentic but

MEDITERRANEAN DIET PYRAMID

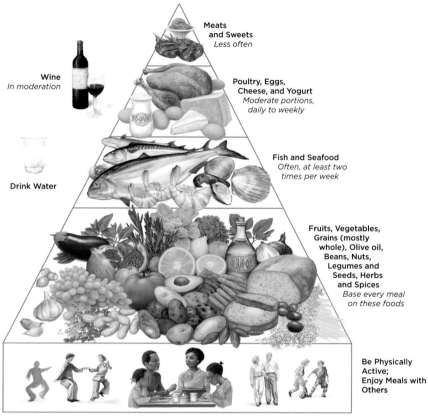

Meats and Sweets
Less often

Wine
In moderation

Poultry, Eggs, Cheese, and Yogurt
Moderate portions, daily to weekly

Fish and Seafood
Often, at least two times per week

Drink Water

Fruits, Vegetables, Grains (mostly whole), Olive oil, Beans, Nuts, Legumes and Seeds, Herbs and Spices
Base every meal on these foods

Be Physically Active; Enjoy Meals with Others

accessible; you won't have to search for esoteric ingredients you'll never use again. Some recipes hew closely to the traditional recipes, and others use ingredients in ways that follow the diet but provide more options. We knew that we could wholeheartedly embrace the tenets of the Mediterranean diet while also translating its vibrant, healthy ingredients, smaller portion sizes, and less-meat-and-more-vegetables approach into interesting, appealing recipes.

By combining ingredients in new and different ways, we produced incredible results: Lemon-Dill Yogurt Cheese (page 30) was one of the simplest things we've ever made—just strain plain yogurt and stir in flavorings—but also decadently creamy, with a pleasant tang. A Macedonian dish of Stewed Chickpeas with Eggplant and Tomatoes (page 178) incorporates simple ingredients we've used hundreds of times before into a complex and savory dish we couldn't stop eating. Tagliatelle with Artichokes and Parmesan (page 143) relies completely on pantry staples—pasta, jarred artichokes, cheese, garlic, and lemon—and elevates them to new heights. Braised Halibut with Leeks and Mustard (page 250), our appealing French-flavored one-pan meal, cooks

the fish on top of the vegetables and then turns the cooking liquid into a sauce. These dishes are perfect for home cooks who want to incorporate more Mediterranean-style dishes into their regular dinner rotation; the ingredients and techniques are straightforward, but the combinations and the resulting flavors and textures are altogether fresh and inspired.

There's also a slew of authentic, slightly more involved recipes, from the sweet-savory Moroccan tart known as B'stilla (page 364), which tops layers of gently spiced chicken and delicate dough with cinnamon sugar (we used stacks of phyllo to replicate the texture of the traditional dough) to Red Wine–Braised Octopus (page 285), a rich, Greek-style dish that coats tender octopus with a velvety red wine sauce (we parcook the octopus in water first to avoid a dish that's overly salty) to Stuffed Grape Leaves (page 35), for which we turned to widely available jarred grape leaves (we show you, step by step, how to successfully roll them around our herb-enhanced rice filling). This book has something for everyone, whether you want to round out your favorite roast chicken with a flavorful grain salad or you're hoping to push the limits of your culinary knowledge with something completely new.

GETTING STARTED

Creating a Mediterranean Table

There is no denying that eating the Mediterranean way requires a shift in thinking: Portion sizes are smaller, less meat defines a serving size, and a meal often has several equally weighted dishes on the plate. The guidelines below are designed to help you put the diet into practice, and the menus that follow show interesting examples of ways to combine recipes for the full Mediterranean dining experience, whether you are creating a weeknight meal for your family or entertaining.

RETHINK YOUR PLATE

While you may normally decide on a central protein first and then choose a vegetable and a starch to accompany it, try choosing a vegetable or grain first. Instead of a main dish with sides, you will be serving more equal "small plates." To this end, most of the recipes in this book are not intended to stand on their own; you'll need one or two complementary dishes to round out a meal. You don't necessarily need to make more dishes than you normally would—just approach the composition of the meal and your planning differently.

MODERATION IS KEY

No matter what you're eating, make sure to moderate your intake. Portions are smaller in the Mediterranean diet, and the yields of our recipes reflect that. A pound of pasta serves six people, not four, and pieces of chicken and meat are in the 4- to 6-ounce range and may be highlighted by a small amount of a light and flavorful sauce. A Mediterranean-style meal is composed of appropriate portions of multiple dishes.

EAT WHAT'S FRESH AND IN SEASON

Eat lots of vegetables and fruits every day. Much of Mediterranean meal planning is based on what vegetables are available and celebrates seasonality. By figuring out what is seasonal and local, you will get better-quality produce that is worthy of being the centerpiece of a meal. Farmers' markets are an excellent source of inspiration. If fresh produce isn't available, we've found that there are certain substitutes that are of reliable quality year-round, such as jarred artichokes, varieties of small tomatoes like cherry and grape, and frozen fava beans and peas.

EAT BEANS AND WHOLE GRAINS EVERY DAY

Since meat and poultry are used more sparingly in the Mediterranean, beans, lentils, nuts, and whole grains are major sources of daily protein. They can be the starring ingredient in soups and stews, salads, and heartier dishes when combined with meat or fish but they can also play a supporting role in vegetable and pasta dishes. Whole grains contain a number of key nutrients, such as antioxidants, but note that not all Mediterranean grains are whole grains (see page 8).

EAT MORE FISH AND LESS RED MEAT

Consuming fresh seafood has long been important in the countries along the Mediterranean Sea. The health benefits of eating fish and shellfish include that they are low in calories and saturated fat and rich in omega-3 fatty acids. Some Mediterranean fish aren't well known in the United States, but there are available substitutes for most of them (see page 248). Fish like sardines and mackerel have the added benefit of being less expensive than many other types of fresh fish. Fish can be pan-roasted, baked, broiled, braised, and grilled and doesn't always have to be an entrée. It can be served as a starter (Provençal-Style Anchovy Dip, page 22, and Chili-Marinated Calamari with Oranges, page 38), as part of a composed salad (Salade Niçoise, page 78, and Fennel and Apple Salad with Smoked Mackerel, page 89), in soups (Provençal Fish Soup, page 63, and Shellfish Soup with Leeks and Turmeric, page 64), and in pasta dishes (Spaghetti with Clams and Roasted Tomatoes, page 154, and Orzo with Shrimp, Feta, and Lemon, page 158).

USE MEAT AS A FLAVORING

Dishes that contain small amounts of meat are common throughout the Mediterranean, since traditionally this was a way to stretch pricey meat further by combining it with less expensive grains or beans. We implemented this idea in creating dishes such as Bulgur with Herbed Lamb and Roasted Red Peppers (page 126) and Orzo with Greek Sausage and Spiced Yogurt (page 159). We made use of more flavorful cuts of meat, such as lamb shanks and shoulder chops, and cured meats like Italian pancetta, Spanish chorizo, and the Turkish sausage *sujuk*, so that a smaller amount would have a big impact.

SERVE FRESH FRUIT AND CAREFULLY CHOSEN SWEETS FOR DESSERT

It is customary in many parts of the region to have a piece of fresh fruit as the ending to a meal. Cakes and cookies are not eaten on a daily basis but are often saved for special family gatherings and celebrations. In keeping with the diet's emphasis on low amounts of saturated fat, we replaced the butter in our cakes, cookies, and pastries with olive oil, but we still wanted to achieve satisfying sweets that would be worthy of serving to guests. This required us to overcome a few challenges; for example, when it came to phyllo-based desserts like Baklava (page 382) and Fig Phyllo Cookies (page 381), replacing the butter with olive oil was not as easy as a one-for-one substitution.

EMBRACE VARIETY

Balance and diversity are hallmarks of Mediterranean meals, so try to serve an array of dishes with different tastes, textures, and temperatures. Many dishes taste great whether they are warm, at room temperature, or even cold out of the fridge. This helps to reduce the pressure to get a completely hot meal on the table. As you can see from our sample menus (page 6), it is easy to mix and match recipes.

MEDITERRANEAN MEAL PLANNING

To help you start thinking about putting the Mediterranean diet into practice, we've compiled a list of recipes that we think work well together and are suitable for busy weeknights. When you have more time, the suggestions on the opposite page show you how to combine small plates and main courses for larger gatherings or special celebrations.

WEEKNIGHT PAIRINGS

Pan-Roasted Halibut with Chermoula (page 250)
Braised Asparagus, Peas, and Radishes with
    Tarragon (page 202)

Lemon-Herb Hake Fillets with Garlic Potatoes (page 246)
Sautéed Cherry Tomatoes (page 228)

Orzo with Shrimp, Feta, and Lemon (page 158)
Green Bean Salad with Cilantro Sauce (page 84)

Za'atar-Rubbed Butterflied Chicken (page 298)
Sautéed Swiss Chard with Currants and Pine
    Nuts (page 226)

Grilled Chicken Kebabs with Tomato-Feta
    Salad (page 300)
Simple Pearl Couscous with Radishes and
    Watercress (page 166)

Flank Steak Peperonata (page 308)
Warm Farro with Lemon and Herbs (page 128)

Spice-Rubbed Pork Tenderloin with Fennel, Tomatoes,
    Artichokes, and Olives (page 315)
Creamy Parmesan Polenta (page 118)

Tagliatelle with Artichokes and Parmesan (page 143)
Tricolor Salad with Balsamic Vinaigrette (page 68)

Bulgur with Herbed Lamb and Roasted Red
    Peppers (page 126)
Spicy Roasted Carrots with Cilantro (page 206)

Stewed Chickpeas with Eggplant and Tomatoes (page 178)
Zucchini Ribbon Salad with Shaved Parmesan (page 99)

ENTERTAINING MENUS

While we used lots of familiar ingredients like chicken, swordfish, couscous, and chickpeas across this book, we also investigated less familiar ingredients and developed recipes for grains like freekeh and farro, beans like cranberry and fava, meats like oxtails and quail, and seafood like monkfish and squid. We learned how to work with finicky ingredients like grape leaves and phyllo dough and flavor builders like sumac, preserved lemons, and pomegranate molasses. You'll find plenty of information on these items throughout the book. What you won't find here, however, are ingredients that aren't native to the Mediterranean region, like quinoa and salmon. Below is information about core pantry ingredients used throughout the book.

CANNED AND DRIED BEANS Legumes are a major source of protein in the Mediterranean diet. They are eaten simply on their own and also paired with diverse other ingredients to add heft and texture, such as Whole-Wheat Spaghetti with Lentils, Pancetta, and Escarole (page 147) and Shrimp with White Beans (page 270). For salads, quicker-cooking soups, and sautés, we've found that canned beans work just as well as or even better than dried; they hold their shape nicely and don't require soaking or extended cooking. We use dried beans in recipes where the cooking of the beans builds body and flavor in the dish such as Hearty Tuscan

Bean Stew (page 192) and Moroccan Braised White Beans with Lamb (page 188). We have found that brining dried beans helps them to hold their shape during cooking and results in fewer blown-out beans (see page 187). Fava beans are one of the only beans that are more frequently used fresh than dried or canned; see page 83 for more information.

RICE AND GRAINS Rice and grains are a vital part of many Mediterranean dishes, from verdant Spanish-Style Brothy Rice (page 111) to savory Creamy Parmesan Polenta (page 118) to multi-textured Egyptian Barley Salad (page 123). In the test kitchen, we determined the best way to cook each grain; grains like farro are best when cooked in a large amount of water like pasta, but finer-grained bulgur needs only to be rehydrated in water. At least half of the grains you eat should be whole grains (those that retain their original kernel); we use barley, bulgur, farro, freekeh, and wheat berries in this book. For more information about rice and other grains, see pages 112 and 117.

PASTA AND COUSCOUS Pasta takes center stage in many Mediterranean dishes but is often used in ways unfamiliar to most American home cooks, as in Rigatoni with Warm-Spiced Beef Ragu (page 156), which gets its distinctive flavor from cinnamon

and cloves. In this book, we also use hearty whole-wheat pasta, which has an earthy flavor that we pair with robust ingredients like pancetta and escarole. In North Africa, couscous, which is made of the same type of wheat as pasta, is popular both as a vehicle to sop up saucy dishes and stews and as a small plate in its own right, as in Couscous with Lamb, Chickpeas, and Orange (page 164). Eastern Mediterranean cuisines often use pearl couscous; its grains are larger than those of regular couscous and are toasted rather than dried, which gives them a nutty flavor perfectly suited for dishes like Hearty Pearl Couscous with Eggplant, Spinach, and Beans (page 167). For more information on pasta and couscous, see pages 152 and 166.

OLIVES AND OLIVE OIL If there is one ingredient that is the emblem of Mediterranean cooking, it is olives. Of course they are best known for their use in olive oil (see page 12). There are countless varieties of eating olives, from French niçoise to Greek kalamata.

Test Kitchen Tip We recommend buying olives from the refrigerated section of your supermarket, since jarred shelf-stable ones tend to be saltier. If you have time, we recommend that you buy unpitted olives and pit them yourself, as they will be less mushy than prepitted ones. To pit olives, place an olive on the counter and hold the flat edge of a knife over it. Press the blade firmly with your hand to loosen the olive meat from the pit, then remove the pit with your fingers.

FRESH AND DRIED HERBS The brightly flavored dishes of the Mediterranean region rely on an abundance of fresh herbs, especially mint, oregano, dill, and basil, so it is helpful to keep your fridge or garden well stocked with these essentials. In this book, we use fresh herbs as a bright garnish for a large number of dishes, but they also act as main flavor components in recipes like Green Bean Salad with Cilantro Sauce (page 84) and Herbed Barley Pilaf (page 120).

Test Kitchen Tip Most fresh herbs are fairly perishable, but if washed and stored correctly they will keep for a week or longer. We recommend gently rinsing and drying herbs (a salad spinner works perfectly) and then loosely rolling them in a few sheets of paper towel. Seal the roll of herbs in a zipper-lock bag and store it in the crisper drawer of your refrigerator.

We also like to keep a variety of dried herbs on hand, which are great for use in long-cooked dishes like stews and braises. Although we usually use only hardy herbs such as rosemary and thyme in dried form, mint is another important dried herb in Mediterranean cuisines, valued for its earthy yet bright flavor. In fact, some dishes such as Turkish Tomato, Bulgur, and Red Pepper

Soup (page 50) use both dried and fresh mint for maximum flavor. Herb blends are also a great way to add complex flavor to dishes; we created our own vibrant Herbes de Provence (page 317), a French herb blend used in Spice-Rubbed Pork Tenderloin with Fennel, Tomatoes, Artichokes, and Olives (page 315).

Test Kitchen Tip Dried herbs lose their potency six to 12 months after opening, so it's important to replace them frequently. You can test dried herbs for freshness by rubbing a small amount between your fingers; if the herbs don't release a bright aroma, it's time to buy a new jar. You can quickly dry hearty herbs (thyme, rosemary, oregano, and bay leaf) in the microwave. Lay a single layer of herbs on a paper towel–lined plate and cover with a second paper towel. Microwave on high for 1 to 3 minutes, checking occasionally, until the herb appears dehydrated. Cool at room temperature and then crumble or store whole in a plastic bag.

SPICES AND SPICE BLENDS AND PASTES The flavor combinations vary, but spices are often what make one Mediterranean cuisine distinct from another. Many of the spices used in Mediterranean cooking are probably already in your pantry, like cinnamon, paprika (both sweet and smoked), and saffron. There are also a number of spices that may be unfamiliar to you, such as sumac, which adds a floral, tangy flavor to recipes like Fattoush (page 92), and Aleppo pepper, which lends subtle heat to dishes like Turkish Pinto Bean Salad with Tomatoes, Eggs, and Parsley (page 187). Spice blends and pastes also add potent flavor: There's North African *ras el hanout*, which can include some 25 spices, seeds, dried flowers, berries, and nuts; *za'atar*, a popular eastern Mediterranean blend that consists of wild thyme, sumac, sesame seeds, and salt and is used as both a seasoning and a condiment; and *harissa*, a North African chili paste made with hot and/or mild chiles, garlic, and oil and often cumin, coriander, and caraway. You can buy these and other spice blends, but if you can't find them you can make your own (see page 316).

Test Kitchen Tip Storing your spices out of the light and heat will extend their shelf life. Check for freshness by observing the aroma and color of your spices (see page 316 for more information). When buying spices, brand makes a difference. Some of our favorites are Penzey's Extra Fancy Vietnamese Cassia Cinnamon, The Spice House Hungarian Sweet Paprika, Simply Organic Smoked Paprika, and Morton & Bassett Saffron Threads.

CHEESES, CURED MEATS, AND NUTS A little cheese (feta or goat cheese), cured meat (pancetta or chorizo), or nuts (almonds or pine nuts) goes a long way in adding rich flavor to Mediterranean

dishes. For example, Paniscia (page 110), a regional Italian risotto, is flavored with bits of salami, and many pastas and vegetable salads rely on a little nutty Parmesan to boost savory flavor. Nuts are common additions to salads and are also an essential element of the North African seasoning blend *dukkah* (page 317).

Test Kitchen Tip For long-term storage in the refrigerator, we find that cheeses are best wrapped in parchment paper and then aluminum foil. The paper allows the cheese to breathe, and the foil keeps out off-flavors and prevents the cheese from drying out. We recommend storing nuts in the freezer to prevent their natural oils from turning rancid. We often toast nuts before using them to bring out more depth of flavor; see page 48 for more information.

CONDIMENTS **Yogurt** You may not think of yogurt as a condiment, but it's used that way in much of the Mediterranean, where a small dollop is used as a topping or it's mixed into sauces and drizzled over Grilled Chicken Kebabs (page 300) and Falafel (page 181). We usually prefer the richer flavor of whole-milk yogurt (our favorite is Brown Cow Cream Top), but some recipes will work with low-fat yogurt as well. Our favorite Greek yogurt, which is perfect for making thick and creamy Tzatziki (page 19), is Fage Total Classic Greek Yogurt.

Tahini Made from ground sesame seeds, tahini is used much like yogurt: It can be used as a topping on its own or as a base for sauces. It's also an essential component of dips like Classic Hummus (page 16) and Baba Ghanoush (page 20). Our favorite brand is Joyva Sesame Tahini.

Pomegranate molasses A reduction of pomegranate juice, pomegranate molasses is thick and syrupy with a unique, sweet-sour flavor. You can buy it or make your own (page 305); pomegranate molasses adds complex tanginess to Muhammara (page 22), Kibbeh (page 305), and many other dishes.

Preserved lemons Preserved lemons (page 252), a specialty of North Africa, add an intense lemon flavor to many dishes. They are easy to make, and they keep for six months in the fridge, but they take several weeks to cure; we offer a quick substitute that you can make in a pinch on page 252.

Dukkah This Egyptian condiment is a blend of nuts, seeds, and spices that can be sprinkled into olive oil as a dip for bread or can be used to add texture and flavor to dishes such as Black-Eyed Peas with Walnuts and Pomegranate (page 182). The ingredients vary depending on the brand, so we prefer to make our own (page 317).

ALL ABOUT OLIVE OIL

Olive oil, which is simply juice pressed from olives, has been an important part of Mediterranean cooking for thousands of years. The highest grade, called extra-virgin, is lively, bright, and full-bodied, with flavors ranging from peppery to buttery depending on the varieties of olives used and how ripe they were when harvested. In the Mediterranean, Spain is the leading producer of olive oil, followed by Italy and Greece. In the United States, California is the top producer (and in fact is the source of our winning supermarket extra-virgin olive oil).

In this book, we use extra-virgin olive oil (EVOO) as our main cooking oil as well as in raw applications. Olive oil supports one of the main pillars of the Mediterranean Diet Pyramid: to eat more healthy fats and fewer saturated fats. It is high in mono-unsaturated fatty acids, which are healthy fats, and also contains important minor components including antioxidants and other beneficial phytochemicals, plant-derived compounds thought to protect against disease. Studies have also shown that people who regularly include olive oil in their diets have lower rates of heart disease, lower blood pressure, and reduced rates of diabetes and some cancers.

Olive oil tastes great when it's fresh. But olives are highly perishable, and their complex flavor degrades quickly, which makes producing—and handling—a top-notch oil time-sensitive, labor-intensive, and expensive.

Although conventional wisdom says that you shouldn't cook with olive oil since its smoke point is low, we have found that this is not the case. With a smoke point of 410 degrees, extra-virgin olive oil is fine for most cooking applications, even frying. However, we don't usually use olive oil for frying because it is not economical to use in large quantities.

Extra-virgin olive oil is of course a starring player in salad dressings, but we also use it as a condiment on vegetables, pastas, bean dishes, and grilled fish, and as a source of richness and body in soups and sauces. Since olive oil is a pricey purchase, we use what we term "supermarket" extra-virgin olive oil for everyday cooked applications and save the most flavorful "high-end" EVOO for drizzling. We replaced butter with olive oil in all of our Mediterranean recipes, both sweet and savory. An olive oil tart crust (page 360) has great savory flavor and a pleasantly tender texture, and a golden Olive Oil–Yogurt Cake (page 386) has amazingly rich flavor, with the olive oil contributing subtle fruity notes.

BUYING AND STORING OLIVE OIL

Buying extra-virgin olive oil in American supermarkets can be a tricky business. The standards of the International Olive Council (IOC), the industry's worldwide governing body, are not enforced in the U.S., and a widely reported 2010 study from the Olive Center at the University of California, Davis, revealed that 69 percent of tested supermarket olive oils sold as "extra-virgin" were actually lesser grades being passed off at premium prices. Since then, the U.S. olive oil industry has taken steps to be more stringent. The state of California, where olive oil production has grown tenfold over the past decade, passed the California Department of Food and Agriculture olive oil standard in 2014. The most stringent standard in the country, it is mandatory for medium- and large-scale California olive oil production. In 2010, the U.S. Department of Agriculture (USDA) adopted chemical and sensory standards for olive oil grades similar to those established by the IOC. The USDA standard, however, is voluntary and rarely enforced, so choosing the right extra-virgin olive oil is a challenge, to say the least.

To find the best "everyday" olive oil, we tasted 10 supermarket extra-virgin olive oils plain, with bread, over tomatoes and mozzarella, and in vinaigrette served on salad greens. We also sent each of the oils to an independent laboratory for chemical evaluation and to 10 trained olive oil tasters to get a second opinion on their flavor quality.

Our tasters were underwhelmed by the supermarket choices, but in the end, one oil stood out above the rest: California Olive Ranch Everyday Extra Virgin Olive Oil. We discovered that this largely boils down to the company's control over every stage of the production process. The company uses a relatively new growing and harvesting process called super-high-density planting, in which the trees are planted together much more tightly than they would be in traditional groves. As a result, the olives can be harvested by machines more efficiently than they would be if they were picked by hand. (Speed is of the essence, since olives begin to change flavor from the moment they are separated from the tree and must be pressed as quickly as possible to ensure that they retain the desired flavor profile.) Then, by bottling very close to the source, the company cuts out the risk

---

TYPES OF OLIVES USED TO MAKE OLIVE OIL

There are over a thousand varieties of olives with a few dozen cultivated varieties that are commercially dominant. Some of the most commonly found varieties in the U.S. market are Arbequina and Picual from Spain, Koroneiki from Greece, and Coratina from Italy. Arbequina is noted for its ripe fruitiness, low bitterness, and pungency. Picual is very fruity with medium bitterness and pungency. Koroneiki is strongly fruity and herbaceous, with mild bitterness and pungency. Coratina is strongly green, herbaceous, bitter, and pungent.

that the oil will oxidize and spoil during transport to another facility. And unlike some producers that sell their oil in clear glass or even plastic bottles, which expose the oil to more damaging light, our winning manufacturer uses dark-green glass bottles that help shield the oil. The upshot of all these factors: fresher and cheaper olive oil. While it costs more than mediocre oils from industrial bottlers, it's far less expensive than our high-end extra-virgin favorite.

When it comes to high-end oils, more expensive ones aren't always better. Our winning high-end oil, Gaea Fresh, hails from Greece and, at half the price of some of the other oils in our tasting lineup, won't break the bank. It won points with tasters for its bold yet nicely balanced flavor. We use this oil in raw applications only.

KEEPING OLIVE OIL FRESH

These three things can help you assess the quality of an extra-virgin olive oil before you buy it.

Harvest Date A "best by" date might be 24 to 32 months after the oil was bottled, which in turn can be one to two years after it was pressed—so by the time that "best by" date rolls around, the oil could be about four years old. A harvest date is a more precise indication of freshness, since olive oil begins to degrade about 18 months after harvest. Look for the most recent date (certainly within the last 12 months), and note that in Europe and the United States, olives are harvested in the fall and winter, so most bottles list the previous year.

Dark Glass Avoid clear glass; dark glass shields the oil from damaging light. Avoid clear plastic, too; it's not a good barrier to light or air.

Oil Origin Bottlers often print where their oil has been sourced from on the label; look for oil that has been sourced from a single country.

TO STORE Never keep olive oil on your kitchen counter, since strong sunlight will oxidize the chlorophyll in the oil, producing stale, harsh flavors. Keeping your olive oil next to the stove is also a bad idea as heat accelerates spoilage. We recommend storing oil in a dark pantry or cupboard; do not store olive oil in the fridge, as it can become cloudy, thick, and viscous and can take a few hours to return to normal. You can keep unopened oil for about a year; but once opened, it lasts only about three months—so don't buy in bulk. And if possible, check the harvest date to ensure the freshest bottle possible.

To check for freshness, pour a little oil in a small glass and sniff it. If it reminds you of crayons or stale walnuts, toss it.

Rating Extra-Virgin Olive Oils

Extra-virgin olive oils range wildly in price, color, and quality, so it's hard to know which to buy. While many things can affect the style and flavor of olive oil, the main factors are the variety of olive and the time of harvest (earlier means greener, more bitter, and pungent); weather and processing also play a part. The best-quality olive oil comes from olives pressed as quickly as possible without heat (which coaxes more oil from the olives at the expense of flavor).

SUPERMARKET
CALIFORNIA OLIVE RANCH
Everyday Extra Virgin Olive Oil
Price: $9.99 for 500 ml ($0.59 per oz)
"Fruity," "fragrant," and "fresh" with a "complex finish," this top-ranked oil is a supermarket standout. In fact, its flavor rivaled that of our favorite high-end extra-virgin oil. Not surprisingly, its lab scores for freshness and quality were also better than those of the other brands across the board.
SOURCE: Northern California
OLIVE VARIETIES: Arbequina, Arbosana, Koroneiki

HIGH-END
GAEA FRESH Extra Virgin Olive Oil
Price: $18.99 for 17 oz ($1.12 per oz)
With its "bright, sweet, grassy, and fresh scent and taste," this oil charmed our tasters in every application. While this was our overall crowd-pleasing favorite, our tasters recommended all of the single-origin premium extra-virgin olive oils we tasted.
SOURCE: Greece
OLIVE VARIETY: Koroneiki

CHAPTER 1

Meze, Antipasti, Tapas, and Other Small Plates

▪ FAST (less than 45 minutes start to finish)   ▪ VEGETARIAN

Photos (clockwise from top left): Marinated Green and Black Olives; Bruschetta; Stuffed Grape Leaves; Muhammara

Classic Hummus

MAKES about 2 cups VEG

WHY THIS RECIPE WORKS Classic hummus, which is made and eaten throughout the eastern Mediterranean, is composed of only a few simple ingredients: chickpeas, tahini, olive oil, garlic, and lemon juice. But many traditional recipes are surprisingly complex: The chickpeas must be soaked overnight and then skinned. We wanted a simple, streamlined recipe for hummus with a light, silky-smooth texture and a balanced flavor profile. We started with convenient canned chickpeas and got out the food processor to make quick work of turning them into a smooth puree. But when we pureed the chickpeas alone, the hummus turned out grainy. The key to the best texture was to create an emulsion: We started by grinding the chickpeas, then slowly added a mixture of water and lemon juice. We whisked the olive oil and a generous amount of tahini together and drizzled the mixture into the chickpeas while processing; this created a lush, light, and flavorful puree. Earthy cumin, garlic, and a pinch of cayenne kept the flavors balanced. If desired, garnish the hummus with 1 tablespoon of minced fresh cilantro or parsley and/or 2 tablespoons of the reserved whole chickpeas. Serve with Olive Oil–Sea Salt Pita Chips (page 22), fresh warm pita, or raw vegetables.

  ¼ cup water
  3 tablespoons lemon juice
  6 tablespoons tahini
  2 tablespoons extra-virgin olive oil, plus extra for serving
  1 (15-ounce) can chickpeas, rinsed
  1 small garlic clove, minced
  ½ teaspoon salt
  ¼ teaspoon ground cumin
    Pinch cayenne pepper

1. Combine water and lemon juice in small bowl. In separate bowl, whisk tahini and oil together.

2. Process chickpeas, garlic, salt, cumin, and cayenne in food processor until almost fully ground, about 15 seconds. Scrape down sides of bowl with rubber spatula. With machine running, add lemon juice mixture in steady stream. Scrape down sides of bowl and continue to process for 1 minute. With machine running, add tahini mixture in steady stream and process until hummus is smooth and creamy, about 15 seconds, scraping down sides of bowl as needed.

3. Transfer hummus to serving bowl, cover with plastic wrap, and let sit at room temperature until flavors meld, about 30 minutes. (Hummus can be refrigerated for up to 5 days; if necessary, loosen hummus with 1 tablespoon warm water before serving.) Drizzle with extra oil to taste before serving.

For a streamlined hummus with a silky texture, we process canned chickpeas with olive oil and tahini.

VARIATIONS

Hummus with Smoked Paprika VEG
Substitute 1 teaspoon smoked paprika for cumin. Garnish hummus with 2 tablespoons toasted pine nuts, 1 tablespoon thinly sliced scallion greens, and extra oil, if desired.

Roasted Red Pepper Hummus VEG
Omit water and cumin. Add ¼ cup jarred roasted red peppers, rinsed and thoroughly patted dry, to food processor with chickpeas. Garnish hummus with 2 tablespoons toasted sliced almonds, 2 teaspoons minced fresh parsley, and extra oil, if desired.

Artichoke-Lemon Hummus VEG
Omit cumin and increase lemon juice to 4 tablespoons (2 lemons). Rinse 1 cup jarred whole baby artichokes packed in water and pat dry with paper towels; chop ¼ cup artichokes and set aside for garnish. Add remaining ¾ cup artichokes and ¼ teaspoon grated lemon zest to food processor with chickpeas. Garnish hummus with reserved chopped artichokes, 2 teaspoons minced fresh parsley or mint, and extra oil, if desired.

Roasted Garlic Hummus `VEG`

Remove outer papery skins from 2 heads garlic; cut top quarters off heads and discard. Wrap garlic in aluminum foil and roast in 350-degree oven until browned and very tender, about 1 hour; let cool, then squeeze out cloves from skins (you should have about ¼ cup). Meanwhile, heat 2 tablespoons extra-virgin olive oil and 2 thinly sliced garlic cloves in 8-inch skillet over medium-low heat. Cook, stirring occasionally, until garlic is golden brown, about 15 minutes; transfer garlic slices to paper towel–lined plate and reserve oil. Substitute garlic cooking oil for olive oil in step 1. Add roasted garlic to food processor with chickpeas. Garnish hummus with toasted garlic slices, 2 teaspoons minced fresh parsley, and extra oil, if desired.

NOTES FROM THE TEST KITCHEN
Tahini 101

Tahini is a thick paste made from ground sesame seeds. It is often used to flavor eastern Mediterranean dishes such as hummus. It is also a popular condiment for Falafel (page 181) and can act as a base for creamy vinaigrettes, as in our Tahini-Lemon Dressing (page 72). You can make your own tahini by grinding sesame seeds in a blender with just enough toasted sesame oil to make a smooth paste. Our favorite store-bought brand is Joyva Sesame Tahini, which has a pleasantly nutty, buttery flavor.

Roasting Garlic

1. Cut off top of head so cloves are exposed. Place head cut side up in the center of square of aluminum foil and seal.

2. Once heads have roasted and cooled, squeeze cloves from skins, starting from root and working up.

MAKES 2 cups `FAST` `VEG`

Toasted nuts are an essential element of many a meze platter, but store-bought seasoned almonds are often stale-tasting or too salty. We wanted to turn out flavorful, crunchy nuts worthy of being served alongside our favorite small plates. We began by toasting raw almonds for just 8 minutes in hot oil, giving them a deeper, more complex flavor. To give the nuts some pizzazz, we came up with several zesty combinations of spices and herbs. Toasting the aromatic additions with the almonds ensured the most potent flavor.

> 1 tablespoon extra-virgin olive oil
> 2 cups skin-on raw whole almonds
> 1 teaspoon salt
> ¼ teaspoon pepper

Heat oil in 12-inch nonstick skillet over medium-high heat until just shimmering. Add almonds, salt, and pepper and reduce heat to medium-low. Cook, stirring often, until almonds are fragrant and their color deepens slightly, about 8 minutes. Transfer almonds to paper towel–lined plate and let cool before serving. (Almonds can be stored at room temperature for up to 5 days.)

VARIATIONS
ROSEMARY ALMONDS `FAST` `VEG`
Add ½ teaspoon dried rosemary to skillet with almonds.

ORANGE-FENNEL ALMONDS `FAST` `VEG`
Add 1 teaspoon grated orange zest and ½ teaspoon ground fennel seeds to skillet with almonds.

SPICED ALMONDS `FAST` `VEG`
Add 2 teaspoons grated lemon zest, 1 teaspoon ground coriander seeds, and ½ teaspoon hot paprika to skillet with almonds.

LEMON-GARLIC ALMONDS `FAST` `VEG`
Add ½ teaspoon grated lemon zest and 1 minced garlic clove to skillet with almonds. Just before serving, toss with another ½ teaspoon grated lemon zest.

Canned cannellini beans make a creamy and savory base for our sun-dried tomato and feta white bean dip.

Garlic and Rosemary White Bean Dip

MAKES about 1¼ cups   `FAST` `VEG`

WHY THIS RECIPE WORKS White beans are a staple ingredient in Mediterranean cuisine, contributing a buttery, creamy quality to soups and salads from Turkey to Tuscany. Their mildly nutty flavor and smooth texture seemed perfectly suited for a hummus-like dip. Our first attempts produced a thick, chunky spread loaded with flavor but lacking the silky-smooth texture we wanted. We tried adding different amounts of water to the dip, soon discovering that 2 tablespoons created just the right consistency. Adding a generous pour of olive oil and processing all of the beans at once helped achieve a rich dip with a sublimely smooth texture, perfect for anything from toasted bread to sliced vegetables. With our dip's groundwork in place, we boosted its flavor with a squeeze of lemon, woodsy rosemary, garlic, and just a pinch of cayenne for some heat. A 30-minute rest before serving let the dip's flavors deepen, and a final drizzle of oil added welcome richness. Serve with Olive Oil–Sea Salt Pita Chips (page 22), slices of toasted baguette, or raw vegetables.

1 (15-ounce) can cannellini beans, rinsed
¼ cup extra-virgin olive oil
2 tablespoons water
2 teaspoons lemon juice
1 teaspoon minced fresh rosemary
1 small garlic clove, minced
　Salt and pepper
　Pinch cayenne pepper

1. Process beans, 3 tablespoons oil, water, lemon juice, rosemary, garlic, ¼ teaspoon salt, ¼ teaspoon pepper, and cayenne in food processor until smooth, about 45 seconds, scraping down sides of bowl as needed.

2. Transfer to serving bowl, cover with plastic wrap, and let sit at room temperature until flavors meld, about 30 minutes. (Dip can be refrigerated for up to 24 hours; if necessary, loosen dip with 1 tablespoon warm water before serving.) Season with salt and pepper to taste and drizzle with remaining 1 tablespoon oil before serving.

VARIATIONS

Caper and Tarragon White Bean Dip   `FAST` `VEG`

Omit salt, substitute 2 teaspoons minced fresh tarragon for rosemary, and add 3 tablespoons rinsed capers to food processor with beans.

Sun-Dried Tomato and Feta White Bean Dip   `FAST` `VEG`

Increase water to ¼ cup, substitute minced fresh oregano for rosemary, and reduce salt to ⅛ teaspoon. Add ½ cup crumbled feta cheese and ¼ cup oil-packed sun-dried tomatoes to food processor with beans.

Mincing Fresh Herbs

To mince fresh herbs, place 1 hand on handle of chef's knife and rest fingers of your other hand on top of knife blade. Use up-and-down rocking motion to evenly mince herbs, pivoting knife as you chop.

Grating and salting both cucumbers and beets eliminates excess moisture and ensures a thick, luscious beet *tzatziki*.

Tzatziki

MAKES about 2 cups VEG

WHY THIS RECIPE WORKS *Tzatziki* is a traditional Greek sauce made from strained yogurt and cucumber, as delicious eaten as a dip for raw vegetables as it is dolloped over grilled chicken or lamb. To make our own classic version, we started by shredding a cucumber on a coarse grater, salting it, and letting it drain to keep any excess liquid from watering down the dip. Greek yogurt gives tzatziki its pleasant tang and richness, but before stirring in our drained cucumber, we enhanced its flavor with minced fresh herbs and garlic. Using Greek yogurt here is key; do not substitute regular plain yogurt or the sauce will be very watery. Serve with Olive Oil–Sea Salt Pita Chips (page 22), fresh warm pita, or raw vegetables.

- 1 (12-ounce) cucumber, peeled, halved lengthwise, seeded, and shredded
  Salt and pepper
- 1 cup whole-milk Greek yogurt
- 2 tablespoons extra-virgin olive oil
- 2 tablespoons minced fresh mint and/or dill
- 1 small garlic clove, minced

1. Toss cucumber with ½ teaspoon salt in colander and let drain for 15 minutes.

2. Whisk yogurt, oil, mint, and garlic together in bowl, then stir in drained cucumber. Cover and refrigerate until chilled, at least 1 hour or up to 2 days. Season with salt and pepper to taste before serving.

VARIATION
Beet Tzatziki VEG
Reduce amount of cucumber to 6 ounces and add 6 ounces raw beets, peeled and grated, to cucumber and salt in step 1.

Caponata

MAKES about 3 cups VEG

WHY THIS RECIPE WORKS Somewhat similar to ratatouille, Sicilian caponata distinguishes itself with boldly flavored eggplant and a sweet-and-sour finish. To make sure the eggplant didn't turn to oil-soaked mush, we salted and microwaved it to eliminate excess moisture. For our sauce, we started with V8 juice, which delivered bright tomato flavor. Brown sugar and red wine vinegar enhanced the traditional sweet-and-sour profile. A scoopful of raisins brought additional sweetness, minced anchovies added a rich umami boost, and briny black olives offered balance. Simmering everything together for just a few minutes allowed the sauce to thicken and the flavors to meld. Although we prefer the complex flavor of V8 juice, tomato juice can be substituted. If coffee filters are not available, food-safe, undyed paper towels can be substituted when microwaving the eggplant. Be sure to remove the eggplant from the microwave immediately so that the steam can escape. Serve caponata with slices of toasted baguette or alongside grilled meat or fish.

- 1 large eggplant (1½ pounds), cut into ½-inch cubes
- ½ teaspoon salt
- ¾ cup V8 juice
- ¼ cup red wine vinegar, plus extra for seasoning
- 2 tablespoons brown sugar
- ¼ cup chopped fresh parsley
- 1½ teaspoons minced anchovy fillets (2 to 3 fillets)
- 1 large tomato, cored, seeded, and chopped
- ¼ cup raisins
- 2 tablespoons minced black olives
- 2 tablespoons extra-virgin olive oil
- 1 celery rib, chopped fine
- 1 red bell pepper, stemmed, seeded, and chopped fine
- 1 small onion, chopped fine (½ cup)
- ¼ cup pine nuts, toasted

1. Toss eggplant with salt in bowl. Line entire surface of large microwave-safe plate with double layer of coffee filters and lightly spray with vegetable oil spray. Spread eggplant in even layer on coffee filters. Microwave until eggplant is dry and shriveled to one-third of its original size, 8 to 15 minutes (eggplant should not brown). Transfer eggplant immediately to paper towel–lined plate.

2. Meanwhile, whisk V8 juice, vinegar, sugar, parsley, and anchovies together in medium bowl. Stir in tomato, raisins, and olives.

3. Heat 1 tablespoon oil in 12-inch nonstick skillet over medium-high heat until shimmering. Add eggplant and cook, stirring occasionally, until edges are browned, 4 to 8 minutes, adding 1 teaspoon more oil if pan appears dry; transfer to bowl.

4. Add remaining 2 teaspoons oil to now-empty skillet and heat over medium-high heat until shimmering. Add celery, bell pepper, and onion and cook, stirring occasionally, until softened and edges are spotty brown, 6 to 8 minutes.

5. Reduce heat to medium-low and stir in eggplant and V8 juice mixture. Bring to simmer and cook until V8 juice is thickened and coats vegetables, 4 to 7 minutes. Transfer to serving bowl and let cool to room temperature. (Caponata can be refrigerated for up to 1 week; bring to room temperature before serving.) Season with extra vinegar to taste and sprinkle with pine nuts before serving.

Creamy Turkish Nut Dip
MAKES about 1 cup FAST VEG

WHY THIS RECIPE WORKS Traditionally made by pureeing nuts, bread, and olive oil to create a velvety-smooth dip, Turkish *tarator* is as simple as it is versatile. For our version, we made the base for the sauce by mashing torn pieces of white bread and water together into a paste. We then pulsed the paste in the blender with nuts, olive oil, garlic, and lemon. A pinch of cayenne contributed some welcome heat. With our simple method in place, we had some choices to make in determining our sauce's flavor profile. Many traditional recipes call for hazelnuts, but our research also turned up versions made with almonds, walnuts, and pine nuts. We made batches with all four nuts and found that they worked equally well in the recipe. Next, we compared toasted and untoasted nuts in a side-by-side tasting. We concluded that toasting the nuts was essential; it brought out their complexity, deepened the sauce's overall flavor, and drew an even greater contrast with the lemon and garlic. Quickly whirred together, the sauce's components blended into a warming, rich accompaniment to our favorite meze platter items. If using

almonds or hazelnuts, make sure they are skinless. Serve with Olive Oil–Sea Salt Pita Chips (page 22), fresh warm pita, raw vegetables, or fresh seafood.

1 slice hearty white sandwich bread, crusts removed, torn into 1-inch pieces
¾ cup water, plus extra as needed
1 cup blanched almonds, blanched hazelnuts, pine nuts, or walnuts, toasted
¼ cup extra-virgin olive oil
2 tablespoons lemon juice, plus extra as needed
1 small garlic clove, minced
Salt and pepper
Pinch cayenne pepper

1. With fork, mash bread and water together in bowl into paste. Process bread mixture, nuts, oil, lemon juice, garlic, ½ teaspoon salt, ⅛ teaspoon pepper, and cayenne in blender until smooth, about 2 minutes. Add extra water as needed until sauce is barely thicker than consistency of heavy cream.

2. Season with salt, pepper, and extra lemon juice to taste. Serve at room temperature. (Sauce can be refrigerated for up to 2 days; bring to room temperature before serving.)

Baba Ghanoush
MAKES about 2 cups VEG

WHY THIS RECIPE WORKS Baba ghanoush is a meze staple across Israel, Lebanon, Palestine, and beyond. It's typically made by concentrating the rich flavors of eggplant over an open flame before scraping and mashing the pulp into a dip seasoned with any number of regional spices and oils. Hoping to bring this recipe indoors, we decided to prepare it in the oven. We pricked the eggplants' skin to encourage moisture to evaporate during cooking, then roasted them whole in a very hot oven until the flesh was very soft and tender. To avoid a watery texture in the finished dish, we scooped the hot pulp into a colander to drain before processing it. We kept the flavorings simple, processing the eggplant with lemon juice, olive oil, garlic, and tahini. Look for eggplants with shiny, taut, and unbruised skins and an even shape (eggplants with a bulbous shape won't cook evenly). We prefer to serve baba ghanoush only lightly chilled; if cold, let it stand at room temperature for about 20 minutes before serving. Serve with Olive Oil–Sea Salt Pita Chips (page 22), fresh warm pita, or raw vegetables.

2 eggplants (1 pound each), pricked all over with fork
2 tablespoons tahini
2 tablespoons extra-virgin olive oil, plus extra for serving
4 teaspoons lemon juice
1 small garlic clove, minced
  Salt and pepper
2 teaspoons chopped fresh parsley

1. Adjust oven rack to middle position and heat oven to 500 degrees. Place eggplants on aluminum foil–lined rimmed baking sheet and roast, turning eggplants every 15 minutes, until uniformly soft when pressed with tongs, 40 to 60 minutes. Let eggplants cool for 5 minutes on baking sheet.

2. Set colander over bowl. Trim top and bottom off each eggplant and slit eggplants lengthwise. Using spoon, scoop hot pulp into colander (you should have about 2 cups pulp); discard skins. Let pulp drain for 3 minutes.

3. Transfer drained eggplant to food processor. Add tahini, oil, lemon juice, garlic, ¾ teaspoon salt, and ¼ teaspoon pepper. Pulse mixture to coarse puree, about 8 pulses. Season with salt and pepper to taste.

4. Transfer to serving bowl, cover tightly with plastic wrap, and refrigerate until chilled, about 1 hour. (Dip can be refrigerated for up to 24 hours; bring to room temperature before serving.) Season with salt and pepper to taste, drizzle with extra oil to taste, and sprinkle with parsley before serving.

Roasting the eggplants until they're completely soft is essential for baba ghanoush with a rich, smooth texture.

Making Baba Ghanoush

1. ROAST EGGPLANTS Roast whole, unpeeled eggplants until skins darken and wrinkle and eggplants are uniformly soft when pressed with tongs.

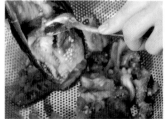

2. REMOVE AND DRAIN PULP Trim top and bottom off each eggplant and slit eggplants lengthwise. Use spoon to scoop hot pulp from skins into colander; let drain for 3 minutes.

3. PULSE DIP Pulse drained eggplant, tahini, oil, lemon juice, garlic, salt, and pepper together in food processor until mixture has coarse texture, about 8 pulses.

4. CHILL Transfer to serving bowl, cover tightly with plastic wrap, and refrigerate until chilled, 45 minutes to 1 hour.

OLIVE OIL–SEA SALT PITA CHIPS

SERVES 8 `FAST` `VEG`

Both white and whole-wheat pita breads will work well here. We prefer the larger crystal size of sea salt or kosher salt here; if using table salt, reduce the amount of salt by half.

4 (8-inch) pita breads
½ cup extra-virgin olive oil
1 teaspoon sea salt or kosher salt

1. Adjust oven racks to upper-middle and lower-middle positions and heat oven to 350 degrees. Using kitchen shears, cut around perimeter of each pita and separate into 2 thin rounds.

2. Working with 1 round at a time, brush rough side generously with oil and sprinkle with salt. Stack rounds on top of one another, rough side up, as you go. Using chef's knife, cut pita stack into 8 wedges. Spread wedges, rough side up and in single layer, on 2 rimmed baking sheets.

3. Bake until wedges are golden brown and crisp, about 15 minutes, rotating and switching sheets halfway through baking. Let cool before serving. (Pita chips can be stored at room temperature for up to 3 days.)

VARIATION

ROSEMARY-PARMESAN PITA CHIPS `FAST` `VEG`
Reduce amount of salt to ½ teaspoon. Toss salt with ½ cup grated Parmesan and 2 tablespoons minced fresh rosemary before sprinkling over pitas.

Preparing Pita for Chips

1. Using kitchen shears or scissors, cut around perimeter of each pita to yield 2 thin rounds.

2. Brush rough sides of each round with oil, season with salt, and stack them. Using chef's knife, cut stack into 8 wedges.

Muhammara

MAKES about 2 cups `FAST` `VEG`

WHY THIS RECIPE WORKS Nutty, rusty-red *muhammara* has deep roots in Aleppo, where Syrian home cooks have been combining nuts, red peppers, and spices into this sweet-and-spicy dip for centuries. Traditional recipes call for Aleppo peppers, but jarred roasted red peppers proved an easy-to-find substitute; we quickly processed them to a spreadable consistency. Toasting the walnuts underscored the peppers' smoky quality. Bread is a standard muhammara ingredient, but we turned to crumbled wheat crackers (Carr's Whole Wheat Crackers worked well) for texture and some extra nutty impact. Finally, we added some pomegranate molasses, which gives the dip its hallmark sweet yet slightly bitter flavor. If you can't find pomegranate molasses, you can make your own (see page 305). Serve with Olive Oil–Sea Salt Pita Chips, fresh warm pita, or raw vegetables.

1½ cups jarred roasted red peppers, rinsed and patted dry
1 cup walnuts, toasted
¼ cup plain wheat crackers, crumbled
3 tablespoons pomegranate molasses
2 tablespoons extra-virgin olive oil
¾ teaspoon salt
½ teaspoon ground cumin
⅛ teaspoon cayenne pepper
Lemon juice, as needed
1 tablespoon minced fresh parsley (optional)

Pulse all ingredients except parsley in food processor until smooth, about 10 pulses. Transfer to serving bowl, cover, and refrigerate for 15 minutes. (Dip can be refrigerated for up to 24 hours; bring to room temperature before serving.) Season with lemon juice, salt, and cayenne to taste and sprinkle with parsley, if using, before serving.

Provençal-Style Anchovy Dip

MAKES about 1½ cups

WHY THIS RECIPE WORKS A Provençal favorite, *anchoïade* is a potently flavorful mixture of anchovies, olive oil, and garlic that can be spread on toast or used as a dip for vegetables. But many versions of this puree can be unappealingly oily or overrun with unnecessary ingredients that drown out the anchovy flavor. To make a smooth, anchovy-rich dip, we started by creating a creamy, neutral-flavored base with another ingredient typical of Provence: almonds. When boiled and pureed, the nuts took on a smooth

Our Provençal anchovy dip gets its velvety texture from boiled and pureed almonds.

consistency that helped to keep our dip cohesive and provided richness without being greasy. We discovered that boiling and then rinsing the blanched almonds ensured that the dip wouldn't turn out grainy. We added the anchovy fillets to the softened almonds, along with raisins for subtle sweetness and a few savory ingredients to round out the flavor. Because extra-virgin olive oil can become bitter if overprocessed, we waited until the dip was mostly smooth before slowly drizzling in the oil. Fresh chives and a final drizzle of olive oil were all this dip needed for a refined presentation to match its sophisticated anchovy flavor. Our favorite brand of anchovies is King Oscar Anchovies—Flat Fillets in Olive Oil. Serve with Olive Oil–Sea Salt Pita Chips (page 22), slices of toasted baguette, or raw vegetables.

¾ cup whole blanched almonds
20 anchovy fillets (1½ ounces), rinsed, patted dry, and minced
¼ cup water
2 tablespoons raisins
2 tablespoons lemon juice, plus extra for serving
1 garlic clove, minced
1 teaspoon Dijon mustard
Salt and pepper
¼ cup extra-virgin olive oil, plus extra for serving
1 tablespoon minced fresh chives

1. Bring 4 cups water to boil in medium saucepan over medium-high heat. Add almonds and cook until softened, about 20 minutes. Drain and rinse well.

2. Process drained almonds, anchovies, water, raisins, lemon juice, garlic, mustard, ¼ teaspoon pepper, and ⅛ teaspoon salt in food processor to mostly smooth paste, about 2 minutes, scraping down sides of bowl as needed. With processor running, slowly add oil and process to smooth puree, about 2 minutes.

3. Transfer mixture to bowl, stir in 2 teaspoons chives, and season with salt and extra lemon juice to taste. (Dip can be refrigerated for up to 2 days; bring to room temperature before serving.) Sprinkle with remaining 1 teaspoon chives and drizzle with extra oil to taste before serving.

NOTES FROM THE TEST KITCHEN
All About Anchovies

Anchovies are small silver-skinned fish usually caught in warm Mediterranean waters. They're used all over the Mediterranean but are especially popular in southern Europe, where they appear in dips, sauces, salads, soups, and more, both as a flavoring and as a main ingredient. In recipes like our Provençal-Style Anchovy Dip (left), the anchovies are the star of the recipe and provide potent, briny flavor. But when used more judiciously, the umami-producing glutamates present in anchovies can help to boost savory notes in a dish without adding fishy flavor.

All preserved anchovies have been cured in salt, but they come to the market in two forms: packed in olive oil or in salt. The salt-packed variety is the least processed, having only the heads and some entrails removed, leaving the filleting and rinsing to the home cook. Oil-packed anchovies have been filleted at the factory and are ready to use.

Our favorite brand is King Oscar Anchovies— Flat Fillets in Olive Oil, which have a firm, meaty texture and pleasantly briny, savory flavor.

Skordalia

MAKES about 2 cups VEG

WHY THIS RECIPE WORKS *Skordalia* is a thick and hearty Greek garlic puree that is usually served as a dip or as an accompaniment for fish or vegetables. For our version, we set our sights on a spreadable dip that could work as a versatile appetizer. Since skordalia is made with raw garlic, we needed only three cloves to give the dip potent garlic flavor. Traditional recipes rely on bread, potatoes, nuts, or a combination thereof to create a velvety, thick-textured base. We tested a variety of combinations and found that bread and potato together had the most pleasing texture: luxuriously thick and creamy without being dense or greasy. A single russet potato was all we needed—any more and our dip started to taste like mashed potatoes—and we discovered that boiling produced a better texture than microwaving or baking. Putting the potato through a ricer ensured that it was fluffy and smooth. To keep our recipe streamlined, we tried combining our ingredients in a blender and a food processor, but the high-speed motion of the blades caused the starches in the potato to become gluey and pasty. Mixing the ingredients by hand produced a much better texture. A generous dose of lemon juice brightened the dip nicely (and letting the garlic marinate in the juice tamed its harsh bite), and a little yogurt added creamy richness. A rasp-style grater can be used to turn the garlic into a paste. We prefer the rich flavor of whole-milk yogurt here; however, low-fat yogurt will also work. Do not use nonfat yogurt. Serve with Olive Oil–Sea Salt Pita Chips (page 22), slices of toasted baguette, or raw vegetables.

Bread and potato create a lusciously creamy Greek *skordalia*, while lemon juice tames the raw garlic flavor.

1 (10- to 12-ounce) russet potato, peeled and cut into
  1-inch chunks
3 garlic cloves, minced to paste
3 tablespoons lemon juice
2 slices hearty white sandwich bread, crusts removed,
  torn into 1-inch pieces
6 tablespoons warm water, plus extra as needed
  Salt and pepper
¼ cup extra-virgin olive oil
¼ cup plain Greek yogurt

1. Place potato in small saucepan and add water to cover by 1 inch. Bring water to boil, then reduce to simmer and cook until potato is tender and paring knife can be inserted into potato with no resistance, 15 to 20 minutes. Drain potato in colander, tossing to remove any excess water.

2. Meanwhile, combine garlic and lemon juice in bowl and let sit for 10 minutes. In separate medium bowl, mash bread, ¼ cup warm water, and ½ teaspoon salt into paste with fork.

3. Transfer potato to ricer (food mill fitted with small disk) and process into bowl with bread mixture. Stir in lemon-garlic mixture, oil, yogurt, and remaining 2 tablespoons warm water until well combined. (Sauce can be refrigerated for up to 3 days; bring to room temperature before serving.) Season with salt and pepper to taste and adjust consistency with extra warm water as needed before serving.

Mincing Garlic to a Paste

Mince garlic, then sprinkle with pinch salt. Scrape side of chef's knife blade across garlic, mashing it into cutting board to make sticky garlic paste.

Lavash Crackers

SERVES 10 to 12 `VEG`

WHY THIS RECIPE WORKS Popular in the eastern Mediterranean, traditional lavash is a little bit nutty and a little bit sweet and has a crisp and airy texture perfect for serving with dips. To get just the right flavor and texture, we used a combination of three flours: fine semolina flour, nutty whole-wheat flour, and all-purpose flour. To make the dough, we mixed the flours (and a little salt) in a stand mixer, then gradually added water and oil until the dough was smooth and elastic. Letting the dough rest for an hour made it much easier to roll out. Once the dough had rested, we rolled it out onto oiled baking sheets, pricked it all over with a fork to prevent air bubbles, brushed it with a beaten egg, and sprinkled it with sesame seeds, salt, and pepper. Finally, we baked the crackers until deeply golden brown and let them cool before breaking the large sheets into crispy, crunchy crackers. We prefer the larger crystal size of sea salt or kosher salt here; if using table salt, reduce the amount of salt by half.

1½ cups (8⅝ ounces) semolina flour
¾ cup (4⅛ ounces) whole-wheat flour
¾ cup (3¾ ounces) all-purpose flour
¾ teaspoon salt
1 cup warm water
⅓ cup extra-virgin olive oil, plus extra for brushing
1 large egg, lightly beaten
2 tablespoons sesame seeds
2 teaspoons sea salt or kosher salt
1 teaspoon coarsely ground pepper

1. Using stand mixer fitted with dough hook, mix semolina flour, whole-wheat flour, all-purpose flour, and salt together on low speed. Gradually add water and oil and knead until dough is smooth and elastic, 7 to 9 minutes. Turn dough out onto lightly floured counter and knead by hand to form smooth, round ball. Divide dough into 4 equal pieces, brush with oil, and cover with plastic wrap. Let rest at room temperature for 1 hour.

2. Adjust oven racks to upper-middle and lower-middle positions and heat oven to 425 degrees. Lightly coat two 18 by 13-inch rimless (or inverted) baking sheets with vegetable oil spray.

3. Working with 2 pieces of dough (keep remaining dough covered with plastic), press dough into small rectangles, then transfer to prepared sheets. Using rolling pin and hands, roll and stretch dough evenly to edges of sheet. Using fork, poke holes in

doughs at 2-inch intervals. Brush doughs with beaten egg, then sprinkle each with 1½ teaspoons sesame seeds, ½ teaspoon salt, and ¼ teaspoon pepper. Press gently on seasonings to help them adhere.

4. Bake crackers until deeply golden brown, 15 to 18 minutes, switching and rotating sheets halfway through baking. Transfer crackers to wire rack and let cool completely. Let baking sheets cool completely before rolling out and baking remaining dough. Break cooled lavash into large crackers and serve. (Lavash can be stored at room temperature for up to 2 weeks.)

Making Lavash Crackers

1. ROLL DOUGH Using rolling pin and hands, roll and stretch 1 piece of dough evenly to edges of sheet.

2. PRICK DOUGH Using fork, poke holes in dough at 2-inch intervals to prevent air bubbles.

3. SEASON DOUGH Brush dough with beaten egg and sprinkle with 1½ teaspoons sesame seeds, ½ teaspoon salt, and ¼ teaspoon pepper, pressing gently to help seasonings adhere.

4. BREAK CRACKERS Once lavash is baked and cooled, break crackers into large pieces using hands.

Marinated Green and Black Olives

SERVES 8 VEG

WHY THIS RECIPE WORKS Homemade marinated olives are simple to make and taste far better than store-bought. Our first task was to choose what type of olives to use. We opted for olives with pits, which have better flavor than pitted ones, and found that tasters preferred brine-cured olives to salt-cured for their subtler flavors. A combination of black and green olives boosted visual appeal. As for the marinade, we found that ¾ cup of good olive oil was just enough to cover the olives without drowning them. Shallot and garlic offered balanced aromatic flavor, and some lemon zest provided a subtle citrus note. Fresh thyme and oregano gave the marinade a fresh, herbal flavor, and a dash of red pepper flakes brought everything into focus. Since our marinated olives were so simple, we also developed a couple of flavorful variations that combined the olives with milky fresh mozzarella and salty feta. Make sure to bring the mixture to room temperature before serving or the oil will look cloudy and congealed. Serve with toothpicks and a thinly sliced baguette or crackers.

    1 cup brine-cured green olives with pits
    1 cup brine-cured black olives with pits
    ¾ cup extra-virgin olive oil
    1 shallot, minced
    1 garlic clove, minced
    2 teaspoons grated lemon zest
    2 teaspoons minced fresh thyme
    2 teaspoons minced fresh oregano
    ½ teaspoon red pepper flakes
    ½ teaspoon salt

Rinse olives thoroughly, then drain and pat dry with paper towels. Toss olives with remaining ingredients in bowl, cover, and refrigerate for at least 4 hours or up to 4 days. Let sit at room temperature for at least 30 minutes before serving.

VARIATIONS

Marinated Olives with Baby Mozzarella VEG

Reduce amount of black and green olives to ½ cup each. Substitute 1 tablespoon shredded fresh basil for oregano. Add 8 ounces fresh mozzarella balls (*bocconcini*), cut into ½-inch pieces (2 cups), to olive mixture.

Marinated Green Olives with Feta VEG

Omit black olives and fresh thyme. Substitute orange zest for lemon zest. Add 8 ounces feta cheese, cut into ½-inch cubes (2 cups), to olive mixture.

NOTES FROM THE TEST KITCHEN
All About Olives

BRINE-CURED VERSUS SALT-CURED

Olives are an important part of nearly every cuisine in the Mediterranean. Jarred olives come in three basic types at the supermarket: brine-cured green, brine-cured black, and salt-cured black (often labeled "oil-cured"). Brine-cured olives are soaked in a salt solution for periods of up to a year to remove bitterness and develop flavor. Salt-cured olives are packed in salt until nearly all their liquid has been extracted, then covered in oil to be replumped. Both processes traditionally take weeks or even months. Generally we find that brine-cured black and green olives can be used interchangeably in any recipe based on personal preference. Among our test cooks, only a few olive aficionados favored the concentrated, bitter taste of salt-cured olives—we don't recommend cooking with them unless a recipe specifically calls for them. And as for canned olives? We avoid them entirely, finding them almost tasteless, with a firm yet oddly slippery texture.

GREEN OLIVES

Often labeled "Spanish" olives, green olives are picked before they fully ripen, and their mild flavor adds a bright, acidic dimension to food. Manzanillas, produced in Spain and California, are the pimento-stuffed olives best known for garnishing martinis. Add these olives at the end of cooking to avoid bitterness.

BLACK OLIVES

Picked when mature, black olives lend a more robust, fruity taste. The most common types are kalamata olives, which have an earthy flavor and creamy flesh, and niçoise olives, which boast an assertive, somewhat bitter flavor. We prefer the fresher kalamatas from the refrigerator section of the supermarket; the jarred shelf-stable ones are bland and mushy in comparison. If you can't find kalamatas in the refrigerator section of your market, look for them at the salad bar.

PITTED VERSUS UNPITTED

Pitted olives are certainly convenient, but they lack the complex, fruity flavors of unpitted olives and often have a mushier texture. After being brined for up to a year, the pitted olives are returned to the brine for packing, which can penetrate the inside of the olive and turn it mushy and pasty, as well as increase the absorption of salt. That saltier taste can mask subtler flavors. If you have the time, we recommend that you buy unpitted olives and pit them yourself.

Marinated Cauliflower and Chickpeas with Saffron

SERVES 6 to 8 `VEG`

WHY THIS RECIPE WORKS The small portions in tapas demand big flavor in every bite, so we set out to enliven creamy chickpeas and earthy cauliflower in a bold, Spanish-inspired marinade. First we blanched the cauliflower, softening it so that it would readily absorb the dressing. We established the marinade's base by blooming saffron in hot water to coax out more of its distinct, complex flavors. Heating smashed garlic cloves in olive oil infused the oil with flavor and tamed the garlic's harsh edge. Along with the saffron, smoked paprika and a sprig of rosemary gave the marinade a vibrant brick-red hue and earthy, aromatic flavor. Thin slices of lemon lent bright citrus flavor and made for a pretty presentation. We stirred together our marinade, adding the saffron and flavor-enhancing sherry vinegar (a go-to ingredient in Spanish cuisine) off the heat. Canned chickpeas were a time-savvy choice, promising reliably tender beans without the wait. We combined our marinade with the chickpeas and cauliflower and let the mixture rest in the refrigerator, allowing the flavors to meld and deepen. The chickpeas and cauliflower emerged with a golden hue, brimming with deep, complex flavor. Use a small sprig of rosemary, or its flavor will be overpowering. Garlic will soften over time. This dish can be served cold or at room temperature.

½ head cauliflower (1 pound), cored and cut into
  1-inch florets
  Salt and pepper
⅛ teaspoon saffron threads, crumbled
⅓ cup extra-virgin olive oil
5 garlic cloves, peeled and smashed
1½ teaspoons sugar
1½ teaspoons smoked paprika
1 small sprig fresh rosemary
2 tablespoons sherry vinegar
1 cup canned chickpeas, rinsed
½ lemon, sliced thin
1 tablespoon minced fresh parsley

1. Bring 2 quarts water to boil in large saucepan. Add cauliflower and 1 tablespoon salt and cook until florets begin to soften, about 3 minutes. Drain florets and transfer to paper towel–lined baking sheet.

2. Combine ¼ cup hot water and saffron in bowl; set aside. Heat oil and garlic in small saucepan over medium-low heat until fragrant and beginning to sizzle but not brown, 4 to 6 minutes. Stir in sugar, paprika, and rosemary and cook until fragrant, about 30 seconds. Off heat, stir in saffron mixture, vinegar, 1½ teaspoons salt, and ¼ teaspoon pepper.

For this Spanish-inspired tapas dish, we infuse cauliflower and chickpeas with a complex, saffron-scented marinade.

3. Combine florets, saffron mixture, chickpeas, and lemon in large bowl. Cover and refrigerate, stirring occasionally, for at least 4 hours or up to 3 days. To serve, discard rosemary sprig, transfer cauliflower and chickpeas to serving bowl with slotted spoon, and sprinkle with parsley.

NOTES FROM THE TEST KITCHEN
Paprika Primer

"Paprika" is a generic term for a spice made from ground dried red peppers. Whether paprika is labeled sweet, smoked, or hot is determined by the variety (or varieties) of pepper used and how the pepper is manipulated. Sweet paprika (sometimes called "Hungarian paprika" or simply "paprika") is made from a combination of mild red peppers and is prized more for its deep scarlet hue than for its subtle flavor; our favorite brand is The Spice House Hungarian Sweet Paprika. Smoked paprika, a Spanish favorite, is produced by drying peppers (either sweet or hot) over smoldering oak embers; we like Simply Organic. We don't often use hot paprika, as heat levels between brands can vary widely.

Marinated Artichokes

SERVES 6 to 8 `VEG`

WHY THIS RECIPE WORKS Marinated artichokes have so many uses that they should be considered a pantry staple; they're perfect for everything from throwing on pizzas, to tossing into a salad or pasta, to eating on an antipasto platter. But store-bought versions tend to be mushy and bland—and expensive. We set out to make our own recipe for easy, inexpensive, and boldly flavorful marinated artichokes. To get the best tender-yet-meaty texture and sweet, nutty artichoke flavor, we started with fresh baby artichokes. We simmered them gently in olive oil with strips of lemon zest, garlic, red pepper flakes, and thyme, then let them sit off the heat until they were perfectly fork-tender and infused with the aromatic flavors. Then we stirred in fresh lemon juice and more zest, minced garlic, and mint before transferring the artichokes to a bowl and topping them with the infused oil for serving and storage.

Simmering baby artichokes in their aromatic marinade before storing them gives them bright and balanced flavor.

2 lemons
2½ cups extra-virgin olive oil
3 pounds baby artichokes (2 to 4 ounces each)
8 garlic cloves, peeled, 6 cloves smashed, 2 cloves minced
¼ teaspoon red pepper flakes
2 sprigs fresh thyme
Salt and pepper
2 tablespoons minced fresh mint

1. Using vegetable peeler, remove three 2-inch strips zest from 1 lemon. Grate ½ teaspoon zest from second lemon and set aside. Halve and juice lemons to yield ¼ cup juice, reserving spent lemon halves.

2. Combine oil and lemon zest strips in large saucepan. Working with 1 artichoke at a time, cut top quarter off each artichoke, snap off outer leaves, and trim away dark parts. Peel and trim stem, then cut artichoke in half lengthwise (quarter artichoke if large). Rub each artichoke half with spent lemon half and place in saucepan.

3. Add smashed garlic, pepper flakes, thyme sprigs, 1 teaspoon salt, and ¼ teaspoon pepper to saucepan and bring to rapid simmer over high heat. Reduce heat to medium-low and simmer, stirring occasionally to submerge all artichokes, until artichokes can be pierced with fork but are still firm, about 5 minutes.

Prepping Baby Artichokes

1. Using chef's knife, cut off top quarter of each artichoke.

2. Snap off tough outer leaves; trim any remaining dark parts using paring knife.

3. Using paring knife, peel stem and trim end.

4. Once trimmed, cut artichoke in half.

Remove from heat, cover, and let sit until artichokes are fork-tender and fully cooked, about 20 minutes.

4. Gently stir in ½ teaspoon reserved grated lemon zest, ¼ cup reserved lemon juice, and minced garlic. Transfer artichokes and oil to serving bowl and let cool to room temperature. Season with salt to taste and sprinkle with mint. Serve. (Artichokes and oil can be refrigerated for up to 4 days.)

Giardiniera

MAKES four 1-pint jars `VEG`

WHY THIS RECIPE WORKS In Italy, *giardiniera* refers to pickled vegetables that are typically eaten as an antipasto. Many versions in the United States consist of a combination of pickled cauliflower, carrots, celery, and sweet and hot peppers—the perfect tangy, spicy foil to rich meats and cheeses. But grocery store versions tend to fall flat, with too-salty brines and washed-out flavors. To make our own quick-pickled version (no sterilization required), we prepped the vegetables, transferred them to jars, and topped them with a hot, flavorful brine. Once the jars were cool, we simply refrigerated them until the vegetables had absorbed the traditional pickling flavors: garlic, dill, sugar, salt, and mild white wine vinegar.

½ head cauliflower (1 pound), cored and cut into ½-inch florets
3 carrots, peeled and sliced ¼ inch thick on bias
3 celery ribs, cut crosswise into ½-inch pieces
1 red bell pepper, stemmed, seeded, and cut into ½-inch-wide strips
2 serrano chiles, stemmed and sliced thin
4 garlic cloves, sliced thin
1 cup chopped fresh dill
2¾ cups white wine vinegar
2¼ cups water
¼ cup sugar
2 tablespoons salt

1. Combine cauliflower, carrots, celery, bell pepper, serranos, and garlic in large bowl, then transfer to four 1-pint jars with tight-fitting lids.

2. Bundle dill in cheesecloth and tie with kitchen twine to secure. Bring dill sachet, vinegar, water, sugar, and salt to boil in large saucepan over medium-high heat. Remove from heat and let steep for 10 minutes. Discard dill sachet.

A hot brine redolent with traditional pickling flavors makes a quick and well-seasoned *giardiniera*.

3. Return brine to brief boil, then pour evenly over vegetables. Let cool to room temperature, then cover and refrigerate until vegetables taste pickled, at least 7 days or up to 1 month.

Cutting Up a Bell Pepper

1. Slice off top and bottom of pepper and remove seeds and stem. Slice down through side of pepper.

2. Lay pepper flat and trim away remaining ribs and seeds. Cut pepper into ½-inch-wide strips.

For our homemade yogurt cheese, we strain plain yogurt through coffee filters; simple stir-ins make great creamy dips.

Yogurt Cheese
MAKES about 1 cup   VEG

WHY THIS RECIPE WORKS Yogurt cheese, also called *labneh*, is not really a cheese at all; rather, it is yogurt that has been strained to remove its whey, giving it a thick, lush consistency and a rich, tangy flavor. Often eaten in the eastern Mediterranean, it can be used plain or mixed with a few simple flavorings to make a light, fresh dip or spread for bread or vegetables. Yogurt cheese couldn't be easier to make at home, requiring only one ingredient and a couple of hours of hands-off time. To end up with about 1 cup of yogurt cheese, we started with 2 cups of traditional yogurt. A strainer lined with several coffee filters or a double layer of cheesecloth was ideal for allowing the whey to drain off. After about 10 hours, a full cup of whey had drained off, leaving us with velvety strained yogurt. Though the tangy yogurt cheese was a treat on its own, we also created a couple of flavorful variations: a bright combination of lemon zest and fresh dill and a sweeter variation made with chopped walnuts and honey. Both regular and low-fat yogurt will work well here; do not use nonfat yogurt. Avoid yogurts containing modified food starch, gelatin, or gums since they prevent the yogurt from draining.

2 cups plain yogurt

1. Line fine-mesh strainer with 3 basket-style coffee filters or double layer of cheesecloth. Set strainer over large measuring cup or bowl (there should be enough room for about 1 cup liquid to drain without touching strainer).

2. Spoon yogurt into strainer, cover tightly with plastic wrap, and refrigerate until yogurt has released about 1 cup liquid and has creamy, cream cheese–like texture, at least 10 hours or up to 2 days.

3. Transfer drained yogurt to clean container; discard liquid. Serve. (Yogurt can be refrigerated for up to 2 days.)

VARIATIONS
Lemon-Dill Yogurt Cheese   VEG
After yogurt cheese has drained, stir in 1 tablespoon minced fresh dill, 2 teaspoons grated lemon zest, ⅛ teaspoon salt, and pinch pepper. Cover and refrigerate until flavors have blended, about 1 hour. Season with salt and pepper to taste before serving.

Honey-Walnut Yogurt Cheese   VEG
After yogurt cheese has drained, stir in 3 tablespoons toasted chopped walnuts, 1 tablespoon honey, and ⅛ teaspoon salt. Cover and refrigerate until flavors have blended, about 1 hour. Season with salt and pepper to taste before serving.

NOTES FROM THE TEST KITCHEN
All About Yogurt
Yogurt is integral to many a Mediterranean dish—from Greek *tzatziki* sauce to Turkish yogurt soups. The word *yogurt* comes from the Turkish word for "condense." To make a basic yogurt, milk is heated and then cooled to just over 100 degrees before a bacteria culture is added. After 4 to 8 hours, the mixture thickens into yogurt. In the Mediterranean, yogurt is often made with sheep's milk, which has a high fat content and makes for a rich, creamy yogurt. In the United States, you're more likely to find yogurt made from cow's (or, sometimes, goat's) milk.

Greek-style yogurt is thicker and creamier than standard yogurt because most of its whey, the watery liquid found in yogurt, is strained out during production. Additionally, it's tangier and has more than twice the fat of regular yogurt. It works well in applications where a velvety, substantial texture is desirable, such as Skordalia (page 24).

Labneh, or yogurt cheese, is the thickest form of strained yogurt. It's often served as part of a meze spread and can be used plain, drizzled with olive oil, or flavored simply with herbs. To make your own yogurt cheese, see our recipe (left).

Spicy Whipped Feta with Roasted Red Peppers

MAKES about 2 cups `FAST` `VEG`

WHY THIS RECIPE WORKS Known in Greece as *htipiti*, this classic meze dish is appealingly simple: Tangy, salty feta cheese is processed to a smooth consistency along with roasted red peppers to make a rich yet light dip. Jarred roasted red peppers offered big flavor with minimal effort. To keep the flavor profile streamlined, we kept the additional flavors simple and straightforward. A hefty dose of cayenne pepper gave the dip a well-rounded heat. Olive oil imparted fruity notes and some richness, and bright lemon juice balanced the saltiness of the cheese. This dip is fairly spicy; to make it less spicy, reduce the amount of cayenne to ¼ teaspoon. Our favorite brand of feta cheese is Mt. Vikos Traditional Feta. Serve with our Olive Oil–Sea Salt Pita Chips (page 22), fresh warm pita, or raw vegetables.

8 ounces feta cheese, crumbled (2 cups)
1 cup jarred roasted red peppers, rinsed, patted dry, and chopped
⅓ cup extra-virgin olive oil, plus extra for serving
1 tablespoon lemon juice
½ teaspoon cayenne pepper
¼ teaspoon pepper

Process feta, red peppers, oil, lemon juice, cayenne, and pepper in food processor until smooth, about 30 seconds, scraping down sides of bowl as needed. Transfer mixture to serving bowl, drizzle with extra oil to taste, and serve. (Dip can be refrigerated for up to 2 days; bring to room temperature before serving.)

Broiled Feta with Olive Oil and Parsley

SERVES 8 to 12 `FAST` `VEG`

WHY THIS RECIPE WORKS We wanted to create an appetizer that would make warm, briny feta cheese the star. We decided to call on the intense heat of the broiler to create a browned exterior on the feta. To keep things simple, we patted ½-inch-thick slabs of feta dry, which encouraged maximum browning. We seasoned the cheese with red pepper flakes and pepper to balance the richness of the cheese. A drizzle of olive oil and a shower of fresh parsley completed our simple appetizer. Broilers can vary in strength dramatically, so use our cooking times as guidelines and check the feta often as it cooks. Slicing the feta into ½-inch-thick slabs is crucial; if sliced thinner, the cheese will crumble, but if sliced thicker, it will not heat through. Be sure to buy a large block of feta so that you can easily slice it into thick slabs. Serve with Olive Oil–Sea Salt Pita Chips (page 22) or fresh warm pita.

The broiler easily transforms thick slices of briny feta cheese into an impressive appetizer.

2 (8-ounce) blocks feta cheese, sliced into ½-inch-thick slabs
¼ teaspoon red pepper flakes
¼ teaspoon pepper
2 tablespoons extra-virgin olive oil
2 teaspoons minced fresh parsley

Adjust oven rack 4 inches from broiler element and heat broiler. Pat feta dry with paper towels and arrange in broiler-safe gratin dish. Sprinkle with red pepper flakes and pepper. Broil until edges of cheese are golden, 3 to 8 minutes. Drizzle with oil, sprinkle with parsley, and serve immediately.

NOTES FROM THE TEST KITCHEN

Buying Feta

In Greece, feta must be made from at least 70 percent sheep's milk. In the United States, this rule doesn't apply, so imitators abound; we found that none of them could beat the real deal. Our favorite brand, Mt. Vikos Traditional Feta, is from Greece and boasts plenty of tang with just enough salt.

Pan-Fried Halloumi

SERVES 6 to 8 `FAST` `VEG`

WHY THIS RECIPE WORKS Named for the small frying pan traditionally used to prepare this dish, Greek *saganaki* is an appetizer made by pan-searing slabs of firm cheese. We chose to create a version using halloumi. To achieve the classic crisp, browned exterior that would offer a satisfying contrast to the chewy interior, we tried pan frying the halloumi plain and dusted with flour, bread crumbs, and cornmeal. A combination of stone-ground cornmeal and a little all-purpose flour provided just the right golden-brown, textured crust. A squeeze of bright lemon juice offered welcome tang. To make a slightly more dressed-up version, we made a quick sauce with thinly sliced garlic, fresh parsley, and red pepper flakes to drizzle over the top. The pan-fried halloumi also tastes great with a drizzle of honey.

- 2 tablespoons cornmeal
- 1 tablespoon all-purpose flour
- 1 (8-ounce) block halloumi cheese, sliced into ½-inch-thick slabs
- 2 tablespoons extra-virgin olive oil
  Lemon wedges

1. Combine cornmeal and flour in shallow dish. Working with 1 piece of cheese at a time, coat both wide sides with cornmeal mixture, pressing to help coating adhere; transfer to plate.

2. Heat oil in 12-inch nonstick skillet over medium heat until shimmering. Arrange halloumi in single layer in skillet and cook until golden brown on both sides, 2 to 4 minutes per side. Transfer to platter and serve with lemon wedges.

NOTES FROM THE TEST KITCHEN

Getting to Know Halloumi

This brined cheese is originally from Cyprus but is now popular throughout the eastern Mediterranean. Made from cow's, sheep's, or goat's milk (or even a combination of the three), it has an elastic quality that is similar to that of mozzarella, but firmer and more dense. Its dairy flavor is mild, and it is typically quite salty. You will often find it packed in brine and sold in blocks.

Because of how it's made, halloumi has a very strong protein network, which means that when it's heated, it softens but doesn't melt. Many recipes, like our recipe for Pan-Fried Halloumi (above), take advantage of this quality by calling for pan frying or grilling cubes or slabs of the cheese, which gives it a crispy, flavorful exterior to contrast with the creamy interior.

Thanks to its high melting point, rich, salty halloumi cheese is ideal for pan-frying to a crisp golden brown.

VARIATION

Pan-Fried Halloumi with Garlic-Parsley Sauce

`FAST` `VEG`

After frying halloumi, discard oil left in skillet and wipe out skillet with paper towels. Add 2 tablespoons extra-virgin olive oil to now-empty skillet and heat over medium heat until shimmering. Add 1 thinly sliced garlic clove, 2 tablespoons chopped fresh parsley, and ¼ teaspoon red pepper flakes and cook until garlic is golden brown and fragrant, about 1 minute. Drizzle oil mixture over pan-fried halloumi and serve with lemon wedges.

Slicing Halloumi

Slice block of halloumi crosswise into ½-inch-thick slabs.

BRUSCHETTA

This classic Italian antipasto starts with slices of simple toasted garlic bread. A combination of chopped tomatoes and olive oil is the most traditional topping, but there are endless variations. Here are a few of our favorites.

Toasted Bread for Bruschetta

SERVES 8 to 10 FAST VEG

Toast the bread just before assembling the bruschetta.

- 1 (10 by 5-inch) loaf country bread with thick crust, ends discarded, sliced crosswise into ¾-inch-thick pieces
- 1 garlic clove, peeled
  Extra-virgin olive oil
  Salt

Adjust oven rack 4 inches from broiler element and heat broiler. Place bread on aluminum foil–lined baking sheet. Broil until bread is deep golden and toasted on both sides, 1 to 2 minutes per side. Lightly rub 1 side of each toast with garlic (you will not use all of garlic). Brush with oil and season with salt to taste.

Bruschetta with Arugula Pesto and Goat Cheese

SERVES 8 to 10 FAST VEG

- 5 ounces (5 cups) baby arugula
- ¼ cup extra-virgin olive oil, plus extra for serving
- ¼ cup pine nuts, toasted
- 1 tablespoon minced shallot
- 1 teaspoon grated lemon zest plus 1 teaspoon juice
  Salt and pepper
- 1 recipe Toasted Bread for Bruschetta
- 2 ounces goat cheese, crumbled

Pulse arugula, oil, pine nuts, shallot, lemon zest and juice, ½ teaspoon salt, and ¼ teaspoon pepper in food processor until mostly smooth, about 8 pulses, scraping down sides of bowl as needed. Spread arugula mixture evenly on toasts, top with goat cheese, and drizzle with extra oil to taste. Serve.

Bruschetta with Ricotta, Tomatoes, and Basil

SERVES 8 to 10 FAST VEG

We prefer the rich flavor of whole-milk ricotta; however, part-skim ricotta can be substituted. Do not use fat-free ricotta.

- 1 pound cherry tomatoes, quartered
  Salt and pepper
- 1 tablespoon extra-virgin olive oil, plus extra for serving
- 5 tablespoons shredded fresh basil
- 10 ounces whole-milk ricotta cheese
- 1 recipe Toasted Bread for Bruschetta

Toss tomatoes with 1 teaspoon salt in colander and let drain for 15 minutes. Transfer drained tomatoes to bowl, toss with oil and ¼ cup basil, and season with salt and pepper to taste. In separate bowl, combine ricotta with remaining 1 tablespoon basil and season with salt and pepper to taste. Spread ricotta mixture evenly on toasts, top with tomato mixture, and drizzle lightly with extra oil to taste. Serve.

Bruschetta with Black Olive Pesto, Ricotta, and Basil

SERVES 8 to 10 FAST VEG

We prefer the rich flavor of whole-milk ricotta; however, part-skim ricotta can be substituted. Do not use fat-free ricotta.

- ¾ cup pitted kalamata olives
- 1 small shallot, minced
- 2 tablespoons extra-virgin olive oil, plus extra for serving
- 1½ teaspoons lemon juice
- 1 garlic clove, minced
- 10 ounces whole-milk ricotta cheese
  Salt and pepper
- 1 recipe Toasted Bread for Bruschetta
- 2 tablespoons shredded fresh basil

Pulse olives, shallot, oil, lemon juice, and garlic in food processor until coarsely chopped, about 10 pulses, scraping down sides of bowl as needed. Season ricotta with salt and pepper to taste. Spread ricotta mixture evenly on toasts, top with olive mixture, and drizzle with extra oil to taste. Sprinkle with basil before serving.

Bruschetta with Artichoke Hearts and Parmesan

SERVES 8 to 10 FAST VEG

While we prefer the flavor and texture of jarred whole baby artichoke hearts, you can substitute 6 ounces frozen artichoke hearts, thawed and patted dry, for the jarred.

- 1 cup jarred whole baby artichoke hearts packed in water, rinsed and patted dry
- 2 tablespoons extra-virgin olive oil, plus extra for serving
- 2 tablespoons chopped fresh basil
- 2 teaspoons lemon juice
- 1 garlic clove, minced
  Salt and pepper
- 2 ounces Parmesan cheese, 1 ounce grated fine, 1 ounce shaved
- 1 recipe Toasted Bread for Bruschetta

Pulse artichoke hearts, oil, basil, lemon juice, garlic, ¼ teaspoon salt, and ¼ teaspoon pepper in food processor until coarsely pureed, about 6 pulses, scraping down sides of bowl as needed. Add grated Parmesan and pulse to combine, about 2 pulses. Spread artichoke mixture evenly on toasts and top with shaved Parmesan. Season with pepper to taste, and drizzle with extra oil to taste. Serve.

We stuff sweet dates with a mixture of chopped walnuts and parsley before wrapping them with buttery prosciutto.

Prosciutto-Wrapped Stuffed Dates

SERVES 6 to 8 FAST

WHY THIS RECIPE WORKS Combining sweet, savory, and salty into one bite-size morsel, stuffed dates make a perfect addition to any appetizer spread. To balance the deep sweetness of the dates, we looked to ultrasavory prosciutto. We wanted to streamline the stuffing as much as possible, so we tried combining the prosciutto with walnuts and parsley in a food processor. We quickly learned that this method wouldn't work; our pricey prosciutto was all but unrecognizable, and the walnut pieces were too small to lend any real texture. We decided instead to wrap the prosciutto around the stuffed dates. This put the prosciutto in the spotlight while still allowing the sweetness of the dates to shine through. As for the stuffing, we found that chopping the walnuts and parsley by hand gave us more control over the final texture of the filling and yielded the best consistency. Orange zest brightened the flavor nicely, and just a bit of olive oil helped bind the mixture together. The stuffing served as a nutty, crunchy counterpoint to the soft, sweet dates and, as an added benefit,

came together in just minutes. High-quality dates and prosciutto are essential to the success of this recipe. Look for dates that are fresh, plump, and juicy; skip over any that look withered or dry. We prefer Medjool dates for this recipe, as they are particularly sweet with a dense texture.

⅔ cup walnuts, toasted and chopped fine
½ cup minced fresh parsley
2 tablespoons extra-virgin olive oil
½ teaspoon grated orange zest
Salt and pepper
12 large pitted dates, halved lengthwise
12 thin slices prosciutto, halved lengthwise

Combine walnuts, parsley, oil, and orange zest in bowl and season with salt and pepper to taste. Mound 1 generous teaspoon filling into center of each date half. Wrap prosciutto securely around dates. Serve. (Dates can be refrigerated for up to 8 hours; bring to room temperature before serving.)

VARIATION

Prosciutto-Wrapped Stuffed Dates with Pistachios and Balsamic Vinegar FAST
Omit orange zest. Substitute ⅔ cup shelled pistachios for walnuts and ¼ cup shredded fresh basil for parsley. Reduce olive oil to 1 tablespoon and add 1 tablespoon balsamic vinegar to nut mixture.

Assembling Prosciutto-Wrapped Dates

1. Mound 1 generous teaspoon filling into center of each date half.

2. Wrap prosciutto securely around date, leaving date ends uncovered.

All About Prosciutto

Italians have been making prosciutto for nearly 2,000 years, most notably in Parma. This city in Emilia-Romagna at the top of Italy's boot is still at it, making Italy's most famous version, Prosciutto di Parma, under the eye of an official consortium that sears Parma's five-pointed crown brand onto every approved ham. Next most renowned: Prosciutto di San Daniele, from the Friuli region in Italy's northeast, with its own consortium and brand shaped like a leg of ham. Both are designated "PDO" by the European Union—Protected Denomination of Origin—meaning that they are exceptional regional products, with exclusive rights to their particular names.

Prosciutto crudo ("raw ham"), as it's called in Italian, is never smoked or cooked. Producers in both regions use the same basic curing method: After slaughtering pigs, they salt and hang the legs for a minimum of 12 months. The meat's flavor concentrates with age, as prosciutto loses up to 30 percent of its weight in moisture during curing. This process gives the prosciutto its signature silky, dense texture and nutty flavor.

If you can't find authentic Italian prosciutto, never fear: In taste tests, we found that Volpi, which is made in Missouri and sold in vacuum-sealed packages at supermarkets, is a viable alternative. They use a series of climate-controlled chambers designed to replicate the curing conditions in northern Italy, which gives the prosciutto a rich, buttery flavor and supple texture.

Stuffed Grape Leaves

MAKES 24 VEG

WHY THIS RECIPE WORKS Stuffed grape leaves, known in Greece as *dolmathes*, should boast seasoned, tender leaves wrapped around a flavorful rice filling, but too often, store-bought versions are drowning in oil and suffer from mushy leaves and overcooked rice. To develop a foolproof recipe that turned out perfect stuffed grape leaves every time, we started with the leaves themselves. Not wanting to be restricted by seasonality, we chose to use jarred grape leaves instead of fresh. Since the jarred leaves were packed in brine, we needed to figure out a way to tame their flavor before using them; blanching them briefly in boiling water did the trick. As for the filling, tasters preferred the slight stickiness of short-grain rice to the texture of long-grain rice. Parcooking the rice before filling the leaves ensured that it would cook to the perfect doneness as the rolled leaves steamed. We chose to simmer the stuffed grape leaves in a skillet since they fit nicely in a single layer; a bit of lemon juice added to the steaming water gave the leaves tangy flavor. Lining the bottom of the skillet with the extra, unused grape leaves ensured that the stuffed leaves were not in direct contact with the heat, preventing scorching. We've had good luck using Peloponnese and Krinos brand grape leaves. Larger grape leaves can be trimmed to 6 inches, and smaller leaves can be overlapped to achieve the correct size. Take care when handling the grape leaves; they can be delicate and easily tear. Long-grain rice can be substituted for short-grain in this recipe, but the filling will not be as cohesive.

1   (16-ounce) jar grape leaves
2   tablespoons extra-virgin olive oil, plus extra for serving
1   large onion, chopped fine
    Salt and pepper
¾   cup short-grain white rice
⅓   cup chopped fresh dill
¼   cup chopped fresh mint
1½ tablespoons grated lemon zest plus 2 tablespoons juice

1. Reserve 24 intact grape leaves, roughly 6 inches in diameter; set aside remaining leaves. Bring 6 cups water to boil in medium saucepan. Add reserved grape leaves and cook for 1 minute. Gently drain leaves and transfer to bowl of cold water to cool, about 5 minutes. Drain again, then transfer leaves to plate and cover loosely with plastic wrap.

2. Heat oil in now-empty saucepan over medium heat until shimmering. Add onion and ½ teaspoon salt and cook until softened and lightly browned, 5 to 7 minutes. Add rice and cook, stirring frequently, until grain edges begin to turn translucent, about 2 minutes. Stir in ¾ cup water and bring to boil. Reduce heat to low, cover, and simmer gently until rice is tender but still firm in center and water has been absorbed, 10 to 12 minutes. Off heat, let rice cool slightly, about 10 minutes. Stir in dill, mint, and lemon zest. (Blanched grape leaves and filling can be refrigerated for up to 24 hours.)

3. Place 1 blanched leaf smooth side down on counter with stem facing you. Remove stem from base of leaf by cutting along both sides of stem to form narrow triangle. Pat leaf dry with paper towels. Overlap cut ends of leaf to prevent any filling from spilling out. Place heaping tablespoon filling ¼ inch from bottom of leaf where ends overlap. Fold bottom over filling and fold in sides. Roll leaf tightly around filling to create tidy roll. Repeat with remaining blanched leaves and filling.

4. Line 12-inch skillet with single layer of remaining leaves. Place rolled leaves seam side down in tight rows in prepared skillet. Combine 1¼ cups water and lemon juice, add to skillet, and bring to simmer over medium heat. Cover, reduce heat to medium-low, and simmer until water is almost completely absorbed and leaves and rice are tender and cooked through, 45 minutes to 1 hour.

5. Transfer stuffed grape leaves to serving platter and let cool to room temperature, about 30 minutes; discard leaves in skillet. Drizzle with extra oil before serving.

VARIATION

Stuffed Grape Leaves with Currants and Pine Nuts VEG

Omit dill and lemon juice. In step 2, add 1½ teaspoons ground allspice and ¼ teaspoon ground cinnamon to cooked onions, and add ¼ cup toasted pine nuts and ¼ cup currants to cooled rice. Increase water in step 4 to 1⅓ cups.

Assembling Grape Leaves

1. Place 1 blanched leaf, smooth side down, on counter. Remove any thick stem from base of grape leaf by cutting along both sides of rib to form narrow triangle.

2. Overlap ends of leaf to prevent any filling from spilling out.

3. Place 1 heaping tablespoon filling ¼ inch from bottom of leaf where ends overlap.

4. Fold bottom over filling and fold in sides. Roll leaf tightly around filling to create tidy roll. Repeat with remaining filling and reserved blanched leaves.

Sizzling Garlic Shrimp
SERVES 8

WHY THIS RECIPE WORKS This classic tapas restaurant dish is known for its dramatic entrances: The potent aroma of garlic and the sound of the sizzling shrimp precede its arrival. For an equally impressive and flavorful version that we could make at home, we began by briefly marinating the shrimp with garlic, olive oil, and salt. Soaking the shrimp for at least half an hour allowed the flavors to permeate completely. Next, we focused on the cooking oil. We infused the oil with fragrant flavor by heating smashed cloves in the oil, then fried up slices of garlic for a crunchy contrast to the shrimp. A bay leaf contributed a savory boost, and dried chile added mild heat. With the flavor down, we introduced the shrimp, cooking them gently before ramping up the heat to achieve a lively sizzle. A splash of sherry vinegar and minced parsley added before the skillet left the stove offered a fresh, tangy finish. You can substitute ¼ teaspoon paprika for the dried chile if necessary. For a true sizzling effect, transfer the cooked shrimp mixture to an 8-inch cast-iron skillet that has been heated for 2 minutes over medium-high heat just before serving. Serve with crusty bread for dipping in the richly flavored olive oil.

  1 pound medium-large shrimp (31 to 40 per pound), peeled, deveined, and tails removed
14 garlic cloves, peeled, 2 cloves minced, 12 cloves left whole
  ½ cup extra-virgin olive oil
  ¼ teaspoon salt
  1 bay leaf
  1 (2-inch) piece mild dried chile, roughly broken, with seeds
1½ teaspoons sherry vinegar
  1 tablespoon minced fresh parsley

1. Toss shrimp with minced garlic, 2 tablespoons oil, and salt in bowl and let marinate at room temperature for at least 30 minutes or up to 1 hour.

2. Meanwhile, using flat side of chef's knife, smash 4 garlic cloves. Heat smashed garlic and remaining 6 tablespoons oil in 12-inch skillet over medium-low heat, stirring occasionally, until garlic is light golden brown, 4 to 7 minutes; let oil cool to room temperature. Using slotted spoon, remove and discard smashed garlic.

3. Thinly slice remaining 8 garlic cloves. Return skillet with cooled oil to low heat and add sliced garlic, bay leaf, and chile. Cook, stirring occasionally, until garlic is tender but not browned, 4 to 7 minutes. (If garlic has not begun to sizzle after 3 minutes, increase heat to medium-low.)

4. Increase heat to medium-low and add shrimp with marinade. Cook, without stirring, until oil starts to bubble gently, about

2 minutes. Using tongs, flip shrimp and continue to cook until almost cooked through, about 2 minutes. Increase heat to high and add vinegar and parsley. Cook, stirring constantly, until shrimp are cooked through and oil is bubbling vigorously, 15 to 20 seconds. Remove and discard bay leaf. Serve immediately.

Mussels Escabèche

SERVES 6 to 8

WHY THIS RECIPE WORKS Mussels *escabèche* calls for pickling briny mussels in an aromatic mixture of vinegar, olive oil, and fragrant spices; we thought this sounded like a unique addition to any tapas spread. The first step in creating our recipe was figuring out how to cook the mussels so that they would be plump and tender. We found that steaming them in a mixture of white wine and water infused them with flavor from the start; bringing the cooking liquid to a boil before adding the mussels ensured that the mussels cooked quickly, reducing the risk of overcooking. After removing the mussels from their shells, we made the marinade by blooming our aromatics in oil; a bay leaf offered depth, and smoked paprika provided earthy nuance. A healthy dose of sherry vinegar was necessary to pickle the mussels; its bright, bold flavor gave this small bite big impact. We suggest serving these mussels with toothpicks and extra bread for dipping in the flavorful marinade. We prefer the bright flavor of these mussels after a quick pickling period of just 15 minutes, but the mussels can be refrigerated for up to 2 days in their vinegar brine. Let the mussels come to room temperature before serving or the oil will look cloudy and congealed. For more information on mussels, see page 279.

⅔ cup white wine
⅔ cup water
2 pounds mussels, scrubbed and debearded
⅓ cup extra-virgin olive oil
½ small red onion, sliced ¼ inch thick
4 garlic cloves, sliced thin
2 bay leaves
2 sprigs fresh thyme
2 tablespoons minced fresh parsley
¾ teaspoon smoked paprika
¼ cup sherry vinegar
    Salt and pepper

1. Bring wine and water to boil in Dutch oven over high heat. Add mussels, cover, and cook, stirring occasionally, until mussels open, 3 to 6 minutes. Strain mussels and discard cooking liquid and any mussels that have not opened. Let mussels cool slightly, then remove mussels from shells and place in large bowl; discard shells.

For our mussels *escabèche*, we first steam mussels in wine, then marinate them in a fragrant sherry vinegar mixture.

2. Heat oil in now-empty Dutch oven over medium heat until shimmering. Add onion, garlic, bay leaves, thyme, 1 tablespoon parsley, and paprika. Cook, stirring often, until garlic is fragrant and onion is slightly wilted, about 1 minute.

3. Off heat, stir in vinegar, ¼ teaspoon salt, and ⅛ teaspoon pepper. Pour mixture over mussels and let sit for 15 minutes. (Mussels can be refrigerated for up to 2 days; bring to room temperature before serving.) Season with salt and pepper to taste and sprinkle with remaining 1 tablespoon parsley before serving.

Debearding Mussels

Occasionally, mussels will have a weedy but harmless piece, called a beard, protruding from their shells. To remove it, grasp beard between your thumb and flat side of paring knife and tug.

Spicy harissa chile paste gives our marinated Mediterranean calamari salad intense and unexpected flavor.

Chili-Marinated Calamari with Oranges

SERVES 6 to 8

WHY THIS RECIPE WORKS Calamari are well-suited to small plates because their mild flavor and pleasing chew are the perfect vehicle for a host of bold flavors. We set our sights on a fresh, aromatic, Spanish-inspired calamari salad. First, we needed to settle on a cooking method for the squid. After trying grilling, broiling, and sautéing, all of which resulted in overcooked, chewy squid, we settled on blanching the squid in boiling water. Soaking the raw squid in a brine of baking soda and salt tenderized the squid so that it was less likely to become rubbery when cooked. To ensure that both the bodies and tentacles were done at the same time, we added the thicker tentacles to the pot 30 seconds before adding the bodies. After blanching, we transferred the squid to an ice water bath to halt the cooking. We dressed the squid with a piquant mixture of tangy red wine vinegar and—looking to Spain's North African neighbors—spicy

harissa chile paste, an intense, aromatic blend of smoky chile peppers and spices. We tossed the squid with our dressing, stirring in pieces of orange, bell pepper, and celery for some contrasting flavors and textures. Marinating the salad in the fridge for at least an hour allowed the flavors to meld. Hazelnuts, stirred in just before serving, gave the salad some crunch. We prefer to use our homemade Harissa (page 316), but you can substitute store-bought harissa if you wish, though spiciness can vary greatly by brand. Be sure to use small squid (with bodies 3 to 4 inches in length) because they cook more quickly and are more tender than larger squid. For the best flavor and texture we recommend allowing the salad to marinate for the full 24 hours before serving.

    2 tablespoons baking soda
      Salt and pepper
    2 pounds squid, bodies sliced crosswise into
      ¼-inch-thick rings, tentacles halved
    ¼ cup extra-virgin olive oil
    3 tablespoons red wine vinegar
  2½ tablespoons harissa
    2 garlic cloves, minced
    1 teaspoon Dijon mustard
    2 oranges
    1 red bell pepper, stemmed, seeded, and cut into
      2-inch-long matchsticks
    2 celery ribs, sliced thin on bias
    1 shallot, sliced thin
    ⅓ cup hazelnuts, toasted, skinned, and chopped
    3 tablespoons chopped fresh mint

Prepping Squid

1. Check squid bodies to make sure plastic-like quill has been completely removed, then slice bodies crosswise into ¼-inch-thick rings.

2. Check tentacles to make sure the hard, sharp beak has been removed, then slice tentacles in half.

1. Dissolve baking soda and 1 tablespoon salt in 3 cups cold water in large container. Submerge squid in brine, cover, and refrigerate for 15 minutes. Remove squid from brine and separate bodies from tentacles.

2. Bring 8 cups water to boil in large saucepan over medium-high heat. Fill large bowl with ice water. Add 2 tablespoons salt and tentacles to boiling water and cook for 30 seconds. Add bodies and cook until bodies are firm and opaque throughout, about 90 seconds. Drain squid, transfer to ice water, and let sit until chilled, about 5 minutes.

3. Whisk oil, vinegar, harissa, garlic, mustard, 1½ teaspoons salt, and ½ teaspoon pepper together in large bowl. Drain squid well and add to bowl with dressing.

4. Cut away peel and pith from oranges. Quarter oranges, then slice crosswise into ½-inch-thick pieces. Add oranges, bell pepper, celery, and shallot to squid and toss to coat. Cover and refrigerate for at least 1 hour or up to 24 hours. Stir in hazelnuts and mint and season with salt and pepper to taste before serving.

Stuffed Sardines

SERVES 8

WHY THIS RECIPE WORKS *Sarde a beccafico* is a popular Sardinian appetizer that is made by rolling fresh sardines around a flavorful bread-crumb stuffing. However, these recipes are often labor intensive—calling for removing the spine, head, and tail of the raw fish before rolling it tightly around the bread-crumb mixture and baking. We wanted to develop a more approachable version. Our first decision was to leave the sardines whole and simply cut a cavity that we could easily fill with a bread-crumb mixture. Laying the fish flat instead of rolling them made for an attractive presentation, and, once cooked, the fish was easy to flake off the bones while eating. Next, we focused on creating a flavorful stuffing for the sardines. The stuffing recipes we found contained a wide range of ingredients, from fresh bread crumbs and citrus to dried fruit and anchovies, so our first task was to figure out a flavor profile. We found that freshly made bread crumbs turned pasty when tucked inside the fish, so we opted for sturdier panko crumbs to keep our stuffing crisp and crunchy. Capers provided a briny backbone, golden raisins and a bit of orange zest offered rounded sweetness, and pine nuts contributed welcome crunch. Our simplified stuffed sardines tasted great and made for a beautiful and impressive presentation that packed a big, flavorful bite. Sardines are often sold whole; if so, ask the fishmonger to scale and gut them for you.

⅓ cup capers, rinsed and minced
¼ cup golden raisins, chopped fine
¼ cup pine nuts, toasted and chopped fine
3 tablespoons extra-virgin olive oil
2 tablespoons minced fresh parsley
2 teaspoons grated orange zest plus wedges for serving
2 garlic cloves, minced
  Salt and pepper
⅓ cup panko bread crumbs
8 fresh sardines (2 to 3 ounces each), scaled, gutted, head and tail on

1. Adjust oven rack to lower-middle position and heat oven to 450 degrees. Line rimmed baking sheet with aluminum foil. Combine capers, raisins, pine nuts, 1 tablespoon oil, parsley, orange zest, garlic, ¼ teaspoon salt, and ¼ teaspoon pepper in bowl. Add panko and gently stir to combine.

2. Using paring knife, slit belly of fish open from gill to tail, leaving spine intact. Gently rinse fish under cold running water and pat dry with paper towels. Rub skin of sardines evenly with remaining 2 tablespoons oil and season with salt and pepper.

3. Place sardines on prepared sheet, spaced 1 inch apart. Stuff cavities of each sardine with 2 tablespoons filling and press on filling to help it adhere; gently press fish closed.

4. Bake until fish flakes apart when gently prodded with paring knife and filling is golden brown, about 15 minutes. Serve with orange wedges.

Stuffing Sardines

1. Using sharp paring knife, slice gutted fish open from gills to tail, leaving spine intact.

2. Stuff cavities of each sardine with 2 tablespoons filling and press on filling to help it adhere; gently press fish closed.

CHAPTER 2

Soups

■ FAST (less than 45 minutes start to finish)   ▦ VEGETARIAN

Photos (clockwise from top left): Greek White Bean Soup; Shellfish Soup with Leeks and Turmeric; Turkish Tomato, Bulgur, and Red Pepper Soup; Chilled Cucumber and Yogurt Soup

A bright sherry vinegar marinade seasons the vegetables throughout for our classic tomato-based gazpacho.

CLASSIC CROUTONS

MAKES about 3 cups `FAST` `VEG`

Either fresh or stale bread can be used in this recipe.

  6 slices hearty white sandwich bread, crusts removed, cut into ½-inch cubes (3 cups)
  3 tablespoons extra-virgin olive oil
    Salt and pepper

Adjust oven rack to middle position and heat oven to 350 degrees. Toss bread with oil, season with salt and pepper, and spread in rimmed baking sheet. Bake until golden brown and crisp, 20 to 25 minutes, stirring halfway through baking. Let cool and serve. (Croutons can be stored at room temperature for up to 3 days.)

VARIATION

GARLIC CROUTONS `FAST` `VEG`

Whisk 1 minced garlic clove into olive oil before tossing with bread.

Classic Gazpacho
SERVES 8 to 10 `VEG`

WHY THIS RECIPE WORKS Served up during the hot, dry summers in the southern Spanish region of Andalusia, gazpacho is a refreshing, tomato-based chilled soup. Although traditional recipes and techniques vary from village to village, the most common ingredients are tomatoes, peppers, cucumbers, and onions, which come together in a bright, surprisingly satisfying soup. Unfortunately, many modern recipes turn out bland, thin gazpachos with little character. We set out to develop an authentic, foolproof recipe with fresh, vibrant vegetables in a bright tomato broth. We started by chopping the classic vegetables by hand (as opposed to using a food processor), which ensured that they retained their color and firm texture. Letting them sit briefly in a sherry vinegar marinade guaranteed well-seasoned vegetables, and a combination of tomato juice and ice cubes, which helped chill the soup, provided the right amount of liquid. Chilling our soup for a minimum of 4 hours was critical to allow the flavors to develop and meld. Use a Vidalia, Maui, or Walla Walla onion here. This recipe makes a large quantity because the leftovers are so good, but it can be halved if you prefer. Traditionally, diners garnish their gazpacho with more of the same diced vegetables that are in the soup, so we cut some extras. Serve with Garlic Croutons, chopped pitted black olives, and chopped hard-cooked eggs. For a finishing touch, serve in chilled bowls.

1½ pounds tomatoes, cored and cut into ¼-inch pieces
  2 red bell peppers, stemmed, seeded, and cut into ¼-inch pieces
  2 small cucumbers (1 peeled, both sliced lengthwise, seeded, and cut into ¼-inch pieces)
  ½ small sweet onion or 2 large shallots, chopped fine
  ⅓ cup sherry vinegar
  2 garlic cloves, minced
    Salt and pepper
  5 cups tomato juice
  8 ice cubes
  1 teaspoon hot sauce (optional)
    Extra-virgin olive oil

1. Combine tomatoes, bell peppers, cucumbers, onion, vinegar, garlic, and 2 teaspoons salt in large bowl (at least 4-quart) and season with pepper to taste. Let stand until vegetables just begin to release their juices, about 5 minutes. Stir in tomato juice, ice cubes, and hot sauce, if using. Cover and refrigerate to blend flavors, at least 4 hours or up to 2 days.

2. Discard any unmelted ice cubes and season soup with salt and pepper to taste. Serve, drizzling individual portions with oil.

White Gazpacho

SERVES 6 to 8 `VEG`

WHY THIS RECIPE WORKS Although both hail from Andalusia, Spain, white gazpacho bears little resemblance to its familiar, vegetable-laden red cousin. White gazpacho, or *ajo blanco*, was originally made by peasants with five simple ingredients at their disposal: stale bread, garlic, vinegar, oil, and salt. They pounded the bread with a mortar and pestle, added slugs of vinegar and olive oil, and then stirred in water to make the mixture drinkable. When the dish made its way onto aristocratic tables, upscale ingredients like almonds and grapes were added, giving the soup nuanced flavor and sophisticated textural contrast. However, the versions we tried were watery and bland or even grainy. We discovered that the order in which we added ingredients to the blender made all the difference: First, we ground almonds, then we added bread (which we had briefly soaked in water), garlic, sherry vinegar, salt, and cayenne. Then we slowly drizzled in the water and olive oil. To amplify the almond flavor without overwhelming the soup, we mixed a tablespoon of the pureed soup with a small amount of almond extract, then added a teaspoon of the mixture back to the soup. Sliced green grapes and toasted almonds added fruitiness and crunch, and a final drizzle of olive oil made for a rich finish and an elegant presentation. This rich soup is best when served in small portions (about 6 ounces). Use a premium-quality extra-virgin olive oil; our favorite is Gaea Fresh Extra-Virgin Olive Oil.

Ground almonds, almond extract, and bread are the keys to our silky and elegant white gazpacho.

6 slices hearty white sandwich bread, crusts removed
4 cups water
2½ cups (8¾ ounces) plus ⅓ cup sliced blanched almonds
1 garlic clove, peeled and smashed
3 tablespoons sherry vinegar
Salt and pepper
Pinch cayenne pepper
½ cup plus 2 teaspoons extra-virgin olive oil, plus extra for serving
⅛ teaspoon almond extract
6 ounces seedless green grapes, sliced thin (1 cup)

1. Combine bread and water in bowl and let soak for 5 minutes. Process 2½ cups almonds in blender until finely ground, about 30 seconds, scraping down sides of blender jar as needed. Using your hands, remove bread from water, squeeze it lightly, and transfer to blender with almonds. Measure out 3 cups soaking water and set aside; transfer remaining soaking water to blender. Add garlic, vinegar, ½ teaspoon salt, and cayenne to blender and process until mixture has consistency of cake batter, 30 to 45 seconds. With blender running, add ½ cup oil in thin, steady stream, about 30 seconds. Add reserved soaking water and process for 1 minute.

2. Season soup with salt and pepper to taste, then strain through fine-mesh strainer into bowl, pressing on solids to extract as much liquid as possible; discard solids.

3. Transfer 1 tablespoon soup to separate bowl and stir in almond extract. Return 1 teaspoon extract-soup mixture to soup; discard remaining mixture. Cover and refrigerate to blend flavors, at least 4 hours or up to 24 hours.

4. Heat remaining 2 teaspoons oil in 8-inch skillet over medium-high heat until shimmering. Add remaining ⅓ cup almonds and cook, stirring constantly, until golden brown, 3 to 4 minutes. Immediately transfer almonds to bowl, stir in ¼ teaspoon salt, and let cool slightly.

5. Ladle soup into shallow bowls. Mound grapes in center of each bowl, sprinkle with almonds, and drizzle with extra oil. Serve immediately.

Pureeing Soup

The texture of a pureed soup should be as smooth and creamy as possible. With this in mind, we tried pureeing several soups with a food processor, a handheld immersion blender, and a regular countertop blender. It pays to use the right appliance to produce a silky-smooth soup. And because pureeing hot soup can be dangerous, follow our safety tips.

BLENDER IS BEST

A standard blender turns out the smoothest pureed soups. The blade on the blender does an excellent job with soups because it pulls ingredients down from the top of the container. No stray bits go untouched by the blade. And as long as plenty of headroom is left at the top of the blender, there is no leakage.

IMMERSION BLENDER LEAVES BITS BEHIND

The immersion blender has appeal because it can be brought to the pot, eliminating the need to ladle hot ingredients from one vessel to another. However, we found that this kind of blender can leave unblended bits of food behind.

PROCESS WITH CAUTION

The food processor does a decent job of pureeing, but some small bits of vegetables can get trapped under the blade and remain unchopped. Even more troubling is the tendency of a food processor to leak hot liquid. Fill the bowl more than halfway and you are likely to see liquid running down the side of the food processor base.

WAIT BEFORE BLENDING, AND BLEND IN BATCHES

When blending hot soup, follow a couple of precautions. Wait 5 minutes for moderate cooling, and fill the blender only two-thirds full; otherwise, the soup can explode out the top.

KEEP LID SECURE

Don't expect the lid on a blender to stay in place. Hold it securely with a folded dish towel to keep it in place and to protect your hand from hot steam. And pulse several times before blending continuously.

Scallion greens, dill, and mint flavor pureed cucumbers and Greek yogurt in this cool and creamy soup.

Chilled Cucumber and Yogurt Soup
SERVES 6 VEG

WHY THIS RECIPE WORKS Called *cacik* in Turkey, *tzatziki* in Greece, and *tarator* in the rest of the Balkans, a mixture of yogurt, cucumber, herbs, and garlic is eaten throughout the eastern Mediterranean. The dish can have nuts, olive oil, lemon juice, or vinegar added and variously takes the form of dip, sauce, side, or soup. We wanted to make a perfect version of this as a soup for a hot summer's evening. But with so few ingredients, we knew that balance and finesse would be key. A food processor turned our soup mushy, and hand chopping all of the cucumber gave us something watery and inconsistent. We found that blending some of the cucumbers and reserving a final chopped handful as a garnish gave us the smooth consistency we wanted with texture to boot. Peeling and seeding the cucumbers removed unpleasantly bitter flavors. We knew that alliums would be important to impart a savory quality but found that garlic, shallots, red onion, and scallions were too astringent; it was only after we left in just the scallion greens that we found the right balance. Tasters preferred dill and mint to other herb combinations as they brought out the freshest aspect of the soup.

5 pounds English cucumbers, peeled and seeded (1 cucumber cut into ½-inch pieces, remaining cucumbers cut into 2-inch pieces)
4 scallions, green parts only, chopped coarse
2 cups water
2 cups plain Greek yogurt
1 tablespoon lemon juice
  Salt and pepper
¼ teaspoon sugar
1½ tablespoons minced fresh dill
1½ tablespoons minced fresh mint
  Extra-virgin olive oil

1. Toss 2-inch pieces of cucumber with scallions. Working in 2 batches, process cucumber-scallion mixture in blender with water until completely smooth, about 2 minutes; transfer to large bowl. Whisk in yogurt, lemon juice, 1½ teaspoons salt, sugar, and pinch pepper. Cover and refrigerate to blend flavors, at least 1 hour or up to 12 hours.

2. Stir in dill and mint and season with salt and pepper to taste. Serve, topping individual portions with remaining ½-inch pieces of cucumber and drizzling with oil.

Classic Chicken Broth
MAKES about 8 cups

WHY THIS RECIPE WORKS Great homemade chicken broth can improve everything you cook with it, not only soup but also risotto, bean dishes, sauces, and more. This broth delivers rich flavor and full body with almost no hands-on work. Our classic approach to making chicken broth calls for gently simmering a mix of chicken backs and wings in water for several hours. The long, slow simmer helped the bones and meat release both deep flavor and gelatin, which created a viscous consistency. We chose a combination of backs and wings not only for their convenience (they didn't need to be hacked into smaller pieces) but because, in addition to a little muscle and fat, these parts contain relatively high levels of collagen, found especially in the skin and joints. The collagen broke down into gelatin during cooking, which added thick richness to the broth. We deliberately left out breasts because they offer little collagen. Because we wanted our broth to taste as chicken-y as possible, we used only chopped onion and bay leaves for flavoring; they added just enough dimension and flavor to the broth without making it taste too vegetal. Chicken backs are often available at supermarket butcher counters during colder months. You can also save and freeze backs if you butcher whole chickens at home. If you have a large pot (at least 12 quarts), you can easily double this recipe to make 1 gallon.

4 pounds chicken backs and wings
14 cups water
1 onion, chopped
2 bay leaves
2 teaspoons salt

1. Heat chicken and water in large stockpot or Dutch oven over medium-high heat until boiling, skimming off any scum that comes to surface. Reduce heat to low and simmer gently for 3 hours.

2. Add onion, bay leaves, and salt and continue to simmer for another 2 hours.

3. Strain broth through fine-mesh strainer into large pot or container, pressing on solids to extract as much liquid as possible. Let broth settle for about 5 minutes, then skim off fat. (Cooled broth can be refrigerated for up to 4 days or frozen for up to 1 month.)

Vegetable Broth Base
MAKES about 1¾ cups base, or about 1¾ gallons broth
FAST **VEG**

WHY THIS RECIPE WORKS Our vegetable broth base delivers on both great flavor and convenience. The broth bases found on supermarket shelves promise an economical alternative to liquid broth, but they usually offer harsh, overwhelming flavors. To make a vegetable concentrate that would pack bold but balanced flavor, we started with a classic mirepoix of onion, carrots, and celery. However, the celery gave the broth a bitter flavor, and the onion was too pungent. We swapped in celery root and leeks, which lent similar but milder flavors. Some parsley added a fresh, herbal note. To amp up the savory flavor and give the broth more depth and complexity, we added dried onion and tomato paste. A hefty dose of salt ensured that the broth was well seasoned and kept the base from freezing solid, so we could store it in the freezer for months and easily remove a tablespoon at a time without having to thaw the container. For the best balance of flavors, measure the prepped vegetables by weight. Kosher salt aids in grinding the vegetables.

1 pound leeks, white and light green parts only, chopped and washed thoroughly (2½ cups)
2 carrots, peeled and cut into ½-inch pieces (⅔ cup)
½ small celery root, peeled and cut into ½-inch pieces (¾ cup)
½ cup (½ ounce) fresh parsley leaves and thin stems
3 tablespoons dried minced onion
3 tablespoons kosher salt
1½ tablespoons tomato paste

1. Process leeks, carrots, celery root, parsley, dried minced onion, and salt in food processor, pausing to scrape down sides of bowl frequently, until paste is as fine as possible, 3 to 4 minutes. Add tomato paste and process for 2 minutes, scraping down sides of bowl every 30 seconds. Transfer mixture to airtight container and tap firmly on counter to remove air bubbles. Press small piece of parchment paper flush against surface of mixture and cover tightly. Freeze for up to 6 months.

2. **TO MAKE 1 CUP BROTH** Stir 1 tablespoon fresh or frozen broth base into 1 cup boiling water. If particle-free broth is desired, let broth steep for 5 minutes, then strain through fine-mesh strainer.

NOTES FROM THE TEST KITCHEN

Buying Broth

Even though homemade broths taste better (page 45), the reality is that the majority of home cooks rely on supermarket broth for most recipes. When selecting store-bought broth, it's important to choose wisely since what you use can have a big impact on your final dish. We prefer chicken broth to beef broth and vegetable broth for its stronger, cleaner flavor, though all have their place in our recipes.

CHICKEN BROTH We like chicken broths with short ingredient lists that include a relatively high percentage of meat-based protein and flavor-boosting vegetables like carrots, celery, and onions. We also like a lower sodium content—less than 700 milligrams per serving. Our favorite is Swanson Chicken Stock.

VEGETABLE BROTH We've found that the top brands of vegetable broth have a hefty amount of salt and enough vegetable content to be listed on the ingredient list. Because store-bought vegetable broths tend to be sweet, we often mix vegetable broth with chicken broth for the best flavor. Orrington Farms Vegan Chicken Flavored Broth Base & Seasoning is almost as good as our Vegetable Broth Base (page 45).

BEEF BROTH We've found the best beef broths have concentrated beef stock and flavor-enhancing ingredients such as tomato paste and yeast extract near the top of their ingredient lists. Our favorite brand is Better Than Bouillon Beef Base.

CLAM JUICE Bottled clam juice conveniently brings a bright and mineral-y flavor to seafood dishes. Our favorite, Bar Harbor Clam Juice, comes from the shores of clam country in Maine.

This classic French soup is loaded with fresh vegetables and enlivened with a traditional pesto.

Provençal Vegetable Soup

SERVES 6 **VEG**

WHY THIS RECIPE WORKS Highlighting the fresh flavors of Provençal cuisine, *soupe au pistou* is a classic French soup composed of seasonal vegetables, creamy white beans, and fragrant herbs. Celebrating colorful, early-summer produce, this soup needed to be chock-full of vegetables and simple to prepare. Leeks, green beans, and zucchini all made the cut; we liked their summery flavors and varying shades of green. Traditional recipes use water for the base, but supplementing the water with vegetable broth promised a more rounded, flavorful base; we cooked orecchiette directly in the broth so that the starch from the pasta would give it more body. Canned white beans tasted great and were far more convenient than long-soaking dried beans. This soup is always served with a dollop of *pistou*, France's answer to pesto, and to make ours we simply whirled basil, Parmesan, olive oil, and garlic in a food processor. If you cannot find haricots verts (thin green beans), substitute regular green beans and cook them for an extra minute or two. You can substitute small shells or ditalini for the orecchiette (the cooking times may vary slightly). Serve with Garlic Toasts (page 56) or crusty bread.

PISTOU

- ½ cup fresh basil leaves
- 1 ounce Parmesan cheese, grated (½ cup)
- ⅓ cup extra-virgin olive oil
- 1 garlic clove, minced

SOUP

- 1 tablespoon extra-virgin olive oil
- 1 leek, white and light green parts only, halved lengthwise, sliced ½ inch thick, and washed thoroughly
- 1 celery rib, cut into ½-inch pieces
- 1 carrot, peeled and sliced ¼ inch thick
  Salt and pepper
- 2 garlic cloves, minced
- 3 cups vegetable broth
- 3 cups water
- ½ cup orecchiette
- 8 ounces haricots verts, trimmed and cut into ½-inch lengths
- 1 (15-ounce) can cannellini or navy beans, rinsed
- 1 small zucchini, halved lengthwise, seeded, and cut into ¼-inch pieces
- 1 large tomato, cored, seeded, and chopped

1. FOR THE PISTOU Process all ingredients in food processor until smooth, about 15 seconds, scraping down sides of bowl as needed. (Pistou can be refrigerated for up to 4 hours.)

2. FOR THE SOUP Heat oil in Dutch oven over medium heat until shimmering. Add leek, celery, carrot, and ½ teaspoon salt and cook until vegetables are softened, 8 to 10 minutes. Stir in garlic and cook until fragrant, about 30 seconds. Stir in broth and water and bring to simmer.

3. Stir in pasta and simmer until slightly softened, about 5 minutes. Stir in haricots verts and simmer until bright green but still crunchy, about 3 minutes. Stir in cannellini beans, zucchini, and tomato and simmer until pasta and vegetables are tender, about 3 minutes. Season with salt and pepper to taste. Serve, topping individual portions with pistou.

Seeding Zucchini

Halve zucchini lengthwise, then gently scrape out seeds using soup spoon.

NOTES FROM THE TEST KITCHEN
Successful Soup Making

Making a great pot of soup requires attention to detail, the right ingredients, well-made equipment, and a good recipe. Whether you're making a homey chicken noodle soup or an elegant pureed vegetable soup, you'll likely build a flavor base the same way and will need a good broth, herbs and spices, and a solid, sturdy pot that can take the heat (and, in some cases, go from the stovetop to the oven).

SAUTÉ AROMATICS The first step in making many soups is sautéing aromatic vegetables such as onion and garlic. Sautéing not only softens their texture so that there is no unwelcome crunch in the soup, it also tames any harsh flavors and develops more complex flavors in the process.

START WITH GOOD BROTH If you're not inclined to pack your freezer with homemade stock, store-bought broth is a convenient option for soup making. Differences among packaged broths are quite significant—some are flavorful, and others taste like salty dishwater. Shop carefully. See Buying Broth on page 46 for further information.

CUT VEGETABLES TO THE RIGHT SIZE Most soups call for chunks of vegetables. Haphazardly cut vegetables will cook unevenly—larger pieces will be underdone and crunchy, and smaller ones will be soft and mushy. Cutting vegetables to the size specified ensures that they will be perfectly cooked.

STAGGER THE ADDITION OF VEGETABLES When a soup contains a variety of vegetables, they often must be added in stages to account for their varied cooking times. Hardy vegetables like potatoes and winter squash can withstand much longer cooking than delicate asparagus or spinach.

SIMMER, DON'T BOIL The fine line between simmering and boiling can make a big difference in your soups. A simmer is a restrained version of a boil; fewer bubbles break the surface. Simmering heats food through more gently and more evenly; boiling can cause vegetables such as potatoes to break apart, and it can toughen meat, too.

SEASON JUST BEFORE SERVING In general, we add salt, pepper, and other seasonings—such as delicate herbs and lemon juice—after cooking, just before serving. The saltiness of the stock and of other ingredients, such as canned tomatoes and beans, can vary greatly, so it's always best to taste and adjust the seasonings once the soup is complete.

Roasted Eggplant and Tomato Soup

SERVES 4 to 6 [VEG]

WHY THIS RECIPE WORKS Eggplants and tomatoes are often found together throughout the eastern Mediterranean in countless dishes, especially soups. For a wonderfully creamy yet hefty soup, we began by dicing and roasting eggplant and found we could skip the task of salting, rinsing, and drying it. We left the skin on for deeper eggplant flavor and broiled it to develop a flavorful char. To build our soup, we started with the usual aromatics—onion and garlic—and added the flavorful North African spice blend *ras el hanout* plus some extra cumin, which gave the soup complex flavor. Using broth gave the soup well-rounded flavor, and we added subtle sweetness with raisins, which once pureed also gave our soup body. Canned tomatoes were easy and offered rich tomato flavor. We reserved some eggplant to add to the pureed soup for a pleasantly chunky texture. Lemon juice provided brightness, almonds gave a pleasant crunch, and cilantro added freshness. We prefer to use our homemade Ras el Hanout (page 316), but you can substitute store-bought ras el hanout if you wish, though flavor and spiciness can vary greatly by brand.

Pureed raisins add body and flavor to our complexly spiced eggplant and tomato soup.

2 pounds eggplant, cut into ½-inch pieces
6 tablespoons extra-virgin olive oil, plus extra for serving
1 onion, chopped
Salt and pepper
2 garlic cloves, minced
1½ teaspoons ras el hanout
½ teaspoon ground cumin
4 cups chicken or vegetable broth, plus extra as needed
1 (14.5-ounce) can diced tomatoes, drained
¼ cup raisins
1 bay leaf
2 teaspoons lemon juice
2 tablespoons slivered almonds, toasted
2 tablespoons minced fresh cilantro

1. Adjust oven rack 4 inches from broiler element and heat broiler. Toss eggplant with 5 tablespoons oil, then spread in aluminum foil–lined rimmed baking sheet. Broil eggplant for 10 minutes. Stir eggplant and continue to broil until mahogany brown, 5 to 7 minutes. Measure out and reserve 2 cups eggplant.

2. Heat remaining 1 tablespoon oil in large saucepan over medium heat until shimmering. Add onion, ¾ teaspoon salt, and ¼ teaspoon pepper and cook until softened and lightly browned, 5 to 7 minutes. Stir in garlic, ras el hanout, and cumin and cook until fragrant, about 30 seconds. Stir in broth, tomatoes, raisins, bay leaf, and remaining eggplant and bring to simmer. Reduce heat to low, cover, and simmer gently until eggplant is softened, about 20 minutes.

3. Discard bay leaf. Working in batches, process soup in blender until smooth, about 2 minutes. Return soup to clean saucepan and stir in reserved eggplant. Heat soup gently over low heat until hot (do not boil) and adjust consistency with extra hot broth as needed. Stir in lemon juice and season with salt and pepper to taste. Serve, sprinkling individual portions with almonds and cilantro and drizzling with extra oil.

NOTES FROM THE TEST KITCHEN
Toasting Nuts and Seeds

Toasting nuts and seeds maximizes their flavor and crunch. To toast less than 1 cup of nuts or seeds, put the nuts or seeds in a dry skillet over medium heat. Shake the skillet occasionally to prevent scorching and toast until they are lightly browned and fragrant, 3 to 8 minutes. Watch them closely since they can go from golden to burnt very quickly. To toast more than 1 cup of nuts or seeds, spread them in a single layer in a rimmed baking sheet and toast in a 350-degree oven. Shake the baking sheet every few minutes, and toast until the nuts or seeds are lightly browned and fragrant, 5 to 10 minutes.

Roasted Red Pepper Soup with Smoked Paprika and Cilantro Yogurt

SERVES 6　VEG

WHY THIS RECIPE WORKS Roasting red peppers turns their raw, sweet crunch into something smoky and rich. We wanted to concentrate that flavor in a silky pureed soup. We started by broiling the peppers until they were charred and puffed. Next, we built an aromatic base for our soup with garlic, red onion, cumin, and smoked paprika. Sautéing some tomato paste and flour gave the soup umami flavor and a velvety thickness. Finally, we whisked in broth, added the peppers, and simmered them until tender before blending the soup smooth. For a garnish, we made a bright cilantro-lime yogurt. The flavor of this soup depends on homemade roasted red peppers; do not substitute jarred. The broiling time for the peppers in step 2 may vary depending on the intensity of your broiler. Sweet paprika can be substituted for the smoked paprika. We prefer the rich flavor of whole-milk yogurt here; however, low-fat yogurt will also work. Do not use nonfat yogurt.

½ cup whole-milk yogurt
3 tablespoons minced fresh cilantro
1 teaspoon lime juice
　Salt and pepper
8 red bell peppers, cored and flattened
1 tablespoon extra-virgin olive oil
2 garlic cloves, minced
1 red onion, chopped
½ teaspoon ground cumin
½ teaspoon smoked paprika
2 tablespoons tomato paste
1 tablespoon all-purpose flour
4 cups chicken or vegetable broth, plus extra as needed
1 bay leaf
½ cup half-and-half
2 tablespoons dry sherry

1. Whisk yogurt, 1 tablespoon cilantro, and lime juice together in bowl. Season with salt and pepper to taste. Cover and refrigerate until needed.

2. Adjust oven rack 3 inches from broiler element and heat broiler. Spread half of peppers skin side up on aluminum foil–lined baking sheet. Broil until skin is charred and puffed but flesh is still firm, 8 to 10 minutes, rotating sheet halfway through broiling. Transfer broiled peppers to bowl, cover with plastic wrap or foil, and let steam until skins peel off easily, 10 to 15 minutes. Repeat with remaining peppers. Peel broiled peppers, discarding skins, and chop coarse.

3. Cook oil and garlic together in Dutch oven over low heat, stirring constantly, until garlic is foamy, sticky, and straw-colored,

6 to 8 minutes. Stir in onion and ¼ teaspoon salt, increase heat to medium, and cook until softened, about 5 minutes.

4. Stir in cumin and paprika and cook until fragrant, about 30 seconds. Stir in tomato paste and flour and cook for 1 minute. Slowly whisk in broth, scraping up any browned bits and smoothing out any lumps. Stir in bay leaf and chopped peppers, bring to simmer, and cook until peppers are very tender, 5 to 7 minutes.

5. Discard bay leaf. Working in batches, process soup in blender until smooth, about 2 minutes. Return soup to clean pot and stir in half-and-half and sherry. Heat soup gently over low heat until hot (do not boil) and adjust consistency with extra hot broth as needed. Stir in remaining 2 tablespoons cilantro and season with salt and pepper to taste. Serve, drizzling individual portions with yogurt mixture.

Roasting Red Peppers

1. Cut off top and bottom of pepper, then remove core and stem. Slice down through side of pepper, then lay flat on cutting board and trim away any remaining ribs.

2. Place flattened peppers, pepper tops, and pepper bottoms on aluminum foil–lined baking sheet. (You can fit up to 4 peppers on sheet.)

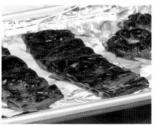

3. Broil peppers until skin is charred and puffed but flesh is still firm, 8 to 10 minutes, rotating sheet halfway through broiling.

4. Transfer broiled peppers to bowl, cover with plastic wrap, and let steam until skins peel off easily, 10 to 15 minutes.

Both dried mint and fresh mint add flavor to this bulgur-enriched smoky Turkish tomato soup.

Turkish Tomato, Bulgur, and Red Pepper Soup

SERVES 6 to 8   VEG

WHY THIS RECIPE WORKS Tomato and red pepper soups have countless variations throughout Turkey, but all are full-flavored and enriched with grains. We started our soup with onion and red bell peppers, softening them before creating a solid flavor backbone with garlic, tomato paste, white wine, dried mint, smoked paprika, and red pepper flakes. For additional smokiness, canned fire-roasted tomatoes did the trick. For the grain, we turned to versatile bulgur, a common ingredient in Turkish and other Mediterranean cuisines. While it plays an important role in salads, it also has a place in soups. When stirred into a soup, bulgur absorbs the surrounding flavors and gives off starch that creates a silky texture. Since bulgur is so quick-cooking, we stirred it in toward the end, giving it just enough time to become tender. A sprinkle of fresh mint gave the soup a final punch of flavor. When shopping, don't confuse bulgur with cracked wheat, which has a much longer cooking time and will not work in this recipe.

2 tablespoons extra-virgin olive oil
1 onion, chopped
2 red bell peppers, stemmed, seeded, and chopped
  Salt and pepper
3 garlic cloves, minced
1 teaspoon dried mint, crumbled
½ teaspoon smoked paprika
⅛ teaspoon red pepper flakes
1 tablespoon tomato paste
½ cup dry white wine
1 (28-ounce) can diced fire-roasted tomatoes
4 cups chicken or vegetable broth
2 cups water
¾ cup medium-grind bulgur, rinsed
⅓ cup chopped fresh mint

1. Heat oil in Dutch oven over medium heat until shimmering. Add onion, bell peppers, ¾ teaspoon salt, and ¼ teaspoon pepper and cook until softened and lightly browned, 6 to 8 minutes. Stir in garlic, dried mint, smoked paprika, and pepper flakes and cook until fragrant, about 30 seconds. Stir in tomato paste and cook for 1 minute.

2. Stir in wine, scraping up any browned bits, and simmer until reduced by half, about 1 minute. Add tomatoes and their juice and cook, stirring occasionally, until tomatoes soften and begin to break apart, about 10 minutes.

3. Stir in broth, water, and bulgur and bring to simmer. Reduce heat to low, cover, and simmer gently until bulgur is tender, about 20 minutes. Season with salt and pepper to taste. Serve, sprinkling individual portions with fresh mint.

Artichoke Soup à la Barigoule

SERVES 4 to 6

WHY THIS RECIPE WORKS Barigoule is a Provençal dish of braised artichokes, mushrooms, and root vegetables. We thought that earthy artichokes and meaty mushrooms would translate well into a satisfying soup. To concentrate the core components, we first seared artichokes to intensify their subtle flavor. Cooking the mushrooms covered and then sautéing them uncovered evaporated their excess moisture before browning, and simmering the parsnips brought out their sweetness. Umami-rich anchovy fillets and garlic supplied depth to the soup, and leek contributed further sweetness and body. White wine and white wine vinegar brightened up the dish, and a little cream brought it all together. A generous amount of tarragon added freshness. While we prefer the flavor and texture of jarred whole baby artichokes, you can substitute 18 ounces frozen artichoke hearts, thawed and patted dry, for the jarred.

To turn simple jarred artichokes into a savory Provençal soup, we sear them to intensify their flavor.

3 tablespoons extra-virgin olive oil
3 cups jarred whole baby artichokes packed in water, quartered, rinsed, and patted dry
12 ounces white mushrooms, trimmed and sliced thin
1 leek, white and light green parts only, halved lengthwise, sliced ¼ inch thick, and washed thoroughly
4 garlic cloves, minced
2 anchovy fillets, rinsed, patted dry, and minced
1 teaspoon minced fresh thyme or ¼ teaspoon dried
3 tablespoons all-purpose flour
¼ cup dry white wine
3 cups chicken broth
3 cups vegetable broth
6 ounces parsnips, peeled and cut into ½-inch pieces
2 bay leaves
¼ cup heavy cream
2 tablespoons minced fresh tarragon
1 teaspoon white wine vinegar, plus extra for seasoning
   Salt and pepper

1. Heat 1 tablespoon oil in Dutch oven over medium heat until shimmering. Add artichokes and cook until browned, 8 to 10 minutes. Transfer to cutting board, let cool slightly, then chop coarse.

2. Heat 1 tablespoon oil in now-empty pot over medium heat until shimmering. Add mushrooms, cover, and cook until they have released their liquid, about 5 minutes. Uncover and continue to cook until mushrooms are dry, about 5 minutes.

3. Stir in leek and remaining 1 tablespoon oil and cook until leek is softened and mushrooms are browned, 8 to 10 minutes. Stir in garlic, anchovies, and thyme and cook until fragrant, about 30 seconds. Stir in flour and cook for 1 minute. Stir in wine, scraping up any browned bits, and cook until nearly evaporated, about 1 minute.

4. Slowly whisk in chicken broth and vegetable broth, smoothing out any lumps. Stir in artichokes, parsnips, and bay leaves and bring to simmer. Reduce heat to low, cover, and simmer gently until parsnips are tender, 15 to 20 minutes. Off heat, discard bay leaves. Stir in cream, tarragon, and vinegar. Season with salt, pepper, and extra vinegar to taste. Serve.

NOTES FROM THE TEST KITCHEN
Storing and Reheating Soups and Stews

Soup and stew recipes often make a generous number of servings, making it convenient to stock your freezer with last night's leftovers so you can reheat them whenever you like. First you'll need to cool the pot. As tempting as it might seem, don't transfer the hot contents straight to the refrigerator. This can increase the fridge's internal temperature to unsafe levels, which is dangerous for all the other food stored there. We find that letting the pot cool on the counter for an hour helps the temperature drop to about 75 degrees, at which point you can transfer it safely to the fridge. If you don't have an hour to cool the whole pot to room temperature, you can divide the contents of the pot into a number of storage containers to allow the heat to dissipate more quickly, or you can cool it rapidly by using a frozen bottle of water to stir the contents of the pot.

To reheat soups and stews, we prefer to simmer them gently on the stovetop in a sturdy, heavy-bottomed pot, but a spin in the microwave works, too. Just be sure to cover the dish to prevent a mess. And note that while most soups and stews store just fine, those that contain dairy or pasta do not—the dairy curdles as it freezes, and the pasta turns bloated and mushy. Instead, make and freeze the dish without including the dairy or pasta component. After you have thawed the soup or stew and it has been heated through, you can stir in the uncooked pasta and simmer until just tender, or stir in the dairy and continue to heat gently until hot (do not boil).

Risi e Bisi

SERVES 6

WHY THIS RECIPE WORKS *Risi e bisi* (translation: rice and peas) is a Venetian risotto-like soup driven by the bright, vegetal sweetness of fresh green peas. We reached for frozen peas for our recipe; because they are processed soon after harvest, frozen peas retain their sugars. Some risi e bisi recipes that we encountered called for making a stock with the leftover pea pods, but we had none to work with. After some rumination, we hit upon the idea of using fresh snow peas in place of pea pods. We simmered chopped snow peas, onion, carrot, garlic, and bay leaves in chicken broth diluted with water to produce a pea-flavored broth. The rice will quickly absorb the soup's liquid as it sits, so add more liquid if necessary. You may also add more liquid if you want a soupier texture; we aimed for right in the middle between soup and risotto.

QUICK PEA BROTH

    6 cups water
 1¾ cups chicken broth
    8 ounces snow peas, chopped
    1 small onion, chopped
    1 carrot, chopped
    1 garlic clove, lightly crushed
    1 teaspoon salt
    2 bay leaves

SOUP

    2 tablespoons extra-virgin olive oil
    1 onion, chopped fine
    2 ounces pancetta, chopped fine
    1 garlic clove, minced
    1 cup Arborio rice
   ½ cup dry white wine
  20 ounces frozen peas
 1½ ounces Parmesan cheese, grated (¾ cup)
    4 teaspoons minced fresh parsley
    2 teaspoons lemon juice
        Salt and pepper

1. FOR THE QUICK PEA BROTH Combine all ingredients in Dutch oven and bring to boil over medium-high heat. Reduce heat to medium-low, partially cover, and simmer for 30 minutes. Strain broth through fine-mesh strainer into medium saucepan, pressing on solids with wooden spoon to extract as much liquid as possible. Cover and keep warm over low heat until ready to use.

2. FOR THE SOUP Heat oil in now-empty pot over medium heat until shimmering. Add onion and pancetta and cook, stirring occasionally, until onion is softened and lightly browned, 5 to 7 minutes. Stir in garlic and cook until fragrant, about 30 seconds.

Add rice and cook, stirring frequently, until grain edges begin to turn translucent, about 3 minutes.

3. Add wine and cook, stirring constantly, until fully absorbed, about 1 minute. Stir in warm broth and bring to boil. Reduce heat to medium-low, cover, and simmer, stirring occasionally, until rice is just cooked, about 15 minutes. Stir in peas and cook until heated through, about 2 minutes. Off heat, stir in Parmesan, parsley, and lemon juice and season with salt and pepper to taste. Serve immediately.

French Lentil Soup

SERVES 4 to 6

WHY THIS RECIPE WORKS *Lentilles du Puy* are known as the caviar of lentils because this small, dark olive green–colored variety possesses a distinctly earthy flavor and firm texture. They appear in dishes from southern France to Turkey, but when used in soups they often turn to unsightly brown mush. To create a hearty and attractive soup, we would need to cook the lentils perfectly. Heating the lentils in a covered pan with aromatics before adding any liquid helped them hold their shape and boosted their flavor; bacon introduced complementary smokiness. Pureeing only some of the soup ensured that the final result had a varied texture. A final splash of balsamic vinegar brightened the dish. Lentilles du Puy, also called French green lentils, are our first choice for this recipe, but brown, black, or regular green lentils are fine, too (note that cooking times will vary depending on the type used).

    3 slices bacon, cut into ¼-inch pieces
    1 large onion, chopped fine
    2 carrots, peeled and chopped
    3 garlic cloves, minced
    1 teaspoon minced fresh thyme or ¼ teaspoon dried
    1 (14.5-ounce) can diced tomatoes, drained
    1 bay leaf
    1 cup lentilles du Puy, picked over and rinsed
        Salt and pepper
   ½ cup dry white wine
 4½ cups chicken broth, plus extra as needed
 1½ cups water
 1½ teaspoons balsamic vinegar
    3 tablespoons minced fresh parsley

1. Cook bacon in Dutch oven over medium-high heat, stirring often, until crisp, about 5 minutes. Stir in onion and carrots and cook until vegetables begin to soften, about 2 minutes. Stir in garlic and thyme and cook until fragrant, about 30 seconds. Stir in tomatoes and bay leaf and cook until fragrant, about 30 seconds. Stir in lentils and ¼ teaspoon salt. Cover, reduce heat to

We puree only some of our French green lentil soup to give it a hearty and varied texture.

medium-low, and cook until vegetables are softened and lentils have darkened, 8 to 10 minutes.

2. Increase heat to high, stir in wine, and bring to simmer. Stir in broth and water and bring to boil. Partially cover pot, reduce heat to low, and simmer gently until lentils are tender but still hold their shape, 30 to 35 minutes.

3. Discard bay leaf. Process 3 cups soup in blender until smooth, about 30 seconds, then return to pot. Heat soup gently over low heat until hot (do not boil) and adjust consistency with extra hot broth as needed. Stir in vinegar and parsley and season with salt and pepper to taste. Serve.

VARIATIONS

French Lentil Soup with Spinach

Substitute 5 cups baby spinach for parsley; cook spinach in soup, stirring often, until wilted, about 3 minutes.

French Lentil Soup with Fragrant Spices

Add 1 teaspoon ground cumin, 1 teaspoon ground coriander, 1 teaspoon ground cinnamon, and ¼ teaspoon cayenne pepper to pot with garlic. Substitute 1½ teaspoons lemon juice for balsamic vinegar and 3 tablespoons minced fresh cilantro for parsley.

Spanish-Style Lentil and Chorizo Soup
SERVES 6 to 8

WHY THIS RECIPE WORKS The sustaining Spanish *sopa de lentejas con chorizo* (lentil and chorizo soup) economically pairs dried lentils with flavor-packed sausage. It's a standout not just for its robust taste—provided by rich, garlicky chorizo, heady smoked paprika, and the bright depth of sherry vinegar—but also for its unique texture: Neither entirely brothy nor creamy, the soup features whole lentils suspended in a thick broth. We prefer French green lentils, or *lentilles du Puy*, for this recipe, but it will work with any type of lentil except red or yellow. If Spanish-style chorizo is not available, kielbasa sausage can be substituted. Red wine vinegar can be substituted for the sherry vinegar. Smoked paprika comes in three varieties: sweet, bittersweet or medium hot, and hot. For this recipe, we prefer the sweet kind.

1 pound (2¼ cups) lentils, picked over and rinsed
   Salt and pepper
1 large onion
5 tablespoons extra-virgin olive oil
1½ pounds Spanish-style chorizo sausage, pricked with fork several times
3 carrots, peeled and cut into ¼-inch pieces
3 tablespoons minced fresh parsley
3 tablespoons sherry vinegar, plus extra for seasoning
2 bay leaves
⅛ teaspoon ground cloves
2 tablespoons sweet smoked paprika
3 garlic cloves, minced
1 tablespoon all-purpose flour

1. Place lentils and 2 teaspoons salt in heatproof container. Cover with 4 cups boiling water and let soak for 30 minutes. Drain well.

2. Meanwhile, finely chop three-quarters of onion (you should have about 1 cup) and grate remaining quarter (you should have about 3 tablespoons). Heat 2 tablespoons oil in Dutch oven over medium heat until shimmering. Add chorizo and cook until browned on all sides, 6 to 8 minutes. Transfer chorizo to large plate. Reduce heat to low and add chopped onion, carrots, 1 tablespoon parsley, and 1 teaspoon salt. Cover and cook, stirring occasionally, until vegetables are very soft but not brown, 25 to 30 minutes. If vegetables begin to brown, add 1 tablespoon water to pot.

3. Add lentils and vinegar to vegetables, increase heat to medium-high, and cook, stirring frequently, until vinegar starts to evaporate, 3 to 4 minutes. Add 7 cups water, chorizo, bay leaves, and cloves; bring to simmer. Reduce heat to low; cover; and cook until lentils are tender, about 30 minutes.

4. Heat remaining 3 tablespoons oil in small saucepan over medium heat until shimmering. Add paprika, grated onion, garlic, and ½ teaspoon pepper; cook, stirring constantly, until fragrant, 2 minutes. Add flour and cook, stirring constantly, 1 minute longer. Remove chorizo and bay leaves from lentils. Stir paprika mixture into lentils and continue to cook until flavors have blended and soup has thickened, 10 to 15 minutes. When chorizo is cool enough to handle, cut in half lengthwise, then cut each half into ¼-inch-thick slices. Return chorizo to soup along with remaining 2 tablespoons parsley and heat through, about 1 minute. Season with salt, pepper, and up to 2 teaspoons vinegar to taste and serve. (Soup can be made up to 3 days in advance.)

Red Lentil Soup with North African Spices

SERVES 4 to 6 `VEG`

WHY THIS RECIPE WORKS Small red lentils are one of our favorite legumes; they do not hold their shape when cooked but break down quickly into a creamy thick puree—perfect for a satisfying soup. Their mild flavor does require a bit of embellishment, so we started by sautéing onion in olive oil and used the warm mixture to bloom some fragrant North African spices. Tomato paste and garlic completed the base before the addition of the lentils, and a mix of broth and water gave the soup a full, rounded character. After only 15 minutes of cooking, the lentils were soft enough to be pureed with a whisk. A generous dose of lemon juice brought the flavors into focus, and a drizzle of spice-infused oil and a sprinkle of fresh cilantro completed the transformation of commonplace ingredients into an exotic yet comforting soup.

¼ cup extra-virgin olive oil
1 large onion, chopped fine
  Salt and pepper
¾ teaspoon ground coriander
½ teaspoon ground cumin
¼ teaspoon ground ginger
⅛ teaspoon ground cinnamon
  Pinch cayenne pepper
1 tablespoon tomato paste
1 garlic clove, minced
4 cups chicken or vegetable broth, plus extra as needed
2 cups water
10½ ounces (1½ cups) red lentils, picked over and rinsed
2 tablespoons lemon juice, plus extra for seasoning
1½ teaspoons dried mint, crumbled
1 teaspoon paprika
¼ cup chopped fresh cilantro

North African spices like cumin, coriander, and dried mint add unique flavor and character to a simple red lentil soup.

1. Heat 2 tablespoons oil in large saucepan over medium heat until shimmering. Add onion and 1 teaspoon salt and cook, stirring occasionally, until softened, about 5 minutes. Stir in coriander, cumin, ginger, cinnamon, ¼ teaspoon pepper, and cayenne and cook until fragrant, about 2 minutes. Stir in tomato paste and garlic and cook for 1 minute.

2. Stir in broth, water, and lentils and bring to vigorous simmer. Cook, stirring occasionally, until lentils are soft and about half are broken down, about 15 minutes.

3. Whisk soup vigorously until broken down to coarse puree, about 30 seconds. Adjust consistency with extra hot broth as needed. Stir in lemon juice and season with salt and extra lemon juice to taste. Cover and keep warm.

4. Heat remaining 2 tablespoons oil in small skillet over medium heat until shimmering. Off heat, stir in mint and paprika. Serve soup, drizzling individual portions with 1 teaspoon spiced oil and sprinkling with cilantro.

Moroccan-Style Chickpea Soup

SERVES 4 to 6   VEG

WHY THIS RECIPE WORKS This warming, evocative soup stands out because the tender, nutty chickpeas are infused with the rich, complex flavors of Moroccan cuisine. To make this soup simple enough to serve up on a weeknight, we turned to convenient canned chickpeas. We created an aromatic base by cooking chopped onion with a little sugar to subtly caramelize it. Plenty of garlic along with paprika, saffron, ginger, and cumin established the soup's potent flavor profile. The saffron lent the soup a distinct aroma and golden color, and the cumin and ginger added a pungent kick that would fool anyone into thinking this soup had been cooked for hours. As soon as the spices' fragrance began wafting from the pot, we stirred in the chickpeas along with potatoes for some starchy, hearty heft, canned diced tomatoes for bright acidity, and chopped zucchini for its contrasting soft texture and a bit of added color. After we poured in some broth and simmered the soup for just 20 minutes, the vegetables were tender and the rich flavors had blended. Mashing some of the potatoes into the soup gave it a rich consistency. You can substitute regular paprika and a pinch of cayenne for the hot paprika.

    3 tablespoons extra-virgin olive oil
    1 onion, chopped fine
    1 teaspoon sugar
      Salt and pepper
    4 garlic cloves, minced
    ½ teaspoon hot paprika
    ¼ teaspoon saffron threads, crumbled
    ¼ teaspoon ground ginger
    ¼ teaspoon ground cumin
    2 (15-ounce) cans chickpeas, rinsed
    1 pound red potatoes, unpeeled, cut into ½-inch pieces
    1 (14.5-ounce) can diced tomatoes
    1 zucchini, cut into ½-inch pieces
  3½ cups chicken or vegetable broth
    ¼ cup minced fresh parsley or mint
      Lemon wedges

1. Heat oil in Dutch oven over medium-high heat until shimmering. Add onion, sugar, and ½ teaspoon salt and cook until onion is softened, about 5 minutes. Stir in garlic, paprika, saffron, ginger, and cumin and cook until fragrant, about 30 seconds. Stir in chickpeas, potatoes, tomatoes and their juice, zucchini, and broth. Bring to simmer and cook, stirring occasionally, until potatoes are tender, 20 to 30 minutes.

2. Using wooden spoon, mash some of potatoes against side of pot to thicken soup. Off heat, stir in parsley and season with salt and pepper to taste. Serve with lemon wedges.

Sicilian Chickpea and Escarole Soup

SERVES 6 to 8   VEG

WHY THIS RECIPE WORKS In Sicily, chickpeas are the favored legume to add some hearty heft to a soup. Of the dozens of chickpea soup recipes we found, one flavor combination struck us as the most intriguing, pairing the mild bean with bright, slightly bitter escarole. We knew that dried beans were the way to go for our traditional soup because we could infuse the chickpeas with lots of flavor as they cooked. For aromatics, we started with classic Sicilian flavors: onion, garlic, oregano, and red pepper flakes. We also added fennel, which grows wild throughout much of the Mediterranean; its mild anise bite complemented the nutty chickpeas. A single strip of orange zest—a nod to the island's abundant citrus fruit crop—added a subtle citrusy note, and a Parmesan rind added a nutty richness and complexity that bolstered the chickpeas' flavor. When stirred in toward the end of cooking, the escarole leaves wilted to a velvety texture and the stems retained a slight crunch. The Parmesan rind can be replaced with a 2-inch chunk of cheese. For more information on soaking beans, see page 187. Serve with Garlic Toasts (page 56) or crusty bread.

      Salt and pepper
    1 pound (2¾ cups) dried chickpeas, picked over and rinsed
    2 tablespoons extra-virgin olive oil, plus extra for serving
    2 fennel bulbs, stalks discarded, bulbs halved, cored, and chopped fine
    1 small onion, chopped
    5 garlic cloves, minced
    2 teaspoons minced fresh oregano or ½ teaspoon dried
    ¼ teaspoon red pepper flakes
    5 cups chicken or vegetable broth
    1 Parmesan cheese rind, plus grated Parmesan for serving
    2 bay leaves
    1 (3-inch) strip orange zest
    1 head escarole (1 pound), trimmed and cut into 1-inch pieces
    1 large tomato, cored and chopped

1. Dissolve 3 tablespoons salt in 4 quarts cold water in large container. Add chickpeas and soak at room temperature for at least 8 hours or up to 24 hours. Drain and rinse well.

2. Heat oil in Dutch oven over medium heat until shimmering. Add fennel, onion, and 1 teaspoon salt and cook until vegetables are softened, 7 to 10 minutes. Stir in garlic, oregano, and pepper flakes and cook until fragrant, about 30 seconds.

3. Stir in 7 cups water, broth, soaked chickpeas, Parmesan rind, bay leaves, and orange zest and bring to boil. Reduce to gentle simmer and cook until chickpeas are tender, 1¼ to 1¾ hours.

4. Stir in escarole and tomato and cook until escarole is wilted, 5 to 10 minutes. Off heat, discard bay leaves and Parmesan rind (scraping off any cheese that has melted and adding it back to pot). Season with salt and pepper to taste. Serve, drizzling individual portions with extra oil and sprinkling with grated Parmesan.

GARLIC TOASTS

MAKES 8 slices `FAST` `VEG`

Be sure to use a high-quality crusty bread, such as a baguette; do not use sliced sandwich bread.

8 (1-inch-thick) slices rustic bread
1 large garlic clove, peeled
3 tablespoons extra-virgin olive oil
Salt and pepper

Adjust oven rack 6 inches from broiler element and heat broiler. Spread bread evenly in rimmed baking sheet and broil, flipping as needed, until well toasted on both sides, about 4 minutes. Briefly rub 1 side of each toast with garlic, drizzle with oil, and season with salt and pepper to taste. Serve.

Greek White Bean Soup

SERVES 6 `VEG`

WHY THIS RECIPE WORKS *Fasolatha*, considered to be one of Greece's national dishes, is a soup consisting of creamy white beans, peppery olive oil, and fresh vegetables. Since this soup is all about the beans, we were determined to avoid tough, exploded beans in our version. So we soaked the beans overnight in salted water, which softened their skins, made them less prone to bursting, and also resulted in creamier beans. As for vegetables, onion and celery created a flavorful base, and using broth instead of water gave additional depth. For a silkier and more cohesive texture, we blended 2 cups of the soup and mixed it back into the pot. Lemon juice added brightness, and stirring in Aleppo pepper at the end provided a hint of spice and warmth. Serving the soup with a drizzle of olive oil and a sprinkle of parsley created an irresistibly fresh flavor and accented the creamy and rich beans. If you can't find Aleppo pepper, you can substitute ¼ teaspoon paprika and ¼ teaspoon finely chopped red pepper flakes. For more information on soaking beans, see page 187.

For the creamiest texture, we brine dried cannellini beans overnight for our take on this traditional Greek soup.

Salt and pepper
1 pound (2½ cups) dried cannellini beans, picked over and rinsed
2 tablespoons extra-virgin olive oil, plus extra for serving
1 onion, chopped
2½ teaspoons minced fresh oregano or ¾ teaspoon dried
6 cups chicken or vegetable broth, plus extra as needed
4 celery ribs, cut into ½-inch pieces
3 tablespoons lemon juice
1 teaspoon ground dried Aleppo pepper
2 tablespoons chopped fresh parsley

1. Dissolve 3 tablespoons salt in 4 quarts cold water in large container. Add beans and soak at room temperature for at least 8 hours or up to 24 hours. Drain and rinse well.

2. Heat oil in Dutch oven over medium heat until shimmering. Add onion, ½ teaspoon salt, and ½ teaspoon pepper and cook until softened and lightly browned, 5 to 7 minutes. Stir in oregano and cook until fragrant, about 30 seconds. Stir in broth, celery, and soaked beans and bring to boil. Reduce heat to low, cover, and simmer until beans are tender, 45 to 60 minutes.

3. Process 2 cups soup in blender until smooth, about 30 seconds, then return to pot. Heat soup gently over low heat until hot (do not boil) and adjust consistency with extra hot broth as needed. Stir in lemon juice, Aleppo, and parsley and season with salt and pepper to taste. Serve, drizzling individual portions with extra oil.

Sorting Dried Beans

 Before cooking dried beans, you should pick them over for any small stones or debris and then rinse them. The easiest way to check for small stones is to spread the beans on a large plate or rimmed baking sheet.

Pasta e Fagioli with Orange and Fennel

SERVES 8 to 10

WHY THIS RECIPE WORKS Though the precise ingredients for Italy's famed *pasta e fagioli* vary from region to region, too many recipes have one thing in common: They turn out bland and mushy and take hours to prepare. For our recipe, we wanted to find a silver bullet—a satisfying soup boasting great flavor and proper texture that didn't take all afternoon to make. We started by cooking some pancetta (bacon worked well, too) in a Dutch oven to create a savory base, then cooked our vegetables in the rendered fat. We established an Italian flavor profile with the help of some fennel seeds, orange zest, dried oregano, red pepper flakes, and plenty of garlic. Minced anchovy fillets contributed a complex, meaty character void of any fishy aftertaste. Turning to canned diced tomatoes (instead of fresh) and sweet, creamy canned cannellini beans (instead of dried) cut hours out of prep time, and using the tomatoes to deglaze our aromatic base intensified the flavor of the soup. A Parmesan rind was an easy way to introduce a subtle umami quality. Cutting our chicken broth with water provided richness without overwhelming the other flavors. For our pasta, we looked to small shapes like ditalini, tubettini, or, our top choice, orzo to complement rather than crowd out the other ingredients. Finally, parsley lent the necessary bright note to finish our soup. The Parmesan rind can be replaced with a 2-inch chunk of cheese. You can substitute ditalini or tubettini for the orzo (the cooking times may vary slightly).

We build lots of flavor in our Italian pasta and bean soup using pancetta, fennel seeds, anchovies, and Parmesan.

1 tablespoon extra-virgin olive oil, plus extra for serving
3 ounces pancetta, chopped fine
1 onion, chopped fine
1 fennel bulb, stalks discarded, bulb halved, cored, and chopped fine
1 celery rib, minced
4 garlic cloves, minced
3 anchovy fillets, rinsed and minced
1 tablespoon minced fresh oregano or 1 teaspoon dried
2 teaspoons grated orange zest
½ teaspoon fennel seeds
¼ teaspoon red pepper flakes
1 (28-ounce) can diced tomatoes
1 Parmesan cheese rind, plus grated Parmesan for serving
2 (15-ounce) cans cannellini beans, rinsed
3½ cups chicken broth
2½ cups water
   Salt and pepper
1 cup orzo
¼ cup minced fresh parsley

1. Heat oil in Dutch oven over medium-high heat until shimmering. Add pancetta and cook, stirring occasionally, until beginning to brown, 3 to 5 minutes. Stir in onion, fennel, and celery and cook until vegetables are softened, 5 to 7 minutes. Stir in garlic, anchovies, oregano, orange zest, fennel seeds, and pepper flakes and cook until fragrant, about 1 minute.

2. Stir in tomatoes and their juice, scraping up any browned bits. Stir in Parmesan rind and beans, bring to simmer, and cook until flavors meld, about 10 minutes.

3. Stir in broth, water, and 1 teaspoon salt. Increase heat to high and bring to boil. Stir in pasta and cook until al dente, about 10 minutes. Off heat, discard Parmesan rind. Stir in parsley and season with salt and pepper to taste. Serve, drizzling individual portions with extra oil and sprinkling with grated Parmesan.

Spiced Fava Bean Soup

SERVES 4 to 6 VEG

WHY THIS RECIPE WORKS *B'ssara* is a traditional Moroccan soup made with dried fava beans that is remarkably simple to make. But even a simple soup can have disastrous pitfalls: undercooked beans, bitter olive oil, overpowering and harsh spices, and flat flavor. We wanted a straightforward, balanced soup that featured the fava bean's characteristic earthy flavor. To start, we focused on the beans, selecting dried split favas to avoid the tedious task of peeling the tough skins off each one. Our first attempts coaxed excellent flavor from the beans, but the soup lacked depth. To build up the flavor without overpowering the beans, we added an onion, sautéing it to bring out its subtle sweetness. We then increased the amount of garlic and bloomed it with fragrant paprika and cumin. Instead of water, we chose broth, which added depth of flavor. After simmering the beans until they were breaking apart, we bypassed the food processor and the blender, which produced soup that was way too thick, and simply whisked our soup, creating a silken broth and looser consistency with pleasant bits of beans for textural contrast. To finish, lemon juice added some necessary brightness, and we topped individual bowls with extra paprika, cumin, and olive oil, which are the customary garnishes.

3 tablespoons extra-virgin olive oil, plus extra for serving
1 onion, chopped
  Salt and pepper
5 garlic cloves, minced
2 teaspoons paprika, plus extra for serving

Cooking dried fava beans with aromatic spices like cumin and paprika gives this Moroccan soup authentic flavor.

2 teaspoons cumin, plus extra for serving
1 pound (3 cups) dried split fava beans, picked over and rinsed
6 cups chicken or vegetable broth, plus extra as needed
2 cups water
¼ cup lemon juice (2 lemons)

1. Heat oil in Dutch oven over medium heat until shimmering. Add onion, ¾ teaspoon salt, and ¼ teaspoon pepper and cook until softened and lightly browned, 5 to 7 minutes. Stir in garlic, paprika, and cumin and cook until fragrant, about 30 seconds.

2. Stir in beans, broth, and water and bring to boil. Cover, reduce heat to low, and simmer gently, stirring occasionally, until beans are soft and broken down, 1½ to 2 hours.

3. Off heat, whisk soup vigorously until broken down to coarse puree, about 30 seconds. Adjust consistency with extra hot broth as needed. Stir in lemon juice and season with salt and pepper to taste. Serve, drizzling individual portions with extra oil and sprinkling with extra paprika and cumin.

Avgolemono

SERVES 6 to 8

WHY THIS RECIPE WORKS The rich, soft texture and bright citrusy flavor of *avgolemono*, a traditional Greek soup, centers around just four humble pantry staples: chicken stock, rice, eggs, and lemons. We started our soup by cooking long-grain white rice in chicken broth; the grains' starches helped to thicken the broth. Bright lemon flavor is central to this soup, so we jump-started the citrusy impact with a dozen strips of lemon zest. Crushed green cardamom pods instantly contributed a slightly sweet, aromatic quality to the soup. Two whole eggs plus two extra yolks produced a perfectly smooth texture, rich flavor, and sunny yellow hue. To ensure that our eggs didn't scramble in the hot soup, we slowly whisked some of the broth into the eggs before adding the mixture to the pot, stirring constantly as the soup thickened. Scallions or fresh mint made for flavorful garnishes. Homemade chicken stock gives this soup the best flavor and body, but in a pinch you can use store-bought chicken broth. Make sure to zest the lemons before juicing them. The longer the final soup cooks after the eggs have been added, the thicker it becomes. Serve the soup immediately; it thickens to a gravylike consistency when reheated.

  8 cups chicken broth
  ½ cup long-grain white rice
 12 (4-inch) strips lemon zest plus ¼ cup juice (2 lemons)
  4 green cardamom pods, crushed, or 2 whole cloves
  1 bay leaf
1½ teaspoons salt
  2 large eggs plus 2 large yolks, room temperature
  1 scallion, sliced thin, or 3 tablespoons chopped fresh mint

1. Bring broth to boil in medium saucepan over high heat. Stir in rice, lemon zest, cardamom pods, bay leaf, and salt. Reduce to simmer and cook until rice is tender and broth is aromatic, 16 to 20 minutes.

2. Gently whisk whole eggs, egg yolks, and lemon juice together in medium bowl until combined. Discard bay leaf, cardamom, and zest strips. Reduce heat to low. Whisking constantly, slowly ladle about 2 cups hot broth into egg mixture and whisk until combined. Pour egg mixture back into saucepan and cook, stirring constantly, until soup is slightly thickened and wisps of steam appear, about 5 minutes (do not simmer or boil). Sprinkle individual portions with scallion and serve immediately.

VARIATIONS

Avgolemono with Chicken

Add two 6-ounce boneless, skinless chicken breasts, cut into ½-inch pieces, to broth along with rice.

Avgolemono with Saffron

Add ¼ teaspoon saffron threads, crumbled, to broth along with rice.

Tempering Eggs

1. To temper eggs so that they won't curdle when added to hot soup, whisk them together in bowl. Then, slowly whisk in some hot broth to gently warm them.

2. Once eggs have been warmed, slowly whisk them into pot and continue to cook gently, stirring constantly, until soup is thickened.

Spicy Moroccan-Style Chicken and Lentil Soup

SERVES 8

WHY THIS RECIPE WORKS *Harira* is an intensely flavored Moroccan soup of lentils, tomatoes, chickpeas, and often chicken or lamb. Best known as a dish with which to break fast during the holy month of Ramadan, it's also served at other celebrations and family get-togethers. Most recipes call for a laundry list of ingredients, many of which are obscure and hard to find in American markets. To simplify our version, we looked to our spice rack for accessible, impactful flavor builders. We chose split chicken breasts as our protein, and after browning them, we bloomed our aromatics in the rendered fat. We began with minced onion, next adding a fragrant combination of fresh ginger, cumin, paprika, cinnamon, cayenne, saffron, and black pepper. The result: a sweet, smoky, deeply flavorful base with just a touch of heat. A bit of flour provided some thickening power. Cooking the chicken through in the broth boosted the base's meaty flavor, and brown lentils held their shape and took on a tender texture when added with the browned chicken. Once the chicken was cooked, we removed it, then shredded it and stirred it back into the pot. Canned chickpeas were convenient while plum tomatoes cut into large, chunky pieces added just the right amount of tomato flavor and acidity. *Harissa*, a superspicy paste of hot chiles, spices, garlic, and olive oil, is a critical finishing touch to every harira recipe; for the best and most potent flavor, we made our own. We stirred plenty of this potent paste into the pot along with bright, fresh cilantro. Large green or brown lentils work well in this recipe; do not use French green lentils, or *lentilles du puy*. We prefer to use our homemade Harissa (page 316), but you can substitute store-bought harissa if you wish, though spiciness can vary greatly by brand.

1½ pounds bone-in split chicken breasts, trimmed
    Salt and pepper
 1 tablespoon extra-virgin olive oil
 1 onion, chopped fine
 1 teaspoon grated fresh ginger
 1 teaspoon ground cumin
 ½ teaspoon paprika
 ¼ teaspoon ground cinnamon
 ¼ teaspoon cayenne pepper
    Pinch saffron threads, crumbled
 1 tablespoon all-purpose flour
10 cups chicken broth
 ¾ cup green or brown lentils, picked over and rinsed
 1 (15-ounce) can chickpeas, rinsed
 4 plum tomatoes, cored and cut into ¾-inch pieces
 ⅓ cup minced fresh cilantro
 ¼ cup harissa, plus extra for serving

1. Pat chicken dry with paper towels and season with salt and pepper. Heat oil in Dutch oven over medium-high heat until just smoking. Brown chicken lightly, about 3 minutes per side; transfer to plate.

2. Add onion to fat left in pot and cook over medium heat until softened, about 5 minutes. Stir in ginger, cumin, paprika, cinnamon, cayenne, ¼ teaspoon pepper, and saffron and cook until fragrant, about 30 seconds. Stir in flour and cook for 1 minute. Slowly whisk in broth, scraping up any browned bits and smoothing out any lumps, and bring to boil.

3. Stir in lentils and chickpeas, then nestle chicken into pot and bring to simmer. Cover, reduce heat to low, and simmer gently until chicken registers 160 degrees, 15 to 20 minutes.

4. Transfer chicken to cutting board, let cool slightly, then shred into bite-size pieces using 2 forks, discarding skin and bones. Meanwhile, continue to simmer lentils, covered, for 25 to 30 minutes.

5. Stir in shredded chicken and cook until heated through, about 2 minutes. Stir in tomatoes, cilantro, and harissa and season with salt and pepper to taste. Serve, passing extra harissa separately.

This hearty Moroccan soup combines chunks of lamb with lentils and a generous dose of spicy harissa.

VARIATION
Spicy Moroccan-Style Lamb and Lentil Soup
SERVES 6 to 8
Large green or brown lentils work well in this recipe; do not use French green lentils, or *lentilles du puy*. We prefer to use our homemade Harissa (page 316), but you can substitute store-bought harissa if you wish, though spiciness can vary greatly by brand.

 1 pound lamb shoulder chops (blade or round bone),
    1 to 1½ inches thick, trimmed and halved
    Salt and pepper
 1 tablespoon extra-virgin olive oil
 1 onion, chopped fine
 1 teaspoon grated fresh ginger
 1 teaspoon ground cumin
 ½ teaspoon paprika
 ¼ teaspoon ground cinnamon
 ¼ teaspoon cayenne pepper
    Pinch saffron threads, crumbled
 1 tablespoon all-purpose flour
10 cups chicken broth
 ¾ cup green or brown lentils, picked over and rinsed

1 (15-ounce) can chickpeas, rinsed
4 plum tomatoes, cored and cut into ¾-inch pieces
⅓ cup minced fresh cilantro
¼ cup harissa, plus extra for serving

1. Adjust oven rack to lower-middle position and heat oven to 325 degrees. Pat lamb dry with paper towels and season with salt and pepper. Heat oil in Dutch oven over medium-high heat until just smoking. Brown lamb, about 4 minutes per side; transfer to plate. Pour off all but 2 tablespoons fat from pot.

2. Add onion to fat left in pot and cook over medium heat until softened, about 5 minutes. Stir in ginger, cumin, paprika, cinnamon, cayenne, ¼ teaspoon pepper, and saffron and cook until fragrant, about 30 seconds. Stir in flour and cook for 1 minute. Slowly whisk in broth, scraping up any browned bits and smoothing out any lumps, and bring to boil.

3. Nestle lamb into pot along with any accumulated juices, bring to simmer, and cook for 10 minutes. Stir in lentils and chickpeas, cover, and place pot in oven. Cook until fork slips easily in and out of lamb and lentils are tender, 50 minutes to 1 hour.

4. Transfer lamb to cutting board, let cool slightly, then shred into bite-size pieces using 2 forks, discarding excess fat and bones. Stir shredded lamb into soup and let sit until heated through, about 2 minutes. Stir in tomatoes, cilantro, and harissa and season with salt and pepper to taste. Serve, passing extra harissa separately.

To give our Libyan *sharba* plenty of meaty, savory flavor, we sear and shred lamb shoulder chops.

Lamb and Mint Sharba

SERVES 6 to 8

WHY THIS RECIPE WORKS *Sharba* is the iconic dish of Libya used to break the daily fast during the holy month of Ramadan. This intensely flavored soup relies on lamb, mint, chickpeas, and often orzo. It traditionally employs *baharat*, a spice mix consisting of sometimes more than 12 ingredients. We wanted to develop a soup reminiscent of this Libyan staple dish without emptying the entire spice cabinet. We started by cooking ground lamb meat with a soup base built on onion, tomatoes, dried mint, and a pared-down blend of spices, finishing the soup with chopped fresh mint. We found the ground lamb a bit dry and chili-like, and the soup lacked any real depth or body. Moreover, the chopped mint proved overpowering, drowning out the other spices. We decided to try braising bigger chunks of seared shoulder meat and then shredding them. Searing the meat produced a significantly more flavorful soup base, and the shredded meat was perfect in texture. But we still needed a more nuanced way of reinforcing mint flavor without making the soup taste like peppermint. We tried varying amounts of dried mint in the soup base, but each version tasted about the same, even when we used up to a full tablespoon. We then reserved some crumbled dried mint that we steeped just at the end. This technique proved successful: The soup took on a subtle but refreshing mint aroma that did not overpower the warmer flavors of the broth. Now we had a comforting, aromatic soup that could stand up to Libyan tradition.

1 pound lamb shoulder chops (blade or round bone), 1 to 1½ inches thick, trimmed and halved
Salt and pepper
1 tablespoon extra-virgin olive oil
1 onion, chopped fine
4 plum tomatoes, cored and cut into ¼-inch pieces
2 tablespoons tomato paste
1½ teaspoons dried mint, crumbled
1 teaspoon ground turmeric
1 teaspoon paprika
½ teaspoon ground cinnamon
¼ teaspoon ground cumin
10 cups chicken broth
1 (15-ounce) can chickpeas, rinsed
1 cup orzo

1. Adjust oven rack to lower-middle position and heat oven to 325 degrees. Pat lamb dry with paper towels and season with salt and pepper. Heat oil in Dutch oven over medium-high heat until just smoking. Brown lamb, about 4 minutes per side; transfer to plate. Pour off all but 2 tablespoons fat from pot.

2. Add onion to fat left in pot and cook over medium heat until softened, about 5 minutes. Stir in tomatoes and cook until softened and juice has evaporated, about 2 minutes. Stir in tomato paste, 1 teaspoon mint, turmeric, paprika, 1 teaspoon salt, cinnamon, cumin, and ¼ teaspoon pepper and cook until fragrant, about 1 minute. Stir in broth, scraping up any browned bits, and bring to boil.

3. Stir in chickpeas, then nestle lamb into pot along with any accumulated juices. Cover, place pot in oven, and cook until fork slips easily in and out of lamb, about 1 hour.

4. Transfer lamb to cutting board, let cool slightly, then shred into bite-size pieces using 2 forks, discarding excess fat and bones. Meanwhile, stir orzo into soup, bring to simmer over medium heat, and cook until tender, 10 to 12 minutes.

5. Stir in shredded lamb and cook until heated through, about 2 minutes. Off heat, stir in remaining ½ teaspoon mint and let sit until fragrant, about 1 minute. Serve.

Spanish-Style Meatball Soup with Saffron
SERVES 6 to 8

WHY THIS RECIPE WORKS Spanish meatball soup boasts a deeply flavorful sunset-colored broth and tender meatballs, but finding the right balance of ingredients is pivotal to its success. We started with the meatballs, opting for a combination of ground pork and beef. A paste made from bread and milk known as a panade helped ensure that the lean meat stayed moist and tender. For extra flavor and texture, we added grated Manchego, a sharp Spanish sheep's-milk cheese, shallot, parsley, and olive oil. We rolled spoon-size ½-inch balls and placed them in the refrigerator to firm up. For a full-flavored broth, we started with a traditional Spanish base, or *sofrito*, of onion, bell pepper, and garlic, then added enough saffron threads for a potent but not overwhelming impact. Paprika contributed some sweetness to the broth while also reinforcing its orange hue, and a bit of red pepper flakes delivered just enough heat. We deglazed the pot with white wine for brightness, poured in chicken broth, and then carefully dropped in the chilled meatballs. Finally, we added body to the soup with a traditional picada, a simple mixture of ground almonds, bread crumbs, and olive oil. We pulsed the ingredients, then gently toasted the mixture in the oven to bring out its nutty flavor. A sprinkling of minced parsley made for a bright, fresh finish. Parmesan or Asiago cheese can be substituted for the Manchego.

Manchego, shallot, parsley, and olive oil add richness and flavor to the pork and beef meatballs in this Spanish soup.

MEATBALLS
2 slices hearty white sandwich bread, torn into quarters
⅓ cup whole milk
8 ounces ground pork
1 ounce Manchego cheese, grated (½ cup)
3 tablespoons minced fresh parsley
1 shallot, minced
2 tablespoons extra-virgin olive oil
½ teaspoon salt
½ teaspoon pepper
8 ounces 80 percent lean ground beef

SOUP
1 tablespoon extra-virgin olive oil
1 onion, chopped fine
1 red bell pepper, stemmed, seeded, and cut into ¾-inch pieces
2 garlic cloves, minced
1 teaspoon paprika
¼ teaspoon saffron threads, crumbled
⅛ teaspoon red pepper flakes
1 cup dry white wine

8 cups chicken broth
1 recipe Picada
2 tablespoons minced fresh parsley
  Salt and pepper

1. FOR THE MEATBALLS Using fork, mash bread and milk together into paste in large bowl. Stir in ground pork, Manchego, parsley, shallot, oil, salt, and pepper until combined. Add ground beef and knead with your hands until combined. Pinch off and roll 2-teaspoon-size pieces of mixture into balls and arrange in rimmed baking sheet (you should have 30 to 35 meatballs). Cover with plastic wrap and refrigerate until firm, at least 30 minutes.

2. FOR THE SOUP Heat oil in large Dutch oven over medium-high heat until shimmering. Add onion and bell pepper and cook until softened and lightly browned, 8 to 10 minutes. Stir in garlic, paprika, saffron, and pepper flakes and cook until fragrant, about 30 seconds. Stir in wine, scraping up any browned bits, and cook until almost completely evaporated, about 1 minute.

3. Stir in broth and bring to simmer. Gently add meatballs and simmer until cooked through, 10 to 12 minutes. Off heat, stir in picada and parsley and season with salt and pepper to taste. Serve.

VARIATION
Spanish-Style Meatball Soup with Saffron and Kale
Add 8 ounces kale, stemmed and chopped, to soup with meatballs.

PICADA

MAKES about 1 cup `FAST` `VEG`

Chopped or whole unsalted almonds can be substituted for the slivered almonds; however, they may require longer processing times.

¼ cup slivered almonds
2 slices hearty white sandwich bread,
  torn into quarters
2 tablespoons extra-virgin olive oil
⅛ teaspoon salt
  Pinch pepper

Adjust oven rack to middle position and heat oven to 375 degrees. Pulse almonds in food processor to fine crumbs, about 20 pulses. Add bread, oil, salt, and pepper and pulse bread to coarse crumbs, about 10 pulses. Spread mixture evenly in rimmed baking sheet and bake, stirring often, until golden brown, about 10 minutes. Set aside to cool. (Picada can be stored in airtight container for up to 2 days.)

To ensure perfectly cooked fish, we gently poach slices of hake off the heat in a richly flavorful broth.

Provençal Fish Soup
SERVES 6 to 8

WHY THIS RECIPE WORKS Every country with a coastline boasts its own version of fish soup; our Provence-inspired version is not only easy to make, it boasts a richly flavored broth fragrant with fennel, paprika, saffron, and orange zest. Fish soup is often a study in culinary frustration: The broth is bland and flavorless, the fish is flaked into tiny pieces, and, worst of all, the fish is criminally overcooked. We chose thick cuts of hake, wanting a firm fish that would not break apart too easily, and orange and fennel to pair with the delicate seafood. The problem then came in building the soup base. Initial tests with premade fish stock produced soups that overpowered the hake's own mild flavor. Water-based versions were more delicate in flavor but lacked any real depth or richness. Deglazing the vegetables and spices with wine and bottled clam juice brought out a more balanced flavor, but tasters wanted even more depth. So we browned some pancetta and cooked the vegetables in the rendered fat. This version had a perfect balance of smokiness, richness, and citrus aroma. To cook the fish perfectly, we left it in big slices so that they wouldn't break apart too much. We tried simmering the fish over low heat, but when we employed direct heat, the fish was overcooked by the time it was served. We decided on a more unconventional method: We placed the fish in the pot, shut off the heat, and let it poach gently. This technique was undeniably successful: The fish was perfectly cooked. Finally we had a hearty, fragrant fish soup with perfect broth and perfect fish. Cod and halibut can be substituted for the hake.

    1 tablespoon extra-virgin olive oil, plus extra for serving
    6 ounces pancetta, chopped fine
    1 fennel bulb, 2 tablespoons fronds minced, stalks
        discarded, bulb halved, cored, and cut into
        ½-inch pieces
    1 onion, chopped
    2 celery ribs, halved lengthwise and cut into
        ½-inch pieces
        Salt and pepper
    4 garlic cloves, minced
    1 teaspoon paprika
    ⅛ teaspoon red pepper flakes
        Pinch saffron threads, crumbled
    1 cup dry white wine or dry vermouth
    4 cups water
    2 (8-ounce) bottles clam juice
    2 bay leaves
    2 pounds skinless hake fillets, 1 to 1½ inches thick,
        sliced crosswise into 6 equal pieces
    2 tablespoons minced fresh parsley
    1 tablespoon grated orange zest

1. Heat oil in Dutch oven over medium heat until shimmering. Add pancetta and cook, stirring occasionally, until beginning to brown, 3 to 5 minutes. Stir in fennel pieces, onion, celery, and 1½ teaspoons salt and cook until vegetables are softened and lightly browned, 12 to 14 minutes. Stir in garlic, paprika, pepper flakes, and saffron and cook until fragrant, about 30 seconds.

2. Stir in wine, scraping up any browned bits. Stir in water, clam juice, and bay leaves. Bring to simmer and cook until flavors meld, 15 to 20 minutes.

3. Off heat, discard bay leaves. Nestle hake into cooking liquid, cover, and let sit until fish flakes apart when gently prodded with paring knife and registers 140 degrees, 8 to 10 minutes. Gently stir in parsley, fennel fronds, and orange zest and break fish into large pieces. Season with salt and pepper to taste. Serve, drizzling individual portions with extra oil.

NOTES FROM THE TEST KITCHEN
Using Bay Leaves

Bay leaves are a key seasoning in many soups. In the test kitchen, we use fresh herbs more often than dried—bay leaves being an exception. We prefer dried bay leaves to fresh; they work just as well in long-cooked recipes, are cheaper, and will keep for 3 months in the freezer in an airtight container. We prefer Turkish bay leaves to those from California. The California bay leaf has a medicinal and potent, eucalyptus-like flavor, but the Turkish bay leaf has a mild, green, and slightly clovelike flavor.

Shellfish Soup with Leeks and Turmeric
SERVES 6 to 8

WHY THIS RECIPE WORKS For a succulent shellfish soup bursting with flavor and chock-full of seafood, we decided to use shrimp, scallops, and squid since these made for an easier-to-eat soup. Since all of the seafood would need to be cooked at the end, we set out to build a flavorful soup base. Initial tests with pancetta and fish stock produced soups that were savory and tasty, but too muddy and rich. We turned to the seafood itself: The shrimp shells were a valuable source of flavor, from which we could extract a potent and aromatic broth. We sautéed the shells and simmered them in white wine and water for a few minutes. After straining out the shells, we used the broth to deglaze the cooked vegetables and to build the soup base. This soup was intensely shrimp-flavored and fragrant. After testing, we found that the broth needed no longer than 10 minutes to simmer with the shells. Building around this concentrated shrimp broth, we chose leeks and spices reminiscent of North Africa—namely, ginger, coriander, and turmeric. A small bit of tomato paste reinforced the more savory aspects of the soup without being distracting, and bottled clam juice added dimension and natural sweetness. Finally we had a potent, shrimp-forward broth that would be the perfect medium for cooking the seafood. To avoid overcooking anything, we added the seafood in stages: Scallops got a 2-minute head start on the shrimp, which cooked in mere minutes. Adding the squid last off heat gently poached it and delivered a perfectly cooked, meaty shellfish soup. If desired, you can omit the squid in this recipe and increase the amount of shrimp to 1½ pounds.

2 tablespoons extra-virgin olive oil, plus extra for serving

12 ounces large shrimp (26 to 30 per pound), peeled and deveined, shells reserved

1 cup dry white wine or dry vermouth

4 cups water

1½ pounds leeks, white and light green parts only, halved lengthwise, sliced thin, and washed thoroughly

4 ounces pancetta, chopped fine

3 tablespoons tomato paste

2 garlic cloves, minced

Salt and pepper

1 teaspoon grated fresh ginger

1 teaspoon ground coriander

½ teaspoon ground turmeric

⅛ teaspoon red pepper flakes

2 (8-ounce) bottles clam juice

12 ounces large sea scallops, tendons removed

12 ounces squid, bodies sliced crosswise into ½-inch-thick rings, tentacles halved

⅓ cup minced fresh parsley

1. Heat 1 tablespoon oil in Dutch oven over medium heat until shimmering. Add shrimp shells and cook, stirring frequently, until beginning to turn spotty brown and pot starts to brown, 2 to 4 minutes. Add wine and simmer, stirring occasionally, for 2 minutes. Stir in water, bring to simmer, and cook for 4 minutes. Strain mixture through fine-mesh strainer into bowl, pressing on solids to extract as much liquid as possible; discard solids.

2. Heat remaining 1 tablespoon oil in now-empty pot over medium heat until shimmering. Add leeks and pancetta and cook until leeks are softened and lightly browned, about 8 minutes. Stir in tomato paste, garlic, 1 teaspoon salt, ginger, coriander, turmeric, and pepper flakes and cook until fragrant, about 1 minute. Stir in wine mixture and clam juice, scraping up any browned bits. Bring to simmer and cook until flavors meld, 15 to 20 minutes.

3. Reduce heat to gentle simmer, add sea scallops, and cook for 2 minutes. Stir in shrimp and cook until just opaque throughout, about 2 minutes. Off heat, stir in squid, cover, and let sit until just opaque and tender, 1 to 2 minutes. Stir in parsley and season with salt and pepper to taste. Serve, drizzling individual portions with extra oil.

Stock made with shrimp shells and wine creates a full-flavored, seafood-rich base for this shellfish soup.

Peeling and Deveining Shrimp

1. Break shell under swimming legs, which will come off as shell is removed. Leave tail intact, if desired, or tug tail to remove shell.

2. Use paring knife to make shallow cut along back of shrimp to expose vein. Use tip of knife to lift out vein. Discard vein by wiping blade against paper towel.

CHAPTER 3

Salads

■ FAST (less than 45 minutes start to finish)   ▦ VEGETARIAN

Photos (clockwise from top left): Fava Bean and Radish Salad; Grilled Vegetable and Halloumi Salad; Fattoush; Moroccan-Style
Carrot Salad with Harissa and Feta

SIMPLE GREEN SALADS

Salads are an integral part of the Mediterranean table, so we developed some interesting simple salads that are easy and quick to put together. They combine various greens with flavorful Italian, Spanish, and Greek ingredients such as nuts, olives, and cheese.

Tricolor Salad with Balsamic Vinaigrette

Basic Green Salad

SERVES 4 `FAST` `VEG`

½ garlic clove, peeled
8 ounces (8 cups) lettuce, torn into bite-size pieces if necessary
 Extra-virgin olive oil
 Vinegar
 Salt and pepper

Rub inside of salad bowl with garlic. Add lettuce. Holding thumb over mouth of olive oil bottle to control flow, slowly drizzle lettuce with small amount of oil. Toss greens very gently. Continue to drizzle with oil and toss gently until greens are lightly coated and just glistening. Sprinkle with small amounts of vinegar, salt, and pepper to taste and toss gently to coat. Serve.

Tricolor Salad with Balsamic Vinaigrette

SERVES 4 to 6 `FAST` `VEG`

1 small head radicchio (6 ounces), cored and cut into 1-inch pieces
1 head Belgian endive (4 ounces), cut into 2-inch pieces
3 ounces (3 cups) baby arugula
1 tablespoon balsamic vinegar
1 teaspoon red wine vinegar
 Salt and pepper
3 tablespoons extra-virgin olive oil

Gently toss radicchio, endive, and arugula together in large bowl. Whisk balsamic vinegar, red wine vinegar, ⅛ teaspoon salt, and pinch pepper together in small bowl. Whisking constantly, slowly drizzle in oil. Drizzle vinaigrette over salad and gently toss to coat. Season with salt and pepper to taste. Serve.

Green Salad with Marcona Almonds and Manchego Cheese

SERVES 4 to 6 `FAST` `VEG`

6 ounces (6 cups) mesclun greens
5 teaspoons sherry vinegar
1 shallot, minced
1 teaspoon Dijon mustard
 Salt and pepper
¼ cup extra-virgin olive oil
⅓ cup Marcona almonds, chopped coarse
2 ounces Manchego cheese, shaved

Place mesclun in large bowl. Whisk vinegar, shallot, mustard, ¼ teaspoon salt, and ¼ teaspoon pepper together in small bowl. Whisking constantly, slowly drizzle in oil. Drizzle vinaigrette over mesclun and gently toss to coat. Season with salt and pepper to taste. Serve, topping individual portions with almonds and Manchego.

BUYING SALAD GREENS

Not only is there a dizzying array of greens available at the supermarket now, but in a good market you can buy the same greens more than one way: full heads, prewashed in a bag, in a clamshell, and loose in bulk bins. Which is the right choice for you? A sturdy lettuce like romaine can be washed and stored for up to a week (see page 71), making it a good option for many nights' worth of salads. Bags of prewashed baby spinach, arugula, and mesclun mix offer great convenience, but be sure to turn over the bags and inspect the greens as closely as you can; the sell-by date alone doesn't ensure quality, so if you see moisture in the bag or hints of blackened leaf edges, move on.

Don't buy bags of already-cut lettuce that you can otherwise buy as whole heads, like romaine, Bibb, or red leaf. Precut lettuce will be inferior in quality because the leaves begin to spoil once they are cut (bagged hearts of romaine are fine but stay away from bags of cut romaine). Endive and radicchio are always sold in heads, and because they are sturdy and will last a while, they are nice to have on hand to complement other greens and just to add more interest to a salad. And when a special salad is planned for company, for the best results you should buy the greens either the day of the party or the day before.

Arugula Salad with Fennel and Shaved Parmesan

SERVES 4 to 6 `FAST` `VEG`

- 6 ounces (6 cups) baby arugula
- 1 large fennel bulb, stalks discarded, bulb halved, cored, and sliced thin
- 1½ tablespoons lemon juice
- 1 small shallot, minced
- 1 teaspoon Dijon mustard
- 1 teaspoon minced fresh thyme
- 1 small garlic clove, minced
  Salt and pepper
- ¼ cup extra-virgin olive oil
- 1 ounce Parmesan cheese, shaved

Gently toss arugula and fennel together in large bowl. Whisk lemon juice, shallot, mustard, thyme, garlic, ⅛ teaspoon salt, and pinch pepper together in small bowl. Whisking constantly, slowly drizzle in oil. Drizzle dressing over salad and gently toss to coat. Season with salt and pepper to taste. Serve, topping individual portions with Parmesan.

Green Salad with Artichokes and Olives

SERVES 4 to 6 `FAST` `VEG`

- 1 romaine lettuce heart (6 ounces), cut into 1-inch pieces
- 3 ounces (3 cups) baby arugula
- 1 cup jarred whole baby artichoke hearts packed in water, quartered, rinsed, and patted dry
- ⅓ cup fresh parsley leaves
- ⅓ cup pitted kalamata olives, halved
- 2 tablespoons white wine vinegar or white balsamic vinegar
- 1 small garlic clove, minced
  Salt and pepper
- 3 tablespoons extra-virgin olive oil
- 1 ounce Asiago cheese, shaved

Gently toss romaine, arugula, artichoke hearts, parsley, and olives together in large bowl. Whisk vinegar, garlic, ¼ teaspoon salt, and pinch pepper together in small bowl. Whisking constantly, slowly drizzle in oil. Drizzle vinaigrette over salad and gently toss to coat. Season with salt and pepper to taste. Serve, topping individual portions with Asiago.

Green Salad with Artichokes and Olives

Making a Simple Green Salad

1. MEASURE OUT AND TOSS GREENS Measure out greens and toss gently with any additional vegetables.

2. MAKE DRESSING BASE Whisk together vinegar or lemon juice and seasonings.

3. WHISK OIL INTO DRESSING BASE To fully emulsify, slowly drizzle oil into base, whisking constantly.

4. DRIZZLE DRESSING OVER SALAD Evenly drizzle vinaigrette over salad and toss gently to coat. Add salt, pepper, and any additions like cheese and nuts and serve.

Here are some of the most common salad greens you'll find at the market. With such a wide array of greens to choose from, it's good to know how to mix and match them to build interesting salads. Many are great on their own, but others are generally best used to add texture or color to other salads. No matter what type of greens you buy, make sure to select the freshest ones possible and avoid any that are wilted, bruised, or discolored.

	TYPE/DESCRIPTION	YIELD	SERVING SUGGESTIONS
	Arugula (also called Rocket or Roquette) Delicate dark green leaves with a peppery bite; sold in bunches, usually with roots attached, or prewashed in cellophane bags; bruises easily and can be very sandy, so wash thoroughly in several changes of water before using.	5-ounce bag (5 cups) 6-ounce bunch (3 cups)	Serve alone for a full-flavored salad, or add to romaine, Bibb, or Boston lettuce to give a spicy punch; for a classic salad, combine with Belgian endive and radicchio.
	Belgian Endive Small, compact head of firm white or pale yellow leaves; should be completely smooth and blemish-free; slightly bitter flavor and crisp texture; one of the few salad greens we routinely cut rather than tear; remove whole leaves from the head and slice crosswise into bite-size pieces.	4-ounce head (1 cup sliced)	Add to watercress or to Bibb, Boston, or loose-leaf lettuce; combine with diced apples, blue cheese, and walnuts; use whole leaves in place of crackers with dips and flavorful soft cheeses.
	Bibb Lettuce Small, compact heads; pale- to medium-green leaves; soft, buttery outer leaves; inner leaves have a surprising crunch and a sweet, mild flavor.	8-ounce head (8 cups)	Combine with watercress or endive, or with Boston, loose-leaf, or romaine lettuce; great tossed with fresh herbs (whole parsley leaves, chives, or dill).
	Boston Lettuce Loose, fluffy head, ranging in color from pale green to red-tipped; similar in texture and flavor to Bibb lettuce, but with softer leaves.	8-ounce head (8 cups)	Combine with baby spinach, watercress, or endive, or with Bibb or romaine lettuce; terrific as a bed for Salade Niçoise (page 78) and pan-fried veggie cakes.
	Chicory (also called Curly Endive) Loose, feathery head of bright green, bitter leaves; texture is somewhat chewy.	10-ounce head (10 cups)	Add to bitter greens salads or use sparingly to add punch to mild mixed greens; great with Balsamic-Mustard or Walnut Vinaigrette (page 72).
	Escarole A kind of chicory with tough, dark green leaves and a mildly bitter flavor; inner leaves are slightly milder.	15-ounce head (15 cups)	Use as an accent to romaine; serve on its own with Balsamic-Mustard Vinaigrette (page 72).
	Frisée A kind of chicory; milder in flavor than other chicories, but with similar feathery leaves; pale green to white in color.	10-ounce head (4 cups)	Combine with arugula or watercress, or with Boston or Bibb lettuce; serve on its own with warm balsamic vinaigrette; great when paired with toasted walnuts and herbed goat cheese.

TYPE/DESCRIPTION	YIELD	SERVING SUGGESTIONS
Iceberg A large, round, tightly packed head of pale green leaves; very crisp and crunchy, with minimal flavor.	1-pound head (12 cups)	Tear into chunks and toss with Bibb, Boston, or loose-leaf lettuce.
Loose-Leaf Lettuces (specifically Red Leaf and Green Leaf) Ruffled dark red or green leaves that grow in big, loose heads; versatile, with a soft yet crunchy texture; green leaf is crisp and mild; red leaf is earthier.	12-ounce head (12 cups)	Pair red leaf with romaine lettuce or watercress; pair green leaf with arugula, radicchio, or watercress; great on sandwiches, or as a bed for grain or bean salads.
Mâche (also called Lamb's Tongue or Lamb's Lettuce) Small heads of three or four stems of small, sweet, deep green leaves; very delicate; usually sold prewashed in bags; if buying heads, wash thoroughly, can be sandy.	4-ounce bag (4 cups)	Combine with arugula or watercress; perfect on its own with crumbled goat cheese and Classic Vinaigrette (page 72).
Mesclun (also called Mesclune, Spring Mix, Field Greens) A mix of up to 14 different baby greens, including spinach, red leaf, oak leaf, frisée, radicchio, green leaf; delicate leaves; flavors range from mild to slightly bitter depending on the blend.	4 ounces bagged or loose (4 cups)	Great as a delicate salad; terrific paired with goat cheese and Lemon Vinaigrette (page 72).
Radicchio Tight heads of red or deep purple leaves streaked with white ribs; bitter flavor.	10-ounce head (3 cups)	Cut into ribbons and mix with arugula, endive, or watercress, or with red or green leaf, Boston, or Bibb lettuce; adds color to any salad.
Romaine Long, full heads with stiff and deep green leaves; crisp, crunchy leaves with a mild, earthy flavor; also sold in bags of three romaine hearts; tough outer leaves should be discarded from full heads.	6-ounce heart (4 cups) 14-ounce head (9 cups)	A great all-purpose lettuce; mix with spinach, watercress, arugula, endive, or radicchio, or with Boston, Bibb, or red leaf lettuce; good on sandwiches and veggie burgers.
Spinach (Flat-Leaf, Curly-Leaf, and Baby) All varieties are vibrant green with an earthy flavor; choose tender flat-leaf or baby spinach for raw salads; tough curly-leaf spinach is better steamed and sautéed; rinse loose spinach well to remove dirt; varieties available prewashed in bags.	5-ounce bag (5 cups) 11-ounce bunch (5 cups)	Delicious mixed with arugula, watercress, or napa cabbage, or with romaine, Bibb, Boston, or loose-leaf lettuce; classic as a wilted salad with creamy dressing or warm lemon vinaigrette.
Watercress Delicate dark green leaves with tough, bitter stems; refreshing mustardlike flavor similar to arugula; usually sold in bunches, sometimes available prewashed in bags; if buying watercress in bunches, take care to wash thoroughly.	2-ounce bunch (2 cups)	Adds flavorful punch and texture to mildly flavored or tender greens such as Bibb or Boston lettuce; delicious on its own with tart green apples, blue cheese, and a mustard-based dressing.

FOOLPROOF SALAD DRESSINGS

The bright flavors of these recipes are perfect for dressing up a simple side salad. For a well-balanced vinaigrette that wouldn't separate, we whisked the oil and vinegar together with a little mayonnaise, which acted as an emulsifier. You can use red wine, white wine, or Champagne vinegar here; however, it is important to use high-quality ingredients. Each vinaigrette makes about ¼ cup, enough to dress 8 to 10 cups of greens; you will need about 1 tablespoon of Tahini-Lemon Dressing for every 2 cups of greens.

Classic Vinaigrette

MAKES ¼ cup FAST VEG

This dressing works well with all types of greens.

- 1 tablespoon wine vinegar
- 1½ teaspoons minced shallot
- ½ teaspoon mayonnaise
- ½ teaspoon Dijon mustard
- ⅛ teaspoon salt
- Pinch pepper
- 3 tablespoons extra-virgin olive oil

Whisk vinegar, shallot, mayonnaise, mustard, salt, and pepper together in bowl until smooth. Whisking constantly, slowly drizzle in oil until emulsified. (Vinaigrette can be refrigerated for up to 2 weeks.)

Lemon Vinaigrette

MAKES ¼ cup FAST VEG

This is best for dressing mild greens.

- ¼ teaspoon grated lemon zest plus 1 tablespoon juice
- ½ teaspoon mayonnaise
- ½ teaspoon Dijon mustard
- ⅛ teaspoon salt
- Pinch pepper
- Pinch sugar
- 3 tablespoons extra-virgin olive oil

Whisk lemon zest and juice, mayonnaise, mustard, salt, pepper, and sugar together in bowl until smooth. Whisking constantly, slowly drizzle in oil until emulsified. (Vinaigrette can be refrigerated for up to 2 weeks.)

Balsamic-Mustard Vinaigrette

MAKES ¼ cup FAST VEG

This is best for dressing assertive greens.

- 1 tablespoon balsamic vinegar
- 2 teaspoons Dijon mustard
- 1½ teaspoons minced shallot
- ½ teaspoon mayonnaise
- ½ teaspoon minced fresh thyme
- ⅛ teaspoon salt
- Pinch pepper
- 3 tablespoons extra-virgin olive oil

Whisk vinegar, mustard, shallot, mayonnaise, thyme, salt, and pepper together in bowl until smooth. Whisking constantly, slowly drizzle in oil until emulsified. (Vinaigrette can be refrigerated for up to 2 weeks.)

Walnut Vinaigrette

MAKES ¼ cup FAST VEG

- 1 tablespoon wine vinegar
- 1½ teaspoons minced shallot
- ½ teaspoon mayonnaise
- ½ teaspoon Dijon mustard
- ⅛ teaspoon salt
- Pinch pepper
- 1½ tablespoons roasted walnut oil
- 1½ tablespoons extra-virgin olive oil

Whisk vinegar, shallot, mayonnaise, mustard, salt, and pepper together in bowl until smooth. Whisking constantly, slowly drizzle in oils until emulsified. (Vinaigrette can be refrigerated for up to 2 weeks.)

Herb Vinaigrette

MAKES ¼ cup FAST VEG

Serve this vinaigrette immediately.

- 1 tablespoon wine vinegar
- 1 tablespoon minced fresh parsley or chives
- 1½ teaspoons minced shallot
- ½ teaspoon minced fresh thyme, tarragon, marjoram, or oregano
- ½ teaspoon mayonnaise
- ½ teaspoon Dijon mustard
- ⅛ teaspoon salt
- Pinch pepper
- 3 tablespoons extra-virgin olive oil

Whisk vinegar, parsley, shallot, thyme, mayonnaise, mustard, salt, and pepper together in bowl until smooth. Whisking constantly, slowly drizzle in oil until emulsified.

Tahini-Lemon Dressing

MAKES about ½ cup FAST VEG

- 2½ tablespoons lemon juice
- 2 tablespoons tahini
- 1 tablespoon water
- 1 garlic clove, minced
- ½ teaspoon salt
- ⅛ teaspoon pepper
- ¼ cup extra-virgin olive oil

Whisk lemon juice, tahini, water, garlic, salt, and pepper together in bowl until smooth. Whisking constantly, slowly drizzle in oil until emulsified. (Dressing can be refrigerated for up to 1 week.)

Arugula Salad with Figs, Prosciutto, Walnuts, and Parmesan

SERVES 6 `FAST`

WHY THIS RECIPE WORKS Arugula has a lively, spicy bite, and so for a salad, it's important to choose accompaniments that can stand up to its assertive character. We found that the sweet and salty notes of figs and prosciutto, both popular in Italian cuisine, paired well with peppery arugula, so we began by frying up thin slices of prosciutto to heighten its flavor and give it some crunch. Dried figs were easier to come by than their fresh counterparts, and chopping them into small pieces ensured that we got bites of fig throughout the salad. A basic vinaigrette, made with mustard and balsamic, was too spicy with the already punchy arugula. A surprise substitution—a spoonful of jam in place of the mustard—added fruity sweetness, pulling the flavors of the salad right in line. Microwaving the vinegar, jam, minced shallot, and chopped figs allowed the fruit to plump and the flavors to meld before we whisked in the olive oil. Toasted walnuts, sprinkled over the dressed arugula, gave the salad an earthy crunch, and Parmesan complemented the walnuts while also reinforcing the prosciutto's salty flavor. Although frying the prosciutto adds crisp texture to the salad, you can simply cut it into ribbons and use it as a garnish. Honey can be substituted for the raspberry jam.

¼ cup extra-virgin olive oil
2 ounces thinly sliced prosciutto, cut into ¼-inch-wide ribbons
3 tablespoons balsamic vinegar
1 tablespoon raspberry jam
1 small shallot, minced
   Salt and pepper
½ cup dried figs, stemmed and chopped
8 ounces (8 cups) baby arugula
½ cup walnuts, toasted and chopped
2 ounces Parmesan cheese, shaved

1. Heat 1 tablespoon oil in 10-inch nonstick skillet over medium heat. Add prosciutto and cook, stirring often, until crisp, about 7 minutes. Using slotted spoon, transfer prosciutto to paper towel–lined plate; set aside.

2. Whisk vinegar, jam, shallot, ¼ teaspoon salt, and ⅛ teaspoon pepper together in large bowl. Stir in figs, cover, and microwave until steaming, about 1 minute. Whisking constantly, slowly drizzle in remaining 3 tablespoons oil. Let sit until figs are softened and vinaigrette has cooled to room temperature, about 15 minutes.

3. Just before serving, whisk vinaigrette to re-emulsify. Add arugula and gently toss to coat. Season with salt and pepper to taste. Serve, topping individual portions with prosciutto, walnuts, and Parmesan.

A spoonful of jam in the dressing guarantees an arugula salad that is lively but not harsh.

VARIATION
Arugula Salad with Pear, Almonds, Goat Cheese, and Apricots

SERVES 6 `FAST` `VEG`

Honey can be substituted for the apricot jam.

3 tablespoons white wine vinegar
1 tablespoon apricot jam
1 small shallot, minced
   Salt and pepper
½ cup dried apricots, chopped
3 tablespoons extra-virgin olive oil
¼ small red onion, sliced thin
8 ounces (8 cups) baby arugula
1 ripe but firm pear, halved, cored, and sliced ¼ inch thick
⅓ cup sliced almonds, toasted
3 ounces goat cheese, crumbled (¾ cup)

1. Whisk vinegar, jam, shallot, ¼ teaspoon salt, and ⅛ teaspoon pepper together in large bowl. Add apricots, cover, and microwave until steaming, about 1 minute. Whisking constantly, slowly drizzle in oil. Stir in onion and let sit until figs are softened and vinaigrette has cooled to room temperature, about 15 minutes.

2. Just before serving, whisk vinaigrette to re-emulsify. Add arugula and pear and gently toss to coat. Season with salt and pepper to taste. Serve, topping individual portions with almonds and goat cheese.

Asparagus and Arugula Salad with Cannellini Beans
SERVES 4 to 6   FAST   VEG

WHY THIS RECIPE WORKS Asparagus has been a favorite vegetable in the Mediterranean since the Greeks and Romans. To incorporate it into a bright, fresh salad, choosing the right cooking method was key. Steaming produced bland, mushy spears, but sautéing the asparagus over high heat delivered deep flavor and tender texture. We sliced the spears on a bias to expose as much of the inner fibers to the cooking surface as possible. With olive oil in a hot pan, we browned some red onion before adding the asparagus pieces. Just 4 minutes of cooking was enough to produce uniformly tender pieces. Creamy cannellini beans provided a subtly nutty and smooth contrast to the asparagus. While the asparagus mixture cooled, we made a simple vinaigrette of balsamic, olive oil, salt, and pepper. For the greens, we knew peppery arugula would hold up well against the other bold flavors, so we dressed and plated it before tossing the asparagus in the dressing as well. Look for asparagus spears no thicker than ½ inch.

5 tablespoons extra-virgin olive oil
½ red onion, sliced thin
1 pound asparagus, trimmed and cut on bias into
   1-inch lengths
   Salt and pepper
1 (15-ounce) can cannellini beans, rinsed
2 tablespoons plus 2 teaspoons balsamic vinegar
6 ounces (6 cups) baby arugula

1. Heat 2 tablespoons oil in 12-inch nonstick skillet over high heat until just smoking. Add onion and cook until lightly browned, about 1 minute. Add asparagus, ¼ teaspoon salt, and ¼ teaspoon pepper and cook, stirring occasionally, until asparagus is browned and crisp-tender, about 4 minutes. Transfer to bowl, stir in beans, and let cool slightly.

2. Whisk vinegar, ¼ teaspoon salt, and ⅛ teaspoon pepper together in small bowl. Whisking constantly, slowly drizzle in remaining 3 tablespoons oil. Gently toss arugula with 2 tablespoons dressing until coated. Season with salt and pepper to taste. Divide arugula among plates. Toss asparagus mixture with remaining dressing, arrange over arugula, and serve.

Asparagus, Red Pepper, and Spinach Salad with Goat Cheese
SERVES 4 to 6   FAST   VEG

Look for asparagus spears no thicker than ½ inch.

5 tablespoons extra-virgin olive oil
1 red bell pepper, stemmed, seeded, and cut into
   2-inch-long matchsticks
1 pound asparagus, trimmed and cut on bias into
   1-inch lengths
   Salt and pepper
1 shallot, halved and sliced thin
1 tablespoon plus 1 teaspoon sherry vinegar
1 garlic clove, minced
6 ounces (6 cups) baby spinach
2 ounces goat cheese, crumbled (½ cup)

1. Heat 1 tablespoon oil in 12-inch nonstick skillet over high heat until just smoking. Add bell pepper and cook until lightly browned, about 2 minutes. Add asparagus, ¼ teaspoon salt, and ⅛ teaspoon pepper and cook, stirring occasionally, until asparagus is browned and almost tender, about 2 minutes. Stir in shallot and cook until softened and asparagus is crisp-tender, about 1 minute. Transfer to bowl and let cool slightly.

2. Whisk vinegar, garlic, ¼ teaspoon salt, and ⅛ teaspoon pepper together in small bowl. Whisking constantly, slowly drizzle in remaining ¼ cup oil. Gently toss spinach with 2 tablespoons dressing until coated. Season with salt and pepper to taste. Divide spinach among plates. Toss asparagus mixture with remaining dressing and arrange over spinach. Sprinkle with goat cheese and serve.

NOTES FROM THE TEST KITCHEN
How to Dress a Salad

Getting a properly dressed salad requires a few simple steps. You never want to dump a set amount of dressing over greens and assume they will be perfectly coated. Once you have overdressed your salad, there is no going back, so it's best to lightly drizzle and toss the salad with tongs a couple of times, tasting as you go. Generally, ¼ cup of vinaigrette dresses 8 to 10 cups of lightly packed greens, enough for four to six side salads or two to three dinner salads. For the freshest salad, make sure to dress your greens just before serving. Also, for just a hint of garlic flavor, rub the inside of the salad bowl with half a clove of peeled garlic before adding the lettuce.

Citrus Salad with Radicchio, Dates, and Smoked Almonds

SERVES 4 to 6 `FAST` `VEG`

WHY THIS RECIPE WORKS Savory salads made with oranges and grapefruit are an impressive way to showcase the colorful citrus fruits that thrive in the sunny, dry Mediterranean climate—but only if you can tame the bitterness of the grapefruit and prevent its ample juice from drowning the other components. We started by treating the grapefruit with salt and sugar to counter its bitter notes and draw out excess liquid. Draining the seasoned fruit enabled us to preemptively remove the excess juice, and reserving some to use in a simple mustard and shallot vinaigrette for the greens helped to make the salad more cohesive. Toasted, salted nuts added richness that contrasted nicely with the fruit and the assertively flavored radicchio, and chopped pitted dates added texture and extra sweetness. We prefer to use navel oranges, tangelos, or Cara Caras in this salad. Blood oranges can also be used, but because they are smaller you'll need four of them.

2 red grapefruits

3 oranges

1 teaspoon sugar

 Salt and pepper

3 tablespoons extra-virgin olive oil

1 small shallot, minced

1 teaspoon Dijon mustard

1 small head radicchio (6 ounces), cored and sliced thin

⅔ cup chopped pitted dates

½ cup smoked almonds, chopped coarse

1. Cut away peel and pith from grapefruits and oranges. Cut each fruit in half from pole to pole, then slice crosswise ¼ inch thick. Transfer to bowl, toss with sugar and ½ teaspoon salt, and let sit for 15 minutes.

2. Drain fruit in fine-mesh strainer set over bowl, reserving 2 tablespoons juice. Arrange fruit on serving platter and drizzle with oil. Whisk reserved juice, shallot, and mustard together in medium bowl. Add radicchio, ⅓ cup dates, and ¼ cup almonds and gently toss to coat. Season with salt and pepper to taste. Arrange radicchio mixture over fruit, leaving 1-inch border of fruit around edges. Sprinkle with remaining ⅓ cup dates and remaining ¼ cup almonds. Serve.

Salting grapefruit and orange slices and draining the excess liquid keeps our citrus salad from being soggy.

VARIATION

Citrus Salad with Arugula, Golden Raisins, and Walnuts `FAST` `VEG`

Substitute 6 ounces baby arugula for radicchio, ½ cup golden raisins for dates, and ½ cup coarsely chopped walnuts for almonds.

Cutting Citrus into Pieces

1. Slice off top and bottom of citrus, then cut away peel and pith using paring knife.

2. Cut peeled fruit from pole to pole as directed, then cut crosswise into slices or pieces.

This traditional Greek salad uses a pleasantly bitter mix of frisée, escarole, and fresh dill.

Bitter Greens Salad with Olives and Feta

SERVES 4 to 6 `FAST` `VEG`

WHY THIS RECIPE WORKS We set out to re-create one of the salads traditionally eaten in Greece, one composed of a seasonal blend of pleasantly peppery, bitter greens that's a far cry from the neighborhood pizza shop version of a Greek salad. We focused first on the greens. Romaine initially seemed like an obvious choice to create a nice neutral base for the salad, but we found that even mixed with peppery chicory greens it didn't have enough of the bitterness we were searching for. We settled on using a combination of escarole and frisée, which had a crisp bite and plenty of spicy, bitter flavor. Dill is a classic component of many bitter greens salads, and we ended up adding a full ⅓ cup to allow its clean, slightly sweet flavor to really shine. We then accented the greens with a bright lemon vinaigrette, a mix of briny feta and kalamata olives, and tangy, slightly spicy pepperoncini peppers. If you prefer more heat, do not seed the pepperoncini.

1 head escarole (1 pound), trimmed and cut into 1-inch pieces
1 small head frisée (4 ounces), trimmed and torn into 1-inch pieces
½ cup pitted kalamata olives, halved
2 ounces feta cheese, crumbled (½ cup)
⅓ cup pepperoncini, seeded and cut into ¼-inch-thick strips
⅓ cup chopped fresh dill
2 tablespoons lemon juice
1 garlic clove, minced
Salt and pepper
3 tablespoons extra-virgin olive oil

Gently toss escarole, frisée, olives, feta, and pepperoncini together in large bowl. Whisk dill, lemon juice, garlic, ¼ teaspoon salt, and ⅛ teaspoon pepper together in small bowl. Whisking constantly, slowly drizzle in oil. Drizzle dressing over salad and gently toss to coat. Serve.

NOTES FROM THE TEST KITCHEN
Putting Together a Perfect Salad

PAIRING LEAFY GREENS WITH VINAIGRETTES
Vinaigrettes are the best choice for dressing leafy greens; heavier, creamier dressings are best on sturdy lettuce such as romaine or iceberg. Most salad greens fall into one of two categories: mellow or assertive. When you're making a green salad, it's important to choose your vinaigrette recipe carefully to complement the greens you are using.

MELLOW-FLAVORED
Boston, Bibb, mâche, mesclun, red and green leaf, red oak, and flat-leaf spinach. Their mild flavors are easily over-powered and are best complemented by a simple dressing such as a classic red wine vinaigrette.

ASSERTIVE OR SPICY GREENS
Arugula, escarole, chicory, Belgian endive, radicchio, frisée, and watercress. These greens can easily stand up to strong flavors like mustard, shallots, and balsamic vinegar and can also be paired with a slightly sweet or creamy vinaigrette.

Kale Salad with Sweet Potatoes and Pomegranate Vinaigrette

SERVES 6 to 8 VEG

WHY THIS RECIPE WORKS We love the earthy flavor of uncooked kale, but the texture of raw kale can be a little tough. Many recipes call for tossing it with dressing and letting it tenderize in the fridge overnight. This method didn't deliver the tender leaves we were after, and the long sitting time wasn't very convenient. Luckily, we found another technique that worked better and faster: massaging. Squeezing and massaging the kale broke down the cell walls in much the same way that heat would, darkening the leaves and turning them silky. Caramelized roasted sweet potatoes, shredded radicchio, crunchy pecans, a sprinkling of Parmesan cheese, and a sweet pomegranate vinaigrette turned our salad into a hearty meal. If you can't find pomegranate molasses, you can make your own (page 305). Tuscan kale (also known as dinosaur or Lacinato kale) is more tender than curly-leaf and red kale; if using curly-leaf or red kale, increase the massaging time to 5 minutes. Do not use baby kale.

SALAD

1½ pounds sweet potatoes, peeled, cut into ½-inch pieces
2 teaspoons extra-virgin olive oil
   Salt and pepper
12 ounces Tuscan kale, stemmed and sliced crosswise into ½-inch-wide strips (7 cups)
½ head radicchio (5 ounces), cored and sliced thin
⅓ cup pecans, toasted and chopped
   Shaved Parmesan cheese

VINAIGRETTE

2 tablespoons water
1½ tablespoons pomegranate molasses
1 small shallot, minced
1 tablespoon honey
1 tablespoon cider vinegar
   Salt and pepper
¼ cup extra-virgin olive oil

1. FOR THE SALAD Adjust oven rack to middle position and heat oven to 400 degrees. Toss sweet potatoes with oil and season with salt and pepper. Arrange potatoes in single layer in rimmed baking sheet and roast until browned, 25 to 30 minutes, flipping potatoes halfway through roasting. Transfer to plate and let cool for 20 minutes. Meanwhile, vigorously squeeze and massage kale with hands until leaves are uniformly darkened and slightly wilted, about 1 minute.

Caramelized sweet potatoes and a tangy pomegranate vinaigrette are the perfect complement to earthy kale.

2. FOR THE VINAIGRETTE Whisk water, pomegranate molasses, shallot, honey, vinegar, ¼ teaspoon salt, and ¼ teaspoon pepper together in large bowl. Whisking constantly, slowly drizzle in oil.

3. Add potatoes, kale, and radicchio to vinaigrette and gently toss to coat. Season with salt and pepper to taste. Transfer to serving platter and sprinkle with pecans and shaved Parmesan to taste. Serve.

Massaging Kale

Vigorously squeeze and massage kale with hands over counter or in large bowl until leaves are uniformly darkened and slightly wilted, about 1 minute for flat-leaf kale (or 5 minutes for curly-leaf or red kale).

Mâche Salad with Cucumber and Mint

SERVES 6 to 8 FAST VEG

WHY THIS RECIPE WORKS Mâche, also called lamb's lettuce, is a soft, tender green that grows in delicate rosettes and is beloved in French kitchens for its sweet, nutty flavor. Hoping to turn this baby lettuce into an elegant side salad, we paired the mâche with the crisp, fresh flavor of thinly sliced cucumber. Chopped mint added brightness, and crunchy pine nuts reinforced the mâche's buttery notes. We kept the dressing simple with just lemon juice, fresh parsley, fresh thyme, and minced garlic, plus capers for some briny contrast to the rest of the salad. Mâche is a very delicate green, so be sure to handle it gently and make sure it is thoroughly dry before tossing it with the vinaigrette. If you can't find mâche, you can substitute either baby spinach or mesclun.

12 ounces (12 cups) mâche
 1 cucumber, sliced thin
 ½ cup chopped fresh mint
 ⅓ cup pine nuts, toasted
 1 tablespoon lemon juice
 1 tablespoon minced fresh parsley
 1 tablespoon capers, rinsed and minced
 1 teaspoon minced fresh thyme
 1 garlic clove, minced
    Salt and pepper
 ¼ cup extra-virgin olive oil

Gently toss mâche, cucumber, mint, and pine nuts together in large bowl. Whisk lemon juice, parsley, capers, thyme, garlic, ¼ teaspoon salt, and ¼ teaspoon pepper together in small bowl. Whisking constantly, slowly drizzle in oil. Drizzle dressing over salad and gently toss to coat. Season with salt and pepper to taste. Serve.

Salade Niçoise

SERVES 6

WHY THIS RECIPE WORKS Along the French Riviera, *salade niçoise*, the fresh and elegant-looking composed salad, is commonplace. But elsewhere renditions of this salad are bland and lifeless, little more than a layer of soggy lettuce with lazily strewn piles of overcooked and underseasoned green beans and potatoes, rubbery eggs, and tuna drowning in dressing. We started by focusing on the right lettuce. Butterhead lettuces such as Boston and Bibb proved more tender than romaine or leaf lettuces. Taking a nod from the French, we dressed our boiled potatoes while warm; they tasted more fully seasoned than those that had cooled. Tuna packed in water let the flavors of the vinaigrette shine through. Taking the time to dress each component separately really paid off; this guaranteed that every bite was fully and evenly seasoned. If you prepare all of the vegetables before you begin cooking the potatoes, this salad comes together easily. Briny niçoise olives are the classic garnish of salade niçoise. If they're not available, substitute another small, black brined olive; do not use canned. Use small red potatoes measuring 2 inches in diameter. You may need to whisk the dressing to re-emulsify. Leave some space between the arranged mounds so that leaves of lettuce show through.

DRESSING

 ¼ cup lemon juice (2 lemons)
 1 shallot, minced
 2 tablespoons minced fresh basil
 2 teaspoons minced fresh thyme
 2 teaspoons minced fresh oregano
 1 teaspoon Dijon mustard
 ½ teaspoon salt
 ¼ teaspoon pepper
 ½ cup extra-virgin olive oil

NOTES FROM THE TEST KITCHEN

Washing and Drying Salad Greens

To make a great salad, the only thing that is more critical than using crisp, fresh greens is using clean, dry greens. Trying to dress a salad while the greens are still wet is a losing battle—the dressing slides off, and the water from the greens will dilute the dressing. We believe that the only foolproof method for drying them is to use a salad spinner.

TO WASH GREENS
Fill a salad spinner bowl with cool water, add cut greens, and gently swish them around. Do not run water directly over the greens, as the force can bruise them. Using your hands,

gently move the greens to loosen grit, which will fall to the bottom of the bowl. Use the sink if you need to clean large amounts of greens.

TO DRY GREENS
Dry greens in a salad spinner, stopping several times to dump out excess moisture. Keep spinning greens until no more moisture accumulates. After spinning them, we like to blot greens dry with paper towels; even the best salad spinners don't dry greens completely.

Dressing each component separately is the key to building a bright, full-flavored *salade niçoise*.

SALAD

1¼ pounds small red potatoes, unpeeled, quartered
Salt and pepper
2 tablespoons dry vermouth
2 heads Boston lettuce or Bibb lettuce (1 pound), torn into bite-size pieces
2 (5-ounce) cans solid white tuna in water, drained and flaked
3 small tomatoes, cored and cut into ½-inch-thick wedges
1 small red onion, sliced thin
8 ounces green beans, trimmed and halved
3 hard-cooked large eggs, peeled and quartered (page 188)
¼ cup pitted niçoise olives
10–12 anchovy fillets, rinsed (optional)
2 tablespoons capers, rinsed (optional)

1. FOR THE DRESSING Whisk lemon juice, shallot, basil, thyme, oregano, mustard, salt, and pepper together in small bowl. Whisking constantly, slowly drizzle in oil.

2. FOR THE SALAD Place potatoes in large saucepan, add water to cover by 1 inch, and bring to boil over high heat. Add 1 tablespoon salt, reduce to simmer, and cook until potatoes are tender and paring knife can be slipped in and out of potatoes with little resistance, 5 to 8 minutes. With slotted spoon, gently transfer potatoes to bowl (do not discard water). Toss warm potatoes with ¼ cup vinaigrette and vermouth. Season with salt and pepper to taste; set aside.

3. While potatoes cook, gently toss lettuce with ¼ cup vinaigrette in bowl until coated. Arrange bed of lettuce on very large, flat serving platter. Place tuna in now-empty bowl and break up with fork. Add ¼ cup vinaigrette and stir to combine. Mound tuna in center of lettuce. In now-empty bowl, toss tomatoes and red onion with 2 tablespoons vinaigrette and season with salt and pepper to taste. Arrange tomato-onion mixture in mound at edge of lettuce bed. Arrange reserved potatoes in separate mound at edge of lettuce bed.

4. Return water to boil and add 1 tablespoon salt and green beans. Cook until crisp-tender, 3 to 5 minutes. Meanwhile, fill large bowl halfway with ice and water. Drain green beans, transfer to ice water, and let sit until just cool, about 30 seconds. Transfer beans to triple layer of paper towels and dry well. In now-empty bowl, toss green beans with remaining 2 tablespoons vinaigrette and season with salt and pepper to taste. Arrange in separate mound at edge of lettuce bed.

5. Arrange eggs, olives, and anchovies, if using, in separate mounds at edge of lettuce bed. Sprinkle entire salad with capers, if using. Serve.

NOTES FROM THE TEST KITCHEN

Storing Salad Greens

Here's the best way to store the most common lettuces.

LETTUCE TYPE	HOW TO STORE
Crisp heads, such as iceberg and romaine	Core lettuce, wrap in moist paper towels, and refrigerate in plastic produce bag or zipper-lock bag left slightly open.
Leafy greens, such as arugula, baby spinach, and mesclun	If prewashed, store in original plastic container or bag. If not prewashed, wash and dry thoroughly in salad spinner and store directly in spinner between layers of paper towels, or lightly roll in paper towels and store in zipper-lock bag left slightly open.
Tender heads, such as Boston and Bibb lettuce	If lettuce comes with root attached, leave lettuce portion attached to root and store in original plastic container, plastic produce bag, or zipper-lock bag left slightly open. If lettuce is without root, wrap in moist paper towels and refrigerate in plastic produce bag or zipper-lock bag left slightly open.

The perfectly wilted curly-leaf spinach in our salad still retains some of its bite.

Warm Spinach Salad with Feta and Pistachios

SERVES 6 FAST VEG

WHY THIS RECIPE WORKS Spinach is a centuries-old staple in Italian cuisine, beloved for its culinary versatility and supercharged nutritional benefits. Served wilted in a salad, spinach takes on a milder flavor, perfect for pairing with bold mix-ins—so long as the leaves aren't reduced to mush. We experimented with various types of spinach and found that flat-leaf and baby spinach became overly soft, but hardier curly-leaf spinach could withstand the heat. To make the dressing, we began by heating 3 tablespoons of fruity extra-virgin olive oil in a Dutch oven along with some minced shallot. For a burst of bright citrus, we also simmered a strip of lemon zest in the oil, then we added fresh lemon juice before tossing in the spinach off the heat. The residual heat in the pot steamed the spinach until it was warm and just wilted. Peppery sliced radishes, crumbled feta, and toasted pistachios rounded out our salad. Be sure to cook the spinach just until it begins to wilt; any longer and the leaves will overcook and clump. Be sure to use curly-leaf spinach here; do not substitute flat-leaf or baby spinach.

1½ ounces feta cheese, crumbled (⅓ cup)
3 tablespoons extra-virgin olive oil
1 (2-inch) strip lemon zest plus 1½ tablespoons juice
1 shallot, minced
2 teaspoons sugar
10 ounces curly-leaf spinach, stemmed and torn into bite-size pieces
6 radishes, trimmed and sliced thin
3 tablespoons chopped toasted pistachios
Salt and pepper

1. Place feta on plate and freeze until slightly firm, about 15 minutes.

2. Cook oil, lemon zest, shallot, and sugar in Dutch oven over medium-low heat until shallot is softened, about 5 minutes. Off heat, discard zest and stir in lemon juice. Add spinach, cover, and let steam off heat until it just begins to wilt, about 30 seconds.

3. Transfer spinach mixture and liquid left in pot to large bowl. Add radishes, pistachios, and chilled feta and toss to combine. Season with salt and pepper to taste. Serve.

Seared Tuna Salad with Olive Dressing

SERVES 4 to 6 FAST

WHY THIS RECIPE WORKS Fresh, quick-cooking tuna steaks are a perfect base for a hearty salad. To make sure we didn't overcook the fish, we patted it dry before searing it in a very hot pan. Slicing it right away ensured that it didn't overcook as it rested. A potent vinaigrette made with chopped green olives, parsley, garlic, and lemon juice stood up to the meaty flavor of the tuna. Cherry tomatoes provided pops of freshness, and cannellini beans added an appealing texture. Peppery arugula provided a perfect vehicle for the rest of our flavorful ingredients. Tuna steaks can be pricey. To get your money's worth, only purchase tuna steaks that are deep purplish red, firm to the touch, and devoid of any "fishy" odor.

½ cup pimento-stuffed green olives, chopped
3 tablespoons lemon juice
1 tablespoon chopped fresh parsley
1 garlic clove, minced
6 tablespoons extra-virgin olive oil
Salt and pepper
2 (12-ounce) tuna steaks, 1 to 1¼ inches thick
5 ounces (5 cups) baby arugula
12 ounces cherry tomatoes, halved
1 (15-ounce) can cannellini beans, rinsed

1. Whisk olives, lemon juice, parsley, and garlic together in large bowl. Whisking constantly, slowly drizzle in 5 tablespoons oil. Season with salt and pepper to taste.

2. Pat tuna dry with paper towels and season with salt and pepper. Heat remaining 1 tablespoon oil in 12-inch nonstick skillet over medium-high heat until just smoking. Cook tuna until well browned and translucent red at center when checked with tip of paring knife and registers 110 degrees (for rare), about 2 minutes per side. Transfer to cutting board and slice into ½-inch-thick slices.

3. Whisk dressing to re-emulsify, then drizzle 1 tablespoon dressing over tuna. Add arugula, tomatoes, and beans to bowl with remaining dressing and gently toss to combine. Season with salt and pepper to taste. Divide salad among plates and top with tuna. Serve.

Asparagus Salad with Oranges, Feta, and Hazelnuts

SERVES 4 to 6   FAST   VEG

WHY THIS RECIPE WORKS Instead of roasting our asparagus, we took a much different approach and made a fresh, vibrant salad with raw asparagus. Slicing the spears thin was key to keeping them crunchy, not woody. An herb-based dressing complemented the freshness of the asparagus. Sweet orange segments, briny feta, and toasted hazelnuts were the finishing touches. For easier slicing, look for large asparagus spears, about ½ inch thick.

PESTO

2 cups fresh mint leaves
¼ cup fresh basil leaves
¼ cup grated Pecorino Romano cheese
1 teaspoon grated lemon zest plus 2 teaspoons juice
1 garlic clove, minced
  Salt and pepper
½ cup extra-virgin olive oil

SALAD

2 pounds asparagus, trimmed
2 oranges
4 ounces feta cheese, crumbled (1 cup)
¾ cup hazelnuts, toasted, skinned, and chopped
  Salt and pepper

1. FOR THE PESTO Process mint, basil, Pecorino, lemon zest and juice, garlic, and ¾ teaspoon salt in food processor until finely chopped, about 20 seconds, scraping down sides of bowl as needed. Transfer to large bowl. Stir in oil and season with salt and pepper to taste.

Thinly sliced raw asparagus spears are mildly sweet and nutty with a delicate crunch.

2. FOR THE SALAD Cut asparagus tips from stalks into ¾-inch-long pieces. Slice asparagus stalks ⅛ inch thick on bias into approximate 2-inch lengths. Cut away peel and pith from oranges. Holding fruit over bowl, use paring knife to slice between membranes to release segments. Add asparagus tips and stalks, orange segments, feta, and hazelnuts to pesto and toss to combine. Season with salt and pepper to taste. Serve.

Cutting Citrus into Segments

1. Slice off top and bottom of citrus, then cut away peel and pith using paring knife.

2. Holding fruit over bowl, slice between membranes to release individual segments.

Roasted Beet Salad with Blood Oranges and Almonds

SERVES 4 to 6 VEG

WHY THIS RECIPE WORKS With their sweet, earthy flavor, juicy texture, and ruby-red hue, beets are a real showstopper. To make them the star of a simple yet elegant salad, we had to find the easiest way to prepare them. Boiling and steaming diluted their flavor, but when wrapped in foil and roasted, the beets were juicy and tender with a concentrated sweetness. Peeling was easier when the beets were still warm—the skins slid off effortlessly. We also tossed the sliced beets with the dressing while still warm, allowing them to absorb maximum flavor. Salty ricotta salata, peppery arugula, and toasted almonds rounded out the dish. You can use either golden or red beets (or a mix of both) in this recipe. To ensure even cooking, use beets that are of similar size—roughly 2 to 3 inches in diameter. If your beets are larger, the cooking time will be longer. Navel oranges, tangelos, or Cara Caras can be substituted for the blood oranges, but because they are larger you'll need just one of them.

  2 pounds beets, trimmed
  4 teaspoons sherry vinegar
     Salt and pepper
  2 tablespoons extra-virgin olive oil
  2 blood oranges
  2 ounces (2 cups) baby arugula
  2 ounces ricotta salata cheese, shaved
  2 tablespoons sliced almonds, toasted

1. Adjust oven rack to middle position and heat oven to 400 degrees. Wrap beets individually in aluminum foil and place in rimmed baking sheet. Roast beets until skewer inserted into center meets little resistance (you will need to unwrap beets to test them), 45 to 60 minutes.

2. Carefully open foil packets and let beets sit until cool enough to handle. Carefully rub off beet skins using paper towel. Slice beets into ½-inch-thick wedges, and, if large, cut in half crosswise.

3. Whisk vinegar, ¼ teaspoon salt, and ¼ teaspoon pepper together in large bowl. Whisking constantly, slowly drizzle in oil. Add beets, toss to coat, and let cool to room temperature, about 20 minutes.

4. Cut away peel and pith from oranges. Quarter oranges, then slice crosswise into ½-inch-thick pieces. Add oranges and arugula to bowl with beets and gently toss to coat. Season with salt and pepper to taste. Transfer to serving platter and sprinkle with ricotta salata and almonds. Serve.

We dress the vegetables in our roasted beet and carrot salad while they're still warm so they can absorb maximum flavor.

Roasted Beet and Carrot Salad with Cumin and Pistachios

SERVES 4 to 6 VEG

WHY THIS RECIPE WORKS Beets and carrots are a winning combination here, and roasting them brings out their earthy sweetness. To turn them into a salad, we tossed them with an equally earthy vinaigrette while they were still hot, which allowed them to absorb maximum flavor. Cumin added warmth to the dressing, honey contributed a touch of sweetness, and shallot gave it a subtle, oniony bite. Pistachios lent nice color and crunch. Adding lemon zest and chopped parsley just before serving resulted in a bright, well-balanced salad. Wrapping the beets in foil allowed them to cook gently, without missing out on the distinct, concentrated flavor of roasting. Steaming them in foil and then slicing the beets also helped to minimize "bleeding" of any liquid. You can use either golden or red beets (or a mix of both) in this recipe. To ensure even cooking, use beets that are of similar size—roughly 2 to 3 inches in diameter. If your beets are larger, the cooking time will be longer.

1 pound beets, trimmed
1 pound carrots, peeled and sliced on bias ¼ inch thick
2½ tablespoons extra-virgin olive oil
   Salt and pepper
1 tablespoon grated lemon zest plus 3 tablespoons juice
1 small shallot, minced
1 teaspoon honey
½ teaspoon ground cumin
½ cup shelled pistachios, toasted and chopped
2 tablespoons minced fresh parsley

1. Adjust oven racks to middle and lowest positions. Place rimmed baking sheet on lower rack and heat oven to 450 degrees.

2. Wrap beets individually in aluminum foil and place in second rimmed baking sheet. Toss carrots with 1 tablespoon oil, ½ teaspoon salt, and ½ teaspoon pepper.

3. Working quickly, arrange carrots in single layer in hot baking sheet and place baking sheet with beets on middle rack. Roast until carrots are tender and well browned on 1 side, 20 to 25 minutes, and skewer inserted into center of beets meets little resistance (you will need to unwrap beets to test them), 35 to 45 minutes.

4. Carefully open foil packets and let beets sit until cool enough to handle. Carefully rub off beet skins using paper towel. Slice beets into ½-inch-thick wedges, and, if large, cut in half crosswise.

5. Whisk lemon juice, shallot, honey, cumin, ¼ teaspoon salt, and ⅛ teaspoon pepper together in large bowl. Whisking constantly, slowly drizzle in remaining 1½ tablespoons oil. Add beets and carrots, toss to coat, and let cool to room temperature, about 20 minutes.

6. Add pistachios, parsley, and lemon zest to bowl with beets and carrots and toss to coat. Season with salt and pepper to taste. Serve.

Fava Bean and Radish Salad
SERVES 4 to 6   FAST   VEG

WHY THIS RECIPE WORKS A highlight of farmers' markets every spring, fava beans are a wonderful fuzzy green pod bean not to be passed by. These Italian-named earthy beans are favored throughout the Mediterranean and date back to ancient times. Since it takes some time to prepare fresh favas, we wanted to use them in a vibrant, interesting salad that would be worth the effort. We added thin half-moons of peppery radishes to provide a nice crunchy bite as well as flecks of color to our salad. Fresh pea shoots supplied another layer of texture and a bit of natural sweetness. Basil and a lemony vinaigrette were the final additions

to this light and flavorful salad that celebrates springtime in every bite. The beans inside their tough outer pod are covered with a waxy translucent sheath that should be removed after shelling (although edible, the sheath can be fibrous—and sometimes bitter—unless from a very young bean). Once the sheath is peeled off, the beans are ready to be enjoyed. While we preferred the brighter flavor of fresh beans, 1 pound (3 cups) of frozen fava beans may be substituted.

3 pounds fava beans, shelled (3 cups)
3 tablespoons lemon juice
2 garlic cloves, minced
½ teaspoon salt
¼ teaspoon pepper
¼ teaspoon ground coriander
¼ cup extra-virgin olive oil
10 radishes, trimmed, halved, and sliced thin
1½ ounces (1½ cups) pea shoots
¼ cup chopped fresh basil

1. Bring 4 quarts water to boil in large pot over high heat. Meanwhile, fill large bowl halfway with ice and water. Add fava beans to boiling water and cook for 1 minute. Drain fava beans, transfer to ice water, and let sit until chilled, about 2 minutes. Transfer fava beans to triple layer of paper towels and dry well. Using paring knife, make small cut along edge of each bean through waxy sheath, then gently squeeze sheath to release bean; discard sheath.

2. Whisk lemon juice, garlic, salt, pepper, and coriander together in large bowl. Whisking constantly, slowly drizzle in oil. Add fava beans, radishes, pea shoots, and basil and gently toss to coat. Serve immediately.

Preparing Fresh Fava Beans

1. To shell favas, use paring knife and thumb to snip off tip of pod and pull apart sides to release beans. Blanch beans and dry well.

2. Use paring knife to make small cut along edge of bean through waxy sheath, then gently squeeze sheath to release bean.

Green Bean Salad with Cilantro Sauce

SERVES 6 to 8 `FAST` `VEG`

WHY THIS RECIPE WORKS To dress up a simple green bean salad, we came up with a fresh take on pesto by swapping the traditional basil for bright, grassy cilantro. A single scallion brightened the green color of the sauce, and walnuts and garlic cloves, briefly toasted in a skillet, added nutty depth. The fruity flavor of extra-virgin olive oil complemented the other flavors in the dressing nicely. Finally, a touch of lemon juice rounded out the flavors and helped to loosen the sauce to just the right consistency. We blanched and shocked the beans to set their vibrant green color and ensure that they were evenly cooked. Don't worry about drying the beans before tossing them with the sauce; any water that clings to the beans will help to thin out the sauce.

¼ cup walnuts
2 garlic cloves, unpeeled
2½ cups fresh cilantro leaves and stems, tough stem ends trimmed (about 2 bunches)
½ cup extra-virgin olive oil
4 teaspoons lemon juice
1 scallion, sliced thin
Salt and pepper
2 pounds green beans, trimmed

1. Cook walnuts and garlic in 8-inch skillet over medium heat, stirring often, until toasted and fragrant, 5 to 7 minutes; transfer to bowl. Let garlic cool slightly, then peel and roughly chop.

2. Process walnuts, garlic, cilantro, oil, lemon juice, scallion, ½ teaspoon salt, and ⅛ teaspoon pepper in food processor until smooth, about 1 minute, scraping down sides of bowl as needed; transfer to large bowl.

3. Bring 4 quarts water to boil in large pot over high heat. Meanwhile, fill large bowl halfway with ice and water. Add 1 tablespoon salt and green beans to boiling water and cook until crisp-tender, 3 to 5 minutes. Drain green beans, transfer to ice water, and let sit until chilled, about 2 minutes. Transfer green beans to bowl with cilantro sauce and gently toss until coated. Season with salt and pepper to taste. Serve. (Salad can be refrigerated for up to 4 hours.)

VARIATION
Green Bean and Potato Salad with Cilantro Sauce
`VEG`

Before cooking beans, place 1 pound red potatoes, unpeeled, sliced ¼ inch thick, in large pot, add water to cover by 1 inch, and bring to boil over high heat. Add 1 tablespoon salt, reduce to simmer, and cook until potatoes are tender and paring knife can be slipped in and out of potatoes with little resistance, about 5 minutes. Drain potatoes, spread out in rimmed baking sheet, and drizzle with some of cilantro sauce. Reduce amount of green beans to 1 pound and cut into 2-inch lengths; cook as directed. Toss green beans and potatoes with remaining sauce, season with salt and pepper to taste, and serve.

A vibrant cilantro-based pesto is a fresh way to dress up blanched green beans.

Trimming Green Beans

Line beans up on cutting board and trim ends with 1 slice.

Brussels Sprout Salad with Pecorino and Pine Nuts

SERVES 4 to 6 FAST VEG

WHY THIS RECIPE WORKS To make Brussels sprouts shine in a salad, we needed to get rid of some of their vegetal rawness. Rather than cooking the sprouts, we sliced them very thin and then marinated them in a bright vinaigrette made with lemon juice and Dijon mustard. The 30-minute soak in the acidic dressing softened and seasoned the sprouts, bringing out and balancing their flavor. Toasted pine nuts and shredded Pecorino Romano added to our salad just before serving added a layer of crunch and nutty richness. Slice the sprouts as thinly as possible. Use the large holes of a box grater to shred the Pecorino Romano.

2 tablespoons lemon juice
1 tablespoon Dijon mustard
1 small shallot, minced
1 garlic clove, minced
  Salt and pepper
¼ cup extra-virgin olive oil
1 pound Brussels sprouts, trimmed, halved, and sliced very thin
2 ounces Pecorino Romano cheese, shredded (⅔ cup)
¼ cup pine nuts, toasted

Whisk lemon juice, mustard, shallot, garlic, and ½ teaspoon salt together in large bowl. Whisking constantly, slowly drizzle in oil. Add Brussels sprouts, toss to coat, and let sit for at least 30 minutes or up to 2 hours. Stir in Pecorino and pine nuts. Season with salt and pepper to taste. Serve.

Shredding Brussels Sprouts for Salad

1. Peel off any loose or discolored leaves and slice off bottom of stem end, leaving leaves attached.

2. Halve Brussels sprouts through stem end, then slice very thin.

Moroccan-Style Carrot Salad

SERVES 4 to 6 FAST VEG

WHY THIS RECIPE WORKS This classic Moroccan salad combines grated carrots with olive oil, citrus, and warm spices like cumin and cinnamon. We tried grating the carrots both with a coarse grater and with a food processor and found that the coarse grater worked better. To complement the earthy carrots, we added juicy orange segments, reserving some of the orange juice to add to the salad dressing. We balanced the sweet orange juice with a squeeze of lemon juice and small amounts of cumin, cayenne, and cinnamon. The musty aroma and slight nuttiness of the cumin nicely complemented the sweetness of the carrots. A touch of honey provided a pleasing floral note. To add color and freshness, we stirred in some minced cilantro before serving. Use the large holes of a box grater to shred the carrots.

2 oranges
1 tablespoon lemon juice
1 teaspoon honey
¾ teaspoon ground cumin
⅛ teaspoon cayenne pepper
⅛ teaspoon ground cinnamon
  Salt and pepper
1 pound carrots, peeled and shredded
3 tablespoons minced fresh cilantro
3 tablespoons extra-virgin olive oil

1. Cut away peel and pith from oranges. Holding fruit over bowl, use paring knife to slice between membranes to release segments. Cut segments in half crosswise and let drain in fine-mesh strainer set over large bowl, reserving juice.

2. Whisk lemon juice, honey, cumin, cayenne, cinnamon, and ½ teaspoon salt into reserved orange juice. Add drained oranges and carrots and gently toss to coat. Let sit until liquid starts to pool in bottom of bowl, 3 to 5 minutes.

3. Drain salad in fine-mesh strainer and return to now-empty bowl. Stir in cilantro and oil and season with salt and pepper to taste. Serve.

VARIATION

Moroccan-Style Carrot Salad with Harissa and Feta
FAST VEG

We prefer to use our homemade Harissa (page 316), but you can substitute store-bought harissa if you wish, though spiciness can vary greatly by brand.

Substitute 2 tablespoons harissa for cumin, cayenne pepper, and cinnamon. Substitute 2 tablespoons chopped fresh mint for cilantro. Stir ½ cup crumbled feta cheese into salad with mint.

Herby Moroccan chermoula lends bright flavor to our salad of deeply browned cauliflower, carrots, and raisins.

North African Cauliflower Salad with Chermoula

SERVES 4 to 6 **VEG**

WHY THIS RECIPE WORKS Chermoula is a traditional Moroccan marinade made with hefty amounts of cilantro, lemon, and garlic that packs a big flavor punch. While this dressing is traditionally used as a marinade for meat and fish, here we decided to make it the flavor base for a zippy cauliflower salad in an effort to zest up a vegetable that can be bland and boring. We focused first on the cooking method of the starring vegetable. Roasting was the best choice to add deep flavor to the cauliflower and balance the bright chermoula. To keep the cauliflower from overbrowning on the exterior before the interior was cooked, we started it covered and let it steam until barely tender. Then we removed the foil, added sliced onions, and returned the pan to the oven to let both the onions and the cauliflower caramelize. Adding the onions to the same pan once the cauliflower was uncovered eased their preparation and ensured that they would finish cooking at the same time. To highlight the natural sweetness of the cooked vegetables, we added shredded carrot and raisins, two traditional North African ingredients. We now had a warm and flavorful salad sure to spice up any meal. Use the large holes of a box grater to shred the carrot.

SALAD
- 1 head cauliflower (2 pounds), cored and cut into 2-inch florets
- 2 tablespoons extra-virgin olive oil
  Salt and pepper
- ½ red onion, sliced ¼ inch thick
- 1 cup shredded carrot
- ½ cup raisins
- 2 tablespoons chopped fresh cilantro
- 2 tablespoons sliced almonds, toasted

CHERMOULA
- ¾ cup fresh cilantro leaves
- ¼ cup extra-virgin olive oil
- 2 tablespoons lemon juice
- 4 garlic cloves, minced
- ½ teaspoon ground cumin
- ½ teaspoon paprika
- ¼ teaspoon salt
- ⅛ teaspoon cayenne pepper

Cutting Cauliflower into Florets

1. Pull off any leaves, then cut out core of cauliflower using paring knife.

2. Separate florets from inner stem using tip of knife.

3. Cut larger florets into smaller pieces by slicing through stem end.

1. FOR THE SALAD Adjust oven rack to lowest position and heat oven to 475 degrees. Toss cauliflower with oil and season with salt and pepper. Arrange cauliflower in single layer in parchment paper–lined rimmed baking sheet. Cover tightly with aluminum foil and roast until softened, 5 to 7 minutes. Remove foil and spread onion evenly in sheet. Roast until vegetables are tender, cauliflower is deep golden brown, and onion slices are charred at edges, 10 to 15 minutes, stirring halfway through roasting. Let cool slightly, about 5 minutes.

2. FOR THE CHERMOULA Process all ingredients in food processor until smooth, about 1 minute, scraping down sides of bowl as needed. Transfer to large bowl.

3. Gently toss cauliflower-onion mixture, carrot, raisins, and cilantro with chermoula until coated. Transfer to serving platter and sprinkle with almonds. Serve warm or at room temperature.

Mediterranean Chopped Salad

SERVES 4 VEG

WHY THIS RECIPE WORKS Throughout the Mediterranean chopped salads are lively, thoughtfully chosen compositions of lettuce and vegetables. To keep our chopped salad from getting soggy, we salted the vegetables to draw out their excess moisture. Seeding the cucumbers and quartering the tomatoes exposed more surface area to the salt for even better results. Then we made a zingy dressing with equal parts oil and vinegar to give the salad bright acidic flavor. Letting the vegetables marinate in the vinaigrette for a few minutes intensified their flavor. Along with the cucumbers and tomatoes, we chose buttery chickpeas, briny kalamata olives, and bright, fresh parsley to give our salad lots of contrasting flavors and textures. Cherry tomatoes can be substituted for the grape tomatoes.

  1 cucumber, peeled, halved lengthwise, seeded, and cut into ½-inch pieces
 10 ounces grape tomatoes, quartered
    Salt and pepper
  3 tablespoons red wine vinegar
  1 garlic clove, minced
  3 tablespoons extra-virgin olive oil
  1 (15-ounce) can chickpeas, rinsed
  ½ cup pitted kalamata olives, chopped
  ½ small red onion, chopped fine
  ½ cup chopped fresh parsley
  1 romaine lettuce heart (6 ounces), cut into ½-inch pieces
  4 ounces feta cheese, crumbled (1 cup)

1. Toss cucumber and tomatoes with 1 teaspoon salt and let drain in colander for 15 minutes.

2. Whisk vinegar and garlic together in large bowl. Whisking constantly, slowly drizzle in oil. Add cucumber-tomato mixture, chickpeas, olives, onion, and parsley and toss to coat. Let sit for at least 5 minutes or up to 20 minutes.

3. Add lettuce and feta and gently toss to combine. Season with salt and pepper to taste. Serve.

NOTES FROM THE TEST KITCHEN
All About Vinegars

Bright, acidic vinegar is essential to making many salad dressings. We also frequently reach for vinegar to add acidity and flavor to sauces, stews, soups, and bean dishes. Because different vinegars have distinctly different flavors, you will want to stock several varieties in your pantry.

BALSAMIC VINEGAR
Traditional Italian balsamic vinegars are aged for years to develop complex flavor—but they're very pricey. They're best saved to drizzle over finished dishes. Our recommended best buy for high-end balsamic is Oliviers & Co. Premium Balsamic Vinegar of Modena. For vinaigrettes and glazes, we use commercial balsamic vinegars, which are younger wine vinegars with added sugar and coloring. Our favorite everyday balsamic is Bertolli Balsamic Vinegar of Modena.

RED WINE VINEGAR
Use this slightly sweet, sharp vinegar for bold vinaigrettes. With its high acidity level, it works well with potent flavors. We prefer red wine vinegars made from a blend of wine and Concord grapes; our favorite brand is Laurent du Clos.

WHITE WINE VINEGAR
This vinegar's refined, fruity bite is perfect for light vinaigrettes. We also use it in dishes like potato salad where the color of red wine vinegar would detract from the presentation. Spectrum Naturals Organic White Wine Vinegar is our favorite.

SHERRY VINEGAR
Sherry vinegar is a Spanish condiment with complex savory flavors. It adds fruity depth to vegetable salads as well as gazpachos. Our favorite is Napa Valley Naturals Reserve.

CIDER VINEGAR
This vinegar has a bite and a fruity sweetness perfect for vinaigrettes; it works well in salads tossed with apple or dried fruits. Our favorite is Spectrum Naturals Organic Apple Cider Vinegar.

Sesame-Lemon Cucumber Salad

SERVES 4 VEG

WHY THIS RECIPE WORKS Cucumbers can make a cool, crisp salad, but often they turn soggy from their own moisture. For a cucumber salad with good crunch, we found that weighting salted cucumbers forced more water from them than salting alone. After many tests, we determined that 1 to 3 hours worked best: Even after 12 hours, the cucumbers gave up no more water than they had after 3 hours. For a bit of zip, we liked pairing the cucumbers with a rice vinegar and lemon juice dressing; sesame seeds added nutty flavor. Toast the sesame seeds in a dry skillet over medium heat until fragrant, about 1 minute, and then remove the skillet from the heat so the sesame seeds won't scorch. This salad is best served within 1 hour of being dressed.

    3 cucumbers, peeled, halved lengthwise, seeded,
        and sliced ¼ inch thick
      Salt and pepper
    ¼ cup rice vinegar
    2 tablespoons toasted sesame oil
    1 tablespoon lemon juice
    1 tablespoon sesame seeds, toasted
    2 teaspoons sugar
    ⅛ teaspoon red pepper flakes, plus extra for seasoning

1. Toss cucumbers with 1 tablespoon salt in colander set over large bowl. Weight cucumbers with 1 gallon-size zipper-lock bag filled with water; drain for 1 to 3 hours. Rinse and pat dry.

2. Whisk vinegar, oil, lemon juice, sesame seeds, sugar, and pepper flakes together in large bowl. Add cucumbers and toss to coat. Season with salt and pepper to taste. Serve at room temperature or chilled.

VARIATION

Yogurt-Mint Cucumber Salad

SERVES 4 VEG

This salad is best served within 1 hour of being dressed.

    3 cucumbers, peeled, halved lengthwise, seeded,
        and sliced ¼ inch thick
    1 small red onion, sliced thin
      Salt and pepper
    1 cup plain low-fat yogurt
    ¼ cup minced fresh mint
    2 tablespoons extra-virgin olive oil
    1 garlic clove, minced
    ½ teaspoon ground cumin

1. Toss cucumbers and onion with 1 tablespoon salt in colander set over large bowl. Weight cucumber-onion mixture with 1 gallon-size zipper-lock bag filled with water; drain for 1 to 3 hours. Rinse and pat dry.

2. Whisk yogurt, mint, oil, garlic, and cumin together in large bowl. Add cucumber-onion mixture and toss to coat. Season with salt and pepper to taste. Serve at room temperature or chilled.

Algerian-Style Fennel, Orange, and Olive Salad

SERVES 4 to 6 FAST VEG

WHY THIS RECIPE WORKS In Algeria and Tunisia, raw fennel is often used to make distinctive salads. We liked the fennel best when it was sliced as thin as possible; this kept the texture from being too tough or chewy. Sweet, juicy oranges were the perfect match for the crisp fennel. To ensure that they were evenly distributed in the salad, we cut the oranges into bite-size pieces and tossed the salad gently to keep the segments from falling apart. To finish off the salad, we added some oil-cured black olives, which are ubiquitous in the region, plus some fresh mint, lemon juice, olive oil, salt, and pepper. Because this dish is so simple, using high-quality ingredients is essential. We prefer to use blood oranges in this salad. Navel oranges, tangelos, or Cara Caras can also be used, but because they are larger, you'll need just three of them.

    4 blood oranges
    2 fennel bulbs, stalks discarded, bulbs halved, cored, and
        sliced thin
    ½ cup pitted oil-cured black olives, quartered
    ¼ cup coarsely chopped fresh mint
    2 tablespoons lemon juice
      Salt and pepper
    ¼ cup extra-virgin olive oil

1. Cut away peel and pith from oranges. Quarter oranges, then slice crosswise into ¼-inch-thick pieces. Combine oranges, fennel, olives, and mint in large bowl.

2. Whisk lemon juice, ¼ teaspoon salt, and ⅛ teaspoon pepper together in small bowl. Whisking constantly, slowly drizzle in oil. Drizzle dressing over salad and gently toss to coat. Season with salt and pepper to taste. Serve.

VARIATION

Algerian-Style Fennel, Orange, and Radish Salad

FAST VEG

Omit olives. Substitute ¼ cup minced fresh tarragon for mint. Add 6 radishes, trimmed and sliced thin, to orange-fennel mixture in step 1.

Thinly sliced raw fennel shines when paired with peppery watercress and earthy smoked mackerel.

Fennel and Apple Salad with Smoked Mackerel
SERVES 4 to 6 FAST

WHY THIS RECIPE WORKS Oftentimes underappreciated, raw fennel has a lively anise flavor and a wonderful crunchy texture that make it a superb salad candidate. Many fennel salad recipes simply have you toss sliced fennel with a little lemon juice and olive oil, but we found those to be overwhelmingly strong in both flavor and texture. We were after a salad in which fennel was the focus but which also included other ingredients to complement the anise flavor and round it out. It occurred to us that some sort of leafy green would help to balance the fennel and improve the overall texture of the salad. To this end, we decided that the peppery flavor and delicate texture of watercress would blend well with the fennel, and tasters agreed. We added Granny Smith apples for a little sweetness and more crunch. A simple lemon and oil–based vinaigrette with fresh tarragon, shallot, and tangy whole-grain mustard really brought everything together. Finally, to turn this light and refreshing salad into a meal, we topped it with smoked mackerel, chosen for its rich, intense flavor.

3 tablespoons lemon juice
1 tablespoon whole-grain mustard
1 small shallot, minced
2 teaspoons minced fresh tarragon
  Salt and pepper
¼ cup extra-virgin olive oil
5 ounces (5 cups) watercress
2 Granny Smith apples, peeled, cored, and cut into 3-inch-long matchsticks
1 fennel bulb, stalks discarded, bulb halved, cored, and sliced thin
6 ounces smoked mackerel, skin and pin bones removed, flaked

1. Whisk lemon juice, mustard, shallot, 1 teaspoon tarragon, ½ teaspoon salt, and ¼ teaspoon pepper together in large bowl. Whisking constantly, slowly drizzle in oil. Add watercress, apples, and fennel and gently toss to coat. Season with salt and pepper to taste.

2. Divide salad among plates and top with flaked mackerel. Drizzle any remaining dressing over mackerel and sprinkle with remaining 1 teaspoon tarragon. Serve immediately.

Preparing Fennel

1. After cutting off stalks and feathery fronds, cut thin slice from base of fennel bulb and remove any tough or blemished layers.

2. Cut bulb in half vertically through base, then use small knife to remove pyramid-shaped core.

3. Slice each half into thin slices to ensure best texture.

Our traditional Greek salad features a mix of fresh vegetables instead of lettuce and is dressed with a lemony vinaigrette.

6 tablespoons extra-virgin olive oil
1½ tablespoons red wine vinegar
2 teaspoons minced fresh oregano
1 teaspoon lemon juice
1 garlic clove, minced
Salt and pepper
2 cucumbers, peeled, halved lengthwise, seeded, and sliced thin
½ red onion, sliced thin
6 large ripe tomatoes, cored, seeded, and cut into ½-inch-thick wedges
1 cup jarred roasted red peppers, rinsed, patted dry, and cut into ½-inch strips
½ cup pitted kalamata olives, quartered
¼ cup chopped fresh parsley
¼ cup chopped fresh mint
5 ounces feta cheese, crumbled (1¼ cups)

1. Whisk oil, vinegar, oregano, lemon juice, garlic, ½ teaspoon salt, and ⅛ teaspoon pepper together in large bowl. Add cucumbers and onion, toss to coat, and let sit for 20 minutes.

2. Add tomatoes, red peppers, olives, parsley, and mint to bowl with cucumber-onion mixture and toss to combine. Season with salt and pepper to taste. Transfer salad to wide, shallow serving bowl or platter and sprinkle with feta. Serve immediately.

Country-Style Greek Salad
SERVES 6 to 8 FAST VEG

WHY THIS RECIPE WORKS Most versions of Greek salad consist of iceberg lettuce, chunks of green pepper, and a few pale wedges of tomato, sparsely dotted with cubes of feta and garnished with one forlorn olive of questionable heritage. For our Greek salad, we aimed higher and left out the lettuce altogether to make a "country style" salad that is popular throughout Greece. We wanted a salad with crisp ingredients and bold flavors, highlighted by briny olives and tangy feta, all blended together with a bright-tasting dressing infused with fresh herbs. For a dressing with balanced flavor, we used a combination of lemon juice and red wine vinegar and added fresh oregano, olive oil, and a small amount of garlic. We poured the dressing over fresh vegetables, including tomatoes, onion, and cucumbers, as well as other ingredients, including fresh mint and parsley, roasted peppers, and a generous sprinkling of feta cheese and olives. Marinating the onion and cucumbers in the vinaigrette toned down the onion's harshness and flavored the cucumbers.

Shaved Mushroom and Celery Salad
SERVES 6 FAST VEG

WHY THIS RECIPE WORKS Earthy mushrooms and vegetal, crunchy celery pair well in many dishes, so we combined them in pursuit of salad perfection. To start, we chose cremini mushrooms for their earthiness as well as full flavor, which would allow them to share the spotlight without losing their identity. Looking to elevate their flavor, we sautéed the mushrooms. Although very flavorful, the cooked mushrooms seemed out of place next to raw celery, and the salad lost its light, fresh appeal. Instead, we sliced the mushrooms very thin and marinated them in a bright lemon vinaigrette. Their 10-minute soak in the acidic dressing softened and seasoned them, bringing out and balancing their flavor. Fresh celery gave our salad the much-needed crunch it would otherwise have been missing. Additional greenery came by way of parsley for its clean taste, and tarragon supplied a pleasant bittersweetness with a hint of anise. Shaved Parmesan added to our salad just before serving added a layer of nutty richness and satisfied the need for additional seasoning. Slice the mushrooms and celery as thinly as possible; this keeps the texture cohesive and allows the dressing to be absorbed more easily. If celery greens (the delicate leaves attached to the celery stalks) are not available, substitute 1 to 2 tablespoons of chopped fresh parsley. Make sure not to marinate the mushrooms for longer than 10 minutes; otherwise the salad will be watery.

¼ cup extra-virgin olive oil
1½ tablespoons lemon juice
    Salt and pepper
  8 ounces cremini mushrooms, trimmed and sliced thin
  1 shallot, halved and sliced thin
  4 celery ribs, sliced thin, plus ½ cup celery leaves
  2 ounces Parmesan cheese, shaved
  ½ cup fresh parsley leaves
  2 tablespoons chopped fresh tarragon

1. Whisk oil, lemon juice, and ¼ teaspoon salt together in large bowl. Add mushrooms and shallot, toss to coat, and let sit for 10 minutes.

2. Add sliced celery and leaves, Parmesan, parsley, and tarragon to mushroom-shallot mixture and toss to combine. Season with salt and pepper to taste. Serve.

Panzanella Salad with White Beans and Arugula
SERVES 6 VEG

WHY THIS RECIPE WORKS *Panzanella*, Italy's beloved bread salad, relies on the crusty, dry quality of stale bread to hold its own alongside juicy tomatoes. Rather than wait for our bread to turn stale, we baked bite-size cubes of hearty Italian bread until they took on a crisp, crunchy texture. As we chopped our tomatoes, we were careful to reserve the seeds and juice, knowing they would contribute intense tomato taste to the vinaigrette. Convenient canned cannellini beans, peppery arugula, and shaved Parmesan offered nice contrast to the bread and tomatoes. It's essential to use high-quality rustic Italian bread for its crusty chew. Avoid sliced white sandwich bread or airy supermarket Italian bread—both will turn to mush once tossed with the dressing. The success of this recipe depends on ripe, in-season tomatoes. Do not discard the seeds or juice as you chop the tomatoes because they add important moisture and flavor to the salad.

 12 ounces rustic Italian bread, cut into 1-inch pieces
    (4 cups)
  5 tablespoons extra-virgin olive oil
    Salt and pepper
  3 tablespoons red wine vinegar
1½ pounds ripe tomatoes, cored and chopped, seeds
    and juice reserved

Toasting hearty cubes of Italian bread helps them maintain their crunch in this classic Italian salad.

  1 (15-ounce) can cannellini beans, rinsed
  1 small red onion, halved and sliced thin
  3 tablespoons chopped fresh basil
  2 tablespoons minced fresh oregano
  3 ounces (3 cups) baby arugula
  2 ounces Parmesan cheese, shaved

1. Adjust oven rack to middle position and heat oven to 350 degrees. Toss bread pieces with 1 tablespoon oil and season with salt and pepper. Arrange bread in single layer in rimmed baking sheet and bake, stirring occasionally, until light golden brown, 15 to 20 minutes. Let cool to room temperature.

2. Whisk vinegar and ¼ teaspoon salt together in large bowl. Whisking constantly, slowly drizzle in remaining ¼ cup oil. Add tomatoes with their seeds and juice, beans, onion, 1½ tablespoons basil, and 1 tablespoon oregano, toss to coat, and let sit for 20 minutes.

3. Add cooled croutons, arugula, remaining 1½ tablespoons basil, and remaining 1 tablespoon oregano and gently toss to combine. Season with salt and pepper to taste. Transfer salad to serving platter and sprinkle with Parmesan. Serve.

Tangy sumac adds bright flavor and baked pita chips add crunch to this traditional eastern Mediterranean salad.

Fattoush

SERVES 4 to 6 `VEG`

WHY THIS RECIPE WORKS *Fattoush* is an eastern Mediterranean salad that combines fresh produce and herbs, toasted pita bread, and bright, tangy sumac. Our goal was to balance the sweetly acidic flavor of sumac with the fresh vegetables, while also preventing the pita from becoming soggy. Sumac is a commonly used spice across the region and traditionally lends its citrusy punch to this salad. We opted to use an ample amount of sumac in the dressing to intensify the flavor, as well as use it as a garnish for the finished salad. Many recipes call for eliminating excess moisture from the salad by taking the time-consuming step of seeding and salting the cucumbers and tomatoes. We skipped these steps in order to preserve the crisp texture of the cucumber and the flavorful seeds and juice of the tomatoes. Instead, we made the pita pieces moisture-repellent by brushing their craggy sides with plenty of olive oil before baking them. The oil prevented the pita from absorbing moisture from the salad and becoming soggy while still allowing them to pick up flavor from the lemony dressing. The success of this recipe depends on ripe, in-season tomatoes.

2 (8-inch) pita breads
7 tablespoons extra-virgin olive oil
  Salt and pepper
3 tablespoons lemon juice
4 teaspoons ground sumac, plus extra for sprinkling
¼ teaspoon minced garlic
1 pound ripe tomatoes, cored and cut into ¾-inch pieces
1 English cucumber, peeled and sliced ⅛ inch thick
1 cup arugula, chopped coarse
½ cup chopped fresh cilantro
½ cup chopped fresh mint
4 scallions, sliced thin

1. Adjust oven rack to middle position and heat oven to 375 degrees. Using kitchen shears, cut around perimeter of each pita and separate into 2 thin rounds. Cut each round in half. Place pitas smooth side down on wire rack set in rimmed baking sheet. Brush 3 tablespoons oil on surface of pitas. (Pitas do not need to be uniformly coated. Oil will spread during baking.) Season with salt and pepper. Bake until pitas are crisp and pale golden brown, 10 to 14 minutes. Let cool to room temperature.

2. Whisk lemon juice, sumac, garlic, and ¼ teaspoon salt together in small bowl and let sit for 10 minutes. Whisking constantly, slowly drizzle in remaining ¼ cup oil.

3. Break pitas into ½-inch pieces and place in large bowl. Add tomatoes, cucumber, arugula, cilantro, mint, and scallions. Drizzle dressing over salad and gently toss to coat. Season with salt and pepper to taste. Serve, sprinkling individual portions with extra sumac.

French Potato Salad with Dijon and Fines Herbes

SERVES 4 to 6 `VEG`

WHY THIS RECIPE WORKS French potato salad should be pleasing not only to the eye but also to the palate. The potatoes (small red potatoes are traditional) should be tender but not mushy, and the flavor of the vinaigrette should permeate the relatively bland potatoes. To eliminate torn skins and broken slices, a common pitfall in boiling skin-on red potatoes, we sliced the potatoes before boiling them. To evenly infuse the potatoes with the garlicky mustard vinaigrette, we spread the warm potatoes on a baking sheet and poured the vinaigrette over the top. Gently folding in fresh herbs just before serving helped keep the potatoes intact. If fresh chervil isn't available, substitute an additional ½ tablespoon of minced parsley and an additional ½ teaspoon of tarragon. Use small red potatoes measuring 1 to 2 inches in diameter.

2 pounds small red potatoes, unpeeled, sliced ¼ inch thick

2 tablespoons salt

1 garlic clove, peeled and threaded on skewer

¼ cup extra-virgin olive oil

1½ tablespoons white wine vinegar or Champagne vinegar

2 teaspoons Dijon mustard

½ teaspoon pepper

1 small shallot, minced

1 tablespoon minced fresh chervil

1 tablespoon minced fresh parsley

1 tablespoon minced fresh chives

1 teaspoon minced fresh tarragon

1. Place potatoes in large saucepan, add water to cover by 1 inch, and bring to boil over high heat. Add salt, reduce heat to simmer, and cook until potatoes are tender and paring knife can be slipped in and out of potatoes with little resistance, about 6 minutes.

2. While potatoes are cooking, lower skewered garlic into simmering water and blanch for 45 seconds. Run garlic under cold running water, then remove from skewer and mince.

3. Reserve ¼ cup cooking water, then drain potatoes and arrange in tight single layer in rimmed baking sheet. Whisk oil, minced garlic, vinegar, mustard, pepper, and reserved potato cooking water together in bowl, then drizzle over potatoes. Let potatoes sit until flavors meld, about 10 minutes.

A garlicky mustard vinaigrette, poured over the potatoes while warm, gives this French-style potato salad great flavor.

Making French Potato Salad

1. COOK SLICED POTATOES Combine sliced potatoes and salt in large saucepan and add water to cover by 1 inch. Bring to boil over high heat, reduce heat to medium-low, and simmer until potatoes are just tender, 5 to 6 minutes.

2. BLANCH GARLIC While potatoes are cooking, lower skewered garlic into simmering water and blanch for 45 seconds. Run garlic under cold running water, then remove from skewer and mince.

3. POUR DRESSING OVER WARM POTATOES Arrange hot potatoes close together in single layer in rimmed baking sheet. Drizzle evenly with dressing and let sit at room temperature until flavors meld, about 10 minutes.

4. ADD HERBS BEFORE SERVING Combine shallot and herbs in small bowl, then sprinkle over potatoes and gently combine using rubber spatula. Serve.

(Potatoes can be refrigerated for up to 8 hours; return to room temperature before serving.)

4. Transfer potatoes to large bowl. Combine shallot and herbs in small bowl, then sprinkle over potatoes and gently toss to coat using rubber spatula. Serve.

VARIATIONS

French Potato Salad with Fennel, Tomatoes, and Olives VEG

If desired, chop 1 tablespoon of the fennel fronds and add it to the salad with the parsley.

Omit chervil, chives, and tarragon. Increase parsley amount to 3 tablespoons. Add ½ fennel bulb, sliced thin, 1 cored and chopped tomato, and ¼ cup pitted oil-cured black olives, quartered, to salad with shallots and parsley.

French Potato Salad with Radishes, Cornichons, and Capers VEG

Omit chervil, chives, tarragon, and parsley. Substitute 2 tablespoons minced red onion for shallot. Add 2 thinly sliced red radishes, ¼ cup rinsed capers, and ¼ cup thinly sliced cornichons to salad with onion.

Roasted Winter Squash Salad with Za'atar and Parsley

SERVES 4 to 6   VEG -

WHY THIS RECIPE WORKS The sweet, nutty flavor of roasted butternut squash pairs best with flavors that are bold enough to balance that sweetness. To fill this role in our roasted butternut squash salad, we chose the traditional eastern Mediterranean spice blend *za'atar* (a pungent combination of toasted sesame seeds, thyme, and sumac). We found that using high heat and placing the oven rack in the lowest position produced perfectly browned squash with a firm center in about 30 minutes. Dusting the za'atar over the hot squash worked much like toasting the spice, boosting its flavor. For a foil to the tender squash, we considered a host of nuts before landing on toasted pumpkin seeds. They provided the textural accent the dish needed and reinforced the squash's flavor. Pomegranate seeds added a burst of tartness and color. We prefer to use our homemade Za'atar (page 316), but you can substitute store-bought za'atar if you wish. You can substitute chopped red grapes or small blueberries for the pomegranate seeds.

3   pounds butternut squash, peeled, seeded, and cut into ½-inch pieces (8 cups)
¼   cup extra-virgin olive oil
    Salt and pepper

1   teaspoon za'atar
1   small shallot, minced
2   tablespoons lemon juice
2   tablespoons honey
¾   cup fresh parsley leaves
⅓   cup roasted, unsalted pepitas
½   cup pomegranate seeds

1. Adjust oven rack to lowest position and heat oven to 450 degrees. Toss squash with 1 tablespoon oil and season with salt and pepper. Arrange squash in single layer in rimmed baking sheet and roast until well browned and tender, 30 to 35 minutes, stirring halfway through roasting. Sprinkle squash with za'atar and let cool for 15 minutes.

2. Whisk shallot, lemon juice, honey, and ¼ teaspoon salt together in large bowl. Whisking constantly, slowly drizzle in remaining 3 tablespoons oil. Add squash, parsley, and pepitas and gently toss to coat. Arrange salad on serving platter and sprinkle with pomegranate seeds. Serve.

Cutting Up Butternut Squash

1. After peeling squash, trim off top and bottom and cut squash in half where narrow neck and wide curved bottom meet.

2. Cut neck of squash into evenly sized planks. Cut planks into evenly sized pieces, according to recipe.

3. Cut squash base in half lengthwise, then scoop out and discard seeds and fibers.

4. Slice each base half into evenly sized lengths, then cut lengths into evenly sized pieces, according to recipe.

Tomato Salad with Feta and Cumin-Yogurt Dressing

SERVES 6 `FAST` `VEG`

WHY THIS RECIPE WORKS Fresh, juicy summer tomatoes make a great salad, so we set out to create one with complementary flavors and a creamy dressing. Tomatoes exude lots of liquid when cut, which can quickly turn a salad into soup. To get rid of some of the tomato juice without losing all its valuable flavor, we looked to a method that had proven successful in our other tomato salad recipes: salting the tomatoes before making the salad. Simply cutting the tomatoes into wedges, tossing them with salt, and letting them sit for 15 minutes provided enough time for the juice to drain. This also seasoned the tomatoes and their juice at the same time. We reserved a measured amount of the flavorful juice to add to the dressing without watering down the salad. Greek yogurt laid the foundation for a creamy, spice-infused dressing, and we boosted its tang with lemon juice and the reserved tomato juice. To that we added fresh oregano, cumin, and garlic, but some tasters found the cumin and garlic too harsh. A quick zap in the microwave was all it took to effectively bloom the spice and cook the garlic, successfully mellowing their flavors. We tossed the tomatoes with the dressing, finishing with just the right amount of briny feta to add richness and another layer of flavor. Both regular and low-fat Greek yogurt will work well here; do not use nonfat yogurt. The success of this recipe depends on ripe, in-season tomatoes.

2½ pounds ripe tomatoes, cored and cut into ½-inch-thick wedges
    Salt and pepper
1 tablespoon extra-virgin olive oil
1 garlic clove, minced
1 teaspoon ground cumin
¼ cup plain Greek yogurt
1 tablespoon lemon juice
1 scallion, sliced thin
1 tablespoon minced fresh oregano
3 ounces feta cheese, crumbled (¾ cup)

1. Toss tomatoes with ½ teaspoon salt and let drain in colander set over bowl for 15 to 20 minutes.

2. Microwave oil, garlic, and cumin in bowl until fragrant, about 30 seconds; let cool slightly. Transfer 1 tablespoon tomato

Salting the tomatoes seasons their juice, which we use to add flavor to the salad dressing.

liquid to large bowl; discard remaining liquid. Whisk in yogurt, lemon juice, scallion, oregano, and oil mixture until combined. Add tomatoes and feta and gently toss to coat. Season with salt and pepper to taste. Serve.

Coring a Tomato

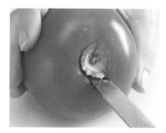

Remove core of tomato using paring knife.

Tomato Salad with Tuna, Capers, and Black Olives

SERVES 6 FAST

WHY THIS RECIPE WORKS We wanted to create a salad reminiscent of *salade niçoise*, only simpler. Fortunately, choosing just one ingredient to build our new salad around was pretty easy; tomatoes stood out as a refreshing and colorful choice, but the treatment of the tomatoes was key in developing this modest salad. Tomato-centric salads tend to be drowning in liquid and suffer from washed-out flavors. To keep our salad from this fate, we tossed the tomato wedges with salt and let them sit to draw out their excess moisture. Not wanting to waste any valuable tomato flavor, we added some of the expelled juice to the base of our dressing and added lemon juice and extra-virgin olive oil to create a light dressing that coated the tomatoes but didn't mask any of their fresh flavor. These well-dressed wedges tasted great but needed a few more ingredients to conjure the spirit of salade niçoise. To keep it simple, we ruled out anything that needed to be blanched or cooked. Since olives, capers, and red onions are boldly flavored Mediterranean standbys, they were in. Using 2½ pounds of tomatoes ensured that they remained the focus. Recalling that our inspiration included both anchovies and tuna, we added a can of tuna to elevate the flavor of our tomato salad and add a little protein. Tuna was a preferred addition over anchovies for its meatier texture and milder flavor. The success of this recipe depends on ripe, in-season tomatoes.

2½ pounds ripe tomatoes, cored and cut into ½-inch-thick wedges
     Salt and pepper
 ¼ cup extra-virgin olive oil
 ⅓ cup pitted kalamata olives, chopped coarse
 ¼ cup capers, rinsed and minced
 ¼ cup finely chopped red onion
 2 tablespoons chopped fresh parsley
 1 tablespoon lemon juice
 1 (5-ounce) can solid white tuna in water, drained and flaked

1. Toss tomatoes with ½ teaspoon salt and let drain in colander set over bowl for 15 to 20 minutes.

2. Transfer 1 tablespoon tomato liquid to large bowl; discard remaining liquid. Whisk in oil, olives, capers, onion, parsley, and lemon juice until combined. Add tomatoes and tuna and gently toss to coat. Season with salt and pepper to taste. Serve.

NOTES FROM THE TEST KITCHEN

Buying and Storing Fresh Tomatoes

Buying tomatoes at the height of summer won't guarantee juicy, flavorful fruit, but keeping these guidelines in mind will help.

CHOOSE LOCALLY GROWN TOMATOES

If at all possible, this is the best way to ensure a flavorful tomato. The shorter the distance a tomato has to travel, the riper it can be when it's picked. And commercial tomatoes are engineered to be sturdier, with thicker walls and less of the flavorful juice and seeds.

LOOKS AREN'T EVERYTHING

When selecting tomatoes, oddly shaped tomatoes are fine, and even cracked skin is OK. Avoid tomatoes that are overly soft or leaking juice. Choose tomatoes that smell fruity and feel heavy. And consider trying heirloom tomatoes; grown from naturally pollinated plants and seeds, they are some of the best local tomatoes you can find.

BUY SUPERMARKET TOMATOES ON THE VINE

If supermarket tomatoes are your only option, look for tomatoes sold on the vine. Although this does not mean that they were fully ripened on the vine, they are better than regular supermarket tomatoes, which are picked when still green and blasted with ethylene gas to develop texture and color.

STORING TOMATOES

Once you've brought your tomatoes home, proper storage is important to preserve their fresh flavor and texture for as long as possible. Here are the rules we follow in the test kitchen:

• Never refrigerate tomatoes; the cold damages enzymes that produce flavor compounds, and it ruins their texture, turning the flesh mealy. Even when cut, tomatoes should be kept at room temperature (wrap them tightly in plastic wrap).

• If the vine is still attached, leave it on and store the tomatoes stem end up. Tomatoes off the vine should be stored stem side down. We have found that this prevents moisture from escaping and bacteria from entering and thus prolongs shelf life.

• To quickly ripen hard tomatoes, store them in a paper bag with a banana or apple, both of which emit ethylene gas, which hastens ripening.

Cherry Tomato Salad with Feta and Olives

SERVES 4 to 6 `VEG`

WHY THIS RECIPE WORKS Cherry tomatoes can make a great salad, but they exude lots of liquid when cut. To get rid of some of the tomato juice without throwing away flavor, we quartered and salted the tomatoes before whirling them in a salad spinner to separate the seeds and juice from the flesh. After we strained the juice and discarded the seeds, we reduced the tomato juice to a flavorful concentrate (adding garlic, oregano, shallot, olive oil, and vinegar) and reunited it with the tomatoes. Feta cheese added richness and another layer of flavor to this great all-season salad. If cherry tomatoes are unavailable, substitute grape tomatoes cut in half along the equator. If you don't have a salad spinner, wrap the bowl tightly with plastic wrap after the salted tomatoes have sat for 30 minutes and gently shake to remove seeds and excess liquid. Strain the liquid and proceed with the recipe as directed. If you have less than ½ cup of juice after spinning, proceed with the recipe using the entire amount of juice and reduce it to 3 tablespoons as directed (the cooking time will be shorter).

- 1½ pounds cherry tomatoes, quartered
- ½ teaspoon sugar
  Salt and pepper
- 1 small cucumber, peeled, halved lengthwise, seeded, and cut into ½-inch pieces
- ½ cup pitted kalamata olives, chopped
- 4 ounces feta cheese, crumbled (1 cup)
- 3 tablespoons chopped fresh parsley
- 1 shallot, minced
- 1 tablespoon red wine vinegar
- 2 garlic cloves, minced
- 2 teaspoons minced fresh oregano
- 2 tablespoons extra-virgin olive oil

1. Toss tomatoes with sugar and ¼ teaspoon salt in bowl and let sit for 30 minutes. Transfer tomatoes to salad spinner and spin until seeds and excess liquid have been removed, 45 to 60 seconds, stopping to redistribute tomatoes several times during spinning. Add tomatoes, cucumber, olives, feta, and parsley to large bowl; set aside.

2. Strain ½ cup tomato liquid through fine-mesh strainer into liquid measuring cup; discard remaining liquid. Bring tomato liquid, shallot, vinegar, garlic, and oregano to simmer in small saucepan over medium heat and cook until reduced to 3 tablespoons, 6 to 8 minutes. Transfer to small bowl and let cool to room temperature, about 5 minutes. Whisking constantly, slowly drizzle in oil. Drizzle dressing over salad and gently toss to coat. Season with salt and pepper to taste. Serve.

VARIATION
Cherry Tomato Salad with Basil and Fresh Mozzarella `VEG`

Omit cucumbers, olives, feta, parsley, garlic, and oregano. Substitute 1 tablespoon balsamic vinegar for red wine vinegar. Add 1½ cups fresh basil leaves, roughly torn, and 8 ounces fresh mozzarella, cut into ½-inch pieces and patted dry with paper towels, to tomatoes with dressing.

Making Cherry Tomato Salad

1. SALT TOMATOES Toss tomatoes, ½ teaspoon sugar, and ¼ teaspoon salt together in bowl and let sit for 30 minutes.

2. DISCARD SEEDS Transfer tomatoes to salad spinner and spin until seeds and excess liquid have been removed, 45 to 60 seconds. Combine seeded tomatoes with cucumber, olives, feta, and parsley.

3. STRAIN TOMATO LIQUID Strain ½ cup tomato liquid into measuring cup. Bring tomato liquid, shallot, vinegar, garlic, and oregano to simmer over medium heat and cook until reduced to 3 tablespoons, 6 to 8 minutes. Once cool, slowly whisk in oil.

4. TOSS TO COAT Drizzle dressing over salad and gently toss to coat.

Garlic bread crumbs, decadent burrata cheese, and a white balsamic dressing jazz up our riff on classic Caprese salad.

Tomato and Burrata Salad with Pangrattato and Basil

SERVES 4 to 6 VEG

WHY THIS RECIPE WORKS Popular in Italy, *burrata* is a deluxe version of fresh mozzarella in which the supple cheese is bound around a filling of cream and soft, stringy curds. We wanted to create a Caprese-inspired salad in which this decadent cheese could star alongside summer's best tomatoes. We quickly realized that just tomatoes, basil, and good extra-virgin olive oil weren't enough to bring out the best in the cheese as they do in a Caprese salad; the richness of the burrata overwhelmed the other components. To maximize the flavor of the tomatoes, we used a combination of standard tomatoes and sweet cherry tomatoes, salting them and letting them sit for 30 minutes to help draw out their watery juices, which intensified the tomato flavor. Blending the olive oil with a little minced shallot and mild, sweet-tart white balsamic vinegar gave us a simple but bold vinaigrette. Finally, we found that a topping of Italian *pangrattato* (garlicky bread crumbs) helped bring the dish together, soaking up both the tomato juice and the burrata cream. The success of this dish depends on using ripe, in-season tomatoes and fresh, high-quality burrata.

1½ pounds ripe tomatoes, cored and cut into 1-inch pieces
8 ounces ripe cherry tomatoes, halved
Salt and pepper
3 ounces rustic Italian bread, cut into 1-inch pieces (1 cup)
6 tablespoons extra-virgin olive oil
1 garlic clove, minced
1 shallot, halved and sliced thin
1½ tablespoons white balsamic vinegar
½ cup chopped fresh basil
8 ounces burrata cheese, room temperature

1. Toss tomatoes with ¼ teaspoon salt and let drain in colander for 30 minutes.

2. Pulse bread in food processor into large crumbs measuring between ⅛ and ¼ inch, about 10 pulses. Combine crumbs, 2 tablespoons oil, pinch salt, and pinch pepper in 12-inch nonstick skillet. Cook over medium heat, stirring often, until crumbs are crisp and golden, about 10 minutes. Clear center of skillet, add garlic, and cook, mashing it into skillet, until fragrant, about 30 seconds. Stir garlic into crumbs. Transfer to plate and let cool slightly.

3. Whisk shallot, vinegar, and ¼ teaspoon salt together in large bowl. Whisking constantly, slowly drizzle in remaining ¼ cup oil. Add tomatoes and basil and gently toss to combine. Season with salt and pepper to taste and arrange on serving platter. Cut buratta into 1-inch pieces, collecting creamy liquid. Sprinkle burrata over tomatoes and drizzle with creamy liquid. Sprinkle with bread crumbs and serve immediately.

Grilled Vegetable and Halloumi Salad

SERVES 4 to 6 FAST VEG

WHY THIS RECIPE WORKS Grilled vegetables are the perfect basis for a summer supper. We set out to match nicely charred pieces of vegetables with chunks of briny halloumi cheese to create a warm and hearty salad. Halloumi cheese, popular in Greece, has a solid consistency and high melting point, making it perfect for grilling. The halloumi becomes beautifully charred and crisp in contrast to its chewy warm interior. To keep with a Greek theme, we chose eggplant, radicchio, and zucchini for the vegetables. After grilling the radicchio for just 5 minutes and the eggplant, zucchini, and cheese for 10 minutes, the vegetables and cheese were perfectly browned, tender, and redolent with smoky flavor. We simply chopped all the grilled goodies before tossing everything with a sweet and herbaceous honey and thyme vinaigrette, which was perfect with the salty cheese and bitter radicchio. This salad is hearty enough to serve as a main dish and pairs well with grilled bread. The halloumi may appear to stick to the grill at first, but as it continues to brown it will naturally release and flip easily.

Grilling turns halloumi cheese and vegetables into a hearty warm and smoky salad.

3 tablespoons honey
1 tablespoon minced fresh thyme
½ teaspoon grated lemon zest plus 3 tablespoons juice
1 garlic clove, minced
  Salt and pepper
1 pound eggplant, sliced into ½-inch-thick rounds
1 head radicchio (10 ounces), quartered
1 zucchini, halved lengthwise
1 (8-ounce) block halloumi cheese, sliced into ½-inch-thick slabs
¼ cup extra-virgin olive oil

1. Whisk honey, thyme, lemon zest and juice, garlic, ⅛ teaspoon salt, and ⅛ teaspoon pepper together in large bowl; set aside. Brush eggplant, radicchio, zucchini, and halloumi with 2 tablespoons oil and season with salt and pepper.

2A. FOR A CHARCOAL GRILL: Open bottom vent completely. Light large chimney starter half filled with charcoal briquettes (3 quarts). When top coals are partially covered with ash, pour evenly over grill. Set cooking grate in place, cover, and open lid vent completely. Heat grill until hot, about 5 minutes.

2B. FOR A GAS GRILL: Turn all burners to high, cover, and heat grill until hot, about 15 minutes. Turn all burners to medium.

3. Clean cooking grate, then repeatedly brush grate with well-oiled paper towels until grate is black and glossy, 5 to 10 times. Place vegetables and cheese on grill. Cook (covered if using gas), flipping as needed, until radicchio is softened and lightly charred, 3 to 5 minutes, and remaining vegetables and cheese are softened and lightly charred, about 10 minutes. Transfer vegetables and cheese to cutting board as they finish cooking, let cool slightly, then cut into 1-inch pieces.

4. Whisking constantly, slowly drizzle remaining 2 tablespoons oil into honey mixture. Add vegetables and cheese and gently toss to coat. Season with salt and pepper to taste. Serve.

Zucchini Ribbon Salad with Shaved Parmesan
SERVES 6 to 8   `FAST`   `VEG`

WHY THIS RECIPE WORKS This elegant alternative to a lettuce-based salad is also a unique way to serve zucchini without losing its crunchy texture or fresh flavor by cooking. Slicing the zucchini into thin ribbons using a peeler or mandoline maximized its surface area for dressing to cling to. We dressed the zucchini simply with olive oil, lemon juice, mint, and shaved Parmesan cheese. The success of this dish depends on using small, in-season zucchini, good olive oil, and high-quality Parmesan.

1½ pounds small zucchini, trimmed and sliced lengthwise into ribbons
  Salt and pepper
½ cup extra-virgin olive oil
¼ cup lemon juice (2 lemons)
6 ounces Parmesan cheese, shaved
2 tablespoons minced fresh mint

Gently toss zucchini with salt and pepper to taste, then arrange attractively on serving platter. Drizzle with oil and lemon juice, then sprinkle with Parmesan and mint. Serve immediately.

Making Zucchini Ribbons

Using vegetable peeler or mandoline, slice zucchini lengthwise into very thin ribbons.

CHAPTER 4

Rice and Grains

■ FAST (less than 45 minutes start to finish)   ▣ VEGETARIAN

Photos (clockwise from top left): Egyptian Barley Salad; Creamy Parmesan Polenta with Broccoli Rabe, Sun-Dried Tomato, and Pine Nut Topping; Bulgur Salad with Carrots and Almonds; Grilled Paella

Basmati Rice Pilaf with Currants and Toasted Almonds

SERVES 4 to 6 `VEG`

WHY THIS RECIPE WORKS In the Mediterranean, rice is rarely served plain—complementary flavorings are added to play off the other dishes on the table. We decided to create a basmati rice pilaf with flavor additions that would pair well with any number of entrées. Rinsing the rice before cooking removed excess starch and ensured fluffy, not clumpy, grains. We sautéed chopped onion to create an aromatic base, then we added the rice. Toasting the rice gave it a nutty, deep flavor, and stirring in garlic, turmeric, and cinnamon along with the rice allowed these big flavors to bloom and meld. Instead of following the traditional ratio of 1 cup of rice to 2 cups of water, we found that using a little less liquid made for a firmer texture that tasters liked. As soon as the grains absorbed the water, we removed the saucepan from the heat so the rice could finish steaming in the gentle residual heat. We stirred in currants for some bursts of sweetness before placing a dish towel under the lid to absorb excess moisture in the pan. Toasted almonds delivered some nice crunch to our jazzed-up pilaf. Long-grain white, jasmine, or Texmati rice can be substituted for the basmati.

Toasting the rice gives our basmati pilaf nutty flavor and using less water makes the rice pleasantly firm.

  1 tablespoon extra-virgin olive oil
  1 small onion, chopped fine
    Salt and pepper
1½ cups basmati rice, rinsed
  2 garlic cloves, minced
  ½ teaspoon ground turmeric
  ¼ teaspoon ground cinnamon
2¼ cups water
  ¼ cup currants
  ¼ cup sliced almonds, toasted

1. Heat oil in large saucepan over medium heat until shimmering. Add onion and ¼ teaspoon salt and cook until softened, about 5 minutes. Add rice, garlic, turmeric, and cinnamon and cook, stirring frequently, until grain edges begin to turn translucent, about 3 minutes.

Making Basmati Rice Pilaf

1. SAUTÉ ONIONS Heat oil in large saucepan and cook onions until softened to create aromatic base.

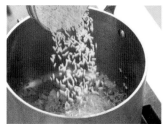

2. TOAST RICE AND SPICES Add rice, garlic, and spices and cook until rice begins to turn translucent. Stir in water, bring to simmer, cover, and cook.

3. STEAM OFF HEAT Remove pot from heat, sprinkle currants over pilaf, and cover, laying dish towel underneath lid. Let sit for 10 minutes.

4. FLUFF RICE Add almonds and fluff pilaf with fork to ensure light, fluffy texture.

2. Stir in water and bring to simmer. Reduce heat to low, cover, and simmer gently until rice is tender and water is absorbed, 16 to 18 minutes.

3. Off heat, sprinkle currants over pilaf. Cover, laying clean dish towel underneath lid, and let pilaf sit for 10 minutes. Add almonds to pilaf and fluff gently with fork to combine. Season with salt and pepper to taste. Serve.

VARIATION

Basmati Rice Pilaf with Peas, Scallions, and Lemon
VEG

Omit turmeric and cinnamon. Stir 1 teaspoon grated lemon zest and ⅛ teaspoon red pepper flakes into pot with rice. Substitute ½ cup thawed frozen peas for currants and 2 thinly sliced scallions and 1 tablespoon lemon juice for almonds.

Spiced Basmati Rice with Cauliflower and Pomegranate
SERVES 8 to 10   VEG

WHY THIS RECIPE WORKS For a fragrant, warm-spiced rice redolent with North African flavors, we started with aromatic basmati. We paired it with sweet, earthy roasted cauliflower, tossed with a generous amount of black pepper for heat and cumin for a deep, warm flavor. Roasting at a high temperature for a short time caramelized and crisped the florets without rendering them limp and mushy. We added the rice to a flavorful mixture of sautéed onion, garlic, and spices, simmered it until tender, then finished the dish with a burst of sweet pomegranate seeds and a mix of fresh herbs. Long-grain white, jasmine, or Texmati rice can be substituted for the basmati. Serve with a cooling yogurt sauce (page 233), if desired; ideally, you should make the sauce before starting the rice to allow the flavors in the sauce to meld.

    1 head cauliflower (2 pounds), cored and cut into
       ¾-inch florets
    ¼ cup extra-virgin olive oil
       Salt and pepper
    ½ teaspoon ground cumin
    1 onion, chopped coarse
  1½ cups basmati rice, rinsed
    4 garlic cloves, minced
    ½ teaspoon ground cinnamon
    ½ teaspoon ground turmeric
  2¼ cups water
    ½ cup pomegranate seeds
    2 tablespoons chopped fresh cilantro
    2 tablespoons chopped fresh mint

Deeply roasting spiced cauliflower gives it a crisp texture and bold flavor that works perfectly with fragrant basmati.

1. Adjust oven rack to lowest position and heat oven to 475 degrees. Toss cauliflower with 2 tablespoons oil, ½ teaspoon salt, ½ teaspoon pepper, and ¼ teaspoon cumin. Arrange cauliflower in single layer in rimmed baking sheet and roast until just tender, 10 to 15 minutes; set aside.

2. Heat remaining 2 tablespoons oil in large saucepan over medium heat until shimmering. Add onion and ¼ teaspoon salt and cook until softened and lightly browned, 5 to 7 minutes. Add rice, garlic, cinnamon, turmeric, and remaining ¼ teaspoon cumin and cook, stirring frequently, until grain edges begin to turn translucent, about 3 minutes.

3. Stir in water and bring to simmer. Reduce heat to low, cover, and simmer gently until rice is tender and water is absorbed, 16 to 18 minutes.

4. Off heat, lay clean dish towel underneath lid and let pilaf sit for 10 minutes. Add roasted cauliflower to pilaf and fluff gently with fork to combine. Season with salt and pepper to taste. Transfer to serving platter and sprinkle with pomegranate seeds, cilantro, and mint. Serve.

Soaking the rice for our Lebanese pilaf in hot water ensures that it's done cooking at the same time as the pasta.

Herbed Basmati Rice and Pasta Pilaf

SERVES 4 to 6   VEG

WHY THIS RECIPE WORKS Classic Lebanese rice and pasta pilaf combines rice with pieces of toasted vermicelli that add richness and a nutty flavor. In order to produce perfectly tender rice and pasta, we needed both elements to cook at the same rate. Jump-starting the rice by soaking it in hot water for a mere 15 minutes softened its outer coating and let it absorb water quickly. Once the pasta and rice were done, we let the pilaf stand in the pot for 10 minutes with a towel under the lid to absorb steam. A handful of fresh parsley lent brightness to the finished pilaf. Long-grain white, jasmine, or Texmati rice can be substituted for the basmati.

1½ cups basmati rice
3 tablespoons extra-virgin olive oil
2 ounces vermicelli pasta, broken into 1-inch lengths
1 onion, chopped fine
1 garlic clove, minced
  Salt and pepper
2½ cups chicken or vegetable broth
3 tablespoons minced fresh parsley

1. Place rice in medium bowl and cover with hot tap water by 2 inches; let stand for 15 minutes.

2. Using your hands, gently swish grains to release excess starch. Carefully pour off water, leaving rice in bowl. Add cold tap water to rice and pour off water. Repeat adding and pouring off cold water 4 to 5 times, until water runs almost clear. Drain rice in fine-mesh strainer.

3. Heat oil in large saucepan over medium heat until shimmering. Add pasta and cook, stirring occasionally, until browned, about 3 minutes. Add onion and garlic and cook, stirring occasionally, until onion is softened but not browned, about 4 minutes. Add rice and cook, stirring occasionally, until edges of rice begin to turn translucent, about 3 minutes. Add broth and 1¼ teaspoons salt and bring to boil. Reduce heat to low, cover, and simmer gently until rice and pasta are tender and broth is absorbed, about 10 minutes. Off heat, lay clean dish towel underneath lid and let pilaf sit for 10 minutes. Add parsley to pilaf and fluff gently with fork to combine. Season with salt and pepper to taste. Serve.

VARIATIONS

Herbed Basmati Rice and Pasta Pilaf with Golden Raisins and Almonds   VEG

Stir 2 bay leaves and 1 teaspoon ground cardamom into rice mixture with broth. Discard bay leaves and sprinkle ½ cup raisins over pilaf before covering with dish towel in step 3. Add ½ cup slivered almonds, toasted and chopped coarse, to pilaf with parsley.

Herbed Basmati Rice and Pasta Pilaf with Pomegranate and Walnuts   VEG

Omit onion. Substitute 2 tablespoons grated fresh ginger and ½ teaspoon ground cumin for garlic. Substitute ½ cup walnuts, toasted and chopped coarse, ½ cup pomegranate seeds, ½ cup chopped fresh cilantro, and 1 tablespoon lemon juice for parsley.

Herbed Basmati Rice and Pasta Pilaf with Yogurt   VEG

Add ¼ cup plain whole-milk yogurt, ¼ cup minced fresh dill, and ¼ cup minced fresh chives to pilaf with parsley.

Rinsing Rice and Grains

In some recipes, rinsing helps rid rice and grains of excess starch. To rinse, place rice or grains in fine-mesh strainer and run under cool water until water runs clear, occasionally stirring lightly with your hand. Let drain briefly.

Spiced Baked Rice with Roasted Sweet Potatoes and Fennel

SERVES 6 to 8 `VEG`

WHY THIS RECIPE WORKS This hearty rice dish combines several flavorful elements of North African cuisine—sweet potatoes, green olives, and fennel—along with the distinctive warmth of the spice blend *ras el hanout*. Roasting yielded sweet potatoes with firm, caramelized exteriors and soft, creamy interiors. We prepared the aromatic base on the stovetop, stirring in the ras el hanout with the rice to ensure that the flavors melded and bloomed. We added enough broth to ensure that our long-grain rice came out tender and not too crunchy, then transferred the pot to the oven. When the rice was cooked, we gently stirred in the potatoes and finished with bright cilantro and lime. We prefer to use our homemade Ras el Hanout (page 316), but you can substitute store-bought ras el hanout if you wish, though spiciness can vary greatly by brand.

1½ pounds sweet potatoes, peeled and cut into 1-inch pieces
¼ cup extra-virgin olive oil
   Salt and pepper
1 fennel bulb, stalks discarded, bulb halved, cored, and chopped fine
1 small onion, chopped fine
1½ cups long-grain white rice, rinsed
4 garlic cloves, minced
2 teaspoons ras el hanout
2¾ cups chicken or vegetable broth
¾ cup large pitted brine-cured green olives, halved
2 tablespoons minced fresh cilantro
   Lime wedges

1. Adjust oven rack to middle position and heat oven to 400 degrees. Toss potatoes with 2 tablespoons oil and ½ teaspoon salt. Arrange potatoes in single layer in rimmed baking sheet and roast until tender and browned, 25 to 30 minutes, stirring potatoes halfway through roasting. Remove potatoes from oven and reduce oven temperature to 350 degrees.

2. Heat remaining 2 tablespoons oil in Dutch oven over medium heat until shimmering. Add fennel and onion and cook until softened, 5 to 7 minutes. Stir in rice, garlic, and ras el hanout and cook, stirring frequently, until grain edges begin to turn translucent, about 3 minutes.

3. Stir in broth and olives and bring to boil. Cover, transfer pot to oven, and bake until rice is tender and liquid is absorbed, 12 to 15 minutes.

4. Remove pot from oven and let sit for 10 minutes. Add potatoes to rice and fluff gently with fork to combine. Season with salt and pepper to taste. Sprinkle with cilantro and serve with lime wedges.

Blooming the North African spice blend *ras el hanout* with the rice is a streamlined way to add complex flavor.

STOVETOP WHITE RICE

SERVES 4 to 6 `FAST` `VEG`

Basmati, jasmine, or Texmati rice can be substituted for the long-grain rice.

1 tablespoon extra-virgin olive oil
2 cups long-grain white rice, rinsed
3 cups water
   Salt and pepper

Heat oil in large saucepan over medium heat until shimmering. Add rice and cook, stirring often, until grain edges begin to turn translucent, about 2 minutes. Add water and 1 teaspoon salt and bring to simmer. Cover, reduce heat to low, and simmer gently until rice is tender and water is absorbed, about 20 minutes. Off heat, lay clean dish towel underneath lid and let rice sit for 10 minutes. Gently fluff rice with fork. Season with salt and pepper to taste. Serve.

Baking brown rice guarantees even cooking, and resting the rice while the add-ins warm through ensures a fluffy texture.

Baked Brown Rice with Roasted Red Peppers and Onions

SERVES 4 to 6 VEG

WHY THIS RECIPE WORKS We set out to bulk up baked brown rice with add-ins that would complement the hearty flavor and texture of the rice. A combination of aromatic browned onions and sweet roasted red peppers made for a simple, refreshing upgrade. To be sure that the aromatics fully penetrated the rice, we sautéed chopped onions until well browned before adding the rice and water to the pot. Once the rice was tender, we stirred in chopped roasted red peppers and let them warm through as the rice rested off the heat. Minced parsley added color and freshness, and we served the dish with a sprinkling of buttery, nutty Parmesan cheese and a squeeze of fresh lemon. Medium-grain or short-grain brown rice can be substituted for the long-grain rice.

- 4 teaspoons extra-virgin olive oil
- 2 onions, chopped fine
- Salt and pepper
- 2¼ cups water

- 1 cup chicken or vegetable broth
- 1½ cups long-grain brown rice, rinsed
- ¾ cup jarred roasted red peppers, rinsed, patted dry, and chopped
- ½ cup minced fresh parsley
- Grated Parmesan cheese
- Lemon wedges

1. Adjust oven rack to middle position and heat oven to 375 degrees. Heat oil in Dutch oven over medium heat until shimmering. Add onions and 1 teaspoon salt and cook, stirring occasionally, until softened and well browned, 12 to 14 minutes.

2. Stir in water and broth and bring to boil. Stir in rice, cover, and transfer pot to oven. Bake until rice is tender and liquid is absorbed, 65 to 70 minutes.

3. Remove pot from oven. Sprinkle red peppers over rice, cover, and let sit for 5 minutes. Add parsley to rice and fluff gently with fork to combine. Season with salt and pepper to taste. Serve with grated Parmesan and lemon wedges.

VARIATION

Baked Brown Rice with Peas, Feta, and Mint VEG
Omit 1 onion and Parmesan. Substitute 1 cup thawed frozen peas for red peppers and ½ cup crumbled feta cheese, ¼ cup minced fresh mint, and ½ teaspoon grated lemon zest for parsley.

FOOLPROOF BAKED BROWN RICE

SERVES 4 VEG

Medium-grain or short-grain brown rice can be substituted for the long-grain rice. For an accurate measurement of boiling water, bring a full kettle of water to a boil, then measure out the desired amount.

- 2⅓ cups boiling water
- 1½ cups long-grain brown rice, rinsed
- 2 teaspoons extra-virgin olive oil
- Salt and pepper

Adjust oven rack to middle position and heat oven to 375 degrees. Combine boiling water, rice, oil, and ½ teaspoon salt in 8-inch square baking dish. Cover dish tightly with double layer of aluminum foil. Bake until rice is tender and water is absorbed, about 1 hour. Remove dish from oven, uncover, and gently fluff rice with fork, scraping up any rice that has stuck to bottom. Cover dish with clean dish towel and let rice sit for 5 minutes. Uncover and let rice sit for 5 minutes longer. Season with salt and pepper to taste. Serve.

Brown Rice with Tomatoes and Chickpeas

SERVES 6 `VEG`

WHY THIS RECIPE WORKS We set out to develop a fresh, flavorful, and easy one-dish meal that put nutty brown rice and alluring Spanish flavors at the fore. Building the entire dish in a 12-inch skillet kept it convenient. To ensure that our brown rice took on plenty of rich flavor, we began with a traditional base of chopped onion and chopped bell peppers. Once both were nicely browned, we stirred in the rice along with three aromatic powerhouses: minced garlic, crumbled saffron threads, and a pinch of cayenne pepper. A generous amount of broth was enough to both cook the rice and add some extra flavor to our mix-ins during cooking. We added canned chickpeas to the skillet halfway through cooking so they could soften slightly while the rice finished cooking. A simple mix of quartered grape tomatoes, bright sliced scallions, and citrusy minced cilantro, united by some olive oil and fresh lime juice, made for a vibrant finishing touch.

12 ounces grape tomatoes, quartered
 5 scallions, sliced thin
 ¼ cup minced fresh cilantro
 4 teaspoons extra-virgin olive oil
 1 tablespoon lime juice
   Salt and pepper
 2 red bell peppers, stemmed, seeded, and chopped fine
 1 onion, chopped fine
 1 cup long-grain brown rice, rinsed
 4 garlic cloves, minced
   Pinch saffron threads, crumbled
   Pinch cayenne pepper
3¼ cups chicken or vegetable broth
 2 (15-ounce) cans chickpeas, rinsed

1. Combine tomatoes, scallions, cilantro, 2 teaspoons oil, and lime juice in bowl. Season with salt and pepper to taste; set aside for serving.

2. Heat remaining 2 teaspoons oil in large saucepan over medium-high heat until shimmering. Add bell peppers and onion and cook until softened and lightly browned, 8 to 10 minutes. Stir in rice, garlic, saffron, and cayenne and cook until fragrant, about 30 seconds.

3. Stir in broth and bring to simmer. Reduce heat to medium-low, cover, and simmer, stirring occasionally, for 25 minutes.

4. Stir in chickpeas, cover, and simmer until rice is tender and broth is almost completely absorbed, 25 to 30 minutes. Season with salt and pepper to taste. Serve, topping individual portions with tomato mixture.

Rice Salad with Oranges, Olives, and Almonds

SERVES 4 to 6 `VEG`

WHY THIS RECIPE WORKS We wanted a citrusy rice salad that paired tender, fluffy rice with briny olives and sweet oranges, a combination beloved in Greek and Italian cooking. To make sure the rice could stand up to a bright vinaigrette and plenty of mix-ins, we sought out a method for cooking long-grain rice that would preserve its fresh-from-the-pan tender texture once cooled. Toasting the rice brought out its nutty flavor and helped to keep the grains distinct and separate even when they were cool. We boiled the rice (like pasta) in plenty of water, which washed away its excess starch and staved off stickiness. Spreading the cooked rice on a baking sheet allowed it to cool quickly and evenly. To flavor the salad, we tossed the cooled rice with a simple orange vinaigrette and some fresh orange segments, chopped green olives, and crunchy toasted almonds. We let the salad sit before serving to give the flavors time to meld. Long-grain white, jasmine, or Texmati rice can be substituted for the basmati. Taste the rice as it nears the end of its cooking time; it should be cooked through and toothsome, but not crunchy. Be careful not to overcook the rice or the grains will "blow out" and fray.

1½ cups basmati rice
   Salt and pepper
 2 oranges, plus ¼ teaspoon grated orange zest plus
   1 tablespoon juice
 2 tablespoons extra-virgin olive oil
 2 teaspoons sherry vinegar
 1 small garlic clove, minced
 ⅓ cup large pitted brine-cured green olives, chopped
 ⅓ cup slivered almonds, toasted
 2 tablespoons minced fresh oregano

1. Bring 4 quarts water to boil in Dutch oven. Meanwhile, toast rice in 12-inch skillet over medium heat until faintly fragrant and some grains turn opaque, 5 to 8 minutes. Add rice and 1½ teaspoons salt to boiling water and cook, stirring occasionally, until rice is tender but not soft, about 15 minutes. Drain rice, spread onto rimmed baking sheet, and let cool completely, about 15 minutes.

2. Cut away peel and pith from oranges. Holding fruit over bowl, use paring knife to slice between membranes to release segments. Whisk oil, vinegar, garlic, orange zest and juice, 1 teaspoon salt, and ½ teaspoon pepper together in large bowl. Add rice, orange segments, olives, almonds, and oregano, gently toss to combine, and let sit for 20 minutes. Serve.

To get the right texture for our brown rice salad, we boil the rice like pasta, then spread it on a baking sheet to cool rapidly.

Brown Rice Salad with Asparagus, Goat Cheese, and Lemon

SERVES 4 to 6   VEG

WHY THIS RECIPE WORKS Nutty, pleasantly chewy brown rice works perfectly in an easy salad, but our favorite method for cooking brown rice—baking—wouldn't work here. In an early test, we discovered that once it was cooled and drizzled with dressing, the baked rice turned gummy. Envisioning a hearty salad bursting with fresh Mediterranean flavors like creamy goat cheese, tender asparagus, and crunchy almonds, we cooked the rice by boiling it in a large pot of water, which washed away its excess starches. Then we spread it out on a baking sheet to cool rapidly, preventing it from overcooking as it sat. To give the rice some bright flavor, we drizzled it with lemon juice while it was still warm. We cooked a pound of asparagus, sliced into 1-inch pieces, in olive oil until it was browned and tender. We wanted the dressing to be zesty but simple, one that would highlight the rustic rice and bright asparagus, so we whisked together olive oil, minced shallot, and

fresh lemon juice and zest. After dressing the rice, we stirred in the sliced asparagus and some crumbled goat cheese and let the dressing's flavors seep into the salad before serving. With a sprinkling of toasted almonds, more goat cheese, and parsley, our salad was loaded with fresh, vibrant flavors, tender rice, and plenty of crunch. Look for asparagus spears no thicker than ½ inch.

1½ cups long-grain brown rice
    Salt and pepper
  1 teaspoon grated lemon zest plus 3 tablespoons juice
3½ tablespoons extra-virgin olive oil
  1 pound asparagus, trimmed and cut into 1-inch lengths
  1 shallot, minced
½ cup goat cheese, crumbled, divided
¼ cup slivered almonds, toasted
¼ cup minced fresh parsley

1. Bring 4 quarts water to boil in Dutch oven. Add rice and 1½ teaspoons salt and cook, stirring occasionally, until rice is tender, 25 to 30 minutes. Drain rice, spread onto rimmed baking sheet, and drizzle with 1 tablespoon lemon juice. Let cool completely, about 15 minutes.

2. Heat 1 tablespoon oil in 12-inch skillet over high heat until just smoking. Add asparagus, ¼ teaspoon salt, and ¼ teaspoon pepper and cook, stirring occasionally, until asparagus is browned and crisp-tender, about 4 minutes; transfer to plate and let cool slightly.

3. Whisk remaining 2½ tablespoons oil, lemon zest and remaining 2 tablespoons juice, shallot, ½ teaspoon salt, and ½ teaspoon pepper together in large bowl. Add rice, asparagus, ¼ cup goat cheese, 3 tablespoons almonds, and 3 tablespoons parsley. Gently toss to combine and let sit for 10 minutes. Season with salt and pepper to taste. Transfer to serving platter and sprinkle with remaining ¼ cup goat cheese, remaining 1 tablespoon almonds, and remaining 1 tablespoon parsley. Serve.

Cooling Brown Rice for Salad

After cooking and draining rice, spread onto rimmed baking sheet and drizzle with 1 tablespoon lemon juice. Let rice cool completely, about 15 minutes; transfer to large bowl.

Buying Goat Cheese

Ubiquitous in French and Spanish cuisine and also used often in Morocco, goat cheese (sometimes labeled chèvre) can be aged or fresh, soft or firm, musky or mild, etc. That said, most of what you can buy in American supermarkets (and the variety we favor in our recipes) is relatively young cheese packaged in a log shape; it has a creamy, slightly grainy texture and a tangy, milky flavor. When shopping for goat cheese, avoid precrumbled cheeses—they tend to be dry and chalky. Our favorite goat cheese is Laura Chenel's Fresh Chèvre Log. Once opened, goat cheese should be wrapped in parchment or wax paper and can be stored in the refrigerator for up to 2 weeks.

Seafood Risotto

SERVES 4 to 6

WHY THIS RECIPE WORKS A classic Italian dish, great seafood risotto is a luxurious mix of flavors and textures against a lush backdrop of creamy Arborio rice. With a wide array of seafood to choose from, the preparation can easily become complicated, so we decided to set some limits. We chose universally appealing shrimp and sweet, meaty bay scallops, perfect for their smaller size. We made a quick broth by simmering the shrimp shells in a base of bottled clam juice, chicken broth, and water with bay leaves and canned tomatoes. As for the seafood, we stirred the shrimp and scallops into the fully cooked risotto and allowed them to steam gently in the warm rice, resulting in flawlessly tender seafood. You can substitute 12 ounces of sea scallops, quartered, for the bay scallops. We recommend "dry" scallops, which don't have chemical additives and taste better than "wet." Dry scallops look ivory or pinkish; wet scallops are bright white.

12 ounces large shrimp (26 to 30 per pound), peeled and deveined, shells reserved
 2 cups chicken broth
2½ cups water
 4 (8-ounce) bottles clam juice
 1 (14.5-ounce) can diced tomatoes, drained
 2 bay leaves
 5 tablespoons extra-virgin olive oil
 1 onion, chopped fine
 2 cups Arborio rice
 5 garlic cloves, minced
 1 teaspoon minced fresh thyme or ¼ teaspoon dried

Letting briny shrimp and sweet bay scallops cook gently in the creamy rice guarantees perfectly cooked seafood.

⅛ teaspoon saffron threads, crumbled
 1 cup dry white wine
12 ounces small bay scallops
 2 tablespoons minced fresh parsley
 1 tablespoon lemon juice
   Salt and pepper

1. Bring shrimp shells, broth, water, clam juice, tomatoes, and bay leaves to boil in large saucepan over medium-high heat. Reduce to simmer and cook for 20 minutes. Strain mixture through fine-mesh strainer into large bowl, pressing on solids to extract as much liquid as possible; discard solids. Return broth to now-empty saucepan, cover, and keep warm over low heat.

2. Heat 2 tablespoons oil in Dutch oven over medium heat until shimmering. Add onion and cook until softened, about 5 minutes. Add rice, garlic, thyme, and saffron and cook, stirring frequently, until grain edges begin to turn translucent, about 3 minutes.

3. Add wine and cook, stirring frequently, until fully absorbed, about 3 minutes. Stir in 3½ cups warm broth, bring to simmer, and cook, stirring occasionally, until almost fully absorbed, 13 to 17 minutes.

4. Continue to cook rice, stirring frequently and adding warm broth, 1 cup at a time, every few minutes as liquid is absorbed, until rice is creamy and cooked through but still somewhat firm in center, 13 to 17 minutes.

5. Stir in shrimp and scallops and cook, stirring frequently, until opaque throughout, about 3 minutes. Remove pot from heat, cover, and let sit for 5 minutes. Adjust consistency with remaining warm broth as needed (you may have broth left over). Stir in remaining 3 tablespoons oil, parsley, and lemon juice and season with salt and pepper to taste. Serve.

Paniscia
SERVES 8

WHY THIS RECIPE WORKS The Italian region of Piedmont is known for its carnaroli rice, its thick-skinned, creamy cranberry beans, its cured meats (*salumi*), and its robust wines (Barolo, Barbaresco, and Barbera, to name a few). It's no wonder that one of the most iconic dishes of the region is a risotto that unites these four elements. In the city of Novara, *paniscia* is made by creating a hearty, brothy vegetable and bean soup and incorporating it into a risotto flavored with *salam d'la duja*, a lard-cured salami. We started with the soup. While traditional recipes vary when it comes to vegetable additions, our tasters liked a combination of leek, carrot, and celery as well as zucchini and red cabbage, which added a satisfying complexity to the dish and served as a perfect foil for the meatier elements. Once our soup was done and the beans were fully tender, we strained out the ultraflavorful broth to make our risotto. Because salam d'la duja is difficult to find outside of Italy, we used a mild, Italian-style salami in its place. The traditional addition of red wine gave the dish a rich backbone, and stirring in the broth in small amounts gave the rice an amazingly velvety consistency. At the end of cooking, we incorporated the vegetables and a splash of red wine vinegar to offset the deep, rich flavors. This dish is traditionally prepared using carnaroli rice, but you can substitute Arborio rice. A medium-bodied dry red wine such as Barbera works well here. For more information on soaking beans, see page 187.

BEANS AND BROTH
    Salt and pepper
  8 ounces (1¼ cups) dried cranberry beans,
      picked over and rinsed
  1 tablespoon extra-virgin olive oil
  2 ounces pancetta, chopped fine
  1 leek, white and light green parts only, halved
      lengthwise, chopped fine, and washed thoroughly
  1 carrot, peeled and chopped fine
  1 celery rib, chopped fine

This hearty Italian risotto gets meaty, savory flavor from a small amount of browned pancetta and salami.

  1 zucchini, cut into ½-inch pieces
  1 cup shredded red cabbage
  1 small sprig fresh rosemary

RISOTTO
  2 tablespoons extra-virgin olive oil
  1 small onion, chopped fine
  2 (½-inch-thick) slices salami (6 ounces), cut into
      ½-inch pieces
      Salt and pepper
1½ cups carnaroli rice
  1 tablespoon tomato paste
  1 cup dry red wine
  2 teaspoons red wine vinegar

1. FOR THE BEANS AND BROTH Dissolve 1½ tablespoons salt in 2 quarts cold water in large container. Add beans and soak at room temperature for at least 8 hours or up to 24 hours. Drain and rinse well.

2. Heat oil in large saucepan over medium-high heat until shimmering. Add pancetta and cook, stirring occasionally, until beginning to brown, 3 to 5 minutes. Stir in leek, carrot, celery, zucchini, and cabbage and cook until softened and lightly browned, 5 to 7 minutes. Stir in drained beans, rosemary, and 8 cups water and bring to boil. Reduce heat to medium-low, cover, and simmer, stirring occasionally, until beans are tender and liquid begins to thicken, 45 minutes to 1 hour. Strain bean-vegetable mixture through fine-mesh strainer into large bowl. Discard rosemary and transfer bean-vegetable mixture to separate bowl; set aside. Return broth to now-empty saucepan, cover, and keep warm over low heat.

3. FOR THE RISOTTO Heat 1 tablespoon oil in Dutch oven over medium heat until shimmering. Add onion, salami, and ½ teaspoon salt and cook until onion is softened, about 5 minutes. Add rice and cook, stirring frequently, until grain edges begin to turn translucent, about 3 minutes.

4. Stir in tomato paste and cook until fragrant, about 1 minute. Add wine and cook, stirring frequently, until fully absorbed, about 2 minutes. Stir in 2 cups warm broth, bring to simmer, and cook, stirring occasionally, until almost fully absorbed, about 5 minutes.

5. Continue to cook rice, stirring frequently and adding warm broth, 1 cup at a time, every few minutes as liquid is absorbed, until rice is creamy and cooked through but still somewhat firm in center, 14 to 16 minutes.

6. Off heat, stir in bean-vegetable mixture, cover, and let sit for 5 minutes. Adjust consistency with remaining warm broth as needed (you may have broth left over). Stir in remaining 1 tablespoon oil and vinegar and season with salt and pepper to taste. Serve.

Spanish-Style Brothy Rice with Clams and Salsa Verde
SERVES 4 to 6

WHY THIS RECIPE WORKS This traditional rice dish from Spain's Mediterranean coast combines the briny sweetness of clams and their liquor with the verdant flavors of leeks, green peppers, and parsley. Unlike paella-style rice dishes, in which the rice absorbs most or all of the cooking liquid, brothy rice has a higher proportion of liquid to rice, so that the finished rice remains surrounded by flavorful liquid. Customarily, when making Spanish brothy rice, all of the liquid is added at once and the rice is simmered for a set amount of time. But using this method tended to yield rice that was starchy and often mushy. To maintain a pleasant chew, we borrowed a technique used for Italian risotto, in which the broth is incorporated little by little and stirred frequently to encourage the rice to release starch and thicken the liquid. We found that the key to achieving the best-tasting dish was to coax as much flavor as possible from each of its simple ingredients. We started by opening our clams in wine and using the cooking liquid to build a deeply flavorful broth. We then set

For a vibrant Spanish rice dish, we steam the clams in wine and stir them into the rice at the end to avoid overcooking them.

the clams aside so they wouldn't overcook and built an aromatic base using leek, green pepper, and garlic. To emphasize these vegetal flavors and the acidic notes of the wine, we finished the dish with a white wine–vinegar enhanced salsa verde. Bomba rice is the most traditional rice for this dish, but you can use any variety of Valencia rice. If you cannot find Valencia rice, you can substitute Arborio rice.

5 tablespoons extra-virgin olive oil
¼ cup minced fresh parsley
6 garlic cloves, minced
1 tablespoon white wine vinegar
2 cups dry white wine
2 pounds littleneck clams, scrubbed
5 cups water
1 (8-ounce) bottle clam juice
1 leek, white and light green parts only, halved lengthwise, chopped fine, and washed thoroughly
1 green bell pepper, stemmed, seeded, and chopped fine
  Salt and pepper
1½ cups Bomba rice
  Lemon wedges

Getting to Know Traditional Mediterranean Rice Varieties

Rice is used all over the Mediterranean region, and different varieties of rice lend distinct qualities to dishes as diverse as Levantine pilafs, Italian risottos, and Spanish paellas. We use a variety of types of rice in this book, many of which are native to the Mediterranean. But we also rely on long-grain white rice and brown rice in many of the Mediterranean-inspired dishes in the book, since they are easily accessible, healthy, and make sense for American home cooks. The rices listed below are used in many of the traditional Mediterranean recipes across the book.

BASMATI RICE

Basmati is a long-grain rice that is prized for its nutty flavor and sweet aroma. Its long, slender grains cook up light, fluffy, and distinct. It's used extensively in the eastern Mediterranean in pilafs, salads, and more. It's also used in North African cooking; some recipes combine the rice with legumes or pasta, such as Koshari (page 173). Our favorite Basmati rice is Tilda.

ARBORIO AND CARNAROLI RICE

Medium-grain rices such as Arborio and carnaroli are often used in Italian risotto dishes; although the grains look similar, their textures differ when cooked. The type of starch in carnaroli rice doesn't break down easily during cooking, which enables it to maintain its shape and texture. Arborio rice, on the other hand, releases more starch during cooking, which creates dishes with a softer, creamier texture. Our favorite Arborio rice is RiceSelect.

VALENCIA AND BOMBA RICE

Short- to medium-grain rices such as Valencia and Bomba are shorter than Arborio and carnaroli rices. Bomba rice (which is a type of Valencia rice grown in Valencia and Calasparra, Spain) is considered the best rice for Spanish paellas and brothy rice dishes because it becomes tender and creamy when cooked but also maintains its shape and chew.

1. Combine 3 tablespoons oil, parsley, half of garlic, and vinegar in bowl; set aside. Bring wine to boil in large saucepan over high heat. Add clams, cover, and cook, stirring occasionally, until clams open, 5 to 7 minutes.

2. Using slotted spoon, transfer clams to large bowl and cover to keep warm; discard any clams that refuse to open. Stir water and clam juice into wine and bring to simmer. Reduce heat to low, cover, and keep warm.

3. Heat remaining 2 tablespoons oil in Dutch oven over medium heat until shimmering. Add leek, bell pepper, and ½ teaspoon salt and cook until softened, 8 to 10 minutes. Add rice and remaining garlic and cook, stirring frequently, until grain edges begin to turn translucent, about 3 minutes.

4. Add 2 cups warm broth and cook, stirring frequently, until almost fully absorbed, about 5 minutes. Continue to cook rice, stirring frequently and adding warm broth, 1 cup at a time, every few minutes as liquid is absorbed, until rice is creamy and cooked through but still somewhat firm in center, 12 to 14 minutes.

5. Off heat, stir in 1 cup warm broth and adjust consistency with extra broth as needed (rice mixture should have thin but creamy consistency; you may have broth left over). Stir in parsley mixture and season with salt and pepper to taste. Nestle clams into rice along with any accumulated juices, cover, and let sit until heated through, 5 to 7 minutes. Serve with lemon wedges.

Indoor Paella
SERVES 6

WHY THIS RECIPE WORKS For a classic paella that could be made year-round, we wanted to stay true to this Spanish rice dish's heritage without relying on specialty equipment or ingredients. First, we substituted a Dutch oven for the traditional paella pan. Paring down the sometimes lengthy ingredient list was next; chorizo, chicken thighs, shrimp, and mussels made the cut. Canned diced tomatoes replaced the typical fresh. As for the rice, we opted for traditional Bomba rice. Chicken broth, white wine, saffron, and a bay leaf were the perfect choices for liquid and seasoning, adding the right amount of flavor without overcomplicating our recipe. Dry-cured Spanish chorizo is the sausage of choice for paella, but fresh chorizo or linguiça sausage is an acceptable substitute. You will need at least a 6-quart Dutch oven for this recipe. Bomba rice is the most traditional rice for this dish, but you can use any variety of Valencia rice. If you cannot find Valencia rice, you can substitute Arborio rice. *Socarrat*, a layer of crusty browned rice that forms on the bottom of the pan, is a traditional part of paella. In this version, socarrat does not develop because most of the cooking is done in the oven; if desired, there are directions for how to make a socarrat before serving in step 7.

1 pound extra-large shrimp (21 to 25 per pound), peeled and deveined

2 tablespoons extra-virgin olive oil, plus extra as needed

8 garlic cloves, minced

Salt and pepper

1 pound boneless, skinless chicken thighs, trimmed and halved crosswise

1 red bell pepper, stemmed, seeded, and cut into ½-inch-wide strips

8 ounces Spanish-style chorizo sausage, sliced on bias ½ inch thick

1 onion, chopped fine

1 (14.5-ounce) can diced tomatoes, drained, minced, and drained again

2 cups Bomba rice

3 cups chicken broth

⅓ cup dry white wine

½ teaspoon saffron threads, crumbled

1 bay leaf

12 mussels, scrubbed and debearded

½ cup frozen peas, thawed

2 teaspoons chopped fresh parsley

Lemon wedges

This ultraflavorful paella is made using streamlined ingredients in a Dutch oven.

1. Adjust oven rack to lower-middle position and heat oven to 350 degrees. Toss shrimp with 1 tablespoon oil, 1 teaspoon garlic, ¼ teaspoon salt, and ¼ teaspoon pepper in bowl until evenly coated. Cover and refrigerate until needed. Pat chicken dry with paper towels and season with salt and pepper.

2. Heat 2 teaspoons oil in Dutch oven over medium-high heat until shimmering. Add bell pepper and cook, stirring occasionally, until skin begins to blister and turn spotty black, about 4 minutes; transfer to bowl.

3. Heat remaining 1 teaspoon oil in now-empty pot until shimmering. Add chicken in single layer and cook, without moving, until browned, about 3 minutes. Turn pieces and cook until browned on second side, about 3 minutes; transfer to separate bowl. Reduce heat to medium and add chorizo to now-empty pot. Cook, stirring frequently, until deeply browned and fat begins to render, about 5 minutes; transfer to bowl with chicken.

4. Add extra oil to fat left in pot to equal 2 tablespoons and heat over medium heat until shimmering. Add onion and cook until softened, about 3 minutes. Stir in remaining garlic and cook until fragrant, about 1 minute. Stir in tomatoes and cook until mixture begins to darken and thicken slightly, about 3 minutes. Stir in rice and cook until grains are well coated with tomato mixture, about 2 minutes.

5. Stir in broth, wine, saffron, bay leaf, and ½ teaspoon salt. Return chicken and chorizo to pot, increase heat to medium-high, and bring to boil, stirring occasionally. Cover, transfer pot to oven, and bake until almost all liquid is absorbed, 15 to 20 minutes.

6. Remove pot from oven. Scatter shrimp and mussels evenly over rice and push hinge side of mussels into rice so they stand up. Cover, return pot to oven, and bake until shrimp are opaque throughout and mussels have opened, 10 to 15 minutes.

7. For optional socarrat, transfer pot to stovetop and remove lid. Cook over medium-high heat for about 5 minutes, rotating pot as needed, until bottom layer of rice is well browned and crisp.

8. Discard any mussels that refuse to open and bay leaf, if it can be easily removed. Arrange bell pepper strips in pinwheel pattern over rice and sprinkle peas over top. Cover and let paella sit for 5 minutes. Sprinkle with parsley and serve with lemon wedges.

VARIATION

Indoor Paella in a Paella Pan

Substitute 14- to 15-inch paella pan for Dutch oven, increase broth to 3¼ cups, and increase wine to ½ cup. Before placing pan in oven, cover tightly with aluminum foil.

Grilling paella gives it a rich, smoky flavor and using traditional Bomba rice creates a perfectly crisp rice crust.

Grilled Paella

SERVES 8

WHY THIS RECIPE WORKS This colorful, flavor-packed Spanish rice dish is a one-pot showpiece that's perfect for entertaining. Most classic paellas rely on medium-grain rice (often Bomba, a type of rice grown in Valencia and Calasparra) that is cooked in a paella pan. As the rice absorbs liquid, the grains in contact with the pan form a prized caramelized crust known as socarrat. We wanted to develop a recipe that would feature tender-chewy rice strewn with moist chicken, sausage, and shellfish; a uniformly golden, crisp crust; and a reliable cooking method—without requiring any special equipment. While many modern recipes are cooked on the stove or in the oven, paella was originally made outside on the grill, so we started there. A large roasting pan was the ideal vessel, since it was easy to maneuver and its plentiful surface area maximized the amount of crisp rice crust. Building a large grill fire and fueling it with fresh coals (which ignited during cooking) ensured that the heat would last throughout cooking. We streamlined the recipe by using roasted red peppers and tomato paste instead of fresh peppers and tomatoes. Staggering the addition of the proteins was essential to ensuring that each element was perfectly cooked. Grilling the

chicken thighs infused them with great smoky flavor and gave them a head start on cooking, and arranging them around the cooler perimeter of the pan helped them stay moist. Nestling the clams and shrimp into the center of the pan allowed them to release their flavorful juices into the rice without overcooking. If littleneck clams are not available, increase the shrimp to 1½ pounds and season the shrimp in step 1 with ½ teaspoon salt. You will need a heavy-duty roasting pan that measures at least 11 by 14 inches for this recipe. If the exterior of your roasting pan is dark, the cooking times will be on the lower side of the ranges given. You can also cook this recipe in a paella pan that is 15 to 17 inches in diameter. Bomba rice is the most traditional rice for this dish, but you can use any variety of Valencia rice. If you cannot find Valencia rice, you can substitute Arborio rice; you will need to reduce the chicken broth amount to 4 cups.

1½ pounds boneless, skinless chicken thighs, trimmed and halved crosswise
Salt and pepper
12 ounces jumbo shrimp (16 to 20 per pound), peeled and deveined
5 tablespoons extra-virgin olive oil
6 garlic cloves, minced
1¾ teaspoons hot smoked paprika
3 tablespoons tomato paste
4½ cups chicken broth
⅔ cup dry sherry
1 (8-ounce) bottle clam juice
Pinch saffron threads, crumbled (optional)
1 onion, chopped fine
½ cup jarred roasted red peppers, rinsed, patted dry, and chopped fine
3 cups Bomba rice
1 pound littleneck clams, scrubbed
8 ounces Spanish-style chorizo sausage, cut into ½-inch pieces
1 cup frozen peas, thawed
Lemon wedges

1. Pat chicken dry with paper towels and season both sides with 1 teaspoon salt and 1 teaspoon pepper. Toss shrimp with 1½ teaspoons oil, ½ teaspoon garlic, ¼ teaspoon paprika, and ¼ teaspoon salt in bowl until evenly coated. Set aside.

2. Heat 1½ teaspoons oil in medium saucepan over medium heat until shimmering. Add remaining garlic and cook, stirring constantly, until garlic sticks to bottom of saucepan and begins to brown, about 1 minute. Add tomato paste and remaining 1½ teaspoons paprika and continue to cook, stirring constantly, until dark brown bits form on bottom of saucepan, about 1 minute. Stir in 4 cups broth, sherry, clam juice, and saffron, if using. Increase heat to high and bring to boil. Remove saucepan from heat and set aside.

3A. FOR A CHARCOAL GRILL Open bottom vent completely. Light large chimney starter mounded with charcoal briquettes (7 quarts). When top coals are partially covered with ash, pour evenly over grill. Using tongs, arrange 20 unlit briquettes evenly over coals. Set cooking grate in place, cover, and open lid vent completely. Heat grill until hot, about 5 minutes.

3B. FOR A GAS GRILL Turn all burners to high, cover, and heat grill until hot, about 15 minutes. Leave all burners on high.

4. Clean and oil cooking grate. Place chicken on grill and cook until both sides are lightly browned, 5 to 7 minutes; transfer chicken to plate and clean cooking grate.

5. Place roasting pan on grill (turning burners to medium-high if using gas) and add remaining ¼ cup oil. When oil begins to shimmer, add onion, red peppers, and ½ teaspoon salt. Cook, stirring frequently, until onion begins to brown, 4 to 7 minutes. Stir in rice (turning burners to medium if using gas) until grains are well coated with oil.

6. Arrange chicken around perimeter of pan. Pour chicken broth mixture and any accumulated chicken juices over rice. Smooth rice into even layer, making sure nothing sticks to sides of pan and no rice rests atop chicken. When liquid reaches gentle simmer, place shrimp in center of pan in single layer. Arrange clams in center of pan, evenly dispersing with shrimp and pushing hinge side of clams into rice slightly so they stand up. Distribute chorizo evenly over surface of rice. Cook, moving and rotating pan to maintain gentle simmer across entire surface of pan, until rice is almost cooked through, 12 to 18 minutes. (If using gas, heat can also be adjusted to maintain simmer.)

7. Sprinkle peas evenly over paella, cover grill, and cook until liquid is fully absorbed and rice on bottom of pan sizzles, 5 to 8 minutes. Continue to cook, uncovered, checking frequently, until uniform golden-brown crust forms on bottom of pan, 8 to 15 minutes longer. (Rotate and slide pan around grill as necessary to ensure even crust formation.) Remove from grill, cover with aluminum foil, and let sit for 10 minutes. Serve with lemon wedges.

All About Saffron

Sometimes known as "red gold," saffron is the world's most expensive spice. It's made from the dried stigmas of *Crocus sativus* flowers; the stigmas are so delicate they must be harvested by hand in a painstaking process. (It takes about 200 hours to pick enough stigmas to produce just 1 pound of saffron, which typically sells for thousands of dollars.)

Luckily, a little saffron goes a long way, adding a distinct reddish-gold color, notes of honey and grass, and a slight hint of bitterness to dishes like bouillabaisse, paella, and risotto. You can find it as powder or threads, but we've found threads are more common. The major producers are Iran and Spain; the saffron you find in the supermarket is usually Spanish. Look for bottles that contain dark red threads—saffron is graded, and the richly hued, high-grade threads from the top of the stigma yield more flavor than the lighter, lesser-grade threads from the base.

When buying saffron, look for dark red threads without any interspersion of yellow or orange threads; our favorite is Morton & Bassett.

Making Grilled Paella

1. GRILL CHICKEN After making cooking liquid, grill chicken until lightly browned on both sides.

2. COOK AROMATICS AND ADD RICE Heat oil in roasting pan on grill and cook onion and roasted red peppers. Stir in rice.

3. ADD PROTEINS Arrange chicken around edge of pan and pour broth mixture over rice. Bring to simmer, then add shrimp and clams to center. Sprinkle chorizo over top.

4. ADD PEAS AND FINISH Sprinkle peas over paella, close grill, and cook until all liquid is absorbed. Continue to cook, uncovered, until uniform golden crust forms on bottom.

We swap the traditional sausage and seafood for bell peppers, fennel, artichokes, and peas in our vegetable paella.

Vegetable Paella
SERVES 6   VEG

WHY THIS RECIPE WORKS Though traditional paella centers on a variety of meat and seafood, we wanted to develop a vegetable-focused version that highlighted the array of hearty vegetables common in Spanish cuisine: artichokes, bell peppers, fennel, and peas. We gave the artichokes and peppers extra flavor by roasting and then tossing them with a bright, lemony sauce. We sautéed the fennel with chopped onion to give it a rich caramelized flavor that gave the dish aromatic backbone. Chopped kalamata olives brought in a distinct pop of briny, contrasting flavor. To infuse the rice with complex, authentic flavor, we bloomed the paprika with the garlic and browned diced tomatoes to give them savory depth. We coated the rice with this potent mixture before adding broth, wine, and saffron and simmering the rice until tender. Cooking on the stovetop alone yielded unevenly cooked rice, so we transferred it to a 350-degree oven where the grains cooked to perfection in the steady, even heat. You will need at least a 6-quart Dutch oven for this recipe. While we prefer the flavor and texture of jarred whole baby artichokes, you can substitute 18 ounces frozen artichoke hearts, thawed and patted dry,

for the jarred. Bomba rice is the most traditional rice for this dish, but you can use any variety of Valencia rice. If you cannot find Valencia rice, you can substitute Arborio rice. *Socarrat*, a layer of crusty browned rice that forms on the bottom of the pan, is a traditional part of paella. In this version, socarrat does not develop because most of the cooking is done in the oven; if desired, there are directions on how to make a socarrat before serving in step 5.

    3 cups jarred whole baby artichokes packed in water, quartered, rinsed, and patted dry
    2 red bell peppers, stemmed, seeded, and chopped coarse
    ½ cup pitted kalamata olives, chopped
    9 garlic cloves, peeled (3 whole, 6 minced)
    6 tablespoons extra-virgin olive oil
      Salt and pepper
    3 tablespoons chopped fresh parsley
    2 tablespoons lemon juice
    1 onion, chopped fine
    1 fennel bulb, stalks discarded, bulb halved, cored, and sliced thin
    ½ teaspoon smoked paprika
    1 (14.5-ounce) can diced tomatoes, drained, minced, and drained again
    2 cups Bomba rice
    3 cups vegetable broth
    ⅓ cup dry white wine
    ½ teaspoon saffron threads, crumbled
    ½ cup frozen peas, thawed

1. Adjust oven rack to lower-middle position, place rimmed baking sheet on rack, and heat oven to 450 degrees. Toss artichokes and peppers with olives, whole garlic cloves, 2 tablespoons oil, ½ teaspoon salt, and ¼ teaspoon pepper in bowl. Spread vegetables in hot sheet and roast until artichokes are browned around edges and peppers are browned, 20 to 25 minutes; let cool slightly.

2. Mince roasted garlic. In large bowl, whisk 2 tablespoons oil, 2 tablespoons parsley, lemon juice, and minced roasted garlic together. Add roasted vegetables and toss to combine. Season with salt and pepper to taste.

3. Reduce oven temperature to 350 degrees. Heat remaining 2 tablespoons oil in Dutch oven over medium heat until shimmering. Add onion and fennel and cook until softened, 8 to 10 minutes.

4. Stir in remaining minced garlic and paprika and cook until fragrant, about 30 seconds. Stir in tomatoes and cook until mixture begins to darken and thicken slightly, about 3 minutes. Stir in rice and cook until grains are well coated with tomato mixture, about 2 minutes. Stir in broth, wine, saffron, and 1 teaspoon salt.

Mediterranean cuisines are heavily reliant on all kinds of whole grains, which are both healthy and filling. The list below highlights the grains that we like to use since they are easy to find in American supermarkets. The list includes cornmeal, which isn't technically a grain, but we include it here since it is prepared and served in a similar way.

Barley

This nutritious high-fiber, high-protein, and low-fat cereal grain is used in Turkey, Morocco, Italy, and beyond. A common ingredient in soups and composed grain dishes or salads, it has a nutty flavor that is similar to that of brown rice. Barley is available in multiple forms. Hulled barley, which is sold with the hull removed and the fiber-rich bran intact, is considered a whole grain and takes a long time to cook; it should be soaked prior to cooking. There is also quick-cooking barley, which may be sold as kernels or flakes. Our favorite is pearl (or pearled) barley, which is hulled barley that has been polished to remove the bran. Pearl barley cooks much more quickly than hulled barley; however, in our testing we have found that there is no consistent standard of labeling to grade the extent to which the barley is pearled, which greatly affects the cooking time. While some brands of pearl barley are barely pearled and take almost 40 minutes to cook, others are thoroughly pearled and take only 20 minutes. To account for this, we give a 20-minute time window in our pearl barley recipes; be sure to check for doneness often while cooking.

Bulgur

Best known as an element in tabbouleh, bulgur is actually quite versatile. It is most commonly used in North Africa and the eastern Mediterranean as an ingredient in salads and pilafs and also to bulk up meat-based stuffings and fillings. Bulgur is made from parboiled or steamed wheat kernels/berries that are then dried, partially stripped of their outer bran layer, and coarsely ground. The result of this process is a highly nutritious grain that cooks relatively quickly—some types require only soaking. Coarse-grind bulgur, which requires simmering, is best suited for making pilaf. Note that medium-grind bulgur can work in either application if you make adjustments to soaking or cooking times. Cracked wheat, on the other hand, often sold alongside bulgur, is not precooked and cannot be substituted for bulgur. Be sure to rinse bulgur, regardless of grain size, to remove excess starches that can turn the grain gluey.

Cornmeal

Cornmeal is the base of Italian polenta and is also used as an ingredient in North African breads. The type you use makes a big difference, so pay close attention to what the recipe calls for and what the label says. At the store, you'll see fine-, medium-, and coarse-ground; instant and quick-cooking; and whole-grain, stone-ground, and regular. For our Creamy Parmesan Polenta (page 118), we like degerminated coarse-ground cornmeal, which produces a soft-textured polenta with great corn flavor.

Farro

A favorite ingredient in Tuscan cuisine, these hulled whole-wheat kernels boast a sweet, nutty flavor and a chewy bite. In Italy, the grain is available in three sizes—*farro piccolo*, *farro medio*, and *farro grande*—but the midsize type is most common in the United States. Although we often turn to the absorption method for quicker-cooking grains, farro takes better to the pasta method because the abundance of water cooks the grains more evenly. When cooked, the grains will be tender but have a slight chew, similar to al dente pasta.

Freekeh

Sometimes spelled *frikeh* or *farik*, freekeh is a nutrient-packed grain that's used in eastern Mediterranean and North African kitchens in pilafs, salads, and more. It has a nutty, slightly smoky flavor. Freekeh is made from durum wheat, which is harvested while immature and soft and then fire-roasted and rubbed to remove the chaff, or husk (*freekeh* means "to rub" in Arabic). It can then be left whole or cracked into smaller pieces. We found that simply boiling the grain like pasta was the most foolproof way to achieve a chewy, firm texture.

Wheat Berries

Wheat berries, often erroneously referred to as "whole wheat," are whole, unprocessed kernels of wheat. Since none of the grain has been removed, wheat berries are an excellent source of nutrition. Compared with more refined forms of wheat (cracked wheat, bulgur, and flour), wheat berries require a relatively long cooking time. In the test kitchen, we like to toast the dry wheat berries until they are fragrant, and then simmer them for about an hour until they are tender but still retain a good bite.

Increase heat to medium-high and bring to boil, stirring occasionally. Cover, transfer pot to oven, and bake until liquid is absorbed and rice is tender, 25 to 35 minutes.

5. For optional socarrat, transfer pot to stovetop and remove lid. Cook over medium-high heat for about 5 minutes, rotating pot as needed, until bottom layer of rice is well browned and crisp.

6. Sprinkle roasted vegetables and peas over rice, cover, and let paella sit for 5 minutes. Sprinkle with remaining 1 tablespoon parsley and serve.

VARIATION

Vegetable Paella in a Paella Pan VEG

Substitute 14- to 15-inch paella pan for Dutch oven, increase broth to 3¼ cups, and increase wine to ½ cup. Before placing pan in oven, cover tightly with aluminum foil.

Creamy Parmesan Polenta

SERVES 4 to 6 VEG

WHY THIS RECIPE WORKS Polenta is an essential element of many an Italian meal; it makes a perfect foil for rich stews and braises, or it can be topped with sautéed vegetables for a simple, satisfying dinner. However, if you don't stir polenta almost constantly to ensure even cooking, it forms intractable lumps, and it can take up to an hour to cook. We wanted to get creamy, smooth polenta with rich corn flavor—but without the fussy process. From the outset, we knew that the right type of cornmeal was essential. Coarse-ground degerminated cornmeal gave us the soft but hearty texture and nutty flavor we were looking for. Adding a pinch of baking soda to the pot helped to soften the cornmeal's endosperm, which cut down on the cooking time. The baking soda also encouraged the granules to break down and release their starch in a uniform way, creating a silky, creamy consistency with minimal stirring. Parmesan cheese and olive oil, stirred in at the last minute, ensured a satisfying, rich flavor. To turn our polenta into a meal, we also created a few vegetable-based toppings, which could be prepared while the polenta cooked (see page 119). If the polenta bubbles or sputters even slightly after the first 10 minutes, the heat is too high and you may need a flame tamer (see page 119).

7½ cups water
　　Salt and pepper
　　Pinch baking soda
1½ cups coarse-ground cornmeal
　2 ounces Parmesan cheese, grated (1 cup), plus extra for serving
　2 tablespoons extra-virgin olive oil

1. Bring water to boil in large saucepan over medium-high heat. Stir in 1½ teaspoons salt and baking soda. Slowly pour cornmeal into water in steady stream while stirring back and forth with wooden spoon or rubber spatula. Bring mixture to boil, stirring constantly, about 1 minute. Reduce heat to lowest setting and cover.

2. After 5 minutes, whisk polenta to smooth out any lumps that may have formed, about 15 seconds. (Make sure to scrape down sides and bottom of saucepan.) Cover and continue to cook, without stirring, until polenta grains are tender but slightly al dente, about 25 minutes longer. (Polenta should be loose and barely hold its shape; it will continue to thicken as it cools.)

3. Off heat, stir in Parmesan and oil and season with pepper to taste. Cover and let sit for 5 minutes. Serve, passing extra Parmesan separately.

Making Creamy Parmesan Polenta

1. BOIL WATER AND ADD BAKING SODA Bring water to boil over medium-high heat. Stir in salt and pinch baking soda.

2. SLOWLY STIR IN CORNMEAL Slowly pour in cornmeal, stirring constantly. Bring to boil, continuing to stir. Reduce heat to lowest setting and cover.

3. WHISK, COVER, AND COOK After 5 minutes, whisk until smooth. Cover and continue to cook until grains are tender.

4. STIR IN CHEESE, THEN LET SIT Remove pot from heat. Stir in cheese, olive oil, and pepper to taste. Cover and let sit for 5 minutes.

Making a Flame Tamer

A flame tamer keeps risotto, polenta, and sauces from simmering too briskly. To make one, shape a sheet of heavy-duty aluminum foil into a 1-inch-thick ring of even thickness the size of your burner.

NOTES FROM THE TEST KITCHEN

Sorting Out Polenta

In the supermarket, cornmeal can be labeled as anything from yellow grits to corn semolina. Forget the names. When shopping for the right product to make polenta, there are three things to consider: "instant" or "quick-cooking" versus the traditional style, degerminated or whole-grain meal, and grind size.

Instant and quick-cooking cornmeals are parcooked and comparatively bland—leave them on the shelf. Though we love the full corn flavor of whole-grain cornmeal, it remains slightly gritty no matter how long you cook it. We prefer degerminated cornmeal, in which the hard hull and germ are removed from each kernel (check the back label or ingredient list to see if your cornmeal is degerminated; if it's not explicitly labeled as such, you can assume it's whole-grain).

As for grind, we found that coarser grains brought the most desirable and pillowy texture to our Creamy Parmesan Polenta. However, grind coarseness can vary dramatically from brand to brand since there are no standards to ensure consistency—one manufacturer's "coarse" may be another's "fine." To identify coarse polenta as really coarse, the grains should be about the size of couscous.

INSTANT VERSUS TRADITIONAL

POLENTA TOPPINGS

SAUTÉED CHERRY TOMATO AND FRESH MOZZARELLA TOPPING
MAKES enough for 4 to 6 servings   VEG

- 3 tablespoons extra-virgin olive oil
- 2 garlic cloves, sliced thin
  Pinch red pepper flakes
  Pinch sugar
- 1½ pounds cherry tomatoes, halved
  Salt and pepper
- 3 ounces fresh mozzarella cheese, shredded (¾ cup)
- 2 tablespoons shredded fresh basil

Cook oil, garlic, pepper flakes, and sugar in 12-inch nonstick skillet over medium-high heat until fragrant and sizzling, about 1 minute. Stir in tomatoes and cook until just beginning to soften, about 1 minute. Season with salt and pepper to taste. Spoon mixture over individual portions of polenta and top with mozzarella and basil. Serve.

BROCCOLI RABE, SUN-DRIED TOMATO, AND PINE NUT TOPPING
MAKES enough for 4 to 6 servings   VEG
Broccolini can be substituted for the broccoli rabe.

- ½ cup oil-packed sun-dried tomatoes, chopped coarse
- 3 tablespoons extra-virgin olive oil
- 6 garlic cloves, minced
- ½ teaspoon red pepper flakes
  Salt and pepper
- 1 pound broccoli rabe, trimmed and cut into 1½-inch pieces
- ¼ cup chicken or vegetable broth
- 2 tablespoons pine nuts, toasted
- ¼ cup grated Parmesan cheese

Cook sun-dried tomatoes, oil, garlic, pepper flakes, and ½ teaspoon salt in 12-inch nonstick skillet over medium-high heat, stirring frequently, until garlic is fragrant and slightly toasted, about 2 minutes. Add broccoli rabe and broth, cover, and cook until broccoli rabe turns bright green, about 2 minutes. Uncover and cook, stirring frequently, until most of broth has evaporated and broccoli rabe is just tender, about 3 minutes. Season with salt and pepper to taste. Spoon mixture over individual portions of polenta and top with pine nuts and Parmesan. Serve.

Herbed Barley Pilaf

SERVES 4 to 6 VEG

WHY THIS RECIPE WORKS You'll often find simple barley dishes in Turkey, Morocco, and beyond, since this hearty, nutrient-rich grain has a firm texture that makes it well suited to accompany anything from robust proteins to delicate vegetables. We chose a judicious mix of bold herbs (fresh thyme, parsley, and chives) for an aromatic, balanced side dish. Cooking an onion and then toasting the barley before adding a measured amount of water enhanced the barley's inherent nuttiness. But during our testing, we uncovered a major inconsistency: One batch of barley was fully tender in 35 minutes, another in 20, and the next in 40. We realized that the extent to which the barley was pearled, or polished to remove the outer bran, was affecting the cooking time—but since there is often no way to tell by the label, the only way to account for the differences was to put a 20-minute range in the cooking time. After the grains were fully cooked and had absorbed the water, we stirred in the herbs. A bit of lemon juice added at the end of cooking brightened the dish for a fresh, vibrant finish. Do not substitute hulled, hull-less, quick-cooking, or presteamed barley (read the ingredient list on the package to determine this) in this recipe.

3 tablespoons extra-virgin olive oil
1 small onion, chopped fine
Salt and pepper
1½ cups pearl barley, rinsed
2 garlic cloves, minced
1½ teaspoons minced fresh thyme or ½ teaspon dried
2½ cups water
¼ cup minced fresh parsley
2 tablespoons minced fresh chives
1½ teaspoons lemon juice

1. Heat oil in large saucepan over medium heat until shimmering. Add onion and ½ teaspoon salt and cook until softened, about 5 minutes. Stir in barley, garlic, and thyme and cook, stirring frequently, until barley is lightly toasted and fragrant, about 3 minutes.

2. Stir in water and bring to simmer. Reduce heat to low, cover, and simmer until barley is tender and water is absorbed, 20 to 40 minutes.

3. Off heat, lay clean dish towel underneath lid and let pilaf sit for 10 minutes. Add parsley, chives, and lemon juice to pilaf and fluff gently with fork to combine. Season with salt and pepper to taste. Serve.

We brighten up a dish of tender barley with sweet pan-roasted carrots and a tangy yogurt-based sauce.

Barley with Roasted Carrots, Snow Peas, and Lemon-Yogurt Sauce

SERVES 4 VEG

WHY THIS RECIPE WORKS For a hearty grain-based entrée ideal for a refreshing supper or substantial lunch, we turned to pearl barley paired with fresh snow peas, spears of sweet pan-roasted carrots, and toasted, spiced sunflower seeds. To keep the cooking method easy and the individual grains distinct and light, we simply boiled the barley until tender, then tossed it with a bright lemon-mint dressing. While the barley cooked, we pan-roasted the carrots and sautéed the snow peas with coriander. Toasted sunflower seeds coated with cardamom, cumin, and a bit more coriander provided a contrasting crunch and warm, aromatic finish. To pull it all together, we created a zesty yogurt sauce infused with lemon and mint to drizzle over the top. Do not substitute hulled barley or hull-less barley in this recipe. If using quick-cooking or presteamed barley (read the ingredient list on the package to determine this), you will need to decrease the barley cooking time in step 1.

ALL ABOUT **COOKING GRAINS**

From bulgur to freekeh, the types of grains and the best methods for cooking them can vary tremendously. Some grains, such as bulgur, cook in minutes, and others, such as barley or wheat berries, take much longer. Here in the test kitchen we have homed in on three basic methods for cooking grains. We then determined which are best for each type of grain. While some grains, such as bulgur, take well to any cooking method, others will turn out best when cooked with a specific method.

Wheat Berries

BOILING DIRECTIONS Bring water to boil in large saucepan. Stir in grain and ½ teaspoon salt. Return to boil, then reduce to simmer and cook until grain is tender, following cooking times given in chart below. Drain.

PILAF-STYLE DIRECTIONS Rinse and then dry grain on towel. Heat 1 tablespoon oil in medium saucepan (preferably nonstick) over medium-high heat until shimmering. Stir in grain and toast until lightly golden and fragrant, 2 to 3 minutes. Stir in water and ¼ teaspoon salt. Bring mixture to simmer, then reduce heat to low, cover, and continue to simmer until grain is tender and has absorbed all of water, following cooking times given below. Off heat, let grain stand for 10 minutes, then fluff with fork.

MICROWAVE DIRECTIONS Rinse grain (see page 104). Combine water, grain, 1 tablespoon oil, and ¼ teaspoon salt in bowl. Cover and cook following times and temperatures given below. Remove from microwave and fluff with fork. Cover bowl with plastic wrap, poke several vent holes with tip of knife, and let sit until completely tender, about 5 minutes.

TYPE OF GRAIN	COOKING METHOD	AMOUNT OF GRAIN	AMOUNT OF WATER	AMOUNT OF SALT	COOKING TIME
Pearl Barley	Pilaf-Style	1 cup	1⅔ cups	¼ teaspoon	20 to 40 minutes
	Boiled	1 cup	4 quarts	1 tablespoon	20 to 40 minutes
	Microwave	X	X	X	X
Bulgur (medium- to coarse-grind)	Pilaf-Style*	1 cup	1½ cups	¼ teaspoon	16 to 18 minutes
	Boiled	1 cup	4 quarts	1½ teaspoons	5 minutes
	Microwave	1 cup	1 cup	¼ teaspoon	5 to 10 minutes
Farro	Pilaf-Style	X	X	X	X
	Boiled	1 cup	4 quarts	1 tablespoon	15 to 30 minutes
	Microwave	X	X	X	X
Freekeh	Pilaf-Style	X	X	X	X
	Boiled	1 cup	4 quarts	1 tablespoon	30 to 45 minutes
	Microwave	X	X	X	X
Wheat Berries	Pilaf-Style	X	X	X	X
	Boiled	1 cup	4 quarts	1½ teaspoons	1 hour to 1 hour 10 minutes
	Microwave	X	X	X	X

* For pilaf, do not rinse, and skip the toasting step, adding the grain to the pot with the liquid.

X = Not recommended

½ cup plain yogurt

1½ teaspoons grated lemon zest plus 1½ tablespoons juice

1½ tablespoons minced fresh mint

   Salt and pepper

1 cup pearl barley

5 carrots, peeled

3 tablespoons extra-virgin olive oil

¾ teaspoon ground coriander

8 ounces snow peas, strings removed, halved lengthwise

⅔ cup raw sunflower seeds

½ teaspoon ground cumin

⅛ teaspoon ground cardamom

1. Whisk yogurt, ½ teaspoon lemon zest and 1½ teaspoons juice, 1½ teaspoons mint, ¼ teaspoon salt, and ⅛ teaspoon pepper together in small bowl; cover and refrigerate until ready to serve.

2. Bring 4 quarts water to boil in Dutch oven. Add barley and 1 tablespoon salt, return to boil, and cook until tender, 20 to 40 minutes. Drain barley, return to now-empty pot, and cover to keep warm.

3. Meanwhile, halve carrots crosswise, then halve or quarter lengthwise to create uniformly sized pieces. Heat 1 tablespoon oil in 12-inch skillet over medium-high heat until just smoking. Add carrots and ½ teaspoon coriander and cook, stirring occasionally, until lightly charred and just tender, 5 to 7 minutes. Add snow peas and cook, stirring occasionally, until spotty brown, 3 to 5 minutes; transfer to plate.

4. Heat 1½ teaspoons oil in now-empty skillet over medium heat until shimmering. Add sunflower seeds, cumin, cardamom, remaining ¼ teaspoon coriander, and ¼ teaspoon salt. Cook, stirring constantly, until seeds are toasted, about 2 minutes; transfer to small bowl.

5. Whisk remaining 1 teaspoon lemon zest and 1 tablespoon juice, remaining 1 tablespoon mint, and remaining 1½ tablespoons oil together in large bowl. Add barley and carrot–snow pea mixture and gently toss to combine. Season with salt and pepper to taste. Serve, topping individual portions with spiced sunflower seeds and drizzling with yogurt sauce.

NOTES FROM THE TEST KITCHEN

Storing Rice, Grains, and Beans

To prevent rice, grains, and beans from spoiling in the pantry, store them in airtight containers; if you can, keep rice and grains in the freezer. This is especially important for whole grains, which turn rancid with oxidation. Use rice and grains within six months. Beans can be kept up to a year, but you will get the best results if you use beans within the first month or two of purchase.

Barley with Lentils, Mushrooms, and Tahini-Yogurt Sauce

SERVES 4 VEG

WHY THIS RECIPE WORKS This super-hearty barley-based dish makes a substantial side or a satisfying vegetarian main, and our creamy Tahini-Yogurt Sauce makes it extra rich. To balance the grains, we decided to use hearty lentils and earthy mushrooms. We tested all types of lentils and found that tasters favored black lentils for their nutty, robust flavor and their ability to hold their shape once cooked. We were happy to find that we could cook the barley and lentils together in one pot, since the sturdy black lentils held their shape as the barley cooked through. Hoping to keep our recipe streamlined, we set the cooked barley and lentils aside and attempted to brown the mushrooms in the same sauce-pan. Unfortunately, the mushrooms were too crowded in the pot, which caused them to steam and overcook. Switching to a large nonstick skillet to cook the mushrooms resulted in more browning and faster cooking, since the increased surface area allowed the mushrooms to make more contact with the pan. We tested many varieties of mushrooms, including white button mushrooms, cremini, porcini, and portobellos; we liked the combination of meaty, plump portobellos along with savory, flavor-rich rehydrated dried porcini. Our tangy Tahini-Yogurt Sauce worked perfectly to balance these hearty flavors, and fresh dill and strips of lemon peel brightened and balanced the earthy notes of the barley and lentils. Do not substitute hulled, hull-less, quick-cooking, or presteamed barley (read the ingredient list on the package to determine this) in this recipe. While we prefer black lentils here, *lentilles du Puy*, brown lentils, and green lentils can be substituted.

½ ounce dried porcini mushrooms, rinsed

1 cup pearl barley

½ cup black lentils, picked over and rinsed

2 tablespoons extra-virgin olive oil

1 onion, chopped fine

2 large portobello mushroom caps, cut into 1-inch pieces

3 (2-inch) strips lemon zest, sliced thin lengthwise

¾ teaspoon ground coriander

   Salt and pepper

2 tablespoons chopped fresh dill

½ cup Tahini-Yogurt Sauce (page 233)

1. Microwave 1½ cups water and porcini mushrooms in covered bowl until steaming, about 1 minute. Let sit until softened, about 5 minutes. Drain mushrooms in fine-mesh strainer lined with coffee filter, reserving soaking liquid, and chop mushrooms.

2. Bring 4 quarts water to boil in Dutch oven. Add barley, lentils, and 1 tablespoon salt, return to boil, and cook until tender, 20 to

40 minutes. Drain barley and lentils, return to now-empty pot, and cover to keep warm.

3. Meanwhile, heat oil in 12-inch nonstick skillet over medium heat until shimmering. Add onion and cook until softened, about 5 minutes. Stir in portobello mushrooms, cover, and cook until portobellos have released their liquid and begin to brown, about 4 minutes.

4. Uncover, stir in lemon zest, coriander, ½ teaspoon salt, and ¼ teaspoon pepper, and cook until fragrant, about 30 seconds. Stir in porcini and porcini soaking liquid, bring to boil, and cook, stirring occasionally, until liquid is thickened slightly and reduced to ½ cup, about 5 minutes. Stir mushroom mixture and dill into barley-lentil mixture and season with salt and pepper to taste. Serve, drizzling individual portions with Tahini-Yogurt Sauce.

Egyptian Barley Salad
SERVES 6 to 8 VEG

WHY THIS RECIPE WORKS We set out to develop a recipe for a vibrantly spiced pearl barley salad with the right balance of sweetness, tang, and nuttiness. Before we could focus on building these exciting flavors, we had to find a consistent cooking method for our barley. We wanted the grains to remain distinct, rather than cohesive as in a pilaf. We turned to what we call the "pasta method," in which we simply boil the grains until tender. With our perfectly cooked barley set aside, we turned our attention back to flavor. Inspired by the flavors of Egypt, we incorporated toasty pistachios, tangy pomegranate molasses, and bright, vegetal cilantro, all balanced by warm, earthy spices and sweet golden raisins. Salty feta cheese, pungent scallions, and pomegranate seeds adorned the top of the dish for a colorful composed salad with dynamic flavors and textures. If you can't find pomegranate molasses, you can make your own (page 305). Do not substitute hulled barley or hull-less barley in this recipe. If using quick-cooking or presteamed barley (read the ingredient list on the package to determine this), you will need to decrease the barley cooking time in step 1.

1½ cups pearl barley
    Salt and pepper
3 tablespoons extra-virgin olive oil, plus extra for serving
2 tablespoons pomegranate molasses
½ teaspoon ground cinnamon
¼ teaspoon ground cumin
⅓ cup golden raisins
½ cup coarsely chopped cilantro
¼ cup shelled pistachios, toasted and chopped coarse
3 ounces feta cheese, cut into ½-inch cubes (¾ cup)
6 scallions, green parts only, sliced thin
½ cup pomegranate seeds

Boiling nutty pearl barley ensures the grains stay separate and distinct in this flavorful Egyptian salad.

1. Bring 4 quarts water to boil in Dutch oven. Add barley and 1 tablespoon salt, return to boil, and cook until tender, 20 to 40 minutes. Drain barley, spread onto rimmed baking sheet, and let cool completely, about 15 minutes.

2. Whisk oil, molasses, cinnamon, cumin, and ½ teaspoon salt together in large bowl. Add barley, raisins, cilantro, and pistachios and gently toss to combine. Season with salt and pepper to taste. Spread barley salad evenly on serving platter and arrange feta, scallions, and pomegranate seeds in separate diagonal rows on top. Drizzle with extra oil and serve.

Barley Risotto
SERVES 4 to 6 VEG

WHY THIS RECIPE WORKS Looking for a different way to enjoy hearty, nutty pearl barley, we found that a risotto cooking method was a great way to bring out a new dimension of the grain. Because the hull and the bran are removed from pearl barley, the starchy interior is exposed, helping to create a supple, velvety sauce when simmered. We used the classic risotto cooking method, adding the liquid in batches and allowing it to be absorbed before adding more. Since barley takes longer to cook than Arborio rice, we found that we needed to use more liquid than we would in a regular risotto. Sautéed onion and carrot gave the risotto a savory-sweet backbone, and white wine added welcome acidity and brightness. Finally, we finished the dish with fresh thyme and Parmesan cheese for richness. Do not substitute hulled, hull-less, quick-cooking, or presteamed barley (read the ingredient list on the package to determine this) in this recipe. Serve with lemon wedges and extra grated Parmesan cheese.

    4 cups chicken or vegetable broth
    4 cups water
    2 tablespoons extra-virgin olive oil
    1 onion, chopped fine
    1 carrot, peeled and chopped fine
 1½ cups pearl barley
    1 cup dry white wine
    1 teaspoon minced fresh thyme or ¼ teaspoon dried
    2 ounces Parmesan cheese, grated (1 cup)
      Salt and pepper

1. Bring broth and water to simmer in medium saucepan. Reduce heat to low and cover to keep warm.

2. Heat 1 tablespoon oil in Dutch oven over medium heat until shimmering. Add onion and carrot and cook until softened, 5 to 7 minutes. Add barley and cook, stirring often, until lightly toasted and aromatic, about 4 minutes.

3. Add wine and cook, stirring frequently, until fully absorbed, about 2 minutes. Stir in 3 cups warm broth and thyme, bring to simmer, and cook, stirring occasionally, until liquid is absorbed and bottom of pot is dry, 22 to 25 minutes. Stir in 2 cups warm broth, bring to simmer, and cook, stirring occasionally, until liquid is absorbed and bottom of pot is dry, 15 to 18 minutes.

4. Continue to cook risotto, stirring often and adding warm broth as needed to prevent pot bottom from becoming dry, until barley is cooked through but still somewhat firm in center, 15 to 20 minutes. Off heat, adjust consistency with remaining warm broth as needed (you may have broth left over). Stir in Parmesan and remaining 1 tablespoon oil and season with salt and pepper to taste. Serve.

VARIATION

Barley Risotto with Mushrooms and Red Wine VEG
A medium-bodied dry red wine blend such as a Côtes du Rhône works nicely here.

Omit carrot. Substitute red wine for white wine and 1 teaspoon minced fresh rosemary for thyme. Before adding barley to saucepan, add 8 ounces cremini mushrooms, trimmed and cut into ½-inch pieces, and ½ ounce dried porcini mushrooms, rinsed and minced, and cook until just beginning to brown, about 4 minutes.

To achieve bulgur with good chew and flavor, we simply soften the grains in lemon juice and water.

Bulgur Salad with Carrots and Almonds
SERVES 4 to 6 VEG

WHY THIS RECIPE WORKS Bulgur is a staple ingredient across the Mediterranean for its nutty flavor and versatility, acting as a nutritious, hearty medium for delivering big, bold flavors. To bulk up this simple cereal into a satisfying salad, we started by softening the bulgur in a mixture of water, lemon juice, and salt for an hour and a half until it had the perfect chew and was thoroughly seasoned. Fresh mint, cilantro, and scallions made our salad crisp and bright, and cumin and cayenne added depth of flavor to our simple lemon vinaigrette. Sweet shredded carrots nicely accented the rich, nutty taste of the bulgur, and toasted almonds provided complementary crunch. We also decided to develop another version of our salad with sweet, juicy grapes and tangy feta. When shopping, do not confuse bulgur with cracked wheat, which has a much longer cooking time and will not work in this recipe.

1½ cups medium-grind bulgur, rinsed
1 cup water
6 tablespoons lemon juice (2 lemons)
  Salt and pepper
⅓ cup extra-virgin olive oil
½ teaspoon ground cumin
⅛ teaspoon cayenne pepper
4 carrots, peeled and shredded
3 scallions, sliced thin
½ cup sliced almonds, toasted
⅓ cup chopped fresh mint
⅓ cup chopped fresh cilantro

1. Combine bulgur, water, ¼ cup lemon juice, and ¼ teaspoon salt in bowl. Cover and let sit at room temperature until grains are softened and liquid is fully absorbed, about 1½ hours.

2. Whisk remaining 2 tablespoons lemon juice, oil, cumin, cayenne, and ½ teaspoon salt together in large bowl. Add bulgur, carrots, scallions, almonds, mint, and cilantro and gently toss to combine. Season with salt and pepper to taste. Serve.

VARIATION
Bulgur Salad with Grapes and Feta
SERVES 4 to 6 VEG
When shopping, do not confuse bulgur with cracked wheat, which has a much longer cooking time and will not work in this recipe.

1½ cups medium-grind bulgur, rinsed
1 cup water
5 tablespoons lemon juice (2 lemons)
  Salt and pepper
¼ cup extra-virgin olive oil
¼ teaspoon ground cumin
  Pinch cayenne pepper
6 ounces seedless red grapes, quartered (1 cup)
½ cup slivered almonds, toasted
2 ounces feta cheese, crumbled (½ cup)
2 scallions, sliced thin
¼ cup chopped fresh mint

1. Combine bulgur, water, ¼ cup lemon juice, and ¼ teaspoon salt in bowl. Cover and let sit at room temperature until grains are softened and liquid is fully absorbed, about 1½ hours.

2. Whisk remaining 1 tablespoon lemon juice, oil, cumin, cayenne, and ¼ teaspoon salt together in large bowl. Add bulgur, grapes, ⅓ cup almonds, ⅓ cup feta, scallions, and mint and gently toss to combine. Season with salt and pepper to taste. Sprinkle with remaining almonds and remaining feta before serving.

Bulgur Pilaf with Cremini Mushrooms
SERVES 4 VEG

WHY THIS RECIPE WORKS We wanted to pair bulgur with bold and flavorful mushrooms in an easy pilaf-style dish. For big mushroom flavor, we chose widely available cremini mushrooms plus a small amount of dried porcini, which underscored the mushroom flavor and provided depth to the dish. Sautéing an onion with the mushrooms offered complementary sweetness; we found it was important to cook the mushrooms until they had released their liquid and begun to brown to deepen their flavor and ensure the best texture. A combination of water and broth gave the bulgur and mushrooms the most well-rounded flavor. Once the bulgur had simmered to tenderness, we removed the pot from the heat, placed a dish towel underneath the lid, and let the bulgur steam gently for an additional 10 minutes, which resulted in perfectly tender, chewy grains. When shopping, don't confuse bulgur with cracked wheat, which has a much longer cooking time and will not work in this recipe.

2 tablespoons extra-virgin olive oil
1 onion, chopped fine
¼ ounce dried porcini mushrooms, rinsed and minced
  Salt and pepper
8 ounces cremini mushrooms, trimmed, halved if small or quartered if large
2 garlic cloves, minced
1 cup medium-grind bulgur, rinsed
¾ cup chicken or vegetable broth
¾ cup water
¼ cup minced fresh parsley

1. Heat oil in large saucepan over medium heat until shimmering. Add onion, porcini mushrooms, and ½ teaspoon salt and cook until onion is softened, about 5 minutes. Stir in cremini mushrooms, increase heat to medium-high, cover, and cook until cremini release their liquid and begin to brown, about 4 minutes. Stir in garlic and cook until fragrant, about 30 seconds.

2. Stir in bulgur, broth, and water and bring to simmer. Reduce heat to low, cover, and simmer gently until bulgur is tender, 16 to 18 minutes.

3. Off heat, lay clean dish towel underneath lid and let pilaf sit for 10 minutes. Add parsley to pilaf and fluff gently with fork to combine. Season with salt and pepper to taste. Serve.

Bulgur with Chickpeas, Spinach, and Za'atar

SERVES 4 to 6   VEG

WHY THIS RECIPE WORKS This dish combines creamy, nutty chickpeas and hearty bulgur with the clean, vegetal punch of fresh spinach. To boost the flavor of this simple side we decided to add the aromatic eastern Mediterranean spice blend *za'atar*, with its fragrant wild herbs, toasted sesame seeds, and tangy sumac. We found that incorporating the za'atar at two distinct points in the cooking process brought out its most complex flavor. First, to release its deep, earthy flavors, we bloomed half of the za'atar in an aromatic base of onion and garlic before adding the bulgur, chickpeas, and cooking liquid. We added the remainder of the za'atar along with the fresh spinach, off the heat; the residual heat in the bulgur was enough to perfectly soften the spinach and to highlight the za'atar's more delicate aromas. The finished dish was a great accompaniment to fish or meat entrées and was even robust enough to serve as a vegetarian main dish. We prefer to use our homemade Za'atar (page 316), but you can substitute store-bought za'atar if you wish. When shopping, don't confuse bulgur with cracked wheat, which has a much longer cooking time and will not work in this recipe.

3 tablespoons extra-virgin olive oil
1 onion, chopped fine
  Salt and pepper
3 garlic cloves, minced
2 tablespoons za'atar
1 cup medium-grind bulgur, rinsed
1 (15-ounce) can chickpeas, rinsed
¾ cup chicken or vegetable broth
¾ cup water
3 ounces (3 cups) baby spinach, chopped
1 tablespoon lemon juice

1. Heat 2 tablespoons oil in large saucepan over medium heat until shimmering. Add onion and ½ teaspoon salt and cook until softened, about 5 minutes. Stir in garlic and 1 tablespoon za'atar and cook until fragrant, about 30 seconds.

2. Stir in bulgur, chickpeas, broth, and water and bring to simmer. Reduce heat to low, cover, and simmer gently until bulgur is tender, 16 to 18 minutes.

3. Off heat, lay clean dish towel underneath lid and let bulgur sit for 10 minutes. Add spinach, lemon juice, remaining 1 tablespoon za'atar, and remaining 1 tablespoon oil and fluff gently with fork to combine. Season with salt and pepper to taste. Serve.

A small amount of ground lamb brings savory depth to a simple bulgur-based dish.

Bulgur with Herbed Lamb and Roasted Red Peppers

SERVES 4 to 6

WHY THIS RECIPE WORKS Looking to Greece for inspiration, we set out to create a bulgur recipe full of character and flavor that could be served alongside any number of dishes—from fresh salads, to hearty soups, to grilled vegetables and meats. Much as pancetta or bacon might be used to flavor a dish, we used ground lamb to create a rich, flavorful base for this pilaf-style bulgur; when we used larger pieces of lamb instead of ground lamb, the meat took on too central a role. We added roasted red peppers to the base with the onion to bring out the peppers' deep sweetness. Fresh marjoram and dill offered a verdant, slightly floral counterpoint to the savory flavors of the lamb and bulgur. We found that adding the marjoram to the aromatics during cooking brought out its fullest flavor, and adding the dill at the end, off the heat, gave us the fresh herbal finish we were after. A squeeze of fresh lemon juice when serving added a burst of brightness and tied the dish together. When shopping, don't confuse bulgur with cracked wheat, which has a much longer cooking time and will not work in this recipe.

1 teaspoon extra-virgin olive oil
8 ounces ground lamb
  Salt and pepper
1 onion, chopped fine
½ cup jarred roasted red peppers, rinsed, patted dry, and chopped
3 garlic cloves, minced
2 teaspoons minced fresh marjoram or ½ teaspoon dried
1 cup medium-grind bulgur, rinsed
1⅓ cups vegetable broth
1 bay leaf
1 tablespoon chopped fresh dill
  Lemon wedges

1. Heat oil in large saucepan over medium-high heat until just smoking. Add lamb, ½ teaspoon salt, and ¼ teaspoon pepper and cook, breaking up meat with wooden spoon, until browned, 3 to 5 minutes. Stir in onion and red peppers and cook until onion is softened, 5 to 7 minutes. Stir in garlic and marjoram and cook until fragrant, about 30 seconds.

2. Stir in bulgur, broth, and bay leaf and bring to simmer. Reduce heat to low, cover, and simmer gently until bulgur is tender, 16 to 18 minutes.

3. Off heat, lay clean dish towel underneath lid and let bulgur sit for 10 minutes. Add dill and fluff gently with fork to combine. Season with salt and pepper to taste. Serve with lemon wedges.

To give our tabbouleh bold flavor, we soak the bulgur in juice we drain from the tomatoes instead of plain water.

Tabbouleh

SERVES 4 to 6 VEG

WHY THIS RECIPE WORKS Tabbouleh is a signature Levantine salad made of bulgur, parsley, tomato, and onion steeped in a penetrating mint and lemon dressing. We started by salting the tomatoes to rid them of excess moisture that otherwise made our salad soggy. Soaking the bulgur in lemon juice and some of the drained tomato liquid, rather than in water, allowed it to absorb lots of flavor as it softened. Chopped onion overwhelmed the salad; two mild scallions added just the right amount of oniony flavor. Parsley, mint, and a bit of cayenne pepper rounded out the dish. Adding the herbs and vegetables while the bulgur was still soaking gave the components time to mingle, resulting in a cohesive dish. Don't confuse bulgur with cracked wheat, which has a much longer cooking time and will not work in this recipe.

3 tomatoes, cored and cut into ½-inch pieces
  Salt and pepper
½ cup medium-grind bulgur, rinsed
¼ cup lemon juice (2 lemons)
6 tablespoons extra-virgin olive oil
⅛ teaspoon cayenne pepper
1½ cups minced fresh parsley
½ cup minced fresh mint
2 scallions, sliced thin

1. Toss tomatoes with ¼ teaspoon salt in fine-mesh strainer set over bowl and let drain, tossing occasionally, for 30 minutes; reserve 2 tablespoons drained tomato juice. Toss bulgur with 2 tablespoons lemon juice and reserved tomato juice in bowl and let sit until grains begin to soften, 30 to 40 minutes.

2. Whisk remaining 2 tablespoons lemon juice, oil, cayenne, and ¼ teaspoon salt together in large bowl. Add tomatoes, bulgur, parsley, mint, and scallions and toss gently to combine. Cover and let sit at room temperature until flavors have blended and bulgur is tender, about 1 hour. Before serving, toss salad to recombine and season with salt and pepper to taste.

VARIATION

Spiced Tabbouleh VEG
Add ¼ teaspoon ground cinnamon and ¼ teaspoon ground allspice to dressing with cayenne.

Warm Farro with Lemon and Herbs

SERVES 4 to 6 `VEG`

WHY THIS RECIPE WORKS Nutty, chewy farro is a popular grain in Italian cuisine and makes for a satisfying side. We used the pasta method to cook our farro; the abundance of water cooked the grains evenly. Sautéed onion and garlic gave the dish savory backbone, and bright lemon and herbs lent it freshness. We prefer the flavor and texture of whole farro; pearled farro can be used, but the texture may be softer. Do not use quick-cooking or presteamed farro (read the ingredient list on the package to determine this) in this recipe. The cooking time for farro can vary greatly among different brands, so we recommend beginning to check for doneness after 10 minutes.

1½ cups whole farro
    Salt and pepper
 3 tablespoons extra-virgin olive oil
 1 onion, chopped fine
 1 garlic clove, minced
¼ cup chopped fresh parsley
¼ cup chopped fresh mint
 1 tablespoon lemon juice

1. Bring 4 quarts water to boil in Dutch oven. Add farro and 1 tablespoon salt, return to boil, and cook until grains are tender with slight chew, 15 to 30 minutes. Drain farro, return to now-empty pot, and cover to keep warm.

2. Heat 2 tablespoons oil in 12-inch skillet over medium heat until shimmering. Add onion and ¼ teaspoon salt and cook until softened, about 5 minutes. Stir in garlic and cook until fragrant, about 30 seconds.

3. Add remaining 1 tablespoon oil and farro and cook, stirring frequently, until heated through, about 2 minutes. Off heat, stir in parsley, mint, and lemon juice. Season with salt and pepper to taste. Serve.

VARIATIONS
Warm Farro with Mushrooms and Thyme

SERVES 4 to 6 `VEG`

We prefer the flavor and texture of whole farro; pearled farro can be used, but the texture may be softer. Do not use quick-cooking or presteamed farro (read the ingredient list on the package to determine this) in this recipe. The cooking time for farro can vary greatly among different brands, so we recommend beginning to check for doneness after 10 minutes.

1½ cups whole farro
    Salt and pepper
 3 tablespoons extra-virgin olive oil

We tested the various forms and prefer the flavor and texture of whole farro for our recipes.

12 ounces cremini mushrooms, trimmed and chopped coarse
 1 shallot, minced
1½ teaspoons minced fresh thyme or ½ teaspoon dried
 3 tablespoons dry sherry
 3 tablespoons minced fresh parsley
1½ teaspoons sherry vinegar, plus extra for serving

1. Bring 4 quarts water to boil in Dutch oven. Add farro and 1 tablespoon salt, return to boil, and cook until grains are tender with slight chew, 15 to 30 minutes. Drain farro, return to now-empty pot, and cover to keep warm.

2. Heat 2 tablespoons oil in 12-inch skillet over medium heat until shimmering. Add mushrooms, shallot, thyme, and ¼ teaspoon salt and cook, stirring occasionally, until moisture has evaporated and vegetables start to brown, 8 to 10 minutes. Stir in sherry and cook, scraping up any browned bits, until skillet is almost dry.

3. Add remaining 1 tablespoon oil and farro and cook, stirring frequently, until heated through, about 2 minutes. Off heat, stir in parsley and vinegar. Season with salt, pepper, and extra vinegar to taste and serve.

Warm Farro with Fennel and Parmesan

SERVES 4 to 6 VEG

We prefer the flavor and texture of whole farro; pearled farro can be used, but the texture may be softer. Do not use quick-cooking or presteamed farro (read the ingredient list on the package to determine this) in this recipe. The cooking time for farro can vary greatly among different brands, so we recommend beginning to check for doneness after 10 minutes.

1½ cups whole farro
   Salt and pepper
3 tablespoons extra-virgin olive oil
1 onion, chopped fine
1 small fennel bulb, stalks discarded, bulb halved, cored, and chopped fine
3 garlic cloves, minced
1 teaspoon minced fresh thyme or ¼ teaspoon dried
1 ounce Parmesan cheese, grated (½ cup)
¼ cup minced fresh parsley
2 teaspoons sherry vinegar

1. Bring 4 quarts water to boil in Dutch oven. Add farro and 1 tablespoon salt, return to boil, and cook until grains are tender with slight chew, 15 to 30 minutes. Drain farro, return to now-empty pot, and cover to keep warm.

2. Heat 2 tablespoons oil in 12-inch skillet over medium heat until shimmering. Add onion, fennel, and ¼ teaspoon salt and cook, stirring occasionally, until softened, 8 to 10 minutes. Add garlic and thyme and cook until fragrant, about 30 seconds.

3. Add remaining 1 tablespoon oil and farro and cook, stirring frequently, until heated through, about 2 minutes. Off heat, stir in Parmesan, parsley, and vinegar. Season with salt and pepper to taste. Serve.

Farro Salad with Asparagus, Snap Peas, and Tomatoes

SERVES 4 to 6 VEG

WHY THIS RECIPE WORKS When we decided to turn farro into a hearty, fresh salad, we wondered if we could bypass the traditional step of soaking the grains overnight and then cooking them gradually for over an hour in favor of a simpler, quicker method. After testing out a few cooking techniques, we learned that boiling the grains in plenty of salted water and then draining them yielded nicely firm but tender farro—no soaking necessary. To make sure this salad looked as good as it tasted, we briefly boiled bite-size pieces of asparagus and snap peas to bring out their vibrant color and crisp-tender bite. A lemon-dill dressing served as a citrusy, herbal complement to the earthy farro. Cherry tomatoes and feta

Cooking farro in plenty of boiling water ensures tender grains that are ready to be paired with fresh vegetables.

cheese offered a fresh, full-flavored finish. For a simple variation, we also created a version with cucumber, yogurt, and mint. We prefer the flavor and texture of whole farro; pearled farro can be used, but the texture may be softer. Do not use quick-cooking or presteamed farro (read the ingredient list on the package to determine this) in this recipe. The cooking time for farro can vary greatly among different brands, so we recommend beginning to check for doneness after 10 minutes.

6 ounces asparagus, trimmed and cut into 1-inch lengths
6 ounces sugar snap peas, strings removed, cut into 1-inch lengths
   Salt and pepper
1½ cups whole farro
3 tablespoons extra-virgin olive oil
2 tablespoons lemon juice
2 tablespoons minced shallot
1 teaspoon Dijon mustard
6 ounces cherry tomatoes, halved
3 tablespoons chopped fresh dill
2 ounces feta cheese, crumbled (½ cup)

1. Bring 4 quarts water to boil in Dutch oven. Add asparagus, snap peas, and 1 tablespoon salt and cook until crisp-tender, about 3 minutes. Using slotted spoon, transfer vegetables to large plate and let cool completely, about 15 minutes.

2. Add farro to water, return to boil, and cook until grains are tender with slight chew, 15 to 30 minutes. Drain farro, spread in rimmed baking sheet, and let cool completely, about 15 minutes.

3. Whisk oil, lemon juice, shallot, mustard, ¼ teaspoon salt, and ¼ teaspoon pepper together in large bowl. Add vegetables, farro, tomatoes, dill, and ¼ cup feta and toss gently to combine. Season with salt and pepper to taste. Transfer to serving platter and sprinkle with remaining ¼ cup feta. Serve.

VARIATION

Farro Salad with Cucumber, Yogurt, and Mint

SERVES 4 to 6   VEG

We prefer the flavor and texture of whole farro; pearled farro can be used, but the texture may be softer. Do not use quick-cooking or presteamed farro (read the ingredient list on the package to determine this) in this recipe. The cooking time for farro can vary greatly among different brands, so we recommend beginning to check for doneness after 10 minutes.

1½ cups whole farro
    Salt and pepper
 3 tablespoons extra-virgin olive oil
 2 tablespoons lemon juice
 2 tablespoons minced shallot
 2 tablespoons plain Greek yogurt
 1 English cucumber, halved lengthwise, seeded, and cut into ¼-inch pieces
 6 ounces cherry tomatoes, halved
 1 cup baby arugula
 3 tablespoons chopped fresh mint

1. Bring 4 quarts water to boil in Dutch oven. Add farro and 1 tablespoon salt, return to boil, and cook until grains are tender with slight chew, 15 to 30 minutes. Drain farro, spread in rimmed baking sheet, and let cool completely, about 15 minutes.

2. Whisk oil, lemon juice, shallot, yogurt, ¼ teaspoon salt, and ¼ teaspoon pepper together in large bowl. Add farro, cucumber, tomatoes, arugula, and mint and toss gently to combine. Season with salt and pepper to taste. Serve.

Pulsing farro in the blender releases its starch to create a rich and creamy Italian farro risotto.

Parmesan Farrotto

SERVES 6   VEG

WHY THIS RECIPE WORKS Italian *farrotto* is essentially a risotto-style dish made with farro in place of the usual Arborio rice. Although it is made with a similar method, farro's more robust, nutty flavor gives the dish new dimension. But because much of farro's starch is trapped inside the outer bran, achieving a creamy, velvety consistency can be a challenge. We tested making farrotto with pearled farro, which has had the outer bran removed, but the flavor was lacking and the sauce turned out thin. Instead, we turned back to whole farro and, to make the starch more accessible without losing farro's hallmark chew, we ran the grains through a blender. After a few pulses, about half of the farro had cracked, freeing up enough starch to create a creamy, risotto-like consistency. Adding most of the liquid up front and cooking the farrotto in a lidded Dutch oven helped the grains cook evenly and meant we didn't have to stir constantly—just twice before stirring in the flavorings. We also created a variation with pancetta, asparagus, and peas, which turned this simple side into a satisfying main course. We prefer the flavor and texture of whole farro. Do not use quick-cooking, presteamed, or pearled farro (read the ingredient list on the package to determine this) in this recipe. The consistency of farrotto is a matter of personal taste; if you prefer a looser texture, add more of the hot broth mixture in step 5.

1½ cups whole farro
3 cups chicken or vegetable broth
3 cups water
3 tablespoons extra-virgin olive oil
½ onion, chopped fine
1 garlic clove, minced
2 teaspoons minced fresh thyme
Salt and pepper
2 ounces Parmesan cheese, grated (1 cup)
2 tablespoons minced fresh parsley
2 teaspoons lemon juice

1. Pulse farro in blender until about half of grains are broken into smaller pieces, about 6 pulses.

2. Bring broth and water to boil in medium saucepan over high heat. Reduce heat to low, cover, and keep warm.

3. Heat 2 tablespoons oil in Dutch oven over medium-low heat. Add onion and cook until softened, about 5 minutes. Stir in garlic and cook until fragrant, about 30 seconds. Add farro and cook, stirring frequently, until grains are lightly toasted, about 3 minutes.

4. Stir 5 cups warm broth mixture into farro mixture, reduce heat to low, cover, and cook until almost all liquid has been absorbed and farro is just al dente, about 25 minutes, stirring twice during cooking.

5. Add thyme, 1 teaspoon salt, and ¾ teaspoon pepper and cook, stirring constantly, until farro becomes creamy, about 5 minutes. Off heat, stir in Parmesan, parsley, lemon juice, and remaining 1 tablespoon oil. Adjust consistency with remaining warm broth mixture as needed (you may have broth left over). Season with salt and pepper to taste. Serve.

VARIATION

Farrotto with Pancetta, Asparagus, and Peas
SERVES 6

We prefer the flavor and texture of whole farro. Do not use quick-cooking, presteamed, or pearled farro (read the ingredient list on the package to determine this) in this recipe. The consistency of farrotto is a matter of personal taste; if you prefer a looser texture, add more of the hot broth mixture in step 5.

1½ cups whole farro
3 cups chicken broth
3 cups water
4 ounces asparagus, trimmed and cut on bias into 1-inch lengths
4 ounces pancetta, cut into ¼-inch pieces
2 tablespoons extra-virgin olive oil
½ onion, chopped fine
1 garlic clove, minced
1 cup frozen peas, thawed
2 teaspoons minced fresh tarragon
Salt and pepper
1½ ounces Parmesan cheese, grated (¾ cup)
1 tablespoon minced fresh chives
1 teaspoon grated lemon zest plus 1 teaspoon juice

Making Parmesan Farrotto

1. CRACK FARRO Pulse farro in blender until half of grains are broken into smaller pieces, about 6 pulses, to release starch.

2. TOAST FARRO Cook farro with softened onion and garlic until lightly toasted.

3. COOK FARRO Stir warm broth into farro mixture and cook until grains are al dente, stirring twice during cooking.

4. ADD FLAVOR Add thyme and cook, stirring constantly, until farro becomes creamy. Off heat, stir in cheese, parsley, lemon juice, and olive oil.

1. Pulse farro in blender until about half of grains are broken into smaller pieces, about 6 pulses.

2. Bring broth and water to boil in medium saucepan over high heat. Add asparagus and cook until crisp-tender, 2 to 3 minutes. Using slotted spoon, transfer asparagus to bowl and set aside. Reduce heat to low, cover broth mixture, and keep warm.

3. Cook pancetta in Dutch oven over medium heat until lightly browned and fat has rendered, about 5 minutes. Add 1 tablespoon oil and onion and cook until softened, about 5 minutes. Stir in garlic and cook until fragrant, about 30 seconds. Add farro and cook, stirring frequently, until grains are lightly toasted, about 3 minutes.

4. Stir 5 cups warm broth mixture into farro mixture, reduce heat to low, cover, and cook until almost all liquid has been absorbed and farro is just al dente, about 25 minutes, stirring twice during cooking.

5. Add peas, tarragon, ¾ teaspoon salt, and ½ teaspoon pepper and cook, stirring constantly, until farro becomes creamy, about 5 minutes. Off heat, stir in Parmesan, chives, lemon zest and juice, remaining 1 tablespoon oil, and reserved asparagus. Adjust consistency with remaining warm broth mixture as needed (you may have broth left over). Season with salt and pepper to taste. Serve.

Freekeh Salad with Butternut Squash, Walnuts, and Raisins
SERVES 4 to 6 VEG

WHY THIS RECIPE WORKS *Freekeh* is a commonly used grain across the eastern Mediterranean and North Africa. We thought its grassy, slightly smoky flavor would work perfectly with sweet roasted winter squash as a hearty lunch or a light dinner. To replace hard-to-find or seasonally restrictive Mediterranean winter squashes, we chose widely available butternut squash. Roasting the squash resulted in lightly charred, beautifully caramelized edges; to give the squash more dimension, we paired it with fenugreek, a slightly sweet and nutty seed with a unique maple-like flavor. To bring all the elements together, we stirred in a rich yet bright tahini-lemon dressing. Chopped walnuts offered complementary crunch. We prefer the texture of whole, uncracked freekeh; cracked freekeh can be substituted, but you will need to decrease the freekeh cooking time in step 2.

1½ pounds butternut squash, peeled, seeded, and cut into ½-inch pieces (4 cups)
  1 tablespoon extra-virgin olive oil
 ½ teaspoon ground fenugreek
     Salt and pepper
1½ cups whole freekeh

We boil whole, uncracked freekeh like pasta to achieve a chewy and firm texture.

 ⅓ cup golden raisins
 ½ cup Tahini-Lemon Dressing (page 72)
  1 cup coarsely chopped cilantro
 ⅓ cup walnuts, toasted and chopped

1. Adjust oven rack to lowest position and heat oven to 450 degrees. Toss squash with oil and fenugreek and season with salt and pepper. Arrange squash in single layer in rimmed baking sheet and roast until well browned and tender, 30 to 35 minutes, stirring halfway through roasting; let cool to room temperature.

2. Meanwhile, bring 4 quarts water to boil in Dutch oven. Add freekeh and 1 tablespoon salt, return to boil, and cook until grains are tender, 30 to 45 minutes. Drain freekeh, transfer to large bowl, and let cool completely, about 15 minutes.

3. Combine raisins and ¼ cup hot tap water in small bowl and let sit until softened, about 5 minutes; drain raisins. Add squash, raisins, dressing, cilantro, and walnuts to bowl with freekeh and gently toss to combine. Season with salt and pepper to taste. Serve.

Freekeh Pilaf with Dates and Cauliflower

SERVES 4 to 6 VEG

WHY THIS RECIPE WORKS For a pilaf that accentuated *freekeh's* unique flavor and chew, we paired it with pan-roasted cauliflower, warm spices and aromatics, and refreshing mint. We found that simply boiling the grain like pasta was the most foolproof cooking method to achieve a chewy, firm texture. Allowing the cauliflower to soften and brown slightly before adding the remaining ingredients to the pan was essential to creating the best flavor and texture. Studded with sweet dates and toasted pistachios, our pilaf was a hearty, healthful option for a unique side dish or satisfying lunch. We prefer the texture of whole, uncracked freekeh; cracked freekeh can be substituted, but you will need to decrease the freekeh cooking time in step 1.

1½ cups whole freekeh
    Salt and pepper
¼ cup extra-virgin olive oil, plus extra for serving
1 head cauliflower (2 pounds), cored and cut into ½-inch florets
3 ounces pitted dates, chopped (½ cup)
1 shallot, minced
1½ teaspoons grated fresh ginger
¼ teaspoon ground coriander
¼ teaspoon ground cumin
¼ cup shelled pistachios, toasted and coarsely chopped
¼ cup chopped fresh mint
1½ tablespoons lemon juice

1. Bring 4 quarts water to boil in Dutch oven. Add freekeh and 1 tablespoon salt, return to boil, and cook until grains are tender, 30 to 45 minutes. Drain freekeh, return to now-empty pot, and cover to keep warm.

2. Heat 2 tablespoons oil in 12-inch nonstick skillet over medium-high heat until shimmering. Add cauliflower, ½ teaspoon salt, and ¼ teaspoon pepper, cover, and cook until florets are softened and start to brown, about 5 minutes.

3. Remove lid and continue to cook, stirring occasionally, until florets turn spotty brown, about 10 minutes. Add remaining 2 tablespoons oil, dates, shallot, ginger, coriander, and cumin and cook, stirring frequently, until dates and shallot are softened and fragrant, about 3 minutes.

4. Reduce heat to low, add freekeh, and cook, stirring frequently, until heated through, about 1 minute. Off heat, stir in pistachios, mint, and lemon juice. Season with salt and pepper to taste and drizzle with extra oil. Serve.

A judicious amount of salt in the cooking water ensures well-seasoned wheat berries that are tender with a good bite.

Warm Wheat Berries with Zucchini, Red Pepper, and Oregano

SERVES 4 to 6 VEG

WHY THIS RECIPE WORKS In Greek culture, wheat represents new life and a bountiful harvest, so we decided to seize on that idea and create a wheat berry salad that would capitalize on fresh, abundant summer vegetables. We cooked the wheat berries using the pasta method to ensure even cooking, but our standard ratio of salt to water (1 tablespoon to 4 quarts) prevented the grains from properly absorbing the water; they stayed hard and crunchy no matter how long we cooked them. Reducing the amount of salt was a simple fix and the grains still turned out nicely seasoned. Sautéing zucchini, red pepper, and red onion gave them great flavor; browning the vegetables in batches was essential to achieving the deep sear we were after. We allowed the warm wheat berries to soak in our bold-flavored vinaigrette while the vegetables were cooking. Do not add more than 1½ teaspoons of salt when cooking the wheat berries; adding more will prevent the grains from softening. If using quick-cooking or presteamed wheat berries (read the ingredient list on the package to determine this), you will need to decrease the wheat berry cooking time in step 1.

1½ cups wheat berries
  Salt and pepper
2 tablespoons extra-virgin olive oil
3 tablespoons red wine vinegar
1 garlic clove, minced
1 tablespoon grated lemon zest
1 tablespoon minced fresh oregano or
  1½ teaspoons dried
1 zucchini, cut into ½-inch pieces
1 red onion, chopped
1 red bell pepper, stemmed, seeded, and cut into
  ½-inch pieces

1. Bring 4 quarts water to boil in Dutch oven. Add wheat berries and 1½ teaspoons salt, return to boil, and cook until tender but still chewy, 60 to 70 minutes.

2. Meanwhile, whisk 1 tablespoon oil, vinegar, garlic, lemon zest, and oregano together in large bowl. Drain wheat berries, add to bowl with dressing, and toss gently to coat.

3. Heat 2 teaspoons oil in 12-inch nonstick skillet over medium-high heat until just smoking. Add zucchini and ¼ teaspoon salt and cook, stirring occasionally, until deep golden brown and beginning to char in spots, 6 to 8 minutes; transfer to bowl with wheat berries.

4. Return now-empty skillet to medium-high heat and add remaining 1 teaspoon oil, onion, bell pepper, and ¼ teaspoon salt. Cook, stirring occasionally, until onion is charred at edges and pepper skin is charred and blistered, 8 to 10 minutes. Add wheat berry–zucchini mixture and cook, stirring frequently, until heated through, about 2 minutes. Season with salt and pepper to taste. Serve.

Grating Zest

Swipe rinsed and dried fruit along microplane grater in one direction—not back and forth—to remove zest and avoid bitter white pith.

The French-inspired combination of orange and tarragon enhances an easy wheat berry salad.

Wheat Berry Salad with Orange and Carrots
SERVES 4 to 6 VEG

WHY THIS RECIPE WORKS In southern France, orange and tarragon is a classic pairing, and it's easy to understand why: sweet-tart orange boosts and brightens tarragon's grassy licorice notes, creating a remarkably vibrant flavor. This combination shone against a backdrop of mildly nutty wheat berries, especially after we added shredded carrots for crunch and orange zest for a deeper citrus flavor. A simple red wine vinaigrette finished off this fresh, crowd-pleasing salad with a sophisticated mix of flavors. Do not add more than 1½ teaspoons of salt when cooking the wheat berries; adding more will prevent the grains from softening. If using quick-cooking or presteamed wheat berries (read the ingredient list on the package to determine this), you will need to decrease the wheat berry cooking time in step 1.

1½ cups wheat berries
  Salt and pepper
1 orange

3 tablespoons red wine vinegar
1½ tablespoons Dijon mustard
1 small shallot, minced
1 garlic clove, minced
⅛ teaspoon grated orange zest
1½ teaspoons honey
2 tablespoons extra-virgin olive oil
3 carrots, peeled and shredded
1 tablespoon minced fresh tarragon

1. Bring 4 quarts water to boil in Dutch oven. Add wheat berries and 1½ teaspoons salt, return to boil, and cook until tender but still chewy, 60 to 70 minutes. Drain wheat berries, spread in rimmed baking sheet, and let cool completely, about 15 minutes.

2. Cut away peel and pith from orange. Quarter orange, then slice crosswise into ¼-inch-thick pieces. Whisk vinegar, mustard, shallot, garlic, orange zest, honey, and ¼ teaspoon salt together in large bowl until combined. Whisking constantly, slowly drizzle in oil. Add wheat berries, carrots, tarragon, and orange pieces and gently toss to coat. Season with salt and pepper to taste. Serve.

Wheat Berry Salad with Figs, Pine Nuts, and Goat Cheese
SERVES 4 to 6 VEG

WHY THIS RECIPE WORKS Figs, a staple of Mediterranean cuisine, have been grown for thousands of years in the region's warm and temperate climate. We wanted to feature their sweet flavor and juicy texture in a hearty summer grain salad. Wheat berries provided the perfect nutty backdrop for the fresh figs; creamy goat cheese contributed a pleasantly rich, tangy element. For the dressing, we chose a zippy vinaigrette made with balsamic vinegar, shallot, mustard, and honey to highlight the figs' natural sweetness. Toasted pine nuts and parsley leaves lent crunch and fragrance to this summery salad. Do not add more than 1½ teaspoons of salt when cooking the wheat berries; adding more will prevent the grains from softening. If using quick-cooking or presteamed wheat berries (read the ingredient list on the package to determine this), you will need to decrease the wheat berry cooking time in step 1.

1½ cups wheat berries
    Salt and pepper
2 tablespoons balsamic vinegar
1 small shallot, minced

A small amount of goat cheese adds just enough rich creaminess to our wheat berry salad.

1 teaspoon Dijon mustard
1 teaspoon honey
3 tablespoons extra-virgin olive oil
8 ounces figs, cut into ½-inch pieces
½ cup fresh parsley leaves
¼ cup pine nuts, toasted
2 ounces goat cheese, crumbled (½ cup)

1. Bring 4 quarts water to boil in Dutch oven. Add wheat berries and 1½ teaspoons salt, return to boil, and cook until tender but still chewy, 60 to 70 minutes. Drain wheat berries, spread onto rimmed baking sheet, and let cool completely, about 15 minutes.

2. Whisk vinegar, shallot, mustard, honey, ¼ teaspoon salt, and ¼ teaspoon pepper together in large bowl. Whisking constantly, slowly drizzle in oil. Add wheat berries, figs, parsley, and pine nuts and toss gently to combine. Season with salt and pepper to taste. Transfer to serving platter and sprinkle with goat cheese. Serve.

Pasta and Couscous

▪ FAST (less than 45 minutes start to finish)   ▥ VEGETARIAN
Photos (clockwise from top left): Spaghetti with Clams and Roasted Tomatoes; Simple Couscous with Carrots, Raisins, and Pine Nuts; Orzo Salad with Pecorino, Radicchio, and Chickpeas; Orecchiette with Broccoli Rabe and White Beans

Penne with Roasted Cherry Tomato Sauce

SERVES 6 VEG

WHY THIS RECIPE WORKS Fresh, simple tomato sauce represents Italian cuisine at its finest—basic ingredients combined with a deft hand to create a final product that is much more than the sum of its parts. We started with cherry tomatoes since they are reliably sweet and available year round, then added more flavor by tossing them with a little sugar, salt, pepper, red pepper flakes, and slivered garlic. A splash of balsamic vinegar, a traditional Italian ingredient, added some color and tang to the mixture. We then roasted them in a single layer on a baking sheet, which allowed their excess liquid to cook off and concentrated the tomatoes' sweetness. Chopped fresh basil and Parmesan cheese were the perfect finishing touches. Grape tomatoes can be substituted for the cherry tomatoes, but because they tend to be sweeter, you will want to reduce or even omit the sugar. Do likewise if your cherry tomatoes are very sweet.

    1 shallot, sliced thin
    ¼ cup extra-virgin olive oil
    2 pounds cherry tomatoes, halved
    3 large garlic cloves, sliced thin
    1 tablespoon balsamic vinegar
    1½ teaspoons sugar, or to taste
       Salt and pepper
    ¼ teaspoon red pepper flakes
    1 pound penne
    ¼ cup coarsely chopped fresh basil
       Grated Parmesan cheese

1. Adjust oven rack to middle position and heat oven to 350 degrees. Toss shallot with 1 teaspoon oil in bowl. In separate bowl, gently toss tomatoes with remaining oil, garlic, vinegar, sugar, ½ teaspoon salt, ¼ teaspoon pepper, and pepper flakes. Spread tomato mixture in even layer in rimmed baking sheet, scatter shallot over tomatoes, and roast until edges of shallot begin to brown and tomato skins are slightly shriveled, 35 to 40 minutes. (Do not stir tomatoes during roasting.) Let cool for 5 to 10 minutes.

2. Meanwhile, bring 4 quarts water to boil in large pot. Add pasta and 1 tablespoon salt and cook, stirring often, until al dente. Reserve ½ cup cooking water, then drain pasta and return it to pot. Using rubber spatula, scrape tomato mixture onto pasta. Add basil and toss to combine. Season with salt and pepper to taste and adjust consistency with reserved cooking water as needed. Serve with Parmesan.

Roasting cherry tomatoes intensifies their sweetness to create an ultraflavorful fresh yet simple sauce for pasta.

VARIATIONS

Penne with Roasted Cherry Tomatoes, Olives, Capers, and Pine Nuts

SERVES 6 VEG

Grape tomatoes can be substituted for the cherry tomatoes, but because they tend to be sweeter, you will want to reduce or even omit the sugar. Do likewise if your cherry tomatoes are very sweet.

    2 pounds cherry tomatoes, halved
    ¼ cup extra-virgin olive oil
    ¼ cup capers, rinsed
    3 large garlic cloves, sliced thin
    1½ teaspoons sugar, or to taste
       Salt and pepper
    ½ teaspoon red pepper flakes
    1 pound penne
    ½ cup pitted kalamata olives, chopped
    ¼ cup pine nuts, toasted
    3 tablespoons chopped fresh oregano
       Grated Pecorino Romano cheese

1. Adjust oven rack to middle position and heat oven to 350 degrees. Gently toss tomatoes with oil, capers, garlic, sugar, ½ teaspoon salt, pepper flakes, and ¼ teaspoon pepper in bowl. Spread tomato mixture in even layer in rimmed baking sheet and roast until tomato skins are slightly shriveled, 35 to 40 minutes. (Do not stir tomatoes during roasting.) Let cool for 5 to 10 minutes.

2. Meanwhile, bring 4 quarts water to boil in large pot. Add pasta and 1 tablespoon salt and cook, stirring often, until al dente. Reserve ½ cup cooking water, then drain pasta and return it to pot. Using rubber spatula, scrape tomato mixture onto pasta. Add olives, pine nuts, and oregano and toss to combine. Season with salt and pepper to taste and adjust consistency with reserved cooking water as needed. Serve with Pecorino Romano.

Penne with Roasted Cherry Tomatoes, Arugula, and Goat Cheese

SERVES 6 VEG

Grape tomatoes can be substituted for the cherry tomatoes, but because they tend to be sweeter, you will want to reduce or even omit the sugar. Do likewise if your cherry tomatoes are very sweet.

    1 shallot, sliced thin
    ¼ cup extra-virgin olive oil
    2 pounds cherry tomatoes, halved
    3 large garlic cloves, sliced thin
    1 tablespoon sherry or red wine vinegar
 1½ teaspoons sugar, or to taste
      Salt and pepper
    ¼ teaspoon red pepper flakes
    1 pound penne
    4 ounces (4 cups) baby arugula
    4 ounces goat cheese, crumbled (1 cup)

1. Adjust oven rack to middle position and heat oven to 350 degrees. Toss shallot with 1 teaspoon oil in bowl. In separate bowl, gently toss tomatoes with remaining oil, garlic, vinegar, sugar, ½ teaspoon salt, ¼ teaspoon pepper, and pepper flakes. Spread tomato mixture in even layer in rimmed baking sheet, scatter shallot over tomatoes, and roast until edges of shallot begin to brown and tomato skins are slightly shriveled, 35 to 40 minutes. (Do not stir tomatoes during roasting.) Let cool for 5 to 10 minutes.

2. Meanwhile, bring 4 quarts water to boil in large pot. Add pasta and 1 tablespoon salt and cook, stirring often, until al dente. Reserve ½ cup cooking water, then drain pasta and return it to pot. Add arugula to pasta and toss until wilted. Using rubber spatula, scrape tomato mixture onto pasta and toss to combine. Season with salt and pepper to taste and adjust consistency with reserved cooking water as needed. Serve, passing goat cheese separately.

Penne and Fresh Tomato Sauce with Fennel and Orange

SERVES 6 FAST VEG

WHY THIS RECIPE WORKS Both Greek and Italian cultures rely on fresh, quick tomato sauces to dress up pasta, which can be eaten as a main dish or served as one of several dishes to make up a meal. We found that ripe tomatoes were key to the best-tasting sauce; we skinned, seeded, chopped, and simmered them in a skillet with garlic and olive oil to boost their flavor. To give our fresh tomato sauce an interesting twist, we wanted to balance the tomatoes with some surprising flavors that are characteristic of Greece. After testing a variety of ingredients, we chose piney fennel, which is indigenous to the region. The combination of this crisp, aromatic vegetable with potent saffron, fruity orange zest, and subtly spicy red pepper flakes kept the sauce in balance. Incorporating just these few robust ingredients provided our sauce with plenty of flavor in a short amount of time—making it perfect for a weeknight meal. Simmering the sauce until the tomatoes just began to break down into chunks kept the flavor of the tomatoes fresh and bright. The success of this recipe depends on ripe, in-season tomatoes.

    ¼ cup extra-virgin olive oil
    1 fennel bulb, stalks discarded, bulb halved, cored, and cut into ¼-inch pieces
    2 garlic cloves, minced
    2 (3-inch) strips orange zest plus 3 tablespoons juice
    ½ teaspoon fennel seeds, crushed
    ⅛ teaspoon red pepper flakes
      Pinch saffron threads, crumbled (optional)
    3 pounds ripe tomatoes, cored, peeled, seeded, and cut into ½-inch pieces
    1 pound penne
      Salt and pepper
    3 tablespoons chopped fresh basil
      Sugar

Crushing Whole Spices

To crush whole seeds or peppercorns, place seeds on cutting board and rock bottom edge of skillet over seeds until they crack.

1. Heat 2 tablespoons oil in 12-inch skillet over medium heat until shimmering. Add fennel and cook until softened and lightly browned, 5 to 7 minutes. Stir in garlic, orange zest, fennel seeds, pepper flakes, and saffron, if using, and cook until fragrant, about 30 seconds. Stir in tomatoes and cook until tomato pieces lose their shape and make chunky sauce, about 10 minutes. Discard orange zest.

2. Meanwhile, bring 4 quarts water to boil in large pot. Add pasta and 1 tablespoon salt and cook, stirring often, until al dente. Reserve ½ cup cooking water, then drain pasta and return it to pot.

3. Stir orange juice, basil, ¼ teaspoon salt, and ⅛ teaspoon pepper into sauce and season with sugar to taste. Add sauce and remaining 2 tablespoons oil to pasta and toss to combine. Season with salt and pepper to taste and adjust consistency with reserved cooking water as needed. Serve.

VARIATION

Penne and Fresh Tomato Sauce with Spinach and Feta
SERVES 6   FAST   VEG

The success of this recipe depends on ripe, in-season tomatoes.

  3 tablespoons extra-virgin olive oil
  2 garlic cloves, minced
  3 pounds ripe tomatoes, cored, peeled, seeded, and
    cut into ½-inch pieces
  5 ounces (5 cups) baby spinach
  1 pound penne
    Salt and pepper
  2 tablespoons chopped fresh mint or oregano
  2 tablespoons lemon juice
    Sugar
  4 ounces feta cheese, crumbled (1 cup)

1. Cook 2 tablespoons oil and garlic in 12-inch skillet over medium heat, stirring often, until garlic turns golden but not brown, about 3 minutes. Stir in tomatoes and cook until tomato pieces begin to lose their shape, about 8 minutes. Stir in spinach, 1 handful at a time, and cook until spinach is wilted and tomatoes have made chunky sauce, about 2 minutes.

2. Meanwhile, bring 4 quarts water to boil in large pot. Add pasta and 1 tablespoon salt and cook, stirring often, until al dente. Reserve ½ cup cooking water, then drain pasta and return it to pot.

3. Stir mint, lemon juice, ¼ teaspoon salt, and ⅛ teaspoon pepper into sauce and season with sugar to taste. Add sauce and remaining 1 tablespoon oil to pasta and toss to combine. Season with salt and pepper to taste and adjust consistency with reserved cooking water as needed. Serve, passing feta separately.

Peeling Tomatoes

1. Cut out stem and core of each tomato, then score small X at base.

2. Lower tomatoes into boiling water and simmer until skins loosen, 30 to 60 seconds.

3. Use paring knife to remove strips of loosened skin starting at X on base of each tomato.

Farfalle with Zucchini, Tomatoes, and Pine Nuts
SERVES 6   VEG

WHY THIS RECIPE WORKS A combination of pasta and summer squash results in a light, flavorful dish that's full of color. We decided against peeling the squash, as the skin helped to keep the pieces intact throughout the cooking process. Because summer squash contains so much liquid, we salted and drained it to keep our sauce from ending up watery and bland. The salted squash also browned beautifully; just 5 minutes in a hot skillet gave a light char to each batch. To accompany the squash, we chose halved grape tomatoes, fresh basil, and pine nuts. We finished the sauce with balsamic vinegar to give it a kick and paired the sauce with farfalle, since its nooks and crannies easily trapped the flavor-packed ingredients. A combination of zucchini and summer squash makes for a more colorful dish, but either may be used exclusively if desired. Cherry tomatoes can be substituted for the grape tomatoes. If farfalle is unavailable, campanelle and fusilli are good substitutes. We prefer using kosher salt because residual grains can be easily wiped away from the squash; if using table salt, be sure to reduce all of the salt amounts in the recipe by half.

Salting the squash removes moisture, allowing us to get lots of flavorful browning to enrich this bright, summery dish.

2 pounds zucchini and/or summer squash, halved lengthwise and sliced ½ inch thick
  Kosher salt and pepper
5 tablespoons extra-virgin olive oil
3 garlic cloves, minced
½ teaspoon red pepper flakes
1 pound farfalle
12 ounces grape tomatoes, halved
½ cup chopped fresh basil
¼ cup pine nuts, toasted
2 tablespoons balsamic vinegar
  Grated Parmesan cheese

1. Toss squash with 1 tablespoon salt and let drain in colander for 30 minutes. Pat squash dry with paper towels and carefully wipe away any residual salt.

2. Heat 1 tablespoon oil in 12-inch nonstick skillet over high heat until just smoking. Add half of squash and cook, stirring occasionally, until golden brown and slightly charred, 5 to 7 minutes, reducing heat if skillet begins to scorch; transfer to large plate. Repeat with 1 tablespoon oil and remaining squash; transfer to plate.

3. Heat 1 tablespoon oil in now-empty skillet over medium heat until shimmering. Add garlic and pepper flakes and cook until fragrant, about 30 seconds. Stir in squash and cook until heated through, about 30 seconds.

4. Meanwhile, bring 4 quarts water to boil in large pot. Add pasta and 1 tablespoon salt and cook, stirring often, until al dente. Reserve ½ cup cooking water, then drain pasta and return it to pot. Add squash mixture, tomatoes, basil, pine nuts, vinegar, and remaining 2 tablespoons oil and toss to combine. Season with salt and pepper to taste and adjust consistency with reserved cooking water as needed. Serve with Parmesan.

VARIATION
Farfalle with Zucchini, Tomatoes, Olives, and Feta
SERVES 6 VEG

A combination of zucchini and summer squash makes for a more colorful dish, but either may be used exclusively if desired. Cherry tomatoes can be substituted for the grape tomatoes. If farfalle is unavailable, campanelle and fusilli are good substitutes. We prefer using kosher salt because residual grains can be easily wiped away from the squash; if using table salt, be sure to reduce all of the salt amounts in the recipe by half.

2 pounds zucchini and/or summer squash, halved lengthwise and sliced ½ inch thick
  Kosher salt and pepper
5 tablespoons extra-virgin olive oil
1 red onion, chopped fine
3 garlic cloves, minced
1 teaspoon grated lemon zest plus 1 tablespoon juice
1 pound farfalle
12 ounces grape tomatoes, halved
½ cup pitted kalamata olives, quartered
¼ cup chopped fresh mint
2 teaspoons red wine vinegar
4 ounces feta cheese, crumbled (1 cup)

1. Toss squash with 1 tablespoon salt and let drain in colander for 30 minutes. Pat squash dry with paper towels and carefully wipe away any residual salt.

2. Heat 1 tablespoon oil in 12-inch nonstick skillet over high heat until just smoking. Add half of squash and cook, stirring occasionally, until golden brown and slightly charred, 5 to 7 minutes, reducing heat if skillet begins to scorch; transfer to large plate. Repeat with 1 tablespoon oil and remaining squash; transfer to plate.

3. Heat 1 tablespoon oil in now-empty skillet over medium heat until shimmering. Add onion and cook until softened and lightly browned, 5 to 7 minutes. Stir in garlic, lemon zest, and ½ teaspoon pepper and cook until fragrant, about 30 seconds. Stir in squash and cook until heated through, about 30 seconds.

4. Meanwhile, bring 4 quarts water to boil in large pot. Add pasta and 1 tablespoon salt and cook, stirring often, until al dente. Reserve ½ cup cooking water, then drain pasta and return it to pot. Add squash mixture, tomatoes, olives, mint, vinegar, lemon juice, and remaining 2 tablespoons oil and toss to combine. Season with salt and pepper to taste and adjust consistency with reserved cooking water as needed. Serve, passing feta seperately.

Spaghetti al Limone

SERVES 6 FAST VEG

WHY THIS RECIPE WORKS *Spaghetti al limone* (spaghetti with lemon) is a classic Italian dish in which just a few high-quality ingredients are combined to make a satisfying meal. In our research, we found that some ingredients for this dish were fairly constant: Lemon juice, lemon zest, pasta, and Parmesan cheese were essentials, and extra-virgin olive oil, butter, heavy cream, and basil were variables. Tasters unanimously declared extra-virgin olive oil the winner—it complemented the lemon flavor beautifully. Plus, using oil had the added benefit of streamlining the recipe; we could simply whisk the oil and lemon juice into a vinaigrette that we tossed with the warm pasta just before serving. Two teaspoons of lemon zest boosted the lemon flavor without adding acidity. A little bit of garlic provided depth but didn't compete with the lemon flavor. Parmesan cheese gave the sauce some body and contributed a nutty flavor that tasters appreciated. Because this recipe is so simple, it is important to use high-quality extra-virgin olive oil, fresh-squeezed lemon juice, and fresh basil here. A rasp-style grater makes quick work of turning the garlic into a paste.

½ cup extra-virgin olive oil
2 teaspoons grated lemon zest plus ⅓ cup lemon juice (2 lemons)
1 small garlic clove, minced to paste
 Salt and pepper
2 ounces Parmesan cheese, grated (1 cup)
1 pound spaghetti
6 tablespoons shredded fresh basil

1. Whisk oil, lemon zest and juice, garlic, ½ teaspoon salt, and ¼ teaspoon pepper together in small bowl, then stir in Parmesan until thick and creamy.

2. Meanwhile, bring 4 quarts water to boil in large pot. Add pasta and 1 tablespoon salt and cook, stirring often, until al dente. Reserve ½ cup cooking water, then drain pasta and return it to pot. Add oil mixture and basil and toss to combine. Season with salt and pepper to taste and adjust consistency with reserved cooking water as needed. Serve.

NOTES FROM THE TEST KITCHEN
All About Parmesan

Produced using traditional methods for the past 800 years in one government-designated area of northern Italy, this hard cow's-milk cheese has a distinctive buttery, nutty, and slightly sharp taste. We frequently reach for it to sprinkle on top of pasta dishes or to add a rich, salty flavor to sauces, soups, and stews.

BUYING PARMESAN
We love authentic Italian Parmigiano-Reggiano in the test kitchen, but it is not vegetarian because it is made with animal rennet. To ensure that you're buying a properly aged cheese, examine the condition of the rind. It should be a few shades darker than the straw-colored interior and should penetrate about ½ inch deep (younger or improperly aged cheeses will have a paler, thinner rind). And closely scrutinize the center of the cheese. Those small white spots found on many samples are actually good things—they signify the presence of calcium phosphate crystals, which are formed only after the cheese has been aged for the proper amount of time.

STORING PARMESAN
We found that the best way to preserve Parmesan's flavor and texture is to wrap it in parchment paper, then aluminum foil. However, if you have just a small piece of cheese, tossing it in a zipper-lock bag works almost as well; just be sure to squeeze out as much air as possible before sealing the bag.

PARMESAN VERSUS PECORINO ROMANO
Parmesan and Pecorino Romano have similar textures and flavors, and often you'll see one as an alternative to the other in recipes. We have found that Parmesan and Pecorino Romano generally can be used interchangeably, especially when the amount called for is moderate. However, when Parmesan is called for in larger quantities, stick with the Parmesan, as Pecorino Romano can be fairly pungent.

CAN YOU PREGRATE YOUR OWN PARMESAN?
We've never been tempted by tasteless powdered Parmesan cheese. But what about grating your own? We found that tasters were hard-pressed to detect any difference between freshly grated Parmesan and cheese that had been grated and stored for up to three weeks. So go ahead and grate your Parmesan ahead; refrigerate in an airtight container.

Tagliatelle with Artichokes and Parmesan
SERVES 6

WHY THIS RECIPE WORKS When combined with a few staple ingredients, artichokes and pasta can defy their simplicity and come together into an elegant and ultraflavorful Italian-inspired dish. To keep our recipe streamlined, we opted to use jarred artichokes since they are available year-round, require only minimal prep, and offer plenty of bold artichoke flavor. To offset any sharp, briny flavor of the artichokes, we trimmed the leaves off the hearts and then gave them a quick soak in water. We cut the artichokes in half and then dried them so they could take on deep browning when sautéed, which brought out their natural nuttiness. Anchovies gave the sauce savory depth without adding a fishy taste; garlic and oregano combined with white wine, olive oil, Parmesan, and some pasta water made up our simple yet flavorful sauce. Fresh parsley and lemon zest kept the pasta light and bright without overwhelming the deep artichoke flavor, and a simple bread-crumb topping enhanced with extra Parmesan gave the dish savory crunch.

 4 cups jarred whole baby artichoke hearts packed in water
 ¼ cup extra-virgin olive oil, plus extra for serving
    Salt and pepper
 4 garlic cloves, minced
 2 anchovy fillets, rinsed, patted dry, and minced
 1 tablespoon minced fresh oregano or 1 teaspoon dried
 ⅛ teaspoon red pepper flakes
 ½ cup dry white wine
 1 pound tagliatelle
 1 ounce Parmesan cheese, grated (½ cup), plus extra for serving
 ¼ cup minced fresh parsley
 1½ teaspoons grated lemon zest
 1 recipe Parmesan Bread Crumbs (page 144)

1. Cut leaves from artichoke hearts. Cut hearts in half and dry with paper towels. Place leaves in bowl and cover with water. Let leaves sit for 15 minutes. Drain well.

2. Heat 1 tablespoon oil in 12-inch nonstick skillet over medium-high heat until shimmering. Add artichoke hearts and ⅛ teaspoon salt and cook, stirring frequently, until spotty brown, 7 to 9 minutes. Stir in garlic, anchovies, oregano, and pepper flakes and cook, stirring constantly, until fragrant, about 30 seconds. Stir in wine and bring to simmer. Off heat, stir in artichoke leaves.

3. Meanwhile, bring 4 quarts water to boil in large pot. Add pasta and 1 tablespoon salt and cook, stirring often, until al dente. Reserve 1½ cups cooking water, then drain pasta and return it to pot. Add 1 cup reserved cooking water, artichoke mixture, Parmesan, parsley, lemon zest, and remaining 3 tablespoons oil and toss to combine. Season with salt and pepper to taste

Jarred artichokes, anchovies, and Parmesan create a luxurious yet light pasta dish.

Buying Processed Artichokes

Artichokes are native to the Mediterranean and are used almost everywhere in the region. They're served fresh, boiled, baked, stuffed, braised, and more. From soups and stews to risotto, paella, and pasta, artichokes are prized everywhere from Spain and France to Turkey and Lebanon and are especially popular in Greece and Italy. But while fresh artichokes have their place, they're limited by seasonality, so many Mediterranean recipes turn to prepared artichokes as a flavorful alternative. When buying processed artichokes, avoid premarinated versions; we prefer to control the seasonings ourselves. We also don't recommend canned hearts, which tend to taste waterlogged and have large, tough leaves. We think that smaller whole jarred artichoke hearts labeled "baby" or "cocktail" are best. (If the label doesn't say this, look for specimens no larger than 1½ inches in length.) Our favorite brand is Pastene Baby Artichokes, which are nicely tender with a sweet, earthy flavor. If you can't find jarred baby artichoke hearts, frozen artichoke hearts will work in certain recipes.

and adjust consistency with remaining ½ cup reserved cooking water as needed. Serve, sprinkling individual portions with bread crumbs and extra Parmesan and drizzling with extra oil.

PARMESAN BREAD CRUMBS

MAKES 1 cup FAST VEG

2 slices hearty white sandwich bread
2 tablespoons extra-virgin olive oil
¼ cup grated Parmesan cheese
Salt and pepper

Pulse bread in food processor until finely ground, 10 to 15 pulses. Heat oil in 12-inch nonstick skillet over medium heat until shimmering. Add bread crumbs and cook, stirring constantly, until crumbs begin to brown, 3 to 5 minutes. Add Parmesan and continue to cook, stirring constantly, until crumbs are golden brown, 1 to 2 minutes. Transfer crumbs to bowl and season with salt and pepper to taste. Serve.

VARIATION
LEMON-CHILI BREAD CRUMBS FAST VEG
Substitute ¼ teaspoon red pepper flakes for Parmesan. Stir 1 tablespoon grated lemon zest into crumbs before seasoning with salt and pepper.

Orecchiette with Broccoli Rabe and White Beans
SERVES 6 FAST VEG

WHY THIS RECIPE WORKS Orecchiette with broccoli rabe is a classic dish from Puglia; lightly dressed with olive oil and Parmesan, this dish makes for a quick and satisfying weeknight meal. To balance out the slightly bitter flavor of the broccoli rabe, we decided to include savory, buttery white beans. To ensure that the thick stalks, tender leaves, and small florets of the broccoli rabe cooked evenly, we boiled them briefly, pulling them from the pot just as they turned crisp-tender. To boost the flavor of the dish, we cooked a shallot with garlic, oregano, and fennel seeds before adding our beans and allowing them to warm through. You can substitute 2 pounds of broccoli, cut into 1-inch florets, for the broccoli rabe.

¼ cup extra-virgin olive oil
1 shallot, minced
6 garlic cloves, minced
1 teaspoon minced fresh oregano or ¼ teaspoon dried

Creamy canned cannellini beans pair with spicy broccoli rabe for an easy weeknight pasta dish.

½ teaspoon fennel seeds, crushed
¼ teaspoon red pepper flakes
1 (15-ounce) can cannellini beans, rinsed
1 pound broccoli rabe, trimmed and cut into 1½-inch pieces
Salt and pepper
1 pound orecchiette
2 ounces Parmesan or Asiago cheese, grated (1 cup)

1. Heat oil in 12-inch nonstick skillet over medium heat until shimmering. Add shallot and cook until softened, about 2 minutes. Stir in garlic, oregano, fennel seeds, and pepper flakes and cook until fragrant, about 30 seconds. Stir in beans and cook until heated through, about 2 minutes; set aside.

2. Meanwhile, bring 4 quarts water to boil in large pot. Add broccoli rabe and 1 tablespoon salt and cook, stirring often, until crisp-tender, about 2 minutes. Using slotted spoon, transfer broccoli rabe to skillet with bean mixture.

3. Return water to boil, add pasta, and cook, stirring often, until al dente. Reserve 1 cup cooking water, then drain pasta and return it to pot. Add bean–broccoli rabe mixture, Parmesan, and ⅓ cup reserved cooking water and toss to combine. Season with salt and pepper to taste and adjust consistency with remaining ⅔ cup reserved cooking water as needed. Serve.

VARIATION

Orecchiette with Broccoli Rabe and Sausage FAST

Omit shallot, oregano, fennel seeds, and cannellini beans and decrease oil to 2 tablespoons. Heat oil in skillet over medium-high heat until just smoking. Add 8 ounces hot or sweet Italian sausage, casings removed, and cook, breaking up meat with wooden spoon, until lightly browned, about 5 minutes. Stir in garlic and pepper flakes and cook until fragrant, about 30 seconds; set aside and continue with recipe as directed.

Whole-Wheat Spaghetti with Greens, Beans, and Pancetta
SERVES 6

WHY THIS RECIPE WORKS Whole-wheat pasta, hearty greens, and savory beans are humble ingredients on their own, but when combined, they can make a rustic, full-flavored Italian dish. We wanted to retain the complex flavor of this satisfying dish but make it an easy and quick midweek meal. To start, we opted to use kale or collard greens, since they require only a quick braise. This meant that we could easily infuse them with aromatic flavors like onion, garlic, spicy red pepper flakes, and chicken broth. The greens, beans, and sauce had to cook with the pasta for only a few minutes to create a harmonious dish. We preferred whole-wheat pasta to regular, as the wheat stood up to the bold flavors of the sauce and complemented the earthiness of the greens. To round out the flavor of the dish, we added crisp, savory pancetta and silky fontina. To give our creamy pasta a bit of textural contrast, we served it with Parmesan bread crumbs. Prosciutto can be substituted for the pancetta. For a spicier dish, use the larger amount of pepper flakes.

    1 tablespoon extra-virgin olive oil
    3 ounces pancetta, cut into ½-inch pieces
    1 onion, chopped fine
    3 garlic cloves, minced
¼–½ teaspoon red pepper flakes
1½ pounds kale or collard greens, stemmed and cut into 1-inch pieces
1½ cups chicken broth
     Salt and pepper
    1 (15-ounce) can cannellini beans, rinsed
    1 pound whole-wheat spaghetti
    4 ounces fontina cheese, shredded (1 cup)
    1 cup Parmesan Bread Crumbs (page 144)

NOTES FROM THE TEST KITCHEN
Cooking Pasta 101

Cooking pasta seems simple, but perfect pasta takes some finesse. Here's how we do it in the test kitchen.

USE PLENTY OF WATER
To prevent sticking, you'll need 4 quarts of water to cook up to 1 pound of dried pasta. Pasta leaches starch as it cooks; without plenty of water to dilute it, the starch will coat the noodles and they will stick. Use a pot with at least a 6-quart capacity so that the water won't boil over.

SALT THE WATER
Adding salt to the pasta cooking water is essential; it seasons and adds flavor to the pasta. Add 1 tablespoon of salt per 4 quarts of water. Be sure to add the salt with the pasta, not before, so it will dissolve and not stain the pot.

SKIP THE OIL
It's a myth that adding oil to pasta cooking water prevents the pasta from sticking together as it cooks. Adding oil to cooking water just creates a slick on the surface of the water, doing nothing for the pasta. And when you drain the pasta, the oil prevents the pasta sauce from adhering. To prevent pasta from sticking, simply stir the pasta for a minute or two when you add it to the boiling water, then stir occasionally while it's cooking.

CHECK OFTEN FOR DONENESS
The timing instructions given on the box are almost always too long and will result in mushy, overcooked pasta. Tasting is the best way to check for doneness. We typically prefer pasta cooked al dente, when it still has a little bite left in the center.

RESERVE SOME WATER
Reserve about ½ cup of cooking water before draining the pasta—the water is flavorful and can help loosen a thick sauce.

DON'T RINSE
Drain the pasta in a colander, but don't rinse the pasta; it washes away starch and makes the pasta taste watery. Do let a little cooking water cling to the cooked pasta to help the sauce adhere.

KEEP IT HOT
If you're using a large serving bowl for the pasta, place it under the colander while draining the pasta. The hot water heats up the bowl, which keeps the pasta warm longer.

1. Heat oil in 12-inch straight-sided sauté pan over medium heat until shimmering. Add pancetta and cook, stirring occasionally, until crisp, 5 to 7 minutes. Using slotted spoon, transfer pancetta to paper towel–lined plate.

2. Add onion to fat left in pan and cook over medium heat until softened and lightly browned, 5 to 7 minutes. Stir in garlic and pepper flakes and cook until fragrant, about 30 seconds. Add half of greens and cook, tossing occasionally, until starting to wilt, about 2 minutes. Add remaining greens, broth, and ¾ teaspoon salt and bring to simmer. Reduce heat to medium, cover (pan will be very full), and cook, tossing occasionally, until greens are tender, about 15 minutes (mixture will be somewhat soupy). Off heat, stir in beans and pancetta.

3. Meanwhile, bring 4 quarts water to boil in large pot. Add pasta and 1 tablespoon salt and cook, stirring often, until just shy of al dente. Reserve ½ cup cooking water, then drain pasta and return it to pot. Add greens mixture and cook over medium heat, tossing to combine, until pasta absorbs most of liquid, about 2 minutes.

4. Off heat, stir in fontina. Season with salt and pepper to taste and adjust consistency with reserved cooking water as needed. Serve, sprinkling individual portions with bread crumbs.

VARIATION

Whole-Wheat Spaghetti with Greens, Beans, Tomatoes, and Garlic Chips

SERVES 6   VEG

For a spicier dish, use the larger amount of pepper flakes.

    3   tablespoons extra-virgin olive oil, plus extra for serving
    8   garlic cloves, peeled (5 sliced thin lengthwise, 3 minced)
        Salt and pepper
    1   onion, chopped fine
¼–½   teaspoon red pepper flakes
  1¼   pounds curly-leaf spinach, stemmed and cut into 1-inch pieces
    ¾   cup vegetable broth
    1   (14.5-ounce) can diced tomatoes, drained
    1   (15-ounce) can cannellini beans, rinsed
    ¾   cup pitted kalamata olives, chopped coarse
    1   pound whole-wheat spaghetti
    2   ounces Parmesan cheese, grated (1 cup), plus extra for serving

1. Cook oil and sliced garlic in 12-inch straight-sided sauté pan over medium heat, stirring often, until garlic turns golden but not brown, about 3 minutes. Using slotted spoon, transfer garlic to paper towel–lined plate and season lightly with salt; set aside.

2. Add onion to oil left in pan and cook over medium heat until softened and lightly browned, 5 to 7 minutes. Stir in minced garlic and pepper flakes and cook until fragrant, about 30 seconds. Add half of spinach and cook, tossing occasionally, until starting to wilt, about 2 minutes. Add remaining spinach, broth, tomatoes, and ¾ teaspoon salt and bring to simmer. Reduce heat to medium, cover (pan will be very full), and cook, tossing occasionally, until spinach is completely wilted, about 10 minutes (mixture will be somewhat soupy). Off heat, stir in beans and olives.

3. Meanwhile, bring 4 quarts water to boil in large pot. Add pasta and 1 tablespoon salt and cook, stirring often, until just shy of al dente. Reserve ½ cup cooking water, then drain pasta and return it to pot. Add greens mixture and cook over medium heat, tossing to combine, until pasta absorbs most of liquid, about 2 minutes.

4. Off heat, stir in Parmesan. Season with salt and pepper to taste and adjust consistency with reserved cooking water as needed. Serve, sprinkling individual portions with garlic chips and extra Parmesan and drizzling with extra oil.

NOTES FROM THE TEST KITCHEN

Buying Whole-Wheat Pasta

Supermarket shelves now carry a wide range of whole-wheat and multigrain pasta. To find the brand with the best nutty, complex flavor and firm, springy texture, we put 18 brands to the test. Some were puzzlingly similar to white pasta, with none of the hearty, nutty flavor we were looking for, and others were heavy, dense, and rough. So what did our tasting panel find? First, most of the 100 percent whole-wheat and 100 percent whole-grain pastas fell quickly to the bottom of the rankings, garnering descriptions like mushy, doughy, sour, and fishy. But there was one dark horse in the bunch, Italian-made Bionaturae Organic 100% Whole Wheat Spaghetti, made entirely of whole wheat but with an appealing chew and firm texture like the pasta with little or no whole grains. The manufacturer's secret? Custom milling (which ensures good flavor), extrusion through a bronze die (which helps build gluten in the dough), and a slower drying process at low temperatures (which yields sturdier pasta).

Sautéed pancetta infuses the vegetables and French lentils in this earthy pasta dish with rich, meaty flavor.

Whole-Wheat Spaghetti with Lentils, Pancetta, and Escarole
SERVES 6

WHY THIS RECIPE WORKS An earthy, hearty, soul-satisfying dish, pasta with lentils has long been a tradition in Italy. But when we developed our own version, we ended up going with a nontraditional choice for the main ingredient: French green lentils, or *lentilles du Puy*, which retained a firm yet tender texture after the long simmering time. Using a combination of water and chicken broth as the cooking liquid imparted a savory backbone without obscuring the lentils' earthy notes. White wine provided a bright punch of acidity, but we couldn't add it until the lentils were softened, lest it prevent them from cooking through. Meaty pancetta, sweet carrots, and spicy escarole rounded out the flavors of this rustic dish. Lentilles du Puy, also called French green lentils, are our first choice for this recipe, but brown, black, or regular green lentils are fine, too (note that cooking times will vary depending on the type used).

¼ cup extra-virgin olive oil
4 ounces pancetta, cut into ¼-inch pieces
1 onion, chopped fine

2 carrots, peeled, halved lengthwise, and sliced ¼ inch thick
2 garlic cloves, minced
¾ cup lentilles du Puy, picked over and rinsed
2 cups chicken broth
1½ cups water
¼ cup dry white wine
1 head escarole (1 pound), trimmed and sliced ½ inch thick
1 pound whole-wheat spaghetti
Salt and pepper
¼ cup chopped fresh parsley
Grated Parmesan cheese

1. Heat 2 tablespoons oil in large saucepan over medium heat until shimmering. Add pancetta and cook, stirring occasionally, until beginning to brown, 3 to 5 minutes. Add onion and carrots and cook until softened, 5 to 7 minutes. Stir in garlic and cook until fragrant, about 30 seconds. Stir in lentils, broth, and water and bring to simmer. Reduce heat to medium-low, cover, and simmer until lentils are fully cooked and tender, 30 to 40 minutes.

2. Stir in wine and simmer, uncovered, for 2 minutes. Stir in escarole, 1 handful at a time, and cook until completely wilted, about 5 minutes.

3. Meanwhile, bring 4 quarts water to boil in large pot. Add pasta and 1 tablespoon salt and cook, stirring often, until al dente. Reserve ¾ cup cooking water, then drain pasta and return it to pot. Add ½ cup reserved cooking water, lentil mixture, parsley, and remaining 2 tablespoons oil and toss to combine. Season with salt and pepper to taste and adjust consistency with remaining ¼ cup reserved cooking water as needed. Serve with Parmesan.

NOTES FROM THE TEST KITCHEN
All About Pancetta

Pancetta is an Italian pork product made from the belly of the pig that is used to add flavor and meaty depth to many Italian stews and braises. Sometimes called Italian bacon, this fatty, succulent cut is also used to make American bacon. However, American bacon is salted, (usually) sugared, and smoked, whereas pancetta is treated with salt, black pepper, and spices and rolled into a cylinder. It is never smoked.

To use bacon in place of pancetta, blanch the uncooked bacon in boiling water to mellow some of its smoky flavor. Because blanching also removes a considerable amount of fat from the bacon, you may need to supplement with additional oil. While the bacon may still impart subtle smokiness, it is an acceptable substitute.

SIMPLE TOMATO SAUCES

Tomato sauce is a Mediterranean staple, from warm-spiced Greek and Egyptian sauces to simple and savory Italian and French versions. Here are a few of our favorite basic tomato sauces, which pair perfectly with pasta. All of these sauces make 4 cups, enough to sauce 1 pound of pasta. Serve with grated Parmesan cheese.

No-Cook Fresh Tomato Sauce
FAST VEG

The success of this recipe depends on ripe, in-season tomatoes. This sauce works well with penne, rotini, or campanelle.

- ¼ cup extra-virgin olive oil
- 2 teaspoons lemon juice, plus extra as needed
- 1 shallot, minced
- 1 garlic clove, minced
  Salt and pepper
  Sugar
- 2 pounds very ripe tomatoes, cored and cut into ½-inch pieces
- 3 tablespoons chopped fresh basil

Stir oil, lemon juice, shallot, garlic, 1 teaspoon salt, ¼ teaspoon pepper, and pinch sugar together in large bowl. Stir in tomatoes and let marinate until very soft and flavorful, about 30 minutes. Before serving, stir in basil and season with salt, pepper, sugar, and extra lemon juice to taste. When tossing sauce with cooked pasta, add some pasta cooking water as needed to adjust consistency.

Quick Tomato Sauce FAST VEG

This sauce works well with any type of pasta.

- 3 tablespoons extra-virgin olive oil
- 3 garlic cloves, minced
- 1 (28-ounce) can crushed tomatoes
- 1 (14.5-ounce) can diced tomatoes
- 3 tablespoons chopped fresh basil
- ¼ teaspoon sugar
  Salt and pepper

Cook oil and garlic in medium saucepan over medium heat, stirring often, until fragrant but not browned, about 2 minutes. Stir in tomatoes and their juice. Bring to simmer and cook until slightly thickened, 15 to 20 minutes. Off heat, stir in basil and sugar. Season with salt and pepper to taste. When tossing sauce with cooked pasta, add some pasta cooking water as needed to adjust consistency.

Classic Marinara Sauce VEG

This sauce works well with any type of pasta. If you prefer a chunkier sauce, give it just three or four pulses in the food processor in step 4.

- 2 (28-ounce) cans whole peeled tomatoes
- 3 tablespoons extra-virgin olive oil
- 1 onion, chopped fine
- 2 garlic cloves, minced
- 2 teaspoons minced fresh oregano or ½ teaspoon dried
- ⅓ cup dry red wine
- 3 tablespoons chopped fresh basil
  Salt and pepper
  Sugar

1. Drain tomatoes in fine-mesh strainer set over large bowl. Using hands, open tomatoes and remove and discard seeds and fibrous cores; let tomatoes drain, about 5 minutes. Reserve ¾ cup tomatoes separately. Reserve 2½ cups drained tomato juice; discard extra juice.

2. Heat 2 tablespoons oil in 12-inch skillet over medium heat until shimmering. Add onion and cook until softened

Classic Marinara Sauce

and lightly browned, 5 to 7 minutes. Stir in garlic and oregano and cook until fragrant, about 30 seconds. Stir in remaining drained tomatoes and increase heat to medium-high. Cook, stirring often, until liquid has evaporated and tomatoes begin to brown and stick to pan, 10 to 12 minutes.

3. Stir in wine and cook until thick and syrupy, about 1 minute. Stir in reserved tomato juice, scraping up any browned bits. Bring to simmer and cook, stirring occasionally, until sauce is thickened, 8 to 10 minutes.

4. Transfer sauce to food processor, add reserved ¾ cup tomatoes, and pulse until slightly chunky, about 8 pulses. Return sauce to now-empty skillet, stir in basil and remaining 1 tablespoon oil, and season with salt, pepper, and sugar to taste. When tossing sauce with cooked pasta, add some pasta cooking water as needed to adjust consistency.

PESTO SAUCES

In Italy, pesto acts as a versatile condiment, dressing up a simple plate of pasta or adorning a piece of simply prepared fish, chicken, or pork. Pestos can be made with lots of different ingredients—from basil and parsley to roasted red peppers, olives, and more. Regardless of the type, a good pesto has two basic requirements: You should use a high-quality extra-virgin olive oil because its flavor will really shine through, and you should toast the garlic to help tame its fiery, raw flavor (toast the unpeeled cloves in a dry skillet over medium heat until their color darkens slightly; let the cloves cool slightly, then peel and mince). Note that the flavor and texture of these pestos vary quite a bit, as does the amount you will need to use to adequately coat your pasta. All the recipes here provide enough pesto to sauce at least 1 pound of pasta; if using as a sauce for fish, chicken, or pork, we recommend using about ¼ cup of pesto per serving.

TO MAKE PESTO Process all ingredients except oil and cheese in food processor until smooth, scraping down bowl as needed. With processor running, slowly add oil until incorporated. Transfer pesto to bowl, stir in cheese, and season with salt and pepper to taste. When tossing pesto with cooked pasta, add some of pasta cooking water as needed (up to ½ cup) to loosen consistency of pesto.

TO MAKE AHEAD Pesto can be refrigerated for up to 3 days or frozen for up to 3 months. To prevent browning, press plastic wrap flush to surface, or top with thin layer of olive oil.

Pesto Sauces

Classic Basil Pesto
MAKES ¾ cup `FAST` `VEG`

Pounding the basil briefly before processing the pesto helps bring out its flavorful oils. To bruise the basil, place it in a large zipper-lock bag and pound lightly with a rolling pin or meat pounder. The optional parsley helps give the pesto a vibrant green hue. For sharper flavor, substitute Pecorino Romano for the Parmesan.

- 2 cups fresh basil leaves, lightly bruised
- 2 tablespoons fresh parsley leaves (optional)
- ¼ cup pine nuts, toasted
- 3 garlic cloves, toasted and minced
- 7 tablespoons extra-virgin olive oil
- ¼ cup grated Parmesan cheese

Roasted Red Pepper Pesto
MAKES 1½ cups `FAST` `VEG`

This pesto tastes great when made with homemade roasted red peppers (see page 49), but jarred roasted red peppers work fine in this recipe. The pesto made with jarred peppers will have a more acidic flavor, so before using them be sure to rinse and dry the jarred peppers well.

- 2 roasted red bell peppers, peeled and chopped (1 cup)
- ¼ cup fresh parsley leaves
- 3 garlic cloves, toasted and minced
- 1 shallot, chopped
- 1 tablespoon fresh thyme leaves
- ½ cup extra-virgin olive oil
- ¼ cup grated Parmesan cheese

Tomato and Almond Pesto
MAKES 1½ cups `FAST` `VEG`

This is a traditional Sicilian pesto known as *Trapanese*. A single pepperoncini adds a nice, spicy kick; however, you can substitute ½ teaspoon of red wine vinegar and ¼ teaspoon of red pepper flakes for the pepperoncini if necessary.

- 12 ounces cherry or grape tomatoes
- ½ cup fresh basil leaves
- ¼ cup slivered almonds, toasted
- 1 small pepperoncini, stemmed, seeded, and minced
- 1 garlic clove, toasted and minced
  Pinch red pepper flakes (optional)
- ⅓ cup extra-virgin olive oil
- 1 ounce Parmesan cheese, grated (½ cup)

Green Olive and Orange Pesto
MAKES 1½ cups `FAST` `VEG`

Using high-quality green olives is crucial to the success of this pesto. Look for fresh green olives (packed in brine) in the supermarket's refrigerated section or at the salad bar.

- 1½ cups fresh parsley leaves
- ½ cup pitted green olives
- ½ cup slivered almonds, toasted
- 2 garlic cloves, toasted and minced
- ½ teaspoon grated orange zest plus 2 tablespoons juice
- ½ cup extra-virgin olive oil
- 1½ ounces Parmesan cheese, grated (¾ cup)

Deeply toasting pieces of vermicelli helps give our Spanish *fideuà* authentic flavor.

Spanish-Style Toasted Pasta with Shrimp
SERVES 4

WHY THIS RECIPE WORKS Traditional recipes for *fideuà*, a Spanish dish akin to paella that uses pasta instead of rice, can take several hours to prepare. We wanted to speed up the process but keep the complex flavors of traditional recipes. To replace the slow-cooked fish stock of classic versions, we made a quick shrimp stock using the shrimp's shells, a combination of chicken broth and water, and a bay leaf. We also streamlined the *sofrito*, the aromatic base commonly used in Spanish cuisine, by using canned, rather than fresh, tomatoes; chopping the tomatoes and finely mincing the onion helped the recipe components soften and brown more quickly. The final tweak to our recipe was boosting the flavor of the shrimp by quickly marinating them in olive oil, garlic, salt, and pepper. In step 5, if your skillet is not broiler-safe, once the pasta is tender transfer the mixture to a greased broiler-safe 13 by 9-inch baking dish; scatter the shrimp over the pasta and stir them in to partially submerge. Broil and serve as directed. Serve with Garlic Aïoli (page 233), if desired.

3 tablespoons plus 2 teaspoons extra-virgin olive oil
3 garlic cloves, minced
  Salt and pepper
1½ pounds extra-large shrimp (21 to 25 per pound), peeled and deveined, shells reserved
2¾ cups water
1 cup chicken broth
1 bay leaf
8 ounces vermicelli pasta or thin spaghetti, broken into 1- to 2-inch lengths
1 onion, chopped fine
1 (14.5-ounce) can diced tomatoes, drained and chopped fine
1 teaspoon paprika
1 teaspoon smoked paprika
½ teaspoon anchovy paste
¼ cup dry white wine
1 tablespoon chopped fresh parsley
  Lemon wedges

1. Combine 1 tablespoon oil, 1 teaspoon garlic, ¼ teaspoon salt, and ⅛ teaspoon pepper in medium bowl. Add shrimp, toss to coat, and refrigerate until ready to use.

2. Place reserved shrimp shells, water, broth, and bay leaf in medium bowl. Cover and microwave until liquid is hot and shells have turned pink, about 6 minutes. Set aside until ready to use.

3. Toss pasta with 2 teaspoons oil in broiler-safe 12-inch skillet until evenly coated. Toast pasta over medium-high heat, stirring frequently, until browned and nutty in aroma (pasta should be color of peanut butter), 6 to 10 minutes. Transfer pasta to bowl. Wipe out skillet with paper towels.

4. Heat remaining 2 tablespoons oil in now-empty skillet over medium-high heat until shimmering. Add onion and ¼ teaspoon salt and cook until softened and beginning to brown around edges, 4 to 6 minutes. Add tomatoes and cook, stirring occasionally, until mixture is thick, dry, and slightly darkened in color, 4 to 6 minutes. Reduce heat to medium, add remaining garlic, paprika, smoked paprika, and anchovy paste, and cook until fragrant, about 1½ minutes. Stir in pasta until combined. Adjust oven rack 5 to 6 inches from broiler element and heat broiler.

5. Pour shrimp broth through fine-mesh strainer into skillet; discard shells. Add wine, ¼ teaspoon salt, and ½ teaspoon pepper and stir well. Increase heat to medium-high and bring to simmer. Cook, stirring occasionally, until liquid is slightly thickened and pasta is just tender, 8 to 10 minutes. Scatter shrimp over pasta and stir to partially submerge. Transfer skillet to oven and broil until shrimp are opaque and surface of pasta is dry with crisped, browned spots, 5 to 7 minutes. Remove from oven and let sit, uncovered, for 5 minutes. Sprinkle with parsley and serve immediately with lemon wedges.

Making Toasted Pasta with Shrimp

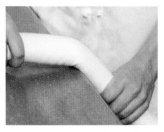

1. BREAK NOODLES Loosely fold half of noodles in dish towel, then press bundle against counter to break pasta into 1- to 2-inch lengths. Repeat with remaining noodles.

2. MAKE BROTH Microwave shrimp shells, water, broth, and bay leaf until liquid is hot and shells turn pink.

3. TOAST NOODLES AND BUILD BASE Toast broken noodles in skillet until well browned; set aside. Make *sofrito* by cooking onion, tomato, and aromatics, then add toasted noodles.

4. ADD LIQUID AND SHRIMP AND BROIL Add shrimp broth and wine to skillet. Bring to simmer and cook until noodles are tender. Nestle shrimp into noodle mixture and broil until shrimp are opaque and top surface of noodles is dry.

Spaghetti with Mussels, Lemon, and White Wine
SERVES 6 FAST

WHY THIS RECIPE WORKS On the coasts of Italy, home cooks transform simple dry pasta and fresh, briny mussels into a beautifully composed meal. Since this classic Italian dish is often eaten as a weeknight meal (but is elegant enough to be served to company), we knew we wanted to keep our recipe fast and easy. To infuse the briny mussels with flavor, we steamed them in white wine; within 5 minutes the mussels opened, indicating they were ready. We reserved the flavorful cooking liquid to add to our sauce, making sure to discard any gritty sediment that had settled

to the bottom of the pan. Sautéed garlic added another layer of flavor to the sauce, red pepper flakes offered subtle heat, and lemon imparted a bright lift. Tossing the hot pasta with the sauce melded all of the flavors and ensured a cohesive finished dish with true Italian flair. A bit of chopped parsley offered a bright, fresh counterpoint to the rich, briny sauce.

    1 pound mussels, scrubbed and debearded
    ½ cup dry white wine
    1 tablespoon extra-virgin olive oil
    2 garlic cloves, minced
    ½ teaspoon red pepper flakes
    1 teaspoon grated lemon zest plus 2 tablespoons juice
    1 pound spaghetti or linguine
      Salt and pepper
    2 tablespoons minced fresh parsley

1. Bring mussels and wine to boil in 12-inch straight-sided sauté pan, cover, and cook, shaking pan occasionally, until mussels open, about 5 minutes. As mussels open, remove them with slotted spoon and transfer to bowl. Discard any mussels that refuse to open. (If desired, remove mussels from shells.) Drain steaming liquid through fine-mesh strainer lined with coffee filter into bowl, avoiding any gritty sediment that has settled on bottom of pan. Wipe skillet clean with paper towels.

2. Cook oil, garlic, and pepper flakes in now-empty pan over medium heat, stirring frequently, until garlic turns golden but not brown, about 3 minutes. Stir in reserved mussel steaming liquid and lemon zest and juice, bring to simmer, and cook until flavors meld, about 4 minutes. Stir in mussels, cover, and cook until heated through, about 2 minutes.

3. Meanwhile, bring 4 quarts water to boil in large pot. Add pasta and 1 tablespoon salt and cook, stirring often, until al dente. Reserve ½ cup cooking water, then drain pasta and return it to pot. Add sauce and parsley and toss to combine. Season with salt and pepper to taste and adjust consistency with reserved cooking water as needed. Serve.

Reserving Pasta Cooking Water

To remind yourself to reserve pasta water, place measuring cup in colander in sink before cooking pasta.

While Italian cuisine is practically synonymous with pasta, Italy is not the only Mediterranean country where pasta is a staple. Greece also has a wide range of pasta shapes, many of which closely resemble Italian pastas, such as orzo, elbows, and spaghetti. Greek recipes use pasta in soups, casseroles, and a variety of other dishes, and the pasta is often cooked in broth, unlike Italian pastas which are more often cooked in water. Egg noodles are also popular in Greek cuisine and may be cut into small squares or long, flat strands like tagliatelle. In Spain, *fideos*, or thin, short noodles, are often toasted and cooked in stock (see page 150). In North Africa and the eastern Mediterranean, couscous is often used like pasta (see page 166 for more information on couscous). In North Africa, vermicelli can also be broken into small pieces and steamed or boiled and served in ways similar to couscous. On these pages, you'll find the Italian-style pastas that are the easiest to find in American supermarkets and the shapes we most often turn to in the test kitchen. When pairing pasta with sauces, there's one basic rule that you should keep in mind: Thick, chunky sauces go with short pastas, and thin, smooth, or light sauces with strand pasta. Although we specify pasta shapes for every recipe in this book, you should feel free to substitute other pasta shapes as long as you follow that rule.

SHORT PASTAS

Short tubular or molded pasta shapes do an excellent job of trapping and holding onto chunky sauces. Sauces with very large chunks are best with rigatoni or other large tubes. Sauces with small chunks pair better with fusilli or penne. Orzo works well as a base for any number of ingredients, from small vegetables like peas to proteins like shrimp and chicken.

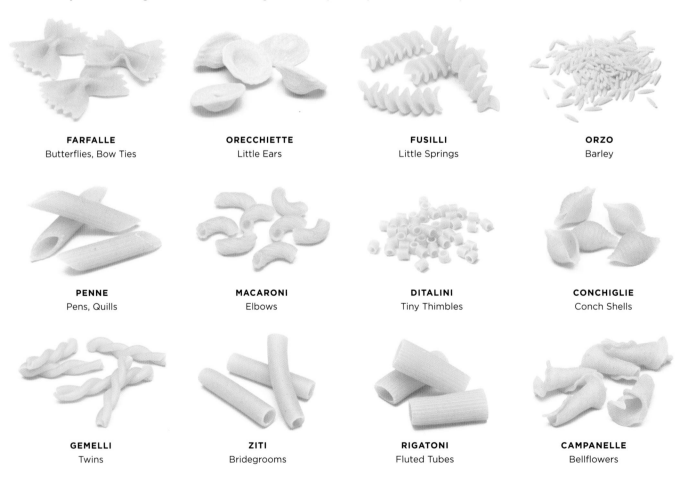

| **FARFALLE** | **ORECCHIETTE** | **FUSILLI** | **ORZO** |
| Butterflies, Bow Ties | Little Ears | Little Springs | Barley |

| **PENNE** | **MACARONI** | **DITALINI** | **CONCHIGLIE** |
| Pens, Quills | Elbows | Tiny Thimbles | Conch Shells |

| **GEMELLI** | **ZITI** | **RIGATONI** | **CAMPANELLE** |
| Twins | Bridegrooms | Fluted Tubes | Bellflowers |

STRAND PASTAS

Long strands are best with smooth sauces or sauces with very small chunks. In general, wider noodles, such as pappardelle and fettuccine, can support slightly chunkier sauces.

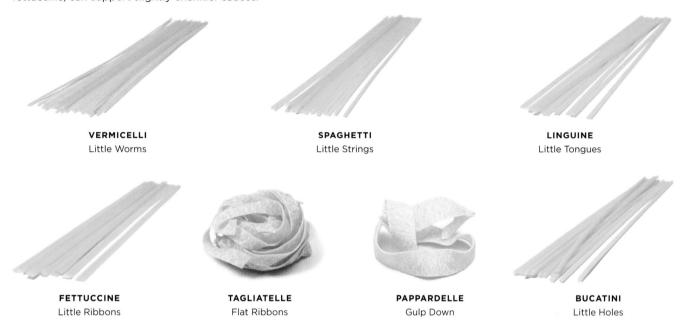

VERMICELLI
Little Worms

SPAGHETTI
Little Strings

LINGUINE
Little Tongues

FETTUCCINE
Little Ribbons

TAGLIATELLE
Flat Ribbons

PAPPARDELLE
Gulp Down

BUCATINI
Little Holes

Measuring Less Than a Pound of Pasta

It's easy enough to measure out a pound of pasta, as most packages are sold in this quantity. But we've included some recipes, such as Spanish-Style Toasted Pasta with Shrimp (page 150), that call for less than 1 pound of pasta. Obviously, you can weigh out partial pounds of pasta using a scale, or you can judge by how full the box is, but we think it's easiest to measure shaped pasta using a dry measuring cup, and strand pasta by determining the diameter.

MEASURING SHORT PASTA

PASTA TYPE*	8 OUNCES	12 OUNCES
Elbow Macaroni and Small Shells	2 cups	3 cups
Orecchiette	2¼ cups	3⅓ cups
Penne, Ziti, and Campanelle	2½ cups	3¾ cups
Rigatoni, Fusilli, Medium Shells, and Wide Egg Noodles	3 cups	4½ cups
Farfalle	3¼ cups	4¾ cups

* These amounts do not apply to whole-wheat pasta.

MEASURING LONG PASTA

When 8 ounces of uncooked strand pasta are bunched together into a tight circle, the diameter measures about 1¼ inches. When 12 ounces of uncooked strand pasta are bunched together, the diameter measures about 1¾ inches.

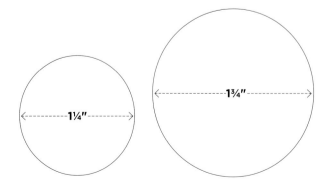

Roasting tomatoes on a wire rack with tomato paste and aromatics creates robust flavor for a sauce with briny clams.

Spaghetti with Clams and Roasted Tomatoes
SERVES 6

WHY THIS RECIPE WORKS Pasta with clams is an Italian classic that rests on the shoulders of simplicity: briny, succulent clams in a delicate but flavorful sauce that dresses perfectly cooked spaghetti. In spite of this simplicity, there are a couple of common pitfalls: The sauce can be bland and flavorless, and the clams are often overcooked and rubbery. We wanted a sauce that could stand up to and complement the brininess of the clams, as well as a foolproof method for cooking the clams. We started with a base of tomatoes, garlic, red pepper flakes, and wine. Though the tomatoes added some depth and a savory quality, we still found this version a bit bland and watery. Moreover, the clams were slightly overcooked by the time we added the pasta, a problem easily solved by pulling the clams out of the pot as they opened. To add more flavor and body to the sauce, we decided to roast the tomatoes in the oven before incorporating them into the sauce, which produced a thicker sauce with deeper flavor.

Still, the tomatoes leached some water into the sauce, and tasters wanted even more robust tomato flavor. Roasting the tomatoes on a wire rack allowed for better air circulation, concentrating the tomatoes' flavor beautifully. Tossing the tomatoes with a mixture of tomato paste, oil, and thyme and scattering whole smashed garlic cloves onto the rack with the tomatoes provided extra aromatic depth. A sprinkle of mint contributed a bright counterpoint to this simple dish.

    2 tablespoons tomato paste
    3 tablespoons extra-virgin olive oil, plus extra for serving
    2 teaspoons minced fresh thyme or ½ teaspoon dried
       Salt and pepper
    3 pounds ripe tomatoes, cored and halved
   12 cloves garlic, peeled (8 smashed, 4 minced)
    1 shallot, sliced thin
   ⅛ teaspoon red pepper flakes
   ½ cup dry white wine
    1 pound spaghetti or linguine
    4 pounds littleneck clams, scrubbed
   ⅓ cup chopped fresh mint or parsley

1. Adjust oven rack to middle position and heat oven to 475 degrees. Combine tomato paste, 1 tablespoon oil, thyme, ¼ teaspoon salt, and ¼ teaspoon pepper in large bowl. Add tomatoes and smashed garlic and gently toss to coat. Place 4-inch square of aluminum foil in center of wire rack set in rimmed baking sheet lined with aluminum foil. Place smashed garlic cloves on foil and arrange tomatoes, cut side down, around garlic. Roast until tomatoes are soft and skins are well charred, 45 to 55 minutes.

2. Heat remaining 2 tablespoons oil in Dutch oven over medium heat until shimmering. Add shallot, pepper flakes, and minced garlic and cook until fragrant, about 1 minute. Stir in wine and cook until almost completely evaporated, about 1 minute. Stir in roasted tomatoes and garlic and bring to boil. Add clams, cover, and cook, shaking pot occasionally, until clams open, 4 to 8 minutes. As clams open, remove them with slotted spoon and transfer to bowl. Discard any clams that refuse to open. (If desired, remove clams from shells.)

3. Meanwhile, bring 4 quarts water to boil in large pot. Add pasta and 1 tablespoon salt and cook, stirring often, until al dente. Reserve ½ cup cooking water, then drain pasta and add to pot with sauce. Add mint and toss to combine. Season with salt and pepper to taste and adjust consistency with reserved cooking water as needed. Transfer pasta to serving bowl, top with clams, and drizzle with extra oil. Serve.

Linguine ai Frutti di Mare
SERVES 6

WHY THIS RECIPE WORKS Traditionally, Italian pasta *ai frutti di mare* incorporates whatever is available in the daily catch into a dish resplendent with flavors of the sea—from briny mollusks to succulent shellfish. We wanted a pasta dish with uncomplicated, clean elements that highlighted and complemented the delicate flavor of the seafood. We chose tomatoes, chili flakes, and saffron—a classic combination—and fortified the sauce with clam juice. For a smooth sauce that nicely coated the pasta and seafood, we found that canned whole tomatoes, pulsed in a food processor, worked best; tasters appreciated the texture of this sauce as opposed to one made with canned crushed tomatoes. We also added tomato paste and anchovies for savory depth. Adding the different types of seafood in stages ensured that each element was cooked perfectly. A sprinkle of toasted lemon-chili bread crumbs served as a perfect aromatic accompaniment to this satisfying seafood dish.

To make sure each type of seafood in our "fruit of the sea" pasta is perfectly cooked, we add them to the pot in stages.

3 tablespoons extra-virgin olive oil, plus extra for serving
8 ounces large shrimp (26 to 30 per pound), peeled and deveined, shells reserved
1 cup dry white wine
1 (28-ounce) can whole peeled tomatoes, drained
2 shallots, sliced thin
6 garlic cloves, sliced thin
2 tablespoons tomato paste
1 anchovy fillet, rinsed and minced
⅛ teaspoon red pepper flakes
⅛ teaspoon saffron threads, crumbled
1 (8-ounce) bottle clam juice
1 pound linguine
8 ounces mussels, scrubbed and debearded
8 ounces large sea scallops, tendons removed
8 ounces squid, bodies sliced crosswise into ¼-inch-thick rings, tentacles halved
⅓ cup minced fresh parsley
1 cup Lemon-Chili Bread Crumbs (page 144)

1. Heat 1 tablespoon oil in Dutch oven over medium heat until shimmering. Add shrimp shells and cook, stirring frequently, until beginning to turn spotty brown and pot starts to brown, 2 to 4 minutes. Add wine and simmer, stirring occasionally, for 5 minutes. Strain mixture through fine-mesh strainer into bowl, pressing on solids to extract as much liquid as possible; discard solids.

2. Pulse tomatoes in food processor until finely ground, about 10 pulses. Heat remaining 2 tablespoons oil in now-empty pot over medium heat until shimmering. Add shallots and cook until softened and lightly browned, 2 to 3 minutes. Stir in garlic, tomato paste, anchovy, pepper flakes, and saffron and cook until fragrant, about 1 minute. Stir in wine mixture, scraping up any browned bits, and cook until nearly evaporated, about 30 seconds. Stir in tomatoes and clam juice, bring to simmer, and cook, stirring occasionally, until thickened and flavors meld, about 20 minutes.

3. Add mussels, bring to boil, cover, and cook, shaking pot occasionally, until mussels open, 3 to 6 minutes. As mussels open, remove them with slotted spoon and transfer to bowl. Discard any mussels that refuse to open.

4. Reduce sauce to simmer, gently stir in scallops, and cook for 2 minutes. Gently stir in shrimp and cook until just opaque throughout, about 2 minutes. Off heat, stir in squid, cover, and let sit until just opaque and tender, 1 to 2 minutes.

5. Meanwhile, bring 4 quarts water to boil in large pot. Add pasta and 1 tablespoon salt and cook, stirring often, until al dente. Reserve ½ cup cooking water, then drain pasta and add to pot with sauce. Add mussels and parsley and toss to combine. Season with salt and pepper to taste and adjust consistency with reserved cooking water as needed. Serve, sprinkling individual portions with bread crumbs and drizzling with extra oil.

Rigatoni with Warm-Spiced Beef Ragu
SERVES 6

WHY THIS RECIPE WORKS Rustic Italian-style ragu is all about low-and-slow simmering—it relies on lots of time but minimal heat to turn the meat, cooked with tomatoes and red wine, fall-apart tender. For this recipe, we liked beef short ribs, which turned tender and moist during braising; they gave the sauce a deep, savory flavor. Tomato sauce and crushed tomatoes made a sauce that was too smooth; although canned diced tomatoes created a chunkier sauce, tasters preferred the rustic texture and appearance of chopped whole canned tomatoes. Cinnamon and cloves, while unexpected, offered a subtle warmth. We also created a Greek-style version using lamb, oregano, and mint in place of beef, thyme, and parsley, increasing the amount of herbs and spices to balance the robust lamb flavor. This recipe will also work with flanken-style short ribs.

1½ pounds bone-in English-style short ribs, trimmed
Salt and pepper
1 tablespoon extra-virgin olive oil
1 onion, chopped fine
3 garlic cloves, minced
1 teaspoon minced fresh thyme or ¼ teaspoon dried
½ teaspoon ground cinnamon
Pinch ground cloves
½ cup dry red wine
1 (28-ounce) can whole peeled tomatoes, drained with juice reserved, chopped fine
1 pound rigatoni
2 tablespoons minced fresh parsley
Grated Parmesan cheese

1. Pat ribs dry with paper towels and season with salt and pepper. Heat oil in 12-inch skillet over medium-high heat until just smoking. Brown ribs on all sides, 8 to 10 minutes; transfer to plate.

2. Pour off all but 1 teaspoon fat from skillet, add onion, and cook over medium heat until softened, about 5 minutes. Stir in garlic, thyme, cinnamon, and cloves and cook until fragrant, about 30 seconds. Stir in wine, scraping up any browned bits, and simmer until nearly evaporated, about 2 minutes.

3. Stir in tomatoes and reserved juice. Nestle ribs into sauce along with any accumulated juices and bring to simmer. Reduce heat to low, cover, and simmer gently, turning ribs occasionally, until meat is very tender and falling off bones, about 2 hours.

Cinnamon and cloves add unexpected warmth to meaty beef short ribs in our modern Italian ragu.

4. Transfer ribs to cutting board, let cool slightly, then shred meat into bite-size pieces using 2 forks; discard excess fat and bones. Using wide, shallow spoon, skim excess fat from surface of sauce. Stir shredded meat and any accumulated juices into sauce and bring to simmer over medium heat. Season with salt and pepper to taste.

5. Meanwhile, bring 4 quarts water to boil in large pot. Add pasta and 1 tablespoon salt and cook, stirring often, until al dente. Reserve ½ cup cooking water, then drain pasta and return it to pot. Add sauce and parsley and toss to combine. Season with salt and pepper to taste and adjust consistency with reserved cooking water as needed. Serve with Parmesan.

VARIATION
Rigatoni with Minted Lamb Ragu
Substitute 1½ pounds bone-in lamb shoulder chops, trimmed, for short ribs, 1 teaspoon minced fresh oregano for thyme, and 3 tablespoons minced fresh mint for parsley. Increase ground cinnamon to ¾ teaspoon and ground cloves to ⅛ teaspoon.

All About Canned Tomatoes

Since canned tomatoes are processed at the height of freshness, they deliver more flavor than off-season fresh tomatoes. But with all the options lining supermarket shelves, it's not always clear what you should buy. We tested a variety of canned tomato products to determine the best uses for each.

WHOLE TOMATOES

Whole tomatoes are peeled tomatoes packed in either their own juice or puree. They are best when fresh tomato flavor is a must. Whole tomatoes are quite soft and break down quickly when cooked. In taste tests, we preferred Muir Glen for their lively, fresh flavor.

DICED TOMATOES

Diced tomatoes are peeled, machine-diced, and packed in either their own juice or puree. Many brands contain calcium chloride, a firming agent that helps the chunks maintain their shape. Diced tomatoes are best for rustic tomato sauces with a chunky texture, and in long-cooked stews and soups in which you want the tomatoes to hold their shape. We favor diced tomatoes packed in juice because they have a fresher flavor than those packed in puree; our favorite is Hunt's.

CRUSHED TOMATOES

Crushed tomatoes are whole tomatoes ground very finely, then enriched with tomato puree. They work well in smoother sauces, and their thicker consistency makes them ideal when you want to make a sauce quickly. We like Tuttorosso, but you can also make your own by crushing canned diced tomatoes in a food processor.

TOMATO PUREE

Tomato puree is made from cooked tomatoes that have been strained to remove their seeds and skins. Tomato puree works well in long-simmered, smooth, thick sauces with a deep, hearty flavor. Our favorite brand is Muir Glen Organic.

TOMATO PASTE

Tomato paste is tomato puree that has been cooked to remove almost all moisture. Because it's naturally full of glutamates, tomato paste brings out subtle depths and savory notes. We use it in a variety of recipes, including both long-simmered sauces and quicker-cooking dishes, to lend a deeper, well-rounded tomato flavor and color. Our preferred brand is Goya.

We toss the orzo in our Greek-inspired salads with olive oil and cool it on a baking sheet to prevent it from clumping.

Orzo Salad with Arugula and Sun-Dried Tomatoes

SERVES 4 to 6 VEG

WHY THIS RECIPE WORKS Orzo, a form of short-cut pasta shaped like a large grain of rice, is particularly popular in Greece and serves as a perfect vehicle for warm or cold salads. Its small shape provides just enough bulk to make a satisfying salad that can act as a foil to any number of other dishes, from spiced grilled meats to simply prepared fish and seafood. We wanted our orzo salad to be bursting with flavors characteristic of Greek cuisine. After cooking and draining the pasta, we transferred the still-warm orzo to a rimmed baking sheet to cool and tossed it with some olive oil to prevent clumping. We then dressed the orzo with a simple vinaigrette made with balsamic vinegar and a bit of garlic; the subtle dressing added flavor but still allowed the rest of the ingredients to shine through. To brighten the dish, we used plenty of fresh arugula along with flavor-packed Parmesan, sweet and tangy sun-dried tomatoes, briny olives, aromatic basil, and toasted pine nuts for a slight nutty crunch.

1¼ cups orzo

Salt and pepper

¼ cup extra-virgin olive oil, plus extra for serving

3 tablespoons balsamic vinegar

2 garlic cloves, minced

2 ounces (2 cups) baby arugula, chopped

1 ounce Parmesan cheese, grated (½ cup)

½ cup oil-packed sun-dried tomatoes, minced

½ cup pitted kalamata olives, halved

½ cup chopped fresh basil

¼ cup pine nuts, toasted

1. Bring 2 quarts water to boil in large pot. Add orzo and 1½ teaspoons salt and cook, stirring often, until al dente. Drain orzo and transfer to rimmed baking sheet. Toss with 1 tablespoon oil and let cool completely, about 15 minutes.

2. Whisk remaining 3 tablespoons oil, vinegar, garlic, ½ teaspoon salt, and ½ teaspoon pepper together in large bowl. Add arugula, Parmesan, tomatoes, olives, basil, pine nuts, and orzo and gently toss to combine. Season with salt and pepper to taste. Let salad sit until flavors meld, about 30 minutes. Serve, drizzled with extra oil. (Salad can be refrigerated for up to 2 days.)

VARIATIONS

Orzo Salad with Pecorino, Radicchio, and Chickpeas VEG

Omit arugula, tomatoes, olives, and pine nuts. Substitute ½ cup grated Pecorino Romano for Parmesan. Add ½ small head radicchio, cored and chopped fine, and 1 (15-ounce) can chickpeas, rinsed, to dressing with arugula.

Orzo Salad with Radishes, Capers, and Anchovies

Omit tomatoes and olives. Substitute 3 tablespoons lemon juice for balsamic vinegar and ½ cup chopped fresh parsley for basil. Whisk 1 minced anchovy fillet into dressing. Add 4 trimmed and thinly sliced radishes and ¼ cup capers to dressing with arugula.

Toasted Orzo with Fennel, Orange, and Olives

SERVES 6 to 8 VEG

WHY THIS RECIPE WORKS Most versions of orzo pilaf are bland at best, little more than a generic starch used to bulk up a meal. We wanted a flavorful orzo pilaf that would hold its own when paired with any main dish. Toasting the orzo until golden brown gave it great flavor, and we turned to modern Greek flavors to round out the pilaf: fennel and onion for an aromatic backbone, fennel seeds to fortify the flavor of the fresh fennel, and a judicious amount of orange zest for a fragrant citrus note. Tasters

liked a combination of white wine and broth as the cooking liquid. Olives made our pilaf more substantial and added some contrasting texture and flavor. Finally, we stirred in some finely grated Parmesan to give the pilaf a creamy texture, as well as a pinch of nutmeg for subtle, complementary warmth.

2 tablespoons extra-virgin olive oil

1 fennel bulb, stalks discarded, bulb halved, cored, and chopped fine

1 onion, chopped fine

Salt and pepper

2 garlic cloves, minced

1 teaspoon grated orange zest

¾ teaspoon fennel seeds

Pinch red pepper flakes

2⅔ cups orzo

2 cups chicken or vegetable broth

1½ cups water

¾ cup dry white wine

½ cup pitted kalamata olives, chopped

1½ ounces Parmesan cheese, grated (¾ cup)

Pinch ground nutmeg

1. Heat oil in 12-inch nonstick skillet over medium heat until shimmering. Add fennel, onion, and ¾ teaspoon salt and cook until softened and lightly browned, 5 to 7 minutes. Stir in garlic, orange zest, fennel seeds, and pepper flakes and cook until fragrant, about 30 seconds. Add orzo and cook, stirring frequently, until orzo is coated with oil and lightly browned, about 5 minutes.

2. Stir in broth, water, and wine and bring to boil. Cook, stirring occasionally, until all liquid has been absorbed and orzo is tender, 10 to 15 minutes. Stir in olives, Parmesan, and nutmeg and season with salt and pepper to taste. Serve.

Orzo with Shrimp, Feta, and Lemon

SERVES 4

WHY THIS RECIPE WORKS In Greece, orzo is used as a base for all types of proteins, so we decided to create a fresh and light shrimp and orzo dish. We tossed the shrimp with salt, pepper, and lemon zest to infuse them with clean citrus flavor. Garlic and onion provided a simple but aromatic base, and toasting the orzo deepened its flavor. Toasting also helped to coat each grain with oil, ensuring that the grains of orzo remained separate and distinct. Chicken broth made for a more savory profile that tasters appreciated. We allowed the shrimp to cook through gently by nestling them into the cooked orzo; this also

For a shrimp skillet dinner with big flavor, we toast orzo with aromatics to give it nutty, savory depth.

1. Combine lemon zest, ½ teaspoon salt, and ½ teaspoon pepper in medium bowl. Add shrimp, toss to coat, and refrigerate until ready to use.

2. Heat 1 tablespoon oil in 12-inch nonstick skillet over medium-high heat until just smoking. Add onion and cook until softened, about 5 minutes. Stir in garlic and cook until fragrant, about 30 seconds. Add orzo and cook, stirring frequently, until orzo is coated with oil and lightly browned, about 5 minutes. Stir in broth and water and bring to boil. Cook, stirring occasionally, until orzo is al dente, about 6 minutes. Stir in olives, ¼ cup feta, and lemon juice. Season with salt and pepper to taste.

3. Reduce heat to medium-low, nestle shrimp into orzo, cover, and cook until shrimp are opaque throughout, about 5 minutes. Sprinkle with parsley and remaining ¼ cup feta and drizzle with extra oil. Serve.

Orzo with Greek Sausage and Spiced Yogurt

SERVES 4 to 6

WHY THIS RECIPE WORKS We wanted a Greek-inspired orzo dish incorporating warm spices that would be perfect as a side or as a quick, easy meal. We started by rendering a small amount of *loukaniko*—a popular Greek sausage composed of lamb and pork and flavored with orange and fennel—and building a broth base (chicken broth added savory depth and wine offered a hint of tartness) with vegetables and warm spices. Cooking the orzo in this flavorful mixture infused each grain with bold flavor. Since pairing brightness and acidity with warm, rich flavors is common practice in Greek cuisine, we decided to incorporate Greek yogurt and stirred in a small amount at the end (off the heat so that the yogurt wouldn't curdle). This version was passable, but the orzo was a bit overcooked and soft, and tasters wanted greater contrast between the savory and bright elements in the dish. To mitigate the risk of overcooking the orzo, we toasted it before simmering to cook off some of the exterior starch. This had the added benefit of lending a nutty aroma to the finished product. We also decreased the amount of cooking liquid. This version was improved, but not as creamy as we had hoped. Stirring the orzo more frequently helped to distribute the starches and resulted in a pleasantly creamy final dish. To balance the warm flavors, we stirred in lemon zest and mint for fresher, brighter notes. Tasters loved the contrasting yet complementary balance of brightness, acidity, and warmth in this convenient, hearty dish. Loukaniko sausage can be found at Greek markets as well as in the international food aisle of many supermarkets; if you cannot find it, substitute kielbasa or Italian sausage. For more information on loukaniko, see page 318.

allowed us to keep the cooking in a single pan. Kalamata olives were a perfect briny counterpoint to the toasty orzo and lemony shrimp, and a judicious amount of feta cheese gave the dish some tang and just enough richness. A sprinkling of parsley freshened everything up.

1 tablespoon grated lemon zest plus 1 tablespoon juice
  Salt and pepper
1½ pounds extra-large shrimp (21 to 25 per pound), peeled and deveined
1 tablespoon extra-virgin olive oil, plus extra for serving
1 onion, chopped fine
2 garlic cloves, minced
2 cups orzo
2 cups chicken broth
2 cups water
½ cup pitted kalamata olives, chopped coarse
2 ounces feta cheese, crumbled (½ cup)
2 tablespoons chopped fresh parsley

1½ cups orzo
1 tablespoon extra-virgin olive oil
4 ounces loukaniko sausage, chopped fine
1 onion, chopped fine
1 red bell pepper, stemmed, seeded, and chopped fine
1 tablespoon tomato paste
2 garlic cloves, minced
1 teaspoon paprika
¼ teaspoon ground cinnamon
⅛ teaspoon red pepper flakes
½ cup dry white wine
2½ cups chicken broth
¼ cup plain whole-milk Greek yogurt
1½ teaspoons grated lemon zest
Salt and pepper
¼ cup chopped fresh mint

1. Toast orzo in 12-inch skillet over medium-high heat until lightly browned, 3 to 5 minutes; transfer to bowl. Heat oil in now-empty skillet over medium heat until shimmering. Add sausage and cook until browned and fat is rendered, 4 to 6 minutes.

2. Stir in onion and bell pepper and cook until softened, 5 to 7 minutes. Stir in tomato paste, garlic, paprika, cinnamon, and pepper flakes and cook until fragrant, about 1 minute. Stir in wine, scraping up any browned bits. Stir in broth and orzo and bring to simmer. Reduce heat to low, cover, and simmer gently until most of liquid is absorbed, about 10 minutes, stirring once halfway through simmering.

3. Uncover and continue to cook, stirring occasionally, until orzo is al dente and creamy, about 4 minutes. Off heat, stir in yogurt and lemon zest. Season with salt and pepper to taste and adjust consistency with hot water as needed. Sprinkle with mint and serve.

Baked Orzo with Eggplant and Tomatoes
SERVES 6 VEG

WHY THIS RECIPE WORKS We wanted to put a modern spin on a classic Greek *manestra*—a simple, hearty baked dish of orzo, tomatoes, and oregano, sometimes adorned with a little cheese and a splash of olive oil. To make our interpretation of this dish into a filling meal, we decided to include a few additional components. Tasters particularly liked the addition of eggplant; pretreating it with salt in a microwave rid the eggplant of excess moisture and allowed us to sauté it using a minimal amount of oil. Tomato paste, garlic, and anchovies gave the dish a rich umami core. Toasting the orzo added a nutty dimension. We found that the dish dried out in the oven unless we topped it

Topping our Greek vegetable casserole with slices of fresh tomato keeps the orzo beneath from drying out.

with an unhealthy amount of cheese; instead, we shingled tomato slices on top to keep the orzo moist while the casserole cooked through. As a final homage to traditional manestra, we topped the dish with feta, oregano, and olive oil.

1 pound eggplant, cut into ½-inch pieces
Salt and pepper
2 cups orzo
3 tablespoons extra-virgin olive oil, plus extra for serving
1 onion, chopped fine
3 garlic cloves, minced
4 teaspoons minced fresh oregano or 1 teaspoon dried
2 teaspoons tomato paste
2 anchovy fillets, rinsed, patted dry, and minced
1¼ cups chicken or vegetable broth
1¼ cups water
1 ounce Parmesan cheese, grated (½ cup)
2 tablespoons capers, rinsed and minced
4 tomatoes, cored and sliced ¼ inch thick
3 ounces feta cheese, crumbled (¾ cup)

Capers

Capers are sun-dried pickled flower buds from the spiny shrub *Capparis spinosa*, and their unique flavor is most commonly found in French and Italian cooking. Capers pack an acidic punch with a lingering sweetness that is both floral and pungent. Capers range in size from tiny nonpareils to large caperberries, and they develop flavor from being cured, either in a salty brine (sometimes with vinegar) or packed in salt. Brined capers are the most commonly available, and we've found that we prefer the smaller nonpareil capers for their compact size and slight crunch.

Toasting couscous before hydrating it with a combination of broth and water delivers separate, flavorful grains.

1. Adjust oven rack to upper-middle position and heat oven to 400 degrees. Line large plate with double layer of coffee filters and spray with vegetable oil spray. Toss eggplant with ½ teaspoon salt and spread evenly on coffee filters. Microwave eggplant, uncovered, until dry to touch and slightly shriveled, 7 to 10 minutes, tossing halfway through microwaving.

2. Toast orzo in 12-inch nonstick skillet over medium-high heat until lightly browned, 3 to 5 minutes; transfer to bowl. Heat 1 tablespoon oil in now-empty skillet over medium-high heat until shimmering. Add eggplant and cook, stirring occasionally, until well browned, 5 to 7 minutes; transfer to separate bowl.

3. Heat remaining 2 tablespoons oil in again-empty skillet over medium heat until shimmering. Add onion and cook until softened and lightly browned, 5 to 7 minutes. Stir in garlic, 1 tablespoon oregano, tomato paste, and anchovies and cook until fragrant, about 30 seconds. Off heat, stir in orzo, eggplant, broth, water, Parmesan, capers, and ¼ teaspoon pepper. Transfer to greased 13 by 9-inch baking dish and spread into even layer.

4. Shingle tomatoes attractively over top, then sprinkle with ¼ teaspoon salt. Bake until all liquid has been absorbed and orzo is tender, 30 to 35 minutes. Let cool for 5 minutes. Sprinkle feta and remaining 1 teaspoon oregano over tomatoes and drizzle with extra oil. Serve.

Simple Couscous
SERVES 6 `FAST` `VEG`

WHY THIS RECIPE WORKS Couscous is one of the fastest and easiest side dishes to prepare. A staple in Morocco and other North African countries, it is traditionally served under stews and braises to soak up the flavorful sauce. But because it often plays sidekick, the grain is too often left bland and unexciting. We knew it had the potential to be a quick and tasty dish, and we were determined to develop a classic version for saucy dishes as well as a handful of flavor-packed variations that would make convenient stand-alone sides. We found that toasting the couscous grains in olive oil before adding liquid deepened their flavor and helped them cook up light and separate. And to bump up the flavor even further, we replaced half of the cooking water with broth. After just 7 minutes of steeping, the couscous was fluffy, tender, and flavorful enough to stand on its own while also ready to accompany any sauce with which it was paired. For our dressed-up variations, dried fruit, nuts, and citrus juice added textural interest and sweet, bright notes.

2 tablespoons extra-virgin olive oil
2 cups couscous
1 cup water
1 cup chicken or vegetable broth
  Salt and pepper

Heat oil in medium saucepan over medium-high heat until shimmering. Add couscous and cook, stirring frequently, until grains are just beginning to brown, 3 to 5 minutes. Stir in water, broth, and 1 teaspoon salt. Cover, remove saucepan from heat, and let sit until couscous is tender, about 7 minutes. Gently fluff couscous with fork and season with pepper to taste. Serve.

Simple Couscous with Dates and Pistachios

FAST **VEG**

Increase oil to 3 tablespoons. Add ½ cup chopped pitted dates, 1 tablespoon grated fresh ginger, and ½ teaspoon ground cardamom to saucepan with couscous. Increase water to 1¼ cups. Before serving, stir in ¾ cup coarsely chopped toasted pistachios, 3 tablespoons minced fresh cilantro, and 2 teaspoons lemon juice.

Simple Couscous with Carrots, Raisins, and Pine Nuts **FAST** **VEG**

Increase oil to 3 tablespoons. Before adding couscous to saucepan, add 2 peeled and grated carrots and ½ teaspoon ground cinnamon and cook until softened, about 2 minutes. Add ½ cup raisins to saucepan with couscous and increase water to 1¼ cups. Before serving, stir in ⅓ cup toasted pine nuts, 3 tablespoons minced fresh cilantro, ½ teaspoon grated orange zest, and 1 tablespoon orange juice.

Spiced Vegetable Couscous

SERVES 6 **VEG**

WHY THIS RECIPE WORKS This easy vegetable couscous dish is inspired by aromatic North African flavors. For our vegetables, we chose a colorful combination of cauliflower, zucchini, and red bell pepper. To encourage deep caramelization on our cauliflower, we cut it into small, even pieces. We started the cauliflower in a cold pan, which ensured that it cooked through before developing a golden exterior. We then quickly sautéed zucchini and bell pepper with garlic, lemon zest, and *ras el hanout*—a flavorful North African spice blend. Marjoram, added at the end, gave a hit of minty freshness. We prefer to use our homemade Ras el Hanout (page 316), but you can substitute store-bought ras el hanout if you wish, though flavor and spiciness can vary greatly by brand.

    1 head cauliflower (2 pounds), cored and cut into
      1-inch florets
    6 tablespoons extra-virgin olive oil, plus extra for serving
      Salt and pepper
 1½ cups couscous
    1 zucchini, cut into ½-inch pieces
    1 red bell pepper, stemmed, seeded, and cut into
      ½-inch pieces
    4 garlic cloves, minced
    2 teaspoons ras el hanout
    1 teaspoon grated lemon zest, plus lemon wedges
      for serving
 1¾ cups chicken or vegetable broth
    1 tablespoon minced fresh marjoram

To achieve perfectly tender, nicely browned cauliflower, we cut the florets small and start them cooking in a cold skillet.

1. Toss cauliflower with 2 tablespoons oil, ¾ teaspoon salt, and ½ teaspoon pepper in 12-inch nonstick skillet. Cover and cook over medium-high heat until florets start to brown and edges just start to become translucent (do not lift lid), about 5 minutes.

2. Remove lid and continue to cook, stirring every 2 minutes, until florets turn golden brown in several spots, about 10 minutes. Transfer to bowl and wipe skillet clean with paper towels.

3. Heat 2 tablespoons oil in now-empty skillet over medium-high heat until shimmering. Add couscous and cook, stirring frequently, until grains are just beginning to brown, 3 to 5 minutes. Transfer to separate bowl and wipe skillet clean with paper towels.

4. Heat remaining 2 tablespoons oil in again-empty skillet over medium-high heat until just smoking. Add zucchini, bell pepper, and ½ teaspoon salt and cook until tender, 6 to 8 minutes. Stir in garlic, ras el hanout, and lemon zest and cook until fragrant, about 30 seconds. Stir in broth and bring to simmer.

5. Stir in couscous. Cover, remove skillet from heat, and let sit until couscous is tender, about 7 minutes. Add cauliflower and marjoram to couscous and gently fluff with fork to combine. Season with salt and pepper to taste and drizzle with extra oil. Serve with lemon wedges.

Moroccan-Style Couscous with Chickpeas

SERVES 6 FAST VEG

WHY THIS RECIPE WORKS We tried a few different approaches for our Moroccan-inspired couscous with chickpeas before coming up with a basic game plan: Toast the couscous to maximize its nutty flavor, sauté the vegetables, toast the spices, add chickpeas, simmer, and finally add the couscous, which we needed only to hydrate with boiling water. We tasted our way through a long list of vegetables and decided in the end to limit our selection to just carrots, onions, and peas, each of which brought a distinctive flavor, texture, and color to the dish. When it came to spices, we narrowed down our choices to classic Moroccan spices: coriander, ground ginger, and a dash of ground anise, each of which supported the vegetables' flavor well. Three cloves of garlic, chicken or vegetable broth, and a hefty amount of herbs stirred in at the end rounded out the dish's flavors.

¼ cup extra-virgin olive oil, plus extra for serving
1½ cups couscous
2 carrots, peeled and chopped fine
1 onion, chopped fine
Salt and pepper
3 garlic cloves, minced
1 teaspoon ground coriander
1 teaspoon ground ginger
¼ teaspoon ground anise seed
1¾ cups chicken or vegetable broth
1 (15-ounce) can chickpeas, rinsed
1½ cups frozen peas
½ cup chopped fresh parsley, cilantro, and/or mint
Lemon wedges

1. Heat 2 tablespoons oil in 12-inch skillet over medium-high heat until shimmering. Add couscous and cook, stirring frequently, until grains are just beginning to brown, 3 to 5 minutes. Transfer to bowl and wipe skillet clean with paper towels.

2. Heat remaining 2 tablespoons oil in now-empty skillet over medium heat until shimmering. Add carrots, onion, and 1 teaspoon salt and cook until softened and lightly browned, 5 to 7 minutes. Stir in garlic, coriander, ginger, and anise and cook until fragrant, about 30 seconds. Stir in broth and chickpeas and bring to simmer.

3. Stir in peas and couscous. Cover, remove skillet from heat, and let sit until couscous is tender, about 7 minutes. Add parsley to couscous and gently fluff with fork to combine. Season with salt and pepper to taste and drizzle with extra oil. Serve with lemon wedges.

Couscous with Turkish Sausage and Preserved Lemon

SERVES 6 FAST

WHY THIS RECIPE WORKS *Sujuk*, a Turkish dry-cured beef sausage, is boldly flavored with spices like cumin and sumac. We thought this robust sausage would pair perfectly with mild couscous. We started by toasting the couscous, which boosted its flavor and helped keep the granules distinct. Because the sujuk was so flavorful, we could forgo a laundry list of spices, choosing to use only a bit of floral ground cardamom. Preserved lemon, which offered an intense citrus flavor, added brightness to the dish, and golden raisins acted as a sweet counterpoint to the spicy sausage. Fluffing the couscous and stirring in fresh cilantro at the end kept the texture light and added freshness to this perfectly balanced dish. Sujuk sausage can be found at Turkish and Middle Eastern markets as well as in the international food aisle of many supermarkets; if you cannot find it, substitute Spanish-style chorizo. For more information on sujuk, see page 318. If you can't find preserved lemons, you can make your own (see page 252).

3 tablespoons extra-virgin olive oil
1½ cups couscous
4 ounces sujuk sausage, chopped fine
1 onion, chopped fine
2 carrots, peeled and chopped fine
Salt and pepper
¼ preserved lemon, pulp and white pith removed, rind rinsed and minced (1 tablespoon)
3 garlic cloves, minced
¼ teaspoon ground cardamom
1¾ cups vegetable broth
½ cup golden raisins
¼ cup chopped fresh cilantro

1. Heat 2 tablespoons oil in 12-inch skillet over medium-high heat until shimmering. Add couscous and cook, stirring frequently, until grains are just beginning to brown, 3 to 5 minutes. Transfer to bowl and wipe skillet clean with paper towels.

2. Heat remaining 1 tablespoon oil in now-empty skillet over medium heat until shimmering. Add sujuk, onion, carrots, ¼ teaspoon salt, and ¼ teaspoon pepper and cook until vegetables are softened and lightly browned, 6 to 8 minutes. Stir in preserved lemon, garlic, and cardamom and cook until fragrant, about 30 seconds. Stir in broth and bring to simmer.

3. Stir in raisins and couscous. Cover, remove skillet from heat, and let sit until couscous is tender, about 7 minutes. Add cilantro to couscous and gently fluff with fork to combine. Season with salt and pepper to taste. Serve.

Couscous with Lamb, Chickpeas, and Orange
SERVES 6

WHY THIS RECIPE WORKS We set out to develop a lively, Moroccan-inspired couscous dish that would be perfect in the cold winter months. We thought that lamb, dried fruit, and warm spices would match nicely, so we began by braising a small amount of lamb in a fragrant wine-based broth enhanced with ginger, coriander, and cinnamon. The lamb imparted a meaty, savory flavor without becoming the star of the dish. Once the lamb was done, we used the ultraflavorful cooking liquid to hydrate the couscous. Chickpeas made the dish more substantial. Raisins provided just the right amount of sweetness without overwhelming the other flavors. Still, we were missing more brightness and depth. Since cinnamon is often paired with orange, we thought that adding strips of aromatic orange zest would lend welcome brightness and dimension. Tasters loved this version and noted that the long braising time had rendered the orange peel completely softened and delicious. To add even more textural contrast, we stirred in toasted almonds. Altogether, this was a satisfying, hearty couscous dish fit for any table.

We braise lamb and chickpeas with wine and warm spices, then use the flavorful braising liquid to hydrate the couscous.

    3 tablespoons extra-virgin olive oil, plus extra for serving
 1½ cups couscous
    1 pound lamb shoulder chops (blade or round bone),
      1 to 1½ inches thick, trimmed and halved
      Salt and pepper
    1 onion, chopped fine
   10 (2-inch) strips orange zest (1 orange)
    1 teaspoon grated fresh ginger
    1 teaspoon ground coriander
   ¼ teaspoon ground cinnamon
   ⅛ teaspoon cayenne pepper
   ½ cup dry white wine
 2½ cups chicken broth
    1 (15-ounce) can chickpeas, rinsed
   ½ cup raisins
   ½ cup sliced almonds, toasted
   ⅓ cup minced fresh parsley

1. Adjust oven rack to lower-middle position and heat oven to 325 degrees. Heat 2 tablespoons oil in Dutch oven over medium-high heat until shimmering. Add couscous and cook, stirring frequently, until grains are just beginning to brown, 3 to 5 minutes. Transfer to bowl and wipe pot clean with paper towels.

2. Pat lamb dry with paper towels and season with salt and pepper. Heat remaining 1 tablespoon oil in now-empty pot over medium-high heat until just smoking. Brown lamb, about 4 minutes per side; transfer to plate.

3. Add onion to fat left in pot and cook over medium heat until softened, about 5 minutes. Stir in orange zest, ginger, coriander, cinnamon, cayenne, and ⅛ teaspoon pepper and cook until fragrant, about 30 seconds. Stir in wine, scraping up any browned bits. Stir in broth and chickpeas and bring to boil.

4. Nestle lamb into pot along with any accumulated juices. Cover, place pot in oven, and cook until fork slips easily in and out of lamb, about 1 hour.

5. Transfer lamb to cutting board, let cool slightly, then shred into bite-size pieces using 2 forks, discarding excess fat and bones. Strain cooking liquid through fine mesh strainer set over bowl. Return solids and 1½ cups cooking liquid to now-empty pot and bring to simmer over medium heat; discard remaining liquid.

6. Stir in couscous and raisins. Cover, remove pot from heat, and let sit until couscous is tender, about 7 minutes. Add shredded lamb, almonds, and parsley to couscous and gently fluff with fork to combine. Season with salt and pepper to taste and drizzle with extra oil. Serve.

Simple Pearl Couscous

SERVES 6 FAST VEG

WHY THIS RECIPE WORKS Pearl couscous, also known as Jerusalem couscous or Israeli couscous, has a chewy texture and toasty flavor that have cemented its popularity in eastern Mediterranean and North African cuisines. We wanted a foolproof method for cooking pearl couscous to serve as a simple side dish or as the base for flavorful salads. To give the pasta as much flavor as possible, we toasted the spheres in oil to bring out their nuttiness. Once they turned golden brown, we added a measured amount of water that the pearls soaked up during cooking. This absorption method helped produce more evenly cooked results than simply boiling the couscous like regular pasta. Plus, once covered, the pot required little attention. When the water was completely absorbed, the warm couscous could be simply tossed with extra-virgin olive oil and salt and pepper before serving or cooled and dressed up with a bold vinaigrette plus plenty of fresh add-ins. Do not substitute regular couscous in this dish, as it requires a different cooking method and will not work in this recipe. If you're making a salad, transfer the couscous to a rimmed baking sheet and let it cool completely, about 15 minutes.

Toasted pearl couscous becomes perfectly cooked using the absorption method and a measured amount of water.

2 cups pearl couscous
1 tablespoon extra-virgin olive oil
2½ cups water
½ teaspoon salt

Heat couscous and oil in medium saucepan over medium heat, stirring frequently, until about half of grains are golden brown, about 5 minutes. Stir in water and salt, increase heat to high, and bring to boil. Reduce heat to medium-low, cover, and simmer, stirring occasionally, until water is absorbed and couscous is tender, 9 to 12 minutes. Off heat, let couscous sit, covered, for 3 minutes. Serve.

VARIATIONS

Simple Pearl Couscous with Tomatoes, Olives, and Ricotta Salata

SERVES 6 VEG

Do not substitute regular couscous in this dish, as it requires a different cooking method and will not work in this recipe. Crumbled feta cheese can be substituted for the ricotta salata.

¼ cup extra-virgin olive oil
2 cups pearl couscous
2½ cups water
   Salt and pepper
3 tablespoons red wine vinegar
1 teaspoon Dijon mustard
12 ounces grape tomatoes, quartered
2 ounces (2 cups) baby spinach, sliced ¼ inch thick
1½ cups coarsely chopped fresh basil
3 ounces ricotta salata cheese, crumbled (¾ cup)
⅔ cup pitted kalamata olives, sliced
½ cup pine nuts, toasted
¼ cup minced fresh chives

1. Heat 1 tablespoon oil and couscous in medium saucepan over medium heat, stirring frequently, until about half of grains are golden brown, about 5 minutes. Stir in water and ½ teaspoon salt, increase heat to high, and bring to boil. Reduce heat to medium-low, cover, and simmer, stirring occasionally, until water is absorbed and couscous is tender, 9 to 12 minutes. Off heat, let couscous sit, covered, for 3 minutes. Transfer couscous to rimmed baking sheet and let cool completely, about 15 minutes.

2. Whisk vinegar, mustard, ⅛ teaspoon salt, and remaining 3 tablespoons oil together in large bowl. Add couscous, tomatoes, spinach, basil, ½ cup ricotta salata, olives, 6 tablespoons pine nuts, and chives and gently toss to combine. Season with salt and pepper to taste and transfer to serving bowl. Let sit for 5 minutes. Sprinkle with remaining ¼ cup ricotta salata and remaining 2 tablespoons pine nuts and serve.

Simple Pearl Couscous with Radishes and Watercress

SERVES 6 `VEG`

Do not substitute regular couscous in this dish, as it requires a different cooking method and will not work in this recipe.

¼ cup extra-virgin olive oil
2 cups pearl couscous
2½ cups water
   Salt and pepper
3 tablespoons sherry vinegar
1 teaspoon Dijon mustard
1 teaspoon smoked paprika
¼ teaspoon sugar
2 ounces (2 cups) watercress, torn into bite-size pieces
6 scallions, sliced thin
6 radishes, trimmed and cut into matchsticks
1½ cups coarsely chopped parsley
½ cup walnuts, toasted and chopped coarse
4 ounces goat cheese, crumbled (1 cup)

NOTES FROM THE TEST KITCHEN

Getting to Know Couscous

Couscous is a starch made from durum semolina, the high-protein wheat flour that is also used to make Italian pasta. However, while pasta is made with ground durum semolina that is mixed with water to form a dough, traditional Moroccan couscous is made by rubbing crushed durum semolina and water between the hands to form small granules. The couscous is then dried and, traditionally, cooked over a simmering stew in a steamer called a *couscoussier*. About the size of bread crumbs, the couscous found in most supermarkets is a precooked version that needs only a few minutes of steeping in hot liquid in order to be fully cooked. Pearl couscous, also known as Israeli couscous, is larger than traditional couscous (about the size of a caper) and, like Italian pasta, is made from durum semolina flour. However, it is toasted, rather than dried, which gives it its unique, nutty flavor.

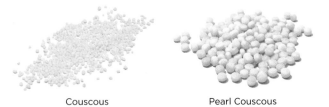

Couscous   Pearl Couscous

---

1. Heat 1 tablespoon oil and couscous in medium saucepan over medium heat, stirring frequently, until about half of grains are golden brown, about 5 minutes. Stir in water and ½ teaspoon salt, increase heat to high, and bring to boil. Reduce heat to medium-low, cover, and simmer, stirring occasionally, until water is absorbed and couscous is tender, 9 to 12 minutes. Off heat, let couscous sit, covered, for 3 minutes. Transfer couscous to rimmed baking sheet and let cool completely, about 15 minutes.

2. Whisk vinegar, mustard, paprika, sugar, ⅛ teaspoon salt, and remaining 3 tablespoons oil together in large bowl. Add couscous, watercress, scallions, radishes, parsley, and 6 tablespoons walnuts and gently toss to combine. Season with salt and pepper to taste and transfer to serving bowl. Let sit for 5 minutes. Sprinkle with goat cheese and remaining 2 tablespoons walnuts and serve.

Simple Pearl Couscous with Peas, Feta, and Pickled Shallots

SERVES 6 `VEG`

Do not substitute regular couscous in this dish, as it requires a different cooking method and will not work in this recipe. For efficiency, let the shallots pickle while you prepare the remaining ingredients.

¼ cup extra-virgin olive oil
2 cups pearl couscous
2½ cups water
   Salt and pepper
⅓ cup red wine vinegar
2 tablespoons sugar
2 shallots, sliced thin
3 tablespoons lemon juice
1 teaspoon Dijon mustard
⅛ teaspoon red pepper flakes
4 ounces (4 cups) baby arugula, coarsely chopped
1 cup fresh mint leaves, torn
½ cup frozen peas, thawed
½ cup shelled pistachios, toasted and chopped
3 ounces feta cheese, crumbled (¾ cup)

1. Heat 1 tablespoon oil and couscous in medium saucepan over medium heat, stirring frequently, until about half of grains are golden brown, about 5 minutes. Stir in water and ½ teaspoon salt, increase heat to high, and bring to boil. Reduce heat to medium-low, cover, and simmer, stirring occasionally, until water is absorbed and couscous is tender, 9 to 12 minutes. Off heat, let couscous sit, covered, for 3 minutes. Transfer couscous to rimmed baking sheet and let cool completely, about 15 minutes.

2. Meanwhile, bring vinegar, sugar, and pinch salt to simmer in small saucepan over medium-high heat, stirring occasionally, until sugar dissolves. Add shallots and stir to combine. Remove from heat, cover, and let cool completely, about 30 minutes. Drain and discard liquid.

3. Whisk remaining 3 tablespoons oil, lemon juice, mustard, pepper flakes, and ⅛ teaspoon salt together in large bowl. Add couscous, arugula, mint, peas, 6 tablespoons pistachios, ½ cup feta, and shallots and gently toss to combine. Season with salt and pepper to taste and transfer to serving bowl. Let sit for 5 minutes. Sprinkle with remaining ¼ cup feta and remaining 2 tablespoons pistachios and serve.

Hearty Pearl Couscous with Eggplant, Spinach, and Beans

SERVES 6 `VEG`

WHY THIS RECIPE WORKS In this simple recipe we used pearl couscous to create a hearty dish with great visual appeal. A superflavorful spice blend made with zesty sumac, nutty-sweet fenugreek, and floral cardamom gave the dish an Israeli-inspired identity. We tossed eggplant with a teaspoon of the blend before microwaving, which bloomed the spices' flavors and quickly cooked off the eggplant's excess moisture, bypassing the need to salt and drain the eggplant. We then seared the eggplant to develop savory browning before building an aromatic broth base in which to cook our couscous. Adding beans and baby spinach made for a more substantial dish. Do not substitute regular couscous in this dish, as it requires a different cooking method and will not work in this recipe.

1 teaspoon ground sumac
1 teaspoon ground fenugreek
  Salt and pepper
¼ teaspoon ground cardamom
1 pound eggplant, cut into ½-inch pieces
1½ cups pearl couscous
5 tablespoons extra-virgin olive oil, plus extra for serving
1 onion, chopped
3 garlic cloves, minced
1 tablespoon tomato paste
2 cups chicken or vegetable broth
1 (15-ounce) can great Northern beans, rinsed
3 ounces (3 cups) baby spinach

1. Combine sumac, fenugreek, ½ teaspoon salt, ½ teaspoon pepper, and cardamom in small bowl. Line large plate with double layer of coffee filters and spray with vegetable oil spray. Toss eggplant with ½ teaspoon spice mixture and spread evenly

Microwaving and sautéing eggplant with Israeli spices adds flavor and keeps it from watering down our hearty couscous.

on coffee filters. Microwave eggplant, uncovered, until dry to touch and slightly shriveled, 7 to 10 minutes, tossing halfway through microwaving.

2. Heat couscous and 2 tablespoons oil in 12-inch nonstick skillet over medium heat, stirring frequently, until about half of grains are golden brown, about 5 minutes. Transfer to bowl and wipe skillet clean with paper towels.

3. Toss eggplant with 1 teaspoon spice mixture. Heat 1 tablespoon oil in now-empty skillet over medium-high heat until shimmering. Add eggplant and cook, stirring occasionally, until well browned, 5 to 7 minutes. Transfer to separate bowl.

4. Heat remaining 2 tablespoons oil in again-empty skillet over medium heat until shimmering. Add onion and cook until softened and lightly browned, 5 to 7 minutes. Stir in garlic, tomato paste, and remaining spice mixture and cook until fragrant, about 1 minute.

5. Stir in broth, beans, and couscous and bring to simmer. Reduce heat to medium-low, cover, and simmer, stirring occasionally, until broth is absorbed and couscous is tender, 9 to 12 minutes. Off heat, stir in spinach and eggplant, cover, and let sit for 3 minutes. Season with salt and pepper to taste and drizzle with extra oil. Serve.

■ FAST (less than 45 minutes start to finish)   ▦ VEGETARIAN
Photos (clockwise from top left): Turkish Pinto Bean Salad with Tomatoes, Eggs, and Parsley; Falafel; Chickpea Salad with Fennel and Arugula; Moroccan Braised White Beans with Lamb

Small *lentilles du Puy* keep their shape and texture during cooking, making them a good base for this simple side dish.

French Lentils with Carrots and Parsley

SERVES 4 to 6   VEG

WHY THIS RECIPE WORKS Smaller and firmer than the more common brown and green varieties, French lentils, or *lentilles du Puy*, are a favorite in the Mediterranean thanks to their rich, complex flavor and tender texture. For a simple side dish that would highlight their sweet, earthy flavors, we took inspiration from their namesake and looked to France, slowly cooking the lentils with carrots, onion, and celery (a classic French combination called a *mirepoix*). We found that soaking the lentils before cooking wasn't necessary, since they held their shape nicely through cooking. Garlic and thyme added aromatic flavors that complemented the lentils. Using water rather than broth let the other flavors come through. Lentilles du Puy, also called French green lentils, are our first choice for this recipe, but brown, black, or regular green lentils are fine, too (note that cooking times will vary depending on the type used).

2 carrots, peeled and chopped fine
1 onion, chopped fine
1 celery rib, chopped fine

2 tablespoons extra-virgin olive oil
  Salt and pepper
2 garlic cloves, minced
1 teaspoon minced fresh thyme or ¼ teaspoon dried
2½ cups water
1 cup lentilles du Puy, picked over and rinsed
2 tablespoons minced fresh parsley
2 teaspoons lemon juice

1. Combine carrots, onion, celery, 1 tablespoon oil, and ½ teaspoon salt in large saucepan. Cover and cook over medium-low heat, stirring occasionally, until vegetables are softened, 8 to 10 minutes. Stir in garlic and thyme and cook until fragrant, about 30 seconds.

2. Stir in water and lentils and bring to simmer. Reduce heat to low, cover, and simmer gently, stirring occasionally, until lentils are mostly tender, 40 to 50 minutes.

3. Uncover and continue to cook, stirring occasionally, until lentils are completely tender, about 8 minutes. Stir in remaining 1 tablespoon oil, parsley, and lemon juice. Season with salt and pepper to taste and serve.

VARIATION

French Lentils with Swiss Chard   VEG

Omit carrots, celery, and parsley. Separate stems and leaves from 12 ounces Swiss chard; finely chop stems and cut leaves into ½-inch pieces. Add chard stems to pot with onion and stir chard leaves into pot after uncovering in step 3.

Lentils with Spinach and Garlic Chips

SERVES 6   VEG

WHY THIS RECIPE WORKS In the eastern Mediterranean, tender-firm lentils are often paired with spinach and garlic to create a simple yet flavorful entrée or side dish. We started by frying sliced garlic in oil; the crunchy golden garlic chips added a nice textural contrast and infused the cooking oil with garlic flavor. Tasters preferred the clean flavor of lentils cooked in water over those cooked in broth. Allowing our sturdy curly-leaf spinach to wilt in the pot with the lentils was simple and avoided using extra dishes; the mineral-y flavor of the spinach complemented the earthy lentils perfectly. As a finishing touch, we stirred in some red wine vinegar for brightness. It's important to cook the garlic until just golden—if it becomes too dark, it will have an unpleasant bitter taste. If you can't find curly-leaf spinach, you can substitute flat-leaf spinach; do not substitute baby spinach. We prefer green or brown lentils for this recipe, but it will work with any type of lentil except red or yellow (note that cooking times will vary depending on the type used).

2 tablespoons extra-virgin olive oil
4 garlic cloves, sliced thin
  Salt and pepper
1 onion, chopped fine
1 teaspoon ground coriander
1 teaspoon ground cumin
2½ cups water
1 cup green or brown lentils, picked over and rinsed
8 ounces curly-leaf spinach, stemmed and chopped coarse
1 tablespoon red wine vinegar

1. Cook oil and garlic in large saucepan over medium-low heat, stirring often, until garlic turns crisp and golden but not brown, about 5 minutes. Using slotted spoon, transfer garlic to paper towel–lined plate and season lightly with salt; set aside.

2. Add onion and ½ teaspoon salt to oil left in saucepan and cook over medium heat until softened and lightly browned, 5 to 7 minutes. Stir in coriander and cumin and cook until fragrant, about 30 seconds.

3. Stir in water and lentils and bring to simmer. Reduce heat to low, cover, and simmer gently, stirring occasionally, until lentils are mostly tender but still intact, 45 to 55 minutes.

4. Stir in spinach, 1 handful at a time. Cook, uncovered, stirring occasionally, until spinach is wilted and lentils are completely tender, about 8 minutes. Stir in vinegar and season with salt and pepper to taste. Transfer to serving dish, sprinkle with toasted garlic, and serve.

Mujaddara
SERVES 4 to 6 `VEG`

WHY THIS RECIPE WORKS This classic Levantine dish is a spectacular example of how a few humble ingredients can add up to a dish that's satisfying and complex. Traditional versions consist of tender basmati rice and lentils seasoned with warm spices and minced garlic and topped with deeply savory fried onions. To give the onions the best crispy texture, we microwaved them to remove some of their liquid, then fried them in oil to a deep golden brown. To ensure that the rice and lentils were done at the same time, we parcooked the lentils and then set them aside while we prepared the rice. We soaked the rice in hot water to ensure that it turned out fluffy, not sticky, and then toasted it along with the spices in some of the flavorful frying oil from the onions. Finished with a bracing garlicky yogurt sauce, this pilaf is comfort food at its best. Large green or brown lentils both work well in this recipe; do not use French green lentils, or *lentilles du Puy*. Long-grain white, jasmine, or Texmati rice can be substituted for the basmati.

NOTES FROM THE TEST KITCHEN
Getting to Know Lentils

Lentils come in many sizes and colors and are integral to many Mediterranean dishes, where they are used both as the starring ingredient and in a supporting role. Listed below are the most commonly available types of lentils.

BROWN AND GREEN LENTILS
These larger lentils are what you'll find in every super-market. They are a uniform drab brown or green. They have a mild yet light and earthy flavor and creamy texture. They hold their shape well when cooked and have tender insides. These are all-purpose lentils, great in soups and salads or tossed with olive oil and herbs.

LENTILLES DU PUY
These French lentils are smaller than the common brown and green varieties. They are a dark olive green, almost black. We love them for their rich, earthy, complex flavor and firm yet tender texture. They keep their shape and look beautiful on the plate when cooked, so they're perfect for salads and dishes where the lentils take center stage.

BLACK LENTILS
Like *lentilles du Puy*, black lentils are slightly smaller than the standard brown lentils. They have a deep black hue similar to the color of caviar. In fact, some markets refer to them as beluga lentils. They have a robust, earthy flavor and hold their shape well when cooked, but their skins can make dishes dark and muddy.

WHITE LENTILS
White lentils are simply skinned and split black lentils. They have a unique flavor similar to that of mung beans. Like red and yellow lentils, they disintegrate as they cook, and they boast a particularly viscous, starchy texture that makes for a great soup.

RED AND YELLOW LENTILS
These small, split orange-red or golden-yellow lentils completely disintegrate when cooked. If you are looking for a lentil that will quickly break down into a thick puree, these are the ones to use.

YOGURT SAUCE

- 1 cup plain whole-milk yogurt
- 2 tablespoons lemon juice
- ½ teaspoon minced garlic
- ½ teaspoon salt

RICE AND LENTILS

8¾ ounces (1¼ cups) green or brown lentils, picked over and rinsed
    Salt and pepper
1¼ cups basmati rice
- 1 recipe Crispy Onions, plus 3 tablespoons reserved oil
- 3 garlic cloves, minced
- 1 teaspoon ground coriander
- 1 teaspoon ground cumin
- ½ teaspoon ground cinnamon
- ½ teaspoon ground allspice
- ⅛ teaspoon cayenne pepper
- 1 teaspoon sugar
- 3 tablespoons minced fresh cilantro

1. FOR THE YOGURT SAUCE Whisk all ingredients together in bowl and refrigerate until ready to serve.

2. FOR THE RICE AND LENTILS Bring lentils, 4 cups water, and 1 teaspoon salt to boil in medium saucepan over high heat. Reduce heat to low and cook until lentils are just tender, 15 to 17 minutes. Drain and set aside.

3. Meanwhile, place rice in medium bowl, cover with hot tap water by 2 inches, and let sit for 15 minutes. Using your hands, gently swish grains to release excess starch. Carefully

---

CRISPY ONIONS

MAKES 1½ cups   VEG

It is crucial to thoroughly dry the microwaved onions after rinsing. Be sure to reserve enough oil to use in Mujaddara or Koshari. Remaining oil may be stored in an airtight container and refrigerated for up to 4 weeks; it tastes great in salad dressings, sautéed vegetables, eggs, and pasta sauces.

- 2 pounds onions, halved and sliced crosswise into ¼-inch-thick pieces
- 2 teaspoons salt
- 1½ cups vegetable oil

1. Toss onions and salt together in large bowl. Microwave for 5 minutes. Rinse thoroughly, transfer to paper towel–lined baking sheet, and dry well.

2. Heat onions and oil in Dutch oven over high heat, stirring frequently, until onions are golden brown, 25 to 30 minutes. Drain onions in colander set in large bowl. Transfer onions to paper towel–lined baking sheet to drain. Serve.

---

pour off water, leaving rice in bowl. Repeat adding and pouring off cold water 4 to 5 times, until water runs almost clear. Drain rice in fine-mesh strainer.

4. Cook reserved onion oil, garlic, coriander, cumin, cinnamon, allspice, ¼ teaspoon pepper, and cayenne in Dutch oven over medium heat until fragrant, about 2 minutes. Add rice and cook, stirring occasionally, until grain edges begin to turn translucent,

Making Mujaddara

1. SOAK RICE Cover rice with hot tap water and let sit for 15 minutes. Rinse rice with cold water until water runs almost clear, then drain.

2. PARCOOK LENTILS Bring lentils, water, and salt to boil and cook until lentils are just tender. Drain and set aside.

3. TOAST RICE AND ADD LENTILS Bloom spices and aromatics in reserved oil from Crispy Onions. Add rice and cook until edges are translucent. Add liquid, bring to boil, then add lentils.

4. REST, FLUFF, AND SERVE Once liquid is absorbed, place dish towel underneath lid and let sit for 10 minutes. Fluff with fork, stir in half of onions, then transfer to platter and top with remaining onions.

about 3 minutes. Stir in 2¼ cups water, sugar, and 1 teaspoon salt and bring to boil. Stir in lentils, reduce heat to low, cover, and simmer gently until all liquid is absorbed, about 12 minutes.

5. Off heat, cover, laying clean dish towel underneath lid, and let sit for 10 minutes. Fluff rice and lentils with fork and stir in cilantro and half of onions. Transfer to serving platter and top with remaining onions. Serve with yogurt sauce.

Koshari
SERVES 4 to 6 VEG

WHY THIS RECIPE WORKS Considered the national dish of Egypt, *koshari* evolved as a way to use up leftovers and is now a popular street food. This hearty dish usually features lentils, rice, pasta, and chickpeas smothered in a spiced tomato sauce and topped with crispy fried onions. Although the dish took some time to put together, each element was fairly simple, and tasters couldn't get enough of the comforting combination. We cooked the lentils and the pasta in pots of salted boiling water, then drained each of them and set them aside while we prepared the rice and sauce. Soaking the rice in hot water before cooking eliminated some of its excess starch so it didn't clump. A few tests revealed that tasters preferred a tomato sauce spiked with vinegar over spicy varieties we came across in our research. Using the same spices (a blend of coriander, cumin, cinnamon, nutmeg, and cayenne) in the sauce and the rice provided a complex flavor profile and made the dish cohesive. We added the chickpeas directly to the sauce to infuse them with flavor. The finishing touch: a generous amount of ultrasavory, crunchy fried onions that brought a satisfying depth and texture to this classic Egyptian comfort food. Large green or brown lentils both work well in this recipe; do not use French green lentils, or *lentilles du Puy*. Long-grain white, jasmine, or Texmati rice can be substituted for the basmati.

    1 cup elbow macaroni
       Salt and pepper
    1 cup green or brown lentils, picked over and rinsed
    1 recipe Crispy Onions, plus ¼ cup reserved oil
       (page 172)
    4 garlic cloves, minced
  1½   teaspoons ground coriander
  1½   teaspoons ground cumin
    ¾ teaspoon ground cinnamon
    ¼ teaspoon ground nutmeg
    ¼ teaspoon cayenne pepper
    1 (28-ounce) can tomato sauce
    1 (15-ounce) can chickpeas, rinsed
    1 cup basmati rice
    1 tablespoon red wine vinegar
    3 tablespoons minced fresh parsley

Warm spices flavor the rice, lentils, pasta, and chickpeas in this traditional Egyptian dish.

1. Bring 2 quarts water to boil in Dutch oven. Add pasta and 1½ teaspoons salt and cook, stirring often, until al dente. Drain pasta, rinse with water, then drain again. Transfer to bowl and set aside.

2. Meanwhile, bring lentils, 4 cups water, and 1 teaspoon salt to boil in medium saucepan over high heat. Reduce heat to low and cook until lentils are just tender, 15 to 17 minutes. Drain and set aside.

3. Cook 1 tablespoon reserved onion oil, 1 teaspoon garlic, ½ teaspoon salt, ½ teaspoon coriander, ½ teaspoon cumin, ¼ teaspoon cinnamon, ⅛ teaspoon nutmeg, and ⅛ teaspoon cayenne in now-empty saucepan over medium heat until fragrant, about 1 minute. Stir in tomato sauce and chickpeas, bring to simmer, and cook until slightly thickened, about 10 minutes. Cover and keep warm.

4. While sauce cooks, place rice in medium bowl, cover with hot tap water by 2 inches, and let sit for 15 minutes. Using your hands, gently swish grains to release excess starch. Carefully pour off water, leaving rice in bowl. Repeat adding and pouring off cold water 4 to 5 times, until water runs almost clear. Drain rice in fine-mesh strainer.

5. Cook remaining 3 tablespoons reserved onion oil, remaining garlic, remaining 1 teaspoon coriander, remaining 1 teaspoon cumin, remaining ½ teaspoon cinnamon, remaining ⅛ teaspoon nutmeg, and remaining ⅛ teaspoon cayenne in now-empty pot over medium heat until fragrant, about 2 minutes. Add rice and cook, stirring occasionally, until grain edges begin to turn translucent, about 3 minutes. Stir in 2 cups water and ½ teaspoon salt and bring to boil. Stir in lentils, reduce heat to low, cover, and simmer gently until all liquid is absorbed, about 12 minutes.

6. Off heat, sprinkle pasta over rice mixture. Cover, laying clean dish towel underneath lid, and let sit for 10 minutes.

7. Return sauce to simmer over medium heat. Stir in vinegar and season with salt and pepper to taste. Fluff rice and lentils with fork and stir in parsley and half of onions. Transfer to serving platter and top with half of sauce and remaining onions. Serve, passing remaining sauce separately.

Spiced Lentil Salad with Winter Squash
SERVES 6 VEG

WHY THIS RECIPE WORKS Winter squash is used throughout the Mediterranean, and we thought its subtle sweetness would work well with earthy lentils to make a balanced side or vegetarian main dish. With just two ingredients sharing the starring role, cooking each of them perfectly was essential. To accentuate the delicate butternut squash flavor, we tossed small pieces with balsamic vinegar and extra-virgin olive oil and roasted them in a hot oven. Putting the rack in the lowest position encouraged deep, even browning, and the caramelized balsamic nicely enhanced the squash's flavor. Satisfied with the squash, we turned to the lentils. For a touch of sophistication, we used black lentils, which hold their shape well during cooking and have a robust flavor. We soaked them in a saltwater solution to season them throughout and ensure fewer blowouts. To infuse them with more flavor as they cooked, we chose a mixture of warm, floral spices that we bloomed in oil and transferred the pot to the oven to ensure even cooking. As for the dressing, we echoed the flavor of the squash by using balsamic vinegar. We also added a small amount of Dijon mustard for depth. Parsley and chopped red onion gave the dish some color and freshness, and toasted pepitas provided just the right amount of textural contrast. Black lentils are our first choice for this recipe, but *lentilles du Puy* (also called French green lentils), brown, or regular green lentils are fine, too (note that cooking times will vary depending on the type used). Salt-soaking helps keep the lentils intact, but if you don't have time, they'll still taste good. You will need a medium ovensafe saucepan for this recipe.

Earthy black lentils are brined before cooking to season them thoroughly and help them hold their shape.

Salt and pepper
1 cup black lentils, picked over and rinsed
1 pound butternut squash, peeled, seeded, and cut into ½-inch pieces (3 cups)
5 tablespoons extra-virgin olive oil
2 tablespoons balsamic vinegar
1 garlic clove, minced
½ teaspoon ground coriander
¼ teaspoon ground cumin
¼ teaspoon ground ginger
⅛ teaspoon ground cinnamon
1 teaspoon Dijon mustard
½ cup fresh parsley leaves
¼ cup finely chopped red onion
1 tablespoon raw pepitas, toasted

1. Dissolve 1 teaspoon salt in 4 cups warm water (about 110 degrees) in bowl. Add lentils and soak at room temperature for 1 hour. Drain well.

2. Meanwhile, adjust oven racks to middle and lowest positions and heat oven to 450 degrees. Toss squash with 1 tablespoon oil, 1½ teaspoons vinegar, ¼ teaspoon salt, and ¼ teaspoon pepper. Arrange squash in single layer in rimmed baking sheet and roast on lower rack until well browned and tender, 20 to 25 minutes, stirring halfway through roasting. Let cool slightly. Reduce oven temperature to 325 degrees.

3. Cook 1 tablespoon oil, garlic, coriander, cumin, ginger, and cinnamon in medium ovensafe saucepan over medium heat until fragrant, about 1 minute. Stir in 4 cups water and lentils. Cover, transfer saucepan to upper rack in oven, and cook until lentils are tender but remain intact, 40 to 60 minutes.

4. Drain lentils well. Whisk remaining 3 tablespoons oil, remaining 1½ tablespoons vinegar, and mustard together in large bowl. Add squash, lentils, parsley, and onion and toss to combine. Season with salt and pepper to taste. Transfer to serving platter and sprinkle with pepitas. Serve warm or at room temperature.

Lentil Salad with Olives, Mint, and Feta
SERVES 4 to 6 VEG

WHY THIS RECIPE WORKS For this Greek-inspired lentil salad, we first needed to ensure that the lentils would stay intact through cooking. French green lentils were the perfect choice, since they are small, firm, and hold their shape better than standard green or brown lentils. A salt soak softened their skins, leading to fewer blowouts. Cooking the lentils in the oven heated them gently and uniformly, and we easily boosted their flavor by simply adding some crushed cloves of garlic and a bay leaf to the pot. With our perfectly cooked lentils in hand, we turned to flavorings. A simple, tart vinaigrette worked perfectly to balance the lentils. We chose several boldly flavored mix-ins to bring our salad to life: fresh mint, minced shallot, and chopped kalamata olives; a sprinkle of rich feta finished the dish. *Lentilles du Puy*, also called French green lentils, are our first choice for this recipe, but brown, black, or regular green lentils are fine, too (note that cooking times will vary depending on the type used). Salt-soaking helps keep the lentils intact, but if you don't have time, they'll still taste good. You will need a medium ovensafe saucepan for this recipe.

Salt and pepper
1 cup lentilles du Puy, picked over and rinsed
5 garlic cloves, lightly crushed and peeled
1 bay leaf
5 tablespoons extra-virgin olive oil
3 tablespoons white wine vinegar
½ cup pitted kalamata olives, chopped coarse
½ cup chopped fresh mint
1 large shallot, minced
1 ounce feta cheese, crumbled (¼ cup)

1. Dissolve 1 teaspoon salt in 4 cups warm water (about 110 degrees) in bowl. Add lentils and soak at room temperature for 1 hour. Drain well.

2. Adjust oven rack to middle position and heat oven to 325 degrees. Combine lentils, 4 cups water, garlic, bay leaf, and ½ teaspoon salt in medium ovensafe saucepan. Cover, transfer saucepan to oven, and cook until lentils are tender but remain intact, 40 to 60 minutes.

3. Drain lentils well, discarding garlic and bay leaf. In large bowl, whisk oil and vinegar together. Add lentils, olives, mint, and shallot and toss to combine. Season with salt and pepper to taste. Transfer to serving dish and sprinkle with feta. Serve warm or at room temperature.

VARIATIONS
Lentil Salad with Hazelnuts and Goat Cheese VEG
Substitute 3 tablespoons red wine vinegar for white wine vinegar and add 2 teaspoons Dijon mustard to dressing. Omit olives and substitute ¼ cup chopped fresh parsley for mint. Substitute ¼ cup crumbled goat cheese for feta and sprinkle salad with ¼ cup coarsely chopped toasted hazelnuts before serving.

Lentil Salad with Carrots and Cilantro VEG
Omit shallot and feta. Toss 2 carrots, peeled and cut into 2-inch-long matchsticks, with 1 teaspoon ground cumin, ½ teaspoon ground cinnamon, and ⅛ teaspoon cayenne pepper in bowl; cover and microwave until carrots are tender but still crisp, 2 to 4 minutes. Substitute 3 tablespoons lemon juice for white wine vinegar, carrots for olives, and ¼ cup chopped fresh cilantro for mint.

Lentil Salad with Spinach, Walnuts, and Parmesan
VEG
Substitute 3 tablespoons sherry vinegar for white wine vinegar. Place 4 cups baby spinach and 2 tablespoons water in bowl. Cover and microwave until spinach is wilted and volume is halved, about 4 minutes. Remove bowl from microwave and keep covered for 1 minute. Transfer spinach to colander and gently press to release liquid. Transfer spinach to cutting board and chop coarse. Return to colander and press again. Substitute chopped spinach for olives and mint and ¼ cup coarsely grated Parmesan cheese for feta. Sprinkle salad with ¼ cup coarsely chopped toasted walnuts before serving.

All About Dried Beans

Canned beans are undeniably convenient, and in many cases they work as well as or even better than dried. However, there are instances when dried beans are central to the success of a recipe. Here's what to know about them.

BUYING

When shopping for beans, it's essential to select "fresh" dried beans. Buy those that are uniform in size and have a smooth exterior. When dried beans are fully hydrated and cooked, they should be plump, with taut skins, and have creamy insides; spent beans will have wrinkled skin and a dry, almost gritty texture.

STORING

Uncooked beans should be stored in a cool, dry place in a sealed plastic or glass container. Beans are less susceptible than rice and grains to pests and spoilage, but it is still best to use them within a month or two. Always pick over dried beans to remove stones and debris, and rinse them before cooking to wash away any dust or impurities.

SUBSTITUTING CANNED BEANS FOR DRIED

Most recipes that call for dried beans require the beans to cook slowly with the other ingredients so that they release their starches and thicken the dish. When you replace the dried beans with canned beans and shorten the cooking time (canned beans are fully cooked and need to cook only long enough to warm through and soak up flavor), you sacrifice both the flavor and the texture of the finished dish. But if you're short on time and want to swap in canned beans, a general rule of thumb is that 1 cup of dried beans equals 3 cups of canned beans.

Chickpeas with Garlic and Parsley

SERVES 4 to 6   FAST   VEG

WHY THIS RECIPE WORKS Chickpeas are an ultraversatile ingredient found in nearly every Mediterranean country. With their buttery, nutty flavor and creamy texture, chickpeas can make a terrific side dish when simply sautéed with a few flavorful ingredients. In search of Mediterranean-inspired flavors that would easily transform our canned chickpeas, we reached for garlic and red pepper flakes. Instead of mincing the garlic, we cut it into thin slices and sautéed them in extra-virgin olive oil to mellow their flavor. The thin slivers maintained their presence

in the finished dish. We softened an onion along with this aromatic base, then added the chickpeas with vegetable broth, which imparted a rich, savory backbone to the dish without overpowering it. As final touches, parsley and lemon juice gave our chickpeas a burst of freshness.

 ¼ cup extra-virgin olive oil
 4 garlic cloves, sliced thin
 ⅛ teaspoon red pepper flakes
 1 onion, chopped fine
  Salt and pepper
 2 (15-ounce) cans chickpeas, rinsed
 1 cup chicken or vegetable broth
 2 tablespoons minced fresh parsley
 2 teaspoons lemon juice

1. Cook 3 tablespoons oil, garlic, and pepper flakes in 12-inch skillet over medium heat, stirring frequently, until garlic turns golden but not brown, about 3 minutes. Stir in onion and ¼ teaspoon salt and cook until softened and lightly browned, 5 to 7 minutes. Stir in chickpeas and broth and bring to simmer. Reduce heat to medium-low, cover, and cook until chickpeas are heated through and flavors meld, about 7 minutes.

2. Uncover, increase heat to high, and continue to cook until nearly all liquid has evaporated, about 3 minutes. Off heat, stir in parsley and lemon juice. Season with salt and pepper to taste and drizzle with remaining 1 tablespoon oil. Serve.

VARIATIONS
Chickpeas with Bell Pepper, Scallions, and Basil
FAST   VEG

Add 1 chopped red bell pepper to skillet with onion. Substitute 2 tablespoons chopped fresh basil for parsley and stir in 2 thinly sliced scallions before serving.

Chickpeas with Smoked Paprika and Cilantro
FAST   VEG

Omit red pepper flakes. Add ½ teaspoon smoked paprika to skillet before chickpeas and cook until fragrant, about 30 seconds. Substitute 2 tablespoons minced fresh cilantro for parsley and 2 teaspoons sherry vinegar for lemon juice.

Chickpeas with Saffron, Mint, and Yogurt
FAST   VEG

Omit red pepper flakes. Add ⅛ teaspoon crumbled saffron threads to skillet before chickpeas and cook until fragrant, about 30 seconds. Add ⅓ cup raisins to skillet with chickpeas. Substitute 2 tablespoons minced fresh mint for parsley and stir in ¼ cup plain yogurt before serving.

The starchy chickpea canning liquid gives this Spanish chickpea and spinach dish body and flavor.

Chickpeas with Spinach, Chorizo, and Smoked Paprika

SERVES 4 to 6 `FAST`

WHY THIS RECIPE WORKS *Espinacas* is a traditional tapas dish found in the southern Spanish region of Andalucia consisting of tender stewed chickpeas, delicate wilted spinach, and bold North African–influenced spices. We set out to develop an adaptation of this dish that could work as part of a larger meal. For the flavor backbone, we stuck with the classic southern Spanish flavors of saffron, garlic, smoked paprika, and cumin. Tasters also liked the traditional addition of chorizo, which added meaty richness. Curly-leaf spinach was the best choice for its sturdy texture in this brothy dish. To keep the recipe streamlined, we opted to wilt the spinach and then set it aside before building the brothy base with canned chickpeas and aromatics. Including the chickpeas' flavorful, starchy canning liquid helped to give the dish more body. Finally, we added a traditional *picada*, which is often used in Spanish cooking as a thickener. The bread crumb–based mixture gave the stewed beans and greens just the right velvety texture and flavor boost. Our finished dish would be equally at home as part of a tapas spread or served as an entrée over rice or with good crusty bread

to sop up the flavorful broth. If you can't find curly-leaf spinach, you can substitute flat-leaf spinach; do not substitute baby spinach. For an accurate measurement of boiling water, bring a full kettle of water to a boil and then measure out the desired amount.

    Pinch saffron threads, crumbled
2 teaspoons extra-virgin olive oil
8 ounces curly-leaf spinach, stemmed
3 ounces Spanish-style chorizo sausage, chopped fine
5 garlic cloves, sliced thin
1 tablespoon smoked paprika
1 teaspoon ground cumin
    Salt and pepper
2 (15-ounce) cans chickpeas
1 recipe Picada (page 63)
1 tablespoon sherry vinegar

1. Combine 2 tablespoons boiling water and saffron in small bowl and let steep for 5 minutes.

2. Heat 1 teaspoon oil in Dutch oven over medium heat until shimmering. Add spinach and 2 tablespoons water, cover, and cook, stirring occasionally, until spinach is wilted but still bright green, about 1 minute. Transfer spinach to colander and gently press to release liquid. Transfer spinach to cutting board and chop coarse. Return to colander and press again.

3. Heat remaining 1 teaspoon oil in now-empty pot over medium heat until shimmering. Add chorizo and cook until lightly browned, about 5 minutes. Stir in garlic, paprika, cumin, and ¼ teaspoon pepper and cook until fragrant, about 30 seconds. Stir in chickpeas and their liquid, 1 cup water, and saffron mixture and bring to simmer. Cook, stirring occasionally, until chickpeas are tender and liquid has thickened slightly, 10 to 15 minutes.

4. Off heat, stir in picada, spinach, and vinegar and let sit until heated through, about 2 minutes. Adjust sauce consistency with hot water as needed. Season with salt and pepper to taste and serve.

NOTES FROM THE TEST KITCHEN
Spanish-Style Chorizo

Spanish chorizo, which comes in links, is generally sold cured and fully cooked. It's made from chopped pork and pork fat and seasoned with garlic, herbs, and smoked paprika, which gives it its trademark red color. Its "jerkylike" texture reminded some tasters of pepperoni; its "pungent smoke" and "vinegary aftertaste" are all its own. You can eat sliced chorizo as an appetizer or add it to dishes like paella (pages 112 and 114) or Chickpeas with Spinach, Chorizo, and Smoked Paprika.

Baking our Greek chickpea and eggplant stew uncovered concentrates its flavors and thickens the sauce.

Stewed Chickpeas with Eggplant and Tomatoes

SERVES 6 VEG

WHY THIS RECIPE WORKS In Greece, fresh eggplant and dried chickpeas are cooked together for hours to create a hearty stew with deep flavor; the silky, luxurious texture of the eggplant is complemented by the firm-tender chickpeas. For a streamlined version of this dish, we started with canned chickpeas, which we've found hold up very well even to long cooking. We chopped canned whole tomatoes to give the dish a rustic texture and a tomatoey backbone. After some initial tests, tasters were amazed at the depth of savory flavor we were able to achieve without using any meat, and they loved the soft and creamy eggplant. However, we wondered whether the hours-long cooking time was really necessary. To find out, we tested cooking methods and times and landed on a combination stovetop-oven method that worked to create the texture we were after. To jump-start the cooking process, we sautéed onions, bell pepper, garlic, oregano, and bay leaves to create an aromatic base. We added our chickpeas, tomatoes, and eggplant (cutting it into 1-inch pieces ensured that it softened but didn't completely break down) and transferred the pot to the oven. Baking the mixture uncovered concentrated the flavors and

allowed any unwanted liquid to evaporate, eliminating the need to pretreat the eggplant. Stirring a couple of times during cooking ensured that the top layer didn't dry out. Some fresh oregano, added at the end, gave this savory dish a welcome burst of herbaceous flavor. We were happy to find that this versatile dish tasted equally good when served warm, at room temperature, or even cold as a side salad.

¼ cup extra-virgin olive oil
2 onions, chopped
1 green bell pepper, stemmed, seeded, and chopped fine
   Salt and pepper
3 garlic cloves, minced
1 tablespoon minced fresh oregano or 1 teaspoon dried
2 bay leaves
1 pound eggplant, cut into 1-inch pieces
1 (28-ounce) can whole peeled tomatoes, drained with juice reserved, chopped coarse
2 (15-ounce) cans chickpeas, drained with 1 cup liquid reserved

1. Adjust oven rack to lower-middle position and heat oven to 400 degrees. Heat oil in Dutch oven over medium heat until shimmering. Add onions, bell pepper, ½ teaspoon salt, and ¼ teaspoon pepper and cook until softened, about 5 minutes. Stir in garlic, 1 teaspoon oregano, and bay leaves and cook until fragrant, about 30 seconds.

2. Stir in eggplant, tomatoes and reserved juice, and chickpeas and reserved liquid and bring to boil. Transfer pot to oven and cook, uncovered, until eggplant is very tender, 45 to 60 minutes, stirring twice during cooking.

3. Discard bay leaves. Stir in remaining 2 teaspoons oregano and season with salt and pepper to taste. Serve.

Spicy Chickpeas with Turnips

SERVES 4 to 6 VEG

WHY THIS RECIPE WORKS Unlike most North African cooking, Tunisian food is known for being quite hot and spicy. We wanted to highlight the flavors of this cuisine with a chickpea dish that could be enjoyed as an accompaniment yet was hearty enough to be served all on its own as an entrée. To start, we created a spicy and savory base of sautéed aromatics. In Tunisia, fresh *Baklouti* chiles are the main source of heat, but we opted for the more widely available jalapeño pepper, which has a similar heat level. We also added extra punch with cayenne pepper. Once the aromatic foundation for this dish was in place, it was time to add the hearty vegetables. In an effort to keep our recipe streamlined, we opted for canned chickpeas; the chickpeas softened slightly with cooking, and the perfectly tender chickpeas were a hit with tasters. Including the starchy, seasoned liquid from the cans gave our sauce good flavor and body. To add bulk and earthy flavor to this dish, we tested a variety of root vegetables and landed on turnips, a common ingredient in Tunisian cuisine. We cut the turnips into bite-size pieces so they would cook quickly and evenly. A final touch of lemon juice was all this zesty bean dish needed before serving.

2 tablespoons extra-virgin olive oil
2 onions, chopped
2 red bell peppers, stemmed, seeded, and chopped
  Salt and pepper
¼ cup tomato paste
1 jalapeño chile, stemmed, seeded, and minced
5 garlic cloves, minced
¾ teaspoon ground cumin
¼ teaspoon cayenne pepper
2 (15-ounce) cans chickpeas
12 ounces turnips, peeled and cut into ½-inch pieces
¾ cup water, plus extra as needed
¼ cup chopped fresh parsley
2 tablespoons lemon juice, plus extra for seasoning

1. Heat oil in Dutch oven over medium heat until shimmering. Add onions, bell peppers, ½ teaspoon salt, and ¼ teaspoon pepper and cook until softened and lightly browned, 5 to 7 minutes. Stir in tomato paste, jalapeño, garlic, cumin, and cayenne and cook until fragrant, about 30 seconds.

2. Stir in chickpeas and their liquid, turnips, and water. Bring to simmer and cook until turnips are tender and sauce has thickened, 25 to 35 minutes.

3. Stir in parsley and lemon juice. Season with salt, pepper, and extra lemon juice to taste. Adjust consistency with extra hot water as needed. Serve.

Chickpea Salad with Carrots, Arugula, and Olives

SERVES 6   FAST   VEG

WHY THIS RECIPE WORKS For a flavorful and easy side salad or light lunch, we combined nutty chickpeas with classic Mediterranean flavors. But simply tossing our ingredients with a lemon vinaigrette resulted in a lackluster salad with a pool of dressing at the bottom of the bowl. We wanted the flavor to go beyond the surface of the chickpeas and fully infuse each one with big, bold flavor. We discovered that the key was to warm the chickpeas before mixing them with the dressing ingredients: The seed coats that cover the chickpeas are rich in pectin, which breaks down when exposed to heat and moisture, creating a more porous inner surface

Warming canned chickpeas helps them to absorb more of the flavorful salad dressing.

that our flavorful dressing could easily penetrate. Letting the dressed chickpeas rest for 30 minutes put the flavor over the top and allowed the chickpeas to cool. Finally, we focused on choosing complementary add-ins for our chickpeas: a combination of sweet carrots, peppery arugula, and briny olives; another with crunchy fennel and arugula; and finally one with sweet, smoky roasted red peppers with tangy feta and fresh parsley.

2 (15-ounce) cans chickpeas, rinsed
¼ cup extra-virgin olive oil
2 tablespoons lemon juice
  Salt and pepper
  Pinch cayenne pepper
3 carrots, peeled and shredded
1 cup baby arugula, chopped coarse
½ cup pitted kalamata olives, chopped coarse

1. Microwave chickpeas in medium bowl until hot, about 2 minutes. Stir in oil, lemon juice, ¾ teaspoon salt, ½ teaspoon pepper, and cayenne and let sit for 30 minutes.

2. Add carrots, arugula, and olives and toss to combine. Season with salt and pepper to taste. Serve.

Chickpea Salad with Fennel and Arugula

FAST VEG

Substitute 1 fennel bulb, stalks discarded, bulb halved, cored, and cut into ¼-inch pieces, for carrots and olives.

Chickpea Salad with Roasted Red Peppers and Feta

FAST VEG

Substitute ½ cup chopped jarred roasted red peppers, ½ cup crumbled feta cheese, and ¼ cup chopped fresh parsley for carrots, arugula, and olives.

Chickpea Cakes

SERVES 6   FAST   VEG

WHY THIS RECIPE WORKS In Greek cuisine, fritters and croquettes are a popular way to use up leftover legumes; home cooks add spices and aromatics to the pureed legumes, form the mixture into patties, and fry them until th e exteriors are crisp and browned. Since we don't often have leftover chickpeas on hand, we decided to use canned chickpeas to make flavorful chickpea cakes that could be served as an appealing main course. Pureeing the chickpeas completely resulted in mushy, homogeneous cakes; instead, we pulsed them until they were coarsely ground but still had some texture. To bind the patties, two eggs and some panko bread crumbs did the trick, and for richness we added two Greek pantry staples: yogurt and olive oil. A combination of coriander, cayenne pepper, scallions, and cilantro ensured that these patties were ultraflavorful, and a cool yogurt sauce was the perfect accompaniment. Avoid overmixing the chickpea mixture in step 1 or the cakes will have a mealy texture.

2 (15-ounce) cans chickpeas, rinsed
½ cup plain Greek yogurt
2 large eggs
6 tablespoons extra-virgin olive oil
1 teaspoon ground coriander
⅛ teaspoon cayenne pepper
⅛ teaspoon salt
1 cup panko bread crumbs
2 scallions, sliced thin
3 tablespoons minced fresh cilantro
1 shallot, minced
1 recipe Cucumber-Yogurt Sauce (page 233)

1. Pulse chickpeas in food processor until coarsely ground, about 8 pulses. Whisk yogurt, eggs, 2 tablespoons oil, coriander, cayenne, and salt together in medium bowl. Gently stir in

Our Greek-inspired pan-fried chickpea patties are held together with eggs, panko crumbs, and yogurt.

chickpeas, panko, scallions, cilantro, and shallot until just combined. Divide mixture into 6 equal portions and gently pack into 1-inch-thick patties.

2. Heat 2 tablespoons oil in 12-inch nonstick skillet over medium heat until shimmering. Carefully lay 3 patties in skillet and cook until well browned and firm, 4 to 5 minutes per side.

3. Transfer cakes to paper towel–lined plate and tent loosely with aluminum foil. Repeat with remaining 2 tablespoons oil and remaining 3 patties. Serve with yogurt sauce.

Rinsing Canned Beans

Place beans in fine-mesh strainer and rinse under cool water to remove excess starchy canning liquid. Let drain briefly.

Falafel

MAKES about 24 `VEG`

WHY THIS RECIPE WORKS Falafel is an eastern Mediterranean specialty of savory fried chickpea balls or patties generously seasoned with herbs and spices. The best falafel have a moist, light interior and a well-browned, crisp crust. Starting with dried chickpeas was essential here; using canned chickpeas resulted in mushy falafel that wouldn't hold their shape. We soaked the dried chickpeas overnight in a saltwater solution, which weakened the cell structure of the chickpeas' skins, giving them a softer texture. We then ground the soaked chickpeas with fresh herbs and warm spices: scallions, parsley, cilantro, garlic, cumin, and cinnamon. Shaping the falafel into small disks ensured that the exteriors developed a crunchy, golden-brown crust while the interiors stayed tender and moist. Shallow frying worked nicely and required far less oil than deep-fried recipes. Both yogurt and tahini sauces are traditional with falafel, and tasters enjoyed them both. The chickpeas in this recipe must be soaked overnight; you cannot substitute canned or quick-soaked chickpeas. Serve the falafel as hors d'oeuvres or in lavash or pita bread with lettuce, chopped tomatoes or cucumbers, and Pink Pickled Turnips (page 182), if desired, with either Tahini-Lemon Dressing (page 72) or Yogurt-Herb Sauce (page 233).

Brining dried chickpeas is essential to creating sturdy falafel with moist and tender interiors.

Salt and pepper
12 ounces (2 cups) dried chickpeas, picked over and rinsed
10 scallions, chopped coarse
1 cup fresh parsley leaves
1 cup fresh cilantro leaves
6 garlic cloves, minced
½ teaspoon ground cumin
⅛ teaspoon ground cinnamon
2 cups vegetable oil

1. Dissolve 3 tablespoons salt in 4 quarts cold water in large container. Add chickpeas and soak at room temperature for at least 8 hours or up to 24 hours. Drain and rinse well.

2. Process chickpeas, scallions, parsley, cilantro, garlic, 1 teaspoon salt, 1 teaspoon pepper, cumin, and cinnamon in food processor until smooth, about 1 minute, scraping down sides

Making Falafel

1. SOAK CHICKPEAS Dissolve 3 tablespoons salt in 4 quarts water. Add chickpeas and soak for at least 8 hours.

2. PROCESS Process soaked chickpeas, herbs, spices, and aromatics in food processor until smooth.

3. SHAPE Pinch off and shape chickpea mixture into 2-tablespoon-size disks, about 1½ inches wide and 1 inch thick.

4. FRY Heat oil to 375 degrees. Fry half of falafel until deep golden brown on both sides. Keep warm in oven.

of bowl as needed. Pinch off and shape chickpea mixture into 2-tablespoon-size disks, about 1½ inches wide and 1 inch thick, and place on parchment paper–lined baking sheet. (Falafel can be refrigerated for up to 2 hours.)

3. Adjust oven rack to middle position and heat oven to 200 degrees. Set wire rack in rimmed baking sheet. Heat oil in 12-inch skillet over medium-high heat to 375 degrees. Fry half of falafel until deep golden brown, 2 to 3 minutes per side. Adjust burner, if necessary, to maintain oil temperature of 375 degrees. Using slotted spoon, transfer falafel to prepared sheet and keep warm in oven. Return oil to 375 degrees and repeat with remaining falafel. Serve.

PINK PICKLED TURNIPS

MAKES 4 cups `VEG`

The turnips need to be refrigerated for two days to fully pickle the vegetables. These are great with falafel, but you can also serve them with Grilled Chicken Souvlaki (page 300), Grilled Whole Mackerel (page 252), or as part of a meze spread with Classic Hummus (page 16).

1¼ cups white wine vinegar
1¼ cups water
2½ tablespoons sugar
1½ tablespoons canning and pickling salt
 3 garlic cloves, smashed and peeled
¾ teaspoon whole allspice berries
¾ teaspoon black peppercorns
 1 pound turnips, peeled and cut into 2 by ½-inch sticks
 1 small beet, trimmed, peeled, and cut into 1-inch pieces

1. Bring vinegar, water, sugar, salt, garlic, allspice, and peppercorns to boil in medium saucepan. Cover, remove from heat, and let steep for 10 minutes. Strain brine through fine-mesh strainer, then return to saucepan.

2. Place two 1-pint jars in bowl and place under hot running water until heated through, 1 to 2 minutes; shake dry. Pack turnips vertically into hot jars with beet pieces evenly distributed throughout.

3. Return brine to brief boil. Using funnel and ladle, pour hot brine over vegetables to cover. Let jars cool to room temperature, cover with lids, and refrigerate for at least 2 days before serving. (Pickled turnips can be refrigerated for up to 1 month; turnips will soften over time.)

The North African nut and seed blend known as *dukkah* provides crunch and flavor to our Egyptian-inspired salad.

Black-Eyed Peas with Walnuts and Pomegranate
SERVES 4 to 6 `FAST` `VEG`

WHY THIS RECIPE WORKS For a black-eyed pea salad that would boast big flavor and be ultrasimple to prepare, we looked to Egyptian cuisine for inspiration. In Egypt, black-eyed peas are a pantry staple, and their delicate skins, creamy interiors, and fairly mild flavor make them a great base for a tart dressing and crunchy additions. To simplify preparation, we used canned black-eyed peas, which had great flavor and texture. We turned to other common Egyptian salad additions like walnuts and pomegranate seeds for their flavor and texture contrasts, along with scallions and parsley for fresh notes. We created a punchy dressing by using equal parts lemon juice and pomegranate molasses, which offered balanced acidity and tang. Finally, we incorporated *dukkah*, a nut and seed blend used as a seasoning across North Africa. The dukkah added a bit more textural contrast as well as a final hit of bold and earthy flavor. We prefer to use our homemade Dukkah (page 317), but you can substitute store-bought dukkah if you wish, though flavor can vary greatly by brand. If you can't find pomegranate molasses, you can make your own (see page 305).

3 tablespoons extra-virgin olive oil

3 tablespoons dukkah

2 tablespoons lemon juice

2 tablespoons pomegranate molasses

  Salt and pepper

2 (15-ounce) cans black-eyed peas, rinsed

½ cup walnuts, toasted and chopped

½ cup pomegranate seeds

½ cup minced fresh parsley

4 scallions, sliced thin

Whisk oil, 2 tablespoons dukkah, lemon juice, pomegranate molasses, ¼ teaspoon salt, and ⅛ teaspoon pepper together in large bowl until smooth. Add peas, walnuts, pomegranate seeds, parsley, and scallions and toss to combine. Season with salt and pepper to taste. Sprinkle with remaining 1 tablespoon dukkah and serve.

Cranberry Beans with Warm Spices

SERVES 6 to 8 `VEG`

WHY THIS RECIPE WORKS Cranberry beans have a delicate flavor and a creamy texture similar to that of pinto or cannellini beans. We wanted to create a dish that would highlight these beans, and since they are common in Turkey, we took inspiration from there to create a gently spiced flavor profile. Since cranberry beans are rarely canned, we knew we'd have to start with dried beans. To help the beans cook up creamy and tender, we soaked them overnight in salt water before thoroughly rinsing them to remove any excess salt. We sautéed aromatic vegetables along with tomato paste for depth of flavor; just a touch of cinnamon imparted a subtle yet distinctly Turkish flavor. White wine offered acidity, and broth gave the dish a hearty backbone. Letting the beans cook through in the gentle heat of the oven ensured that they were perfectly cooked without the need for constant monitoring. We completed our comforting side dish with lemon juice and fresh mint, which nicely balanced the warm, rich flavors of the beans. If cranberry beans are unavailable, you can substitute pinto beans. For more information on soaking beans, see page 187.

  Salt and pepper

1 pound (2½ cups) dried cranberry beans, picked over and rinsed

¼ cup extra-virgin olive oil

1 onion, chopped fine

2 carrots, peeled and chopped fine

4 garlic cloves, sliced thin

Soaking dried cranberry beans overnight ensures that they stay intact when slowly cooked in the oven.

1 tablespoon tomato paste

½ teaspoon ground cinnamon

½ cup dry white wine

4 cups chicken or vegetable broth

2 tablespoons lemon juice, plus extra for seasoning

2 tablespoons minced fresh mint

1. Dissolve 3 tablespoons salt in 4 quarts cold water in large container. Add beans and soak at room temperature for at least 8 hours or up to 24 hours. Drain and rinse well.

2. Adjust oven rack to lower-middle position and heat oven to 350 degrees. Heat oil in Dutch oven over medium heat until shimmering. Add onion and carrots and cook until softened, about 5 minutes. Stir in garlic, tomato paste, cinnamon, and ¼ teaspoon pepper and cook until fragrant, about 1 minute. Stir in wine, scraping up any browned bits. Stir in broth, ½ cup water, and beans and bring to boil. Cover, transfer pot to oven, and cook until beans are tender, about 1½ hours, stirring every 30 minutes.

3. Stir in lemon juice and mint. Season with salt, pepper, and extra lemon juice to taste. Adjust consistency with extra hot water as needed. Serve.

We reduce red wine vinegar and sugar for a sweet and sour dressing for our Italian bean salad.

Cranberry Beans with Fennel, Grapes, and Pine Nuts

SERVES 6 to 8   VEG

WHY THIS RECIPE WORKS *Agrodolce* is an Italian sweet-and-sour sauce made by reducing vinegar and sugar. This boldly flavored condiment can accompany a range of dishes, from chicken to pasta to beans. Here we chose to use this classic sauce in a light and flavorful cranberry bean salad. We started with dried beans since canned cranberry beans are hard to find. We first brined the beans overnight to ensure fewer blowouts before rinsing and gently simmering them until tender. Next, we built a flavorful foundation for our salad. We sautéed chopped fennel until it had softened and added fennel seeds to reinforce the fresh fennel's flavor. We reduced red wine vinegar and sugar until they thickened into a syrupy glaze that beautifully coated the salad. Grapes and pine nuts—both common Italian ingredients—provided pops of sweetness and extra crunch. A sprinkling of fennel fronds gave the dish some color and further underscored the fennel flavor. If cranberry beans are unavailable, you can substitute pinto beans. For more information on soaking beans, see page 187.

Salt and pepper
1 pound (2½ cups) dried cranberry beans, picked over and rinsed
3 tablespoons extra-virgin olive oil
½ fennel bulb, 2 tablespoons fronds chopped, stalks discarded, bulb cored and chopped
1 cup plus 2 tablespoons red wine vinegar
½ cup sugar
1 teaspoon fennel seeds
6 ounces seedless red grapes, halved (1 cup)
½ cup pine nuts, toasted

1. Dissolve 3 tablespoons salt in 4 quarts cold water in large container. Add beans and soak at room temperature for at least 8 hours or up to 24 hours. Drain and rinse well.

2. Bring beans, 4 quarts water, and 1 teaspoon salt to boil in Dutch oven. Reduce to simmer and cook, stirring occasionally, until beans are tender, 1 to 1½ hours. Drain beans and set aside.

3. Wipe Dutch oven clean with paper towels. Heat oil in now-empty pot over medium heat until shimmering. Add fennel, ¼ teaspoon salt, and ¼ teaspoon pepper and cook until softened, about 5 minutes. Stir in 1 cup vinegar, sugar, and fennel seeds until sugar is dissolved. Bring to simmer and cook until liquid is thickened to syrupy glaze and edges of fennel are beginning to brown, about 10 minutes.

4. Add beans to vinegar-fennel mixture and toss to coat. Transfer to large bowl and let cool to room temperature. Add grapes, pine nuts, fennel fronds, and remaining 2 tablespoons vinegar and toss to combine. Season with salt and pepper to taste and serve.

Mashed Fava Beans with Cumin and Garlic

SERVES 4 to 6   FAST   VEG

WHY THIS RECIPE WORKS Fava beans are hugely popular in Egypt, so it's no surprise that *ful medames*, a simple dish composed of mashed fava beans flavored with cumin and garlic and topped with a host of fresh ingredients, is one of the nation's most beloved dishes. Despite being Egyptian in origin, many versions of the dish now exist across the Mediterranean, so we set out to create a simplified recipe that was loyal to the dish's ancient roots. The traditional dish is made by cooking dried fava beans in a pear-shaped pot for hours until the beans are soft enough to be mashed. We took a hint from many modern recipes and opted to use canned beans, eliminating both the long cooking time and the need to procure a piece of specialty cookware. We cooked the unrinsed beans in their own seasoned liquid until they were tender and then mashed them gently with a potato masher. We added lemon juice for brightness and cumin for its token warm flavor. As for toppings, recipes we found varied widely, so we opted for the customary additions of chopped tomato, raw onion, and chopped hard-cooked eggs, along with some parsley and a drizzle of extra-virgin olive oil for richness. Traditionally, this dish is served as a hearty breakfast dish, as a dip, or as a side for lunch or dinner; tasters liked it best as a side dish with meat or vegetables or as a flavor-packed snack served with pita. When mashing, keep in mind that the beans do not need to be completely smooth. The finished texture should be similar to that of refried beans. Adjust the consistency while mashing by adding water 1 tablespoon at a time. We had good luck using a single 30-ounce can of Costa brand fava beans.

- 4 garlic cloves, minced
- 1 tablespoon extra-virgin olive oil, plus extra for serving
- 1 teaspoon ground cumin
- 2 (15-ounce) cans fava beans
- 3 tablespoons tahini
- 2 tablespoons lemon juice, plus lemon wedges for serving
  Salt and pepper
- 1 tomato, cored and cut into ½-inch pieces
- 1 small onion, chopped fine
- 2 tablespoons minced fresh parsley
- 2 hard-cooked large eggs, chopped (optional; page 188)

1. Cook garlic, oil, and cumin in medium saucepan over medium heat until fragrant, about 2 minutes. Stir in beans and their liquid and tahini. Bring to simmer and cook until liquid thickens slightly, 8 to 10 minutes.

2. Off heat, mash beans to coarse consistency using potato masher. Stir in lemon juice and 1 teaspoon pepper. Season with salt and pepper to taste. Transfer to serving dish, top with tomato, onion, parsley, and eggs, if using, and drizzle with extra oil. Serve with lemon wedges.

VARIATIONS
Mashed Fava Beans with Cucumbers, Olives, and Feta FAST VEG
Omit onion and egg. Sprinkle ½ cucumber, peeled, halved lengthwise, seeded, and cut into ½-inch pieces, ¼ cup pitted kalamata olives, halved, and ¼ cup crumbled feta cheese over beans along with tomatoes and parsley.

Spicy Mashed Fava Beans with Yogurt FAST VEG
Omit parsley and egg. Add 1 thinly sliced jalapeño chile and ¼ teaspoon cayenne pepper to saucepan with garlic. Substitute 3 chopped scallions for onion. Mix ⅓ cup plain yogurt with additional 1 tablespoon lemon juice and drizzle over beans before serving.

This classic Italian dish features silky mashed dried fava beans topped with a hefty amount of escarole.

Mashed Fava Beans with Sautéed Escarole and Parmesan
SERVES 4 VEG

WHY THIS RECIPE WORKS In wintertime and early spring in the Italian region of Puglia, locals combine their winter stores of dried fava beans with peppery wild chicory into a satisfying, hearty dish, suitable as a vegetarian main or vegetable accompaniment to a meat dish. Dried fava beans are typically cooked down until they can be mashed into a smooth puree and are then topped with chicory dressed simply with olive oil and salt. Unfortunately, wild chicory is not commonplace in American markets, so we designed a recipe that embraced the dish's humble roots using more readily available escarole, which is a member of the chicory family. It was easy to find, quick to cook, and offered a pleasant bitterness. To amp up the flavor and add brightness to the dish, we added chili flakes and lemon zest to the greens, which balanced out the bitter notes. With the greens settled, we turned our attention to creating a smooth, silky puree from our fava beans. Potato is a traditional addition to lend a smoother, more unctuous texture; we found that adding just one potato to the pot with the beans was enough to achieve the texture we were after. We processed the cooked fava beans and potato through a food mill to help prevent a gummy texture. Finally, we finished the dish with shaved Parmesan cheese for a salty bite that brought out all of the complex, earthy flavors of the fava beans.

2½ cups chicken or vegetable broth
2½ cups water, plus extra as needed
  8 ounces (1½ cups) dried split fava beans
  1 Yukon Gold potato, peeled and cut into 1-inch pieces
  3 tablespoons extra-virgin olive oil, plus extra for serving
    Salt and pepper
  3 garlic cloves, minced
  ¼ teaspoon red pepper flakes
  1 head escarole (1 pound), cored and cut into 1-inch pieces
  1 tablespoon grated lemon zest
  1 ounce Parmesan cheese, shaved

1. Bring broth, water, and beans to boil in large saucepan. Reduce to simmer and cook until beans are softened and beginning to break down, about 15 minutes. Stir in potato, return to simmer, and cook until potato is tender and almost all liquid is absorbed, 25 to 30 minutes. Process bean-potato mixture through food mill or ricer into medium bowl. Stir in 2 tablespoons oil and season with salt and pepper to taste. Adjust consistency with extra hot water as needed. (Mixture should be consistency of thin mashed potatoes.) Cover to keep warm.

2. Meanwhile, heat remaining 1 tablespoon oil in 12-inch skillet over medium heat until shimmering. Add garlic, pepper flakes, and ¼ teaspoon salt and cook until fragrant, about 30 seconds. Stir in escarole, cover, and cook until wilted, 3 to 5 minutes. Stir in lemon zest and season with salt and pepper to taste.

Shaving Parmesan

Run vegetable peeler over block of Parmesan, making sure to use light touch to ensure even shavings.

3. Spread fava bean mixture into even layer on serving platter and arrange escarole on top. Sprinkle with Parmesan and drizzle with extra oil. Serve.

Gigante Beans with Spinach and Feta
SERVES 6 to 8 VEG

WHY THIS RECIPE WORKS Popular throughout Greece, gigante beans are similar in size and texture to large lima beans. They're usually about 1½ inches long, with a velvety, creamy texture and earthy flavor. In Greece, they are used in a variety of ways, from soups and stews to salads and sides, to create rustic, full-flavored dishes. Greens are ubiquitous in Greek cuisine as well, present at almost every meal, so we set our sights on combining these two ingredients into a hearty, satisfying side dish that could be served alongside a garlicky leg of lamb or with a piece of crusty bread as a light lunch or vegetarian main course. We cooked down the spinach in a large Dutch oven using a combination steam-sauté method, which gave the spinach more flavor as it wilted. We then stirred in our soaked and cooked beans (soaking was essential to preventing blowouts) along with flavor-boosting tomatoes and dill. To make the dish even more impressive, we took a cue from some recipes we had found in our research and baked the greens and beans with some fresh bread crumbs on top to give the dish some crunch. A sprinkle of feta cheese offered salty, tangy contrast. If you can't find curly-leaf spinach, you can substitute flat-leaf spinach; do not substitute baby spinach. Dried gigante beans can be found at Greek and Middle Eastern markets as well as in the international food aisle of many supermarkets; if you cannot find them, substitute dried large lima beans. For more information on soaking beans, see page 187.

    Salt and pepper
  8 ounces (1½ cups) dried gigante beans, picked over and rinsed
  6 tablespoons extra-virgin olive oil
  2 onions, chopped fine
  3 garlic cloves, minced
 20 ounces curly-leaf spinach, stemmed
  2 (14.5-ounce) cans diced tomatoes, drained
  ¼ cup minced fresh dill
  2 slices hearty white sandwich bread, torn into quarters
  6 ounces feta cheese, crumbled (1½ cups)
    Lemon wedges

1. Dissolve 3 tablespoons salt in 4 quarts cold water in large container. Add beans and soak at room temperature for at least 8 hours or up to 24 hours. Drain and rinse well.

2. Bring beans and 2 quarts water to boil in Dutch oven. Reduce to simmer and cook, stirring occasionally, until beans are tender, 1 to 1½ hours. Drain beans and set aside.

3. Wipe Dutch oven clean with paper towels. Heat 2 tablespoons oil in now-empty pot over medium heat until shimmering. Add onions and ½ teaspoon salt and cook until softened, about 5 minutes. Stir in garlic and cook until fragrant, about 30 seconds. Stir in half of spinach, cover, and cook until beginning to wilt, about 2 minutes. Stir in remaining spinach, cover, and cook until wilted, about 2 minutes. Off heat, gently stir in beans, tomatoes, dill, and 2 tablespoons oil. Season with salt and pepper to taste.

4. Meanwhile, adjust oven rack to middle position and heat oven to 400 degrees. Pulse bread and remaining 2 tablespoons oil in food processor to coarse crumbs, about 5 pulses. Transfer bean mixture to 13 by 9-inch baking dish and sprinkle with feta, then bread crumbs. Bake until bread crumbs are golden brown and edges are bubbling, about 20 minutes. Serve with lemon wedges.

NOTES FROM THE TEST KITCHEN

The Science of Salt-Soaking Beans

Most people think of brining as a way to keep lean meat juicy and tender, but brining isn't just for meat. When you soak dried beans in salted water, they cook up with softer skins and are less likely to blow out and disintegrate. Why? It has to do with how the sodium ions in salt interact with the cells of the bean skins. As the beans soak, the sodium ions replace some of the calcium and magnesium ions in the skins. Because sodium ions are more weakly charged than calcium and magnesium ions, they allow more water to penetrate into the skins, leading to a softer texture. During soaking, the sodium ions filter only partway into the beans, so their greatest effect is on the cells in the outermost part of the beans. Softening the skins also makes them less likely to split as the beans cook, keeping the beans intact. For 1 pound of dried beans, dissolve 3 tablespoons of table salt in 4 quarts of cold water. Soak the beans at room temperature for 8 to 24 hours. Drain and rinse them well before using.

FOR A QUICK SALT-SOAK

If you are pressed for time, you can "quick-soak" your beans. Simply combine the salt, water, and beans in a large Dutch oven and bring to a boil over high heat. Remove the pot from the heat, cover, and let stand for 1 hour. Drain and rinse the beans well before using.

A toasted garlic broth infuses canned pinto beans with flavor in this Turkish salad.

Turkish Pinto Bean Salad with Tomatoes, Eggs, and Parsley

SERVES 4 to 6 FAST VEG

WHY THIS RECIPE WORKS *Fasulye piyazi* is a traditional Turkish bean salad that is often served with *kofte*, or Turkish meatballs (page 321). Frequently made with small white beans, this hearty salad usually contains tomatoes, parsley, hard-cooked eggs, and more. For our version, we started with the beans. To give our salad a more robust flavor, we opted for pinto beans instead of white beans. To further elevate flavor, we infused the beans with aromatics by warming them briefly in a toasted garlic broth. The traditional dressing of olive oil and lemon juice proved underwhelming when paired with the stronger-flavored pinto beans, so we decided to incorporate another staple eastern Mediterranean ingredient: tahini. A generous amount of Aleppo pepper, with its sweet, gently spicy, and mildly smoky undertones, complemented the tart acidity of the dressing. Tossing the beans with the dressing while they were still warm allowed for better flavor absorption. Keeping with tradition, we added cherry tomatoes, onion, and parsley, which contributed to our salad's bright, fresh flavor. A sprinkle of sesame seeds provided textural contrast and emphasized the tahini nicely. Last, the traditional addition of hard-cooked eggs provided extra protein, giving the dish enough substance to act as an entrée as well as a complexly flavored side. If you can't find Aleppo pepper, you can substitute ¾ teaspoon of paprika and ¾ teaspoon of finely chopped red pepper flakes.

¼ cup extra-virgin olive oil
3 garlic cloves, lightly crushed and peeled
2 (15-ounce) cans pinto beans, rinsed
  Salt and pepper
¼ cup tahini
3 tablespoons lemon juice
1 tablespoon ground dried Aleppo pepper, plus extra for serving
8 ounces cherry tomatoes, halved
¼ red onion, sliced thin
½ cup fresh parsley leaves
2 hard-cooked large eggs, quartered
1 tablespoon toasted sesame seeds

EASY-PEEL HARD-COOKED EGGS

MAKES 6 eggs `VEG`

Be sure to use large eggs that have no cracks and are cold from the refrigerator. If you don't have a steamer basket, use a spoon or tongs to gently place the eggs in the water. It does not matter if the eggs are above the water or partially submerged. You can use this method for fewer than six eggs without altering the timing. You can also double this recipe as long as you use a pot and steamer basket large enough to hold the eggs in a single layer. There's no need to peel the eggs right away. They can be stored in their shells and peeled when needed.

6 large eggs

1. Bring 1 inch water to rolling boil in medium saucepan over high heat. Place eggs in steamer basket. Transfer basket to saucepan. Cover, reduce heat to medium-low, and cook eggs for 13 minutes.

2. When eggs are almost finished cooking, combine 2 cups ice cubes and 2 cups cold water in medium bowl. Using tongs or spoon, transfer eggs to ice bath; let sit for 15 minutes. Peel before using.

---

1. Cook 1 tablespoon oil and garlic in medium saucepan over medium heat, stirring often, until garlic turns golden but not brown, about 3 minutes. Add beans, 2 cups water, and 1 teaspoon salt and bring to simmer. Remove from heat, cover, and let sit for 20 minutes.

2. Drain beans and discard garlic. Whisk remaining 3 tablespoons oil, tahini, lemon juice, Aleppo, 1 tablespoon water, and ¼ teaspoon salt together in large bowl. Add beans, tomatoes, onion, and parsley and gently toss to combine. Season with salt and pepper to taste. Transfer to serving platter and arrange eggs on top. Sprinkle with sesame seeds and extra Aleppo and serve.

Moroccan Braised White Beans with Lamb
SERVES 6 to 8

WHY THIS RECIPE WORKS *Loubia* is a dish of stewed white beans that is well loved in Morocco. Traditionally, the beans are cooked in a warm-spiced tomatoey base and scooped up with good bread, making for a comforting meal. *Khlii*, a Moroccan preserved meat, is often used as a flavorful seasoning, leaving the beans to take center stage. But khlii is difficult to find in the United States, so we decided to use a lamb shank to enhance the meaty flavor of the dish. We seared and then slowly braised the lamb in the oven with the beans. A healthy dose of Moroccan-inspired spices gave the dish a deeply flavorful backbone, and some white wine provided acidity. A combination of mostly chicken broth and a little water gave the dish some savory depth without making it too salty. We chose dried beans over canned so that the beans would cook at the same rate as the lamb shank, leaving us with creamy, richly flavored beans and melt-in-your-mouth tender pieces of lamb. You can substitute 1 pound of lamb shoulder chops (blade or round bone), 1 to 1½ inches thick, trimmed and halved, for the lamb shank; reduce the browning time in step 2 to 8 minutes. For more information on soaking beans, see page 187.

  Salt and pepper
1 pound (2½ cups) dried great Northern beans, picked over and rinsed
1 (12- to 16-ounce) lamb shank
1 tablespoon extra-virgin olive oil, plus extra for serving
1 onion, chopped
1 red bell pepper, stemmed, seeded, and chopped fine
2 tablespoons tomato paste
3 garlic cloves, minced
2 teaspoons paprika
2 teaspoons ground cumin
1½ teaspoons ground ginger
¼ teaspoon cayenne pepper

A rich lamb shank flavors dried white beans in this savory Moroccan stewed dish.

½ cup dry white wine
4 cups chicken broth
2 tablespoons minced fresh parsley

1. Dissolve 3 tablespoons salt in 4 quarts cold water in large container. Add beans and soak at room temperature for at least 8 hours or up to 24 hours. Drain and rinse well.

2. Adjust oven rack to lower-middle position and heat oven to 350 degrees. Pat lamb dry with paper towels and season with salt and pepper. Heat oil in Dutch oven over medium-high heat until just smoking. Brown lamb on all sides, 10 to 15 minutes; transfer to plate. Pour off all but 2 tablespoons fat from pot.

3. Add onion and bell pepper to fat left in pot and cook over medium heat until softened and lightly browned, 5 to 7 minutes. Stir in tomato paste, garlic, paprika, cumin, ginger, cayenne, and ⅛ teaspoon pepper and cook until fragrant, about 30 seconds. Stir in wine, scraping up any browned bits. Stir in broth, 1 cup water, and beans and bring to boil.

4. Nestle lamb into beans along with any accumulated juices. Cover, transfer pot to oven, and cook until fork slips easily in and out of lamb and beans are tender, 1½ to 1¾ hours, stirring every 30 minutes.

5. Transfer lamb to cutting board, let cool slightly, then shred into bite-size pieces using 2 forks; discard excess fat and bone. Stir shredded lamb and parsley into beans and season with salt and pepper to taste. Adjust consistency with extra hot water as needed. Serve, drizzling individual portions with extra oil.

Sicilian White Beans and Escarole
SERVES 4 FAST VEG

WHY THIS RECIPE WORKS White beans and escarole are a classic pairing in Italian cooking: Combining the buttery texture of cannellini beans with tender, slightly bitter escarole results in a well-balanced and simple side dish. Canned beans made this dish simple, and their texture was a perfect counterpoint to the greens. Sautéed onions gave the dish a rich, deep flavor base without requiring too much time at the stove. Red pepper flakes lent a slight heat without overwhelming the other ingredients, and a combination of broth and water provided a flavorful backbone. We added the escarole and beans along with the liquid, and then we cooked the greens just until the leaves were wilted before cranking up the heat so the liquid would quickly evaporate. This short stint on the heat prevented the beans from breaking down and becoming mushy. Once we took the pot off the heat, we stirred in lemon juice for a bright finish and drizzled on some extra olive oil for richness. Chicory can be substituted for the escarole; however, its flavor is stronger.

1 tablespoon extra-virgin olive oil, plus extra for serving
2 onions, chopped fine
  Salt and pepper
4 garlic cloves, minced
⅛ teaspoon red pepper flakes
1 head escarole (1 pound), trimmed and sliced 1 inch thick
1 (15-ounce) can cannellini beans, rinsed
1 cup chicken or vegetable broth
1 cup water
2 teaspoons lemon juice

1. Heat oil in Dutch oven over medium heat until shimmering. Add onions and ½ teaspoon salt and cook until softened and lightly browned, 5 to 7 minutes. Stir in garlic and pepper flakes and cook until fragrant, about 30 seconds.

2. Stir in escarole, beans, broth, and water and bring to simmer. Cook, stirring occasionally, until escarole is wilted, about 5 minutes. Increase heat to high and cook until liquid is nearly evaporated, 10 to 15 minutes. Stir in lemon juice and season with salt and pepper to taste. Drizzle with extra oil and serve.

Creamy canned cannellini beans make a perfect base for ultrasimple Mediterranean-flavored salads.

¼ cup extra-virgin olive oil
3 garlic cloves, peeled and smashed
2 (15-ounce) cans cannellini beans, rinsed
  Salt and pepper
2 teaspoons sherry vinegar
1 small shallot, minced
1 red bell pepper, stemmed, seeded, and cut into ¼-inch pieces
¼ cup chopped fresh parsley
2 teaspoons chopped fresh chives

1. Cook 1 tablespoon oil and garlic in medium saucepan over medium heat, stirring often, until garlic turns golden but not brown, about 3 minutes. Add beans, 2 cups water, and 1 teaspoon salt and bring to simmer. Remove from heat, cover, and let sit for 20 minutes.

2. Meanwhile, combine vinegar and shallot in large bowl and let sit for 20 minutes. Drain beans and remove garlic. Add beans, remaining 3 tablespoons oil, bell pepper, parsley, and chives to shallot mixture and gently toss to combine. Season with salt and pepper to taste. Let sit for 20 minutes. Serve.

VARIATION

White Bean Salad with Tomatoes and Olives VEG
Substitute 1 cup quartered cherry tomatoes for bell pepper and ½ cup chopped fresh basil for parsley and chives. Add ⅓ cup chopped kalamata olives to salad before tossing to combine.

White Bean Salad
SERVES 6 to 8 VEG

WHY THIS RECIPE WORKS White beans are used in a host of recipes across the Mediterranean region, and one of our favorites is a simple salad preparation that allows the creamy-sweet beans to shine. This well-balanced, ultraflavorful white bean salad is the perfect way to add some protein and substance to a meal; we used classic Spanish flavors and ingredients to give the salad an identity. Cannellini beans worked perfectly, since they have a savory, buttery flavor that tasters enjoyed. We steeped the beans in a garlicky broth, which infused them with flavor. While the beans sat, we had enough time to rid our shallots of any harsh flavors by briefly marinating them in nutty, complex sherry vinegar. Red bell pepper offered sweetness and crunch. Parsley provided grassy, herby flavor, and chives gave the salad some subtle onion notes, rounding out the dish nicely. Our ultrasimple salad had a surprisingly complex flavor profile, and we were happy to find that it was as versatile as it was easy to put together.

White Bean Salad with Sautéed Squid and Pepperoncini
SERVES 4 to 6

WHY THIS RECIPE WORKS Recipes that pair savory white beans with lean, mild squid are common in Italy, and it's easy to understand why: The delicate flavor of the beans complements but doesn't overpower the subtle seafood flavor of the squid. But recipes vary widely in both cooking method and ingredient additions, so we knew we had our work cut out for us. We started with the squid. Since we wanted to achieve some flavorful browning, we immediately ruled out steaming and boiling. We also decided that grilling was too fussy for just a pound of squid, so we settled on sautéing. In past recipes, we've used a baking soda brine to tenderize the squid and make it less likely to overcook, and we wondered if it was necessary here. A side-by-side test determined that it was: The unbrined squid had turned rubbery by the time we achieved any browning, but the brined squid stayed beautifully tender even after spending several minutes in the skillet. Cooking

To achieve well-browned, tender squid, we soak it quickly in a baking soda brine, then sauté it over high heat.

the squid in two batches encouraged more even browning. Using canned beans kept the overall cooking time short, and simmering them in an aromatic liquid infused them with flavor. After a few tests, we determined that tasters preferred simpler salads that allowed the tender squid and beans to shine. Nutty sherry vinegar and tangy pepperoncini were winning additions, and to bring out more of the pepperoncini flavor, we also added some of the brine. Scallions and whole parsley leaves provided a finishing touch of freshness. Be sure to use small squid (with bodies 3 to 4 inches in length) because they cook more quickly and are more tender than larger squid.

1 tablespoon baking soda
  Salt and pepper
1 pound squid, bodies sliced crosswise into ½-inch-thick rings, tentacles halved
6 tablespoons extra-virgin olive oil
1 red onion, chopped fine
3 garlic cloves, minced
2 (15-ounce) cans cannellini beans, rinsed
⅓ cup pepperoncini, stemmed and sliced into ¼-inch-thick rings, plus 2 tablespoons brine
2 tablespoons sherry vinegar
½ cup fresh parsley leaves
3 scallions, green parts only, sliced thin

1. Dissolve baking soda and 1 tablespoon salt in 3 cups cold water in medium container. Add squid, cover, and refrigerate for 15 minutes. Dry squid thoroughly with paper towels and toss with 1 tablespoon oil.

2. Heat 1 tablespoon oil in medium saucepan over medium heat until shimmering. Add onion and ¼ teaspoon salt and cook, stirring occasionally, until softened and lightly browned, 5 to 7 minutes. Stir in garlic and cook until fragrant, about 30 seconds. Stir in beans and ¼ cup water and bring to simmer. Reduce heat to low, cover, and continue to simmer, stirring occasionally, for 2 to 3 minutes; set aside.

3. Heat 1 tablespoon oil in 12-inch nonstick skillet over high heat until just smoking. Add half of squid in single layer and cook, without moving, until well browned, about 3 minutes. Flip squid and continue to cook, without moving, until well browned on second side, about 2 minutes; transfer to bowl. Wipe skillet clean with paper towels and repeat with 1 tablespoon oil and remaining squid.

4. Whisk remaining 2 tablespoons oil, pepperoncini brine, and vinegar together in large bowl. Add beans and any remaining cooking liquid, squid, parsley, scallions, and pepperoncini and toss to combine. Season with salt and pepper to taste. Serve.

NOTES FROM THE TEST KITCHEN
Buying White Beans

White beans are a staple in France, Spain, Italy, and beyond in everything from creamy dips and salads to soups to braises. While dried beans are essential for certain recipes, we've found that in many cases canned beans are just as good as or even better than dried. In fact, in our tasting of canned and dried white beans, canned Goya Cannellini took top honors: The nutty flavor and uniformly tender texture won tasters over. However, when a recipe requires dried white beans, we'll turn to Rancho Gordo Classic Cassoulet Beans, which have a creamy, smooth texture and fresh, clean taste.

For optimal texture, we soak dried beans and cook our Tuscan stew in the gentle heat of the oven.

Hearty Tuscan Bean Stew
SERVES 8

WHY THIS RECIPE WORKS Rustic bean soups and stews are a hallmark of Tuscan cuisine, so we set out to develop a recipe with big flavor, tender beans and greens, and a streamlined method. To make an aromatic base, we combined pancetta, carrots, onion, celery, and garlic before adding the beans and cooking liquid. Transferring the pot to the oven encouraged even cooking and avoided the need for constant stirring. We added tomatoes toward the end of cooking, since their acid would otherwise prevent the beans from softening. Adding the kale with the tomatoes ensured that it didn't overcook and turn to mush. Finally, we briefly steeped a sprig of rosemary in the stew to provide herbal notes without overpowering the other flavors. If pancetta is unavailable, substitute four slices of bacon. For more information on soaking beans, see page 187. Serve with Garlic Toasts (page 56) or crusty bread.

    Salt and pepper
1 pound (2½ cups) dried cannellini beans, picked over and rinsed

1 tablespoon extra-virgin olive oil, plus extra for serving
6 ounces pancetta, cut into ¼-inch pieces
1 large onion, chopped
2 carrots, peeled and cut into ½-inch pieces
2 celery ribs, cut into ½-inch pieces
8 garlic cloves, peeled and smashed
4 cups chicken broth
3 cups water
2 bay leaves
1 pound kale or collard greens, stemmed and chopped
1 (14.5-ounce) can diced tomatoes, drained
1 sprig fresh rosemary

Making Hearty Tuscan Bean Stew

1. CREATE AROMATIC BASE Cook pancetta until browned and fat is rendered, then add onion, carrots, and celery and cook until lightly browned. Stir in garlic.

2. ADD BEANS AND TRANSFER TO OVEN Stir in broth, water, soaked beans, and bay leaf and bring to boil. Cover pot and transfer to oven. Cook until beans are almost tender.

3. ADD KALE AND TOMATOES Stir in kale and canned tomatoes and return pot to oven. Let cook until beans and kale are completely tender.

4. STEEP ROSEMARY AND FINISH Remove pot from oven and submerge rosemary sprig in stew for 15 minutes. If desired, press some beans against side of pot to thicken stew.

1. Dissolve 3 tablespoons salt in 4 quarts cold water in large container. Add beans and soak at room temperature for at least 8 hours or up to 24 hours. Drain and rinse well.

2. Adjust oven rack to lower-middle position and heat oven to 250 degrees. Heat oil and pancetta in Dutch oven over medium heat. Cook, stirring occasionally, until pancetta is lightly browned and fat has rendered, 6 to 10 minutes. Add onion, carrots, and celery and cook, stirring occasionally, until softened and lightly browned, 10 to 16 minutes. Stir in garlic and cook until fragrant, about 1 minute. Stir in broth, water, bay leaves, and beans and bring to boil. Cover, transfer pot to oven, and cook until beans are almost tender (very center of beans will still be firm), 45 minutes to 1 hour.

3. Stir in kale and tomatoes, cover, and cook until beans and greens are fully tender, 30 to 40 minutes.

4. Remove pot from oven and submerge rosemary sprig in stew. Cover and let sit for 15 minutes. Discard bay leaves and rosemary sprig and season stew with salt and pepper to taste. If desired, use back of spoon to press some beans against side of pot to thicken stew. Serve, drizzling individual portions with extra oil.

North African Vegetable and Bean Stew
SERVES 6 to 8 **VEG**

WHY THIS RECIPE WORKS North African stews combine heady, potent spices with hearty, filling vegetables, pasta, and beans. We set out to create a rich-tasting vegetable stew in the manner of Tunisian and Moroccan cookery; a combination of chickpeas and butter beans gave our stew a balance of earthiness and creaminess. For the vegetables, we chose Swiss chard and chunks of carrot, and tiny dried pasta like ditalini worked nicely in place of the traditional handmade North African noodles. *Harissa*, a ubiquitous North African spice paste made with ground chiles, cumin, coriander, garlic, and olive oil, added both heat and depth of flavor to the stew. You can substitute one 10-ounce bag of frozen baby lima beans for the butter beans. We prefer to use our homemade Harissa (page 316), but you can substitute store-bought harissa if you wish, though spiciness can vary greatly by brand.

1 tablespoon extra-virgin olive oil
1 onion, chopped fine
8 ounces Swiss chard, stems chopped fine, leaves cut into ½-inch pieces
4 garlic cloves, minced
1 teaspoon ground cumin
½ teaspoon paprika
½ teaspoon ground coriander
¼ teaspoon ground cinnamon
2 tablespoons tomato paste
2 tablespoons all-purpose flour

This traditional North African vegetarian stew gets body and substance from two types of beans and tiny pasta.

7 cups vegetable broth
2 carrots, peeled and cut into ½-inch pieces
1 (15-ounce) can chickpeas, rinsed
1 (15-ounce) can butter beans, rinsed
½ cup small pasta, such as ditalini, tubettini, or elbow macaroni
⅓ cup minced fresh parsley
6 tablespoons harissa
Salt and pepper

1. Heat oil in Dutch oven over medium heat until shimmering. Add onion and chard stems and cook until softened, about 5 minutes. Stir in garlic, cumin, paprika, coriander, and cinnamon and cook until fragrant, about 30 seconds. Stir in tomato paste and flour and cook for 1 minute.

2. Slowly stir in broth and carrots, scraping up any browned bits and smoothing out any lumps, and bring to boil. Reduce to gentle simmer and cook for 10 minutes. Stir in chard leaves, chickpeas, beans, and pasta and simmer until vegetables and pasta are tender, 10 to 15 minutes. Stir in parsley and ¼ cup harissa. Season with salt and pepper to taste. Serve, passing remaining harissa separately.

Vegetables

■ FAST (less than 45 minutes start to finish)   ■ VEGETARIAN

Photos (clockwise from top left): Sautéed Spinach with Yogurt and Dukkah; Spicy Roasted Carrots with Cilantro; Roasted Celery Root with Yogurt and Sesame Seeds

Roasted Artichokes with Lemon Vinaigrette

SERVES 4 `VEG`

WHY THIS RECIPE WORKS A staple of both Greek and Italian cuisines, delicately nutty artichokes need little adornment. We decided to try roasting them to concentrate their flavor. We prepped the artichokes for the oven by trimming the leaves, halving the artichokes, and removing the fuzzy chokes. Submerging the prepped artichokes in water and lemon juice kept them from oxidizing. Because they have so much surface area, artichokes can quickly dry out and toughen in the oven, so we covered them with aluminum foil to let them steam in their own juice. This simple step tenderized the artichokes from leaves to heart. Tossing the artichokes with oil and roasting them cut side down encouraged flavorful browning. The fresh tang of citrus pairs well with artichokes' earthy flavor, so we roasted some halved lemons alongside the artichokes and used the deeply flavorful juice in a vinaigrette. We whisked the juice with grated garlic and Dijon before drizzling in and emulsifying some olive oil to create a bright, intense dressing. If your artichokes are larger than 8 to 10 ounces, strip away another layer or two of the toughest outer leaves. The tender inner leaves, heart, and stem are entirely edible. To eat the tough outer leaves, use your teeth to scrape the flesh from the underside of each leaf. A rasp-style grater makes quick work of turning the garlic into a paste. These artichokes taste great warm or at room temperature.

- 3 lemons
- 4 artichokes (8 to 10 ounces each)
- 9 tablespoons extra-virgin olive oil
  Salt and pepper
- ½ teaspoon garlic, minced to paste
- ½ teaspoon Dijon mustard
- 2 teaspoons chopped fresh parsley

Roasting fresh artichokes in a covered dish steams them to tenderness while concentrating their flavor.

1. Adjust oven rack to lower-middle position and heat oven to 475 degrees. Cut 1 lemon in half, squeeze halves into container filled with 2 quarts water, then add spent halves.

2. Working with 1 artichoke at a time, trim stem to about ¾ inch and cut off top quarter of artichoke. Break off bottom 3 or 4 rows

Making Roasted Artichokes

1. PREP Trim artichokes, cut in half, and remove fuzzy chokes. Submerge prepped artichokes in prepared lemon water.

2. SEASON Remove artichokes from lemon water, leaving some water clinging to leaves. Toss with oil, salt, and pepper and arrange in dish.

3. ROAST Trim and halve lemons and place in dish with artichokes. Cover with foil and roast until artichokes begin to brown and are tender.

4. MAKE DRESSING Squeeze cooled lemons into strainer set over bowl. Whisk in seasonings, then oil, then parsley. Serve.

of tough outer leaves by pulling them downward. Using paring knife, trim outer layer of stem and base, removing any dark green parts. Cut artichoke in half lengthwise, then remove fuzzy choke and any tiny inner purple-tinged leaves using small spoon. Submerge prepped artichokes in lemon water.

3. Coat bottom of 13 by 9-inch baking dish with 1 tablespoon oil. Remove artichokes from lemon water and shake off water, leaving some water still clinging to leaves. Toss artichokes with 2 tablespoons oil, ¾ teaspoon salt, and pinch pepper; gently rub oil and seasonings between leaves. Arrange artichokes cut side down in prepared dish. Trim ends off remaining 2 lemons, halve crosswise, and arrange cut side up next to artichokes. Cover tightly with aluminum foil and roast until cut sides of artichokes begin to brown and bases and leaves are tender when poked with tip of paring knife, 25 to 30 minutes.

4. Transfer artichokes to serving platter. Let lemons cool slightly, then squeeze into fine-mesh strainer set over bowl, extracting as much juice and pulp as possible; press firmly on solids to yield 1½ tablespoons juice. Whisk garlic, mustard, and ½ teaspoon salt into juice. Whisking constantly, slowly drizzle in remaining 6 tablespoons oil until emulsified. Whisk in parsley and season with salt and pepper to taste. Serve artichokes with dressing.

Braised Artichokes with Tomatoes and Thyme
SERVES 4 to 6

WHY THIS RECIPE WORKS We wanted to use fresh whole artichokes to create an everyday side that would keep the focus on these seasonal gems. Gently braising the artichokes to perfect tenderness seemed to fit the bill—and we decided to create a rich, flavorful sauce at the same time. To avoid drab-looking, flat-tasting, and fibrous artichokes, we trimmed them so that only their most tender inner leaves remained. A braising liquid of white wine and chicken broth imparted acidity and depth of flavor. Subtle and earthy thyme complemented the artichokes' delicate flavor, and anchovies amplified the savory qualities of the dish. Canned tomatoes are common in braises, but when we used them, tasters detected an unpleasant metallic note; replacing them with halved cherry tomatoes at the end of cooking preserved the brightness of the sauce and added welcome splashes of color. If your artichokes are larger than 8 to 10 ounces, strip away another layer or two of the toughest outer leaves.

1 lemon
4 artichokes (8 to 10 ounces each)
2 tablespoons extra-virgin olive oil
1 onion, chopped fine
  Salt and pepper
3 garlic cloves, minced
2 anchovy fillets, rinsed, patted dry, and minced
1 teaspoon minced fresh thyme or ¼ teaspoon dried
½ cup dry white wine
1 cup chicken broth
6 ounces cherry tomatoes, halved
2 tablespoons chopped fresh parsley

1. Cut lemon in half, squeeze halves into container filled with 2 quarts water, then add spent halves. Working with 1 artichoke at a time, trim stem to about ¾ inch and cut off top quarter of artichoke. Break off bottom 3 or 4 rows of tough outer leaves by pulling them downward. Using paring knife, trim outer layer of stem and base, removing any dark green parts. Cut artichoke in half lengthwise, remove fuzzy choke and any tiny inner purple-tinged leaves using small spoon, then cut each half into 1-inch-thick wedges. Submerge prepped artichokes in lemon water.

2. Heat oil in 12-inch skillet over medium heat until shimmering. Add onion, ¾ teaspoon salt, and ¼ teaspoon pepper and cook until softened and lightly browned, 5 to 7 minutes. Stir in garlic, anchovies, and thyme and cook until fragrant, about 30 seconds. Stir in wine and cook until almost evaporated, about 1 minute. Stir in broth and bring to simmer.

3. Remove artichokes from lemon water, shaking off excess water, and add to skillet. Cover, reduce heat to medium-low, and simmer until artichokes are tender, 20 to 25 minutes.

4. Stir in tomatoes, bring to simmer, and cook until tomatoes start to break down, 3 to 5 minutes. Off heat, stir in parsley and season with salt and pepper to taste. Serve.

NOTES FROM THE TEST KITCHEN
Assessing Artichokes

When selecting fresh artichokes at the market, examine the leaves for some clues that will help you pick the best specimens. The leaves should look tight, compact, and bright green; they should not appear dried out or feathery at the edges. If you give an artichoke a squeeze, its leaves should squeak as they rub together (evidence that the artichoke still possesses much of its moisture). The leaves should also snap off cleanly; if they bend, the artichoke is old.

Greek yogurt adds richness to the flavorful broth of our hearty vegetarian tagine.

Artichoke, Pepper, and Chickpea Tagine

SERVES 4 to 6 VEG

WHY THIS RECIPE WORKS Slow-cooked, hearty tagines are synonymous with North African cuisine and traditionally boast a range of vegetables and meats. We wanted to turn out a satisfying meatless version packed with big bites of artichokes and peppers and tender chickpeas, flavored with pungent garlic, lots of warm spices, briny olives, and tangy lemon. Using only quick-cooking vegetables kept this tagine from being an all-day affair. First we drained and rinsed jarred artichokes, then we sautéed them to drive off any remaining moisture. Next we lightly browned bell peppers and onion. Canned chickpeas needed only to be simmered in the flavorful broth. For the aromatic lemon flavor that distinguishes authentic tagines, we used lots of lemon zest. Finally, we enriched the broth by stirring in Greek yogurt just before serving. While we prefer the richer, fuller flavor of whole-milk Greek yogurt, regular plain whole-milk yogurt can be substituted; the sauce will be slightly thinner. A rasp-style grater makes quick work of turning the garlic into a paste. While we prefer the flavor and texture of jarred whole baby artichoke hearts, you can substitute 18 ounces frozen artichoke hearts, thawed and patted dry, for the jarred. Serve with Simple Couscous (page 161).

¼ cup extra-virgin olive oil, plus extra for serving
3 cups jarred whole baby artichoke hearts packed in water, quartered, rinsed, and patted dry
2 yellow or red bell peppers, stemmed, seeded, and cut into ½-inch-wide strips
1 onion, halved and sliced ¼ inch thick
4 (2-inch) strips lemon zest plus 1 teaspoon grated zest (2 lemons)
8 garlic cloves, minced
1 tablespoon paprika
½ teaspoon ground cumin
¼ teaspoon ground ginger
¼ teaspoon ground coriander
¼ teaspoon ground cinnamon
⅛ teaspoon cayenne pepper
2 tablespoons all-purpose flour
3 cups vegetable broth
2 (15-ounce) cans chickpeas, rinsed
½ cup pitted kalamata olives, halved
½ cup golden raisins
2 tablespoons honey
½ cup plain whole-milk Greek yogurt
½ cup minced fresh cilantro
Salt and pepper

1. Heat 1 tablespoon oil in Dutch oven over medium heat until shimmering. Add artichokes and cook until golden brown, 5 to 7 minutes; transfer to bowl.

2. Add bell peppers, onion, lemon zest strips, and 1 tablespoon oil to now-empty pot and cook over medium heat until vegetables are softened and lightly browned, 5 to 7 minutes. Stir in two-thirds of garlic, paprika, cumin, ginger, coriander, cinnamon, and cayenne and cook until fragrant, about 30 seconds. Stir in flour and cook for 1 minute.

3. Slowly whisk in broth, scraping up any browned bits and smoothing out any lumps. Stir in artichoke hearts, chickpeas, olives, raisins, and honey and bring to simmer. Reduce heat to low, cover, and simmer gently until vegetables are tender, about 15 minutes.

4. Off heat, discard lemon zest strips. Combine ¼ cup hot liquid and yogurt in bowl to temper, then stir yogurt mixture into pot. Stir in remaining 2 tablespoons oil, remaining garlic, cilantro, and grated lemon zest. Season with salt and pepper to taste. Serve, drizzling individual portions with extra oil.

Pan-Roasted Asparagus with Cherry Tomatoes and Kalamata Olives

SERVES 6 `FAST` `VEG`

WHY THIS RECIPE WORKS We set out to create a pan-roasted asparagus dish enhanced with the flavors of Italy. Pan roasting is a simple stovetop cooking method that delivers crisp, evenly browned asparagus spears without the need to turn on the oven. We started with thicker spears because thin ones overcooked before they browned. To help the asparagus release moisture, which encouraged caramelization and better flavor, we parcooked it, covered, with oil and water before browning it. The evaporating water helped to steam the asparagus, producing bright green, crisp-tender spears. At this point, we removed the lid and cranked up the heat until the spears were evenly browned on the bottom. We found there was no need to brown the asparagus all over; tasters preferred the flavor of spears browned on only one side, and, as a bonus, the partially browned spears never had a chance to go limp. With our asparagus cooked to perfection, we decided on a combination of tomatoes, olives, and garlic to create a simple yet flavorful relish. A final dusting of Parmesan cheese and shredded basil rounded out our Italian-inspired flavor profile. This recipe works best with thick asparagus spears that are between ½ and ¾ inch in diameter. If using thinner spears, reduce the covered cooking time to 3 minutes and the uncovered cooking time to 5 minutes. Do not use pencil-thin asparagus; it overcooks too easily. You will need a 12-inch skillet with a tight-fitting lid for this recipe.

- 2 tablespoons extra-virgin olive oil
- 2 garlic cloves, minced
- 12 ounces cherry tomatoes, halved
- ½ cup pitted kalamata olives, chopped coarse
- 2 pounds thick asparagus, trimmed
- 2 tablespoons shredded fresh basil
- ¼ cup grated Parmesan cheese
  Salt and pepper

1. Cook 1 tablespoon oil and garlic in 12-inch skillet over medium heat, stirring often, until garlic turns golden but not brown, about 3 minutes. Add tomatoes and olives and cook until tomatoes begin to break down, about 3 minutes; transfer to bowl.

2. Heat remaining 1 tablespoon oil in now-empty skillet over medium-high heat until shimmering. Add half of asparagus with tips pointed in 1 direction and remaining asparagus with tips pointed in opposite direction. Shake skillet gently to help distribute spears evenly (they will not quite fit in single layer). Add 1 teaspoon water, cover, and cook until asparagus is bright green and still crisp, about 5 minutes.

Deeply browning asparagus on just one side gives it great flavor while maintaining its crisp texture.

3. Uncover, increase heat to high, and cook, moving spears around with tongs as needed, until asparagus is well browned on 1 side and tip of paring knife inserted at base of largest spear meets little resistance, 5 to 7 minutes. Season with salt and pepper to taste. Transfer asparagus to serving platter, top with tomato mixture, and sprinkle with basil and Parmesan. Serve.

VARIATION

Pan-Roasted Asparagus with Toasted Garlic and Parmesan `FAST` `VEG`

Omit tomatoes, olives, and basil. Increase garlic to 3 cloves and slice thin. Before cooking asparagus, cook 2 tablespoons extra-virgin olive oil and sliced garlic in 12-inch skillet over medium-low heat, stirring often, until garlic turns crisp and golden but not brown, about 5 minutes. Using slotted spoon, transfer garlic to paper towel–lined plate and season lightly with salt. Add asparagus to oil left in skillet and cook as directed. Sprinkle asparagus with toasted garlic and Parmesan before serving.

Vegetables are an essential part of the Mediterranean way of eating and should be included in your meals as often as possible. Sometimes you want to prepare your vegetables in the simplest (and quickest) way by steaming, boiling, or microwaving them. Just follow the times in the chart for perfectly cooked vegetables every time.

TYPE OF VEGETABLE	AMOUNT/YIELD	PREPARATION	BOILING TIME (AMOUNT OF WATER AND SALT)	STEAMING TIME	MICROWAVING TIME (AMOUNT OF WATER)
Asparagus	1 bunch (1 pound)/ serves 3	tough ends trimmed	2 to 4 minutes (4 quarts water plus 1 tablespoon salt)	3 to 5 minutes	3 to 6 minutes (3 tablespoons water)
Beets	1½ pounds (6 medium)/ serves 4	greens discarded and beets scrubbed well	X	35 to 55 minutes	18 to 24 minutes (¾ cup water)
Broccoli	1 bunch (1½ pounds)/ serves 4	florets cut into 1- to 1½-inch pieces and stalks peeled and cut into ¼-inch-thick pieces	2 to 4 minutes (4 quarts water plus 1 tablespoon salt)	4 to 6 minutes	4 to 6 minutes (3 tablespoons water)
Brussels Sprouts	1 pound/ serves 4	stem ends trimmed, discolored leaves removed, and halved through stem	6 to 8 minutes (4 quarts water plus 1 tablespoon salt)	7 to 9 minutes	X
Carrots	1 pound/ serves 4	peeled and sliced ¼ inch thick on bias	3 to 4 minutes (4 quarts water plus 1 tablespoon salt)	5 to 6 minutes	4 to 7 minutes (2 tablespoons water)
Cauliflower	1 head (2 pounds)/ serves 4 to 6	cored and florets cut into 1-inch pieces	5 to 7 minutes (4 quarts water plus 1 tablespoon salt)	7 to 9 minutes	4 to 7 minutes (¼ cup water)
Green Beans	1 pound/ serves 4	stem ends trimmed	3 to 5 minutes (4 quarts water plus 1 tablespoon salt)	6 to 8 minutes	4 to 6 minutes (3 tablespoons water)
Red Potatoes	2 pounds (6 medium)/ serves 4	scrubbed and poked several times with fork	16 to 22 minutes (4 quarts water plus 1 tablespoon salt)	18 to 24 minutes	6 to 10 minutes (no water and uncovered)
Russet Potatoes	2 pounds (4 medium)/ serves 4	scrubbed and poked several times with fork	X	X	8 to 12 minutes (no water and uncovered)
Snap Peas	1 pound/ serves 4	stems trimmed and strings removed	2 to 4 minutes (4 quarts water plus 1 tablespoon salt)	4 to 6 minutes	3 to 6 minutes (3 tablespoons water)
Snow Peas	1 pound/ serves 4	stems trimmed and strings removed	2 to 3 minutes (4 quarts water plus 1 tablespoon salt)	4 to 6 minutes	3 to 6 minutes (3 tablespoons water)
Squash (Winter)	2 pounds/ serves 4	peeled, seeded, and cut into 1-inch chunks	X	12 to 14 minutes	8 to 11 minutes (¼ cup water)
Sweet Potatoes	2 pounds (3 medium) serves 4	peeled and cut into 1-inch chunks	X	12 to 14 minutes	8 to 10 minutes (¼ cup water)

X = Not recommended

Roasted Asparagus

SERVES 4 to 6 `FAST` `VEG`

WHY THIS RECIPE WORKS Italian cooking brings out the best in seasonal vegetables, and one of the most elegant yet simple preparations is roasting. But when it comes to delicate asparagus, simply tossing the spears with oil, salt, and pepper and spreading them on a baking sheet doesn't always produce reliably crisp-tender spears. After a few tests, we discovered that thicker spears (½ inch in diameter) held up better to roasting, but they required some prep. Trimming off the woody stems wasn't even a question, but what to do with the tough skins? Though it seemed a little fussy, we found that peeling the bottom halves of the stalks—just enough to expose the creamy white flesh— delivered consistently tender and visually appealing asparagus. To ensure a hard sear on our spears, we preheated the baking sheet and resisted the urge to give it a shake during roasting. The result? Intense, flavorful browning on one side of the asparagus and vibrant green on the other. For some complementary seasoning, we again took our cue from Italian cuisine, preparing a bright garnish of minced fresh herbs called a *gremolata*. Fresh mint, fresh parsley, orange zest, minced garlic, and a hit of cayenne constituted our first version, and the more classic combination of tarragon, parsley, lemon zest, and garlic our second. Both reinforced the stalks' vibrant flavor and gave our simple side a more distinct presence. This recipe works best with thick asparagus spears that are between ½ and ¾ inch in diameter. Do not use pencil-thin asparagus; it overcooks too easily.

    2 pounds thick asparagus, trimmed
    2 tablespoons plus 2 teaspoons extra-virgin olive oil
    ½ teaspoon salt
    ¼ teaspoon pepper

1. Adjust oven rack to lowest position, place rimmed baking sheet on rack, and heat oven to 500 degrees. Peel bottom halves of asparagus spears until white flesh is exposed, then toss with 2 tablespoons oil, salt, and pepper.

Peeling Asparagus

Trim woody ends of asparagus spears. Peel bottom halves of spears until white flesh is exposed.

For perfectly crisp-tender asparagus, we peel the bottom half of the stalks before roasting them in the oven.

2. Transfer asparagus to preheated sheet and spread into single layer. Roast, without moving asparagus, until undersides of spears are browned, tops are bright green, and tip of paring knife inserted at base of largest spear meets little resistance, 8 to 10 minutes. Transfer asparagus to serving platter and drizzle with remaining 2 teaspoons oil. Serve.

VARIATIONS

Roasted Asparagus with Mint-Orange Gremolata
`FAST` `VEG`

Combine 2 tablespoons minced fresh mint, 2 tablespoons minced fresh parsley, 2 teaspoons grated orange zest, 1 minced garlic clove, and pinch cayenne pepper in bowl. Sprinkle gremolata over asparagus before serving.

Roasted Asparagus with Tarragon-Lemon Gremolata
`FAST` `VEG`

Combine 2 tablespoons minced fresh tarragon, 2 tablespoons minced fresh parsley, 2 teaspoons grated lemon zest, and 1 minced garlic clove in bowl. Sprinkle gremolata over asparagus before serving.

Gently simmering a bright mix of spring vegetables amplifies their fresh flavors.

Braised Asparagus, Peas, and Radishes with Tarragon

SERVES 4 to 6   FAST   VEG

WHY THIS RECIPE WORKS While raw and roasted vegetables certainly have their place, many Mediterranean recipes capitalize on the freshness of spring vegetables in another, more unexpected way: braising. To turn our early-season produce into a warm side dish, we started by softening a minced shallot in olive oil with additional aromatics for a savory base. To build a flavorful braising liquid, we poured in water and lemon and orange zest and dropped in a bay leaf. Adding the vegetables in stages ensured that each cooked at its own rate and maintained a crisp texture. Peppery radishes, which turned soft and sweet with cooking, were nicely complemented by the more vegetal notes of asparagus and peas (frozen peas were reliably sweet, and adding them off the heat prevented overcooking). In no time at all, we had a simple side of radiant vegetables in an invigorating,

complex broth, proof positive that braising can bring out the best in even the most delicate flavors. A toss of chopped fresh tarragon gave a final nod to spring. Look for asparagus spears no thicker than ½ inch.

¼ cup extra-virgin olive oil
1 shallot, sliced into thin rounds
2 garlic cloves, sliced thin
3 fresh thyme sprigs
 Pinch red pepper flakes
10 radishes, trimmed and quartered lengthwise
1¼ cups water
2 teaspoons grated lemon zest
2 teaspoons grated orange zest
1 bay leaf
 Salt and pepper
1 pound asparagus, trimmed and cut into 2-inch lengths
2 cups frozen peas
4 teaspoons chopped fresh tarragon

1. Cook oil, shallot, garlic, thyme sprigs, and pepper flakes in Dutch oven over medium heat until shallot is just softened, about 2 minutes. Stir in radishes, water, lemon zest, orange zest, bay leaf, and 1 teaspoon salt and bring to simmer. Reduce heat to medium-low, cover, and cook until radishes can be easily pierced with tip of paring knife, 3 to 5 minutes. Stir in asparagus, cover, and cook until tender, 3 to 5 minutes.

2. Off heat, stir in peas, cover, and let sit until heated through, about 5 minutes. Discard thyme sprigs and bay leaf. Stir in tarragon and season with salt and pepper to taste. Serve.

Stuffed Bell Peppers with Spiced Beef, Currants, and Feta

SERVES 4

WHY THIS RECIPE WORKS Stuffed bell peppers are a simple entrée enjoyed throughout the Mediterranean. Balance in both flavor and texture is paramount to the success of this dish. We found that briefly blanching the peppers curbed their raw crunch but ensured that they were sturdy enough to hold our hearty filling; since we couldn't rid green peppers of their bitterness, we stuck with red, orange, and yellow varieties. To keep our recipe streamlined, we used the same water to blanch the peppers and cook the rice (simple long-grain white rice was preferred). Ground beef made for a simple and savory element of our filling.

A generous dose of spices ensured that our stuffing wasn't bland, and some sautéed garlic and onion rounded out the aromatic profile. Chopped toasted almonds brought some welcome crunch, and a little feta helped bind everything together and further boosted flavor. We found that we could make our stuffing while the peppers and rice cooked, keeping the process efficient. For a unique twist on the finished recipe, we also created a version using lamb; we found that the meat's robust flavor required upping the spices to balance the dish.

 4 red, yellow, or orange bell peppers, ½ inch trimmed off
    tops, cores and seeds discarded
    Salt and pepper
 ½ cup long-grain white rice
 1 tablespoon extra-virgin olive oil, plus extra for serving
 1 onion, chopped fine
 3 garlic cloves, minced
 2 teaspoons grated fresh ginger
 2 teaspoons ground cumin
 ¾ teaspoon ground cardamom
 ½ teaspoon red pepper flakes
 ¼ teaspoon ground cinnamon
10 ounces 90 percent lean ground beef
 1 (14.5-ounce) can diced tomatoes, drained with
    2 tablespoons juice reserved
 ¼ cup currants
 2 teaspoons chopped fresh oregano or ½ teaspoon dried
 2 ounces feta cheese, crumbled (½ cup)
 ¼ cup slivered almonds, toasted and chopped

1. Bring 4 quarts water to boil in large pot. Add bell peppers and 1 tablespoon salt and cook until just beginning to soften, 3 to 5 minutes. Using tongs, remove peppers from pot, drain excess water, and place peppers cut side up on paper towels. Return water to boil, add rice, and cook until tender, about 13 minutes. Drain rice and transfer to large bowl; set aside.

2. Adjust oven rack to middle position and heat oven to 350 degrees. Heat oil in 12-inch skillet over medium-high heat until shimmering. Add onion and ¼ teaspoon salt and cook until softened and lightly browned, 5 to 7 minutes. Stir in garlic, ginger, cumin, cardamom, pepper flakes, and cinnamon and cook until fragrant, about 30 seconds. Add ground beef and cook, breaking up meat with wooden spoon, until no longer pink, about 4 minutes. Off heat, stir in tomatoes and reserved juice, currants, and oregano, scraping up any browned bits. Transfer mixture to bowl with rice. Add ¼ cup feta and almonds and gently toss to combine. Season with salt and pepper to taste.

3. Place peppers cut side up in 8-inch square baking dish. Pack each pepper with rice mixture, mounding filling on top. Bake until filling is heated through, about 30 minutes. Sprinkle remaining ¼ cup feta over peppers and drizzle with extra oil. Serve.

VARIATION
Stuffed Bell Peppers with Spiced Lamb, Currants, and Feta
Substitute 10 ounces ground lamb for ground beef. Increase ginger to 1 tablespoon, cumin to 1 tablespoon, cardamom to 1 teaspoon, and cinnamon to ½ teaspoon.

Preparing Peppers for Stuffing

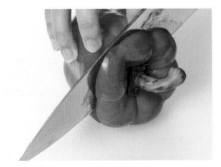

1. Trim ½ inch off tops of peppers.

2. Pull out core, seeds, and ribs and discard.

3. Cook peppers until just beginning to soften. Using tongs, remove peppers from pot, drain off excess water, and place cut side up on paper towels.

All About Garlic

The pungent, aromatic flavor of garlic is great in everything from pasta sauces to vinaigrettes to steamed vegetables. Here's everything you need to know about buying, storing, and cooking with garlic.

BUYING GARLIC

When shopping for garlic, look for unpackaged loose garlic heads so you can examine them closely. Pick heads without spots, mold, or sprouting. Squeeze them to make sure they're not rubbery, have no soft spots, and aren't missing cloves. The garlic shouldn't have much of a scent; if it does, you're risking spoilage. Of the various garlic varieties, your best bet is soft-neck garlic, since it stores well and is heat tolerant. This variety features a circle of large cloves surrounding a small cluster at the center. Hard-neck garlic has a stiff center staff surrounded by large, uniform cloves and boasts a more intense, complex flavor. But since it's easily damaged and doesn't store as well as soft-neck garlic, buy it at the farmers' market.

STORING GARLIC

With proper storage, whole heads of garlic should last for at least a few weeks. Store heads in a cool, dark place with plenty of air circulation to prevent spoiling and sprouting. (A small basket in the pantry is ideal.)

PREPARING GARLIC

When preparing garlic, keep in mind that garlic's pungency emerges only after its cell walls are ruptured, triggering the creation of a compound called allicin. The more a clove is broken down, the more allicin is produced. Thus you can control the amount of bite garlic contributes to a recipe by how fine or coarse you cut it. It's also best not to cut garlic in advance; the longer cut garlic sits, the harsher its flavor.

COOKING GARLIC

Garlic's flavor is sharpest when raw. Once heated above 150 degrees, its enzymes are destroyed and no new flavor is produced. This is why roasted garlic, which is cooked slowly and takes longer to reach 150 degrees, has a mellow, slightly sweet flavor. Alternatively, garlic browned at very high temperatures (300 to 350 degrees) has a more bitter flavor. To avoid the creation of bitter compounds, wait to add garlic to the pan until other aromatics or ingredients have softened. And don't cook garlic over high heat for much longer than 30 seconds; you want to cook it, stirring constantly, only until it turns fragrant.

Blanching broccoli rabe and then sautéing it gives this robust green well-rounded flavor.

Broccoli Rabe with Garlic and Red Pepper Flakes
SERVES 4 FAST VEG

WHY THIS RECIPE WORKS Many Italians have a taste for bitter greens, so it's no surprise that broccoli rabe is so popular in that country. But when developing our recipe, we knew that broccoli rabe's bitterness can be overwhelming to some, so we set out to develop a quick and dependable method of cooking this aggressive vegetable that would tamp down the bitterness in favor of rounder, more balanced flavor. We found that blanching the rabe in a large amount of salted water tamed its bitterness without eliminating its depth of flavor. Then we sautéed the blanched rabe with garlic and red pepper flakes, Italian standbys that complemented the vegetable's strong flavor beautifully. Using a salad spinner makes easy work of drying the cooled blanched broccoli rabe.

14 ounces broccoli rabe, trimmed and cut into 1-inch pieces
   Salt and pepper
 2 tablespoons extra-virgin olive oil
 3 garlic cloves, minced
¼ teaspoon red pepper flakes

1. Bring 3 quarts water to boil in large saucepan. Fill large bowl halfway with ice and water. Add broccoli rabe and 2 teaspoons salt to boiling water and cook until wilted and tender, about 2½ minutes. Drain broccoli rabe, then transfer to ice water and let sit until chilled. Drain again and thoroughly pat dry.

2. Cook oil, garlic, and pepper flakes in 10-inch skillet over medium heat, stirring often, until garlic begins to sizzle, about 2 minutes. Increase heat to medium-high, add broccoli rabe, and cook, stirring to coat with oil, until heated through, about 1 minute. Season with salt and pepper to taste and serve.

VARIATIONS

Broccoli Rabe with Sun-Dried Tomatoes and Pine Nuts FAST VEG

Add ¼ cup oil-packed sun-dried tomatoes, cut into thin strips, to skillet with oil. Sprinkle broccoli rabe with 3 tablespoons toasted pine nuts before serving.

Broccoli Rabe with Red Bell Pepper, Olives, and Feta FAST VEG

Substitute 1 teaspoon minced fresh oregano for pepper flakes. Add 1 red bell pepper, stemmed, seeded, and cut into ½-inch pieces, to skillet with oil and oregano. Add ¼ cup chopped kalamata olives to skillet with broccoli rabe. Sprinkle broccoli rabe with ¼ cup crumbled feta cheese before serving.

Trimming Broccoli Rabe

1. Trim off and discard very thick stalk ends, about 2 inches from bottom of stalks.

2. Cut remaining stems and florets into pieces according to recipe directions.

Sautéed Cabbage with Parsley and Lemon

SERVES 4 to 6 FAST VEG

WHY THIS RECIPE WORKS We wanted a simple preparation for humble green cabbage that would bring out the vegetable's natural sweetness and maintain its crisp-tender texture. Instead of boiling or braising, we pan-steamed and sautéed the cabbage over relatively high heat to cook it quickly and add an extra layer of flavor from browning. A precooking step of soaking the cabbage reduced bitterness while providing extra moisture to help the cabbage steam. Cooked onion helped reinforce sweetness, and lemon juice provided punch. Fresh parsley offered a bright finish.

1   small head green cabbage (1¼ pounds), cored and sliced thin
2   tablespoons extra-virgin olive oil
1   onion, halved and sliced thin
    Salt and pepper
¼   cup chopped fresh parsley
1½ teaspoons lemon juice

1. Place cabbage in large bowl and cover with cold water. Let sit for 3 minutes; drain well.

2. Heat 1 tablespoon oil in 12-inch nonstick skillet over medium-high heat until shimmering. Add onion and ¼ teaspoon salt and cook until softened and lightly browned, 5 to 7 minutes; transfer to bowl.

3. Heat remaining 1 tablespoon oil in now-empty skillet over medium-high heat until shimmering. Add cabbage and sprinkle with ½ teaspoon salt and ¼ teaspoon pepper. Cover and cook, without stirring, until cabbage is wilted and lightly browned on bottom, about 3 minutes. Stir and continue to cook, uncovered, until cabbage is crisp-tender and lightly browned in places, about 4 minutes, stirring once halfway through cooking. Off heat, stir in onion, parsley, and lemon juice. Season with salt and pepper to taste and serve.

VARIATION

Sautéed Cabbage with Fennel and Garlic FAST VEG

Omit pepper. Substitute 1 small head savoy cabbage for green cabbage and 1 fennel bulb, fronds minced, stalks discarded, bulb halved, cored, and sliced thin, for onion. Cook fennel until softened, 8 to 10 minutes, then add 2 minced garlic cloves and ¼ teaspoon red pepper flakes and cook until fragrant, about 30 seconds. Substitute fennel fronds for parsley and increase lemon juice to 2 teaspoons. Drizzle cabbage with extra 1 tablespoon oil and sprinkle with 2 tablespoons grated Parmesan cheese before serving.

Tossing carrots with olive oil and a little brown sugar encourages them to brown in the oven.

Spicy Roasted Carrots with Cilantro

SERVES 4 to 6 FAST VEG

WHY THIS RECIPE WORKS From France to Morocco, carrots are used in salads, sides, and meze, and roasting is one of the best ways to maximize their sweet, earthy flavor. The high heat caramelizes the carrots' sugars and browns the exteriors, leaving the interiors tender and moist. To ensure that the carrots were cooked through evenly, we first steamed them in their own juice by covering them for the first part of roasting. To encourage the exteriors to turn a beautiful golden brown, we tossed the carrots with a little brown sugar before cooking. A complex, spicy mix of Aleppo pepper, earthy cumin, warm cinnamon, and bright cilantro provided lots of high-impact, Turkish-inspired flavor. Fresh orange juice provided a bit of brightness to offset the bold flavors. If you can't find Aleppo pepper, you can substitute ⅛ teaspoon paprika and ⅛ teaspoon finely chopped red pepper flakes.

    2 tablespoons extra-virgin olive oil
    1 tablespoon packed dark brown sugar
      Salt and pepper
 1½ pounds carrots, peeled

 ¼ cup chopped fresh cilantro
  2 tablespoons orange juice
 ½ teaspoon ground dried Aleppo pepper
 ¼ teaspoon ground cumin
 ⅛ teaspoon ground cinnamon

1. Adjust oven rack to middle position and heat oven to 450 degrees. Whisk oil, sugar, ½ teaspoon salt, and ½ teaspoon pepper together in large bowl.

2. Cut carrots in half crosswise, then cut lengthwise into halves or quarters as needed to create uniformly sized pieces. Add carrots to oil mixture and toss to coat. Transfer to aluminum foil–lined rimmed baking sheet and spread into single layer.

3. Cover sheet tightly with foil and roast for 12 minutes. Remove foil and continue to roast until carrots are well browned and tender, 16 to 22 minutes, stirring halfway through roasting.

4. Whisk orange juice, Aleppo, cumin, and cinnamon together in large bowl. Add carrots and cilantro and gently toss to combine. Season with salt and pepper to taste and serve.

Cutting Carrots for Roasting

1. First, cut carrots in half crosswise.

2. Then cut each half lengthwise into halves or quarters as needed to create uniformly sized pieces.

Slow-Cooked Whole Carrots

SERVES 4 to 6 VEG

WHY THIS RECIPE WORKS Cooking carrots brings out a new dimension of sweetness and flavor, so we wanted to develop a recipe for slow-cooked carrots that would yield a sweet and meltingly tender vegetable from one end to the other without the carrots becoming waterlogged. Gently steeping the carrots in warm water before cooking them firmed up the vegetable's cell walls so that the carrots could be cooked for a long time without falling apart. We also topped the carrots with a *cartouche* (a circle of parchment that sits directly on the food) during cooking to ensure that the moisture in the pan cooked the carrots evenly. Finishing cooking at a simmer evaporated the liquid and concentrated the carrots' flavor so that they tasted great when served on their own or with a flavorful relish. Use carrots that measure ¾ to 1¼ inches across at the thickest end.

    1 tablespoon extra-virgin olive oil
    ½ teaspoon salt
    1½ pounds carrots, peeled

1. Cut parchment paper into 11-inch circle, then cut 1-inch hole in center, folding paper as needed.

2. Bring 3 cups water, oil, and salt to simmer in 12-inch skillet over high heat. Off heat, add carrots, top with parchment, cover skillet, and let sit for 20 minutes.

3. Uncover, leaving parchment in place, and bring to simmer over high heat. Reduce heat to medium-low and cook until most of water has evaporated and carrots are very tender, about 45 minutes.

4. Discard parchment, increase heat to medium-high, and cook carrots, shaking skillet often, until lightly glazed and no water remains, 2 to 4 minutes. Serve.

VARIATIONS

Slow-Cooked Whole Carrots with Green Olive and Raisin Relish VEG

Microwave ⅓ cup raisins and 1 tablespoon water in medium bowl until hot, about 1 minute; let sit for 5 minutes. Stir in ½ cup chopped green olives, 1 minced shallot, 2 tablespoons extra-virgin olive oil, 1 tablespoon red wine vinegar, 1 tablespoon minced fresh parsley, ½ teaspoon ground fennel, and ¼ teaspoon salt. Spoon relish over carrots before serving.

Slow-Cooked Whole Carrots with Pine Nut Relish VEG

Combine ⅓ cup toasted pine nuts, 1 minced shallot, 1 tablespoon sherry vinegar, 1 tablespoon minced fresh parsley, 1 teaspoon honey, ½ teaspoon minced fresh rosemary, ¼ teaspoon smoked paprika, ¼ teaspoon salt, and pinch cayenne pepper in bowl. Spoon relish over carrots before serving.

Slow-Cooked Whole Carrots with Onion-Balsamic Relish VEG

Heat 3 tablespoons extra-virgin olive oil in medium saucepan over medium heat until shimmering. Add 1 finely chopped red onion and ¼ teaspoon salt and cook until soft and well browned, about 15 minutes. Stir in 2 minced garlic cloves and cook until fragrant, about 30 seconds. Stir in 2 tablespoons balsamic vinegar and cook for 1 minute. Let cool for 15 minutes. Stir in 2 tablespoons minced fresh mint. Spoon relish over carrots before serving.

Folding Parchment for Slow-Cooked Carrots

1. Cut parchment into 11-inch circle, then cut 1-inch hole in center, folding paper as needed to cut out hole.

2. Lay parchment circle on top of carrots, underneath lid, to help retain and evenly distribute moisture during cooking.

Skillet-Roasted Cauliflower
SERVES 4 to 6 FAST VEG

WHY THIS RECIPE WORKS In Turkey, Greece, and Italy, cauliflower florets are often battered and fried to give them a crisp exterior; we wanted to seize on this idea without the need for messy battering and unhealthy deep frying. Pan roasting seemed like the perfect way to achieve the texture we were after and give the florets an irresistibly nutty, caramelized flavor. We began by cutting cauliflower into planks and then into flat-sided florets to maximize their exposed surface area for plenty of flavorful browning. Starting in a cold covered pan allowed the slices to gradually steam in their own moisture before we removed the lid and let them brown. To give our side dish some standout flavor, we finished cooking the florets with minced garlic, lemon zest, and fresh parsley, and to add some crunch, we sprinkled on toasted fresh bread crumbs. For the first 5 minutes of cooking, the cauliflower steams in its own released moisture, so it is important not to lift the lid from the skillet during this time.

    1 head cauliflower (2 pounds)
    1 slice hearty white sandwich bread, torn into
        1-inch pieces
    5 tablespoons extra-virgin olive oil
        Salt and pepper
    1 garlic clove, minced
    1 teaspoon grated lemon zest, plus lemon wedges
        for serving
    ¼ cup chopped fresh parsley

1. Trim outer leaves of cauliflower and cut stem flush with bottom of head. Turn head so stem is facing down and cut head into ¾-inch-thick slices. Cut around core to remove florets; discard

Starting cauliflower in a cold covered skillet allows the florets to gradually steam in their own moisture.

mixture into cauliflower and continue to cook, stirring occasionally, until cauliflower is tender but still firm, about 3 minutes. Off heat, stir in parsley and season with salt and pepper to taste. Transfer cauliflower to serving platter and sprinkle with bread crumbs. Serve with lemon wedges.

VARIATIONS

Skillet-Roasted Cauliflower with Capers and Pine Nuts FAST VEG

Omit bread and reduce oil to ¼ cup. Reduce salt in step 3 to ¾ teaspoon. Substitute 2 tablespoons capers, rinsed and minced, for garlic. Substitute 2 tablespoons minced fresh chives for parsley, and stir ¼ cup toasted pine nuts into cauliflower with chives.

Skillet-Roasted Spiced Cauliflower with Pistachios FAST VEG

Omit bread and reduce oil to ¼ cup. Heat 1 teaspoon cumin seeds and 1 teaspoon coriander seeds in 12-inch nonstick skillet over medium heat, stirring frequently, until lightly toasted and fragrant, about 2 minutes. Transfer to spice grinder or mortar and pestle and coarsely grind. Wipe skillet clean with paper towels. Substitute ground cumin-coriander mixture, ½ teaspoon paprika, and pinch cayenne pepper for garlic, 1 teaspoon grated lime zest for lemon zest, and 3 tablespoons chopped fresh mint for parsley. Sprinkle cauliflower with ¼ cup pistachios, toasted and chopped, before serving with lime wedges.

core. Cut large florets into 1½-inch pieces. Transfer florets to bowl, including any small pieces that may have been created during trimming, and set aside.

2. Pulse bread in food processor to coarse crumbs, about 10 pulses. Heat bread crumbs, 1 tablespoon oil, pinch salt, and pinch pepper in 12-inch nonstick skillet over medium heat, stirring frequently, until bread crumbs are golden brown, 3 to 5 minutes. Transfer crumbs to bowl and wipe skillet clean with paper towels.

3. Combine 2 tablespoons oil and cauliflower florets in now-empty skillet and sprinkle with 1 teaspoon salt and ½ teaspoon pepper. Cover skillet and cook over medium-high heat until florets start to brown and edges just start to become translucent (do not lift lid), about 5 minutes. Remove lid and continue to cook, stirring every 2 minutes, until florets turn golden brown in many spots, about 12 minutes.

4. Push cauliflower to sides of skillet. Add remaining 2 tablespoons oil, garlic, and lemon zest to center and cook, stirring with rubber spatula, until fragrant, about 30 seconds. Stir garlic

Braised Cauliflower with Garlic and White Wine
SERVES 4 to 6   FAST VEG

WHY THIS RECIPE WORKS When properly cooked and imaginatively flavored, braised cauliflower can be toothsome, nutty, and slightly sweet—a perfect backdrop for a variety of Mediterranean flavors. However, too many recipes result in cauliflower that is waterlogged and bland or, worse, sulfurous and unappealing. To avoid these problems (which stem from overcooking), we knew we would need to quickly braise the florets. To this end, we cut the florets into small, 1½-inch pieces, which reduced the total cooking time. Sautéing the cauliflower in olive oil imparted nuttiness. Because we wanted the cauliflower to cook in our braising liquid for only a short amount of time, we maximized its impact by creating an ultraflavorful broth that the porous vegetable could absorb. White wine and broth made for a complexly flavored base, and a generous amount of garlic along with a pinch of red pepper flakes added punch and deeper flavor. For the best texture and taste, make sure to brown the cauliflower well in step 1.

3 tablespoons plus 1 teaspoon extra-virgin olive oil
3 garlic cloves, minced
⅛ teaspoon red pepper flakes
1 head cauliflower (2 pounds), cored and cut into
  1½-inch florets
  Salt and pepper
⅓ cup chicken or vegetable broth
⅓ cup dry white wine
2 tablespoons minced fresh parsley

1. Combine 1 teaspoon oil, garlic, and pepper flakes in small bowl. Heat remaining 3 tablespoons oil in 12-inch skillet over medium-high heat until shimmering. Add cauliflower and ¼ teaspoon salt and cook, stirring occasionally, until florets are golden brown, 7 to 9 minutes.

2. Push cauliflower to sides of skillet. Add garlic mixture to center and cook, mashing mixture into skillet, until fragrant, about 30 seconds. Stir garlic mixture into cauliflower.

3. Stir in broth and wine and bring to simmer. Reduce heat to medium-low, cover, and cook until cauliflower is crisp-tender, 4 to 6 minutes. Off heat, stir in parsley and season with salt and pepper to taste. Serve.

VARIATIONS

Braised Cauliflower with Capers and Anchovies
FAST

Add 2 anchovy fillets, rinsed and minced, and 1 tablespoon rinsed and minced capers to oil mixture in step 1. Stir 1 tablespoon lemon juice into cauliflower with parsley.

Braised Cauliflower with Sumac and Mint
FAST VEG

Omit wine. Substitute 2 teaspoons ground sumac for pepper flakes and increase broth to ½ cup. In step 3, once cauliflower is crisp-tender, uncover and continue to cook until liquid is almost evaporated, about 1 minute. Substitute 2 tablespoons chopped fresh mint for parsley and stir ¼ cup plain yogurt into cauliflower with mint.

Cauliflower Cakes
SERVES 4 VEG

WHY THIS RECIPE WORKS In eastern Mediterranean countries, vegetable cakes are a common addition to the dinner table; they're simple, filling, and a unique way to serve vegetables. For cauliflower cakes with complex flavors, a creamy interior, and a crunchy browned exterior, we started with the cauliflower itself. To ensure that the flavor of the cauliflower didn't get lost and to

drive off excess moisture that would otherwise make our cakes fall apart, we cut the cauliflower into florets and roasted them until they were well browned and tender. Tossing the florets with warm spices like turmeric, coriander, and ground ginger bloomed the spices' flavors and gave the cakes an aromatic backbone. Next we needed a binder to hold the shaped cakes together. Egg and flour are standard additions, but we also added some goat cheese to provide extra binding, creaminess, and tangy flavor. Though these cakes held together, they were very soft and tricky to flip in the pan. Refrigerating the cakes for 30 minutes before cooking them proved to be the best solution. The chilled cakes transferred from baking sheet to skillet without a problem and were much sturdier when it came time to flip them. In addition to the lemon wedges, serve with Cucumber-Yogurt Sauce or Yogurt-Herb Sauce (page 233).

1 head cauliflower (2 pounds), cored and cut into
  1-inch florets
¼ cup extra-virgin olive oil
1 teaspoon ground turmeric
1 teaspoon ground coriander
1 teaspoon salt
½ teaspoon ground ginger
¼ teaspoon pepper
4 ounces goat cheese, softened
2 scallions, sliced thin
1 large egg, lightly beaten
2 garlic cloves, minced
1 teaspoon grated lemon zest, plus lemon wedges
  for serving
¼ cup all-purpose flour

1. Adjust oven rack to middle position and heat oven to 450 degrees. Toss cauliflower with 1 tablespoon oil, turmeric, coriander, salt, ginger, and pepper. Transfer to aluminum foil–lined rimmed baking sheet and spread into single layer. Roast until cauliflower is well browned and tender, about 25 minutes. Let cool slightly, then transfer to large bowl.

2. Line clean rimmed baking sheet with parchment paper. Mash cauliflower coarsely with potato masher. Stir in goat cheese, scallions, egg, garlic, and lemon zest until well combined. Sprinkle flour over cauliflower mixture and stir to incorporate. Using wet hands, divide mixture into 4 equal portions, pack gently into ¾-inch-thick cakes, and place on prepared sheet. Refrigerate cakes until chilled and firm, about 30 minutes.

3. Line large plate with paper towels. Heat remaining 3 tablespoons oil in 12-inch nonstick skillet over medium heat until shimmering. Gently lay cakes in skillet and cook until deep golden brown and crisp, 5 to 7 minutes per side. Drain cakes briefly on prepared plate. Serve with lemon wedges.

For caramelized exteriors and creamy interiors, we roast sliced celery root at a high temperature on a low oven rack.

Roasted Celery Root with Yogurt and Sesame Seeds

SERVES 6 VEG

WHY THIS RECIPE WORKS Celery root is native to the Mediterranean, but it is often overlooked as a vegetable side. We wanted to bring this root vegetable to the table and highlight its herbal flavor and pleasant, creamy texture. To unlock the unique flavor of the celery root, we found that roasting was best. By cooking slices on the bottom oven rack at a high temperature, we were able to caramelize the exteriors and concentrate the flavor perfectly. Tangy yogurt, with reinforced brightness from both lemon juice and zest, complemented the rich and savory celery root. To finish, we sprinkled an aromatic combination of toasted sesame seeds, coriander, and dried thyme over the top before adding whole cilantro leaves to freshen the dish.

3 celery roots (2½ pounds), peeled, halved, and sliced ½ inch thick
3 tablespoons extra-virgin olive oil
 Salt and pepper
¼ cup plain yogurt

¼ teaspoon grated lemon zest plus 1 teaspoon juice
1 teaspoon sesame seeds, toasted
1 teaspoon coriander seeds, toasted and crushed
¼ teaspoon dried thyme
¼ cup fresh cilantro leaves

1. Adjust oven rack to lowest position and heat oven to 425 degrees. Toss celery root with oil, ½ teaspoon salt, and ¼ teaspoon pepper and arrange in rimmed baking sheet in single layer. Roast celery root until sides touching sheet toward back of oven are well browned, 25 to 30 minutes. Rotate sheet and continue to roast until sides touching sheet toward back of oven are well browned, 6 to 10 minutes.

2. Use metal spatula to flip each piece and continue to roast until celery root is very tender and sides touching sheet are browned, 10 to 15 minutes.

3. Transfer celery root to serving platter. Whisk yogurt, lemon zest and juice, and pinch salt together in bowl. In separate bowl, combine sesame seeds, coriander seeds, thyme, and pinch salt. Drizzle celery root with yogurt sauce and sprinkle with seed mixture and cilantro. Serve.

Peeling Celery Root

1. Using chef's knife, cut ½ inch from both root end and opposite end of celery root.

2. Turn celery root so 1 cut side rests on board. To peel, cut from top to bottom, rotating celery root while removing wide strips of skin.

Marinated Eggplant with Capers and Mint

SERVES 4 to 6 VEG

WHY THIS RECIPE WORKS Marinated eggplant, a highlight of Greek meze platters, has a surprisingly creamy texture and a deep yet tangy flavor. However, many recipes we tried turned out overly greasy, with accompanying flavors that were either muted and dull or so strong that they overwhelmed the eggplant. We wanted a recipe that would keep the eggplant in the spotlight, with a complementary, brightly flavored marinade. To start, we experimented

This classic Greek dish features tender eggplant marinated with bold, tangy red wine vinegar.

with cooking techniques: We tried frying but found that the eggplant absorbed too much oil; pan frying in batches required too much time for a simple side dish, and roasting yielded either leathery eggplant skin or undercooked and tough flesh. We found that broiling was perfect; we could achieve flavorful browning on the eggplant and it cooked through perfectly. To encourage even more browning, we first salted the eggplant, which drew out excess moisture. As for the marinade, a Greek-inspired combination of extra-virgin olive oil (using only a few tablespoons kept the eggplant from turning greasy), red wine vinegar, capers, lemon zest, oregano, garlic, and mint worked perfectly. This dish is great as part of an assortment of appetizers or as a vegetable side to any protein. We prefer using kosher salt because residual grains can be easily wiped away from the eggplant; if using table salt, be sure to reduce all of the salt amounts in the recipe by half.

1½ pounds Italian eggplant, sliced into 1-inch-thick rounds
    Kosher salt and pepper
¼ cup extra-virgin olive oil
4 teaspoons red wine vinegar
1 tablespoon capers, rinsed and minced
1 garlic clove, minced

½ teaspoon grated lemon zest
½ teaspoon minced fresh oregano
3 tablespoons minced fresh mint

1. Spread eggplant on paper towel–lined baking sheet, sprinkle both sides with ½ teaspoon salt, and let sit for 30 minutes.

2. Adjust oven rack 4 inches from broiler element and heat broiler. Thoroughly pat eggplant dry with paper towels, arrange on aluminum foil–lined rimmed baking sheet in single layer, and lightly brush both sides with 1 tablespoon oil. Broil eggplant until mahogany brown and lightly charred, 6 to 8 minutes per side.

3. Whisk remaining 3 tablespoons oil, vinegar, capers, garlic, lemon zest, oregano, and ¼ teaspoon pepper together in large bowl. Add eggplant and mint and gently toss to combine. Let eggplant cool to room temperature, about 1 hour. Season with pepper to taste and serve.

Broiled Eggplant with Basil
SERVES 4 to 6 FAST VEG

WHY THIS RECIPE WORKS Eggplant is one of the most widely used vegetables in the Mediterranean region, but it can be challenging to prepare. Its creamy flesh readily takes to a wide range of flavors, but it can easily become mushy and oily if not treated correctly. If you simply slice and broil eggplant, it will steam in its own juice rather than brown. So to get broiled eggplant with great color and texture, we started by salting the eggplant to draw out its moisture. After 30 minutes, we patted the eggplant slices dry, moved them to a baking sheet (lined with aluminum foil for easy cleanup), and brushed them with oil. With the excess moisture taken care of, a few minutes per side under the blazing-hot broiler turned the eggplant a beautiful mahogany color. With its concentrated roasted flavor, all the eggplant needed was a sprinkling of fresh basil. It is important to slice the eggplant thin so that the slices will cook through by the time the exterior is browned. We prefer using kosher salt because residual grains can be easily wiped away from the eggplant; if using table salt, be sure to reduce all of the salt amounts in the recipe by half.

1½ pounds eggplant, sliced into ¼-inch-thick rounds
    Kosher salt and pepper
3 tablespoons extra-virgin olive oil
2 tablespoons chopped fresh basil

1. Spread eggplant on paper towel–lined baking sheet, sprinkle both sides with 1½ teaspoons salt, and let sit for 30 minutes.

2. Adjust oven rack 4 inches from broiler element and heat broiler. Thoroughly pat eggplant dry with paper towels, arrange on aluminum foil–lined rimmed baking sheet in single layer, and

brush both sides with oil. Broil eggplant until mahogany brown and lightly charred, about 4 minutes per side. Transfer eggplant to serving platter, season with pepper to taste, and sprinkle with basil. Serve.

NOTES FROM THE TEST KITCHEN

All About Eggplant

One of the most widely used vegetables in the Mediterranean, eggplant can be stuffed, baked, broiled, grilled, pureed, and more. Eggplants are available year-round. When shopping, look for eggplants that are firm, with smooth skin and no soft or brown spots. They should feel heavy for their size. Eggplants are very perishable and will get bitter if they overripen, so aim to use them within a day or two. They can be stored in a cool, dry place short-term, but for more than one or two days, refrigeration is best.

There are many varieties of eggplant, ranging anywhere from 2 to 12 inches long, from round to oblong, and from dark purple to white. Here are the two most common Mediterranean varieties that can be found in American supermarkets:

GLOBE

The most common variety in the United States, globe eggplant has a mild flavor and a tender texture that works well in most cooked applications. It can be sautéed, broiled, grilled, and pureed. Because of its high water content, it's often best to salt and drain it before cooking.

ITALIAN

Also called baby eggplant, Italian eggplant looks like a smaller version of a globe eggplant. It has moderately moist flesh and a distinct spicy flavor and can be sautéed, broiled, grilled, and more.

SALTING EGGPLANT

We often recommend salting eggplant before cooking. Salting eggplant not only draws out excess moisture, it also draws out flavor molecules that are tightly bound to proteins that make them inaccessible to our tastebuds. The salt draws flavor compounds out of the cell walls while forcing the proteins to separate from these molecules, resulting in eggplant with more intense flavor that won't water down your dish.

Slicing eggplant into thin rounds is essential to achieving good color and char on the grill.

Grilled Eggplant with Yogurt Sauce

SERVES 4 to 6 VEG

WHY THIS RECIPE WORKS Grilling is a popular way to prepare eggplant in Greece, Italy, Turkey, and beyond, since eggplant's creamy, tender flesh takes well to smoke and char. Unfortunately, grilled eggplant can easily turn out leathery or spongy. After a series of tests, we found that ¼-inch-thick rounds worked best; the interiors became tender by the time the exteriors were nicely grill marked. Since it was necessary to brush the rounds with olive oil so they didn't stick to the grill, we infused that oil with minced garlic and red pepper flakes. Microwaving the garlic and pepper flakes in the oil bloomed and enhanced their flavors. We strained the oil, reserving the garlic mixture to sprinkle over the finished dish. Finally, we prepared a flavorful Turkish-inspired sauce, mixing tangy yogurt with lemon juice and zest, cumin, mint, and a bit of the garlic oil. It is important to slice the eggplant thin so that the slices will cook through by the time the exterior is browned.

6 tablespoons extra-virgin olive oil

5 garlic cloves, minced

⅛ teaspoon red pepper flakes

½ cup plain whole-milk yogurt

3 tablespoons chopped fresh mint

1 teaspoon grated lemon zest plus 2 teaspoons juice

1 teaspoon ground cumin

Salt and pepper

2 pounds eggplant, sliced into ¼-inch-thick rounds

1. Combine oil, garlic, and pepper flakes in bowl. Microwave until garlic is golden brown and crisp, about 2 minutes. Strain garlic oil through fine-mesh strainer into small bowl. Reserve garlic oil and garlic separately.

2. Whisk 1 tablespoon garlic oil, yogurt, mint, lemon zest and juice, cumin, and ¼ teaspoon salt together in separate bowl; set aside for serving.

3A. FOR A CHARCOAL GRILL Open bottom vent completely. Light large chimney starter filled with charcoal briquettes (6 quarts). When top coals are partially covered with ash, pour evenly over grill. Set cooking grate in place, cover, and open lid vent completely. Heat grill until hot, about 5 minutes.

3B. FOR A GAS GRILL Turn all burners to high, cover, and heat grill until hot, about 15 minutes. Turn all burners to medium-high.

4. Clean and oil cooking grate. Brush eggplant with remaining garlic oil and season with salt and pepper. Place half of eggplant on grill and cook (covered if using gas) until browned and tender, about 4 minutes per side; transfer to serving platter. Repeat with remaining eggplant; transfer to platter. Drizzle yogurt sauce over eggplant and sprinkle with garlic. Serve.

Preparing Eggplant for Grilling

1. To ensure that eggplant cooks through on grill, thinly slice eggplant into ¼-inch-thick rounds.

2. After microwaving and straining garlic oil, brush rounds with remaining oil and season with salt and pepper.

Scoring and roasting eggplant halves cut side down on a hot baking sheet prepares them for stuffing.

Stuffed Eggplant with Bulgur

SERVES 4   VEG

WHY THIS RECIPE WORKS There are countless variations on stuffed eggplant from nearly every country in the Mediterranean region, but we found ourselves enamored of a classic Turkish preparation known as *Imam Bayildi*. Most recipes for it are similar: Eggplant is cooked in olive oil and then stuffed with onions, garlic, and tomatoes. For our version, we wanted to make sure that the eggplants were rich and creamy and that the filling was hearty and satisfying. Italian eggplants are the perfect size for stuffing, so we started there. Roasting the eggplants prior to stuffing was key to preventing them from turning watery and tasteless. The slight caramelizing effect of roasting them on a preheated baking sheet added depth of flavor, too. We then let the eggplants drain briefly on paper towels (which got rid of excess liquid) before adding the stuffing. Nutty bulgur made a perfect filling base, plum tomatoes lent bright flavor and a bit of moisture, and Pecorino Romano and pine nuts provided richness. When shopping, do not confuse bulgur with cracked wheat, which has a much longer cooking time and will not work in this recipe. For more information on bulgur, see page 117.

4 (10-ounce) Italian eggplants, halved lengthwise
2 tablespoons extra-virgin olive oil
   Salt and pepper
½ cup medium-grind bulgur, rinsed
¼ cup water
1 onion, chopped fine
3 garlic cloves, minced
2 teaspoons minced fresh oregano or ½ teaspoon dried
¼ teaspoon ground cinnamon
   Pinch cayenne pepper
1 pound plum tomatoes, cored, seeded, and chopped
2 ounces Pecorino Romano cheese, grated (1 cup)
2 tablespoons pine nuts, toasted
2 teaspoons red wine vinegar
2 tablespoons minced fresh parsley

Making Stuffed Eggplant

1. PREPARE EGGPLANT Using tip of knife, score each eggplant half in 1-inch diamond pattern, about 1 inch deep. Brush scored sides with oil, season with salt and pepper, and roast cut side down on preheated baking sheet.

2. MAKE STUFFING Soak bulgur until softened. Meanwhile, cook onion, garlic, oregano, and spices. Off heat, stir in soaked bulgur, tomatoes, Pecorino, pine nuts, and vinegar.

3. STUFF EGGPLANT Using 2 forks, gently press eggplant flesh to sides. Mound bulgur mixture into eggplant halves; pack lightly with back of spoon.

4. BAKE Sprinkle with remaining Pecorino and bake until cheese is melted. Sprinkle with parsley and serve.

1. Adjust oven racks to upper-middle and lowest positions, place parchment paper–lined rimmed baking sheet on lowest rack, and heat oven to 400 degrees.

2. Score flesh of each eggplant half in 1-inch diamond pattern, about 1 inch deep. Brush scored sides of eggplant with 1 tablespoon oil and season with salt and pepper. Lay eggplant cut side down on hot sheet and roast until flesh is tender, 40 to 50 minutes. Transfer eggplant cut side down to paper towel–lined baking sheet and let drain.

3. Toss bulgur with water in bowl and let sit until grains are softened and liquid is fully absorbed, 20 to 40 minutes.

4. Heat remaining 1 tablespoon oil in 12-inch skillet over medium heat until shimmering. Add onion and cook until softened, 5 minutes. Stir in garlic, oregano, ½ teaspoon salt, cinnamon, and cayenne and cook until fragrant, about 30 seconds. Off heat, stir in bulgur, tomatoes, ¾ cup Pecorino, pine nuts, and vinegar and let sit until heated through, about 1 minute. Season with salt and pepper to taste.

5. Return eggplant cut side up to rimmed baking sheet. Using 2 forks, gently push eggplant flesh to sides to make room for filling. Mound bulgur mixture into eggplant halves and pack lightly with back of spoon. Sprinkle with remaining ¼ cup Pecorino. Bake on upper rack until cheese is melted, 5 to 10 minutes. Sprinkle with parsley and serve.

Braised Fennel with Radicchio and Parmesan
SERVES 6 VEG

WHY THIS RECIPE WORKS Slow-cooked fennel makes a great accompaniment to meat, fish, or polenta, so we set out to turn this ubiquitous Mediterranean ingredient into a richly flavorful side dish. We cut the fennel into thick slabs and braised them with wine and aromatics. To achieve deeper flavor, we opted to leave the fennel in the skillet even after the braising liquid had evaporated to achieve a deeply golden, caramelized crust. To take advantage of the fond left in the pan and to balance the sweetness of the fennel, we stirred in sliced radicchio, cooking it briefly with water and honey to tame its bitter edge and create a complex pan sauce. A sprinkle of Parmesan cheese and toasted pine nuts added richness and crunch, and some minced fennel fronds provided brightness.

3 tablespoons extra-virgin olive oil
3 fennel bulbs (12 ounces each), 2 tablespoons fronds minced, stalks discarded, bulbs cut vertically into ½-inch-thick slabs
½ teaspoon grated lemon zest plus 2 teaspoons juice
   Salt and pepper
½ cup dry white wine
1 head radicchio (10 ounces), cored and sliced thin

¼ cup water

2 teaspoons honey

2 tablespoons pine nuts, toasted and chopped
   Shaved Parmesan cheese

1. Heat oil in 12-inch skillet over medium heat until shimmering. Add fennel pieces, lemon zest, ½ teaspoon salt, and ¼ teaspoon pepper, then pour wine over fennel. (Skillet will be slightly crowded at first, but fennel will fit into single layer as it cooks.) Cover, reduce heat to medium-low, and cook until fennel is just tender, about 20 minutes.

2. Increase heat to medium, flip fennel pieces, and continue to cook, uncovered, until fennel is well browned on first side and liquid is almost completely evaporated, 5 to 8 minutes. Flip fennel pieces and continue to cook until well browned on second side, 2 to 4 minutes. Transfer fennel to serving platter and tent loosely with aluminum foil.

3. Add radicchio, water, honey, and pinch salt to now-empty skillet and cook over low heat, scraping up any browned bits, until wilted, 3 to 5 minutes. Off heat, stir in lemon juice and season with salt and pepper to taste. Arrange radicchio over fennel and sprinkle with pine nuts, minced fennel fronds, and shaved Parmesan. Serve.

Slicing Fennel for Braising

1. Cut off tops and feathery fronds, trim very thin slice from bottom of base, and remove any tough or blemished outer layers.

2. Place trimmed fennel bulb upright on base and cut vertically into ½-inch-thick slabs.

Fava Beans with Artichokes, Asparagus, and Peas

SERVES 6 VEG

WHY THIS RECIPE WORKS Italian *vignole* is a vibrant braise that highlights the best of spring produce. Since fresh fava beans are traditional, we started there. The favas are usually eaten skin on, but tasters found their fibrous skins tough and unpleasant. We

For this vibrant Italian braise, we tenderize fresh skin-on fava beans by boiling them in a baking soda solution.

were happy to find that we could tenderize the skins by blanching the beans in a baking soda solution. After testing various ratios of water to baking soda, we landed on 2 cups of water and a teaspoon of baking soda; this resulted in nicely tender beans without any bitter, soapy aftertaste. However, the baking soda solution had one drawback: The high pH of the water caused the favas to slowly turn purple during cooking—and they continued to change color after draining. We found that the most effective way to counteract this was to simply rinse them thoroughly after cooking. With our skin-on favas perfected, we turned to the remaining vegetables. Sweet peas, savory baby artichokes, and grassy asparagus added layers of springtime flavor. A speedy stovetop braise was the ideal method for cooking each vegetable perfectly; we added the artichokes first to allow them time to cook almost all the way through before adding the more delicate asparagus and peas, and finally the favas to warm through. We finished the dish with fresh herbs and lemon zest to reinforce the lively flavor profile. This recipe works best with fresh, in-season vegetables; however, if you can't find fresh fava beans and peas, you can substitute 1 cup of frozen, thawed fava beans and 1¼ cups of frozen peas; add the peas to the skillet with the beans in step 4.

2 teaspoons grated lemon zest, plus 1 lemon
4 baby artichokes (3 ounces each)
1 teaspoon baking soda
1 pound fava beans, shelled (1 cup)
1 tablespoon extra-virgin olive oil, plus extra for serving
1 leek, white and light green parts only, halved lengthwise, sliced thin, and washed thoroughly
   Salt and pepper
3 garlic cloves, minced
1 cup chicken or vegetable broth
1 pound asparagus, trimmed and cut on bias into 2-inch lengths
1 pound fresh peas, shelled (1¼ cups)
2 tablespoons shredded fresh basil
1 tablespoon chopped fresh mint

1. Cut 1 lemon in half, squeeze halves into container filled with 2 quarts water, then add spent halves. Working with 1 artichoke at a time, trim stem to about ¾ inch and cut off top quarter of artichoke. Break off bottom 3 or 4 rows of tough outer leaves by pulling them downward. Using paring knife, trim outer layer of stem and base, removing any dark green parts. Cut artichoke into quarters and submerge in lemon water.

2. Bring 2 cups water and baking soda to boil in small saucepan. Add beans and cook until edges begin to darken, 1 to 2 minutes. Drain and rinse well with cold water.

3. Heat oil in 12-inch skillet over medium heat until shimmering. Add leek, 1 tablespoon water, and 1 teaspoon salt and cook until softened, about 3 minutes. Stir in garlic and cook until fragrant, about 30 seconds.

4. Remove artichokes from lemon water, shaking off excess water, and add to skillet. Stir in broth and bring to simmer. Reduce heat to medium-low, cover, and cook until artichokes are almost tender, 6 to 8 minutes. Stir in asparagus and peas, cover, and cook until crisp-tender, 5 to 7 minutes. Stir in beans and cook until heated through and artichokes are fully tender, about 2 minutes. Off heat, stir in basil, mint, and lemon zest. Season with salt and pepper to taste and drizzle with extra oil. Serve immediately.

Roasted Green Beans with Pecorino and Pine Nuts

SERVES 4 to 6 FAST VEG

WHY THIS RECIPE WORKS Roasted green beans can be dry and leathery; we wanted earthy, sweet beans with moist interiors and just the right amount of browning. We started by roasting the beans covered to allow them to steam and soften slightly. A mixture of oil, salt, pepper, and sugar seasoned them thoroughly; the sugar also promoted flavorful browning once we

A hybrid moist-then-dry roasting method is a foolproof way to achieve tender green beans with a hint of flavorful browning.

uncovered the sheet. To add a lively bite to the blistered beans, we tossed them with a lemony vinaigrette, microwaving garlic and lemon zest with oil to bloom their flavors and tame the garlic's raw bite. We topped the beans with salty, sharp Pecorino and crunchy toasted pine nuts. Use the large holes of a box grater to shred the Pecorino.

1½ pounds green beans, trimmed
¼ cup extra-virgin olive oil
¾ teaspoon sugar
   Salt and pepper
2 garlic cloves, minced
1 teaspoon grated lemon zest plus 1 tablespoon juice
1 teaspoon Dijon mustard
2 tablespoons chopped fresh basil
¼ cup shredded Pecorino Romano cheese
2 tablespoons pine nuts, toasted

1. Adjust oven rack to lowest position and heat oven to 475 degrees. Toss green beans with 1 tablespoon oil, sugar, ¼ teaspoon salt, and ½ teaspoon pepper. Transfer to rimmed baking sheet and spread into single layer.

2. Cover sheet tightly with aluminum foil and roast for 10 minutes. Remove foil and continue to roast until green beans are spotty brown, about 10 minutes, stirring halfway through roasting.

3. Meanwhile, combine garlic, lemon zest, and remaining 3 tablespoons oil in medium bowl and microwave until bubbling, about 1 minute. Let mixture steep for 1 minute, then whisk in lemon juice, mustard, ⅛ teaspoon salt, and ¼ teaspoon pepper until combined.

4. Transfer green beans to bowl with dressing, add basil, and toss to combine. Season with salt and pepper to taste. Transfer green beans to serving platter and sprinkle with Pecorino and pine nuts. Serve.

VARIATION

Roasted Green Beans with Almonds and Mint
FAST VEG

Omit Pecorino. Substitute 1 teaspoon lime zest and 1 tablespoon juice for lemon zest and juice, ¼ cup torn fresh mint leaves for basil, and 2 tablespoons toasted and chopped whole blanched almonds for pine nuts.

Braised Green Beans with Potatoes and Basil
SERVES 6 VEG

WHY THIS RECIPE WORKS Unlike crisp-tender green beans that have been steamed or sautéed, Greece's traditional braised green beans boast a uniquely soft, velvety texture without being mushy. Unfortunately, achieving this can require 2 hours of simmering. To get ultratender braised green beans in half the time, we first simmered them with a pinch of baking soda to weaken their cell walls. Once the beans were partially softened, we stirred in canned diced tomatoes to add sweet flavor; their acid also neutralized the baking soda and prevented the beans from oversoftening. The beans turned meltingly tender after less than an hour of simmering in a low oven. Sautéed garlic and onion plus some lemon juice, basil, and a drizzle of olive oil delivered bright flavor and richness. Finally, to make the dish more substantial, we added chunks of potatoes; 1-inch pieces turned tender in the same amount of time as the beans.

5 tablespoons extra-virgin olive oil
1 onion, chopped fine
2 tablespoons minced fresh oregano or 2 teaspoons dried
4 garlic cloves, minced
1½ cups water
1½ pounds green beans, trimmed and cut into 2-inch lengths
1 pound Yukon Gold potatoes, peeled and cut into 1-inch pieces
½ teaspoon baking soda

For velvety green beans, we simmer them with a little baking soda, then add canned tomatoes partway through cooking.

1 (14.5-ounce) can diced tomatoes, drained with juice reserved, chopped
1 tablespoon tomato paste
Salt and pepper
3 tablespoons chopped fresh basil
Lemon juice

1. Adjust oven rack to lower-middle position and heat oven to 275 degrees. Heat 3 tablespoons oil in Dutch oven over medium heat until shimmering. Add onion and cook until softened, about 5 minutes. Stir in oregano and garlic and cook until fragrant, about 30 seconds. Stir in water, green beans, potatoes, and baking soda, bring to simmer, and cook, stirring occasionally, for 10 minutes.

2. Stir in tomatoes and their juice, tomato paste, 2 teaspoons salt, and ¼ teaspoon pepper. Cover, transfer pot to oven, and cook until sauce is slightly thickened and green beans can be cut easily with side of fork, 40 to 50 minutes.

3. Stir in basil and season with salt, pepper, and lemon juice to taste. Transfer green beans to serving bowl and drizzle with remaining 2 tablespoons oil. Serve.

Wilting kale in broth instead of water infuses the greens with savory flavor as they cook.

Garlicky Braised Kale

SERVES 8 | VEG

WHY THIS RECIPE WORKS Hearty winter greens like kale are frequently prepared in Mediterranean countries such as Italy and Spain. For a one-pot recipe that would make the most of a generous harvest or market haul, we first briefly cooked the kale with broth. Onion and a substantial amount of garlic gave the greens some aromatic character. Adding the greens in three batches allowed them to wilt down so they fit in the pot. When the kale had nearly reached the tender-firm texture we wanted, we removed the lid and raised the heat to allow the liquid to cook off. This will look like a mountain of raw kale before it's cooked, but it wilts down and will eventually all fit into the pot.

6 tablespoons extra-virgin olive oil
1 large onion, chopped fine
10 garlic cloves, minced
¼ teaspoon red pepper flakes
2 cups chicken or vegetable broth
1 cup water
Salt and pepper
4 pounds kale, stemmed and cut into 3-inch pieces
1 tablespoon lemon juice, plus extra for seasoning

1. Heat 3 tablespoons oil in Dutch oven over medium heat until shimmering. Add onion and cook until softened and lightly browned, 5 to 7 minutes. Stir in garlic and pepper flakes and cook until fragrant, about 1 minute. Stir in broth, water, and ½ teaspoon salt and bring to simmer.

2. Add one-third of kale, cover, and cook, stirring occasionally, until wilted, 2 to 4 minutes. Repeat with remaining kale in 2 batches. Continue to cook, covered, until kale is tender, 13 to 15 minutes.

3. Remove lid and increase heat to medium-high. Cook, stirring occasionally, until most liquid has evaporated and greens begin to sizzle, 10 to 12 minutes. Off heat, stir in remaining 3 tablespoons oil and lemon juice. Season with salt, pepper, and extra lemon juice to taste. Serve.

Making Garlicky Braised Kale

1. COOK AROMATICS In Dutch oven, cook onion until softened, then add garlic and pepper flakes.

2. ADD LIQUID AND KALE Add broth, water, and salt; bring to simmer. Add kale in batches and cook, covered, until wilted.

3. UNCOVER AND EVAPORATE Remove lid and increase heat to medium-high. Cook until most of liquid has evaporated.

4. SEASON AND SERVE Off heat, add rest of oil and lemon juice. Season with salt, pepper, and additional lemon juice. Serve.

Hearty greens figure into many Mediterranean dishes. Their sturdy leaves offer earthy flavor and texture as well as an abundance of nutrients—iron, fiber, vitamins K, A, and C, and magnesium, just to name a few. The season for hearty greens spans from early fall until late spring, sometimes stretching into summer. A large bunch of greens will reduce dramatically when cooked, so don't be intimidated if the greens initially dominate the pan.

Selecting Hearty Greens

There are many types of hearty greens, but the ones below are the ones we use most often since they are widely available in American markets.

SWISS CHARD

Swiss chard has dark, ruffled leaves and a tough stem that can be crimson red, orange, yellow, or white. The leaves and stems need to be cooked separately, as the stems take much longer to soften. Look for bunches with bright-stemmed leaves that are firm and undamaged.

COLLARD GREENS

Collard greens have dark green, very wide leaves and a thick stem. Look for bunches with trimmed stems and no sign of yellowing or wilting. Unless you plan to slice the leaves thinly, it is best to braise collard greens until tender. They pair well with strongly flavored ingredients. Be sure to strip the leaves from the stems, which are tough and woody.

KALE

Kale comes in many varieties: curly green kale, red kale, more delicate Tuscan kale, and baby kale. Its hearty leaves have a surprisingly sweet undertone. Kale is easy to find both in bunches and in prewashed bags. Tender baby kale can be eaten raw in salads without any special treatment, but mature kale is tougher. To eat it raw, cut it into pieces, then vigorously knead it for about 5 minutes.

MUSTARD GREENS

There are many varieties of mustard greens, but the most common has crisp, bright green leaves and thin stems. These greens have a medium-hot flavor with a fairly strong bite.

Storing Hearty Greens

To preserve freshness, store greens loosely in a dry plastic bag in the refrigerator. Kept this way, the greens can last for five to seven days.

Prepping Hearty Greens

1A. Hold leaf at base of stem and use knife to slash leafy portion from either side of tough stem.

1B. Alternatively, fold each leaf in half and cut along edge of rib to remove thickest part of rib and stem.

2. After separating leaves, stack several and either cut into strips or roll pile into cigar shape and coarsely chop.

3. Fill salad spinner bowl with cool water, add cut greens, and gently swish them around. Let grit settle to bottom of bowl, then lift greens out and drain water. Repeat until greens no longer release any dirt.

With their substantial, meaty texture and great flavor, mushrooms are favored throughout France, Italy, and Spain, where they add complex meatiness to soups, sauces, and stuffings. They are also enjoyed simply sautéed, stuffed, marinated, or grilled on their own. Here's everything you need to know about buying, storing, and preparing mushrooms.

Buying Mushrooms

There are many varieties of fresh mushrooms available at the supermarket now: the humble white button mushroom, as well as cremini, shiitake, oyster, and portobello mushrooms, for starters. We find cremini mushrooms to be firmer and more flavorful than less expensive white button mushrooms, but the two are interchangeable in any recipe. If possible, always buy mushrooms loose so that you can inspect their quality. When buying button or cremini mushrooms, look for mushrooms with whole, intact caps; avoid those with discoloration or dry, shriveled patches. Pick mushrooms with large caps and minimal stems.

Storing Mushrooms

Because of their high moisture content, mushrooms are very perishable; most mushrooms can be kept fresh for only a few days. To extend their shelf life as long as possible, store loose mushrooms in the crisper drawer in a partially open zipper-lock bag. Store packaged mushrooms in their original containers, as these are designed to "breathe," maximizing the life of the mushrooms. Once the package has been opened, simply rewrap it with plastic wrap.

Cleaning Mushrooms

When it comes to cleaning, you can ignore the advice against washing mushrooms, which exaggerates their ability to absorb water. As long as they are washed before they are cut, we found that 6 ounces of mushrooms gain only about a quarter-ounce of water. However, rinsing can cause discoloration, so don't wash mushrooms that will be eaten raw; simply brush dirt away with a soft pastry brush or cloth. If you are cooking the mushrooms, rinse away dirt and grit with cold water just before using, then spin dry in a salad spinner.

Preparing Mushrooms

For mushrooms with tender stems, such as white button and cremini, trim the stems, then prep and cook the stems alongside the caps.

For mushrooms with tough, woody stems, such as shiitakes and portobellos, the stems should be removed.

Buying and Preparing Dried Porcini

We often turn to dried porcini to add potent savory flavor to dishes. Because the mushrooms are dried, their flavor is concentrated and they are conveniently shelf-stable. When buying dried porcini, always inspect the mushrooms. Avoid those with small holes, which indicate the mushrooms may have been subjected to pinworms. Look for large, smooth porcini free of holes, dust, and grit. Because porcini mushrooms are foraged, not farmed, they vary in cleanliness. Always remove any grit before using; we like to swish them in a bowl of water to loosen dirt, then rinse them.

Buying and Preparing Portobellos

Portobellos are the giants of the mushroom family, ranging from 4 to 6 inches in diameter. They are the mature form of cremini mushrooms, and, as a result of the extra growing time, they have a particularly intense, meaty flavor and a steaklike texture. They are ideal sautéed, roasted, grilled, or stuffed. Look for mushrooms with fully intact caps and dry gills. Wet, damaged gills are a sign of spoilage. The stems are woody and are often discarded, so buy mushrooms with stems only if you plan to use them (such as in soup or stock). To clean portobellos, simply wipe them with a damp towel. When cooking portobellos in soups or stews, you may want to remove the gills on the underside of the cap so that your dish won't taste or look muddy.

Roasted Mushrooms with Parmesan and Pine Nuts

SERVES 4 VEG

WHY THIS RECIPE WORKS From earthy and smoky to deep and woodsy, mushrooms have an amazing range of flavors and textures. We decided to develop a simple side that showcased this versatile ingredient along with some key Mediterranean flavors. A combination of full-flavored cremini and meaty shiitakes gave us the deepest, most well-rounded flavor. Sautéing the mushrooms required cooking them in multiple batches to achieve good browning, so we opted instead to roast them in a hot oven. But this presented a new problem: Since roasting concentrates flavor, it became clear that our mushrooms were unevenly seasoned—some were inedibly salty, and others were quite bland. To remedy this, we brined the mushrooms briefly before cooking. The salted water ensured even and thorough seasoning, and the excess water easily evaporated during cooking. Finally, we dressed the mushrooms in olive oil and lemon juice before adding flavorful Italian-inspired mix-ins: Parmesan, parsley, and pine nuts. Cremini mushrooms, also called Baby Bella, vary in diameter. Quarter large (more than 2 inches) mushrooms, halve medium (1 to 2 inches) ones, and leave small (under 1 inch) ones whole.

Salt and pepper
1½ pounds cremini mushrooms, trimmed and left whole if small, halved if medium, or quartered if large
1 pound shiitake mushrooms, stemmed, caps larger than 3 inches halved
3 tablespoons extra-virgin olive oil
1 teaspoon lemon juice
1 ounce Parmesan cheese, grated (½ cup)
2 tablespoons pine nuts, toasted
2 tablespoons chopped fresh parsley

1. Adjust oven rack to lowest position and heat oven to 450 degrees. Dissolve 5 teaspoons salt in 2 quarts room-temperature water in large container. Add cremini mushrooms and shiitake mushrooms, cover with plate or bowl to submerge, and soak at room temperature for 10 minutes.

2. Drain mushrooms and pat dry with paper towels. Toss mushrooms with 2 tablespoons oil, then spread into single layer in rimmed baking sheet. Roast until liquid from mushrooms has completely evaporated, 35 to 45 minutes.

3. Remove sheet from oven (be careful of escaping steam when opening oven) and, using metal spatula, carefully stir mushrooms. Return to oven and continue to roast until mushrooms are deeply browned, 5 to 10 minutes.

4. Whisk remaining 1 tablespoon oil and lemon juice together in large bowl. Add mushrooms and toss to coat. Stir in Parmesan,

We brine a combination of cremini and shiitake mushrooms to make a well-seasoned, full-flavored side dish.

pine nuts, and parsley and season with salt and pepper to taste. Serve immediately.

VARIATIONS

Roasted Mushrooms with Harissa and Mint VEG

We prefer to use our homemade Harissa (page 316), but you can substitute store-bought harissa if you wish, though spiciness can vary greatly by brand.

Omit Parmesan and pine nuts and increase lemon juice to 2 teaspoons. Whisk 1 minced garlic clove, 2 teaspoons harissa, ¼ teaspoon ground cumin, and ¼ teaspoon salt into oil mixture in step 4. Substitute 2 tablespoons mint for parsley.

Roasted Mushrooms with Roasted Garlic and Smoked Paprika VEG

Omit Parmesan and pine nuts. Add 3 unpeeled whole garlic cloves to sheet with mushrooms. Remove garlic from sheet in step 3 when stirring mushrooms. When garlic is cool enough to handle, peel and mash. Substitute 2 teaspoons sherry vinegar for lemon juice. Whisk mashed garlic, ½ teaspoon smoked paprika, and ¼ teaspoon salt into oil mixture in step 4.

Grilled Portobello Mushrooms and Shallots with Rosemary-Dijon Vinaigrette

SERVES 4 to 6   FAST   VEG

WHY THIS RECIPE WORKS Meaty portobello mushrooms are a great match for the heat and smoke of the grill, which concentrates their flavor and produces perfect charred-on-the-outside, tender-on-the-inside mushrooms. To give our Italian-inspired vegetable entrée some extra interest, we decided to grill some aromatic shallots and create a lively dressing. We were happy to find that the shallots and mushrooms cooked in the same amount of time and had just enough smoky flavor after roughly 20 minutes on the grill. We drizzled our vegetables with the vinaigrette while they were still warm, which boosted their flavor without overpowering them. You will need two 12-inch metal skewers for this recipe.

6 tablespoons extra-virgin olive oil
1 small garlic clove, minced
2 teaspoons lemon juice
1 teaspoon Dijon mustard
1 teaspoon minced fresh rosemary
   Salt and pepper
8 shallots, peeled
6 portobello mushroom caps (4 to 5 inches in diameter)

1. Whisk 2 tablespoons oil, garlic, lemon juice, mustard, rosemary, and ¼ teaspoon salt together in small bowl. Season with salt and pepper to taste; set aside for serving.

2. Thread shallots through roots and stem ends onto two 12-inch metal skewers. Using paring knife, cut ½-inch crosshatch pattern, ¼ inch deep, on tops of mushroom caps. Brush shallots and mushroom caps with remaining ¼ cup oil and season with salt and pepper.

3A. FOR A CHARCOAL GRILL Open bottom vent completely. Light large chimney starter half filled with charcoal briquettes (3 quarts). When top coals are partially covered with ash, pour evenly over grill. Set cooking grate in place, cover, and open lid vent completely. Heat grill until hot, about 5 minutes.

3B. FOR A GAS GRILL Turn all burners to high, cover, and heat grill until hot, about 15 minutes. Turn all burners to medium.

4. Clean and oil cooking grate. Place shallots and mushrooms, gill side up, on grill. Cook (covered if using gas) until mushrooms have released their liquid and vegetables are charred on first side, about 8 minutes. Flip mushrooms and shallots and continue to cook (covered if using gas) until vegetables are tender and charred on second side, about 8 minutes. Transfer vegetables to serving platter. Remove skewers from shallots and discard any charred outer layers. Whisk vinaigrette to recombine and drizzle over vegetables. Serve.

Greek-Style Garlic-Lemon Potatoes

SERVES 4 to 6   FAST   VEG

WHY THIS RECIPE WORKS In Greece, potato wedges are cooked in plenty of olive oil until browned and crisp and are accented by classic Greek flavors like lemon and oregano. For our version, we chose Yukon Golds, which hold their shape nicely and cook up with pleasantly fluffy interiors, and browned them in a nonstick skillet in olive oil to give them deep flavor and color. We then covered the pan to allow the potatoes to finish cooking through. A combination of juice and zest gave them full lemon flavor, and we added a modest amount of garlic to give them an aromatic backbone. Letting the lemon, garlic, and oregano cook briefly with the potatoes gave the dish a rounded, cohesive flavor profile. A final sprinkling of parsley added welcome freshness.

3   tablespoons extra-virgin olive oil
1½ pounds Yukon Gold potatoes, peeled and cut lengthwise into ¾-inch-thick wedges
1½ tablespoons minced fresh oregano
3   garlic cloves, minced
2   teaspoons grated lemon zest plus 1½ tablespoons juice
    Salt and pepper
1½ tablespoons minced fresh parsley

1. Heat 2 tablespoons oil in 12-inch nonstick skillet over medium-high heat until shimmering. Add potatoes cut side down in single layer and cook until golden brown on first side (skillet should sizzle but not smoke), about 6 minutes. Using tongs, flip potatoes onto second cut side and cook until golden brown, about 5 minutes. Reduce heat to medium-low, cover, and cook until potatoes are tender, 8 to 12 minutes.

2. Meanwhile, whisk remaining 1 tablespoon oil, oregano, garlic, lemon zest and juice, ½ teaspoon salt, and ½ teaspoon pepper together in small bowl. When potatoes are tender, gently stir in garlic mixture and cook, uncovered, until fragrant, about 2 minutes. Off heat, gently stir in parsley and season with salt and pepper to taste. Serve.

VARIATION

Greek-Style Garlic-Lemon Potatoes with Olives and Feta   FAST   VEG
Stir ½ cup crumbled feta cheese and 2 tablespoons chopped pitted kalamata olives into potatoes with parsley.

Understanding Potato Types

Since potatoes have varying textures (determined by starch level), you can't just reach for any potato and expect great results. Potatoes fall into three main categories—baking, boiling, and all-purpose—depending on texture.

ALL-PURPOSE POTATOES

These potatoes contain a moderate amount of starch (18 to 20 percent)—less than dry, floury baking potatoes but more than firm boiling potatoes. Although they are considered "in-between" potatoes, in comparison to boiling potatoes, their texture is more mealy, putting them closer to baking potatoes. All-purpose potatoes can be mashed or baked but won't be as fluffy as baking potatoes. They can be used in salads and soups but won't be quite as firm as boiling potatoes. Common varieties: Yukon Gold, Yellow Finn, Purple Peruvian, Kennebec, and Katahdin.

BOILING POTATOES

These potatoes contain a relatively low amount of starch (16 to 18 percent), which means they have a firm, smooth, and waxy texture. Often they are called "new" potatoes because they are less-mature potatoes harvested in late spring and summer. They are less starchy than "old" potatoes because they haven't had time to convert their sugar to starch. They also have thinner skins. Firm, waxy potatoes are perfect when you want the potatoes to hold their shape. They are also a good choice when roasting or boiling. Common varieties: Red Bliss, French Fingerling, Red Creamer, and White Rose.

BAKING POTATOES

These dry, floury potatoes contain more starch (20 to 22 percent) than those in other categories, giving these varieties a dry, mealy texture. These potatoes are the best choice when baking or mashing. They work well when you want to thicken a stew or soup, but not when you want distinct chunks of potatoes. Common varieties: russet, Russet Burbank, and Idaho.

Strategically arranging our root vegetables on the baking sheet ensures that they all cook through at the same rate.

Roasted Root Vegetables with Lemon-Caper Sauce

SERVES 4 to 6 VEG

WHY THIS RECIPE WORKS We set out to create a hearty winter side that would elevate humble root vegetables. We chose a combination of Brussels sprouts, red potatoes, and carrots to create a balance of flavors and textures. To ensure that the vegetables would roast evenly, we cut them into equal-size pieces. Arranging the Brussels sprouts in the center of the baking sheet, with the hardier potatoes and carrots around the perimeter, kept the more delicate sprouts from charring in the hot oven. Before roasting, we tossed the vegetables with olive oil, thyme, rosemary, and a little sugar (to promote browning). Whole garlic cloves and halved shallots softened and mellowed in the oven, lending great flavor to the finished dish. Once all of the vegetables were perfectly tender and caramelized, we tossed them with a bright, Mediterranean-inspired dressing of parsley, capers, and lemon juice.

1 pound Brussels sprouts, trimmed and halved
1 pound red potatoes, unpeeled, cut into 1-inch pieces
8 shallots, peeled and halved
4 carrots, peeled and cut into 2-inch lengths, thick ends halved lengthwise
6 garlic cloves, peeled
3 tablespoons extra-virgin olive oil
2 teaspoons minced fresh thyme
1 teaspoon minced fresh rosemary
1 teaspoon sugar
  Salt and pepper
2 tablespoons minced fresh parsley
1½ tablespoons capers, rinsed and minced
1 tablespoon lemon juice, plus extra for seasoning

1. Adjust oven rack to middle position and heat oven to 450 degrees. Toss Brussels sprouts, potatoes, shallots, and carrots with garlic, 1 tablespoon oil, thyme, rosemary, sugar, ¾ teaspoon salt, and ¼ teaspoon pepper.

2. Spread vegetables into single layer in rimmed baking sheet, arranging Brussels sprouts cut side down in center of sheet. Roast until vegetables are tender and golden brown, 30 to 35 minutes, rotating sheet halfway through roasting.

3. Whisk parsley, capers, lemon juice, and remaining 2 tablespoons oil together in large bowl. Add roasted vegetables and toss to combine. Season with salt, pepper, and extra lemon juice to taste. Serve.

VARIATION

Roasted Radicchio, Fennel, and Parsnips with Lemon-Basil Sauce VEG

Substitute 2 fennel bulbs, halved, cored, and sliced into ½-inch wedges, 8 ounces parsnips, peeled and cut into 2-inch pieces, and 1 head radicchio, cored and cut into 2-inch wedges, for Brussels sprouts and carrots. Arrange radicchio in center of baking sheet before roasting. Omit capers and parsley and add 2 tablespoons chopped fresh basil and 2 tablespoons minced fresh chives to oil mixture in step 3.

Cutting Brussels Sprouts in Half

Cut sprouts in half through stem end so that leaves stay intact.

Grilled Radicchio with Garlic and Rosemary–Infused Oil
SERVES 4 to 6 FAST VEG

WHY THIS RECIPE WORKS Radicchio is popular in Italy, where it's often cooked and served as an accompaniment to meat or fish. When grilled, the purple leaves become lightly crisp and smoky tasting. To keep the radicchio from falling apart on the grill, we cut it through the core end into thick wedges. To avoid singed leaves, we found it was necessary to coat the leaves liberally with olive oil; we infused the oil with extra flavor by microwaving it with garlic and rosemary before brushing it on the radicchio. For maximum browning, we turned each wedge of radicchio twice so that each flat side of the wedges could rest directly against the grill grate.

6 tablespoons extra-virgin olive oil
1 garlic clove, minced
1 teaspoon minced fresh rosemary
3 heads radicchio (10 ounces each), quartered
  Salt and pepper

1. Microwave oil, garlic, and rosemary in bowl until bubbling, about 1 minute; let mixture steep for 1 minute. Brush radicchio with ¼ cup oil mixture and season with salt and pepper.

2A. FOR A CHARCOAL GRILL Open bottom vent completely. Light large chimney starter half filled with charcoal briquettes (3 quarts). When top coals are partially covered with ash, pour evenly over grill. Set cooking grate in place, cover, and open lid vent completely. Heat grill until hot, about 5 minutes.

2B. FOR A GAS GRILL Turn all burners to high, cover, and heat grill until hot, about 15 minutes. Turn all burners to medium.

3. Clean and oil cooking grate. Place radicchio on grill. Cook (covered if using gas), flipping as needed, until radicchio is softened and lightly charred, 3 to 5 minutes. Transfer to serving platter and drizzle with remaining oil mixture. Serve.

Cutting Radicchio for Grilling

1. Cut radicchio in half through core.

2. Cut each half again through core so that quarters stay intact.

How to Grill Vegetables

To easily grill a simple vegetable to serve with dinner, use this chart as a guide. Brush or toss the vegetables with oil and season with salt and pepper before grilling. Grill vegetables over a medium-hot fire (you can comfortably hold your hand 5 inches above the cooking grate for 3 to 4 seconds).

VEGETABLE	PREPARATION	GRILLING DIRECTIONS
Asparagus	Snap off tough ends.	Grill, turning once, until streaked with light grill marks, 5 to 7 minutes.
Bell Pepper	Core, seed, and cut into large wedges.	Grill, turning often, until streaked with dark grill marks, 8 to 10 minutes.
Eggplant	Remove ends. Cut into ¾-inch-thick rounds or strips.	Grill, turning once, until flesh is darkly colored, 8 to 10 minutes.
Endive	Halve lengthwise through stem end.	Grill, flat side down, until streaked with dark grill marks, 5 to 7 minutes.
Fennel	Slice bulb through base into ¼-inch-thick pieces.	Grill, turning once, until streaked with dark grill marks and quite soft, 7 to 9 minutes.
Portobello Mushrooms	Discard stems and wipe caps clean.	Grill, turning once, until streaked with dark grill marks and quite soft, 7 to 9 minutes.
White or Cremini Mushrooms	Trim thin slice from stems, then thread onto skewers.	Grill, turning several times, until golden brown, 6 to 7 minutes.
Onions	Peel, cut into ½-inch-thick slices, and skewer.	Grill, turning occasionally, until lightly charred, 10 to 12 minutes.
Cherry Tomatoes	Remove stems, then thread onto skewers.	Grill, turning often, until streaked with dark grill marks, 3 to 6 minutes.
Plum Tomatoes	Halve lengthwise and seed if desired.	Grill, turning once, until streaked with dark grill marks, about 6 minutes.
Zucchini or Yellow Summer Squash	Remove ends. Slice lengthwise into ½-inch-thick strips.	Grill, turning once, until streaked with dark grill marks, 8 to 10 minutes.

We sauté curly-leaf spinach and then squeeze out excess moisture before dressing it with a warm garlic-infused oil.

Sautéed Spinach with Yogurt and Dukkah

SERVES 4 **FAST** **VEG**

WHY THIS RECIPE WORKS A combination found throughout the eastern Mediterranean region, earthy, tender spinach and creamy, tangy yogurt are a perfect match. To make a successful side dish using this pair of ingredients, we started with the spinach. We found that we greatly preferred the hearty flavor and texture of curly-leaf spinach to baby spinach, which wilted down into mush. We cooked the spinach in extra-virgin olive oil and, once it was cooked, used tongs to squeeze the excess moisture out of the leaves. Lightly toasted minced garlic, cooked after the spinach in the same pan, added a sweet nuttiness. We emphasized the yogurt's tanginess with lemon zest and juice and drizzled it over our garlicky spinach, but tasters thought the dish seemed incomplete. To elevate the flavor and give it some textural contrast, we sprinkled on some *dukkah*, an Egyptian blend of ground chickpeas, nuts, and spices. Two pounds of flat-leaf spinach (about three bunches) can be substituted for the curly-leaf spinach. We prefer to use our homemade Dukkah (page 317), but you can substitute store-bought dukkah if you wish.

½ cup plain yogurt

1½ teaspoons grated lemon zest plus 1 teaspoon juice

3 tablespoons extra-virgin olive oil

20 ounces curly-leaf spinach, stemmed

2 garlic cloves, minced

Salt and pepper

¼ cup dukkah

1. Combine yogurt and lemon zest and juice in bowl; set aside for serving. Heat 1 tablespoon oil in Dutch oven over high heat until shimmering. Add spinach, 1 handful at a time, stirring and tossing each handful to wilt slightly before adding more. Cook spinach, stirring constantly, until uniformly wilted, about 1 minute. Transfer spinach to colander and squeeze between tongs to release excess liquid.

2. Wipe pot dry with paper towels. Add remaining 2 tablespoons oil and garlic to now-empty pot and cook over medium heat until fragrant, about 30 seconds. Add spinach and toss to coat, gently separating leaves to evenly coat with garlic oil. Off heat, season with salt and pepper to taste. Transfer spinach to serving platter, drizzle with yogurt sauce, and sprinkle with dukkah. Serve.

Sautéed Swiss Chard with Garlic

SERVES 4 FAST VEG

WHY THIS RECIPE WORKS Swiss chard is a leafy green beloved from the Côte d'Azur to Turkey, offering a bitter, beetlike flavor that mellows when cooked. The key to sautéing this hearty vegetable is to get the stems to finish cooking at the same time as the leaves. Unlike spinach's quick-cooking stems and kale's inedibly tough ribs, Swiss chard stems fall somewhere in the middle. To encourage the stems to cook efficiently and evenly, we sliced them thin on the bias. We gave the stems a head start, sautéing them with garlic over relatively high heat to create a crisp-tender texture and complex, lightly caramelized flavor. We introduced the tender leaves later and in two stages, allowing the first batch to begin wilting before adding the rest. Served with a squeeze of lemon, the result was a bright, nuanced side of greens with a range of appealing textures in every bite. You can use any variety of Swiss chard for this recipe.

2 tablespoons extra-virgin olive oil

3 garlic cloves, sliced thin

1½ pounds Swiss chard, stems sliced ¼ inch thick on bias, leaves sliced into ½-inch-wide strips

Salt and pepper

2 teaspoons lemon juice

1. Heat oil in 12-inch nonstick skillet over medium-high heat until just shimmering. Add garlic and cook, stirring constantly, until lightly browned, 30 to 60 seconds. Add chard stems and ⅛ teaspoon salt and cook, stirring occasionally, until spotty brown and crisp-tender, about 6 minutes.

2. Add two-thirds of chard leaves and cook, tossing with tongs, until just starting to wilt, 30 to 60 seconds. Add remaining chard leaves and continue to cook, stirring frequently, until leaves are tender, about 3 minutes. Off heat, stir in lemon juice and season with salt and pepper to taste. Serve.

VARIATIONS

Sautéed Swiss Chard with Pancetta and Caramelized Shallots FAST

Omit garlic. Heat 1 tablespoon of oil in 12-inch nonstick skillet over medium heat until shimmering. Add 3 thinly sliced shallots and cook, stirring frequently, until well browned and softened, 10 to 12 minutes. Transfer shallots to bowl and wipe skillet clean with paper towels. Cook 2 ounces pancetta, cut into ¼-inch pieces, and remaining 1 tablespoon oil in now-empty skillet over medium-high heat, stirring occasionally, until rendered and crisp, 6 to 8 minutes. Using slotted spoon, transfer pancetta to paper towel–lined plate. Pour off all but 2 tablespoons fat from skillet and return to medium-high heat. Proceed with recipe, adding ⅛ teaspoon red pepper flakes to skillet with chard stems. Substitute 1 tablespoon balsamic vinegar for lemon juice and stir pancetta and shallots into chard with vinegar.

Sautéed Swiss Chard with Currants and Pine Nuts FAST VEG

Reduce garlic to 1 minced clove and add ¼ teaspoon ground cumin to skillet with garlic. Substitute 2 teaspoons sherry vinegar for lemon juice and stir 3 tablespoons dried currants and 3 tablespoons toasted pine nuts into chard with vinegar.

Roasted Winter Squash with Tahini and Feta

SERVES 6 VEG

WHY THIS RECIPE WORKS Winter squashes are eaten throughout the Mediterranean, and we sought to create a savory recipe for roasted butternut squash that was simple and presentation-worthy. We chose to peel the squash to remove not only the tough outer skin but also the rugged fibrous layer of white flesh just beneath, ensuring supremely tender squash. To encourage the squash slices to caramelize, we used a hot 425-degree oven, placed the squash on the lowest oven rack, and increased the baking time to evaporate moisture. Finally, we selected a mix of

Greek-inspired toppings that added crunch, creaminess, fresh flavor, and a little sweetness: pistachios, feta, mint, and tahini spiked with honey and lemon juice. This dish can be served warm or at room temperature. For the best texture, be sure to peel the squash thoroughly, removing all of the fibrous flesh just below the squash's skin.

- 3 pounds butternut squash
- 3 tablespoons extra-virgin olive oil
- Salt and pepper
- 1 tablespoon tahini
- 1½ teaspoons lemon juice
- 1 teaspoon honey
- 1 ounce feta cheese, crumbled (¼ cup)
- ¼ cup shelled pistachios, toasted and chopped fine
- 2 tablespoons chopped fresh mint

1. Adjust oven rack to lowest position and heat oven to 425 degrees. Using sharp vegetable peeler or chef's knife, remove squash skin and fibrous threads just below skin (squash should be completely orange with no white flesh). Halve squash lengthwise and scrape out seeds. Place squash cut side down on cutting board and slice crosswise into ½-inch-thick pieces.

2. Toss squash with 2 tablespoons oil, ½ teaspoon salt, and ½ teaspoon pepper and arrange in rimmed baking sheet in single layer. Roast squash until sides touching sheet toward back of oven are well browned, 25 to 30 minutes. Rotate sheet and continue to roast until sides touching sheet toward back of oven are well browned, 6 to 10 minutes.

3. Use metal spatula to flip each piece and continue to roast until squash is very tender and sides touching sheet are browned, 10 to 15 minutes.

To achieve tender and beautifully caramelized butternut squash, we roast slices in a hot oven.

4. Transfer squash to serving platter. Whisk tahini, lemon juice, honey, remaining 1 tablespoon oil, and pinch salt together in bowl. Drizzle squash with tahini dressing and sprinkle with feta, pistachios, and mint. Serve.

Cutting Up Squash for Roasting

1. Using sharp vegetable peeler or chef's knife, remove squash skin and fibrous threads just below skin.

2. Carefully drive tip of chef's knife into center of peeled squash. Place folded dish towel on top of squash, over tip of knife.

3. Drive rest of knife down through end of squash. Turn squash around and repeat from opposite side to cut squash in half.

4. Scrape out seeds using spoon, then place squash flat side down on cutting board and slice into ½-inch-thick pieces.

Roasting sliced tomatoes in extra-virgin olive oil speeds up their cooking time.

Roasted Tomatoes

SERVES 4 VEG

WHY THIS RECIPE WORKS When tomatoes are in season, oven roasting is a great way to intensify their flavor while increasing their shelf life. Many recipes call for a low oven and hours of cooking, only to yield leathery tomatoes. We were able to cut down on the cooking time without sacrificing quality of flavor by cutting the tomatoes into thick slices to create lots of exposed surface area from which water could escape. Oil transfers heat with great efficiency, so we poured some over the slices to help drive more moisture away and to concentrate the tomatoes' flavor. We started roasting the tomatoes in a 425-degree oven and then reduced the temperature to 300 degrees to gently finish cooking. Leftover tomato oil can be used to make salad dressings or as a dipping oil for bread. The success of this recipe depends on ripe, in-season tomatoes.

    3 pounds large tomatoes, cored, bottom ⅛ inch trimmed,
      and sliced ¾ inch thick
    2 garlic cloves, peeled and smashed

¼ teaspoon dried oregano
  Kosher salt and pepper
¾ cup extra-virgin olive oil

1. Adjust oven rack to middle position and heat oven to 425 degrees. Line rimmed baking sheet with aluminum foil. Arrange tomatoes in even layer in prepared sheet, with larger slices around edge and smaller slices in center. Place garlic cloves on tomatoes. Sprinkle with oregano and ¼ teaspoon salt and season with pepper to taste. Drizzle oil evenly over tomatoes.

2. Bake for 30 minutes, rotating sheet halfway through baking. Remove sheet from oven. Reduce oven temperature to 300 degrees and prop open door with wooden spoon to cool oven. Using thin spatula, flip tomatoes.

3. Return tomatoes to oven, close oven door, and continue to cook until spotty brown, skins are blistered, and tomatoes have collapsed to ¼ to ½ inch thick, 1 to 2 hours. Remove from oven and let cool completely, about 30 minutes. Discard garlic and transfer tomatoes and oil to airtight container. (Tomatoes can be refrigerated for up to 5 days or frozen for up to 2 months.)

Sautéed Cherry Tomatoes

SERVES 4 to 6 FAST VEG

WHY THIS RECIPE WORKS Cherry tomatoes are often used raw in salads, but sautéing turns them into a terrific vegetable side that can be enjoyed year-round. When shopping for cherry tomatoes, we looked for plump numbers with smooth skin—signs that the tomatoes were fully ripe. Because they contain a lot of liquid, these tomatoes cook very quickly, and it took only a minute for them to soften in a hot skillet. Tossing the halved tomatoes with sugar and salt encouraged some light caramelization. Before removing the tomatoes from the heat, we seasoned them with some minced garlic and then stirred in fresh basil to complement their sweetness. Grape tomatoes can be substituted for the cherry tomatoes, but because they tend to be sweeter, you will want to reduce or even omit the sugar. Do likewise if your cherry tomatoes are very sweet. Don't toss the tomatoes with the sugar and salt ahead of time or you will draw out their juice and make them overly soft.

    1 tablespoon extra-virgin olive oil
 1½ pounds cherry tomatoes, halved
    2 teaspoons sugar, or to taste
      Salt and pepper
    1 garlic clove, minced
    2 tablespoons chopped fresh basil

Heat oil in 12-inch skillet over medium-high heat until shimmering. Toss tomatoes with sugar and ¼ teaspoon salt, then add to skillet and cook, stirring often, for 1 minute. Stir in garlic and cook until fragrant, about 30 seconds. Off heat, stir in basil and season with salt and pepper to taste. Serve.

VARIATION

Sautéed Cherry Tomatoes with Capers and Anchovies FAST

Heat 2 anchovy fillets, rinsed and minced, with oil until beginning to sizzle, about 2 minutes. Increase garlic to 2 cloves and add 2 tablespoons rinsed capers to tomatoes with garlic. Substitute 2 tablespoons minced fresh parsley for basil.

Stuffed Tomatoes with Couscous, Olives, and Orange

SERVES 6 VEG

To make a flavor-packed stuffing for tomatoes, we hydrate the couscous with some of the tomatoes' juice.

WHY THIS RECIPE WORKS Stuffed tomatoes are eaten everywhere from Italy and France to Greece and Turkey, and the fillings vary as much as the countries themselves. We wanted a foolproof recipe for stuffed tomatoes that would be bursting with uniquely Mediterranean flavors. To concentrate flavor and eliminate excess moisture, we seasoned hollowed-out tomatoes with salt and sugar and let them drain. We started the filling by wilting spinach over browned aromatics before adding couscous (tasters preferred the nutty flavor of couscous to the more neutral flavor of rice). For intense tomato flavor, we hydrated the couscous with the tomatoes' reserved juice. Orange zest and kalamata olives added citrusy, briny flavors. After stuffing the tomatoes, we sprinkled on a topping of browned panko bread crumbs and Manchego cheese for crunch and richness. We drizzled the baked stuffed tomatoes with a bright vinaigrette made by whisking red wine vinegar into the cooking liquid left behind in the baking dish. Look for large tomatoes, about 3 inches in diameter. We prefer using kosher salt because residual grains can be easily wiped away from the tomatoes; if using table salt, be sure to reduce all of the salt amounts in the recipe by half. Use the large holes of a box grater to shred the Manchego.

6 large ripe tomatoes (8 to 10 ounces each)
1 tablespoon sugar
   Kosher salt and pepper
4½ tablespoons extra-virgin olive oil
¼ cup panko bread crumbs
3 ounces Manchego cheese, shredded (¾ cup)
1 onion, halved and sliced thin
2 garlic cloves, minced
⅛ teaspoon red pepper flakes

8 ounces (8 cups) baby spinach, chopped coarse
1 cup couscous
½ teaspoon grated orange zest
¼ cup pitted kalamata olives, chopped
1 tablespoon red wine vinegar

1. Adjust oven rack to middle position and heat oven to 375 degrees. Cut top ½ inch off stem end of tomatoes and set aside. Using melon baller or teaspoon measure, scoop out tomato pulp and transfer to fine-mesh strainer set over bowl. Press on pulp with wooden spoon to extract juice; set aside juice and discard pulp. (You should have about ⅔ cup tomato juice; if not, add water as needed to equal ⅔ cup.)

2. Combine sugar and 1 tablespoon salt in bowl. Sprinkle each tomato cavity with 1 teaspoon sugar mixture, then turn tomatoes upside down on plate to drain for 30 minutes.

3. Combine 1½ teaspoons oil and panko in 10-inch skillet and toast over medium-high heat, stirring frequently, until golden brown, about 3 minutes. Transfer to bowl and let cool for 10 minutes. Stir in ¼ cup Manchego.

4. Heat 2 tablespoons oil in now-empty skillet over medium heat until shimmering. Add onion and ½ teaspoon salt and cook until softened, about 5 minutes. Stir in garlic and pepper flakes and cook until fragrant, about 30 seconds. Add spinach, 1 handful at a time, and cook until wilted, about 3 minutes. Stir in couscous, orange zest, and reserved tomato juice. Cover, remove skillet from heat, and let sit until couscous is tender, about 7 minutes. Add olives and remaining ½ cup Manchego to couscous and gently fluff with fork to combine. Season with salt and pepper to taste.

5. Coat bottom of 13 by 9-inch baking dish with remaining 2 tablespoons oil. Blot tomato cavities dry with paper towels and season with salt and pepper. Pack each tomato with couscous mixture, about ½ cup per tomato, mounding excess. Top stuffed tomatoes with 1 heaping tablespoon panko mixture. Place tomatoes in prepared dish. Season reserved tops with salt and pepper and place in empty spaces in dish.

6. Bake, uncovered, until tomatoes have softened but still hold their shape, about 20 minutes. Using slotted spoon, transfer to serving platter. Whisk vinegar into oil remaining in dish, then drizzle over tomatoes. Place tops on tomatoes and serve.

VARIATIONS

Stuffed Tomatoes with Couscous, Capers, and Pine Nuts VEG

Substitute ¾ cup shredded mozzarella cheese for Manchego. Stir 2 tablespoons rinsed capers and 2 tablespoons toasted pine nuts into cooked couscous mixture with mozzarella.

Stuffed Tomatoes with Couscous, Currants, and Pistachios VEG

Substitute ¾ cup crumbled feta cheese for Manchego. Stir 2 tablespoons dried currants and 2 tablespoons chopped pistachios into cooked couscous mixture with feta.

Sautéed Zucchini Ribbons
SERVES 4 to 6   FAST   VEG

WHY THIS RECIPE WORKS Quick-cooking and delicately flavored, yellow summer squash and zucchini are favorites in Mediterranean cuisines and perfect for a light side dish. To create a fresh, simple recipe, we started with very thinly sliced squash, using a peeler to make even "ribbons" and discarding the waterlogged seeds. The ultrathin ribbons browned and cooked so quickly that they didn't have time to break down and release their liquid, eliminating the need to salt them before cooking. The cooked squash needed little embellishment; a quick, tangy vinaigrette of extra-virgin olive oil, garlic, and lemon and a sprinkle of fresh parsley rounded out the flavors. We like a mix of yellow summer squash and zucchini, but you can use just one or the other. The thickness of the squash ribbons may vary depending on the peeler used; we developed this recipe with our winning Kuhn Rikon Original Swiss peeler, which produces ribbons that are 1/32 inch thick. Steeping the minced garlic in lemon juice mellows the garlic's bite; do not skip this step. To avoid overcooking the squash, start checking for doneness at the lower end of the cooking time.

1 small garlic clove, minced
1 teaspoon grated lemon zest plus 1 tablespoon juice
4 (6- to 8-ounce) zucchini or yellow summer squash, trimmed
2 tablespoons plus 1 teaspoon extra-virgin olive oil
Salt and pepper
1½ tablespoons chopped fresh parsley

1. Combine garlic and lemon juice in large bowl and set aside for at least 10 minutes. Using vegetable peeler, shave off 3 ribbons

Preparing Tomatoes for Stuffing

1. Using sharp knife, slice top ½ inch off each tomato.

2. Using melon baller or teaspoon measure, remove pulp and transfer to fine-mesh strainer set over bowl. Press on pulp with wooden spoon to extract juice.

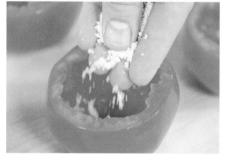

3. Sprinkle inside of each tomato with 1 teaspoon sugar-salt mixture, place upside down on plate, and let drain for 30 minutes.

We eliminate the need to salt and drain raw zucchini and summer squash by shaving them into ribbons with a peeler.

from 1 side of summer squash, then turn squash 90 degrees and shave off 3 more ribbons. Continue to turn and shave ribbons until you reach seeds; discard core. Repeat with remaining squash.

2. Whisk 2 tablespoons oil, ¼ teaspoon salt, ⅛ teaspoon pepper, and lemon zest into garlic–lemon juice mixture.

3. Heat remaining 1 teaspoon oil in 12-inch nonstick skillet over medium-high heat until just smoking. Add summer squash and cook, tossing occasionally with tongs, until squash has softened and is translucent, 3 to 4 minutes. Transfer squash to bowl with dressing, add parsley, and gently toss to coat. Season with salt and pepper to taste. Serve.

VARIATION

Sautéed Zucchini Ribbons with Mint and Pistachios
FAST VEG

Omit lemon zest and substitute 1½ teaspoons cider vinegar for lemon juice. Substitute ⅓ cup chopped fresh mint for parsley and sprinkle squash with 2 tablespoons toasted and chopped pistachios before serving.

Grilled Zucchini and Red Onion with Lemon-Basil Dressing
SERVES 4 FAST VEG

WHY THIS RECIPE WORKS Perfectly tender grilled zucchini is a Greek specialty, and it makes a great pairing for just about any grilled fish or meat dish. To double up on flavor, we combined two vegetables in our recipe. Mindful of complementary cooking times, we paired mild-flavored zucchini with sweet red onion. We cooked the onion slices on skewers to make sure they wouldn't fall apart. For a bright finish, we whisked up a quick lemon-basil dressing to flavor the vegetables after they came off the grill. After about 5 minutes, faint grill marks should begin to appear on the undersides of the vegetables; if necessary, adjust their position on the grill or adjust the heat level. The vegetables can be served hot, warm, or at room temperature. You will need two 12-inch metal skewers for this recipe.

    1 large red onion, peeled and sliced into ½-inch-
       thick rings
    1 pound zucchini, sliced lengthwise into ¾-inch-
       thick planks
    6 tablespoons extra-virgin olive oil
       Salt and pepper
    1 teaspoon grated lemon zest plus 1 tablespoon juice
    1 small garlic clove, minced
    ¼ teaspoon Dijon mustard
    1 tablespoon chopped fresh basil

1. Thread onion rounds from side to side onto two 12-inch metal skewers. Brush onion and zucchini with ¼ cup oil, sprinkle with 1 teaspoon salt, and season with pepper. Whisk remaining 2 tablespoons oil, lemon zest and juice, garlic, mustard, and ¼ teaspoon salt together in bowl; set aside for serving.

2A. FOR A CHARCOAL GRILL Open bottom vent completely. Light large chimney starter half filled with charcoal briquettes (3 quarts). When top coals are partially covered with ash, pour evenly over grill. Set cooking grate in place, cover, and open lid vent completely. Heat grill until hot, about 5 minutes.

2B. FOR A GAS GRILL Turn all burners to high, cover, and heat grill until hot, about 15 minutes. Turn all burners to medium.

3. Clean and oil cooking grate. Place vegetables cut side down on grill. Cook (covered if using gas), turning as needed, until tender and caramelized, 18 to 22 minutes; transfer vegetables to serving platter as they finish cooking. Remove skewers from onion and discard any charred outer rings. Whisk dressing to recombine, then drizzle over vegetables. Sprinkle with basil and serve.

All About Squash

Generally, squash is divided into two categories: winter squash and summer squash. Zucchini and yellow squash are the most common varieties of summer squash. They both have thin, edible skins and a high moisture content, so they cook quickly whether steamed, baked, or sautéed. Winter squashes have hard, thick peels and firm flesh that requires longer cooking to turn tender. The flesh can vary from deep yellow to orange in color.

BUYING WINTER SQUASH

Whether acorn, butternut, delicata, or another variety, winter squash should feel hard; soft spots are an indication that the squash has been mishandled. Squash should also feel heavy for its size, a sign that the flesh is moist and ripe. Most supermarkets sell butternut squash that has been completely or partially prepped. Whole squash you peel yourself has the best flavor and texture, but if you are looking to save a few minutes of prep, we have found that the peeled and halved squash is fine. We don't like the butternut squash sold in chunks; while it's a timesaver, the flavor is wan and the texture stringy.

BUYING ZUCCHINI AND SUMMER SQUASH

Choose zucchini and summer squash that are firm and without soft spots. Smaller squashes are more flavorful and less watery than larger specimens; they also have fewer seeds. Look for zucchini and summer squash no heavier than 8 ounces, and preferably just 6 ounces.

STORING SQUASH

You can store winter squash in a cool, well-ventilated spot for several weeks. Zucchini and summer squash are more perishable; store them in the refrigerator in a partially sealed zipper-lock bag for up to five days.

A couple of eggs and a bit of flour bind our zucchini fritters together while allowing the vegetable's flavor to shine.

Zucchini and Feta Fritters

SERVES 4 to 6   VEG

WHY THIS RECIPE WORKS In the eastern Mediterranean, vegetables are often made into crisp, flavorful fritters. We packed our zucchini fritters with the classic Greek flavors of feta cheese and dill to make an appealing appetizer or entrée. Shredding and salting the zucchini, letting it drain, and then squeezing it in a clean dish towel eliminated excess moisture, which can make the fritters soggy. To allow the zucchini's delicate flavor to shine, we bound the zucchini with just a couple of eggs and a little flour. A simple yogurt-based sauce offered the perfect finish. Use a coarse grater or the shredding disk of a food processor to shred the zucchini. Make sure to squeeze the zucchini until it is completely dry, or the fritters will fall apart in the skillet. Do not let the zucchini sit on its own for too long after it has been squeezed dry or it will turn brown. In addition to the lemon wedges, serve with Cucumber-Yogurt Sauce or Yogurt-Herb Sauce (page 233). Fritters can be served warm or at room temperature.

EASY MEDITERRANEAN SAUCES

Refreshing and light Mediterranean sauces can bring a dish to life with just a few simple ingredients. These easy sauces can be dolloped over anything from vegetables to meat to pilafs.

Tahini Sauce
MAKES about 1¼ cups `FAST` `VEG`

½ cup tahini
½ cup water
¼ cup lemon juice (2 lemons)
2 garlic cloves, minced
   Salt and pepper

Whisk tahini, water, lemon juice, and garlic together in bowl until combined. Season with salt and pepper to taste. Let sit until flavors meld, about 30 minutes. (Sauce can be refrigerated for up to 4 days.)

Tahini-Yogurt Sauce
MAKES about 1 cup `FAST` `VEG`

⅓ cup tahini
⅓ cup plain Greek yogurt
¼ cup water
3 tablespoons lemon juice
1 garlic clove, minced
   Salt and pepper

Whisk tahini, yogurt, water, lemon juice, garlic, and ¾ teaspoon salt together in bowl until combined. Season with salt and pepper to taste. Let sit until flavors meld, about 30 minutes. (Sauce can be refrigerated for up to 4 days.)

Yogurt-Herb Sauce
MAKES about 1 cup `FAST` `VEG`

1 cup plain yogurt
2 tablespoons minced fresh cilantro
2 tablespoons minced fresh mint
1 garlic clove, minced
   Salt and pepper

Whisk yogurt, cilantro, mint, and garlic together in bowl until combined. Season with salt and pepper to taste. Let sit until flavors meld, about 30 minutes. (Sauce can be refrigerated for up to 2 days.)

Lemon-Yogurt Sauce
MAKES about 1 cup `FAST` `VEG`

1 cup plain yogurt
1 tablespoon minced fresh mint
1 teaspoon grated lemon zest plus
   2 tablespoons juice
1 garlic clove, minced
   Salt and pepper

Whisk yogurt, mint, lemon zest and juice, and garlic together in bowl until combined. Season with salt and pepper to taste. Let sit until flavors meld, about 30 minutes. (Sauce can be refrigerated for up to 2 days.)

Cucumber-Yogurt Sauce
MAKES about 2½ cups `FAST` `VEG`
Cilantro, mint, parsley, or tarragon can be substituted for the dill if desired.

1 cup plain Greek yogurt
2 tablespoons extra-virgin olive oil
2 tablespoons minced fresh dill
1 garlic clove, minced
1 cucumber, peeled, halved
   lengthwise, seeded, and shredded
   Salt and pepper

Whisk yogurt, oil, dill, and garlic together in medium bowl until combined. Stir in cucumber and season with salt and pepper to taste. (Sauce can be refrigerated for up to 1 day.)

Cucumber-Yogurt Sauce

Garlic Aïoli
MAKES about 1¼ cups `FAST` `VEG`
A combination of vegetable oil and extra-virgin olive oil is crucial to the flavor of the aïoli.

2 large egg yolks
2 teaspoons Dijon mustard
2 teaspoons lemon juice
1 garlic clove, minced
¾ cup vegetable oil
1 tablespoon water
   Salt and pepper
¼ cup extra-virgin olive oil

Process egg yolks, mustard, lemon juice, and garlic in food processor until combined, about 10 seconds. With processor running, slowly drizzle in vegetable oil, about 1 minute. Transfer mixture to medium bowl and whisk in water, ½ teaspoon salt, and ¼ teaspoon pepper. Whisking constantly, slowly drizzle in olive oil until emulsified. (Aïoli can be refrigerated for up to 4 days.)

1 pound zucchini, shredded
  Salt and pepper
4 ounces feta cheese, crumbled (1 cup)
2 scallions, minced
2 large eggs, lightly beaten
2 tablespoons minced fresh dill
1 garlic clove, minced
¼ cup all-purpose flour
6 tablespoons extra-virgin olive oil
  Lemon wedges

1. Adjust oven rack to middle position and heat oven to 200 degrees. Toss zucchini with 1 teaspoon salt and let drain in fine-mesh strainer for 10 minutes.

2. Wrap zucchini in clean dish towel, squeeze out excess liquid, and transfer to large bowl. Stir in feta, scallions, eggs, dill, garlic, and ¼ teaspoon pepper. Sprinkle flour over mixture and stir to incorporate.

3. Heat 3 tablespoons oil in 12-inch nonstick skillet over medium heat until shimmering. Drop 2-tablespoon-size portions of batter into skillet and use back of spoon to press batter into 2-inch-wide fritter (you should fit about 6 fritters in skillet at a time). Fry until golden brown, about 3 minutes per side.

4. Transfer fritters to paper towel–lined baking sheet and keep warm in oven. Wipe skillet clean with paper towels and repeat with remaining 3 tablespoons oil and remaining batter. Serve with lemon wedges.

Squeezing Zucchini Dry

1. Shred zucchini on large holes of box grater.

2. Squeeze shredded zucchini in clean dish towel or several layers of paper towels until dry.

Parcooking the zucchini halves before stuffing them eliminates excess moisture and ensures they cook through.

Stuffed Zucchini with Spiced Lamb, Dried Apricots, and Pine Nuts
SERVES 4

WHY THIS RECIPE WORKS We wanted a recipe for perfectly cooked zucchini boats filled with a rich, gently spiced lamb stuffing. To balance the distinct flavor of the lamb, we chose a trio of elements popular in Moroccan cuisine: sweet dried apricots, buttery pine nuts, and aromatic *ras el hanout*, the North African spice blend that includes coriander, cardamom, cinnamon, and more. After browning the lamb, we poured off all but a small amount of the fat to keep our filling from tasting too greasy; to offset the filling's meaty texture and add a mild, wheaty chew, we incorporated a small amount of bulgur. We took several steps to avoid overcooked and flavorless zucchini: We scooped out the seeds to reduce moisture; we roasted the unstuffed zucchini cut side down to achieve a flavorful sear and give the vegetable a head start on cooking; and we returned the zucchini to the hot oven—packed with our robust filling—for a final burst of heat before serving. We prefer to use our homemade Ras el Hanout (page 316), but you can substitute store-bought ras el hanout if you wish, though flavor and spiciness can vary greatly by brand. Serve with Cucumber-Yogurt Sauce or Yogurt-Herb Sauce (page 233), if desired.

4 zucchini (8 ounces each), halved lengthwise and seeded
2 tablespoons plus 1 teaspoon extra-virgin olive oil
   Salt and pepper
8 ounces ground lamb
1 onion, chopped fine
4 garlic cloves, minced
2 teaspoons ras el hanout
⅔ cup chicken broth
½ cup medium-grind bulgur, rinsed
¼ cup dried apricots, chopped fine
2 tablespoons pine nuts, toasted
2 tablespoons minced fresh parsley

1. Adjust oven racks to upper-middle and lowest positions, place rimmed baking sheet on lower rack, and heat oven to 400 degrees.

2. Brush cut sides of zucchini with 2 tablespoons oil and season with salt and pepper. Lay zucchini cut side down in hot sheet and roast until slightly softened and skins are wrinkled, 8 to 10 minutes. Remove zucchini from oven and flip cut side up on sheet; set aside.

3. Meanwhile, heat remaining 1 teaspoon oil in large saucepan over medium-high heat until just smoking. Add lamb, ½ teaspoon salt, and ¼ teaspoon pepper and cook, breaking up meat with wooden spoon, until browned, 3 to 5 minutes. Using slotted spoon, transfer lamb to paper towel–lined plate.

4. Pour off all but 1 tablespoon fat from saucepan. Add onion to fat left in saucepan and cook over medium heat until softened, about 5 minutes. Stir in garlic and ras el hanout and cook until fragrant, about 30 seconds. Stir in broth, bulgur, and apricots and bring to simmer. Reduce heat to low, cover, and simmer gently until bulgur is tender, 16 to 18 minutes.

5. Off heat, lay clean dish towel underneath lid and let pilaf sit for 10 minutes. Add pine nuts and parsley to pilaf and gently fluff with fork to combine. Season with salt and pepper to taste.

6. Pack each zucchini half with bulgur mixture, about ½ cup per zucchini half, mounding excess. Place baking sheet on upper rack and bake zucchini until heated through, about 6 minutes. Serve.

For firm and flavorful stewed zucchini, we seed large pieces of zucchini and brown them on the stovetop.

Greek Stewed Zucchini

SERVES 6 to 8 VEG

WHY THIS RECIPE WORKS Stewed vegetable dishes are popular across Greece, but they vary widely from region to region: They can depend on as few as two vegetables or as many as 20; they can be cooked exclusively in a skillet or a pot, on the stove or in the oven. One pitfall we found again and again, whatever the method, was watery, bland vegetables. We wanted our vegetables to retain their character while still coming together to create a deeply flavored, cohesive stew. After testing a variety of recipes, we landed on a combination of zucchini and tomatoes as our starting point. As for the method, we started by browning seeded zucchini on the stovetop (in batches to ensure thorough, even browning), then set it aside while we built our savory tomato sauce. Tasters found canned diced tomatoes mealy, canned crushed tomatoes sludgy and cloying, and fresh tomatoes inconsistent in quality. Canned whole peeled tomatoes, processed until smooth, gave the dish the right balance of tomato flavor and silky texture. A smattering of olives complemented the sauce without dominating it. Once our sauce had simmered and thickened, we stirred in the browned zucchini and transferred the pot to the oven to allow the dish to gently finish cooking and develop deep, concentrated flavor. A traditional garnish of shredded fresh mint, stirred in at the end, added brightness.

1 (28-ounce) can whole peeled tomatoes
3 tablespoons extra-virgin olive oil
5 zucchini (8 ounces each), trimmed, quartered lengthwise, seeded, and cut into 2-inch lengths
1 onion, chopped fine
   Salt and pepper
3 garlic cloves, minced
1 teaspoon minced fresh oregano or ¼ teaspoon dried
¼ teaspoon red pepper flakes
2 tablespoons chopped pitted kalamata olives
2 tablespoons shredded fresh mint

1. Adjust oven rack to lower-middle position and heat oven to 325 degrees. Process tomatoes and their juice in food processor until completely smooth, about 1 minute; set aside.

2. Heat 2 teaspoons oil in Dutch oven over medium-high heat until just smoking. Brown one-third of zucchini, about 3 minutes per side; transfer to bowl. Repeat with 4 teaspoons oil and remaining zucchini in 2 batches.

3. Add remaining 1 tablespoon oil, onion, and ¾ teaspoon salt to now-empty pot and cook, stirring occasionally, over medium-low heat until onion is very soft and golden brown, 9 to 11 minutes. Stir in garlic, oregano, and pepper flakes and cook until fragrant, about 30 seconds. Stir in olives and tomatoes, bring to simmer, and cook, stirring occasionally, until sauce has thickened, about 30 minutes.

4. Stir in zucchini and any accumulated juice, cover, and transfer pot to oven. Bake until zucchini is very tender, 30 to 40 minutes. Stir in mint and adjust sauce consistency with hot water as needed. Season with salt and pepper to taste. Serve.

Preparing Zucchini for Stewing

Trim off top and bottom of zucchini, then quarter lengthwise. Rest each quarter on trimmed side and cut through core to remove seeds. Cut cored zucchini quarters into 2-inch lengths.

Summer Vegetable Gratin
SERVES 6 to 8 VEG

WHY THIS RECIPE WORKS A gratin is a classic French preparation that can transform simple summer produce into something spectacular. We chose to create a bread crumb–topped gratin of zucchini, yellow summer squash, and ripe tomatoes. To prevent the juicy vegetables from turning our gratin into a soupy mess, we salted and then drained them before assembling the casserole. Baking the dish uncovered encouraged excess moisture to evaporate in the oven. Layering the tomatoes on top maximized their heat exposure and helped them roast and caramelize. To flavor the vegetables, we tossed them with an aromatic garlic-thyme oil, then drizzled more oil over the top. Fresh bread crumbs tossed with Parmesan and shallots made a simple but elegant topping. The success of this recipe depends on fresh, in-season vegetables. Look for zucchini and yellow summer squash of roughly the same diameter. We like a mix of yellow summer squash and zucchini, but you can use just one or the other.

1 pound zucchini, sliced ¼ inch thick
1 pound yellow summer squash, sliced ¼ inch thick
   Salt and pepper
1½ pounds ripe tomatoes, cored and sliced ¼ inch thick
6 tablespoons extra-virgin olive oil
2 onions, halved and sliced thin
2 garlic cloves, minced
1 tablespoon minced fresh thyme
1 slice hearty white sandwich bread, torn into quarters
2 ounces Parmesan cheese, grated (1 cup)
2 shallots, minced
¼ cup chopped fresh basil

1. Toss zucchini and summer squash with 1 teaspoon salt and let drain in colander set over bowl until vegetables release at least 3 tablespoons liquid, about 45 minutes. Thoroughly pat zucchini and summer squash dry with paper towels.

2. Meanwhile, spread tomatoes on paper towel–lined baking sheet, sprinkle with ½ teaspoon salt, and let sit for 30 minutes. Thoroughly pat tomatoes dry with paper towels.

3. Heat 1 tablespoon oil in 12-inch nonstick skillet over medium heat until shimmering. Add onions and ½ teaspoon salt and cook, stirring occasionally, until softened and dark golden brown, 20 to 25 minutes; set aside.

4. Adjust oven rack to upper-middle position and heat oven to 400 degrees. Coat bottom of 13 by 9-inch baking dish with 1 tablespoon oil. Combine 3 tablespoons oil, garlic, thyme, and ½ teaspoon pepper in bowl. Process bread in food processor until finely ground, about 10 seconds, then combine with remaining 1 tablespoon oil, Parmesan, and shallots in separate bowl.

5. Toss zucchini and summer squash with half of garlic-oil mixture and arrange in prepared dish. Sprinkle evenly with onions, then arrange tomatoes on top, overlapping them slightly. Spoon remaining garlic-oil mixture evenly on tomatoes. Bake until vegetables are tender and tomatoes are starting to brown on edges, 40 to 45 minutes.

6. Remove dish from oven and increase oven temperature to 450 degrees. Sprinkle bread-crumb mixture evenly over top and continue to bake gratin until bubbling and cheese is lightly browned, 5 to 10 minutes. Let cool for 10 minutes, then sprinkle with basil. Serve.

Assembling a Summer Vegetable Gratin

1. Arrange zucchini and yellow squash in greased baking dish.

2. Sprinkle caramelized onions evenly over top.

3. Lay tomato slices over onions, overlapping them slightly, and spoon remaining garlic-oil mixture evenly over top.

4. Bake until vegetables are tender and tomatoes are starting to brown on edges, then sprinkle bread-crumb mixture evenly over top. Bake until cheese is lightly browned, 5 to 10 minutes.

Dressing the vegetables both before and after cooking gives them bold, balanced flavor.

Grilled Vegetable Kebabs with Grilled Lemon Dressing

SERVES 4 to 6   FAST   VEG

WHY THIS RECIPE WORKS Kebabs are a staple across much of the eastern Mediterranean and North Africa, but vegetables are often added as an afterthought or as a filler on meat kebabs. We wanted the vegetables to be the star of this dish, so we set our sights on achieving veggies with nicely crisp, charred exteriors and pleasantly tender interiors. We chose sweet bell peppers, hearty zucchini, and meaty portobello mushrooms, since their varying flavors and textures complemented each other nicely. We tossed them with half of our boldly flavored dressing base before skewering and grilling them, infusing them with great flavor from the start. Grilling lemon quarters toned down their bright acidity and gave the juice a deeper, more complex flavor when added to the dressing. You will need eight 12-inch metal skewers for this recipe.

¼ cup extra-virgin olive oil

1 teaspoon Dijon mustard

1 teaspoon minced fresh rosemary

1 garlic clove, minced

Salt and pepper

6 portobello mushroom caps (4 to 5 inches in diameter), quartered

2 zucchini, halved lengthwise and sliced ¾ inch thick

2 red bell peppers, stemmed, seeded, and cut into 1½-inch pieces

2 lemons, quartered

1. Whisk oil, mustard, rosemary, garlic, ½ teaspoon salt, and ¼ teaspoon pepper together in large bowl. Measure out and reserve half of oil mixture for serving. Toss mushrooms, zucchini, and bell peppers with remaining oil mixture, then thread in alternating order onto eight 12-inch metal skewers.

2A. FOR A CHARCOAL GRILL Open bottom vent completely. Light large chimney starter half filled with charcoal briquettes (3 quarts). When top coals are partially covered with ash, pour evenly over grill. Set cooking grate in place, cover, and open lid vent completely. Heat grill until hot, about 5 minutes.

2B. FOR A GAS GRILL Turn all burners to high, cover, and heat grill until hot, about 15 minutes. Turn all burners to medium.

3. Clean and oil cooking grate. Place kebabs and lemons on grill. Cook (covered if using gas), turning as needed, until vegetables are tender and well browned and lemons are juicy and slightly charred, 16 to 18 minutes.

4. Transfer kebabs and lemons to serving platter and remove skewers. Juice 2 lemon quarters and whisk juice into reserved oil mixture. Drizzle vegetables with dressing and serve with remaining lemon quarters.

Mechouia

SERVES 4 to 6 VEG

WHY THIS RECIPE WORKS For our take on the robustly flavored Tunisian grilled vegetable salad *mechouia*, we started by prepping the vegetables for the grill. To maximize surface area for flavorful charring, we halved the eggplant, zucchini, and plum tomatoes lengthwise and stemmed and flattened the bell peppers. We also scored the eggplant and zucchini so they would release their excess moisture as they cooked. We used a potent combination of Tunisian spices to infuse our vegetables with flavor, and more of the spices plus garlic, lemon, and a trio of herbs provided a bright, fresh-tasting dressing. Equal amounts of ground coriander and cumin can be substituted for the whole spices. Serve with grilled pita bread or with Easy-Peel Hard-Cooked Eggs (page 188) and olives.

Peeling most of the vegetables after grilling gives them the best texture for our Tunisian vegetable salad.

DRESSING

2 teaspoons coriander seeds

1½ teaspoons caraway seeds

1 teaspoon cumin seeds

5 tablespoons extra-virgin olive oil

½ teaspoon paprika

⅛ teaspoon cayenne pepper

3 garlic cloves, minced

¼ cup chopped fresh parsley

¼ cup chopped fresh cilantro

2 tablespoons chopped fresh mint

1 teaspoon grated lemon zest plus 2 tablespoons juice

Salt

VEGETABLES

2 red or green bell peppers, tops and bottoms trimmed, stemmed and seeded, and peppers flattened

1 small eggplant, halved lengthwise and scored on cut side

1 zucchini (8 to 10 ounces), halved lengthwise and scored on cut side

4 plum tomatoes, cored and halved lengthwise

Salt and pepper

2 shallots, unpeeled

1. FOR THE DRESSING Grind coriander seeds, caraway seeds, and cumin seeds in spice grinder until finely ground. Whisk ground spices, oil, paprika, and cayenne together in bowl. Reserve 3 tablespoons oil mixture for brushing vegetables before grilling. Heat remaining oil mixture and garlic in 8-inch skillet over low heat, stirring occasionally, until fragrant and small bubbles appear, 8 to 10 minutes. Transfer to large bowl, let cool for 10 minutes, then whisk in parsley, cilantro, mint, and lemon zest and juice and season with salt to taste; set aside for serving.

2. FOR THE VEGETABLES Brush interior of bell peppers and cut sides of eggplant, zucchini, and tomatoes with reserved oil mixture and season with salt.

3A. FOR A CHARCOAL GRILL Open bottom vent completely. Light large chimney starter three-quarters filled with charcoal briquettes (4½ quarts). When top coals are partially covered with ash, pour evenly over grill. Set cooking grate in place, cover, and open lid vent completely. Heat grill until hot, about 5 minutes.

3B. FOR A GAS GRILL Turn all burners to high, cover, and heat grill until hot, about 15 minutes. Turn all burners to medium-high.

4. Clean and oil cooking grate. Place bell peppers, eggplant, zucchini, tomatoes, and shallots cut side down on grill. Cook (covered if using gas), turning as needed, until tender and slightly charred, 8 to 16 minutes. Transfer eggplant, zucchini, tomatoes, and shallots to baking sheet as they finish cooking; place bell peppers in bowl, cover with plastic wrap, and let steam to loosen skins.

5. Let vegetables cool slightly. Peel bell peppers, tomatoes, and shallots. Chop all vegetables into ½-inch pieces, then toss gently with dressing in bowl. Season with salt and pepper to taste. Serve warm or at room temperature.

Prepping Vegetables for Mechouia

1. To flatten bell pepper, trim off top and bottom, then remove stem and seeds. Cut through 1 side of pepper, then press flat and trim away any remaining ribs.

2. Using tip of chef's knife (or paring knife), score cut sides of halved zucchini and eggplant in ½-inch diamond pattern, cutting down to but not through skin.

Adding bell peppers and zucchini to our ratatouille towards the end of cooking gives the stew nice textural contrast.

Ratatouille

SERVES 4 to 6 `VEG`

WHY THIS RECIPE WORKS A traditional Provençal dish of stewed summer vegetables, ratatouille is one of the ultimate examples of simple ingredients adding up to more than the sum of their parts. We wanted to develop a streamlined recipe that would be flavorful enough to stand on its own or act as a side dish. We started by sautéing our aromatics on the stovetop; once we added the eggplant and tomatoes, we moved the cooking to the ambient heat of the oven to concentrate the stew's flavor. Zucchini and bell peppers went into the pot last so that they retained some texture. Finishing the dish with fresh herbs, sherry vinegar, and extra-virgin olive oil tied everything together. This dish is best prepared using ripe, in-season tomatoes. If good tomatoes are not available, substitute one 28-ounce can of whole peeled tomatoes that have been drained and chopped coarse. We prefer to use our homemade Herbes de Provence (page 317), but you can substitute store-bought herbes de Provence if you wish, though flavor can vary by brand. As an entrée, serve ratatouille with crusty bread, topped with an egg, or over pasta or rice. This dish can be served warm, at room temperature, or chilled.

⅓ cup plus 1 tablespoon extra-virgin olive oil

2 large onions, cut into 1-inch pieces

8 large garlic cloves, peeled and smashed
   Salt and pepper

1½ teaspoons herbes de Provence

¼ teaspoon red pepper flakes

1 bay leaf

1½ pounds eggplant, peeled and cut into 1-inch pieces

2 pounds plum tomatoes, peeled, cored, and chopped coarse

2 small zucchini, halved lengthwise and cut into 1-inch pieces

1 red bell pepper, stemmed, seeded, and cut into 1-inch pieces

1 yellow bell pepper, stemmed, seeded, and cut into 1-inch pieces

2 tablespoons chopped fresh basil

1 tablespoon minced fresh parsley

1 tablespoon sherry vinegar

1. Adjust oven rack to middle position and heat oven to 400 degrees. Heat ⅓ cup oil in Dutch oven over medium-high heat until shimmering. Add onions, garlic, 1 teaspoon salt, and ¼ teaspoon pepper and cook, stirring occasionally, until onions are translucent and starting to soften, about 10 minutes. Add herbes de Provence, pepper flakes, and bay leaf and cook, stirring frequently, for 1 minute. Stir in eggplant and tomatoes. Sprinkle with ½ teaspoon salt and ¼ teaspoon pepper and stir to combine. Transfer pot to oven and cook, uncovered, until vegetables are very tender and spotty brown, 40 to 45 minutes.

2. Remove pot from oven and, using potato masher or heavy wooden spoon, smash and stir eggplant mixture until broken down to saucelike consistency. Stir in zucchini, bell peppers, ¼ teaspoon salt, and ¼ teaspoon pepper and return to oven. Cook, uncovered, until zucchini and bell peppers are just tender, 20 to 25 minutes.

3. Remove pot from oven, cover, and let sit until zucchini is translucent and easily pierced with tip of paring knife, 10 to 15 minutes. Using wooden spoon, scrape any browned bits from sides of pot and stir back into ratatouille. Discard bay leaf. Stir in 1 tablespoon basil, parsley, and vinegar. Season with salt and pepper to taste. Transfer ratatouille to serving platter, drizzle with remaining 1 tablespoon oil, and sprinkle with remaining 1 tablespoon basil. Serve.

Ciambotta
SERVES 6 VEG

WHY THIS RECIPE WORKS The combination of eggplant, tomatoes, and peppers is found all over the Mediterranean, and *ciambotta* is Italy's stewlike answer to this trifecta of summer vegetables. It makes for a hearty, one-bowl meal with nary a trace of meat. To keep the zucchini and peppers from diluting the stew, we used a skillet to cook off their juices before adding them to the pot. To thicken the broth, we embraced the eggplant's natural tendency to fall apart, simmering it until it completely broke down into the tomato-enriched sauce (microwaving it first banished excess moisture). To deepen the stew's flavor, we browned the eggplant along with the onion and potatoes, then sautéed tomato paste to develop lots of flavorful fond before adding the liquid to the pot. Finally, we found that a quick basil and oregano pesto—whirled in the food processor and stirred into the zucchini and peppers before we added them to the pot—gave the stew a bold, bright herbal flavor. Serve with crusty bread.

PESTO

⅓ cup chopped fresh basil

⅓ cup fresh oregano leaves

6 garlic cloves, minced

2 tablespoons extra-virgin olive oil

¼ teaspoon red pepper flakes

STEW

12 ounces eggplant, peeled and cut into ½-inch pieces
   Salt

¼ cup extra-virgin olive oil

1 large onion, chopped

1 pound russet potatoes, peeled and cut into ½-inch pieces

2 tablespoons tomato paste

2¼ cups water

1 (28-ounce) can whole peeled tomatoes, drained with juice reserved, chopped coarse

2 zucchini, halved lengthwise, seeded, and cut into ½-inch pieces

2 red or yellow bell peppers, stemmed, seeded, and cut into ½-inch pieces

1 cup shredded fresh basil

1. FOR THE PESTO Process all ingredients in food processor until finely ground, about 1 minute, scraping down sides of bowl as needed; set aside.

2. FOR THE STEW Line large plate with double layer of coffee filters and spray with vegetable oil spray. Toss eggplant with 1½ teaspoons salt and spread evenly on coffee filters. Microwave

We coax big flavor out of watery vegetables like eggplant, zucchini, peppers, and onions in this hearty Italian stew.

eggplant, uncovered, until dry to touch and slightly shriveled, 8 to 12 minutes, tossing halfway through microwaving.

3. Heat 2 tablespoons oil in Dutch oven over high heat until shimmering. Add eggplant, onion, and potatoes and cook, stirring frequently, until eggplant is browned, about 2 minutes.

4. Push vegetables to sides of pot. Add 1 tablespoon oil and tomato paste to center and cook, stirring often, until brown fond develops on bottom of pot, about 2 minutes. Stir in 2 cups water and tomatoes and their juice, scraping up any browned bits, and bring to simmer. Reduce heat to medium-low, cover, and simmer gently until eggplant is completely broken down and potatoes are tender, 20 to 25 minutes.

5. Meanwhile, heat remaining 1 tablespoon oil in 12-inch skillet over high heat until just smoking. Add zucchini, bell peppers, and ½ teaspoon salt and cook, stirring occasionally, until vegetables are browned and tender, 10 to 12 minutes. Push vegetables to sides of skillet. Add pesto to center and cook until fragrant, about 1 minute. Stir pesto into vegetables and transfer to bowl. Off heat, add remaining ¼ cup water to skillet and scrape up any browned bits.

6. Off heat, stir vegetable mixture and water from skillet into pot. Cover and let sit until flavors meld, about 20 minutes. Stir in basil and season with salt to taste. Serve.

All About Onions

Many supermarkets stock a half-dozen types of onions. They don't all look the same or taste the same. Here are the onions and their close relatives that you will find in most markets.

YELLOW ONIONS

These strong-flavored onions maintain their potency when cooked, making them our first choice for cooking.

WHITE ONIONS

These pungent onions are similar to yellow onions but lack some of their complexity.

RED ONIONS

These crisp onions have a sweet, peppery flavor when raw and are often used in salads.

SWEET ONIONS

Vidalia, Maui, and Walla Walla are three common sweet varieties. Their texture can become stringy when cooked, so these sugary onions are best used raw.

PEARL ONIONS

These crunchy small onions are generally used in soups, stews, and side dishes. Peeling them is a chore, so we recommend buying frozen pearl onions that are already peeled.

SHALLOTS

Shallots have a complex, subtly sweet flavor. When cooked, they become very soft and almost melt away, making them the perfect choice for sauces.

SCALLIONS

Scallions have an earthy flavor and a delicate crunch that work best in dishes that involve little or no cooking.

BUYING ONIONS

Choose onions with dry, papery skins. They should be rock hard, with no soft spots or powdery mold on the skin. Avoid onions with green sprouts.

STORING ONIONS

Store onions and shallots at cool room temperature, away from light. Delicate scallions are the exception; they belong in the refrigerator. Stand them up in 1 inch of water in a tall container and cover them loosely with a plastic bag.

CHAPTER 8

Seafood

■ FAST (less than 45 minutes start to finish)   ■ VEGETARIAN

Photos (clockwise from top left): Grilled Whole Sardines; Greek-Style Shrimp with Tomatoes and Feta; Grilled Sea Bass with Citrus and Black Olive Salad; Sautéed Sole with Fresh Tomato Relish

Mayonnaise helps the lemony coating adhere to the bluefish fillets and a little sugar speeds up the browning.

Broiled Bluefish with Preserved Lemon and Zhoug

SERVES 4 FAST

WHY THIS RECIPE WORKS Bluefish is a fatty, firm-fleshed fish that is especially popular in Turkey. We wanted a bluefish recipe that was supereasy and resulted in fillets with assertive but not overpowering flavor. Buying the freshest fish was of the utmost importance, since the longer bluefish sits on ice, the more pronounced its "fishy" flavor becomes. We used a coating of bold, floral preserved lemon, garlic, and mayonnaise to stand up to the oiliness of the bluefish and paired it with vibrant green *zhoug*, an Israeli hot sauce made from fresh herbs and chiles. The mayonnaise helped the preserved lemon cling to the fillets while they cooked, and a little sugar helped the fish brown quickly under the broiler. The gray-brown flesh of bluefish turns white once it is cooked through. Mackerel is a good substitute for bluefish. If you can't find preserved lemons, you can make your own (page 252).

4 (4- to 6-ounce) skinless bluefish fillets, 1 to 1½ inches thick
   Salt and pepper
¼ cup mayonnaise
¼ preserved lemon, pulp and white pith removed, rind rinsed and minced (1 tablespoon)
1 garlic clove, minced
¼ teaspoon sugar
¼ cup Green Zhoug (page 316)
   Lemon wedges

1. Adjust oven rack 4 inches from broiler element and heat broiler. Pat bluefish dry with paper towels, season with salt and pepper, and place skinned side down in greased rimmed baking sheet.

2. Combine mayonnaise, preserved lemon, garlic, and sugar in bowl, then spread mixture evenly on tops of fillets. Broil until bluefish flakes apart when gently prodded with paring knife and registers 140 degrees, about 5 minutes. Serve with Green Zhoug and lemon wedges.

Broiled Grape Leaf–Wrapped Grouper

SERVES 4

WHY THIS RECIPE WORKS Wrapping fish in grape leaves is a thoroughly Mediterranean cooking technique; the leaves form a protective packet around either fillets or whole fish, holding the fish together and insulating it during grilling, baking, or broiling. In some preparations the leaves are not meant to be eaten, but we wanted the leaves in our rustic dish to be both utilitarian and delicious. Starting with the fish, we chose grouper for its firm, mild flesh and let it sit in a briny and fragrant caper and lemon zest marinade while we assembled the grape leaf packets. We found brined grape leaves straight out of the jar to be unpleasantly thick and chewy; blanching the leaves briefly got us the soft texture we wanted. Then we looked to simplify: Most recipes call for the leaves to be individually patted dry, and with 24 leaves in this recipe, that was a time-consuming endeavor. We wondered if we could skip that step and use the extra moisture to provide a steamy cooking environment for the fish; the fish did indeed benefit from the wet leaves. We cooked the fish and let it rest briefly on a wire rack set in a baking sheet, allowing any excess moisture to drain off. A light coating of oil and the broiler produced a beautifully charred exterior for our packets. Our Tahini-Lemon Dressing was the perfect creamy and bright foil for our fillets. We've had good luck using Peloponnese and Krinos brand grape leaves. Take care when handling the grape leaves; they can be delicate and tear easily. Larger grape leaves can be trimmed to 6 inches. If using smaller leaves (about 4 inches in diameter), reserve 40 leaves and cook as directed in step 2; overlap nine leaves to create a 9-inch circle in step 3. Snapper and sea bass are good substitutes for the grouper.

    3 tablespoons extra-virgin olive oil, plus extra
        for brushing
    2 tablespoons minced fresh parsley
    1 tablespoon capers, rinsed and minced
    1 teaspoon grated lemon zest
    ½ teaspoon salt
    ½ teaspoon pepper
    4 (4- to 6-ounce) skinless grouper fillets, ¾ to 1 inch thick
    1 (16-ounce) jar grape leaves
    ½ cup Tahini-Lemon Dressing (page 72)

1. Whisk oil, parsley, capers, lemon zest, salt, and pepper together in medium bowl. Add grouper and gently turn to coat. Cover and refrigerate while preparing grape leaves.

2. Reserve 24 intact grape leaves, roughly 6 inches in diameter; set aside remaining leaves for another use. Bring 8 cups water to boil in large saucepan. Add grape leaves and cook for 5 minutes. Gently drain leaves and transfer to bowl of cold water to cool, about 5 minutes. Drain again thoroughly.

3. Adjust oven rack 8 inches from broiler element and heat broiler. Set wire rack in rimmed baking sheet and spray with vegetable oil spray. Shingle 5 leaves smooth side down on counter into 9-inch circle with stems pointing toward center of circle, then place 1 leaf smooth side down over opening in center. Place 1 fillet in center of leaf circle and spoon portion of remaining marinade on top. Fold sides of leaf circle over grouper, then fold up bottom of circle and continue to roll tightly into packet. Transfer packet seam side down to prepared rack. Repeat with remaining grape leaves, fillets, and marinade.

We quickly blanch jarred grape leaves so they are easier to roll around the fish and are softer to eat.

4. Pat tops of grouper packets dry with paper towels and brush with extra oil. Broil until grape leaves are crisp and lightly charred and grouper registers 140 degrees, 12 to 18 minutes, rotating sheet halfway through broiling. Serve with Tahini-Lemon Dressing.

Making Broiled Grape Leaf–Wrapped Grouper

1. BLANCH LEAVES Reserve 24 intact grape leaves, roughly 6 inches in diameter. Blanch leaves in boiling water, then gently drain and cool.

2. SHINGLE LEAVES Shingle 5 leaves smooth side down into 9-inch circle, then place 1 leaf smooth side down over opening in center.

3. FOLD PACKET Fold sides of leaf circle over grouper, then fold up bottom of circle and continue to roll tightly into packet.

4. BROIL Pat tops of packets dry and brush with oil. Broil until grape leaves are crisp and lightly charred and grouper registers 140 degrees.

Lemon-Herb Hake Fillets with Garlic Potatoes

SERVES 4 **FAST**

WHY THIS RECIPE WORKS Hake is a popular Mediterranean member of the cod family. Its firm texture and mild flavor make it suitable for many different preparations; it is also rich in beneficial fatty oils. We wanted to use hake fillets in a bright-tasting and fuss-free fish dinner that was suitable for a weeknight meal yet impressive enough to serve guests. For a simple hake and potato recipe, we gave thinly sliced russet potatoes a head start by microwaving them with oil and garlic until just tender. We then nestled the fillets on top of the potatoes in a casserole dish. Lemon slices placed atop the hake basted it as it baked, and sprigs of thyme added subtle seasoning to the fish. In the oven, the potatoes got nicely crisped and infused with flavor while the fish cooked through gently and evenly. Best of all, the side dish and entrée were ready at the same time. Haddock and cod are good substitutes for the hake.

1½ pounds russet potatoes, unpeeled, sliced into ¼-inch-thick rounds
¼ cup extra-virgin olive oil
3 garlic cloves, minced
   Salt and pepper
4 (4- to 6-ounce) skinless hake fillets, 1 to 1½ inches thick
4 sprigs fresh thyme
1 lemon, sliced thin

1. Adjust oven rack to lower-middle position and heat oven to 425 degrees. Toss potatoes with 2 tablespoons oil and garlic in bowl and season with salt and pepper. Microwave, uncovered,

until potatoes are just tender, 12 to 14 minutes, stirring halfway through microwaving.

2. Transfer potatoes to 13 by 9-inch baking dish and press gently into even layer. Pat hake dry with paper towels, season with salt and pepper, and arrange skinned side down on top of potatoes. Drizzle hake with remaining 2 tablespoons oil, then place thyme sprigs and lemon slices on top. Bake until hake flakes apart when gently prodded with paring knife and registers 140 degrees, 15 to 18 minutes. Slide spatula underneath potatoes and hake and carefully transfer to individual plates. Serve.

Hake in Saffron Broth with Chorizo and Potatoes

SERVES 4

WHY THIS RECIPE WORKS Saffron is a beloved ingredient in Mediterranean cuisine, and its distinctive aroma and bright yellow-orange color pair especially well with seafood. We set out to create a Spanish-inspired seafood dish that highlighted this prized ingredient. Versatile hake is a favorite white fish in Spain, and its mild flavor was the perfect backdrop for the saffron. We created a flavorful saffron broth with aromatics, white wine, and clam juice in which we braised the fish, then ladled the broth over the fillets for serving. For additional flavor, we added spicy Spanish-style chorizo to the pan with the onions and sautéed the sausage until browned, lending a subtle heat and smoky flavor to the broth. Tasters thought the dish was delicious, but they wanted a starchy element in the mix to round out the meal. Waxy red potatoes, sliced into coins to mirror the slices of chorizo, brought in just the right creaminess to soak up the flavorful broth. A hit of lemon added brightness to the broth at the end of cooking, and a sprinkle of parsley and drizzle of olive oil on the flaky fish, swimming in the fragrant saffron liquid, brought it all together. Haddock and cod are good substitutes for the hake. Use small red potatoes measuring 1 to 2 inches in diameter. Serve with crusty bread to dip into the broth.

1 tablespoon extra-virgin olive oil, plus extra for serving
1 onion, chopped fine
3 ounces Spanish-style chorizo sausage, sliced ¼ inch thick
4 garlic cloves, minced
¼ teaspoon saffron threads, crumbled
1 (8-ounce) bottle clam juice
¾ cup water
½ cup dry white wine
4 ounces small red potatoes, unpeeled, sliced ¼ inch thick
1 bay leaf

Assembling Hake Fillets and Potatoes

1. Transfer microwaved potatoes to 13 by 9-inch baking dish and press gently into even layer.

2. Arrange hake skinned side down on top of potatoes, drizzle with oil, and top with thyme sprigs and lemon slices.

Thick slices of hake poach to perfection in a fragrant garlic and saffron broth for a simple one-bowl meal.

4 (4- to 6-ounce) skinless hake fillets, 1 to 1½ inches thick
   Salt and pepper
1 teaspoon lemon juice
2 tablespoons minced fresh parsley

1. Heat oil in 12-inch skillet over medium heat until shimmering. Add onion and chorizo and cook until onion is softened and lightly browned, 5 to 7 minutes. Stir in garlic and saffron and cook until fragrant, about 30 seconds. Stir in clam juice, water, wine, potatoes, and bay leaf and bring to simmer. Reduce heat to medium-low, cover, and cook until potatoes are almost tender, about 10 minutes.

2. Pat hake dry with paper towels and season with salt and pepper. Nestle hake skinned side down into skillet and spoon some broth over top. Bring to simmer, cover, and cook until potatoes are fully tender and hake flakes apart when gently prodded with paring knife and registers 140 degrees, 10 to 12 minutes.

3. Carefully transfer hake to individual shallow bowls. Using slotted spoon, divide potatoes and chorizo evenly among bowls. Discard bay leaf. Stir lemon juice into broth and season with salt and pepper to taste. Spoon broth over hake, sprinkle with parsley, and drizzle with extra oil. Serve.

Provençal Braised Hake

SERVES 4

WHY THIS RECIPE WORKS Turning to the flavors of Provence for inspiration, we envisioned tender, moist hake napped in an aromatic, garlicky tomato sauce that we could mop up with a good loaf of crusty bread. To build the sauce, we started by sautéing a sliced onion in extra-virgin olive oil, then added a generous four cloves of garlic and sautéed them briefly. Canned diced tomatoes added bright tomato flavor, and draining them before adding them to the skillet kept the sauce concentrated. White wine added brightness and fennel contributed a clean, refreshing punch with its subtle anise flavor. The key to braising our fish was twofold: Low heat ensured that nothing burned, and a skillet with a tight-fitting lid trapped the heat so that the sauce gently simmered and the fish cooked properly. We nestled the hake into the simmering sauce, then cooked it over medium-low heat, covered, for just 10 minutes. The fish emerged succulent and moist, and the sauce had good body. Fresh thyme and parsley and a final drizzle of fruity extra-virgin olive oil rounded out the flavors. Haddock and cod are good substitutes for the hake. Serve with crusty bread to dip into the sauce.

2 tablespoons extra-virgin olive oil, plus extra for serving
1 onion, halved and sliced thin
1 fennel bulb, stalks discarded, bulb halved, cored, and sliced thin
   Salt and pepper
4 garlic cloves, minced
1 teaspoon minced fresh thyme or ¼ teaspoon dried
1 (14.5-ounce) can diced tomatoes, drained
½ cup dry white wine
4 (4- to 6-ounce) skinless hake fillets, 1 to 1½ inches thick
2 tablespoons minced fresh parsley

1. Heat oil in 12-inch skillet over medium heat until shimmering. Add onion, fennel, and ½ teaspoon salt and cook until softened, about 5 minutes. Stir in garlic and thyme and cook until fragrant, about 30 seconds. Stir in tomatoes and wine and bring to simmer.

2. Pat hake dry with paper towels and season with salt and pepper. Nestle hake skinned side down into skillet, spoon some sauce over top, and bring to simmer. Reduce heat to medium-low, cover, and cook until hake flakes apart when gently prodded with paring knife and registers 140 degrees, 10 to 12 minutes.

3. Carefully transfer hake to individual shallow bowls. Stir parsley into sauce and season with salt and pepper to taste. Spoon sauce over hake and drizzle with extra oil. Serve.

We know that buying fish can be confusing and that markets don't always stock the type of fish (or cut) you desire. This chart will help to explain what Mediterranean varieties of fish you can generally find at the market; the recipes list what you can substitute for them when they aren't available. And since we believe that some fish are suitable for sautéing, baking, or poaching and some are not, we've listed what we think are the best cooking methods for all the fish below.

TYPE OF FISH	WHAT YOU'LL FIND AT THE MARKET	TEXTURE	FLAVOR	BEST COOKING METHODS
Bluefish	Whole fish and fillets	Medium-firm, dark-fleshed fish	Pronounced, well suited to robust sauces and accompaniments	Stuffing and roasting or grilling (whole fish); steaming, braising, broiling, baking (fillets)
Cod	Whole and portioned fillets (both with and without skin)	Medium-firm, meaty white fish	Clean, mild flavor; suited to most any preparation and flavor combination	Steaming, braising, baking, oven frying, deep frying, grilling; also great for soups and stews
Flounder	Whole fish and very thin fillets, interchangeable with sole	Delicate and flaky white fish	Sweet and mild, identical to sole	Stuffing and baking (whole fish); steaming, sautéing, pan frying (fillets)
Grouper	Whole fish and fillets	Medium-firm, meaty white fish	Mild to bland	Stuffing and baking (whole fish); steaming, pan searing, sautéing, baking, pan frying (fillets)
Haddock	Fillets, usually with skin on; ask fishmonger to remove skin	Medium-firm white fish	Very mild, well suited to robust flavors	Steaming, poaching, braising, sautéing, baking, oven frying, pan frying
Hake	Whole and portioned fillets (both with and without skin)	Medium-firm, meaty white fish	Clean, mild flavor; suited to most any preparation and flavor combination	Steaming, braising, baking, oven frying, deep frying, grilling; also great for soups and stews
Halibut	Whole steaks, belly steaks, fillets	Very firm, lean white fish	Mild but rich, well suited to robust flavors	Steaming, pan searing, roasting, grilling (steaks); steaming, pan searing, sautéing, braising, poaching, baking, roasting, deep frying, grilling (fillets)
Mackerel	Steaks, fillets, whole fish; best for practicing filleting, as bones are easily removed	Medium-firm, off-white, flaky, oily fish	Full, rich, pronounced flavor	Braising, poaching, pan frying (small whole fish, fillets, steaks); pan searing, broiling, grilling, smoking, stuffing and baking (whole fish)
Mahi-Mahi	Steaks, fillets, whole fish; usually without skin	Medium-firm, off-white, flaky fish	Sweet and mild; well suited to robust flavors	Baking (fillets); braising, pan frying, grilling (small whole fish, fillets with skin); soups and stews

TYPE OF FISH	WHAT YOU'LL FIND AT THE MARKET	TEXTURE	FLAVOR	BEST COOKING METHODS
Mako Shark	Steaks, fillets, chunks; usually without skin	Firm and meaty pinkish-white fish	Mild, clean, and slightly sweet; similar to swordfish	Braising, pan frying, pan searing, deep frying, grilling (steaks or kebabs); soups and stews; avoid overcooking
Monkfish	Skinless, boneless loin-shaped pieces cut from tail; ask fishmonger to remove gray membrane	Very meaty, firm, pinkish-white fish	Hearty and rich, slightly muskier than lobster	Steaming, poaching, braising, sautéing, baking, oven frying, pan frying
Sardine	Whole fish	Medium-firm, off-white, flaky, oily fish	Full, rich, and pronounced	Stuffing and baking or grilling (whole fish)
Sea Bass	Whole fish and fillets	Medium-firm white fish with translucent quality	Sweet and mild	Steaming, deep frying, grilling, stuffing and roasting (whole fish); steaming, poaching, braising, pan searing, pan roasting, sautéing, grilling (fillets)
Snapper	Whole fish (with colorful skin and many bones), fillets, occasionally steaks	Medium-firm, flaky white fish	Mild to moderate, stands up well to bold flavors	Baking, deep frying, grilling, stuffing and roasting (whole fish); steaming, poaching, braising, pan searing, sautéing, broiling, baking, pan frying, grilling (fillets)
Sole	Fillets, interchangeable with flounder	Very delicate, flaky white fish	Sweet and mild, best suited to simple preparations	Steaming, sautéing, stuffing and baking
Swordfish	Steaks	Very firm and meaty	Mild to moderate, well suited to robust flavors	Pan searing, braising, broiling, grilling, soups and stews
Trout	Whole fish and fillets	Delicate and flaky, ranges in color from pale golden to pink	Rich and flavorful	Pan frying, grilling, stuffing and roasting (whole fish); sautéing, pan frying (fillets)
Tuna	Steaks	Very firm, meaty fish that ranges in color from pink to deep ruby red	Mild to moderate	Braising, pan searing, grilling; best cooked rare to medium, not beyond

Pan-Roasted Halibut with Chermoula

SERVES 8 FAST

WHY THIS RECIPE WORKS Cooks often pan-roast or sauté halibut because browning adds great flavor, but it can be a challenge to keep the fish from drying out. We didn't want to compromise on either texture or flavor, so we set out to develop a technique for cooking halibut that would produce perfectly cooked and tender fish with good browning. A combination of pan searing and oven roasting proved best. To be sure the halibut steaks wouldn't over-cook, we seared one side in a hot skillet, then turned the steaks over before placing them in the oven to finish cooking. When they were done, the steaks were browned but still moist inside. We took our fish to the next level by serving it with *chermoula*, a zesty Moroccan dressing. If halibut isn't available, you can substitute four 4- to 6-ounce skin-on swordfish steaks, 1 to 1½ inches thick; be sure to adjust the cooking time in step 2 as needed. You will need a 12-inch ovensafe nonstick skillet for this recipe.

CHERMOULA

- ¾ cup fresh cilantro leaves
- ¼ cup extra-virgin olive oil
- 2 tablespoons lemon juice
- 4 garlic cloves, minced
- ½ teaspoon ground cumin
- ½ teaspoon paprika
- ¼ teaspoon salt
- ⅛ teaspoon cayenne pepper

FISH

- 2 (1¼-pound) skin-on full halibut steaks, 1 to 1½ inches thick and 10 to 12 inches long, trimmed
  Salt and pepper
- 2 tablespoons extra-virgin olive oil

1. FOR THE CHERMOULA Process all ingredients in food processor until smooth, about 1 minute, scraping down sides of bowl as needed; set aside for serving.

2. FOR THE FISH Adjust oven rack to middle position and heat oven to 325 degrees. Pat halibut dry with paper towels and season with salt and pepper. Heat oil in 12-inch ovensafe nonstick skillet over medium-high heat until just smoking. Place halibut in skillet and cook until well browned on first side, about 5 minutes.

3. Gently flip halibut using 2 spatulas and transfer skillet to oven. Roast until halibut flakes apart when gently prodded with paring knife and registers 140 degrees, 6 to 9 minutes.

4. Carefully transfer halibut to cutting board, tent loosely with aluminum foil, and let rest for 5 minutes. Remove skin from steaks and separate each quadrant of meat from bones by slipping knife or spatula between them. Serve with chermoula.

Our braising method for fish delivers perfectly cooked fillets along with a vegetable side and silky sauce.

Braised Halibut with Leeks and Mustard

SERVES 4

WHY THIS RECIPE WORKS When it comes to methods for cooking fish, braising is often overlooked. But this approach, which requires cooking the fish in a small amount of liquid so that it gently simmers and steams, has a lot going for it. As a moist-heat cooking method, braising is gentle and thus forgiving, all but guaranteeing tender fish. Plus, it makes a great one-pot meal since the cooking liquid becomes a sauce, and it's easy to add vegetables to the pan to cook at the same time. We chose halibut for its sweet, delicate flavor and firm texture that made for easier handling and paired it with the classic French flavors of leeks, white wine, and Dijon mustard. Because the portion of the fillets submerged in liquid cooks more quickly than the upper half that cooks through in the steam, we cooked the fillets for a few minutes in the pan on just one side and then braised them parcooked side up to even out the cooking. For the cooking liquid, wine supplemented by the juices released by the fish and vegetables during cooking delivered a sauce with balanced flavor and just the right amount of brightness. If halibut isn't available, you can substitute sea bass in this recipe.

4 (4- to 6-ounce) skinless halibut fillets,
  ¾ to 1 inch thick
  Salt and pepper
¼ cup extra-virgin olive oil, plus extra for serving
1 pound leeks, white and light green parts only, halved
  lengthwise, sliced thin, and washed thoroughly
1 teaspoon Dijon mustard
¾ cup dry white wine
1 tablespoon minced fresh parsley
  Lemon wedges

1. Pat halibut dry with paper towels and sprinkle with ½ teaspoon salt. Heat oil in 12-inch skillet over medium heat until warm, about 15 seconds. Place halibut skinned side up in skillet and cook until bottom half of halibut begins to turn opaque (halibut should not brown), about 4 minutes. Carefully transfer halibut raw side down to large plate.

2. Add leeks, mustard, and ¼ teaspoon salt to oil left in skillet and cook over medium heat, stirring frequently, until softened, 10 to 12 minutes. Stir in wine and bring to simmer. Place halibut raw side down on top of leeks. Reduce heat to medium-low, cover, and simmer gently until halibut flakes apart when gently prodded with paring knife and registers 140 degrees, 6 to 10 minutes. Carefully transfer halibut to serving platter, tent loosely with aluminum foil, and let rest while finishing leeks.

3. Return leeks to high heat and simmer briskly until mixture is thickened slightly, 2 to 4 minutes. Season with salt and pepper to taste. Arrange leek mixture around halibut, drizzle with extra oil, and sprinkle with parsley. Serve with lemon wedges.

VARIATIONS

Braised Halibut with Carrots and Coriander
Substitute 1 pound carrots, peeled and shaved with vegetable peeler into ribbons, and 4 shallots, halved and sliced thin, for leeks. Substitute ½ teaspoon ground coriander for Dijon mustard and stir 1½ teaspoons lemon juice into carrot mixture before seasoning with salt and pepper. Substitute 1 tablespoon minced fresh cilantro for parsley.

Braised Halibut with Fennel and Tarragon
Substitute two 10-ounce fennel bulbs, stalks discarded, bulbs halved, cored, and sliced thin, and 4 shallots, halved and sliced thin, for leeks. Omit Dijon mustard and stir 1 teaspoon lemon juice into fennel mixture before seasoning with salt and pepper. Substitute 1 tablespoon minced fresh tarragon for parsley.

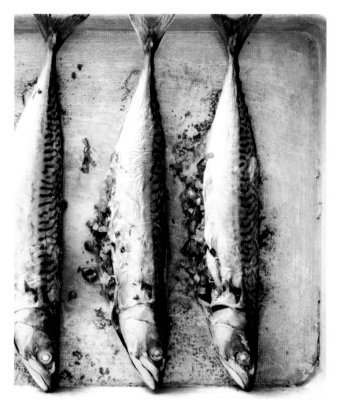

We stuff mackerel whole and roast them directly on a baking sheet for the best flavor and texture.

Baked Stuffed Mackerel with Red Pepper and Preserved Lemon
SERVES 4

WHY THIS RECIPE WORKS Mackerel, like many other oily fish, can get a bad reputation, fueled by memories of greasy smoked fillets or dry, overpowering fresh preparations. But when cooked properly, mackerel is moist and silky and a great canvas for strong Moroccan flavors. We decided to roast the fish whole, which not only created a dramatic presentation but was also a good way to protect the flesh and keep it moist—sometimes too moist. We found that both baking dishes and roasting pans caused the fish to exude moisture and steam in their juices, which proved detrimental to the fish's flavor and texture. Roasting the fish on a rimmed baking sheet delivered far better results due to good air circulation. Since mackerel stands up so well to bold flavors, we weren't timid with our approach. We chose the powerful flavor of preserved lemon, putting its fragrant and floral notes front and center. Red pepper added sweetness, and green olives added a tangy brininess. If you can't find preserved lemons, you can make your own (page 252). If mackerel isn't available, you can substitute trout. The mackerel heads can be removed before serving, if desired.

PRESERVED LEMONS

MAKES 4 preserved lemons

It is important to wash, scrub, and dry the lemons well before preserving.

12 lemons, preferably Meyer
½ cup Diamond Crystal Kosher Salt or 6 tablespoons Morton Kosher Salt

1. Wash and dry 4 lemons, then cut lengthwise into quarters, stopping 1 inch from bottom so lemons stay intact at base. Juice remaining lemons to yield 1½ cups juice; reserve extra juice to use as needed.

2. Working over bowl, gently stretch 1 cut lemon open and pour 2 tablespoons salt into center. Gently rub cut surfaces of lemon together, then place in 1-quart jar. Repeat with remaining cut lemons and salt. Add any accumulated salt and juice in bowl to jar.

3. Pour 1½ cups lemon juice into jar and press gently to submerge lemons. (Add more lemon juice to jar if needed to cover lemons completely.) Cover jar tightly with lid and shake. Refrigerate lemons, shaking jar once per day for first 4 days to redistribute salt and juice. Let lemons cure in refrigerator until glossy and softened, 6 to 8 weeks. (Preserved lemons can be refrigerated for at least 6 months.)

4. To use, cut off desired amount of preserved lemon. If desired, use knife to remove pulp and white pith from rind before using.

NOTE It takes at least 6 weeks to make your own preserved lemons; however, if necessary you can make a quick substitute: Combine four 2-inch strips lemon zest, minced, 1 teaspoon lemon juice, ½ teaspoon water, ¼ teaspoon sugar, and ¼ teaspoon salt. Microwave mixture at 50 percent power until liquid evaporates, about 1½ minutes, stirring and mashing lemon with back of spoon every 30 seconds. Makes about 1 tablespoon.

Preparing Preserved Lemons

Gently stretch open quartered lemon, pour salt into center, and rub cut surfaces together; place in 1-quart jar. Pour lemon juice into jar and press gently to submerge lemons.

3 tablespoons extra-virgin olive oil
1 red bell pepper, stemmed, seeded, and chopped fine
1 red onion, chopped fine
½ preserved lemon, pulp and white pith removed, rind rinsed and minced (2 tablespoons)
⅓ cup pitted brine-cured green olives, chopped
1 tablespoon minced fresh parsley
   Salt and pepper
4 (8- to 10-ounce) whole mackerel, gutted, fins snipped off with scissors
   Lemon wedges

1. Adjust oven rack to middle position and heat oven to 500 degrees. Heat 2 tablespoons oil in 12-inch skillet over medium-high heat until shimmering. Add bell pepper and onion and cook until vegetables are softened and well browned, 8 to 10 minutes. Stir in preserved lemon and cook until fragrant, about 30 seconds. Off heat, stir in olives and parsley and season with salt and pepper to taste.

2. Grease rimmed baking sheet with remaining 1 tablespoon oil. Rinse each mackerel under cold running water and pat dry with paper towels inside and out. Open cavity of each mackerel, season flesh with salt and pepper, and spoon one-quarter of filling into opening. Place mackerel on prepared sheet, spaced at least 2 inches apart. Bake until thickest part of mackerel registers 130 to 135 degrees, 10 to 12 minutes. Carefully transfer mackerel to serving platter and let rest for 5 minutes. Serve with lemon wedges.

Grilled Whole Mackerel with Lemon and Marjoram

SERVES 4 FAST

WHY THIS RECIPE WORKS We wanted to pair earthy grilled mackerel with sweet, aromatic marjoram, a member of the mint family found throughout the Mediterranean. To get the mackerel from grill to plate before the interior overcooked, we applied a mixture of honey and mayonnaise to the exterior of the fish. This coating encouraged speedy browning without offering any competing flavors. A sprinkling of marjoram, lemon zest, and salt made for a perfectly seasoned and subtly flavored fish. Though it seemed counterintuitive at first, we discovered that the hotter the grill, the easier the fish released from the grate. We placed the mackerel on the hot grate and after just a few minutes per side, we had beautifully browned fish that released with ease. If mackerel isn't available, you can substitute trout. We prefer marjoram in this recipe, but thyme or oregano can be substituted. Do not flip the fish over in one motion. Instead, gently lift the fish with a thin metal spatula, then support the fish with a second spatula to flip it back onto the grate. The mackerel heads can be removed before serving, if desired.

2 teaspoons chopped fresh marjoram
1 teaspoon grated lemon zest, plus lemon wedges for serving
  Salt and pepper
4 (8- to 10-ounce) whole mackerel, gutted, fins snipped off with scissors
2 tablespoons mayonnaise
½ teaspoon honey
1 (13 by 9-inch) disposable aluminum roasting pan (if using charcoal)

1. Place marjoram, lemon zest, and 1 teaspoon salt on cutting board and chop until finely minced and well combined. Rinse each mackerel under cold running water and pat dry with paper towels inside and out. Open cavity of each mackerel, season flesh with pepper, and sprinkle evenly with marjoram mixture; let sit for 10 minutes. Combine mayonnaise and honey, then brush mixture evenly on exterior of each fish.

2A. FOR A CHARCOAL GRILL Using kitchen shears, poke twelve ½-inch holes in bottom of disposable pan. Open bottom vent completely and place prepared pan in center of grill. Light large chimney starter two-thirds filled with charcoal briquettes (4 quarts). When top coals are partially covered with ash, pour into even layer in pan. Set cooking grate over coals with bars parallel to long side of pan, cover, and open lid vent completely. Heat grill until hot, about 5 minutes.

2B. FOR A GAS GRILL Turn all burners to high, cover, and heat grill until hot, about 15 minutes. Leave all burners on high.

3. Clean cooking grate, then repeatedly brush grate with well-oiled paper towels until grate is black and glossy, 5 to 10 times. Place mackerel on grill (directly over coals if using charcoal) and cook (covered if using gas) until skin is browned and beginning to blister on first side, 2 to 4 minutes. Using spatula, lift bottom of thick backbone edge of mackerel from cooking grate just enough to slide second spatula under fish. Remove first spatula, then use it to support raw side of mackerel as you use second spatula to flip fish over. Cook until second side is browned and beginning to blister and thickest part of mackerel registers 130 to 135 degrees, 2 to 4 minutes. Carefully transfer mackerel to serving platter and let rest for 5 minutes. Serve with lemon wedges.

VARIATIONS

Grilled Mackerel with Orange and Fennel `FAST`

Substitute 1 teaspoon ground fennel seeds for marjoram and 1 teaspoon grated orange zest for lemon zest.

Grilled Mackerel with Lime and Coriander `FAST`

Substitute 1 teaspoon ground coriander for marjoram and 1 teaspoon grated lime zest and wedges for lemon zest and wedges.

In order to achieve moist and flaky monkfish, we use the stovetop and oven to cook it to the ideal temperature.

Pan-Roasted Monkfish with Oregano– Black Olive Relish

SERVES 4 `FAST`

WHY THIS RECIPE WORKS Monkfish has a lobsterlike firm texture and slightly sweet flavor that are prized in Greek and other Mediterranean cuisines. Unlike other white fish, the chewier flesh of monkfish fillets comes from the hardworking tail, rather than the belly, which means it has long, sinewy muscle fibers that run its length. Because of this structural difference, we found that we had to approach cooking it differently than other fish. Typically, we cook white fish to an internal temperature of 140 degrees, but when we pan-roasted monkfish to this temperature, tasters found it unappealingly fibrous, mealy, and spongy. To improve the texture, we tested cooking the fish to incrementally higher temperatures and found 160 degrees to be the ideal internal temperature for our monkfish fillets—this higher temperature made the fish flaky and moist, while still retaining a firm and meaty texture. This made sense: Much like cooking cuts of meat from active muscles, such as pork butt or beef chuck, more cooking was needed to soften and break down the muscle fibers for tender results. Sprinkling the fillets with a bit of sugar helped them brown quickly on the stovetop, and finishing them in the oven ensured even cooking and moist flesh. With our fish cooked to perfection, we put together a bright, briny relish made with kalamata olives, red wine vinegar, and fresh oregano steeped in olive oil. The punchy Greek-flavored relish was the ideal counterpoint to the sweet monkfish. Monkfish fillets are surrounded by a thin membrane that needs to be removed before cooking. Your fishmonger can do this for you, but if your fillets still have the membrane attached, see below for more information on how to remove it.

¼ cup extra-virgin olive oil
2 tablespoons minced fresh oregano
2 tablespoons red wine vinegar
1 small shallot, minced
1 teaspoon Dijon mustard
Salt and pepper
¼ cup pitted kalamata olives, minced
4 (4- to 6-ounce) skinless monkfish fillets, 1 to 1½ inches thick, trimmed
½ teaspoon sugar

1. Combine 2 tablespoons oil and oregano in medium bowl and microwave until bubbling, about 30 seconds. Let mixture steep for 5 minutes, then whisk in vinegar, shallot, mustard, and ¼ teaspoon pepper. Stir in olives and set aside for serving.

2. Adjust oven rack to middle position and heat oven to 425 degrees. Pat monkfish dry with paper towels, season with salt and pepper, and sprinkle evenly with sugar.

3. Heat remaining 2 tablespoons oil in 12-inch ovensafe skillet over medium-high heat until just smoking. Place monkfish in skillet and press lightly to ensure even contact with skillet. Cook until browned on first side, about 2 minutes. Gently flip monkfish using 2 spatulas and cook until browned on second side, about 2 minutes. Transfer skillet to oven and roast until monkfish is opaque in center and registers 160 degrees, 8 to 12 minutes. Carefully transfer monkfish to serving platter, tent loosely with aluminum foil, and let rest for 5 minutes. Serve with relish.

Trimming Monkfish

To remove membrane from monkfish, slip knife underneath it, angle knife slightly upward, and use back-and-forth motion to cut it away from fish.

Coating sardines with a mix of honey and mayonnaise helps them to brown more quickly and release from the hot grill.

Grilled Whole Sardines
SERVES 4 to 6 **FAST**

WHY THIS RECIPE WORKS Grilled sardines are a popular outdoor tradition all along the Mediterranean, where these fish are fresh and plentiful. In the simplest preparation, whole sardines are oiled, quickly charred on a hot grill, and served with regional accompaniments. We found variations that included skewering to hold the delicate fish together, marinating the fish for more flavor, and even filleting and sandwiching the fish together before grilling in an attempt to further insulate the flesh. But we found that the sardines were prone to breaking off the skewers, the oily fish had plenty of innate flavor without a marinade, and, if cooked correctly, they were unlikely to overcook. So we went back to basics and set out to perfect the grilling method for whole fish. We found that when just oiled, even on a very hot grill, some of our sardines stuck, and the skin tore when we flipped them. We applied a technique we had developed for grilled mackerel to address just this problem: We used a mixture of honey and mayonnaise on their exteriors, allowing the sardines to achieve beautiful browning quickly, and when their skin was charred and crisp, they naturally released from the grill. The trick, we found, was being patient; if we didn't move the sardines until they offered no resistance, we were able to get perfectly intact skin. If fresh sardines aren't available, you can substitute frozen, though you will likely need to clean them yourself. We enjoy these sardines paired simply with lemon wedges or with our Tomato and Almond Pesto or Green Olive and Orange Pesto (page 149).

12 (2- to 3-ounce) whole sardines, scaled, gutted, fins snipped off with scissors
Pepper
2 tablespoons mayonnaise
½ teaspoon honey
Lemon wedges

1. Rinse each sardine under cold running water and pat dry with paper towels inside and out. Open cavity of each sardine and season flesh with pepper. Combine mayonnaise and honey, then brush mixture evenly on exterior of each fish.

2A. FOR A CHARCOAL GRILL Open bottom vent completely. Light large chimney starter filled with charcoal briquettes (6 quarts). When top coals are partially covered with ash, pour evenly over grill. Set cooking grate in place, cover, and open lid vent completely. Heat grill until hot, about 5 minutes.

2B. FOR A GAS GRILL Turn all burners to high, cover, and heat grill until hot, about 15 minutes. Leave all burners on high.

3. Clean cooking grate, then repeatedly brush grate with well-oiled paper towels until grate is black and glossy, 5 to 10 times. Place sardines on grill and cook (covered if using gas) until skin is browned and beginning to blister, 2 to 4 minutes. Gently flip sardines using spatula and continue to cook until second side is browned and beginning to blister, 2 to 4 minutes. Serve with lemon wedges.

Pan-Roasted Sea Bass

SERVES 4 FAST

WHY THIS RECIPE WORKS Pan-roasted fish seems like a simple dish, but in reality it takes some practice to get it right. At home, many attempts result in dry, overbaked fillets. We set out to develop a foolproof recipe for producing moist, well-browned fillets with a bright-meets-briny Greek relish. We quickly learned we needed thick fillets and chose semifirm sea bass; thinner fish overcooked by the time they achieved a serious sear. We then turned to a common restaurant method to cook the fish: We seared the fillets in a hot pan, flipped them, then transferred the pan to the oven to finish cooking. Sprinkling the fillets with sugar accelerated browning on the stovetop, shortening the cooking time and thus ensuring that the fish didn't dry out. After a short stay in the oven to finish cooking through, the fish emerged well browned, tender, and moist. Creating a complementary relish was as simple as whirling nuts, green olives or roasted red peppers, garlic, and citrus zest in the food processor before stirring in oil and fresh herbs. Cod and snapper are good substitutes for the sea bass.

4 (4- to 6-ounce) skinless sea bass fillets, 1 to 1½ inches thick
Salt and pepper
½ teaspoon sugar
1 tablespoon extra-virgin olive oil
Lemon wedges

1. Adjust oven rack to middle position and heat oven to 425 degrees. Pat sea bass dry with paper towels, season with salt and pepper, and sprinkle sugar evenly on 1 side of each fillet.

2. Heat oil in 12-inch ovensafe skillet over medium-high heat until just smoking. Place sea bass sugared side down in skillet and press lightly to ensure even contact with skillet. Cook until browned on first side, about 2 minutes. Gently flip sea bass using 2 spatulas, transfer skillet to oven, and roast until fish flakes apart when gently prodded with paring knife and registers 140 degrees, 7 to 10 minutes. Serve with lemon wedges.

VARIATIONS

Pan-Roasted Sea Bass with Green Olive, Almond, and Orange Relish FAST

Pulse ½ cup toasted slivered almonds, ½ cup pitted brine-cured green olives, chopped coarse, 1 small minced garlic clove, and 1 teaspoon grated orange zest in food processor until finely chopped, 10 to 12 pulses. Transfer to bowl and stir in ¼ cup orange juice, ¼ cup extra-virgin olive oil, ¼ cup minced fresh mint, and 2 teaspoons white wine vinegar. Season with salt and cayenne to taste. Serve with fish.

Pan-Roasted Sea Bass with Roasted Red Pepper, Hazelnut, and Thyme Relish FAST

Pulse ½ cup toasted and skinned hazelnuts, ½ cup jarred roasted red peppers, rinsed, patted dry, and chopped coarse, 1 minced garlic clove, and ½ teaspoon grated lemon zest in food processor until finely chopped, 10 to 12 pulses. Transfer to bowl and stir in ¼ cup extra-virgin olive oil, 2 tablespoons chopped fresh parsley, 4 teaspoons lemon juice, 1 teaspoon minced fresh thyme, and ¼ teaspoon smoked paprika. Season with salt and pepper to taste. Serve with fish.

Pan-Roasted Sea Bass with Wild Mushrooms
SERVES 4

WHY THIS RECIPE WORKS Sea bass, with its large, firm, moist flakes, is a perfect complement to chewy mushrooms. For this pan-roasted sea bass recipe, we liked a combination of full-flavored cremini and portobellos, with a small amount of dried porcini for a deep, woodsy flavor. We first tried sautéing the mushrooms and fish separately, but the result lacked unity. We decided to add the fish to the sautéed mushrooms in a hot skillet and then slide the pan into the oven, so the fish and the mushrooms melded in flavor, and the porcini liquid reduced to a light, flavorful sauce. Cod and snapper are good substitutes for the sea bass.

½ cup water
⅓ ounce dried porcini mushrooms
4 (4- to 6-ounce) skinless sea bass fillets, 1 to
    1½ inches thick
¼ cup extra virgin olive oil, plus extra for serving
    Salt and pepper
1 sprig fresh rosemary
1 red onion, halved and sliced thin
12 ounces portobello mushroom caps, halved and sliced
    ½ inch thick
1 pound cremini mushrooms, trimmed and halved if small
    or quartered if large
2 garlic cloves, minced
1 tablespoon minced fresh parsley
    Lemon wedges

1. Microwave water and porcini mushrooms in covered bowl until steaming, about 1 minute. Let sit until softened, about 5 minutes. Drain mushrooms in fine-mesh strainer lined with coffee filter, reserve porcini liquid, and mince mushrooms.

2. Adjust oven rack to lower-middle position and heat oven to 475 degrees. Pat sea bass dry with paper towels, rub with 2 tablespoons oil, and season with salt and pepper.

3. Heat remaining 2 tablespoons oil and rosemary in 12-inch ovensafe skillet over medium-high heat until shimmering. Add onion, portobello mushrooms, cremini mushrooms, and ½ teaspoon salt. Cook, stirring occasionally, until mushrooms have released their liquid and are beginning to brown, 8 to 10 minutes. Stir in garlic and porcini mushrooms and cook until fragrant, about 30 seconds.

4. Off heat, stir in reserved porcini liquid. Nestle sea bass skinned side down into skillet, transfer to oven, and roast until fish flakes apart when gently prodded with paring knife and registers 140 degrees, 10 to 12 minutes. Sprinkle with parsley and drizzle with extra oil. Serve with lemon wedges.

Tucking a Fish Tail

If using any tail-end fillets, simply tuck the thinner end under itself before cooking so that it will cook at the same rate as thicker fillets.

Grilled Sea Bass with Citrus and Black Olive Salad
SERVES 4 **FAST**

WHY THIS RECIPE WORKS At its best, grilled sea bass boasts firm, moist flesh under a crisp, seared exterior, but many recipes turn out underdone, fishy-tasting fillets. To bring out the best in our grilled sea bass, we started by seeking out thick fillets. Sea bass skin is too tough to eat, so we removed it and rubbed the fish with oil to keep it from sticking to the grill. Unlike other meaty cuts of fish, cooking this fillet all the way through—cooking over the hottest part of the grill for up to 10 minutes before finishing on the cooler side—produced the best flavor; salting the fish before grilling also helped prevent any off-flavors. In under 20 minutes, the sea bass had taken on great flavorful char, but these rich fillets deserved a bright, fresh accompaniment. A zesty citrus salad of orange and grapefruit segments, balanced out with chopped kalamata olives and a blend of cumin and paprika, paired perfectly with the fish. Cod and snapper are good substitutes for the sea bass. Use only the citrus pieces in the relish, not the juices, which will water down the flavor and texture.

2 oranges
1 red grapefruit
¼ cup pitted kalamata olives, chopped
2 tablespoons minced fresh parsley
½ teaspoon ground cumin
½ teaspoon paprika
    Pinch cayenne pepper
    Salt and pepper
4 (4- to 6-ounce) skinless sea bass fillets, 1 to
    1½ inches thick
2 tablespoons extra-virgin olive oil

1. Cut away peel and pith from oranges and grapefruit. Quarter oranges, then slice crosswise into ½-inch-thick pieces. Cut grapefruit into 8 wedges, then slice wedges crosswise into ½-inch-thick pieces. Combine oranges, grapefruit, olives, parsley, cumin,

paprika, and cayenne in bowl. Season with salt to taste, cover, and set aside for serving.

2. Pat sea bass dry with paper towels, rub with oil, and season with salt and pepper.

3A. FOR A CHARCOAL GRILL Open bottom vent completely. Light large chimney starter filled with charcoal briquettes (6 quarts). When top coals are partially covered with ash, pour evenly over half of grill. Set cooking grate in place, cover, and open lid vent completely. Heat grill until hot, about 5 minutes.

3B. FOR A GAS GRILL Turn all burners to high, cover, and heat grill until hot, about 15 minutes. Leave primary burner on high and turn other burner(s) to medium-low.

4. Clean cooking grate, then repeatedly brush grate with well-oiled paper towels until grate is black and glossy, 5 to 10 times. Place sea bass on hotter part of grill and cook, uncovered, until well browned, about 10 minutes, gently flipping fillets using 2 spatulas halfway through cooking.

5. Gently move sea bass to cooler part of grill and cook, uncovered, until fish flakes apart when gently prodded with paring knife and registers 140 degrees, 3 to 6 minutes. Serve with salad.

Grilled Whole Sea Bass with Salmoriglio Sauce
SERVES 4 FAST

WHY THIS RECIPE WORKS *Salmoriglio* is a citrusy, herbal sauce spooned over grilled fish at tables throughout southern Italy and particularly in Sicily. To re-create this fresh combination at home, we started with the sauce, whisking together garlic, lemon juice, minced oregano and olive oil. For perfectly grilled fish that didn't stick to the grate, we opted for sea bass for its sturdy, semifirm texture. Making shallow diagonal slashes on the skin helped ensure even cooking and enabled us to gauge doneness more easily. To prevent the skin from sticking, we greased the cooking grate and coated the fish with a film of oil. We used two thin metal spatulas to flip the delicate fish once the first side was done. They also made it easier to remove the cooked fish from the grill. The cooked fish needed only a few cuts to enable us to lift away the meat from the bones on each side in a single piece with a spatula (see page 260). Drizzled with our homemade salmoriglio sauce, the bass was perfectly cooked and bursting with bright, fresh flavors. If sea bass isn't available, you can substitute snapper. Fish weighing more than 2 pounds will be hard to maneuver on the grill and should be avoided.

SALMORIGLIO SAUCE
1 small garlic clove, minced
1 tablespoon lemon juice
⅛ teaspoon salt

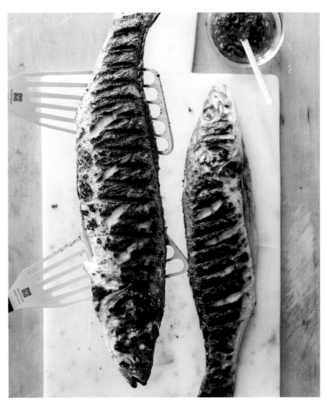

Making shallow slashes in the skin helps the fish to cook more evenly and also makes it easy to check if it's done.

⅛ teaspoon pepper
1½ tablespoons minced fresh oregano
¼ cup extra-virgin olive oil

FISH
2 (1½- to 2-pound) whole sea bass, scaled, gutted, fins snipped off with scissors
3 tablespoons extra-virgin olive oil
Salt and pepper

1. FOR THE SALMORIGLIO SAUCE Whisk all ingredients together in bowl until combined; cover and set aside for serving.

2A. FOR A CHARCOAL GRILL Open bottom vent completely. Light large chimney starter filled with charcoal briquettes (6 quarts). When top coals are partially covered with ash, pour evenly over grill. Set cooking grate in place, cover, and open lid vent completely. Heat grill until hot, about 5 minutes.

2B. FOR A GAS GRILL Turn all burners to high, cover, and heat grill until hot, about 15 minutes. Leave all burners on high.

3. Rinse each sea bass under cold running water and pat dry with paper towels inside and out. Using sharp knife, make 3 or

4 shallow slashes, about 2 inches apart, on both sides of sea bass. Rub sea bass with oil and season generously with salt and pepper inside and outside.

4. Clean cooking grate, then repeatedly brush grate with well-oiled paper towels until black and glossy, 5 to 10 times. Place sea bass on grill and cook (covered if using gas) until skin is browned and beginning to blister on first side, 6 to 8 minutes. Using spatula, lift bottom of thick backbone edge of sea bass from cooking grate just enough to slide second spatula under fish. Remove first spatula, then use it to support raw side of sea bass as you use second spatula to flip fish over. Cook (covered if using gas) until second side is browned, beginning to blister, and sea bass registers 140 degrees, 6 to 8 minutes.

5. Carefully transfer sea bass to carving board and let rest for 5 minutes. Fillet sea bass by making vertical cut just behind head from top of fish to belly. Make another cut on top of sea bass from head to tail. Use spatula to lift meat from bones, starting at head end and running spatula over bones to lift out fillet. Repeat on other side of sea bass. Discard head and skeleton. Serve with sauce.

Grilling Whole Fish

1. SLASH SKIN Using sharp knife, make shallow diagonal slashes every 2 inches on both sides of fish, beginning just behind dorsal fin.

2. USE 2 SPATULAS TO FLIP Cook until first side is browned and crisp, 6 to 8 minutes, then flip fish over using 2 spatulas and continue to cook on second side.

3. DON'T OVERCOOK When both sides are browned and crisp, gently transfer fish to platter using 2 spatulas.

Poached Snapper with Crispy Artichokes and Sherry-Tomato Vinaigrette
SERVES 4

WHY THIS RECIPE WORKS Poaching fish fillets in olive oil is a popular Italian and French technique that delivers supermoist, delicately cooked fish. In our recipe the oil pulled triple duty: We used it to crisp artichokes and garlic for a garnish, poached the fish in it, and then blended the oil into a creamy vinaigrette for serving. To get the oil temperature just right, we first fried the garnish, then added more room-temperature oil to quickly cool the oil. We placed half an onion in the skillet to displace the oil so it would come up higher in the pan—and we could use less of it. After adding the fish, we moved the skillet to the even heat of the oven. While we prefer the flavor and texture of jarred whole baby artichokes, you can substitute 6 ounces frozen artichoke hearts, thawed and patted dry, for the jarred. Sea bass and cod are good substitutes for snapper. You will need a 10-inch ovensafe nonstick skillet for this recipe.

FISH
 4 (4- to 6-ounce) skinless red snapper fillets, about 1 inch thick
   Salt
 1 cup jarred whole baby artichokes packed in water, quartered, rinsed, and patted dry
 1 tablespoon cornstarch
 ¾ cup extra-virgin olive oil
 3 garlic cloves, minced
 ½ onion, peeled

VINAIGRETTE
 6 ounces cherry tomatoes (2 ounces cut into ⅛-inch-thick rounds)
 ½ small shallot, peeled
 4 teaspoons sherry vinegar
   Salt and pepper
 1 tablespoon minced fresh parsley

1. FOR THE FISH Adjust oven racks to middle and lower-middle positions and heat oven to 250 degrees. Pat snapper dry with paper towels and season each fillet with ⅛ teaspoon salt. Let sit at room temperature for 20 minutes.

2. Meanwhile, toss artichokes with cornstarch in bowl to coat. Heat ½ cup oil in 10-inch ovensafe nonstick skillet over medium heat until shimmering. Shake excess cornstarch from artichokes and add to skillet. Cook, stirring occasionally, until crisp and golden, 2 to 4 minutes. Add garlic and continue to cook until garlic is golden, 30 to 60 seconds. Strain oil through fine-mesh strainer into bowl. Transfer artichokes and garlic to ovensafe paper towel–lined plate and season with salt. Do not wash strainer.

Oil poaching is a foolproof technique for cooking delicate fish, plus the oil is used to make both the sauce and garnish.

3. Return strained oil to now-empty skillet and add remaining ¼ cup oil. Place onion half in center of skillet. Let oil cool until it registers about 180 degrees, 5 to 8 minutes. Arrange fillets skinned side up around onion (oil should come roughly halfway up fillets) and spoon some oil over each fillet. Cover, transfer skillet to upper rack, and cook for 15 minutes.

4. Using potholders, remove skillet from oven. Being careful of hot skillet handle, gently flip fillets using 2 spatulas. Cover, return skillet to upper rack, and place plate with artichokes and garlic on lower rack. Continue to bake snapper until it registers 130 to 135 degrees, 9 to 14 minutes. Carefully transfer snapper to serving platter, reserving ½ cup oil, and tent loosely with aluminum foil. Turn off oven, leaving plate of artichokes in oven.

5. FOR THE VINAIGRETTE Process reserved ½ cup fish cooking oil, whole tomatoes, shallot, vinegar, ½ teaspoon pepper, and ¼ teaspoon salt in blender until smooth, about 2 minutes, scraping down sides of bowl as needed. Add any accumulated fish juices, season with salt to taste, and blend for 10 seconds. Strain sauce through fine-mesh strainer into bowl; discard solids. To serve, spoon vinaigrette around fish. Garnish each fillet with warmed crisped artichokes and garlic, parsley, and tomato rounds. Serve.

NOTES FROM THE TEST KITCHEN
Buying and Storing Fish

WHAT TO LOOK FOR The most important factor when buying fish is making sure the fish is fresh. Always buy fish from a trusted source (preferably one with high volume to help ensure freshness). The store, and the fish in it, should smell like the sea, not fishy or sour. And all the fish should be on ice or properly refrigerated. Fillets and steaks should look bright, shiny, and firm, not dull or mushy. Whole fish should have moist, taut skin, clear eyes, and bright red gills.

WHAT TO ASK FOR It is always better to have your fishmonger slice steaks and fillets to order rather than buying precut pieces that may have been sitting around. Don't be afraid to be picky at the seafood counter; a ragged piece of hake or a tail end of sea bass will be difficult to cook properly. It is important to keep your fish cold, so if you have a long ride home, ask your fishmonger for a bag of ice.

BUYING FROZEN FISH Thin fish fillets like flounder and sole are the best choice if you have to buy your fish frozen, because they freeze quickly, minimizing moisture loss. Firm fillets like halibut, snapper, and swordfish are acceptable to buy frozen if cooked beyond medium-rare, but at lower degrees of doneness they will have a dry, stringy texture. When buying frozen fish, make sure it is frozen solid, with no signs of freezer burn or excessive crystallization around the edges and no blood in the packaging. The ingredients should include only the name of the fish you are buying.

DEFROSTING FISH To defrost fish in the refrigerator overnight, remove the fish from its packaging, place it in a single layer on a rimmed plate or dish (to catch any water), and cover it with plastic wrap. You can also do a "quick thaw" by leaving the vacuum-sealed bags under cool running tap water for 30 minutes. Do not use a microwave to defrost fish; it will alter the texture of the fish or, worse, partially cook it. Dry the fish thoroughly with paper towels before seasoning and cooking it.

HOW TO STORE IT Because fish is so perishable, it's best to buy it the day it will be cooked. If that's not possible, it's important to store it properly. When you get home, unwrap the fish, pat it dry, put it in a zipper-lock bag, press out the air, and seal the bag. Then set the fish on a bed of ice in a bowl or other container (one that can hold the water once the ice melts) and place it in the back of the fridge, where it is coldest. If the ice melts before you use the fish, replenish it. The fish should keep for one day.

Whole Roasted Snapper with Citrus Vinaigrette

SERVES 4 `FAST`

WHY THIS RECIPE WORKS Cooking fish whole is commonplace in the Mediterranean, and roasting easily delivers deep flavor. We found mild red snapper to be perfectly suited to this technique. Roasting the fish on a rimmed baking sheet allowed for plenty of air circulation, which gave the snapper a firm, flaky texture; a brief stint in a hot oven helped the fish stay moist. Shallow slashes in the skin ensured even cooking and seasoning and also allowed us to gauge the doneness of the fish easily. We rubbed the fish with an intensely citrusy salt to infuse it with flavor. A quick citrus vinaigrette added a final punch of flavor. If snapper isn't available, you can substitute sea bass. Fish weighing more than 2 pounds will be hard to maneuver on the sheet and should be avoided.

6 tablespoons extra-virgin olive oil
¼ cup minced fresh cilantro
2 teaspoons grated lime zest plus 2 tablespoons juice
2 teaspoons grated orange zest plus 2 tablespoons juice
1 small shallot, minced
⅛ teaspoon red pepper flakes
   Salt and pepper
2 (1½- to 2-pound) whole red snapper, scaled, gutted, fins snipped off with scissors

1. Adjust oven rack to middle position and heat oven to 500 degrees. Line rimmed baking sheet with parchment paper and grease parchment. Whisk ¼ cup oil, cilantro, lime juice, orange juice, shallot, and pepper flakes together in bowl. Season with salt and pepper to taste; set aside for serving.

2. In separate bowl, combine lime zest, orange zest, 1½ teaspoons salt, and ½ teaspoon pepper. Rinse each snapper under cold running water and pat dry with paper towels inside and out. Using sharp knife, make 3 or 4 shallow slashes, about 2 inches apart, on both sides of snapper. Open cavity of each snapper and sprinkle 1 teaspoon salt mixture on flesh. Brush 1 tablespoon oil on outside of each snapper and season with remaining salt mixture; transfer to prepared sheet and let sit for 10 minutes.

3. Roast until snapper flakes apart when gently prodded with paring knife and registers 140 degrees, 15 to 20 minutes. (To check for doneness, peek into slashed flesh or into interior through opened bottom area of each fish.)

4. Carefully transfer snapper to carving board and let rest for 5 minutes. Fillet snapper by making vertical cut just behind head from top of fish to belly. Make another cut along top of snapper from head to tail. Use spatula to lift meat from bones, starting at head end and running spatula over bones to lift out fillet. Repeat on other side of snapper. Discard head and skeleton. Whisk dressing to recombine and serve with snapper.

Serving Whole Fish

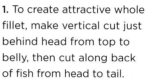

1. To create attractive whole fillet, make vertical cut just behind head from top to belly, then cut along back of fish from head to tail.

2. Starting at head and working toward tail, use metal spatula to lift meat away from bones. Repeat on second side.

Sautéed Sole

SERVES 4 `FAST`

WHY THIS RECIPE WORKS Simply prepared fish is a hallmark of Mediterranean cuisines. Sole is especially well suited to this type of treatment since its delicate texture is preserved and its sweet and mild flavor is enhanced by just a quick turn in a hot nonstick skillet. A light coating of flour protected the fish and created just a bit of a browned crust during sautéing. Although the cooked fish is perfect unadorned or with just a squeeze of lemon, we also developed two fresh relishes that can be served over it. If sole isn't available, you can substitute flounder. Fish fillets are sold in a range of sizes. Do not use fillets thinner than ¼ inch, as they will overcook very quickly.

½ cup all-purpose flour
8 (2- to 3-ounce) skinless sole fillets, ¼ to ½ inch thick
   Salt and pepper
¼ cup extra-virgin olive oil
   Lemon wedges

1. Place flour in shallow dish. Pat sole dry with paper towels and season with salt and pepper. Working with 1 fillet at a time, dredge in flour to coat, shaking off any excess.

2. Heat 2 tablespoons oil in 12-inch nonstick skillet over medium-high heat until shimmering. Place half of sole in skillet and cook until lightly browned on first side, 2 to 3 minutes. Gently flip sole using 2 spatulas and continue to cook until fish flakes apart when gently prodded with paring knife, 30 to 60 seconds.

3. Carefully transfer sole to serving platter and tent loosely with aluminum foil. Wipe skillet clean with paper towels and repeat with remaining 2 tablespoons oil and fillets. Serve with lemon wedges.

Sautéed Sole with Fresh Tomato Relish FAST

This relish is a great accompaniment to simple seafood dishes.

Combine 2 ripe tomatoes, cored, seeded, and cut into ¼-inch pieces, 1 small minced shallot, 2 tablespoons chopped fresh basil, 1 tablespoon extra-virgin olive oil, 1 small minced garlic clove, and 1 teaspoon red wine vinegar in bowl. Let sit for 15 minutes. Season with salt and pepper to taste. Serve over sole.

Sautéed Sole with Grapefruit and Basil Relish FAST

This relish is a great accompaniment to simple seafood dishes.

Cut away peel and pith from 2 red grapefruits. Cut each grapefruit into 8 wedges, then slice wedges crosswise into ½-inch-thick pieces. Place grapefruit in strainer set over bowl and let drain for 15 minutes; reserve 1 tablespoon drained juice. Combine reserved juice, 2 tablespoons chopped fresh basil, 1 small minced shallot, 2 teaspoons lemon juice, and 2 teaspoons extra-virgin olive oil in bowl. Stir in drained grapefruits and let sit for 15 minutes. Season with salt, pepper, and sugar to taste. Serve over sole.

Swordfish en Cocotte with Shallots, Cucumber, and Mint

SERVES 4

WHY THIS RECIPE WORKS The premise behind the French method of cooking *en cocotte* (or casserole roasting) is to slow down the cooking process in order to concentrate flavor. Fish cooked for an extended period of time usually winds up dry, but a combination of low oven temperature, moist-heat environment, and the right cut of fish allows it to remain juicy and tender. We found that meaty swordfish steaks were particularly well suited to cooking en cocotte. The fresh Mediterranean flavors of mint, parsley, lemon, and garlic easily combined with sliced cucumber to make an insulating layer on which to cook the fish; we then turned the cucumber mixture into a complementary flavorful topping for serving. It is important to choose steaks that are similar in size and thickness to ensure that each piece will cook at the same rate. If swordfish isn't available, you can substitute halibut.

¾ cup fresh mint leaves
¼ cup fresh parsley leaves
5 tablespoons extra-virgin olive oil
2 tablespoons lemon juice
4 garlic cloves, minced
1 teaspoon ground cumin
¼ teaspoon cayenne pepper
  Salt and pepper
3 shallots, sliced thin

Cooking swordfish steaks on a bed of cucumbers covered in a low oven concentrates all of the flavors.

1 cucumber, peeled, seeded, and sliced thin
4 (4- to 6-ounce) skin-on swordfish steaks, 1 to 1½ inches thick

1. Adjust oven rack to lowest position and heat oven to 250 degrees. Process mint, parsley, 3 tablespoons oil, lemon juice, garlic, cumin, cayenne, and ¼ teaspoon salt in food processor until smooth, about 20 seconds, scraping down sides of bowl as needed.

2. Heat remaining 2 tablespoons oil in Dutch oven over medium-low heat until shimmering. Add shallots, cover, and cook, stirring occasionally, until softened, about 5 minutes. Off heat, stir in processed mint mixture and cucumber.

3. Pat swordfish dry with paper towels and season with salt and pepper. Place swordfish on top of cucumber-mint mixture. Place large sheet of aluminum foil over pot and press to seal, then cover tightly with lid. Transfer pot to oven and cook until swordfish flakes apart when gently prodded with paring knife and registers 140 degrees, 35 to 40 minutes.

4. Carefully transfer swordfish to serving platter. Season cucumber-mint mixture with salt and pepper to taste, then spoon over swordfish. Serve.

We rub chunks of swordfish with coriander then grill them alongside eggplant, cherry tomatoes, and scallions.

Grilled Swordfish Skewers with Tomato-Scallion Caponata

SERVES 4 to 6 FAST

WHY THIS RECIPE WORKS Swordfish is a favorite fish to grill along the Mediterranean and beyond. It has a robust taste all its own and needs costarring ingredients with just as much oomph. For our skewers, we paired swordfish with a Sicilian-inspired grilled caponata. As a base for the caponata, we grilled cherry tomatoes, lemons, and scallions alongside the swordfish and added an aromatic blend of warm spices for a potent sauce to complement the fish. Once grilled, the lemon transformed from tart and acidic to sweet and rich. Rubbing the swordfish with a bit of ground coriander added complexity and provided flavor that popped with the tomato, scallions, and a final sprinkling of fresh basil. If swordfish isn't available, you can substitute halibut. You will need six 12-inch metal skewers for this recipe.

1½ pounds skinless swordfish steaks, 1¼ to 1½ inches thick, cut into 1¼-inch pieces
5 teaspoons ground coriander
Salt and pepper
12 ounces cherry tomatoes
1 small eggplant (12 ounces), cut crosswise on bias into ½-inch-thick ovals
6 scallions, trimmed
¼ cup extra-virgin olive oil
1 tablespoon grated lemon zest, plus 2 lemons, halved
1½ tablespoons honey
2 garlic cloves, minced
1 teaspoon ground cumin
¼ teaspoon ground cinnamon
⅛ teaspoon ground nutmeg
¼ cup pitted kalamata olives, chopped
2 tablespoons minced fresh basil

1. Pat swordfish dry with paper towels, rub with 1 tablespoon coriander, and season with salt and pepper. Thread fish onto three 12-inch metal skewers. Thread tomatoes onto three 12-inch metal skewers. Brush swordfish, tomatoes, eggplant, and scallions with 2 tablespoons oil.

2A. FOR A CHARCOAL GRILL Open bottom vent completely. Light large chimney starter filled with charcoal briquettes (6 quarts). When top coals are partially covered with ash, pour evenly over grill. Set cooking grate in place, cover, and open lid vent completely. Heat grill until hot, about 5 minutes.

Cutting Up Swordfish for Skewers

1. Using sharp knife, trim skin and dark lines from flesh.

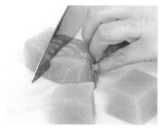

2. Cut trimmed flesh into 1¼-inch pieces.

2B. FOR A GAS GRILL Turn all burners to high, cover, and heat grill until hot, about 15 minutes. Leave all burners on high.

3. Clean cooking grate, then repeatedly brush grate with well-oiled paper towels until black and glossy, 5 to 10 times. Place swordfish, tomatoes, eggplant, scallions, and lemon halves on grill. Cook (covered if using gas), turning as needed, until swordfish flakes apart when gently prodded with paring knife and registers 140 degrees and tomatoes, eggplant, scallions, and lemon halves are softened and lightly charred, 5 to 15 minutes. Transfer items to serving platter as they finish grilling and tent loosely with aluminum foil. Let swordfish rest while finishing caponata.

4. Whisk remaining 2 teaspoons coriander, remaining 2 tablespoons oil, lemon zest, honey, garlic, cumin, ¾ teaspoon salt, ¼ teaspoon pepper, cinnamon, and nutmeg together in large bowl. Microwave, stirring occasionally, until fragrant, about 1 minute. Once lemons are cool enough to handle, squeeze into fine-mesh strainer set over bowl with oil-honey mixture, extracting as much juice as possible; whisk to combine. Stir in olives.

5. Using tongs, slide tomatoes off skewers onto cutting board. Coarsely chop tomatoes, eggplant, and scallions, transfer to bowl with dressing, and gently toss to combine. Season with salt and pepper to taste. Remove swordfish from skewers, sprinkle with basil, and serve with caponata.

Grilled Swordfish with Italian Salsa Verde
SERVES 4 FAST

WHY THIS RECIPE WORKS When developing our grilled swordfish recipe, our first step was to choose thicker steaks because thinner steaks overcooked easily. (It's the dense, meaty flesh that keeps the steaks from falling apart.) Since they can stay on the grill longer, the thicker steaks also picked up more smoky flavor. We found it was important to leave the fish in place long enough that it developed good grill marks before moving it. A two-level fire was necessary so the fish could sear over the hot fire and then cook through on the cooler part of the grill. Classic green Italian salsa verde, a piquant mix of parsley, mint, anchovies, capers, and garlic, was perfect with our grilled swordfish. If swordfish isn't available, you can substitute halibut.

4 (4- to 6-ounce) skin-on swordfish steaks, 1 to
   1½ inches thick
2 tablespoons extra-virgin olive oil
   Salt and pepper
½ cup Italian Salsa Verde (page 310)

These simple swordfish steaks get their flavor both from the grill and a sauce full of classic Italian ingredients.

1. Pat swordfish dry with paper towels, rub with oil, and season with salt and pepper.

2A. FOR A CHARCOAL GRILL Open bottom vent completely. Light large chimney starter filled with charcoal briquettes (6 quarts). When top coals are partially covered with ash, pour two-thirds evenly over half of grill, then pour remaining coals over other half of grill. Set cooking grate in place, cover, and open lid vent completely. Heat grill until hot, about 5 minutes.

2B. FOR A GAS GRILL Turn all burners to high, cover, and heat grill until hot, about 15 minutes. Leave primary burner on high and turn other burner(s) to medium-high.

3. Clean cooking grate, then repeatedly brush grate with well-oiled paper towels until black and glossy, 5 to 10 times. Place swordfish on hotter part of grill and cook, uncovered, until streaked with dark grill marks, 6 to 9 minutes, gently flipping steaks using 2 spatulas halfway through cooking.

4. Gently move swordfish to cooler part of grill and continue to cook, uncovered, until fish flakes apart when gently prodded with paring knife and registers 140 degrees, 1 to 3 minutes per side. Serve with Italian Salsa Verde.

A potent mixture of cilantro and warm spices flavors swordfish steaks and also dresses the grilled eggplant salad.

Grilled Swordfish with Eggplant, Tomato, and Chickpea Salad

SERVES 4 **FAST**

WHY THIS RECIPE WORKS Since meaty swordfish stands up so well to grilling, we decided to cook swordfish steaks simultaneously with some eggplant for a quick and elegant grilled dinner. We gave a flavor boost to the fish by coating it with a paste of cilantro, onion, garlic, and warm spices which bloomed over the hot fire, reserving part of the paste to dress the eggplant salad. We removed the fish when the interior was just opaque since it would cook a little more from residual heat as it rested while we prepared the accompanying vegetables. After grilling the eggplant until soft and charred, we chopped it into chunks and mixed it with juicy cherry tomatoes and canned chickpeas, then dressed it with the remaining cilantro mixture for an easy and vibrant salad. If swordfish isn't available, you can substitute halibut.

  1 cup fresh cilantro leaves
 ½ red onion, chopped coarse
  6 tablespoons extra-virgin olive oil

  3 tablespoons lemon juice
  4 garlic cloves, chopped
  1 teaspoon ground cumin
  1 teaspoon paprika
 ¼ teaspoon cayenne pepper
 ⅛ teaspoon ground cinnamon
    Salt and pepper
  4 (4- to 6-ounce) skin-on swordfish steaks, 1 to 1½ inches thick
  1 large eggplant, sliced into ½-inch-thick rounds
  6 ounces cherry tomatoes, halved
  1 (15-ounce) can chickpeas, rinsed

1. Process cilantro, onion, 3 tablespoons oil, lemon juice, garlic, cumin, paprika, cayenne, cinnamon, and ½ teaspoon salt in food processor until smooth, about 2 minutes, scraping down sides of bowl as needed. Measure out and reserve ½ cup cilantro mixture. Transfer remaining cilantro mixture to large bowl and set aside.

2. Brush swordfish with reserved ½ cup cilantro mixture. Brush eggplant with remaining 3 tablespoons oil and season with salt and pepper.

3A. FOR A CHARCOAL GRILL Open bottom vent completely. Light large chimney starter filled with charcoal briquettes (6 quarts). When top coals are partially covered with ash, pour two-thirds evenly over half of grill, then pour remaining coals over other half of grill. Set cooking grate in place, cover, and open lid vent completely. Heat grill until hot, about 5 minutes.

NOTES FROM THE TEST KITCHEN

Reheating Fish

Fish is notoriously susceptible to overcooking, so reheating previously cooked fillets is something that makes nearly all cooks balk. But since almost everyone has leftover fish from time to time, we decided to figure out the best approach to warming it up.

As we had suspected, we had far more success reheating thick fillets and steaks than thin ones. Both swordfish and halibut steaks reheated nicely, retaining their moisture well and with no detectable change in flavor. There was little we could do to prevent mackerel from drying out and overcooking when heated a second time.

To reheat thicker fish fillets, use this gentle approach: Place the fillets on a wire rack set in a rimmed baking sheet, cover them with foil (to prevent the exteriors of the fish from drying out), and heat them in a 275-degree oven until they register 125 to 130 degrees, about 15 minutes for 1-inch-thick fillets (timing varies according to fillet size). We recommend serving leftover cooked thin fish in cold applications like salads.

3B. FOR A GAS GRILL Turn all burners to high, cover, and heat grill until hot, about 15 minutes. Leave primary burner on high and turn other burner(s) to medium-high.

4. Clean cooking grate, then repeatedly brush grate with well-oiled paper towels until black and glossy, 5 to 10 times. Place swordfish and eggplant on hotter part of grill. Cook swordfish, uncovered, until streaked with dark grill marks, 6 to 9 minutes, gently flipping steaks using 2 spatulas halfway through cooking. Cook eggplant, flipping as needed, until softened and lightly charred, about 8 minutes; transfer to serving platter and tent loosely with aluminum foil.

5. Gently move swordfish to cooler part of grill and continue to cook, uncovered, until fish flakes apart when gently prodded with paring knife and registers 140 degrees, 1 to 3 minutes per side; transfer to platter and tent loosely with foil. Let swordfish rest while finishing salad.

6. Coarsely chop eggplant and add to bowl with cilantro mixture along with tomatoes and chickpeas. Gently toss to combine and season with salt and pepper to taste. Serve.

Grilled Tuna Steaks with Romesco
SERVES 4 **FAST**

WHY THIS RECIPE WORKS Like swordfish, tuna is well suited to grilling. Perfectly grilled tuna steaks should combine a hot, smoky, charred exterior with a cool, rare center. For a home cook, this ideal can be elusive. To achieve grilled tuna steaks with an intense smoky char and a tender interior, we started with a hot grill. We moistened the tuna steaks with olive oil to penetrate the meat and keep it juicy. To promote browning, we added honey to the oil; sugar worked as well but honey created browning faster, which was important since the tuna spends only a brief time on the grate. To add a touch of brightness and heat, we finished the dish with a pungent Spanish romesco sauce, made with sweet and smoky roasted red peppers. In addition to being an excellent accompaniment to fish, this sauce is also terrific spread on toasted bread or used as a dip for crudités. We prefer our tuna served rare or medium-rare. If you like your tuna cooked medium, observe the timing for medium-rare, then tent the steaks with foil for 5 minutes before serving.

1 slice hearty white sandwich bread, crusts removed, bread lightly toasted and cut into ½-inch pieces (½ cup)
1½ tablespoons slivered almonds, toasted
1 cup jarred roasted red peppers, rinsed, patted dry, and chopped coarse
1 plum tomato, cored, seeded, and chopped

To help thick tuna steaks brown faster we coat them with extra-virgin olive oil and honey before they hit the grill.

¼ cup extra-virgin olive oil
2¼ teaspoons sherry vinegar
1 garlic clove, minced
⅛ teaspoon cayenne pepper
Salt and pepper
2 teaspoons honey
1 teaspoon water
2 (8- to 12-ounce) skinless tuna steaks, 1 inch thick, halved crosswise

1. Process bread and almonds in food processor until nuts are finely ground, 10 to 15 seconds. Add red peppers, tomato, 1 tablespoon oil, vinegar, garlic, cayenne, and ½ teaspoon salt. Process until smooth and mixture has texture similar to mayonnaise, 20 to 30 seconds, scraping down sides of bowl as needed. Season with salt to taste; set aside for serving.

2. Whisk remaining 3 tablespoons oil, honey, water, ½ teaspoon salt, and pinch pepper together in bowl. Pat tuna dry with paper towels and generously brush with oil mixture.

3A. FOR A CHARCOAL GRILL Open bottom vent completely. Light large chimney starter filled with charcoal briquettes (6 quarts). When top coals are partially covered with ash, pour evenly over half of grill. Set cooking grate in place, cover, and open lid vent completely. Heat grill until hot, about 5 minutes.

3B. FOR A GAS GRILL Turn all burners to high, cover, and heat grill until hot, about 15 minutes. Leave all burners on high.

4. Clean cooking grate, then repeatedly brush grate with well-oiled paper towels until grate is black and glossy, 5 to 10 times. Place tuna on grill (on hotter side if using charcoal) and cook (covered if using gas) until opaque and streaked with dark grill marks on first side, 1 to 3 minutes. Gently flip tuna using 2 spatulas and continue to cook until opaque at perimeter and translucent red at center when checked with tip of paring knife and registers 110 degrees (for rare), about 1½ minutes, or until opaque at perimeter and reddish pink at center when checked with tip of paring knife and registers 125 degrees (for medium-rare), about 3 minutes. Serve with sauce.

Bouillabaisse
SERVES 6 to 8

WHY THIS RECIPE WORKS Bouillabaisse is a classic Provençal dish with humble origins, a fisherman's cost-effective family meal turned upscale seafood stew, that will bring the flavors and aroma of the French seaside into your kitchen. It relies on a deeply flavored fish stock (or *fumet*) made from scratch. After the broth has simmered for hours, a variety of fish and shellfish are poached in the complex broth. Bouillabaisse is always served with thick slices of French bread or garlic croutons and with *rouille*, a luxuriant saffron and garlic mayonnaise. Our goal was to create a simpler adaptation of this French classic that was still authentic in flavor, without being overly time-consuming. Traditional bouillabaisse relies on a medley of upward of six different species of seafood. In the interest of time and expense, we limited our variety to diverse but widely available shrimp, scallops, and halibut. Wishing to have at least one shell-on mollusk in the mix, we added mussels for their delicate flavor and shorter cooking time. While we loved the idea of using homemade fish stock, we wondered if with everything else going on in the pot we could get away with using bottled clam juice to streamline things. Fortified with sautéed aromatics, fennel, white wine, and a generous amount of garlic, we created a solidly flavorful broth on which to build the rest of our dish. We added diced tomatoes and just enough saffron to perfume the broth with its distinctive flavor, color, and aroma and added fresh thyme and bay leaves as well. As the shrimp, scallops, halibut, and mussels cooked, their juices combined with the saffron-infused tomato base to produce the ideal amount of cooking liquid with plenty left to serve in a soup plate. If halibut isn't available, you can substitute swordfish. Serve with a touch of Rouille (page 302) and Garlic Toasts (page 56), if desired.

We streamline the preparation of a deeply flavored Provençal stew by using supermarket seafood and bottled clam juice.

¼ cup extra-virgin olive oil
1 small fennel bulb, stalks discarded, bulb halved, cored, and chopped fine
1 onion, chopped fine
8 garlic cloves, minced
1 teaspoon minced fresh thyme or ¼ teaspoon dried
¼ teaspoon saffron threads, crumbled
⅛ teaspoon red pepper flakes
¾ cup dry white wine or dry vermouth
2 (8-ounce) bottles clam juice
1 (14.5-ounce) can whole peeled tomatoes, drained with juice reserved, chopped
2 bay leaves
1 pound skinless halibut fillets, ¾ to 1 inch thick, cut into 3- to 4-inch pieces
   Salt and pepper
12 ounces mussels, scrubbed and debearded
1 pound large sea scallops, tendons removed
8 ounces medium-large shrimp (31 to 40 per pound), peeled and deveined
2 tablespoons minced fresh tarragon

1. Heat oil in Dutch oven over medium-high heat until shimmering. Add fennel and onion and cook until softened, about 5 minutes. Stir in garlic, thyme, saffron, and pepper flakes and cook until fragrant, about 30 seconds. Stir in wine and cook until slightly reduced, about 30 seconds.

2. Stir in clam juice, tomatoes with their juice, and bay leaves. Bring to simmer and cook until liquid has reduced by about half, 7 to 9 minutes.

3. Pat halibut dry with paper towels and season with salt and pepper. Nestle halibut into pot, spoon some cooking liquid over top, and bring to simmer. Reduce heat to medium-low, cover, and simmer gently for 2 minutes. Nestle mussels and scallops into pot, cover, and continue to cook until halibut is almost cooked through, about 3 minutes.

4. Arrange shrimp evenly over stew, cover, and continue to cook until halibut flakes apart when gently prodded with paring knife, shrimp and scallops are firm and opaque in center, and mussels have opened, about 2 minutes.

5. Off heat, discard bay leaves and any mussels that refuse to open. Gently stir in tarragon and season with salt and pepper to taste. Serve in wide, shallow bowls.

Sicilian Fish Stew

SERVES 4 to 6

WHY THIS RECIPE WORKS In Sicily, fish is combined with tomatoes and favorite local ingredients to create a simple stew. Although easy to prepare, this stew requires a balancing act of sweet, sour, and salty flavors. Many Sicilian dishes exhibit the strong influence of Arabic cooking through the use of dried fruits and nuts. Although these flavors are delicious, they must be used judiciously to keep them from upstaging each other and the fish. This stew is typically made with firm white-fleshed fillets, such as snapper. However, tasters felt that the snapper's mild flavor was lost amid the bold flavors of the stew and preferred the stronger flavor and meaty texture of swordfish. To prevent the fish from overcooking and drying out, we found it best to add the fish when the stew was nearly done, simmering it until partially cooked and letting it finish cooking by residual heat with the stove off and the pot covered. For the base of the stew, we created a quick stock using aromatic onions, celery, and garlic simmered with white wine, whole peeled tomatoes, and clam juice and mixed in golden raisins and capers for sweet and briny pops of flavor. To finish our stew, we put together a twist on *gremolata*, a classic Italian herb condiment usually made with lemon zest and parsley. Here, we swapped those elements for orange zest and mint to underline the sweet and fragrant flavors in the dish and stirred in toasted pine nuts for added crunch. Tuna and halibut are good substitutes for the swordfish. Serve with crusty bread to dip into the broth.

To perfectly cook pieces of swordfish, we simmer the fish until partially done then let it finish cooking off the heat.

¼ cup pine nuts, toasted
¼ cup chopped fresh mint
4 garlic cloves, minced
1 teaspoon grated orange zest
2 tablespoons extra-virgin olive oil
2 onions, chopped fine
1 celery rib, minced
  Salt and pepper
1 teaspoon minced fresh thyme or ¼ teaspoon dried
  Pinch red pepper flakes
½ cup dry white wine
1 (28-ounce) can whole peeled tomatoes, drained with juice reserved, chopped coarse
2 (8-ounce) bottles clam juice
¼ cup golden raisins
2 tablespoons capers, rinsed
1½ pounds skinless swordfish steaks, 1 to 1 ½ inches thick, cut into 1-inch pieces

1. Combine pine nuts, mint, one-quarter of garlic, and orange zest in bowl; set aside for serving. Heat oil in Dutch oven over medium heat until shimmering. Add onions, celery, ½ teaspoon salt, and ¼ teaspoon pepper and cook until softened, about 5 minutes. Stir in thyme, pepper flakes, and remaining garlic and cook until fragrant, about 30 seconds.

2. Stir in wine and reserved tomato juice, bring to simmer, and cook until reduced by half, about 4 minutes. Stir in tomatoes, clam juice, raisins, and capers, bring to simmer, and cook until flavors meld, about 15 minutes.

3. Pat swordfish dry with paper towels and season with salt and pepper. Nestle swordfish into pot and spoon some cooking liquid over top. Bring to simmer and cook for 4 minutes. Off heat, cover and let sit until swordfish flakes apart when gently prodded with paring knife, about 3 minutes. Season with salt and pepper to taste. Serve, sprinkling individual bowls with pine nut mixture.

Monkfish Tagine
SERVES 4 to 6

WHY THIS RECIPE WORKS A traditional North African specialty, a tagine is both the name for a conical cooking vessel and the stew that is cooked inside it. The special shape of a tagine allows steam from the cooking meat and vegetables to condense and drip back down onto the stew, keeping it moist and concentrated in flavor. While a tagine is an attractive and unique piece of cooking equipment, we found that we could get similar results for trapping steam when using a Dutch oven with a heavy lid. We set out to create a Moroccan-style fish tagine with the signature sweet and sour flavors of the region. Meaty monkfish fillets were our go-to choice for this dish, as their firm texture would help them keep their shape while simmering in the pot. For sweetness, we turned to orange zest, onion, carrots, and tomato paste, which, along with fragrant paprika, cumin, dried mint, and saffron, built the base for the tagine's broth. Deglazing the sautéed aromatics with a bottle of clam juice brought in a salty, briny element and created a rich broth in which to braise the fish. Nestling the fillets into the broth, covering the pot, and turning down the heat allowed all of the flavors to meld while the fish and carrots cooked through. For a salty, sour punch, we finished the sauce by stirring in pungent Moroccan oil-cured olives and a teaspoon of sherry vinegar. Fresh mint completed the dish with bright flavor. Sweet, tangy, vibrantly colored, and perfectly moist, our monkfish tagine offered intense Moroccan flavors in just half an hour. Monkfish fillets are surrounded by a thin membrane that needs to be removed before cooking. Your fishmonger can do this for you, but if your fillets still have the membrane attached, see page 254 for more information on how to remove it.

We braise meaty monkfish and spices in a covered Dutch oven to create a flavorful Moroccan-style fish tagine.

3 (2-inch) strips orange zest
5 garlic cloves, minced
2 tablespoons extra-virgin olive oil
1 large onion, halved and sliced ¼ inch thick
3 carrots, peeled, halved lengthwise, and sliced ¼ inch thick
   Salt and pepper
1 tablespoon tomato paste
1¼ teaspoons paprika
1 teaspoon ground cumin
½ teaspoon dried mint
¼ teaspoon saffron threads, crumbled
1 (8-ounce) bottle clam juice
1½ pounds skinless monkfish fillets, 1 to 1½ inches thick, trimmed and cut into 3-inch pieces
¼ cup pitted oil-cured black olives, quartered
2 tablespoons minced fresh mint
1 teaspoon sherry vinegar

1. Mince 1 strip orange zest and combine with 1 teaspoon garlic in bowl; set aside.

2. Heat oil in Dutch oven over medium heat until shimmering. Add onion, carrots, ¼ teaspoon salt, and remaining 2 strips orange zest and cook until vegetables are softened and lightly browned, 10 to 12 minutes. Stir in remaining garlic, tomato paste, paprika, cumin, dried mint, and saffron and cook until fragrant, about 30 seconds. Stir in clam juice, scraping up any browned bits.

3. Pat monkfish dry with paper towels and season with salt and pepper. Nestle monkfish into pot, spoon some cooking liquid over top, and bring to simmer. Reduce heat to medium-low, cover, and simmer gently until monkfish is opaque in center and registers 160 degrees, 8 to 12 minutes.

4. Discard orange zest. Gently stir in olives, fresh mint, vinegar, and garlic–orange zest mixture. Season with salt and pepper to taste. Serve.

Greek-Style Shrimp with Tomatoes and Feta

SERVES 4 to 6

WHY THIS RECIPE WORKS In the traditional Greek dish shrimp *saganaki*, sweet, briny shrimp are covered with a garlic- and herb-accented tomato sauce and topped with crumbles of creamy, salty feta cheese. Restaurant versions, however, can be a gamble. The shrimp can be tough and rubbery, the tomato sauce can turn out dull or overwhelming, and the feta is often lackluster. We set out to develop a foolproof recipe for home cooks. Canned diced tomatoes along with sautéed onion and garlic provided the base for the sauce. Dry white wine added acidity, and ouzo, the slightly sweet anise-flavored Greek liqueur, added welcome complexity. While the shrimp are typically layered with the tomato sauce and feta and baked, we were after a quick and easy dish. We opted to cook the shrimp right in the sauce; adding the shrimp raw to the sauce helped infuse them with the sauce's bright flavor. And for even more flavor, we first marinated the shrimp with olive oil, ouzo, garlic, and lemon zest while we made the sauce. A generous sprinkling of feta and chopped fresh dill over the sauced shrimp finished our recipe. The cooking time is for extra-large shrimp (about 21 to 25 per pound). If using smaller or larger shrimp, be sure to adjust the cooking time as needed. If you don't have ouzo, you can substitute an equal amount of Pernod or 1 tablespoon vodka plus ⅛ teaspoon anise seeds. Serve with Stovetop White Rice (page 105) and/or crusty bread.

For the most tender and succulent Greek-style shrimp, we simmer them gently in a sweet-tart tomato sauce in a skillet.

1½ pounds extra-large shrimp (21 to 25 per pound), peeled and deveined
¼ cup extra-virgin olive oil
3 tablespoons ouzo
5 garlic cloves, minced
1 teaspoon grated lemon zest
  Salt and pepper
1 small onion, chopped
1 red or green bell pepper, stemmed, seeded, and chopped
½ teaspoon red pepper flakes
1 (28-ounce) can diced tomatoes, drained with ⅓ cup juice reserved
¼ cup dry white wine
2 tablespoons coarsely chopped fresh parsley
6 ounces feta cheese, crumbled (1½ cups)
2 tablespoons chopped fresh dill

1. Toss shrimp in bowl with 1 tablespoon oil, 1 tablespoon ouzo, 1 teaspoon garlic, lemon zest, ¼ teaspoon salt, and ⅛ teaspoon pepper; set aside.

2. Heat 2 tablespoons oil in 12-inch skillet over medium heat until shimmering. Add onion, bell pepper, and ¼ teaspoon salt, cover, and cook, stirring occasionally, until vegetables release their liquid, 3 to 5 minutes. Uncover and continue to cook, stirring occasionally, until liquid evaporates and vegetables are softened, about 5 minutes. Stir in remaining garlic and pepper flakes and cook until fragrant, about 1 minute.

3. Stir in tomatoes and reserved juice, wine, and remaining 2 tablespoons ouzo. Bring to simmer and cook, stirring occasionally, until flavors meld and sauce is slightly thickened (sauce should not be completely dry), 5 to 8 minutes. Stir in parsley and season with salt and pepper to taste.

4. Reduce heat to medium-low and add shrimp along with any accumulated juices; stir to coat and distribute evenly. Cover and cook, stirring occasionally, until shrimp are opaque throughout, 6 to 9 minutes, adjusting heat as needed to maintain bare simmer. Off heat, sprinkle with feta and dill and drizzle with remaining 1 tablespoon oil. Serve.

Shrimp with White Beans

SERVES 4 **FAST**

WHY THIS RECIPE WORKS Northern Italians combine their beloved white, or cannellini, beans with a seemingly infinite variety of ingredients. Shrimp and white beans may seem like an unusual combination, but it is utterly traditional. The dish consists of beans lightly cooked with shrimp, vegetables, and herbs until the flavors blend. The combination works to great effect; the sweetness of the mild, creamy beans is the perfect foil to the briny, chewy shrimp. Canned beans passed muster and are the heart of this dish, but the shrimp play the starring role. We looked for a cooking method that would boost the flavor of the shrimp and found that searing on the stovetop worked best. We seasoned the shrimp with sugar, salt, and pepper, then added them to a smoking-hot skillet. Within a minute and a half, they were perfectly cooked, seared on the outside as if they'd been grilled and moist on the inside. We also briefly cooked red onion, red bell pepper, and garlic, which kept their flavors fresh and their texture appealingly crunchy. Tasters loved arugula in this dish as opposed to herbs like basil and rosemary. Its gentle peppery bite successfully married all of the other flavors. Although we prefer

We quickly sear seasoned shrimp in a hot skillet then mix them with cannellini beans in this traditional Italian dish.

this dish warm, it may be eaten chilled as a salad or antipasto. The cooking time is for extra-large shrimp (about 21 to 25 per pound). If using smaller or larger shrimp, be sure to adjust the cooking time as needed.

   1 pound extra-large shrimp (21 to 25 per pound), peeled and deveined
     Pinch sugar
     Salt and pepper
   5 tablespoons extra-virgin olive oil
   1 red bell pepper, stemmed, seeded, and chopped fine
   1 small red onion, chopped fine
   2 garlic cloves, minced
  ¼ teaspoon red pepper flakes
   2 (15-ounce) cans cannellini beans, rinsed
   2 ounces (2 cups) baby arugula, chopped coarse
   2 tablespoons lemon juice

1. Pat shrimp dry with paper towels and season with sugar, salt, and pepper. Heat 1 tablespoon oil in 12-inch nonstick skillet over high heat until just smoking. Add shrimp to skillet in single layer and cook, without stirring, until spotty brown and edges turn pink on first side, about 1 minute.

2. Off heat, flip shrimp and let sit until opaque throughout, about 30 seconds. Transfer shrimp to bowl and cover to keep warm.

3. Heat remaining ¼ cup oil in now-empty skillet over medium heat until shimmering. Add bell pepper, onion, and ½ teaspoon salt and cook until softened, about 5 minutes. Stir in garlic and pepper flakes and cook until fragrant, about 30 seconds. Stir in beans and cook until heated through, about 5 minutes.

4. Add arugula and shrimp along with any accumulated juices and gently toss until arugula is wilted, about 1 minute. Stir in lemon juice and season with salt and pepper to taste. Serve.

Garlicky Roasted Shrimp with Parsley and Anise
SERVES 4 to 6   FAST

WHY THIS RECIPE WORKS Roasting quick-cooking shrimp until they developed deep browning seemed like an easy route to a flavorful weeknight Mediterranean recipe. We were surprised, then, when we ended up with pale shrimp without even a hint of flavor. We knew we could do better. Quickly brining the shrimp kept them plump and moist and seasoned them throughout. To further protect them as they cooked, and to produce a more roasted flavor, we left their shells on. For maximum flavor, we tossed the shrimp with a savory mixture of spices and herbs and then broiled them in a single layer on a wire rack. Don't be tempted to use smaller shrimp with this cooking technique; they will be overseasoned and prone to overcook.

¼ cup salt
2 pounds shell-on jumbo shrimp (16 to 20 per pound)
¼ cup extra-virgin olive oil
6 garlic cloves, minced
1 teaspoon anise seeds
½ teaspoon red pepper flakes
¼ teaspoon pepper
2 tablespoons minced fresh parsley
   Lemon wedges

A quick brine keeps these shrimp moist and flavorful and keeping their shells on protects them as they broil.

1. Dissolve salt in 4 cups cold water in large container. Using kitchen shears or sharp paring knife, cut through shell of shrimp and devein but do not remove shell. Using paring knife, continue to cut shrimp ½ inch deep, taking care not to cut in half completely. Submerge shrimp in brine, cover, and refrigerate for 15 minutes.

2. Adjust oven rack 4 inches from broiler element and heat broiler. Combine oil, garlic, anise seeds, pepper flakes, and pepper in large bowl. Remove shrimp from brine and pat dry with paper towels. Add shrimp and parsley to oil mixture and toss well, making sure oil mixture gets into interior of shrimp. Arrange shrimp in single layer on wire rack set in rimmed baking sheet.

3. Broil shrimp until opaque and shells are beginning to brown, 2 to 4 minutes, rotating sheet halfway through broiling. Flip shrimp and continue to broil until second side is opaque and shells are beginning to brown, 2 to 4 minutes, rotating sheet halfway through broiling. Serve with lemon wedges.

Shrimp Basics

BUYING SHRIMP Virtually all of the shrimp sold in supermarkets today have been previously frozen, either in large blocks of ice or by a method called "individually quick-frozen," or IQF for short. Supermarkets simply defrost the shrimp before displaying them on ice at the fish counter. We highly recommend purchasing bags of still-frozen shrimp and defrosting them as needed at home, since there is no telling how long "fresh" shrimp may have been kept on ice at the market. IQF shrimp have a better flavor and texture than shrimp frozen in blocks, and they are convenient because it's easy to defrost just the amount you need. Shrimp are sold both with and without their shells, but we find shell-on shrimp to be firmer and sweeter. Also, shrimp should be the only ingredient listed on the bag; some packagers add preservatives, but we find treated shrimp to have an unpleasant, rubbery texture.

SORTING OUT SHRIMP SIZES Shrimp are sold both by size (small, medium, etc.) and by the number needed to make 1 pound, usually given in a range. Choosing shrimp by the numerical rating is more accurate, because the size labels vary from store to store. Here's how the two sizing systems generally compare:

Small	51 to 60 per pound
Medium	41 to 50 per pound
Medium-Large	31 to 40 per pound
Large	26 to 30 per pound
Extra-Large	21 to 25 per pound
Jumbo	16 to 20 per pound

DEFROSTING SHRIMP You can thaw frozen shrimp overnight in the refrigerator in a covered bowl. For a quicker thaw, place them in a colander under cold running water; they will be ready in a few minutes. Thoroughly dry the shrimp before cooking.

We tightly pack peeled shrimp alternating heads and tails on metal skewers so they can stay on the grill longer.

Grilled Marinated Shrimp Skewers
SERVES 4 to 6

WHY THIS RECIPE WORKS Jolts of grill flavor and subtle heat can enhance the delicately sweet and briny flavor of shrimp, but it's easy to overdo it. Most recipes overcook the shrimp and finish them in a bath of mouth-numbing sauce; we wanted juicy shrimp with a smoky crust and flavor that was more than just superficial. We looked to the spices of Morocco and found just the right blend: lime zest for tang, paprika to accent the smoky grill flavor, ginger and cayenne for complex heat, and cumin and plenty of garlic for a rounded earthy-sharp flavor. We left the fresh lime juice for finishing, since an acidic marinade can degrade the shrimp's texture. To get browning without overcooking, we sprinkled one side of the shrimp with sugar and grilled this side for a few minutes. Then we flipped the skewers to finish gently cooking on the cooler side of the grill. Butterflying the shrimp before marinating and grilling them opened up more shrimp flesh for the marinade and finishing sauce to flavor. We also packed the shrimp very tightly onto the skewers so they would cook more slowly. The cooking time is for extra-large shrimp (about 21 to 25 per pound). If using smaller or larger shrimp, be sure to adjust the cooking time as needed. You will need four 12-inch metal skewers for this recipe. Serve with Yogurt-Herb Sauce (page 233), if desired.

MARINADE

- 3 tablespoons extra-virgin olive oil
- 6 garlic cloves, minced
- 1 teaspoon grated lime zest
- ½ teaspoon smoked paprika
- ½ teaspoon ground ginger
- ½ teaspoon ground cumin
- ½ teaspoon salt
- ¼ teaspoon cayenne pepper

SHRIMP

- 1½ pounds extra-large shrimp (21 to 25 per pound), peeled and deveined
- ½ teaspoon sugar
- 1 tablespoon minced fresh cilantro
  Lime wedges

1. FOR THE MARINADE Whisk all ingredients together in medium bowl.

2. FOR THE SHRIMP Pat shrimp dry with paper towels. Using sharp paring knife, make shallow cut down outside curve of shrimp. Add shrimp to bowl with marinade and toss to coat. Cover and refrigerate for at least 30 minutes or up to 1 hour.

3A. FOR A CHARCOAL GRILL Open bottom vent completely. Light large chimney starter filled with charcoal briquettes (6 quarts). When top coals are partially covered with ash, pour evenly over half of grill. Set cooking grate in place, cover, and open lid vent completely. Heat grill until hot, about 5 minutes.

3B. FOR A GAS GRILL Turn all burners to high, cover, and heat grill until hot, about 15 minutes. Leave all burners on high.

4. Clean and oil cooking grate. Thread shrimp tightly onto four 12-inch metal skewers (about 12 shrimp per skewer), alternating direction of heads and tails. Sprinkle 1 side of skewered shrimp with sugar. Place shrimp skewers sugared side down on grill (on hotter side if using charcoal). Cook (covered if using gas), without moving them, until lightly charred on first side, 3 to 4 minutes. Flip skewers and move to cooler side of grill (if using charcoal) or turn all burners off (if using gas) and cook, covered, until shrimp are opaque throughout, 1 to 2 minutes. Using tongs, slide shrimp off skewers onto serving platter and season with salt and pepper to taste. Sprinkle with cilantro and serve with lime wedges.

We make sure our scallops are really dry before browning them in batches to give them a perfect golden crust.

Seared Scallops with Orange-Lime Dressing
SERVES 4 to 6 `FAST`

WHY THIS RECIPE WORKS Seared scallops make for an ideal quick meal, as they cook in just a few minutes on the stovetop and have a mild flavor that works well with a wide variety of other ingredients. For this dish, we decided to punch up the scallops' mellow sweetness with a bold vinaigrette made with citrus, cilantro, and red pepper flakes. When searing the scallops, we found that trying to cook them all at once made the pan too crowded and caused them to steam. We found that waiting to add the scallops to the skillet until the oil was beginning to smoke, cooking the scallops in two batches instead of one, and switching to a nonstick skillet allowed them all to achieve a deep golden-brown crust. Sweet, bright, and tangy, these scallops are the perfect centerpiece for a light meal—even on a busy weeknight. Be sure to purchase dry scallops for this recipe. If you can find only wet scallops, or if your scallops are not labeled, see page 275 for more information on buying scallops.

1½ pounds large sea scallops, tendons removed

6 tablespoons extra-virgin olive oil

2 tablespoons orange juice

2 tablespoons lime juice

1 small shallot, minced

1 tablespoon minced fresh cilantro

⅛ teaspoon red pepper flakes

Salt and pepper

1. Place scallops in rimmed baking sheet lined with clean kitchen towel. Place second clean kitchen towel on top of scallops and press gently on towel to blot liquid. Let scallops sit at room temperature, covered with towel, for 10 minutes.

2. Whisk ¼ cup oil, orange juice, lime juice, shallot, cilantro, and pepper flakes together in bowl. Season with salt to taste and set aside for serving.

3. Heat 1 tablespoon oil in 12-inch nonstick skillet over medium-high heat until just smoking. Add half of scallops to skillet in single layer and cook, without moving them, until well browned on first side, about 1½ minutes. Flip scallops and continue to cook, without moving them, until well browned on second side, about 1½ minutes. Transfer scallops to serving platter and tent loosely with aluminum foil. Repeat with remaining 1 tablespoon oil and remaining scallops. Whisk dressing to recombine and serve with scallops.

Grilled Scallop and Zucchini Skewers with Basil Vinaigrette

SERVES 4 to 6

WHY THIS RECIPE WORKS In theory, scallops are tailor-made for the grill. The blazing-hot fire should deeply brown the bivalves' exteriors while leaving their centers plump and moist, with a hint of smoke. Unfortunately, in reality, by the time the scallops develop a good sear, they're usually overcooked and rubbery. And then there's the problem of trying to flip them when they inevitably stick to the cooking grate. To avoid overcooking the scallops but

Prepping Scallops

Use your fingers to peel away the small, crescent-shaped muscle that is sometimes attached to scallops, as this tendon becomes incredibly tough when cooked.

A thin coating of oil, flour, cornstarch, and sugar keeps the scallops from sticking to the grill and promotes browning.

still have them develop a brown crust, we needed a quick blast of blazing heat. So we built the hottest fire possible by corralling the coals in a disposable aluminum pan set in the bottom of the grill. We found that using large dry scallops kept them from falling through the grate and avoided the soapy flavor that afflicts wet scallops. To make flipping easier, we incorporated a couple of techniques into our recipe: We lightly coated the scallops with a slurry of extra-virgin olive oil, flour, cornstarch, and sugar and threaded them onto doubled metal skewers. The slurry kept the scallops from sticking to the grill grate, the sugar promoted browning, and the two skewers prevented the scallops from spinning when turned. Thoroughly oiling the grate also helped get our scallops off the grill in one piece. For a perfect complement, we whipped up a sweet basil vinaigrette and grilled fresh zucchini to serve alongside the juicy, smoky scallops. Be sure to purchase dry scallops for this recipe. If you can find only wet scallops, or if your scallops are not labeled, see page 275 for more information on buying scallops. You will need eight 12-inch metal skewers for this recipe.

1½ pounds large sea scallops, tendons removed

¾ cup fresh basil leaves

2 tablespoons minced fresh chives

1 tablespoon white wine vinegar
2 garlic cloves, minced
1¾ teaspoons sugar
  Salt and pepper
½ cup extra-virgin olive oil
2 zucchini, halved lengthwise and sliced ¾ inch thick
1 (13 by 9-inch) disposable aluminum roasting pan (if using charcoal)
1 tablespoon all-purpose flour
1 teaspoon cornstarch

1. Place scallops in rimmed baking sheet lined with clean kitchen towel. Place second clean kitchen towel on top of scallops and press gently on towel to blot liquid. Let scallops sit at room temperature, covered with towel, for 10 minutes.

2. Meanwhile, pulse basil, chives, vinegar, garlic, ¾ teaspoon sugar, ¾ teaspoon salt, and ¼ teaspoon pepper in food processor until roughly chopped, about 5 pulses. With processor running, slowly drizzle in 6 tablespoons oil and process until emulsified, about 30 seconds, scraping down sides of bowl as necessary. Measure out and reserve 2 tablespoons vinaigrette in large bowl. Set aside remaining vinaigrette for serving. Toss zucchini with reserved 2 tablespoons vinaigrette, then thread onto two 12-inch metal skewers.

3. With scallops on flat work surface, thread onto doubled skewers so that flat sides will directly touch grill grate, 4 to 6 scallops per doubled skewer (3 doubled skewers total). Return skewered scallops to towel-lined sheet and refrigerate, covered with second towel, while preparing grill.

4A. FOR A CHARCOAL GRILL Using kitchen shears, poke twelve ½-inch holes in bottom of disposable pan. Open bottom vent completely and place prepared pan in center of grill. Light large chimney starter mounded with charcoal briquettes (7 quarts). When top coals are partially covered with ash, pour into even layer in pan. Set cooking grate over coals with bars parallel to long side of pan, cover, and open lid vent completely. Heat grill until hot, about 5 minutes.

Skewering Scallops for the Grill

To double-skewer scallops, which makes flipping them much easier, thread 4 to 6 scallops onto one 12-inch metal skewer, then place second skewer through scallops parallel to and about ¼ inch from first skewer.

4B. FOR A GAS GRILL Turn all burners to high, cover, and heat grill until hot, about 15 minutes. Leave all burners on high.

5. Whisk remaining 2 tablespoons oil, remaining 1 teaspoon sugar, flour, and cornstarch together in small bowl. Remove towels from scallops. Brush both sides of scallops with oil mixture and season with salt and pepper.

6. Clean cooking grate, then repeatedly brush grate with well-oiled paper towels until grate is black and glossy, 5 to 10 times. Place scallops and zucchini on grill (directly over coals if using charcoal). Cook (covered if using gas), without moving them, until lightly browned on first side, 2½ to 4 minutes. Gently flip skewers and continue to cook, without moving them, until zucchini is tender and lightly browned and scallop sides are firm and centers are opaque, 2 to 4 minutes. Using tongs, slide zucchini and scallops off skewers onto serving platter. Serve with remaining vinaigrette.

NOTES FROM THE TEST KITCHEN
Buying Scallops

In general, most recipes use only one type of scallop—sea scallops. The other scallop varieties, bay and Calico (the latter often mislabeled as bay), are much smaller and often too rare and expensive or very cheap and rubbery.

DRY VERSUS WET SCALLOPS Wet scallops are dipped in preservatives (a solution of water and sodium tripolyphosphate, known as STP) to extend their shelf life. Unfortunately, these watery preservatives dull the scallops' flavor and ruin their texture. Unprocessed, or dry, scallops have much more flavor and a creamy, smooth texture, plus they brown very nicely. Dry scallops look ivory or pinkish; wet scallops are bright white.

DISTINGUISHING DRY FROM WET If your scallops are not labeled, you can find out if they are wet or dry with this quick microwave test: Place one scallop on a paper towel–lined plate and microwave for 15 seconds. A dry scallop will exude very little water, but a wet scallop will leave a sizable ring of moisture on the paper towel. (The microwaved scallop can be cooked as is.)

TREATING WET SCALLOPS When you can find only wet scallops, you can hide the offputting taste of the preservative by soaking the scallops in a solution of 1 quart of cold water, ¼ cup of lemon juice, and 2 tablespoons of salt for 30 minutes. Be sure to pat the scallops very dry after soaking them. Even after this treatment, these scallops will be harder to brown than untreated dry scallops.

A lot of Mediterranean cooking takes place over a live charcoal fire. (We've found that even the best gas grills don't brown and sear as well as charcoal.) A charcoal grill offers some other advantages over gas, including more options for creating custom fires (see page 277) and a better capability for imparting smoke and wood flavor. That said, using a charcoal grill does require some extra effort. Setting up the grill and properly heating and cleaning it before cooking are as important to successful grilling as getting the food just right.

Setting Up A Charcoal Grill

1. USE A CHIMNEY STARTER We strongly recommend using a chimney starter because lighter fluid imparts an off-flavor to grilled foods. Plus, this simple device gets all of the charcoal ready at once; a large starter holds about 6 quarts of charcoal. Remove the cooking grate and open the bottom vent. Fill the bottom of the starter with crumpled newspaper, set it on the charcoal grate, and fill the top with charcoal.

2. GET THE COALS HOT Ignite the newspaper and allow the charcoal to burn until the briquettes on top are partly covered with a thin layer of gray ash. Fine gray ash is a sign that the coals are fully lit and hot and are ready to be turned out into the grill. Don't pour out the coals prematurely; you will be left with both unlit coals at the bottom of the pile that may never ignite as well as a cooler fire.

3. POUR OUT THE COALS Once the coals are covered with gray ash, empty the briquettes onto the grill and distribute them in one of the custom grill setups. Different types of food require different types of fire, so arrange the coals as called for in the recipe.

4. GET THE COOKING GRATE HOT Set the cooking grate in place, cover, and heat the grate until hot, about 5 minutes. A hot cooking grate jump-starts the cooking process and reduces sticking once you place food on the grill. Also, a blast of heat will make it easier to clean the grate.

5. SCRUB THE COOKING GRATE CLEAN Use a grill brush to scrape the cooking grate clean. Some cooks think a dirty cooking grate "seasons" the food. This makes no sense; you wouldn't cook in a dirty pan. If you skip the cleaning step, food is more likely to stick and to pick up off-flavors.

6. OIL THE COOKING GRATE Using tongs, dip a wad of paper towels in vegetable oil and wipe the cooking grate several times. The oil offers another layer of protection against sticking. But the oil burns off and so needs to be reapplied every time you grill. Pouring the oil into a small bowl makes it easier to dip the paper towels.

Building the Right Fire

Two of the biggest mistakes outdoor grillers make happen before the food even hits the grill: creating too much fire and setting up the fire incorrectly. The first problem is easy to avoid—add the amount of charcoal called for in recipes or, if cooking on a gas grill, adjust the burner temperatures as directed. The second problem is more complicated. Depending on the food being cooked, we use one of the four grill setups outlined below. You might have to adapt these setups based on the shape, depth, and/or circumference of your grill.

	TYPE/DESCRIPTION	CHARCOAL	GAS
	**Single-Level Fire** A single-level fire delivers a uniform level of heat across the entire cooking surface and is often used for small, quick-cooking pieces of food, such as sausages, some fish, and some vegetables.	Distribute the lit coals in an even layer across the bottom of the grill.	After preheating the grill, turn all the burners to the heat setting as directed in the recipe.
	**Two-Level Fire** This setup creates two cooking zones: a hotter area for searing and a slightly cooler area to cook food more gently. It is often used for thick chops and bone-in chicken pieces.	Evenly distribute two-thirds of the lit coals over half of the grill, then distribute the remainder of the coals in an even layer over the other half of the grill.	After preheating the grill, leave the primary burner on high and turn the other(s) to medium. The primary burner is the one that must be left on; see your owner's manual if in doubt.
	**Modified Two-Level (Half-Grill) Fire** Like a two-level fire, this fire has two cooking zones, but the difference in heat level is more dramatic. One side is intensely hot, and the other side is comparatively cool. It's great for cooking fatty foods because the coal- or flame-free zone provides a place to set food while flare-ups die down. For foods that require long cooking times, you can brown the food on the hotter side, then set it on the cooler side to finish with indirect heat. It's also good for cooking chicken breasts over the cooler side gently, then giving them a quick sear on the hotter side.	Distribute the lit coals over half of the grill, piling them in an even layer. Leave the other half of the grill free of coals.	After preheating the grill, adjust the primary burner as directed in the recipe and turn off the other burner(s).
	**Concentrated Fire** A concentrated fire creates a blazing-hot fire for food like scallops or lamb that needs to quickly get a good sear to avoid overcooking the delicate meat.	Poke 12 holes in the bottom of a 13 by 9-inch disposable aluminum roasting pan. Open the bottom and lid vents completely and place the pan in the center of the grill. Pour the lit coals into the pan, set the cooking grate in place, and preheat the grill.	Turn all burners to high and preheat the grill; leave all burners on high.

For perfectly cooked mussels, we easily steam a big batch in a large roasting pan in the gentle heat of the oven.

Oven-Steamed Mussels

SERVES 4 to 6   FAST

WHY THIS RECIPE WORKS Mussels are enjoyed all across the Mediterranean from Spain to Israel. We thought steaming would be a quick and easy way to enjoy mussels, as they come with their own built-in, briny-sweet broth. But they come in all different sizes, so they cook at different rates, especially when piled on top of each other in a pot. To get them to cook evenly, we opted to cook the mussels in a wide roasting pan in the oven so that the heat surrounded the mussels on all sides, leading to more even (and gentle) cooking than was possible on the stove. Even in a 500-degree oven, the mussels took just a few minutes longer and were plump and moist. With wine, thyme, and bay leaves as a base, the mussels' liquid made a tasty broth. Discard any mussels with an unpleasant odor or with a cracked shell or a shell that won't close. For information on debearding mussels, see page 37. Serve with crusty bread to dip into the broth.

  3 tablespoons extra-virgin olive oil
  3 garlic cloves, minced
    Pinch red pepper flakes
  1 cup dry white wine
  3 sprigs fresh thyme
  2 bay leaves
  4 pounds mussels, scrubbed and debearded
  ¼ teaspoon salt
  2 tablespoons minced fresh parsley

1. Adjust oven rack to lowest position and heat oven to 500 degrees. Heat 1 tablespoon oil, garlic, and pepper flakes in large roasting pan over medium heat and cook, stirring constantly, until fragrant, about 30 seconds. Stir in wine, thyme sprigs, and bay leaves, bring to boil, and cook until wine is slightly reduced, about 1 minute.

Making Oven-Steamed Mussels

1. COOK AROMATICS AND ADD WINE Cook oil, garlic, and pepper flakes in roasting pan until fragrant. Add wine, thyme sprigs, and bay leaves and cook until wine is slightly reduced.

2. ADD MUSSELS AND COVER Add mussels and salt. Cover tightly with aluminum foil and transfer to oven.

3. COOK UNTIL MUSSELS OPEN Cook until mussels have opened (a few may remain closed), about 15 to 18 minutes. Remove pan from oven.

4. FINISH BROTH Discard thyme sprigs, bay leaves, and any unopened mussels. Drizzle with remaining oil, sprinkle with parsley, and toss to combine before serving.

2. Stir in mussels and salt. Cover pan tightly with aluminum foil and transfer to oven. Cook until most mussels have opened (a few may remain closed), 15 to 18 minutes.

3. Remove pan from oven. Discard thyme sprigs, bay leaves, and any mussels that refuse to open. Drizzle with remaining 2 tablespoons oil, sprinkle with parsley, and toss to combine. Serve.

VARIATION

Oven-Steamed Mussels with Leeks and Pernod FAST

Omit pepper flakes and thyme sprigs. Add 1 pound leeks, white and light green parts only, halved lengthwise, sliced thin, and washed thoroughly, to pan with garlic and cook until leeks are wilted, about 3 minutes. Substitute ½ cup Pernod and ¼ cup water for wine. After removing pan from oven in step 3, push mussels to sides of pan. Add ¼ cup crème fraîche and oil to center and whisk until combined. Substitute 2 tablespoons chives for parsley.

Clams Steamed in White Wine

SERVES 4 to 6 FAST

WHY THIS RECIPE WORKS It doesn't take a lot of embellishment to turn fresh clams into an exceptional dish, but as we found, it does take proper technique. We wanted a simple preparation that would complement the clams' natural briny flavor without overshadowing it. Equally important, we wanted them perfectly cooked; clams quickly turn from tender to tough and rubbery. To flavor our clams, we developed a quick broth made with white wine, shallots, garlic, and bay leaf. As the clams steamed in the flavorful liquid, they opened up and released their juices into the pot. A drizzle of olive oil, parsley, and lemon finished the dish.

  1½ cups dry white wine
   3 shallots, minced
   4 garlic cloves, minced
   1 bay leaf
   4 pounds littleneck clams, scrubbed
   3 tablespoons extra-virgin olive oil
   2 tablespoons minced fresh parsley
      Lemon wedges

1. Bring wine, shallots, garlic, and bay leaf to simmer in Dutch oven over high heat and cook for 3 minutes. Add clams, cover, and cook, stirring twice, until clams open, 4 to 8 minutes. Using slotted spoon, transfer clams to serving bowl, discarding any that refuse to open.

2. Off heat, whisk oil into cooking liquid until combined. Pour sauce over clams and sprinkle with parsley. Serve with lemon wedges.

It is simple and fast to steam clams on the stovetop in a flavorful broth.

NOTES FROM THE TEST KITCHEN

Buying Mussels and Clams

For the best flavor and texture, mussels and clams should be as fresh as possible. They should smell clean, not sour or sulfurous, and the shells should look moist. Look for tightly closed mussels and clams—avoid any that are broken or sitting in a puddle of water. Some shells may gape slightly, but they should close when they are tapped. Discard any that won't close; they may be dead and should not be eaten. Most mussels and clams today are farmed and free of grit. Soft-shell clams, however, almost always contain a lot of sand and should be submerged in a large bowl of cold water and drained several times before cooking. Both clams and mussels need to be scrubbed and rinsed before cooking; simply use a brush to scrub away any sand trapped in the outer shell. Some mussels may also need to be debearded. The best way to store mussels and clams is in the refrigerator in a colander of ice set over a bowl; discard any water that accumulates so that the shellfish are never submerged.

For a quick one-pan supper, we steam clams in a fragrant mixture of leeks, tomatoes, Spanish chorizo, and vermouth.

Clams with Pearl Couscous, Chorizo, and Leeks
SERVES 4 to 6   FAST

WHY THIS RECIPE WORKS To infuse this simple clam dish with big flavor, we added Spanish chorizo, thyme, and dry vermouth for a potent broth in which to steam our shellfish. We added larger-grain pearl couscous instead of traditional small-grain couscous, as it is the perfect vehicle for soaking up flavors and also adds textural appeal. Pearl couscous, also known as Israeli couscous, is about the size of a caper and is not precooked, unlike the smaller grains. It has a unique, nutty flavor that gives this dish just the right boost. We like the punch that dry vermouth adds, but dry white wine will also work. Do not substitute regular couscous in this dish, as it requires a different cooking method and will not work in this recipe.

2 cups pearl couscous
  Salt and pepper
2 tablespoons extra-virgin olive oil

1½ pounds leeks, white and light green parts only, halved lengthwise, sliced thin, and washed thoroughly
6 ounces Spanish-style chorizo sausage, halved lengthwise and sliced thin
3 garlic cloves, minced
1 tablespoon minced fresh thyme or 1 teaspoon dried
1 cup dry vermouth or dry white wine
3 tomatoes, cored, seeded, and chopped
4 pounds littleneck clams, scrubbed
½ cup minced fresh parsley

1. Bring 2 quarts water to boil in medium saucepan. Stir in couscous and 2 teaspoons salt and cook until al dente, about 8 minutes; drain.

2. Meanwhile, heat oil in Dutch oven over medium heat. Add leeks and chorizo and cook until leeks are tender, about 4 minutes. Stir in garlic and thyme and cook until fragrant, about 30 seconds. Stir in vermouth and cook until slightly reduced, about 1 minute. Stir in tomatoes and clams, cover, and cook until clams open, 8 to 12 minutes.

3. Use slotted spoon to transfer clams to large serving bowl, discarding any that refuse to open. Stir couscous and parsley into cooking liquid and season with salt and pepper to taste. Portion couscous mixture into individual bowls, top with clams, and serve.

Spanish Shellfish Stew
SERVES 4 to 6

WHY THIS RECIPE WORKS Less well-known than France's bouillabaisse is Spain's version of shellfish stew, *zarzuela*. Chock-full of shellfish like lobsters, clams, and mussels, this tomato-based stew is seasoned with saffron and paprika and thickened with a *picada*, a flavorful mixture of ground almonds, bread crumbs, and olive oil. Unlike many seafood stews, this one contains no fish stock or clam juice—instead, the shellfish release their rich liquors into the pot as they cook. To create our version of this dish, we followed Spanish tradition and began with a *sofrito* of onion, red bell pepper, and garlic and next added paprika, saffron, red pepper flakes, and bay leaves to create a rich foundation. Canned tomatoes and dry white wine formed the liquid base of our broth, and a little brandy lent depth of flavor. When selecting the shellfish, we focused on building more flavor. Knowing that shells contribute significant flavor to dishes, we enriched the broth by steeping the shrimp shells in wine while we prepared the other ingredients. Since each of the shellfish was a different size, we knew we'd have to stagger the time when we added each variety.

After some trial and error, we determined that the clams should be added to the stew first, followed by the mussels and scallops, and finally the shrimp. Stirring in the picada at the end gave the stew added richness and also thickened it; do not omit it. All that was left to do was sprinkle the dish with fresh parsley and a squeeze of lemon for a bright, fresh finish. Be sure to buy shrimp with their shells on and reserve the shells when cleaning the shrimp; they add important flavor to the cooking liquid in step 1.

¼ cup extra-virgin olive oil
8 ounces medium-large shrimp (31 to 40 per pound), peeled and deveined, shells reserved
1½ cups dry white wine or dry vermouth
1 onion, chopped fine
1 red bell pepper, stemmed, seeded, and chopped fine
3 garlic cloves, minced
1 teaspoon paprika
¼ teaspoon saffron threads, crumbled
⅛ teaspoon red pepper flakes
2 tablespoons brandy
1 (28-ounce) can whole peeled tomatoes, drained with juice reserved, chopped
2 bay leaves
1½ pounds littleneck clams, scrubbed
8 ounces mussels, scrubbed and debearded
12 ounces large sea scallops, tendons removed
1 recipe Picada (page 63)
1 tablespoon minced fresh parsley
Salt and pepper
Lemon wedges

1. Heat 1 tablespoon oil in medium saucepan over medium heat until shimmering. Add shrimp shells and cook, stirring frequently, until they begin to turn spotty brown and pot starts to brown, 2 to 4 minutes. Off heat, stir in wine, cover, and let steep until ready to use.

2. Heat remaining 3 tablespoons oil in large Dutch oven over medium-high heat until shimmering. Add onion and bell pepper and cook until softened and lightly browned, 5 to 7 minutes. Stir in garlic, paprika, saffron, and pepper flakes and cook until fragrant, about 30 seconds. Stir in brandy, scraping up any browned bits. Stir in tomatoes and their juice and bay leaves and cook until slightly thickened, 5 to 7 minutes.

3. Strain wine mixture into Dutch oven, pressing on solids to extract as much liquid as possible; discard solids. Bring to simmer and cook until flavors meld, 3 to 5 minutes.

The broth of our Spanish stew relies on the flavor of shrimp shells steeped in white wine and the liquors of the shellfish.

4. Nestle clams into pot, cover, and cook for 4 minutes. Nestle mussels and scallops into pot, cover, and continue to cook until most clams have opened, about 3 minutes. Arrange shrimp evenly over stew, cover, and continue to cook until shrimp are opaque throughout, scallops are firm and opaque in center, and clams and mussels have opened, 1 to 2 minutes.

5. Off heat, discard bay leaves and any clams and mussels that refuse to open. Stir in picada and parsley and season with salt and pepper to taste. Serve in wide, shallow bowls with lemon wedges.

VARIATION
Spanish Shellfish Stew with Lobster
In Spain, this stew is often made with *langostinos*, or prawns. Fresh prawns are difficult to find stateside, so we chose to use lobster instead.

Reduce number of clams and mussels to 12 each. Stir 8 ounces cooked lobster meat, cut into ½-inch pieces, into stew with picada; cover and let sit until heated through, about 1 minute, before serving.

Simmering the squid in flavorful white wine makes it tender and green olives and capers add a briny element to this stew.

Calamari Stew with Garlic and Tomatoes
SERVES 4 to 6

WHY THIS RECIPE WORKS Stewed calamari with tomatoes, garlic, and white wine is a classic Mediterranean dish. This stewed preparation puts the sweet, subtle flavor of the squid front and center. We started building our stew's flavor with onions, a generous amount of garlic, and the fresh vegetal addition of celery, then added white wine to these aromatics. After much testing, we found that around the 45-minute mark was when the squid became tender enough for our liking; any longer and they became tough and rubbery. As for the tomatoes, we had the best luck with canned whole tomatoes, which not only gave the stew a fresh tomato flavor but broke down just enough to thicken the stew while remaining a distinct component. To make our stew substantial, we balanced the 2 pounds of squid with three large cans of tomatoes. Because the tomatoes tended to lose their fresh flavor the longer they cooked, we added them to the pot after the squid had simmered for 15 minutes. Green olives and capers lent a welcome briny

element, and red pepper flakes provided just the right amount of heat. Finished with fresh parsley and a drizzle of extra-virgin olive oil, our stew was the perfect calamari showcase. Be sure to use small squid (with bodies 3 to 4 inches in length) because they cook more quickly and are more tender than larger squid. This brothy stew can be served with Creamy Parmesan Polenta (page 118) for a hearty meal or with crusty bread to dip into the broth.

¼ cup extra-virgin olive oil, plus extra for serving
2 onions, chopped fine
2 celery ribs, sliced thin
8 garlic cloves, minced
¼ teaspoon red pepper flakes
½ cup dry white wine or dry vermouth
2 pounds small squid, bodies sliced crosswise into 1-inch-thick rings, tentacles halved
Salt and pepper
3 (28-ounce) cans whole peeled tomatoes, drained and chopped coarse
⅓ cup pitted brine-cured green olives, chopped coarse
1 tablespoon capers, rinsed
3 tablespoons minced fresh parsley

1. Heat oil in Dutch oven over medium-high heat until shimmering. Add onions and celery and cook until softened, about 5 minutes. Stir in garlic and pepper flakes and cook until fragrant, about 30 seconds. Stir in wine, scraping up any browned bits, and cook until nearly evaporated, about 1 minute.

2. Pat squid dry with paper towels and season with salt and pepper. Stir squid into pot. Reduce heat to medium-low, cover, and simmer gently until squid has released its liquid, about 15 minutes. Stir in tomatoes, olives, and capers, cover, and continue to cook until squid is very tender, 30 to 35 minutes.

3. Off heat, stir in parsley and season with salt and pepper to taste. Serve, drizzling individual portions with extra oil.

Stuffed Squid
SERVES 4

WHY THIS RECIPE WORKS Before developing our recipe for this Greek-style stuffed squid, we tested all of the renditions of this dish we could get our hands on. Whether stuffed with rice, bread crumbs, or milk-soaked white bread, or studded with salt pork, capers, or currants, the squid were all just rubbery packages of dry and either bland or overwhelming conflicting flavors. We unanimously found the bread-crumb base most appealing as our stuffing platform, for its homogeneous texture and subtle presence. In order to fortify the sweet, delicate flavor of the squid bodies, we chopped the tentacles and incorporated them into the stuffing. Subtle pine nuts, dried mint, sweet golden raisins, and a bit of anchovy rounded out the filling into a balanced, dynamic mix. Next, we had to solve the issue of rubber band–like squid casings. In most of the recipes we found, the stuffed squid were boiled, broiled, or baked for 20 to 40 minutes, resulting in inedibly chewy squid. We found that to prevent its muscle fibers from tightening and becoming tough, squid needs to be cooked either very briefly or much longer, giving the collagen time to break down into gelatin and tenderize. For silky, succulent squid bodies encasing our filling, we simmered them in a simple tomato sauce for an hour. Not only did this tenderize the squid, but it also ensured a moist, rich filling. Be sure not to overstuff the squid; the bodies shrink and the filling swells while cooking, so they burst open if packed too full. Look for medium squid (with bodies 4 to 6 inches in length) for this recipe to make stuffing them easier.

2 tablespoons extra-virgin olive oil
3 onions, chopped fine
16 medium squid bodies, plus 6 ounces tentacles, chopped (¾ cup)
¼ cup pine nuts, toasted
1 tablespoon dried mint
  Salt and pepper
½ cup plain dried bread crumbs
5 tablespoons minced fresh parsley
¼ cup golden raisins
4 anchovy fillets, rinsed and minced
1 garlic clove, minced
½ cup dry white wine
1 (15-ounce) can tomato sauce

1. Heat 1 tablespoon oil in 12-inch nonstick skillet over medium-high heat until shimmering. Add two-thirds of onions and cook until softened, about 5 minutes. Stir in squid tentacles and cook until no longer translucent, 1 to 2 minutes. Stir in pine nuts, mint, and ¼ teaspoon pepper and cook until fragrant, about 1 minute. Transfer mixture to large bowl and stir in bread crumbs, ¼ cup parsley, raisins, and anchovies. Season with salt and pepper to taste and let cool slightly.

2. Using small soup spoon, portion 2 tablespoons filling into each squid body, pressing on filling gently to create 1-inch space at top. Thread toothpick through opening of each squid to secure closed.

3. Heat remaining 1 tablespoon oil in now-empty skillet over medium-high heat until shimmering. Add remaining onions and cook until softened, about 5 minutes. Stir in garlic, ¼ teaspoon salt, and ¼ teaspoon pepper and cook until fragrant, about 30 seconds. Stir in wine and tomato sauce and bring to simmer.

4. Nestle squid into sauce. Reduce heat to low, cover, and simmer gently until sauce has thickened slightly and squid is easily pierced with paring knife, about 1 hour, turning squid halfway through cooking. Season sauce with salt and pepper to taste. Remove toothpicks from squid and sprinkle with remaining 1 tablespoon parsley. Serve.

Making Stuffed Squid

1. ASSEMBLE FILLING Transfer onion-squid mixture to large bowl. Stir in bread crumbs, parsley, raisins, and anchovies. Season with salt and pepper to taste.

2. STUFF SQUID Portion 2 tablespoons filling into each squid body, leaving 1-inch space at top. Thread toothpick through opening of each squid to secure closed.

3. MAKE SAUCE Stir garlic, salt, and pepper into sautéed onion and cook until fragrant. Stir in wine and tomato sauce and bring to simmer.

4. COOK SQUID UNTIL TENDER Gently simmer squid until easily pierced with paring knife, about 1 hour. Remove toothpicks and sprinkle with parsley.

We quickly brine small squid in baking soda, salt, and water to tenderize them and prevent them from overcooking.

Grilled Squid with Lemon and Garlic
SERVES 4

WHY THIS RECIPE WORKS With the country's thousands of miles of coastline, it's no surprise that fresh seafood is a mainstay of Greek cuisine, an abundance of which is squid. We loved the idea of simple grilled squid tossed with a lemony vinaigrette. To promote maximum browning and even cooking, we found it best to slit the squid bodies lengthwise and then open them to create a single plank so these squid "steaks" would lie flat on the grill; skewering the tentacles prevented them from falling through the grates. Good charring can't occur if there's moisture in the squid, but if the squid is cooked for too long it becomes rubbery and tough. By quickly brining the squid in an alkaline solution of baking soda, salt, and water, we ensured that the proteins tenderized before hitting the grill. Then we layered the squid between dish towels to help dry any excess moisture, giving our ideal char marks a head start. A superhot grill setup helped us get tasty browning while our squid remained tender. Be sure to use small squid (with bodies 3 to 4 inches in length) because they cook more quickly and are more tender than larger squid. You will need 2 metal skewers for this recipe.

5 tablespoons extra-virgin olive oil
1 tablespoon lemon juice, plus lemon wedges for serving
2 teaspoons minced fresh parsley
1 garlic clove, minced
  Salt and pepper
1 pound small squid
2 tablespoons baking soda

1. Combine 3 tablespoons oil, lemon juice, parsley, garlic, and ¼ teaspoon pepper in large bowl; set aside for serving.

2. Using kitchen shears, cut squid bodies lengthwise down one side. Open squid bodies and flatten into planks. Dissolve baking soda and 2 tablespoons salt in 3 cups cold water in large container. Submerge squid bodies and tentacles in brine, cover, and refrigerate for 15 minutes. Remove squid from brine and spread in even layer in rimmed baking sheet lined with clean kitchen towel. Place second clean kitchen towel on top of squid and press gently on towel to blot liquid. Let squid sit at room temperature, covered with towel, for 10 minutes.

3. Toss squid with remaining 2 tablespoons oil and season with pepper. Thread tentacles onto two 12-inch metal skewers.

4A. FOR A CHARCOAL GRILL Open bottom vent completely. Light large chimney starter mounded with charcoal briquettes (7 quarts). When top coals are partially covered with ash, pour evenly over half of grill. Set cooking grate in place, cover, and open lid vent completely. Heat grill until hot, about 5 minutes.

4B. FOR A GAS GRILL Turn all burners to high, cover, and heat grill until hot, about 15 minutes. Leave all burners on high.

5. Clean cooking grate, then repeatedly brush grate with well-oiled paper towels until black and glossy, 5 to 10 times. Place squid bodies and tentacles on grill (directly over coals if using charcoal), draping long tentacles over skewers to prevent them from falling through grates. Cook (covered if using gas) until squid is opaque and lightly charred, about 5 minutes, flipping halfway through cooking. Transfer bodies to plate and tent loosely with aluminum foil. Continue to grill tentacles until ends are browned and crisp, about 3 minutes; transfer to plate with bodies.

6. Using tongs, remove tentacles from skewers. Transfer bodies to cutting board and slice into ½-inch-thick strips. Add tentacles and bodies to bowl with oil mixture and toss to coat. Serve with lemon wedges.

We simmer octopus in water before braising to rid it of all of the salt water it contains.

Red Wine–Braised Octopus

SERVES 4

WHY THIS RECIPE WORKS Following a Greek tradition, we wanted to create a braised octopus dish with an intense, silky red wine sauce. Octopus flesh is a dense array of thin muscle fibers reinforced by a network of collagen and connective tissue, so it is all too often tough and chewy. Most of the octopus you can buy in the United States is frozen, and we found that simply defrosting it helped lead to tender octopus; the ice crystals tore through the tough muscle fibers and helped them break down during cooking. Thinking the octopus collagen and connective tissue would break down with gentle, low-heat cooking as meat does, we cooked the octopus in red wine over low heat. But because octopus is made up of almost half salt water by weight, it released its salty juices into the sauce, making it unpalatable. We found that the best way to desalinate our braise was to cook the octopus in water first; however, since octopus contains a lot of collagen, which transforms into gelatin as it cooks, we also lost the viscosity and velvety texture provided by the collagen. To counteract this, we added powdered gelatin to our wine sauce. Octopus can be found cleaned and frozen in the seafood section of specialty grocery stores and Asian markets. Be sure to rinse the defrosted octopus

well, as sand can collect in the suckers. The octopus's membrane-like skin is easiest to peel while still warm, so be sure to do so as soon as it's cool enough to handle. You can thaw frozen octopus in a large container under cold running water; it will be ready in about 2 hours. For more information about preparing octopus, see pages 286 and 287. Serve over Creamy Parmesan Polenta (page 118) or with crusty bread to dip into the sauce.

1 (4-pound) octopus, rinsed
1 tablespoon extra-virgin olive oil
2 tablespoons tomato paste
4 garlic cloves, peeled and smashed
1 sprig fresh rosemary
2 bay leaves
  Pepper
  Pinch ground cinnamon
  Pinch ground nutmeg
1 cup dry red wine
2 tablespoons red wine vinegar
2 tablespoons unflavored gelatin
2 teaspoons chopped fresh parsley

1. Using sharp knife, separate octopus mantle (large sac) and body (lower section with tentacles) from head (midsection containing eyes); discard head. Place octopus in large pot, cover with water by 2 inches, and bring to simmer over high heat. Reduce heat to low, cover, and simmer gently, flipping octopus occasionally, until skin between tentacle joints tears easily when pulled, 45 minutes to 1¼ hours.

2. Transfer octopus to cutting board and let cool slightly. Measure out and reserve 3 cups octopus cooking liquid; discard remaining liquid and wipe pot dry with paper towels.

3. While octopus is still warm, use paring knife to cut mantle into quarters, then trim and scrape away skin and interior fibers; transfer to bowl. Using your fingers, remove skin from body, being careful not to remove suction cups from tentacles. Cut tentacles from around core of body in three sections; discard core. Separate tentacles and cut into 2-inch lengths; transfer to bowl.

4. Heat oil in now-empty pot over medium-high heat until shimmering. Add tomato paste and cook, stirring constantly, until beginning to darken, about 1 minute. Stir in garlic, rosemary sprig, bay leaves, ½ teaspoon pepper, cinnamon, and nutmeg and cook until fragrant, about 30 seconds. Stir in reserved octopus cooking liquid, wine, vinegar, and gelatin, scraping up any browned bits. Bring to boil and cook, stirring occasionally, for 20 minutes.

5. Stir in octopus and any accumulated juices and bring to simmer. Cook, stirring occasionally, until octopus is tender and sauce has thickened slightly and coats back of spoon, 20 to 25 minutes. Off heat, discard rosemary sprig and bay leaves. Stir in parsley and season with pepper to taste. Serve.

Spanish Grilled Octopus Salad with Orange and Bell Pepper

SERVES 4 to 6

WHY THIS RECIPE WORKS We wanted a way to bring octopus home in a Spanish-style grilled octopus salad with vibrant flavors and crisp vegetables. Having found that octopus collagen and connective tissue break down with gentle, low-heat cooking, we slowly simmered the octopus in an aromatic mix of water, wine, garlic, and bay leaves. After successfully tenderizing our octopus, we quickly charred it on a superhot grill, sliced it thin, and tossed it into a marinade redolent with the flavors of Spain: lemon juice and zest, extra-virgin olive oil, sherry vinegar, smoked paprika, and garlic. The marinade transformed into the salad's dressing when tossed with refreshing celery and orange segments, salty green olives, and parsley. Octopus can be found cleaned and frozen in the seafood section of specialty grocery stores and Asian markets. Be sure to rinse the defrosted octopus well, as sand can collect in the suckers. The octopus's membranelike skin is easiest to peel while still warm, so be sure to do so as soon as it's cool enough to handle. You can thaw frozen octopus in a large container under cold running water; it will be ready in about 2 hours.

1 (4-pound) octopus, rinsed
2 cups dry white wine
6 garlic cloves (4 peeled and smashed, 2 minced)
2 bay leaves
1 teaspoon grated lemon zest plus ⅓ cup juice (2 lemons)

7 tablespoons extra-virgin olive oil
3 tablespoons sherry vinegar
2 teaspoons smoked paprika
1 teaspoon sugar
  Salt and pepper
1 large orange
2 celery ribs, sliced thin on bias
1 red bell pepper, stemmed, seeded, and cut into 2-inch-long matchsticks
½ cup pitted brine-cured green olives, halved
2 tablespoons chopped fresh parsley

1. Using sharp knife, separate octopus mantle (large sac) and body (lower section with tentacles) from head (midsection containing eyes); discard head. Place octopus, wine, smashed garlic, and bay leaves in large pot, add water to cover octopus by 2 inches, and bring to simmer over high heat. Reduce heat to low, cover, and simmer gently, flipping octopus occasionally, until skin between tentacle joints tears easily when pulled, 45 minutes to 1¼ hours.

2. Transfer octopus to cutting board and let cool slightly; discard cooking liquid. Using paring knife, cut mantle in half, then trim and scrape away skin and interior fibers; transfer to bowl. Using your fingers, remove skin from body, being careful not to remove suction cups from tentacles. Cut tentacles from around core of body in three sections; discard core. Separate tentacles and transfer to bowl.

3. Whisk lemon juice and zest, 6 tablespoons oil, vinegar, paprika, minced garlic, sugar, ¼ teaspoon salt, and ¼ teaspoon pepper together in bowl; transfer to 1-gallon zipper-lock bag and set aside.

Preparing Octopus for Braising and Grilling

1. Using sharp knife, separate octopus mantle (large sac) and body (lower section with tentacles) from head (midsection containing eyes); discard head.

2. While octopus is still warm, use paring knife to cut mantle into quarters (or halves), then trim and scrape away skin and interior fibers.

3. Using your fingers, grasp skin at base of each tentacle and pull toward tips to remove. Be careful not to remove suction cups from tentacles.

4. Cut tentacles from around core of body in three sections; discard core. Separate tentacles and cut into pieces (if directed).

We gently simmer our octopus in a flavorful broth before quickly charring it and tossing it with a Spanish marinade.

4A. FOR A CHARCOAL GRILL Open bottom vent completely. Light large chimney starter filled with charcoal briquettes (6 quarts). When top coals are partially covered with ash, pour evenly over half of grill. Set cooking grate in place, cover, and open lid vent completely. Heat grill until hot, about 5 minutes.

4B. FOR A GAS GRILL Turn all burners to high, cover, and heat grill until hot, about 15 minutes. Leave all burners on high.

5. Toss octopus with remaining 1 tablespoon oil. Clean cooking grate, then repeatedly brush grate with well-oiled paper towels until black and glossy, 5 to 10 times. Place octopus on grill (directly over coals if using charcoal). Cook (covered if using gas) until octopus is streaked with dark grill marks and lightly charred at tips of tentacles, 8 to 10 minutes, flipping halfway through grilling; transfer to cutting board.

6. While octopus is still warm, slice ¼ inch thick on bias, then transfer to zipper-lock bag with oil-lemon mixture and toss to coat. Press out as much air from bag as possible and seal bag. Refrigerate for at least 2 hours or up to 24 hours, flipping bag occasionally.

7. Transfer octopus and marinade to large bowl and let come to room temperature, about 2 hours. Cut away peel and pith from orange. Holding fruit over bowl with octopus, use paring knife to slice between membranes to release segments. Add celery, bell pepper, olives, and parsley and gently toss to coat. Season with salt and pepper to taste. Serve.

VARIATION
Greek Grilled Octopus Salad with Celery and Fennel
Omit orange. Substitute 1 tablespoon dried oregano for paprika, 1 fennel bulb, stalks discarded, bulb halved, cored, and sliced thin, for bell pepper, and 2 tablespoons chopped fresh dill for parsley.

NOTES FROM THE TEST KITCHEN
All About Octopus
Octopus is consumed throughout the Mediterranean, most notably in Greece, Italy, and Spain. It is low in calories, high in vitamins, and not expensive to buy. Octopus belongs to the class of marine mollusks known as cephalopods, and there are more than 300 different species. An immediately recognizable creature, it has a large sac on its head, which is surrounded by eight muscular, sucker-bearing arms. The Mediterranean species of octopus tend to be larger than the Asian species. We had the most success using frozen octopus from either Spain or Portugal. (Frozen octopus is actually preferable to fresh because the ice crystals help to break down the tough muscle fibers.) Asian species of octopus will also work; however, they tend to have thinner tentacles, which cook more quickly. Frozen octopus is easy to find, and it usually has been cleaned and the organs and eyes removed during processing. It is necessary to rinse the suckers well to rid them of any remaining dirt.

The octopus has no skeleton so no bones. The mantle is the large sac on top; it contains organs and the ink sac, and it is edible once cleaned. The head is the central midsection and contains the eyes and brain; it is not edible. The beak is cartilage in the center of the tentacles and is visible from underneath. The tentacles are the arms, and they are covered with suckers; the tentacles contain most of the meat.

Octopus is made up of 50 to 80 percent salt water, which is released during cooking. It is important to note that the finished volume of your dish could turn out to be less than half of what you started with and very salty if you don't follow the recipe.

CHAPTER 9

Poultry and Meat

■ FAST (less than 45 minutes start to finish)   ■ VEGETARIAN
Photos (from left): Pan-Seared Chicken Breasts with Chickpea Salad; Kibbeh

Jarred roasted red peppers make our Spanish-style romesco sauce quick and easy to make.

Sautéed Chicken Cutlets with Romesco Sauce
SERVES 4 **FAST**

WHY THIS RECIPE WORKS Looking to create a simple sauce that would provide a boost of flavor and richness to quick-cooking chicken cutlets, we found inspiration in the classic Spanish sauce romesco. To keep things simple, we used a combination of boldly flavored jarred and no-cook ingredients to build our sauce. Our version was a thick, coarse mixture of roasted red peppers, toasted hazelnuts and cubed bread, sherry vinegar, olive oil, smoked paprika, and garlic that we whirled together in the food processor. The roasted red peppers and paprika provided a sweet smokiness, the sherry vinegar gave the sauce an acidic punch, and the underpinning of nuts and bread lent texture and body, as well as brought all the other ingredients together. A teaspoon of honey helped bring all the flavors into focus. Best of all, this complexly flavored sauce could be made in about 5 minutes. Finding that most sautéed chicken cutlet recipes produced dry, bland, tough

chicken, we were determined to produce our own recipe that would guarantee juicy, flavorful results. For even cooking, we halved the breasts horizontally before pounding them until they were ¼ inch thick and then seasoned them with salt and pepper. After just 2½ minutes in the skillet, the cutlets were juicy and cooked through. You will need at least a 12-ounce jar of roasted red peppers for this recipe.

SAUCE
- ½ slice hearty white sandwich bread, cut into ½ inch pieces
- ¼ cup hazelnuts, toasted and skinned
- 2 tablespoons extra-virgin olive oil
- 2 garlic cloves, sliced thin
- 1 cup jarred roasted red peppers, rinsed and patted dry
- 1½ tablespoons sherry vinegar
- 1 teaspoon honey
- ½ teaspoon smoked paprika
- ½ teaspoon salt
  Pinch cayenne pepper

CHICKEN
- 4 (4- to 6-ounce) boneless, skinless chicken breasts, trimmed
  Salt and pepper
- 4 teaspoons extra-virgin olive oil

1. FOR THE SAUCE Cook bread, hazelnuts, and 1 tablespoon oil in 12-inch skillet over medium heat, stirring constantly, until bread and hazelnuts are lightly toasted, about 3 minutes. Add garlic and cook, stirring constantly, until fragrant, about 30 seconds. Transfer mixture to food processor and pulse until coarsely chopped, about 5 pulses. Add red peppers, vinegar, honey, paprika, salt, cayenne, and remaining 1 tablespoon oil to processor. Pulse until finely chopped, 5 to 8 pulses. Transfer sauce to bowl and set aside for serving. (Sauce can be refrigerated for up to 2 days.)

2. FOR THE CHICKEN Cut chicken horizontally into 2 thin cutlets, then cover with plastic wrap and pound to uniform ¼-inch thickness. Pat cutlets dry with paper towels and season with salt and pepper. Heat 2 teaspoons oil in 12-inch skillet over medium-high heat until just smoking. Place 4 cutlets in skillet and cook, without moving, until browned on first side, about 2 minutes. Flip cutlets and continue to cook until opaque on second side, about 30 seconds. Transfer chicken to serving platter and tent loosely with aluminum foil. Repeat with remaining 4 cutlets and remaining 2 teaspoons oil. Serve with sauce.

Sautéed Chicken Cutlets with Sun-Dried Tomato Sauce `FAST`

Omit honey, smoked paprika, and cayenne. Substitute ¼ cup pine nuts for hazelnuts, 1 small tomato, cored and cut into ½-inch pieces, and ½ cup oil-packed sun-dried tomatoes for red peppers, and 2 tablespoons balsamic vinegar for sherry vinegar. Add 2 tablespoons chopped fresh basil to food processor with tomato.

Sautéed Chicken Cutlets with Olive-Orange Sauce `FAST`

Omit smoked paprika and cayenne. Cut away peel and pith from 1 orange. Quarter orange, then slice crosswise into ½-inch-thick pieces. Substitute ¼ cup slivered almonds for hazelnuts, orange pieces and ¾ cup pitted kalamata olives for red peppers, and 1½ tablespoons red wine vinegar for sherry vinegar. Add ¼ teaspoon fennel seeds to skillet with garlic and 2 tablespoons chopped fresh mint to food processor with orange.

Preparing Chicken Cutlets

1. If small strip of meat (tenderloin) is loosely attached to underside of breast, pull it off and reserve for another use.

2. Lay chicken smooth side up on cutting board. With your hand on top of chicken, carefully slice it in half horizontally to yield 2 pieces between ⅜ and ½ inch thick.

3. Lay each cutlet between 2 sheets of plastic wrap and pound with meat pounder or small skillet until roughly ¼ inch thick.

Buying Chicken

Here's what you need to know when buying chicken.

DECIPHERING LABELS A lot of labeling doesn't (necessarily) mean much. Companies can exploit loopholes to qualify for "Natural/All-Natural," "Hormone-Free," and "Vegetarian Diet/Fed" labeling. "USDA Organic," however, isn't all hype: The chickens must eat all organic feed without animal byproducts, be raised without antibiotics, and have access to the outdoors.

PAY ATTENTION TO PROCESSING Our research showed that processing is the major player in chicken's texture and flavor. We found that brands labeled "water-chilled" (soaked in a water bath in which they absorb up to 14 percent of their weight in water, which you pay for since chicken is sold by the pound) or "enhanced" (injected with broth and flavoring) are unnaturally spongy and are best avoided. Labeling laws say water gain must be shown on the product label, so these should be easily identifiable. When buying whole chickens or chicken parts, look for those that are labeled "air-chilled." Without the excess water weight, these brands are less spongy in texture (but still plenty juicy) and have more chicken flavor.

BONELESS, SKINLESS BREASTS AND CUTLETS Try to pick a package with breasts of similar size, and pound them to an even thickness so they will cook at the same rate. You can buy cutlets ready to go at the grocery store, but we don't recommend it. These cutlets are usually ragged and of various sizes; it's better to cut your own cutlets from breasts.

BONE-IN PARTS You can buy a whole chicken or chicken parts at the supermarket, but sometimes it's hard to tell by looking at the package if it's been properly butchered. If you have a few minutes of extra time, consider buying a whole chicken and butchering it yourself.

WHOLE CHICKENS Whole chickens come in various sizes. Broilers and fryers are younger chickens that weigh 2½ to 4½ pounds. A roaster (or "oven-stuffer roaster") is an older chicken and usually clocks in between 5 and 7 pounds. Stewing chickens, which are older laying hens, are best used for stews since the meat is tougher and more stringy. A 3½- to 4-pound bird will feed four people.

Poultry Safety and Handling

It's important to follow some basic safety procedures when storing, handling, and cooking chicken, turkey, and other poultry.

REFRIGERATING Keep poultry refrigerated until just before cooking. Bacteria thrive at temperatures between 40 and 140 degrees. This means leftovers should also be promptly refrigerated.

FREEZING AND THAWING Poultry can be frozen in its original packaging or after repackaging. If you are freezing it for longer than two months, rewrap (or wrap over the packaging) with aluminum foil or plastic wrap, or place it inside a zipper-lock bag. You can keep poultry frozen for several months, but after two months the texture and flavor will suffer. Don't thaw frozen poultry on the counter; this puts it at risk of growing bacteria. Thaw it in its packaging in the refrigerator (in a container to catch its juices), or in the sink under cold running water. Count on one day of defrosting in the refrigerator for every 4 pounds of bird.

HANDLING RAW POULTRY When handling raw poultry, make sure to wash hands, knives, cutting boards, and counters (and anything else that has come into contact with the raw bird, its juices, or your hands) with hot, soapy water. Be careful not to let the poultry, its juices, or your unwashed hands touch foods that will be eaten raw. When seasoning raw poultry, touching the saltshaker or pepper mill can lead to cross-contamination. To avoid this, set aside the necessary salt and pepper before handling the poultry.

RINSING The U.S. Department of Agriculture advises against washing poultry. Rinsing poultry will not remove or kill much bacteria, and the splashing of water around the sink can spread the bacteria found in raw poultry.

COOKING AND LEFTOVERS Poultry should be cooked to an internal temperature of 160 degrees to ensure that any bacteria have been killed (however, we prefer the flavor and texture of thigh meat cooked to 175 degrees). Leftover cooked poultry should be refrigerated and consumed within three days.

A smoking-hot skillet does double duty, quickly cooking boneless chicken breasts, then a medley of fresh vegetables.

Sautéed Chicken Breasts with Cherry Tomatoes, Zucchini, and Yellow Squash

SERVES 4 **FAST**

WHY THIS RECIPE WORKS Boneless, skinless chicken breasts are a go-to choice for weeknight cooking. Adding some Mediterranean vegetables and flavorings created a great easy dinner for any day of the week. First off, the star ingredient needed to be cooked correctly. To sauté the chicken, one thing was key: The pan needed to be smoking hot. A thin, delicate item like a boneless, skinless chicken breast must be cooked through quickly. Cooking over low heat brings the juices to the surface, and once that happens, the chicken will never brown. To keep the meal to one pan, we sautéed cherry tomatoes and quick-cooking zucchini and summer squash in the same pan in which we cooked the chicken to create a flavorful medley of vegetables. Seasoning the chicken with herbes de Provence and finishing with basil gave our dish Mediterranean-fresh flavor. We prefer to use our homemade Herbes de Provence (page 317), but you can substitute store-bought herbes de Provence if you wish, though flavor can vary by brand.

½ cup all-purpose flour

4 (4- to 6-ounce) boneless, skinless chicken breasts, trimmed

1 teaspoon herbes de Provence

 Salt and pepper

3 tablespoons plus 2 teaspoons extra-virgin olive oil

2 zucchini, quartered lengthwise and sliced ½ inch thick

2 yellow summer squash, quartered lengthwise and sliced ½ inch thick

2 garlic cloves, minced

12 ounces cherry tomatoes, halved

2 tablespoons capers, rinsed

¼ cup shredded fresh basil or mint

1. Spread flour in shallow dish. Pound thicker ends of chicken breasts between 2 sheets of plastic wrap to uniform ½-inch thickness. Pat chicken dry with paper towels, sprinkle with herbes de Provence, and season with salt and pepper. Working with 1 chicken breast at a time, dredge in flour to coat, shaking off any excess.

2. Heat 2 tablespoons oil in 12-inch nonstick skillet over medium-high heat until just smoking. Place chicken in skillet and cook, turning as needed, until golden brown on both sides and chicken registers 160 degrees, about 10 minutes. Transfer chicken to plate, tent loosely with aluminum foil, and let rest while preparing vegetables.

3. Heat 2 teaspoons oil in now-empty skillet over medium-high heat until shimmering. Add zucchini and squash and cook until well browned, about 10 minutes. Stir in garlic and cook until fragrant, about 30 seconds. Stir in tomatoes and capers and cook until tomatoes are just softened, about 2 minutes. Off heat, stir in basil and remaining 1 tablespoon oil. Season with salt and pepper to taste. Serve chicken with vegetables.

Pounding Chicken Breasts

To create chicken breasts of even thickness, simply pound the thicker ends of the breasts until they are all of uniform thickness. Though some breasts will still be larger, at least they will cook at the same rate.

Pan-Seared Chicken Breasts with Chickpea Salad
SERVES 4 **FAST**

WHY THIS RECIPE WORKS Hearty chickpeas are ideal as a salad component because they absorb flavors easily and provide texture and substance. We added the classic Mediterranean flavors of lemon, smoked paprika, cumin, and fresh mint to canned chickpeas for an easy accompaniment to quick-cooking pan-seared chicken breasts. Reserving a few tablespoons of the dressing for drizzling on the chicken before serving helped to reinforce the smoky, tangy flavors of the chickpea salad. Smoked sweet or smoked hot paprika can be used interchangeably in this recipe.

6 tablespoons extra-virgin olive oil

¼ cup lemon juice (2 lemons)

1 teaspoon honey

1 teaspoon smoked paprika

½ teaspoon ground cumin

 Salt and pepper

2 (15-ounce) cans chickpeas, rinsed

½ red onion, sliced thin

¼ cup chopped fresh mint

½ cup all-purpose flour

4 (4- to 6-ounce) boneless, skinless chicken breasts, trimmed

1. Whisk ¼ cup oil, lemon juice, honey, paprika, cumin, ½ teaspoon salt, and ½ teaspoon pepper together in large bowl until combined. Reserve 3 tablespoons dressing for serving. Add chickpeas, onion, and mint to remaining dressing and toss to combine. Season with salt and pepper to taste and set aside for serving.

2. Spread flour in shallow dish. Pound thicker ends of chicken breasts between 2 sheets of plastic wrap to uniform ½-inch thickness. Pat chicken dry with paper towels and season with salt and pepper. Working with 1 chicken breast at a time, dredge in flour to coat, shaking off any excess.

3. Heat remaining 2 tablespoons oil in 12-inch skillet over medium-high heat until just smoking. Place chicken in skillet and cook, turning as needed, until golden brown on both sides and chicken registers 160 degrees, about 10 minutes. Transfer chicken to serving platter, tent loosely with aluminum foil, and let rest for 5 minutes. Drizzle reserved dressing over chicken and serve with salad.

Chicken in Turkish Walnut Sauce

SERVES 4 `FAST`

WHY THIS RECIPE WORKS Circassian chicken is a dish of tender poached chicken served in a creamy walnut sauce and drizzled with chile or olive oil. It is commonly prepared on special occasions in Turkey and is often served at room temperature as a meze with wedges of pita bread. We were intrigued by its rich, nutty flavors and decided to develop our own version. We started with the chicken. Our favorite was boneless, skinless chicken breasts; they were easier to shred without any skin and bones in the way, and they cooked more quickly than bone-in, skin-on chicken. Looking for the right cooking method, we found our answer in a half-sautéing and half-poaching method. We browned the breasts on one side only, turned them, poured in some chicken broth, then gently simmered them until they were done. The broth that remained after cooking came into play not only to facilitate pureeing but also to add depth and chicken-y flavor to the sauce. This dish is mostly about the sauce, and we found that toasted walnuts added a deep nuttiness to it. The simple combination of sautéed onion and garlic, spiced with paprika for complexity and cayenne for a little heat, perfectly complemented the nuts. To give the sauce the right viscosity, we borrowed a traditional Turkish technique of pureeing bread with the other ingredients. A sprinkle of parsley and a bit of extra oil were the perfect simple garnish. This dish is commonly served at room temperature. To serve hot, transfer the sauce and chicken mixture to a large skillet and reheat over medium heat. Serve with fresh warm pitas.

4 (4- to 6-ounce) boneless, skinless chicken breasts, trimmed
  Salt and pepper
3 tablespoons extra-virgin olive oil, plus extra for serving
3 cups chicken broth
1 onion, chopped fine
4 teaspoons paprika
3 garlic cloves, minced
½ teaspoon cayenne pepper
2 slices hearty white sandwich bread, crusts removed, torn into 1-inch pieces
2 cups walnuts, toasted
2 tablespoons minced fresh parsley

1. Pound thicker ends of chicken breasts between 2 sheets of plastic wrap to uniform ½-inch thickness. Pat chicken dry with paper towels and season with salt and pepper. Heat 1 tablespoon oil in 12-inch skillet over medium-high heat until just smoking.

Pureeing pieces of bread with toasted walnuts and broth ensures a lush and creamy Turkish sauce for chicken.

Place chicken in skillet and cook until golden brown on first side, about 4 minutes. Flip chicken, add broth, and bring to simmer. Reduce heat to medium-low, cover, and cook until chicken registers 160 degrees, about 8 minutes.

2. Transfer chicken to cutting board, let cool slightly, then shred into bite-size pieces using 2 forks. Transfer chicken to large bowl and set aside. Strain and reserve broth, discarding white foam.

3. Wipe skillet clean with paper towels. Heat remaining 2 tablespoons oil in now-empty skillet over medium heat until shimmering. Add onion and ½ teaspoon salt and cook until softened, about 5 minutes. Stir in paprika, garlic, and cayenne and cook until fragrant, about 30 seconds.

4. Process onion mixture, bread, walnuts, and 2½ cups reserved broth in food processor until smooth, about 20 seconds, scraping down sides of bowl as needed. Adjust sauce consistency with remaining reserved broth as needed. (Sauce should be slightly thicker than heavy cream.) Add sauce to chicken and toss to coat. Season with salt and pepper to taste. Transfer chicken to serving platter, sprinkle with parsley, and drizzle with extra oil. Serve.

Spanish-Style Braised Chicken and Almonds

SERVES 8

WHY THIS RECIPE WORKS *Pollo en pepitoria* is a classic chicken dish from Spain's saffron-producing Castilla–La Mancha region that has a sherry-based sauce thickened with ground almonds and egg yolks. To balance the richness of the nuts and hard-cooked yolks in our version, we brightened the lush sauce with canned tomatoes (more consistent year-round than fresh tomatoes) and a little lemon juice. Adding some of the braising liquid to the nut mixture when we blended it to make the sauce helped it puree thoroughly but still retain a pleasantly coarse consistency. Chicken thighs are fully cooked when they reach 175 degrees, but we purposely overcooked them—and did it slowly—which allowed collagen in the meat to break down into gelatin, making the meat ultratender. We finished our dish with a sprinkle of chopped egg white. Any dry sherry, such as fino or Manzanilla, will work in this dish. Serve with crusty bread.

8 (5- to 7-ounce) bone-in chicken thighs, trimmed
  Salt and pepper
1 tablespoon extra-virgin olive oil
1 onion, chopped fine
3 garlic cloves, minced
1 bay leaf
¼ teaspoon ground cinnamon
⅔ cup dry sherry
1 cup chicken broth
1 (14.5-ounce) can whole peeled tomatoes, drained
  and chopped fine
2 hard-cooked large eggs, yolks and whites separated,
  whites chopped fine
½ cup slivered almonds, toasted
  Pinch saffron threads, crumbled
2 tablespoons chopped fresh parsley
1½ teaspoons lemon juice

1. Adjust oven rack to middle position and heat oven to 300 degrees. Pat chicken dry with paper towels and season with salt and pepper. Heat oil in 12-inch skillet over medium-high heat until just smoking. Brown thighs, 5 to 6 minutes per side. Transfer thighs to plate and pour off all but 2 teaspoons fat from skillet.

2. Add onion and ¼ teaspoon salt to fat left in skillet and cook over medium heat until just softened, about 3 minutes. Stir in two-thirds of garlic, bay leaf, and cinnamon and cook until

The rich flavor and consistency of this classic Spanish dish depends on a sherry-based sauce thickened with almonds.

fragrant, about 1 minute. Stir in sherry and cook, scraping up any browned bits, until sherry starts to thicken, about 2 minutes. Stir in broth and tomatoes and bring to simmer. Nestle thighs into skillet, cover, and transfer to oven. Cook until chicken registers 195 degrees, 45 to 50 minutes.

3. Using potholders, remove skillet from oven. Being careful of hot skillet handle, transfer thighs to serving platter, discard skin, and tent loosely with aluminum foil.

4. Discard bay leaf. Transfer ¾ cup cooking liquid, egg yolks, almonds, saffron, and remaining garlic to blender. Process until smooth, about 2 minutes, scraping down sides of jar as needed. Return almond mixture to skillet along with 1 tablespoon parsley and lemon juice. Bring to simmer over medium heat and cook, whisking frequently, until sauce has thickened, 3 to 5 minutes. Season with salt and pepper to taste. Spoon sauce over chicken and sprinkle with remaining 1 tablespoon parsley and egg whites. Serve.

Braised Chicken with Mushrooms and Tomatoes
SERVES 8

WHY THIS RECIPE WORKS Classic chicken *cacciatore*, an Italian stew that includes earthy mushrooms, tomatoes, and red wine, should boast moist meat and a silken, robust sauce. Too often, though, the chicken is dry and the sauce greasy and unbalanced. Using chicken thighs and removing the skin after rendering the fat solved the problems of dry meat, soggy skin, and greasy sauce in our Italian-inspired braise. Cooking the chicken in a combination of red wine, chicken broth, and diced tomatoes, seasoned with fresh thyme, yielded moist, well-seasoned chicken. Portobello mushrooms gave the dish a meatier flavor, and fresh sage, to finish, highlighted our braise's woodsy notes. The Parmesan cheese rind is optional, but we highly recommend it for the rich, savory flavor it adds to the dish.

8 (5- to 7-ounce) bone-in chicken thighs, trimmed
    Salt and pepper
1 tablespoon extra-virgin olive oil
1 onion, chopped
6 ounces portobello mushroom caps, cut into
    ¾-inch pieces
4 garlic cloves, minced
2 teaspoons minced fresh thyme
1½ tablespoons all-purpose flour
1½ cups dry red wine
½ cup chicken broth
1 (14.5-ounce) can diced tomatoes, drained
1 Parmesan cheese rind (optional)
2 teaspoons minced fresh sage

1. Adjust oven rack to middle position and heat oven to 300 degrees. Pat chicken dry with paper towels and season with salt and pepper. Heat oil in Dutch oven over medium-high heat until just smoking. Brown thighs, 5 to 6 minutes per side. Transfer thighs to plate and discard skin. Pour off all but 1 tablespoon fat from pot.

2. Add onion, mushrooms, and ½ teaspoon salt to fat left in pot and cook, stirring occasionally, until softened and beginning to brown, 6 to 8 minutes. Stir in garlic and thyme and cook until fragrant, about 30 seconds. Stir in flour and cook for 1 minute. Slowly whisk in wine, scraping up any browned bits and smoothing out any lumps.

3. Stir in broth, tomatoes, and cheese rind, if using, and bring to simmer. Nestle thighs into pot, cover, and transfer to oven. Cook until chicken registers 195 degrees, 35 to 40 minutes.

4. Remove pot from oven and transfer chicken to serving platter. Discard cheese rind, if using. Stir sage into sauce and season with salt and pepper to taste. Spoon sauce over chicken and serve.

We capture the essence of a traditional Moroccan dish using crisp-skinned chicken thighs and a savory serving sauce.

Roasted Chicken Thighs with Moroccan Pistachio and Currant Sauce
SERVES 8

WHY THIS RECIPE WORKS *B'stilla* is the dish with which to start a celebration in Morocco—a sweet and savory pie filled with meltingly tender game or chicken simmered in oil, cinnamon, nuts, and orange blossom water. It traditionally takes two days to make, but we loved the idea of capturing the essence of b'stilla in a weeknight meal. To mimic the shattering crispness of the pastry covering tender juicy meat, we turned to chicken thighs. We cooked them, skin side down, on a preheated baking sheet until the skin was browned and rendered. We then flipped the thighs over and put them under the broiler briefly to dry and crisp the skin. The result was chicken thighs with succulent and juicy meat under a sheer layer of crackly crisp, deeply browned skin. To pull together a sauce, we quick-caramelized shallots by jump-starting their cooking in the microwave and then finishing them in a foil packet in the oven while the chicken was cooking. For best results, trim all visible fat from the thighs. Use a heavy-duty rimmed baking sheet and fully preheat the oven and baking sheet before adding the chicken.

3 shallots, sliced thin (½ cup)
5 tablespoons extra-virgin olive oil
8 (5- to 7-ounce) bone-in chicken thighs, trimmed
   Salt and pepper
½ cup fresh parsley leaves
6 tablespoons water
¼ cup dried currants
¼ cup shelled pistachios, toasted
1 tablespoon lime juice
½ teaspoon ground cinnamon
¼ teaspoon orange blossom water

1. Adjust oven racks to middle and lowest positions, place rimmed baking sheet on lower rack, and heat oven to 450 degrees.

2. Toss shallots with 1 tablespoon oil in bowl. Cover and microwave until shallots are softened, about 3 minutes, stirring once halfway through microwaving. Place shallots in center of 12-inch square of aluminum foil. Cover with second 12-inch square of foil and fold edges together to create packet about 7 inches square; set aside.

3. Using metal skewer, poke skin side of chicken thighs 10 to 12 times. Pat thighs dry with paper towels, rub skin with 1 tablespoon oil, and season with salt and pepper. Place thighs skin side down on hot sheet and place foil packet on upper rack. Roast chicken until skin side is beginning to brown and chicken registers 160 degrees, 17 to 22 minutes, rotating sheet and removing foil packet after 10 minutes. Remove chicken from oven and heat broiler.

4. Flip chicken skin side up and broil on upper rack until skin is crisp and well browned and chicken registers 175 degrees, about 5 minutes, rotating sheet as needed for even browning. Transfer chicken to serving platter and let rest while preparing sauce.

5. Pulse shallots, parsley, water, currants, pistachios, lime juice, cinnamon, orange blossom water, and ¼ teaspoon salt in food processor until finely chopped, about 10 pulses. With processor running, slowly drizzle in remaining 3 tablespoons oil and process until incorporated, scraping down sides of bowl as needed. Season with salt and pepper to taste. Serve chicken with sauce.

VARIATION
Roasted Chicken Thighs with Fennel, Olive, and Orange Sauce
SERVES 8
For best results, trim all visible fat from the thighs. Use a heavy-duty baking sheet and fully preheat the oven and baking sheet before adding the chicken.

3 shallots, sliced thin (½ cup)
5 tablespoons extra-virgin olive oil
8 (5- to 7-ounce) bone-in chicken thighs, trimmed

   Salt and pepper
¾ cup fresh parsley leaves
¼ cup pitted oil-cured black olives, chopped
¼ cup water
2 teaspoons red wine vinegar
1 anchovy fillet, rinsed
1 teaspoon grated orange zest
½ teaspoon ground fennel seeds
¼ teaspoon red pepper flakes

1. Adjust oven racks to middle and lowest positions, place rimmed baking sheet on lower rack, and heat oven to 450 degrees.

2. Toss shallots with 1 tablespoon oil in bowl. Cover and microwave until shallots have softened, about 3 minutes, stirring once

Making Roasted Chicken Thighs

1. MAKE FOIL PACKET Place microwaved shallots in center of 12-inch square of aluminum foil. Cover with second 12-inch square of foil and fold edges together to create packet about 7 inches square.

2. POKE AND SEASON CHICKEN Using metal skewer, poke skin side of chicken thighs 10 to 12 times. Pat thighs dry with paper towels, rub skin with oil, and season with salt and pepper.

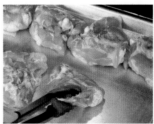

3. ROAST AND BROIL CHICKEN Place thighs skin side down on preheated sheet and roast until skin side is beginning to brown. Flip chicken and broil until skin is crisp and well browned.

4. PREPARE SAUCE Pulse shallots, parsley, water, currants, pistachios, lime juice, cinnamon, and orange blossom water until finely chopped, then slowly drizzle in oil and process until incorporated.

halfway through microwaving. Place shallots in center of 12-inch square of aluminum foil. Cover with second 12-inch square of foil and fold edges together to create packet about 7 inches square; set aside.

3. Using metal skewer, poke skin side of chicken thighs 10 to 12 times. Pat thighs dry with paper towels, rub skin with 1 tablespoon oil, and season with salt and pepper. Place thighs skin side down on hot sheet and place foil packet on upper rack. Roast chicken until skin side is beginning to brown and chicken registers 160 degrees, 17 to 22 minutes, rotating sheet and removing foil packet after 10 minutes. Remove chicken from oven and heat broiler.

4. Flip chicken skin side up and broil on upper rack until skin is crisp and well browned and chicken registers 175 degrees, about 5 minutes, rotating sheet as needed for even browning. Transfer chicken to serving platter and let rest while preparing sauce.

5. Pulse shallots, parsley, olives, water, vinegar, anchovy, orange zest, fennel seeds, pepper flakes, and ¼ teaspoon salt in food processor until finely chopped, about 10 pulses. With processor running, slowly drizzle in remaining 3 tablespoons oil and process until incorporated, scraping down sides of bowl as needed. Season with salt and pepper to taste. Serve chicken with sauce.

Za'atar-Rubbed Butterflied Chicken
SERVES 4

WHY THIS RECIPE WORKS For an easy but impressive weeknight dinner, we turned to a simple dish of chicken rubbed with *za'atar*. Za'atar is the Arabic name for wild thyme but now commonly denotes an addictive spice mixture of thyme, sumac, and sesame. So the fat would render quickly and the skin crisp, we borrowed an Italian technique of cooking under a brick (or a pot in this case). A thick za'atar paste contributed a strong complementary flavor to the chicken as it cooked through. Finishing the chicken breast side up in a hot oven turned the paste into a crust. While the chicken cooked, we created a zesty vinaigrette that brightened up the finished dish. We prefer to use our homemade Za'atar (page 316), but you can substitute store-bought za'atar if you wish, though flavor can vary by brand. If you can't find preserved lemons, you can make your own (page 252).

2 tablespoons za'atar
5 tablespoons plus 1 teaspoon extra-virgin olive oil
1 (3½- to 4-pound) whole chicken, giblets discarded
  Salt and pepper
1 tablespoon minced fresh mint
¼ preserved lemon, pulp and white pith removed, rind rinsed and minced (1 tablespoon)

A layer of the eastern Mediterranean spice blend *za'atar* adds a flavorful crust to simple roast chicken.

2 teaspoons white wine vinegar
½ teaspoon Dijon mustard

1. Adjust oven rack to lowest position and heat oven to 450 degrees. Combine za'atar and 2 tablespoons oil in small bowl. With chicken breast side down, use kitchen shears to cut through bones on either side of backbone. Discard backbone and trim away excess fat and skin around neck. Flip chicken and tuck wingtips behind back. Press firmly on breastbone to flatten, then pound breast to be same thickness as legs and thighs. Pat chicken dry with paper towels and season with salt and pepper.

2. Heat 1 teaspoon oil in 12-inch ovensafe skillet over medium-high heat until just smoking. Place chicken skin side down in skillet, reduce heat to medium, and place heavy pot on chicken to press it flat. Cook chicken until skin is crisp and browned, about 25 minutes. (If chicken is not crisp after 20 minutes, increase heat to medium-high.)

3. Off heat, remove pot and carefully flip chicken. Brush skin with za'atar mixture, transfer skillet to oven, and roast until breast registers 160 degrees and thighs register 175 degrees, 10 to 20 minutes.

4. Transfer chicken to carving board and let rest for 10 minutes. Meanwhile, whisk mint, preserved lemon, vinegar, mustard, ⅛ teaspoon salt, and ⅛ teaspoon pepper together in bowl until combined. Whisking constantly, slowly drizzle in remaining 3 tablespoons oil until emulsified. Carve chicken and serve with dressing.

Grilled Chicken alla Diavola

SERVES 4

WHY THIS RECIPE WORKS In Italian, *alla diavola* means "in the style of the devil," or in this case with heat from a good amount of red pepper flakes. Butterflying a chicken is a win-win when it comes to grilling. It allows the chicken to cook through more quickly and evenly and also exposes more skin to the grill so it can brown and become ultracrisp. But crisp skin and tender meat are only half the battle—the chicken has to be flavorful, too. To that end, we set out to infuse our bird with bold heat and garlicky flavor. Adding two heads of garlic to a brine was our first move. Next, we created a potent garlic-pepper oil and rubbed some under the skin of the chicken before grilling. For one last punch of flavor, we reserved some of the garlicky oil to serve with the chicken. If using a kosher chicken, do not brine in step 1. This dish is very spicy; for milder heat, reduce the amount of red pepper flakes.

- 2 garlic heads, plus 4 cloves minced
- 3 bay leaves
  Salt and pepper
- 1 (3½- to 4-pound) whole chicken, giblets discarded
- ¼ cup extra-virgin olive oil
- 2 teaspoons red pepper flakes
- 1 (13 by 9-inch) disposable aluminum roasting pan (if using charcoal)
  Lemon wedges

1. Combine garlic heads, bay leaves, and ½ cup salt in 1-gallon zipper-lock bag, crush gently with meat pounder, and transfer to large container. Stir in 2 quarts water to dissolve salt. With chicken breast side down, use kitchen shears to cut through bones on either side of backbone. Discard backbone and trim away excess fat and skin around neck. Flip chicken, press firmly on breastbone to flatten, then pound breast to be same thickness as legs and thighs. Submerge chicken in brine, cover, and refrigerate for 1 hour.

2. Meanwhile, cook oil, minced garlic, pepper flakes, and 2 teaspoons pepper in small saucepan over medium heat until fragrant, about 3 minutes. Let oil cool, then reserve 2 tablespoons for serving.

3. Remove chicken from brine and pat dry with paper towels. Gently loosen skin covering breast and thighs and rub remaining garlic-pepper oil underneath skin. Tuck wingtips behind back.

4A. FOR A CHARCOAL GRILL Open bottom vent completely and place disposable pan in center of grill. Light large chimney starter filled with charcoal briquettes (6 quarts). When top coals are partially covered with ash, pour into 2 even piles on either side of disposable pan. Set cooking grate in place, cover, and open lid vent completely. Heat grill until hot, about 5 minutes.

4B. FOR A GAS GRILL Turn all burners to high, cover, and heat grill until hot, about 15 minutes. Turn all burners to medium-low. (Adjust burners as needed to maintain grill temperature of 350 degrees.)

5. Clean and oil cooking grate. Place chicken skin side down in center of grill (over pan if using charcoal). Cover and cook until skin is crisp, breast registers 160 degrees, and thighs register 175 degrees, 30 to 45 minutes.

6. Transfer chicken to carving board and let rest for 5 to 10 minutes. Carve chicken and serve with reserved garlic oil and lemon wedges.

Butterflying a Chicken

1. Cut through bones on either side of backbone and trim any excess fat and skin around neck.

2. Flip chicken over and use heel of your hand to flatten breastbone.

3. Cover chicken with plastic wrap and pound breast to be same thickness as legs and thighs.

The chicken pieces in these kebabs are coated with a yogurt marinade to keep them from drying out on the grill.

Grilled Chicken Kebabs with Tomato-Feta Salad

SERVES 4 to 6

WHY THIS RECIPE WORKS Grilled meat on skewers is a popular form of Mediterranean fast food. We wanted an easy and foolproof recipe for chicken skewers. Since breast meat can dry out on the grill, we coated the chicken with a yogurt marinade to protect it. A fresh and quickly made salad using cherry tomatoes, feta, and red onion turned our kebabs into a meal. The yogurt dressing doubles as a finishing sauce for the chicken. You will need four 12-inch metal skewers for this recipe.

¼ cup extra-virgin olive oil
1 teaspoon grated lemon zest plus 3 tablespoons juice
3 garlic cloves, minced
1 tablespoon minced fresh oregano
  Salt and pepper
1 pound cherry tomatoes, halved
4 ounces feta cheese, crumbled (1 cup)

¼ cup thinly sliced red onion
¼ cup plain yogurt
1½ pounds boneless, skinless chicken breasts, trimmed and cut into 1-inch pieces

1. Whisk oil, lemon zest and juice, garlic, oregano, ½ teaspoon salt, and ½ teaspoon pepper together in medium bowl. Reserve half of oil mixture in second medium bowl. Add tomatoes, feta, and onion to remaining oil mixture and toss to coat. Season with salt and pepper to taste and set aside for serving.

2. Whisk yogurt into reserved oil mixture. Set aside half of yogurt dressing for serving. Add chicken to remaining yogurt dressing and toss to coat. Thread chicken onto four 12-inch metal skewers.

3A. FOR A CHARCOAL GRILL Open bottom vent completely. Light large chimney starter filled with charcoal briquettes (6 quarts). When top coals are partially covered with ash, pour evenly over grill. Set cooking grate in place, cover, and open lid vent completely. Heat grill until hot, about 5 minutes.

3B. FOR A GAS GRILL Turn all burners to high, cover, and heat grill until hot, about 15 minutes. Leave all burners on high.

4. Place skewers on grill and cook, turning occasionally, until chicken is well browned and registers 160 degrees, about 10 minutes. Using tongs, slide chicken off skewers onto serving platter. Serve chicken with salad and reserved dressing.

Grilled Chicken Souvlaki

SERVES 4 to 6

WHY THIS RECIPE WORKS Souvlaki is a Greek specialty consisting of chunks of marinated meat threaded onto skewers, sometimes with chunks of vegetables such as green pepper and onion, and grilled. Chicken souvlaki is almost always made with boneless, skinless breasts, which have a marked tendency to dry out when grilled. To prevent this, we swapped the traditional overnight soak in an acidic marinade for a quick 30-minute brine while the grill heated. We then tossed the chunks of chicken with a classic and flavorful mixture of lemon, olive oil, herbs, and honey right before grilling. To prevent the end pieces from overcooking, we protected the chicken by threading pepper and onion pieces on the ends of the skewers. Once the chicken was cooked, we tossed it with the reserved marinade to ensure that the exterior was brightly flavored and just as tender and moist as the interior. We like the chicken in a wrap, but you may skip the pita and serve the chicken, vegetables, and Tzatziki with rice. If using kosher chicken, do not brine in step 1. You will need four 12-inch metal skewers for this recipe. We prefer to use our homemade Pita Bread (page 344), but you can use store-bought.

Salt and pepper

1½ pounds boneless, skinless chicken breasts, trimmed and cut into 1-inch pieces

⅓ cup extra-virgin olive oil

2 tablespoons minced fresh parsley

1 teaspoon finely grated lemon zest plus ¼ cup juice (2 lemons)

1 teaspoon honey

1 teaspoon dried oregano

1 green bell pepper, quartered, stemmed, seeded, and each quarter cut into 4 pieces

1 small red onion, halved through root end, each half cut into 4 chunks

4-6 (8-inch) pita breads

1 cup Tzatziki (page 19)

1. Dissolve 2 tablespoons salt in 1 quart cold water in large container. Submerge chicken in brine, cover, and refrigerate for 30 minutes. Combine oil, parsley, lemon zest and juice, honey, oregano, and ½ teaspoon pepper in medium bowl. Reserve ¼ cup oil mixture in large bowl.

2. Remove chicken from brine and pat dry with paper towels. Toss chicken with remaining oil mixture. Thread 4 pieces of bell pepper, concave side up, onto one 12-inch metal skewer. Thread one-quarter of chicken onto skewer. Thread 2 chunks of onion onto skewer and place skewer on plate. Repeat skewering remaining chicken and vegetables on 3 more skewers. Lightly moisten 2 pita breads with water. Sandwich unmoistened pitas between moistened pitas and wrap stack tightly in lightly greased heavy-duty aluminum foil.

3A. FOR A CHARCOAL GRILL Open bottom vent completely. Light large chimney starter mounded with charcoal briquettes (7 quarts). When top coals are partially covered with ash, pour evenly over half of grill. Set cooking grate in place, cover, and open lid vent completely. Heat grill until hot, about 5 minutes.

3B. FOR A GAS GRILL Turn all burners to high, cover, and heat grill until hot, about 15 minutes. Leave primary burner on high and turn off other burner(s).

4. Clean and oil cooking grate. Place skewers on hotter side of grill and cook, turning occasionally, until chicken and vegetables are well browned and chicken registers 160 degrees, 15 to 20 minutes. Using tongs, slide chicken and vegetables off skewers into bowl of reserved oil mixture. Toss gently, breaking up onion chunks. Cover loosely with foil and let sit while heating pitas.

5. Place packet of pitas on cooler side of grill and flip occasionally until heated through, about 5 minutes. Lay each warm pita on 12-inch square of foil. Spread each pita with 2 tablespoons Tzatziki. Place one-quarter of chicken and vegetables in middle of each pita. Roll into cylindrical shape and serve.

To keep the chicken skin crisp we rest the chicken pieces on the potatoes above the liquid as they cook in the oven.

Chicken Bouillabaisse
SERVES 6

WHY THIS RECIPE WORKS Bouillabaisse is a traditional French stew bursting with fish and shellfish and the flavors of Provence. We thought its potent flavors would work just as well with chicken. Adapting the recipe for this famous stew involved several steps: We substituted canned chicken broth for fish stock and added flour and tomato paste to the saffron and cayenne before adding the broth to give the sauce extra body. White wine and orange zest brought complexity to the broth, and adding the pastis, an anise-flavored liqueur, early on gave the alcohol time to cook off and leave behind a hint of sweetness. To help the chicken skin stay crisp after browning, we switched from stovetop to oven cooking. We rested the chicken on the potatoes as the bouillabaisse cooked in the oven so that the skin stayed out of the liquid and remained crisp. A finishing blast from the broiler before serving further enhanced the crispness. Serve with Rouille (page 302) and Garlic Toasts (page 56), if desired.

ROUILLE

MAKES 1 cup `FAST` `VEG`

Leftover Rouille will keep refrigerated for up to 1 week and can be used as a sauce for vegetables and fish.

  3 tablespoons boiling water
  ¼ teaspoon saffron threads, crumbled
  1 (3-inch) piece baguette, crusts removed, torn into 1-inch pieces (1 cup)
  4 teaspoons lemon juice
  1 large egg yolk
  2 teaspoons Dijon mustard
  2 small garlic cloves, minced
  ¼ teaspoon cayenne pepper
  ½ cup vegetable oil
  ½ cup extra-virgin olive oil
    Salt and pepper

Combine boiling water and saffron in medium bowl and let steep for 5 minutes. Stir bread pieces and lemon juice into saffron-infused water and let soak for 5 minutes. Using whisk, mash soaked bread mixture until uniform paste forms, 1 to 2 minutes. Whisk in egg yolk, mustard, garlic, and cayenne until smooth, about 15 seconds. Whisking constantly, slowly drizzle in vegetable oil until smooth mayonnaise-like consistency is reached, scraping down bowl as necessary. Slowly whisk in olive oil in steady stream until smooth. Season with salt and pepper to taste.

  3 pounds bone-in chicken pieces (split breasts cut in half, drumsticks, and/or thighs), trimmed
    Salt and pepper
  2 tablespoons extra-virgin olive oil
  1 large leek, white and light green parts only, halved lengthwise, sliced thin, and washed thoroughly
  1 small fennel bulb, stalks discarded, bulb halved, cored, and sliced thin
  4 garlic cloves, minced
  1 tablespoon tomato paste
  1 tablespoon all-purpose flour
  ¼ teaspoon saffron threads, crumbled
  ¼ teaspoon cayenne pepper
  3 cups chicken broth
  1 (14.5-ounce) can diced tomatoes, drained
 12 ounces Yukon Gold potatoes, unpeeled, cut into ¾-inch pieces
  ½ cup dry white wine
  ¼ cup pastis or Pernod
  1 (3-inch) strip orange zest
  1 tablespoon chopped fresh tarragon or parsley

1. Adjust oven racks to upper-middle and lowest positions and heat oven to 375 degrees. Pat chicken dry with paper towels and season with salt and pepper. Heat oil in Dutch oven over medium-high heat until just smoking. Brown chicken well, 5 to 8 minutes per side; transfer to plate.

2. Add leek and fennel to fat left in pot and cook, stirring often, until beginning to soften and turn translucent, about 4 minutes. Stir in garlic, tomato paste, flour, saffron, and cayenne and cook

Making Chicken Bouillabaisse

1. BUILD BASE Brown chicken, then cook leeks, fennel, and aromatics. Stir in broth, tomatoes, potatoes, wine, pastis, and orange zest and bring to simmer.

2. NESTLE CHICKEN AND BAKE Place chicken on potatoes with skin above surface of liquid and bake until breasts register 145 degrees and thighs/drumsticks register 160 degrees.

3. BROIL Return pot to oven and broil until chicken skin is crisp and breasts register 160 degrees and drumsticks/thighs register 175 degrees.

4. FINISH AND SERVE Skim excess fat from surface of stew, then stir in tarragon and season with salt and pepper to taste.

until fragrant, about 30 seconds. Slowly whisk in broth, scraping up any browned bits and smoothing out any lumps. Stir in tomatoes, potatoes, wine, pastis, and orange zest. Bring to simmer and cook for 10 minutes.

3. Nestle chicken thighs and drumsticks into pot with skin above surface of liquid. Cook, uncovered, for 5 minutes. Nestle breast pieces into pot, adjusting pieces as necessary to ensure that skin stays above surface of liquid. Transfer pot to upper rack and cook, uncovered, until breasts register 145 degrees and thighs/drumsticks register 160 degrees, 10 to 20 minutes.

4. Remove pot from oven and heat broiler. Return pot to oven and broil until chicken skin is crisp and breasts register 160 degrees and drumsticks/thighs register 175 degrees, 5 to 10 minutes (smaller pieces may cook faster than larger pieces; remove individual pieces as they reach correct temperature and return to pot before serving).

5. Using large spoon, skim excess fat from surface of stew. Stir in tarragon and season with salt and pepper to taste. Serve in wide, shallow bowls.

Chicken Tagine with Chickpeas and Apricots
SERVES 8

WHY THIS RECIPE WORKS Tagines are a North African specialty: exotically spiced, assertively flavored stews slow-cooked in earthenware vessels of the same name. They can include all manner of meats, vegetables, and fruit. Traditional recipes usually require a time-consuming cooking method, a special pot (the tagine), and hard-to-find ingredients; we wanted to make tagine more accessible. First off, we found that braising in a Dutch oven was a serviceable substitute for stewing for hours in a tagine. Almost all of the recipes we collected called for a whole chicken, cut into pieces. The batches we made with both white and dark meat had more depth and character than those with just white meat. We gave the dark meat a head start to ensure that all of the chicken was ready at the same time. Chickpeas, carrots, onion, and garlic rounded out the stew. Next we tackled the defining spices. The spice blend for tagines can contain upward of 30 spices; we experimented until we landed on a blend that was short on ingredients but long on flavor. Cumin and ginger lent depth, cinnamon brought warmth that tempered a little cayenne heat, and citrusy coriander boosted the stew's lemon flavor (as did a couple of broad ribbons of lemon zest); paprika colored the broth a deep, attractive red and lent a pleasant sweetness, as did dried apricots. Serve with Simple Couscous (page 161).

3 (2-inch) strips lemon zest plus 3 tablespoons juice
5 garlic cloves, minced
4 pounds bone-in chicken pieces (split breasts cut in half, drumsticks, and/or thighs), trimmed

We fill our chicken tagine with heady North African spices but temper them with a little honey and dried apricots.

   Salt and pepper
2 tablespoons extra-virgin olive oil
1 large onion, halved and sliced ¼ inch thick
1¼ teaspoons paprika
½ teaspoon ground cumin
¼ teaspoon cayenne pepper
¼ teaspoon ground ginger
¼ teaspoon ground coriander
¼ teaspoon ground cinnamon
2 cups chicken broth
2 carrots, peeled, halved lengthwise, and sliced ½ inch thick
1 (15-ounce) can chickpeas, rinsed
1 tablespoon honey
1 cup dried apricots, halved
2 tablespoons chopped fresh cilantro

1. Mince 1 strip lemon zest and combine with 1 teaspoon garlic in bowl; set aside.

2. Pat chicken dry with paper towels and season with salt and pepper. Heat oil in Dutch oven over medium-high heat until just smoking. Brown half of chicken well, 5 to 8 minutes per side;

transfer to large plate. Repeat with remaining chicken; transfer to plate. Pour off all but 1 tablespoon fat from pot.

3. Add onion and remaining 2 lemon zest strips to fat left in pot and cook over medium heat until softened, about 5 minutes. Stir in remaining garlic, paprika, cumin, cayenne, ginger, coriander, and cinnamon and cook until fragrant, about 1 minute. Stir in broth, scraping up any browned bits. Stir in carrots, chickpeas, and honey and bring to simmer.

4. Nestle chicken into pot along with any accumulated juices and bring to simmer. Reduce heat to medium-low, cover, and cook until breasts register 160 degrees and drumsticks/thighs register 175 degrees, about 20 minutes for breasts and 1 hour for thighs and drumsticks. (If using both types of chicken, simmer thighs and drumsticks for 40 minutes before adding breasts.)

5. Transfer chicken to bowl, tent loosely with aluminum foil, and let rest while finishing sauce. Discard lemon zest. Using large spoon, skim excess fat from surface of sauce. Stir in apricots, return sauce to simmer over medium heat, and cook until apricots are heated through, about 5 minutes. Return chicken and any accumulated juices to pot. Stir in cilantro, lemon juice, and garlic–lemon zest mixture. Season with salt and pepper to taste. Serve.

VARIATION

Lamb Tagine with Olives and Lemon
If desired, the lamb can be pulled off the bone and shredded before it is returned to the pot in step 5.

Omit chickpeas. Substitute 3½ pounds lamb shoulder chops (blade or round bone), 1 to 1½ inches thick, trimmed and halved, for chicken pieces and 1 cup pitted brine-cured green olives, halved, for apricots. Brown lamb as directed in step 2, then simmer until tender, about 1 hour, in step 4.

Pomegranate-Glazed Roasted Quail
SERVES 4

WHY THIS RECIPE WORKS These tiny game birds are prized throughout the Mediterranean for their delicate flavor, which is milder and sweeter than that of many other game birds. As they can be so small, we found the major challenge was to get the skin golden brown before the flesh overcooked. Brining and drying the skin well insured us somewhat against this latter risk at the expense of the former. Direct heat from a just-smoking skillet allowed all the surface moisture to be shed and jump-started our browning process. Finishing the birds in a 500-degree oven furthered the bronzing and didn't allow enough time for the quail to dry out. Turning to a classic eastern Mediterranean staple, we glazed the skin with pomegranate molasses in two applications. This not only richly burnished the skin but offered complementary

Pomegranate molasses makes a great glaze for quail because it clings nicely and its sugars help the skin brown.

sweet, sour, and fruity notes. Cinnamon and thyme contributed a warming woodsiness that paired well with our perfectly cooked meat. Quail is often sold with the neck still attached; you can remove it with kitchen shears, if desired. If you can't find pomegranate molasses, you can make your own (page 305).

    Salt and pepper
8 (5- to 7-ounce) whole quail, giblets discarded
2 tablespoons extra-virgin olive oil
6 tablespoons pomegranate molasses
1 tablespoon minced fresh thyme
1 teaspoon ground cinnamon

1. Adjust oven rack to upper-middle position and heat oven to 500 degrees. Set wire rack in aluminum foil–lined rimmed baking sheet and spray with vegetable oil spray. Dissolve ½ cup salt in 2 quarts water in large container. Submerge quail in brine and refrigerate for 20 minutes.

2. Remove quail from brine, pat dry with paper towels, and season with pepper. Working with 1 quail at a time, make incision through meat of one drumstick, using tip of paring knife, about

½ inch from tip of drumstick bone. Carefully insert other drumstick through incision so legs are securely crossed. Tuck wingtips behind back.

3. Heat 1 tablespoon oil in 12-inch skillet over medium-high heat until just smoking. Brown 4 quail on all sides, about 4 minutes; transfer to prepared rack. Repeat with remaining 1 tablespoon oil and remaining 4 quail.

4. Combine pomegranate molasses, thyme, cinnamon, and ⅛ teaspoon salt in bowl. Brush quail evenly with half of pomegranate molasses mixture and roast for 5 minutes. Brush quail with remaining pomegranate molasses mixture and continue to roast until well browned and breasts register 160 degrees and thighs register 175 degrees, 7 to 13 minutes. Transfer quail to serving platter and let rest for 5 minutes. Serve.

POMEGRANATE MOLASSES

MAKES ⅔ cup `FAST` `VEG`

If you overreduce the syrup in step 2, you can slowly whisk in warm water as needed to measure ⅔ cup.

 2 tablespoons water
 1 tablespoon sugar
 4 cups unsweetened pomegranate juice
 2 teaspoons lemon juice

1. Combine water and sugar in medium saucepan until sugar is completely moistened. Bring to boil over medium-high heat and cook until sugar begins to turn golden, 2 to 3 minutes, gently swirling saucepan as needed to ensure even cooking. Continue to cook until sugar begins to smoke and is color of peanut butter, about 1 minute. Off heat, let caramel sit until mahogany brown, 45 to 60 seconds. Carefully swirl in 2 tablespoons pomegranate juice until incorporated; mixture will bubble and steam. Slowly whisk in remaining pomegranate juice and lemon juice, scraping up any caramel.

2. Bring mixture to boil over high heat and cook, stirring occasionally, until tight, slow-popping bubbles cover surface and syrup measures ⅔ cup, 30 to 35 minutes. Let cool slightly, then transfer to container and continue to cool to room temperature. (Pomegranate molasses can be refrigerated in airtight container for up to 1 month.)

Preparing Quail for Roasting

1. Using tip of paring knife, make incision through meat of 1 drumstick, about ½ inch from tip of drumstick bone.

2. Carefully insert other drumstick through incision so legs are securely crossed.

3. Tuck wingtips behind back.

Kibbeh
MAKES 16

WHY THIS RECIPE WORKS *Kibbeh*—a mixture of bulgur, onion, finely ground meat, and spices—is a central part of Lebanese and Syrian cuisines and is popular throughout the eastern Mediterranean. There are many preparations: Kibbeh *nayyeh* is served raw, like a tartare, with greens, herbs, bread, and condiments; kibbeh *bil sanieh* is layered with filling and baked; and kibbeh *bil laban* is formed into balls and cooked in a yogurt sauce. The most popular kibbeh, however, is a hearty croquette, made by stuffing the kibbeh mixture with a filling of meat, onions, pine nuts, and spices, which is then deep-fried. Our goal was to develop an easy recipe for these crowd-pleasing, protein-packed morsels that was at once rich and satisfying, but also delicate and relatively light. Traditionally, meat, bulgur, onions, and spices are pounded in a mortar and pestle to create a very smooth, doughlike paste. We opted for 1 minute in the food processor, and then chilled our dough while we made a flavorful filling of lamb, onion, pine nuts, spices, and a touch of pomegranate molasses. We carefully stuffed our kibbeh, molded them into the traditional torpedo shape, and then, rather than deep-frying them, we found we could achieve a crisp, golden crust by shallow-frying them in a skillet. Note that the dough and the filled kibbeh require 30 minutes of chilling time each. When shopping, do not confuse bulgur with cracked wheat, which has a much longer cooking time and will not work in this recipe. If you can't find pomegranate molasses, you can make your own (see page 305). Serve with Yogurt-Herb Sauce (page 233), if desired.

DOUGH

- 1 cup medium-grind bulgur, rinsed
- 1 cup water
- 8 ounces ground lamb
- 1 small onion, chopped
- ½ teaspoon ground cinnamon
- ½ teaspoon salt
- ¼ teaspoon pepper

FILLING

- 1 teaspoon extra-virgin olive oil
- 8 ounces ground lamb
  Salt and pepper
- 1 small onion, chopped fine
- ½ cup pine nuts, toasted
- ½ teaspoon ground cinnamon
- ⅛ teaspoon ground allspice
- 1 tablespoon pomegranate molasses
- 2 cups vegetable oil

1. FOR THE DOUGH Combine bulgur and water in bowl and let sit until grains begin to soften, 30 to 40 minutes. Drain bulgur well and transfer to bowl of food processor. Add lamb, onion, cinnamon, salt, and pepper and process to smooth paste, about 1 minute, scraping down sides of bowl as needed. Transfer dough to bowl, cover, and refrigerate until chilled, about 30 minutes.

2. FOR THE FILLING Heat oil in 12-inch skillet over medium-high heat until just smoking. Add lamb, ½ teaspoon salt, and ¼ teaspoon pepper and cook, breaking up meat with wooden spoon, until browned, 3 to 5 minutes. Using slotted spoon, transfer meat to paper towel–lined plate. Pour off all but 1 tablespoon fat from skillet.

3. Add onion to fat left in skillet and cook over medium heat until softened, about 5 minutes. Stir in pine nuts, cinnamon, and allspice and cook until fragrant, about 30 seconds. Off heat, stir in lamb and pomegranate molasses and season with salt and pepper to taste.

4. Line rimmed baking sheet with parchment paper and grease parchment. Pinch off and roll dough into 2-inch balls (16 balls total). Working with 1 dough ball at a time, use your lightly oiled hands to press and stretch dough into rough cup with ¼-inch-thick sides. Spoon 1 tablespoon filling into cup, pressing gently to pack filling, and pinch seam closed. Gently form kibbeh into 3 by 1½-inch torpedo shape with tapered ends and transfer to prepared sheet. Cover and refrigerate kibbeh until firm, at least 30 minutes or up to 24 hours.

5. Adjust oven rack to middle position and heat oven to 200 degrees. Set wire rack in second rimmed baking sheet and line with triple layer of paper towels. Heat oil in clean 12-inch skillet over medium-high heat to 375 degrees. Fry half of kibbeh until deep golden brown, 2 to 3 minutes per side. Adjust burner, if necessary, to maintain oil temperature of 375 degrees. Using slotted spoon, transfer kibbeh to prepared rack and keep warm in oven. Return oil to 375 degrees and repeat with remaining kibbeh. Serve.

Forming Kibbeh

1. Using your lightly oiled hands, press and stretch dough ball into rough cup with ¼-inch-thick sides.

2. Spoon 1 tablespoon filling into cup, pressing gently to pack filling, and pinch seam closed.

3. Gently form kibbeh into 3 by 1½-inch torpedo shape with tapered ends.

Grilled Beef Kebabs with Lemon and Rosemary Marinade

SERVES 4 to 6

WHY THIS RECIPE WORKS Well-marbled steak tips, with their beefy flavor and tender texture, proved the best choice for our grilled beef kebabs. We created a robust marinade using several key elements: Beef broth and tomato paste added rich, umami tones, salt helped brine the meat and keep it moist, a bit of sugar helped with caramelization, and rosemary and lemon zest added bright aromas. (For a spicy North African variation, we used cilantro, paprika, cumin, and cayenne.) We cut the meat into large pieces and packed it tightly onto the skewers to help keep it moist and tender while grilling and also patted it dry to help prevent steaming. We paired our beef with a trio of firm and flavorful vegetables that came into their own when grilled: peppers, red onions, and zucchini. If you can't find sirloin steak tips, sometimes labeled "flap meat," substitute 2 pounds of blade steak (if using, cut each steak in half to remove the gristle). You will need six 12-inch metal skewers for this recipe. If you have long, thin pieces of meat, roll or fold them into approximate 2-inch cubes before skewering. We prefer these kebabs cooked to medium-rare, but if you prefer them more or less done, see the chart on page 310.

MARINADE

- 1 onion, chopped
- ⅓ cup beef broth
- ⅓ cup extra-virgin olive oil
- 3 tablespoons tomato paste
- 6 garlic cloves, chopped
- 2 tablespoons chopped fresh rosemary
- 2 teaspoons grated lemon zest
- 2 teaspoons salt
- 1½ teaspoons sugar
- ¾ teaspoon pepper

BEEF AND VEGETABLES

- 1½ pounds sirloin steak tips, trimmed and cut into 2-inch pieces
- 2 zucchini or yellow summer squash, halved lengthwise and sliced 1 inch thick
- 2 red or green bell peppers, stemmed, seeded, and cut into 1½-inch pieces
- 2 red onions, cut into 1-inch pieces, 3 layers thick

1. FOR THE MARINADE Process all ingredients in blender until smooth, about 45 seconds, scraping down sides of blender jar as needed. Transfer ¾ cup marinade to large bowl and set aside.

2. FOR THE BEEF AND VEGETABLES Place remaining marinade and beef in 1-gallon zipper-lock bag and toss to coat. Press

Skewering the beef and vegetables separately for these kebabs ensures that each of the components cooks perfectly.

out as much air as possible and seal bag. Refrigerate for at least 1 hour or up to 2 hours, flipping bag every 30 minutes.

3. Add zucchini, bell peppers, and onions to bowl with reserved marinade and toss to coat. Cover and let sit at room temperature for at least 30 minutes.

4. Remove beef from bag and pat dry with paper towels. Thread beef tightly onto two 12-inch metal skewers. In alternating pattern of zucchini, bell pepper, and onion, thread vegetables onto four 12-inch metal skewers.

5A. FOR A CHARCOAL GRILL Open bottom vent completely. Light large chimney starter mounded with charcoal briquettes (7 quarts). When top coals are partially covered with ash, pour evenly over center of grill, leaving 2-inch gap between grill wall and charcoal. Set cooking grate in place, cover, and open lid vent completely. Heat grill until hot, about 5 minutes.

5B. FOR A GAS GRILL Turn all burners to high, cover, and heat grill until hot, about 15 minutes. Leave primary burner on high and turn other burner(s) to medium-low.

6. Clean and oil cooking grate. Place beef skewers on grill (directly over coals if using charcoal or over hotter side of grill if using gas). Place vegetable skewers on grill (near edge of coals but still over coals if using charcoal or on cooler side of grill if using gas). Cook (covered if using gas), turning skewers every 3 to 4 minutes, until beef is well browned and registers 120 to 125 degrees (for medium-rare), 12 to 16 minutes. Transfer beef skewers to serving platter, tent loosely with aluminum foil, and let rest while finishing vegetables.

7. Continue to cook vegetable skewers until tender and lightly charred, about 5 minutes; transfer to platter. Using tongs, slide beef and vegetables off skewers onto platter. Serve.

VARIATION

Grilled Beef Kebabs with North African Marinade

Substitute 20 cilantro sprigs, 2 teaspoons paprika, 1½ teaspoons ground cumin, and ½ teaspoon cayenne pepper for rosemary and lemon zest.

Preparing Onions for Kebabs

1. Peel onion, trim off root and stem ends, then quarter onion.

2. Pull apart onion into sections that are 3 layers thick; discard core.

3. Cut each 3-layer section into 1-inch pieces.

4. Skewer onion through center of each piece.

Sweet peppers quickly cooked in olive oil make the perfect Italian condiment with tender slices of spice-rubbed steak.

Flank Steak Peperonata
SERVES 4 to 6

WHY THIS RECIPE WORKS *Peperonata* is an Italian mixture of sweet peppers, onion, tomato, and garlic cooked in fruity olive oil until the peppers are soft and the flavors have melded. To pair with it, we cut flank steak with the grain into three equal pieces, seasoned all sides with salt, pepper, and oregano, and wrapped the pieces in plastic for up to 24 hours to fully season the meat. Then we cooked red and yellow bell peppers, onion, and garlic in a hefty amount of extra-virgin olive oil until softened, added diced tomatoes, capers, and red pepper flakes, and cooked the mixture until the vegetables were softened. After wiping out the skillet, we seared the seasoned steak pieces on all sides to a perfect medium-rare. While the meat rested, we stirred fresh basil into the peperonata mixture. To serve, we sliced the meat into smaller pieces, against the grain, seasoned the slices with salt and pepper and the accumulated meat juices, and arranged the meat with the peperonata. A drizzle of extra-virgin olive oil balanced the tangy, meaty flavors. We prefer flank steak cooked to medium-rare, but if you prefer it more or less done, see the chart on page 310.

2 teaspoons dried oregano
  Salt and pepper
1 (1½-pound) flank steak, trimmed
⅓ cup plus 1 tablespoon extra-virgin olive oil, plus extra
  for serving
4 red or yellow bell peppers, quartered, stemmed,
  seeded, and cut crosswise into ¼-inch-wide strips
1 onion, quartered through root end and sliced crosswise
  into ¼-inch-wide strips
6 garlic cloves, lightly crushed and peeled
1 (14.5-ounce) can diced tomatoes
2 tablespoons capers plus 4 teaspoons caper brine
⅛ teaspoon red pepper flakes
½ cup chopped fresh basil

1. Combine oregano and 1 teaspoon salt in bowl. Cut steak with grain into 3 equal pieces. Sprinkle steak with oregano mixture, wrap tightly in plastic wrap, and refrigerate for at least 30 minutes or up to 24 hours.

2. Heat ⅓ cup oil in 12-inch nonstick skillet over medium-high heat until just smoking. Add bell peppers, onion, garlic, and ½ teaspoon salt. Cover and cook, stirring occasionally, until vegetables are soft, about 10 minutes.

3. Stir in tomatoes and their juice, capers and brine, and pepper flakes and cook, uncovered, until slightly thickened, about 5 minutes. Season with salt and pepper to taste. Transfer peperonata to bowl, cover, and keep warm.

4. Wipe skillet clean with paper towels. Pat steaks dry with paper towels and season with pepper. Heat remaining 1 tablespoon oil in now-empty skillet over medium-high heat until just smoking. Cook steaks until well browned and meat registers 120 to 125 degrees (for medium-rare), 5 to 7 minutes per side. Transfer steaks to carving board, tent loosely with aluminum foil, and let rest for 10 minutes.

5. Stir basil into peperonata. Slice steaks thin against grain on bias. Season steak slices with salt and pepper and drizzle with extra oil. Serve steak with peperonata.

Grilled Flank Steak with Grilled Vegetables and Salsa Verde

SERVES 4 to 6

WHY THIS RECIPE WORKS Rich and beefy flank steak is thin, flat, and quick-cooking, making it ideal for grilling. It is also relatively inexpensive, so you can serve it at a dinner party without breaking the bank. We paired it with our pungent, easy-to-make

A fresh Italian green sauce packed with herbs, capers, and anchovies is an ideal accent to grilled flank steak.

Italian Salsa Verde (page 310)—packed with fresh parsley and mint, capers, anchovies, and garlic—and elevated this simple char-grilled steak to company-worthy status. Following the Italian garden-party theme, we chose fresh zucchini, earthy eggplant, aromatic red onion, and sweet cherry tomatoes for our vegetable skewers, taking care to grill each element to perfection. You will need four 12-inch metal skewers for this recipe. We prefer flank steak cooked to medium-rare, but if you prefer it more or less done, see the chart on page 310.

1 red onion, sliced into ½-inch-thick rounds
8 ounces cherry tomatoes
2 zucchini, sliced lengthwise into ¾-inch-thick planks
1 pound eggplant, sliced lengthwise into ¾-inch-
  thick planks
2 tablespoons extra-virgin olive oil
1½ pounds flank steak, trimmed
  Salt and pepper
½ cup Italian Salsa Verde (page 310)

1. Thread onion rounds from side to side onto two 12-inch metal skewers. Thread cherry tomatoes onto two 12-inch metal skewers. Brush onion rounds, tomatoes, zucchini, and eggplant with oil and season with salt and pepper. Pat steak dry with paper towels and season with salt and pepper.

2A. FOR A CHARCOAL GRILL Open bottom grill vent completely. Light large chimney starter filled with charcoal briquettes (6 quarts). When top coals are partially covered with ash, pour evenly over grill. Set cooking grate in place, cover, and open lid vent completely. Heat grill until hot, about 5 minutes.

2B. FOR A GAS GRILL Turn all burners to high, cover, and heat grill until hot, about 15 minutes. Leave all burners on high.

3. Clean and oil cooking grate. Place steak, onion and tomato skewers, zucchini, and eggplant on grill. Cook (covered if using gas), flipping steak and turning vegetables as needed, until steak is well browned and registers 120 to 125 degrees (for medium-rare) and vegetables are slightly charred and tender, 7 to 12 minutes. Transfer steak and vegetables to carving board as they finish grilling and tent loosely with aluminum foil. Let steak rest for 10 minutes.

4. Meanwhile, slide tomatoes and onions off skewers using tongs. Cut onion rounds, zucchini, and eggplant into 2- to 3-inch pieces. Arrange vegetables on serving platter and season with salt and pepper to taste. Slice steak thin against grain on bias and arrange on platter with vegetables. Drizzle steak with ¼ cup Salsa Verde. Serve, passing remaining sauce separately.

ITALIAN SALSA VERDE

MAKES 1 cup FAST

    3 cups fresh parsley leaves
    1 cup fresh mint leaves
    ½ cup extra-virgin olive oil
    3 tablespoons white wine vinegar
    2 tablespoons capers, rinsed
    3 anchovy fillets, rinsed
    1 garlic clove, minced
    ⅛ teaspoon salt

Pulse all ingredients in food processor until mixture is finely chopped (mixture should not be smooth), about 10 pulses, scraping down sides of bowl as needed. Transfer mixture to bowl and serve. (Sauce can be refrigerated for up to 2 days; bring to room temperature before serving.)

NOTES FROM THE TEST KITCHEN

Taking the Temperature of Meat and Poultry

Since the temperature of beef and pork will continue to rise as the meat rests—an effect called carryover cooking—they should be removed from the oven, grill, or pan when they are 5 to 10 degrees below the desired serving temperature. Carryover cooking doesn't apply to poultry and fish (they lack the dense muscle structure of beef and pork and don't retain heat as well), so they should be cooked to the desired serving temperature. The following temperatures should be used to determine when to stop the cooking process.

FOR THIS INGREDIENT...	COOK TO THIS TEMPERATURE
BEEF/LAMB	
Rare	115 to 120 degrees (120 to 125 degrees after resting)
Medium-Rare	120 to 125 degrees (125 to 130 degrees after resting)
Medium	130 to 135 degrees (135 to 140 degrees after resting)
Medium-Well	140 to 145 degrees (145 to 150 degrees after resting)
Well-Done	150 to 155 degrees (155 to 160 degrees after resting)
PORK	
Chops and Tenderloin	145 degrees (150 degrees after resting)
Loin Roasts	140 degrees (145 degrees after resting)
CHICKEN	
White Meat	160 degrees
Dark Meat	175 degrees

We start this Turkish meat and white bean braise by roasting beefy oxtails to render their fat and then brown them.

Braised Oxtails with White Beans, Tomatoes, and Aleppo Pepper

SERVES 6 to 8

WHY THIS RECIPE WORKS A popular Turkish dish, *etli kuru fasulye*, which means "white beans with meat," is often served with rice pilaf and pickled vegetables. It is the starting point for this hearty braise, only in this case the meat—succulent, beefy oxtails—plays the starring role, and the white beans offer a creamy, nutty counterpoint. To be sure our braise did not turn out too greasy, we started by roasting the oxtails in the oven for an hour, rather than quickly browning them in a pan; this way we rendered and discarded a significant amount of fat (about a half-cup). We then transferred the oxtails to a Dutch oven and deglazed the roasting pan with chicken broth to create a flavorful liquid for braising. We added a simple yet flavorful trio of eastern Mediterranean elements to give the braising liquid its character: sweet whole tomatoes, warm and earthy Aleppo pepper, and pungent oregano. After braising, we were careful to remove the fat (about another half-cup) from the cooking liquid using a fat separator. We added canned navy beans, sherry vinegar, and fresh oregano to create a hearty

sauce in which we reheated the oxtails. Try to buy oxtails that are approximately 2 inches thick and 2 to 4 inches in diameter. Oxtails can often be found in the freezer section of the grocery store; if using frozen oxtails, be sure to thaw them completely before using. If you can't find Aleppo pepper, you can substitute 1½ teaspoons paprika and 1½ teaspoons finely chopped red pepper flakes.

    4 pounds oxtails, trimmed
       Salt and pepper
    4 cups chicken broth
    2 tablespoons extra-virgin olive oil
    1 onion, chopped fine
    1 carrot, peeled and chopped fine
    6 garlic cloves, minced
    2 tablespoons tomato paste
    2 tablespoons ground dried Aleppo pepper
    1 tablespoon minced fresh oregano
    1 (28-ounce) can whole peeled tomatoes
    1 (15-ounce) can navy beans, rinsed
    1 tablespoon sherry vinegar

1. Adjust oven rack to lower-middle position and heat oven to 450 degrees. Pat oxtails dry with paper towels and season with salt and pepper. Arrange oxtails cut side down in single layer in large roasting pan and roast until meat begins to brown, about 45 minutes.

2. Discard any accumulated fat and juices in pan and continue to roast until meat is well browned, 15 to 20 minutes. Transfer oxtails to bowl and tent loosely with aluminum foil; set aside. Stir chicken broth into pan, scraping up any browned bits; set aside.

3. Reduce oven temperature to 300 degrees. Heat oil in Dutch oven over medium heat until shimmering. Add onion and carrot and cook until softened, about 5 minutes. Stir in garlic, tomato paste, Aleppo, and 1 teaspoon oregano and cook until fragrant, about 30 seconds.

4. Stir in broth mixture from roasting pan and tomatoes and their juice and bring to simmer. Nestle oxtails into pot and bring to simmer. Cover, transfer pot to oven, and cook until oxtails are tender and fork slips easily in and out of meat, about 3 hours.

5. Transfer oxtails to bowl and tent loosely with aluminum foil. Strain braising liquid through fine-mesh strainer into fat separator; return solids to now-empty pot. Let braising liquid settle for 5 minutes, then pour defatted liquid into pot with solids.

6. Stir in beans, vinegar, and remaining 2 teaspoons oregano. Return oxtails and any accumulated juices to pot, bring to gentle simmer over medium heat, and cook until oxtails and beans are heated through, about 5 minutes. Season with salt and pepper to taste. Transfer oxtails to serving platter and spoon 1 cup sauce over top. Serve, passing remaining sauce separately.

Pomegranate-Braised Beef Short Ribs with Prunes and Sesame
SERVES 6 to 8

WHY THIS RECIPE WORKS This braise takes its cue from a popular combination in Moroccan tagines: meltingly tender beef and sweet, tangy prunes. We found that using pomegranate juice—another Moroccan element—as the braising liquid gave our sauce the perfect touch of tartness to balance the meatiness of the beef and the sweetness of the prunes. A good dose of *ras el hanout* added a pleasing, piquant aroma. We chose short ribs for their intense, beefy flavor but found we needed to remove the fat throughout the cooking process. Rather than simply browning the ribs, we started by roasting them in the oven; this enabled us to render and discard a significant amount of fat. After braising, we defatted the cooking liquid, then blended it with the vegetables and part of the prunes to create a velvety sauce. We added the remaining prunes to the sauce and garnished the dish with toasted sesame seeds and cilantro. Short ribs come in two styles: English-style ribs contain a single rib bone and a thick piece of meat. Flanken-style ribs are cut thinner and have several smaller bones. While either will work here, we prefer the less expensive and more readily available English-style ribs. If using flanken-style ribs, flip the ribs halfway through roasting in step 1. We prefer to use our Ras el Hanout (page 316), but you can substitute store-bought ras el hanout if you wish, though flavor and spiciness can vary greatly by brand.

Our Moroccan-inspired take on beef short ribs uses chopped prunes to enrich the velvety sauce.

4 pounds bone-in English-style short ribs, trimmed
  Salt and pepper
4 cups unsweetened pomegranate juice
1 cup water
2 tablespoons extra-virgin olive oil
1 onion, chopped fine
1 carrot, peeled and chopped fine
2 tablespoons ras el hanout
4 garlic cloves, minced
¾ cup prunes, halved
1 tablespoon red wine vinegar
2 tablespoons toasted sesame seeds
2 tablespoons chopped fresh cilantro

1. Adjust oven rack to lower-middle position and heat oven to 450 degrees. Pat short ribs dry with paper towels and season with salt and pepper. Arrange ribs bone side down in single layer in large roasting pan and roast until meat begins to brown, about 45 minutes.

2. Discard any accumulated fat and juices in pan and continue to roast until meat is well browned, 15 to 20 minutes. Transfer ribs to bowl and tent loosely with aluminum foil; set aside. Stir pomegranate juice and water into pan, scraping up any browned bits; set aside.

3. Reduce oven temperature to 300 degrees. Heat oil in Dutch oven over medium heat until shimmering. Add onion, carrot, and ¼ teaspoon salt and cook until softened, about 5 minutes. Stir in ras el hanout and garlic and cook until fragrant, about 30 seconds.

4. Stir in pomegranate mixture from roasting pan and half of prunes and bring to simmer. Nestle short ribs bone side up into pot and bring to simmer. Cover, transfer pot to oven, and cook until ribs are tender and fork slips easily in and out of meat, about 2½ hours.

5. Transfer short ribs to bowl, discard any loose bones, and tent loosely with aluminum foil. Strain braising liquid through fine-mesh strainer into fat separator; transfer solids to blender. Let braising liquid settle for 5 minutes, then pour defatted liquid into blender with solids and process until smooth, about 1 minute.

6. Transfer sauce to now-empty pot and stir in vinegar and remaining prunes. Return short ribs and any accumulated juices to pot, bring to gentle simmer over medium heat, and cook, spooning sauce over ribs occasionally, until heated through, about 5 minutes. Season with salt and pepper to taste. Transfer short ribs to serving platter, spoon 1 cup sauce over top, and sprinkle with sesame seeds and cilantro. Serve, passing remaining sauce separately.

Grilled Spiced Pork Skewers with Onion and Caper Relish

SERVES 4 to 6

WHY THIS RECIPE WORKS For grilled pork skewers that were moist and flavorful, we turned to boneless country-style ribs, which are quick-cooking and tender, yet have enough fat to keep them from drying out. A flavorful North African–inspired spice rub with garlic, lemon, coriander, cumin, nutmeg, and cinnamon did double duty, first as a marinade and later, mixed with honey, to create a basting sauce. As a base for the relish, we grilled onions, which needed a head start on the grill before being finished alongside the pork. We mixed the grilled onions with a zesty combination of olives, capers, balsamic vinegar, and parsley for a bright, potent sauce that perfectly complemented the skewers. You will need six 12-inch metal skewers for this recipe.

 6 tablespoons extra-virgin olive oil
 5 garlic cloves, minced
 1 tablespoon grated lemon zest
 1 tablespoon ground coriander
 2 teaspoons ground cumin
    Salt and pepper
 ½ teaspoon ground nutmeg
 ½ teaspoon ground cinnamon
 1½ pounds boneless country-style pork ribs, trimmed and cut into 1-inch pieces
 2 tablespoons honey
 2 onions, sliced into ½-inch-thick rounds
 ½ cup pitted kalamata olives, chopped
 ¼ cup capers, rinsed
 3 tablespoons balsamic vinegar
 2 tablespoons minced fresh parsley

1. Whisk ¼ cup oil, garlic, lemon zest, coriander, cumin, 1½ teaspoons salt, ½ teaspoon pepper, nutmeg, and cinnamon together in medium bowl. Transfer 2 tablespoons marinade to small bowl and set aside. Combine remaining marinade and pork in 1-gallon zipper-lock bag and toss to coat. Press out as much air as possible and seal bag. Refrigerate for at least 1 hour or up to 2 hours, flipping bag every 30 minutes.

2. Whisk honey into reserved marinade and microwave until fragrant, 15 to 30 seconds. Remove pork from bag and pat dry with paper towels. Thread pork tightly onto four 12-inch metal skewers. Thread onion rounds from side to side onto two 12-inch metal skewers, brush with 1 tablespoon oil, and season with salt and pepper.

3A. FOR A CHARCOAL GRILL Open bottom vent completely. Light large chimney starter three-quarters filled with charcoal briquettes (4½ quarts). When top coals are partially covered with

For flavorful and juicy pork kebabs, we use boneless country-style ribs and marinate them in warm spices.

NOTES FROM THE TEST KITCHEN
Natural Versus Enhanced Pork

Because modern pork is so lean and therefore somewhat bland and prone to dryness if overcooked, many producers now inject their fresh pork products with a sodium solution. So-called enhanced pork is now the only option at many supermarkets, especially when buying lean cuts like tenderloin. (To be sure, read the label; if the pork has been enhanced, it will have an ingredient label.) Enhanced pork is injected with a solution of water, salt, sodium phosphates, sodium lactate, potassium lactate, sodium diacetate, and varying flavor agents, generally adding 7 to 15 percent extra weight. While enhanced pork does cook up juicier (it has been pumped full of water!), we find the texture almost spongy, and the flavor is often unpleasantly salty. We prefer the genuine pork flavor of natural pork and rely on brining to keep it juicy. Also, enhanced pork loses six times more moisture than natural pork when frozen and thawed—yet another reason to avoid enhanced pork. If you do buy enhanced pork, do not brine it.

---

ash, pour evenly over grill. Set cooking grate in place, cover, and open lid vent completely. Heat grill until hot, about 5 minutes.

3B. FOR A GAS GRILL Turn all burners to high, cover, and heat grill until hot, about 15 minutes. Turn all burners to medium-high.

4. Clean and oil cooking grate. Place pork and onion skewers on grill and cook (covered if using gas), turning skewers every 2 minutes and basting pork with honey mixture, until pork is browned and registers 140 degrees and onions are slightly charred and tender, 10 to 15 minutes. Transfer pork and onions to cutting board as they finish grilling and tent loosely with aluminum foil. Let pork rest while preparing relish.

5. Coarsely chop onions and combine with remaining 1 tablespoon oil, olives, capers, vinegar, and parsley. Season with salt and pepper to taste. Using tongs, slide pork off skewers onto serving platter. Serve pork with relish.

Greek-Style Braised Pork with Leeks
SERVES 4 to 6

WHY THIS RECIPE WORKS Pork braised with an abundant amount of leeks in white wine is a classic Greek dish. For our version, we browned the pork pieces to add deep flavor. Because leeks are milder than onions, we went with a full 2 pounds to ensure that we got a ton of flavor. After sautéing the leeks in the fat left from searing the pork, we built our aromatic base by cooking diced tomatoes and garlic. We then combined everything with white wine, chicken broth, and a bay leaf and put it all in the oven to cook low and slow until the pork was meltingly tender and the leeks were soft. A sprinkle of fresh oregano added pleasant earthy and minty notes. Pork butt roast is often labeled "Boston butt" in the supermarket.

2 pounds boneless pork butt roast, trimmed and cut into 1-inch pieces
  Salt and pepper
3 tablespoons extra-virgin olive oil
2 pounds leeks, white and light green parts only, halved lengthwise, sliced 1 inch thick, and washed thoroughly
2 garlic cloves, minced
1 (14.5-ounce) can diced tomatoes
1 cup dry white wine
½ cup chicken broth
1 bay leaf
2 teaspoons chopped fresh oregano

1. Adjust oven rack to lower-middle position and heat oven to 325 degrees. Pat pork dry with paper towels and season with salt and pepper. Heat 1 tablespoon oil in Dutch oven over medium-high heat until just smoking. Brown half of pork on all sides, about 8 minutes; transfer to bowl. Repeat with 1 tablespoon oil and remaining pork; transfer to bowl.

2. Add remaining 1 tablespoon oil, leeks, ½ teaspoon salt, and ½ teaspoon pepper to fat left in pot and cook over medium heat, stirring occasionally, until softened and lightly browned, 5 to 7 minutes. Stir in garlic and cook until fragrant, about 30 seconds. Stir in tomatoes and their juice, scraping up any browned bits, and cook until tomato liquid is nearly evaporated, 10 to 12 minutes.

3. Stir in wine, broth, bay leaf, and pork with any accumulated juices and bring to simmer. Cover, transfer pot to oven, and cook until pork is tender and falls apart when prodded with fork, 1 to 1½ hours. Discard bay leaf. Stir in oregano and season with salt and pepper to taste. Serve.

Preparing Leeks

1. Trim and discard root and dark green leaves.

2. Cut trimmed leek in half lengthwise, then slice into pieces according to recipe.

3. Rinse cut leeks thoroughly using salad spinner or bowl of water to remove dirt and sand.

A dry rub of herbes de Provence easily adds both great flavor and color to mild-mannered pork tenderloin.

Spice-Rubbed Pork Tenderloin with Fennel, Tomatoes, Artichokes, and Olives
SERVES 6

WHY THIS RECIPE WORKS When done right, nothing can match the fine-grained, buttery-smooth texture of pork tenderloin. Since it has a tendency to be bland, it benefits from bold seasoning. We wondered if a dry rub might allow us to skip the step of browning, adding both flavor and color to our tenderloins without the extra work. We were looking for a distinct flavor profile and reasoned that herbes de Provence would easily give a distinctly Mediterranean flavor to our pork. A little of this spice goes a long way; a mere 2 teaspoons were sufficient to flavor and coat two tenderloins without overwhelming the pork. For a vegetable that would complement both the rub and the pork, we thought of sweet, mild fennel and supplemented it with artichokes, kalamata olives, and cherry tomatoes. After jump-starting the fennel in the microwave, we cooked the tenderloins on top of the vegetables in a roasting pan. In less than an hour, we were transported to Provence with a weeknight dinner that was low on fuss but high on flavor. We prefer to use our homemade Herbes de Provence (page 317), but you can substitute store-bought herbes de Provence if you wish, though flavor can vary by brand. While we prefer the flavor and texture of jarred whole baby artichoke hearts, you can substitute 12 ounces of frozen artichoke hearts, thawed and patted dry, for the jarred.

2 large fennel bulbs, stalks discarded, bulbs halved, cored, and sliced ½ inch thick
2 cups jarred whole baby artichoke hearts packed in water, quartered, rinsed, and patted dry
½ cup pitted kalamata olives, halved
3 tablespoons extra-virgin olive oil
2 (12- to 16-ounce) pork tenderloins, trimmed
2 teaspoons herbes de Provence
Salt and pepper
1 pound cherry tomatoes, halved
1 tablespoon grated lemon zest
2 tablespoons minced fresh parsley

1. Adjust oven rack to lower-middle position and heat oven to 450 degrees. Combine fennel and 2 tablespoons water in bowl, cover, and microwave until softened, about 5 minutes. Drain fennel well, then toss with artichoke hearts, olives, and oil.

2. Pat tenderloins dry with paper towels, sprinkle with herbes de Provence, and season with salt and pepper. Spread vegetables in large roasting pan, then place tenderloins on top. Roast tenderloins and vegetables until pork registers 145 degrees, 25 to 30 minutes, turning tenderloins over halfway through roasting.

3. Transfer tenderloins to carving board, tent loosely with aluminum foil, and let rest for 10 minutes. Meanwhile, stir tomatoes and lemon zest into vegetables and continue to roast until fennel is tender and tomatoes have softened, about 10 minutes. Stir in parsley and season with salt and pepper to taste. Slice pork into ½-inch-thick slices and serve with vegetables.

Removing Pork Silverskin

Silverskin is a swath of connective tissue located between the meat and the fat that covers its surface. To remove silverskin, simply slip a knife under it, angle slightly upward, and use a gentle back-and-forth motion.

MEDITERRANEAN SPICE BLENDS AND PASTES

These spice blends and condiments serve as a great starting point or finishing touch to many flavorful Mediterranean recipes and are used throughout the book. Whether to contribute robust heat, nutty earthiness, or rounded, floral notes, these are handy additions to keep in your pantry or fridge.

Green Zhoug

Green Zhoug

MAKES about ½ cup `FAST` `VEG`

Zhoug is an Israeli hot sauce that can be either red or green. Our vibrant green version is made with fresh herbs, chiles, and spices. We like it with fish or drizzled on sandwiches.

- 6 tablespoons extra-virgin olive oil
- ½ teaspoon ground coriander
- ¼ teaspoon ground cumin
- ¼ teaspoon ground cardamom
- ¼ teaspoon salt
  Pinch ground cloves
- ¾ cup fresh cilantro leaves
- ½ cup fresh parsley leaves
- 2 green Thai chiles, stemmed and chopped
- 2 garlic cloves, minced

1. Microwave oil, coriander, cumin, cardamom, salt, and cloves in covered bowl until fragrant, about 30 seconds; let cool to room temperature.

2. Pulse oil-spice mixture, cilantro, parsley, chiles, and garlic in food processor until coarse paste forms, about 15 pulses, scraping down sides of bowl as needed. (Green Zhoug can be refrigerated for up to 4 days.)

Harissa

MAKES about ½ cup `FAST` `VEG`

Harissa is a traditional North African condiment that is great for flavoring soups, sauces, and dressings or dolloping on lamb, hummus, eggs, and sandwiches. If you can't find Aleppo pepper, you can substitute ¾ teaspoon paprika and ¾ teaspoon finely chopped red pepper flakes.

- 6 tablespoons extra-virgin olive oil
- 6 garlic cloves, minced
- 2 tablespoons paprika
- 1 tablespoon ground coriander
- 1 tablespoon ground dried Aleppo pepper
- 1 teaspoon ground cumin
- ¾ teaspoon caraway seeds
- ½ teaspoon salt

Combine all ingredients in bowl and microwave until bubbling and very fragrant, about 1 minute, stirring halfway through microwaving; let cool to room temperature. (Harissa can be refrigerated for up to 4 days.)

Ras el Hanout

MAKES about ½ cup `FAST` `VEG`

Ras el hanout is a complex Moroccan spice blend that traditionally features a host of warm spices. We use it to give robust flavor to couscous dishes, soups, stews, braises, and more. If you can't find Aleppo pepper, you can substitute ½ teaspoon paprika and ½ teaspoon red pepper flakes.

- 16 cardamom pods
- 4 teaspoons coriander seeds
- 4 teaspoons cumin seeds
- 2 teaspoons anise seeds
- ½ teaspoon allspice berries
- ¼ teaspoon black peppercorns
- 4 teaspoons ground ginger
- 2 teaspoons ground nutmeg
- 2 teaspoons ground dried Aleppo pepper
- 2 teaspoons ground cinnamon

1. Toast cardamom, coriander, cumin, anise, allspice, and peppercorns in small skillet over medium heat until fragrant, shaking skillet occasionally to prevent scorching, about 2 minutes. Let cool to room temperature.

2. Transfer toasted spices, ginger, nutmeg, Aleppo, and cinnamon to spice grinder and process to fine powder. (Ras el hanout can be stored at room temperature in airtight container for up to 1 year.)

Za'atar

MAKES about ½ cup `FAST` `VEG`

Za'atar is an aromatic eastern Mediterranean spice blend that is used as both a seasoning and a condiment. Try sprinkling it in olive oil as a dip for bread, or use it in grain dishes or as a flavorful topping for hummus or other dips.

- ½ cup dried thyme, ground
- 2 tablespoons sesame seeds, toasted
- 1½ tablespoons ground sumac

Combine all ingredients in bowl. (Za'atar can be stored at room temperature in airtight container for up to 1 year.)

Dukkah

MAKES 2 cups `VEG`

Dukkah is a North African blend that contains spices, nuts, and seeds. It's traditionally sprinkled on olive oil as a dip for bread, but it also makes a great crunchy coating for goat cheese, a garnish for soup, or a topping for grain and bean salads.

- 1 (15-ounce) can chickpeas, rinsed
- 1 teaspoon extra-virgin olive oil
- ½ cup shelled pistachios, toasted
- ⅓ cup black sesame seeds, toasted
- 2½ tablespoons coriander seeds, toasted
- 1 tablespoon cumin seeds, toasted
- 2 teaspoons fennel seeds, toasted
- 1½ teaspoons pepper
- 1¼ teaspoons salt

1. Adjust oven rack to middle position and heat oven to 400 degrees. Pat chickpeas dry with paper towels and toss with oil. Spread chickpeas into single layer in rimmed baking sheet and roast until browned and crisp, 40 to 45 minutes, stirring every 5 to 10 minutes; let cool completely.

2. Process chickpeas in food processor until coarsely ground, about 10 seconds; transfer to medium bowl. Pulse pistachios and sesame seeds in now-empty food processor until coarsely ground, about 15 pulses; transfer to bowl with chickpeas. Process coriander, cumin, and fennel seeds in again-empty food processor until finely ground, 2 to 3 minutes; transfer to bowl with chickpeas. Add pepper and salt and whisk until mixture is well combined. (Dukkah can be refrigerated for up to 1 month.)

Herbes de Provence

MAKES about ½ cup `FAST` `VEG`

Herbes de Provence is an aromatic blend of dried herbs from the south of France. It can be used as a rub for poultry or pork.

- 2 tablespoons dried thyme
- 2 tablespoons dried marjoram
- 2 tablespoons dried rosemary
- 2 teaspoons fennel seeds, toasted

Combine all ingredients in bowl. (Herbes de Provence can be stored at room temperature in airtight container for up to 1 year.)

Ingredients for Dukkah

MAKING AND STORING SPICE BLENDS AND PASTES

When making your own spice blends and pastes, it's important to start with the freshest spices and dried herbs. Here are some tips for how to determine freshness and how to store your blends to maximize their shelf life.

SHELF LIFE OF DRIED HERBS AND SPICES

Ground spices and dried herbs last about a year when properly stored. Don't store spices and herbs on the counter close to the stove; heat, light, and moisture shorten their shelf life. When possible, buy whole spices and grind them just before using instead of buying preground spices. Not only do whole spices last longer in the pantry (about two years), but grinding releases the volatile compounds that give a spice its flavor and aroma. The longer the spice sits around (or is stored), the more compounds disappear.

CHECKING DRIED HERBS AND SPICES FOR FRESHNESS

To check the freshness of dried herbs or spices, rub a small amount between your fingers and take a whiff. If it releases a lively aroma, it's still good to go. If the aroma and color have faded, it's time to restock.

STORING SPICE BLENDS AND PASTES

Dry spice blends can keep for about a year if kept away from heat and light. When storing spice pastes, store them in the fridge; pastes that contain raw garlic that is submerged in oil, such as *zhoug* or *harissa*, should be stored for no more than four days to prevent the growth of potentially harmful bacteria.

All About Mediterranean Sausages

Throughout the Mediterranean, sausages are browned, braised, or grilled and served whole or are cut up and used as more of a flavoring than a main ingredient. Here are the sausages that we used throughout this book:

LOUKANIKO

Loukaniko is a traditional Greek sausage typically made of pork and flavored with orange peel, fennel, and spices; it is not very spicy. It is most often found fresh and must be cooked before eating. Loukaniko can be bought in specialty markets; if you cannot find it, you can substitute hot or sweet Italian sausage.

MERGUEZ

Merguez is a spicy sausage from North Africa made with lamb or beef or a combination of the two and is flavored with spicy red peppers among other spices. It can be purchased raw or dried.

SUJUK

Sujuk is typically found in Turkey and is the eastern Mediterranean equivalent of merguez. It is made with beef, lamb, or a combination of the two; vary rarely, pork or horse is used to make it. It is generally sold cured or fermented but can also be found cooked or smoked. Sujuk is a dry sausage, so it doesn't give off a lot of fat when cooked.

SPANISH CHORIZO

Spanish *chorizo* is spicy and is typically sold already cooked, either smoked or cured. It is made with pork or a combination of meats. It is red in color as it usually contains a lot of paprika. For more information on Spanish chorizo, see page 177.

ITALIAN SAUSAGE

Italian sausage comes either hot or sweet. Both are made with coarsely ground fresh pork flavored with garlic and fennel seeds; the hot variety is also seasoned with red pepper flakes. Since Italian sausage is very flavorful, and readily available, we found it was a good substitute for harder-to-find authentic sausages.

Braised Greek Sausages with Peppers

SERVES 4 to 6

WHY THIS RECIPE WORKS In Greece, *spetsofai* is a classic dish of savory sausages braised with wine and peppers. A traditional Greek pork sausage with fennel and orange called *loukaniko* is often used in it. For our version, we started by searing whole loukaniko to create flavorful browning. We then sautéed a colorful assortment of sweet bell peppers, spicy jalapeños, and bold onion. For our aromatics, we quickly cooked garlic, tomato paste, grated orange zest, and ground fennel to bring out their flavors before adding the tomatoes, white wine, and chicken broth. We cut our sausage into pieces and added them to the skillet. Once the sausages were completely cooked and the flavors were beginning to meld, we uncovered the skillet and let the peppers finish cooking through while also reducing our sauce, concentrating its flavor. A final sprinkle of fresh oregano rounded out this flavorful braise. Loukaniko sausage can be found in specialty markets; if you cannot find it, you can substitute hot or sweet Italian sausage.

1½ pounds loukaniko sausage
2 tablespoons extra-virgin olive oil
4 bell peppers (red, yellow, and/or green), stemmed, seeded, and cut into 1½-inch pieces
1 onion, chopped
2 jalapeño chiles, stemmed, seeded, and minced
Salt and pepper
3 garlic cloves, minced
1 tablespoon tomato paste
2 teaspoons grated orange zest
1 teaspoon ground fennel
½ cup dry white wine
1 (14.5-ounce) can diced tomatoes
¾ cup chicken broth
1 tablespoon minced fresh oregano

1. Prick sausages with fork in several places. Heat 1 tablespoon oil in 12-inch nonstick skillet over medium-high heat until just smoking. Brown sausages well on all sides, about 8 minutes. Transfer sausages to cutting board, let cool slighty, then cut into quarters.

2. Heat remaining 1 tablespoon oil in now-empty skillet over medium heat until shimmering. Add peppers, onion, jalapeños, ½ teaspoon salt, and ½ teaspoon pepper and cook until peppers are beginning to soften, about 5 minutes. Stir in garlic, tomato paste, orange zest, and fennel and cook until fragrant, about 1 minute. Stir in wine, scraping up any browned bits.

3. Stir in tomatoes and their juice, broth, and sausages and any accumulated juices and bring to simmer. Cover, reduce heat to low, and simmer gently until sausages are cooked through, about 5 minutes.

4. Uncover, increase heat to medium, and cook until sauce has thickened slightly, about 10 minutes. Stir in oregano and season with salt and pepper to taste. Serve.

Sausage and White Beans with Mustard Greens
SERVES 4 to 6

WHY THIS RECIPE WORKS The south of France is known for its rich stews that combine meaty sausage, creamy white beans, and fresh greens. Drawing inspiration from them, we wanted to make a stew that put the sausage in the forefront. Since authentic French garlic sausage was difficult to find, we cast around for an alternative. Sweet Italian sausage, which is very flavorful and easy to get, was a perfect substitute. We started by creating flavorful browning on the sausage before sweating our aromatics—onion, tomatoes, garlic, and thyme—in the leftover fat. We then cooked down savory chicken broth and a healthy splash of white wine before adding the beans. Using canned cannellini beans eliminated an overnight soak. For the greens, we enjoyed the peppery spice of mustard greens, which we gently wilted before braising them. To finish, a sprinkle of cheesy bread crumbs and parsley added pleasant crunch and freshness. You can substitute kale for the mustard greens.

1 pound hot or sweet Italian sausage
2 tablespoons extra-virgin olive oil
1 onion, chopped fine
  Salt and pepper
2 tablespoons minced fresh thyme or 2 teaspoons dried
6 garlic cloves, minced
½ cup dry white wine
1 (14.5-ounce) can diced tomatoes, drained with juice reserved
1½ cups chicken broth
1 (15-ounce) can cannellini beans, rinsed
12 ounces mustard greens, stemmed and cut into 2-inch pieces
½ cup Parmesan Bread Crumbs (page 144)
2 tablespoons minced fresh parsley

We brown then braise easy-to-find Italian sausages on top of hearty greens in this rich French white bean dish.

1. Prick sausages with fork in several places. Heat 1 tablespoon oil in Dutch oven over medium-high heat until just smoking. Brown sausages well on all sides, about 8 minutes; transfer to plate.

2. Heat remaining 1 tablespoon oil in now-empty pot over medium heat until shimmering. Add onion and ¼ teaspoon salt and cook until softened and lightly browned, 5 to 7 minutes. Stir in thyme and garlic and cook until fragrant, about 30 seconds. Stir in wine and reserved tomato juice, scraping up any browned bits, and cook until nearly evaporated, about 5 minutes. Stir in broth, beans, and tomatoes and bring to simmer.

3. Stir in mustard greens and cook until slightly wilted, about 1 minute. Place sausages on top of greens. Reduce heat to low, cover, and cook until greens are wilted and reduced in volume by about half, about 10 minutes.

4. Uncover, increase heat to medium-low, and continue to cook, stirring occasionally, until sausages are cooked through and greens are tender, about 15 minutes. Off heat, using back of spoon, mash portion of beans against side of pot to thicken sauce. Serve, sprinkling individual portions with bread crumbs and parsley.

Lamb Meatballs with Leeks and Yogurt Sauce
SERVES 4

WHY THIS RECIPE WORKS Lamb meatballs are a staple throughout the Mediterranean. Our version features a hefty dose of chopped mint, warm spices, and a lemony leek-yogurt sauce made in the skillet. Combining tender lamb with aromatic spices seems straightforward, but there is a lot that can go wrong, from dry and tough meatballs to flavorless ones; we wanted to avoid those pitfalls. We started with ground lamb and found that making a quick panade from bread crumbs and Greek yogurt and adding an egg yolk not only helped bind our meatballs together but also kept them from drying out. A flavorful eastern Mediterranean–inspired combination of spices—cumin, cinnamon, and cloves—along with garlic, packed a lot of flavor into our meatballs. To make this an entrée-worthy dish, we wanted to create a flavorful sauce to go along with the meatballs. Sautéing leeks, garlic, and lemon zest built the flavor backbone of the sauce before the addition of savory chicken broth. We bulked up the meaty flavor of the sauce by using it to braise the meatballs, and to give the sauce extra clinging power and pleasant tang, we finished it by whisking in additional Greek yogurt. Serve with orzo or Simple Couscous (page 161).

1 cup whole Greek yogurt
3 tablespoons panko bread crumbs
2 tablespoons water
1 pound ground lamb
3 tablespoons minced fresh mint
1 large egg yolk
2 garlic cloves, minced
1 teaspoon ground cumin
¾ teaspoon ground cinnamon
　Salt and pepper
⅛ teaspoon ground cloves
2 tablespoons extra-virgin olive oil
8 ounces leeks, white and light green parts only, chopped and washed thoroughly
½ teaspoon grated lemon zest plus ½ teaspoon juice
1 cup chicken broth

1. Mash ⅓ cup yogurt, panko, and water together with fork in large bowl to form paste. Add ground lamb, 2 tablespoons mint, egg yolk, half of garlic, cumin, cinnamon, ¾ teaspoon salt, ⅛ teaspoon pepper, and cloves and knead with your hands until thoroughly combined. Pinch off and roll mixture into twelve 1½-inch meatballs.

A quick binder made from panko and Greek yogurt keeps our lamb meatballs light and holds them together.

2. Heat oil in 12-inch skillet over medium-high heat until just smoking. Brown meatballs on all sides, 6 to 8 minutes; transfer to plate. Pour off all but 1 tablespoon fat from skillet.

3. Add leeks and cook over medium heat until softened and lightly browned, 5 to 7 minutes. Stir in lemon zest and remaining garlic and cook until fragrant, about 30 seconds. Stir in broth, scraping up any browned bits, and bring to simmer.

4. Return meatballs to skillet and bring to simmer. Reduce heat to medium-low, cover, and simmer, turning meatballs occasionally, for 5 minutes. Uncover and continue to cook until liquid has reduced slightly, about 2 minutes.

5. Off heat, transfer meatballs to serving platter and tent loosely with aluminum foil. Whisking constantly, slowly ladle about 1 cup hot liquid into remaining ⅔ cup yogurt in bowl until combined. Stir yogurt mixture into skillet along with lemon juice until combined. Season with salt and pepper to taste. Pour sauce over meatballs and sprinkle with remaining 1 tablespoon mint. Serve.

Grilled Lamb Kofte

SERVES 4 to 6

WHY THIS RECIPE WORKS In the Middle East, kebabs called *kofte* feature ground meat, not chunks, mixed with lots of spices and fresh herbs. These ground lamb patties are typically grilled over high heat on long metal skewers, making them tender and juicy on the inside and encasing them in a smoky, crunchy coating of char. Our challenge was to get their sausagelike texture just right. While kofte is traditionally made by mincing the meat by hand with a cleaver, we wanted to make our recipe as streamlined as possible, so we decided to use store-bought ground lamb. We typically use a panade (a paste of bread and milk) to keep ground meat patties moist, but the starchy panade gave our kofte an unwelcome pastiness. We found that replacing the panade with a small amount of powdered gelatin helped the meat firm up and hold fast to the skewer, resulting in tender, juicy kofte. Ground pine nuts added to the meat prevented toughness and contributed their own pleasant texture and a boost in richness. A concentrated charcoal fire setup (see page 277) mimicked the concentrated heat of a traditional kofte grill. Our Tahini-Yogurt Sauce (page 233) was the perfect finishing touch. You will need eight 12-inch metal skewers for this recipe. Serve with rice pilaf or make sandwiches with warm pita bread, sliced red onion, and chopped fresh mint.

Replacing the bread panade with a little powdered gelatin keeps our lamb *kofte* moist and more flavorful.

½ cup pine nuts
4 garlic cloves, peeled and smashed
1½ teaspoons hot smoked paprika
1 teaspoon salt
1 teaspoon ground cumin
½ teaspoon pepper
¼ teaspoon ground coriander
¼ teaspoon ground cloves
⅛ teaspoon ground nutmeg
⅛ teaspoon ground cinnamon
1½ pounds ground lamb
½ cup grated onion, drained
⅓ cup minced fresh parsley
⅓ cup minced fresh mint
1½ teaspoons unflavored gelatin
1 (13 by 9-inch) disposable aluminum roasting pan (if using charcoal)
1 recipe Tahini-Yogurt Sauce (page 233)

1. Process pine nuts, garlic, paprika, salt, cumin, pepper, coriander, cloves, nutmeg, and cinnamon in food processor until coarse paste forms, 30 to 45 seconds; transfer to large bowl. Add ground lamb, onion, parsley, mint, and gelatin and knead with your hands until thoroughly combined and mixture feels slightly sticky, about 2 minutes.

2. Divide mixture into 8 equal portions. Shape each portion into 5-inch-long cylinder about 1 inch in diameter. Using eight 12-inch metal skewers, thread 1 cylinder onto each skewer, pressing gently to adhere. Transfer skewers to lightly greased baking sheet, cover with plastic wrap, and refrigerate for at least 1 hour or up to 24 hours.

3A. FOR A CHARCOAL GRILL Using kitchen shears, poke twelve ½-inch holes in bottom of disposable pan. Open bottom vent completely and place pan in center of grill. Light large chimney starter filled two-thirds with charcoal briquettes (4 quarts). When top coals are partially covered with ash, pour into pan. Set cooking grate in place, cover, and open lid vent completely. Heat grill until hot, about 5 minutes.

3B. FOR A GAS GRILL Turn all burners to high, cover, and heat grill until hot, about 15 minutes. Leave all burners on high.

4. Clean and oil cooking grate. Place skewers on grill (directly over coals if using charcoal) at 45-degree angle to grate. Cook (covered if using gas) until browned and meat easily releases from grill, 4 to 7 minutes. Flip skewers and continue to cook until browned on second side and meat registers 160 degrees, about 6 minutes. Transfer skewers to serving platter and serve with Tahini-Yogurt Sauce.

Adding a paste of pita crumbs and lemon juice to our ground lamb patties makes them moist and sturdier for grilling.

Grilled Greek-Style Lamb Pita Sandwiches
SERVES 4

WHY THIS RECIPE WORKS What's not to love about a Greek gyro, a sandwich of seasoned, marinated lamb, tomato, lettuce, and cucumber-yogurt *tzatziki* sauce stuffed inside a soft pita? The traditional method for cooking the meat employs an electric vertical rotisserie on which layers of sliced and marinated leg of lamb are stacked. After cooking for hours, the meat is shaved with a long slicing knife, revealing pieces with crisp exteriors and moist interiors infused with garlic and oregano. We wanted to translate this recipe for the home kitchen. Surprisingly, using ground lamb—which we formed into patties and grilled—was easy and came close to reproducing the texture of rotisserie lamb. A modified panade, or wet binder, of pita bread crumbs, lemon juice, and garlic gave our patties a sturdier structure and fuller, more savory flavor. For a crisp outside and moist inside, we browned our patties on the grill until a crust formed on each side. Then we grilled the pitas as well to warm them and add a little smoky flavor.

We prefer to use our homemade Pita Bread (page 344), but you can use store-bought. If using pocketless pitas, do not cut off the tops in step 1; instead, use a portion of a fifth pita to create crumbs.

4 (8-inch) pita breads
½ onion, chopped coarse
1 tablespoon minced fresh oregano or 1 teaspoon dried
4 teaspoons lemon juice
2 garlic cloves, minced
½ teaspoon salt
¼ teaspoon pepper
1 pound ground lamb
2 teaspoons extra-virgin olive oil
1 cup Tzatziki (page 19)
1 large tomato, cored and sliced thin
2 cups shredded iceberg lettuce
2 ounces feta cheese, crumbled (½ cup)

1. Cut top quarter off each pita bread. Tear quarters into 1-inch pieces. (You should have ¾ cup pita pieces.) Lightly moisten 2 pita breads with water. Sandwich unmoistened pitas between moistened pitas and wrap stack tightly in lightly greased heavy-duty aluminum foil; set aside.

2. Process pita bread pieces, onion, oregano, lemon juice, garlic, salt, and pepper in food processor until smooth paste forms, about 30 seconds; transfer to large bowl. Add ground lamb and knead with your hands until thoroughly combined. Divide mixture into 12 equal portions. Shape each portion into ball, then gently flatten into round disk about ½ inch thick and 2½ inches in diameter.

3A. FOR A CHARCOAL GRILL Open bottom vent completely. Light large chimney starter three-quarters filled with charcoal (4½ quarts). When top coals are partially covered with ash, pour evenly over half of grill. Set cooking grate in place, cover, and open lid vent completely. Heat grill until hot, about 5 minutes.

3B. FOR A GAS GRILL Turn all burners to high, cover, and heat grill until hot, about 15 minutes. Turn primary burner to medium-high and turn off other burner(s).

4. Clean and oil cooking grate. Place patties on hotter side of grill, cover (if using gas), and cook until well browned and crust forms, 4 to 6 minutes per side. Transfer patties to paper towel–lined plate, cover loosely with foil, and let sit while heating pitas.

5. Place packet of pitas on cooler side of grill and flip occasionally until heated through, about 5 minutes. Using spoon, spread ¼ cup Tzatziki inside each warm pita. Divide patties evenly among pitas and fill each sandwich with tomato slices, ½ cup shredded lettuce, and 2 tablespoons feta. Serve immediately.

Grilled Lamb Shish Kebabs

SERVES 4 to 6

WHY THIS RECIPE WORKS Lamb and vegetable shish kebab is perhaps the best-known "barbecue" dish from Turkey. When done right, the lamb is well browned and the vegetables are crisp and tender. But shish kebab has its challenges, from overcooked meat to bland flavors; we wanted a foolproof method that would give us flavorful and perfectly cooked vegetables and meat every time. We opted to use a boneless leg of lamb: It's inexpensive, has bold lamb flavor, and cooks up tender in just minutes. After extensive testing, we found three vegetables that worked well: bell peppers, red onions, and zucchini. They have similar textures and cook through at about the same rate when cut appropriately. Marinating the lamb ensured that it stayed moist throughout cooking. As little as 1 hour of marinating was enough to give the kebabs good flavor. Reserving some of the marinade allowed us to flavor our vegetables while they cooked. You will need six 12-inch metal skewers for this recipe. If you have long, thin pieces of meat, roll or fold them into approximate 2-inch cubes before skewering. We prefer these kebabs cooked to medium-rare, but if you prefer them more or less done, see the chart on page 310.

MARINADE

    6 tablespoons extra-virgin olive oil
    7 large fresh mint leaves
    2 teaspoons chopped fresh rosemary
    2 garlic cloves, peeled
    1 teaspoon salt
    ½ teaspoon grated lemon zest plus 2 tablespoons juice
    ¼ teaspoon pepper

LAMB AND VEGETABLES

    2 pounds boneless leg of lamb, pulled apart at seams, trimmed, and cut into 2-inch pieces
    2 zucchini or yellow summer squash, halved lengthwise and sliced 1 inch thick
    2 red or green bell peppers, stemmed, seeded, and cut into 1½-inch pieces
    2 red onions, cut into 1-inch pieces, 3 layers thick

1. FOR THE MARINADE Process all ingredients in food processor until smooth, about 1 minute, scraping down sides of bowl as needed. Transfer 3 tablespoons marinade to large bowl and set aside.

2. FOR THE LAMB AND VEGETABLES Place remaining marinade and lamb in 1-gallon zipper-lock bag and toss to coat. Press out as much air as possible and seal bag. Refrigerate for at least 1 hour or up to 2 hours, flipping bag every 30 minutes.

We cut our own chunks of meat from flavorful boneless leg of lamb and marinate them for just an hour before grilling.

3. Add zucchini, bell peppers, and onions to bowl with reserved marinade and toss to coat. Cover and let sit at room temperature for at least 30 minutes.

4. Remove lamb from bag and pat dry with paper towels. Thread lamb tightly onto two 12-inch metal skewers. In alternating pattern of zucchini, bell pepper, and onion, thread vegetables onto four 12-inch metal skewers.

5A. FOR A CHARCOAL GRILL Open bottom vent completely. Light large chimney starter mounded with charcoal briquettes (7 quarts). When top coals are partially covered with ash, pour evenly over center of grill, leaving 2-inch gap between grill wall and charcoal. Set cooking grate in place, cover, and open lid vent completely. Heat grill until hot, about 5 minutes.

5B. FOR A GAS GRILL Turn all burners to high, cover, and heat grill until hot, about 15 minutes. Leave primary burner on high and turn other burner(s) to medium-low.

6. Clean and oil cooking grate. Place lamb skewers on grill (directly over coals if using charcoal or over hotter side of grill if using gas). Place vegetable skewers on grill (near edge of coals but still over coals if using charcoal or on cooler side of grill if using gas). Cook (covered if using gas), turning skewers every 3 to 4 minutes, until lamb is well browned and registers 120 to

125 degrees (for medium-rare), 10 to 15 minutes. Transfer lamb skewers to serving platter, tent loosely with aluminum foil, and let rest while finishing vegetables.

7. Continue to cook vegetable skewers until tender and lightly charred, 5 to 7 minutes; transfer to platter. Using tongs, slide lamb and vegetables off skewers onto platter. Serve.

Grilled Marinated Lamb Shoulder Chops with Asparagus
SERVES 4 to 6

WHY THIS RECIPE WORKS Lamb shoulder chops are significantly less expensive than rib or loin chops, and their flavor is much more complex due to their delicate networks of fat and collagen-rich connective tissue—an appealing option, we thought, for a quick, economical, anytime meal from the grill. What we found, however, is that producing a grilled shoulder chop with a beautifully browned exterior and a moist and tender interior can be a challenge. Because the chops are relatively thin, we had trouble achieving good color on the outside of our chops before they overcooked. We also found that the texture of our cooked chops was uneven—meatier parts might be tender while other parts stayed chewy and tough. We knew from past recipes that a quick soak in a baking soda brine can help speed up the browning process and also tenderize meat, but when we tried it with our shoulder chops, we detected an unappealing aftertaste. We needed a gentler approach, so we tried a simple marinade of oil, garlic, salt, oregano, and just a small amount of baking soda. In under 10 minutes on a hot grill, our chops were perfectly browned, juicy, and full of flavor. We paired them with grilled asparagus (which cooked while our chops were resting) and a bright, refreshing vinaigrette. This recipe works best with thick asparagus spears that are between ½ and ¾ inch in diameter. Do not use pencil-thin asparagus; it overcooks too easily. We prefer these chops cooked to medium-rare, but if you prefer them more or less done, see the chart on page 310.

½ cup extra-virgin olive oil
3 tablespoons red wine vinegar
2 tablespoons chopped fresh mint
1 small shallot, minced
1 teaspoon Dijon mustard
  Salt and pepper
2 garlic cloves, minced
2 teaspoons minced fresh oregano
1 teaspoon baking soda
4 (8- to 12-ounce) lamb shoulder chops (blade or round bone), ¾ to 1 inch thick, trimmed
1½ pounds thick asparagus, trimmed

A little baking soda in the marinade helps lamb shoulder chops to brown on the grill and remain perfectly tender.

1. Whisk ¼ cup oil, vinegar, mint, shallot, mustard, ¼ teaspoon salt, and ⅛ teaspoon pepper together in bowl; set aside for serving.

2. Whisk remaining ¼ cup oil, garlic, oregano, baking soda, ½ teaspoon salt, and ½ teaspoon pepper together in bowl. Place marinade and chops in 1-gallon zipper-lock bag and toss to coat. Press out as much air as possible and seal bag. Refrigerate for at least 30 minutes or up to 1 hour, flipping bag halfway through. Remove lamb and let excess marinade drip off but do not pat dry.

3A. FOR A CHARCOAL GRILL Open bottom vent completely. Light large chimney starter filled with charcoal briquettes (6 quarts). When top coals are partially covered with ash, pour evenly over grill. Set cooking grate in place, cover, and open lid vent completely. Heat grill until hot, about 5 minutes.

3B. FOR A GAS GRILL Turn all burners to high, cover, and heat grill until hot, about 15 minutes. Leave all burners on high.

4. Clean and oil cooking grate. Place chops on grill and cook until well browned and meat registers 120 to 125 degrees (for medium-rare), 2 to 4 minutes per side. Transfer chops to serving platter, tent loosely with aluminum foil, and let rest while preparing asparagus.

5. Place asparagus on grill and cook, turning as needed, until crisp-tender and lightly browned, about 5 minutes; transfer to platter with lamb. Drizzle with vinaigrette and serve.

Roast Butterflied Leg of Lamb with Coriander, Cumin, and Mustard Seeds

SERVES 8 to 10

WHY THIS RECIPE WORKS There is no better centerpiece for a Mediterranean-style feast than an aromatic roasted leg of lamb. Here we swapped in a butterflied leg of lamb for the usual bone-in or boned, rolled, and tied leg options, which kept things easy and allowed more thorough seasoning, a great ratio of crust to meat, and faster, more even cooking. By first roasting the lamb in a 250-degree oven, we were able to keep the meat juicy, and a final blast under the broiler was all it took to crisp and brown the exterior. We ditched the usual spice rub (which had a tendency to scorch under the broiler) in favor of a slow-cooked spice-infused oil that seasoned the lamb during cooking. We prefer the subtler flavor of lamb labeled "domestic" or "American" for this recipe. We prefer this lamb cooked to medium-rare, but if you prefer it more or less done, see the chart on page 310. Serve with Lemon-Yogurt Sauce (page 233), if desired.

1 (3½- to 4-pound) butterflied leg of lamb
  Kosher salt
⅓ cup extra-virgin olive oil
3 shallots, sliced thin
4 garlic cloves, peeled and smashed
1 (1-inch) piece ginger, peeled, sliced into ½-inch-thick rounds, and smashed
1 tablespoon coriander seeds
1 tablespoon cumin seeds
1 tablespoon mustard seeds
3 bay leaves
2 (2-inch) strips lemon zest

1. Place lamb on cutting board with fat cap facing down. Using sharp knife, trim any pockets of fat and connective tissue from underside of lamb. Flip lamb over, trim fat cap to between ⅛ and ¼ inch thick, and pound roast to even 1-inch thickness. Cut slits, spaced ½ inch apart, in fat cap in crosshatch pattern, being careful to cut down to but not into meat. Rub 1 tablespoon salt over entire roast and into slits. Let sit, uncovered, at room temperature for 1 hour.

2. Meanwhile, adjust oven rack to lower-middle position and second rack 4 to 5 inches from broiler element and heat oven to 250 degrees. Stir together oil, shallots, garlic, ginger, coriander seeds, cumin seeds, mustard seeds, bay leaves, and lemon zest in rimmed baking sheet and bake on lower rack until spices are softened and fragrant and shallots and garlic turn golden, about 1 hour. Remove sheet from oven and discard bay leaves.

3. Pat lamb dry with paper towels and transfer fat side up to sheet (directly on top of spices). Roast on lower rack until lamb registers 120 degrees, 20 to 25 minutes. Remove sheet from oven and heat broiler. Broil lamb on upper rack until surface is well browned and charred in spots and lamb registers 125 degrees (for medium-rare), 3 to 8 minutes.

4. Remove sheet from oven and transfer lamb to carving board (some spices will cling to bottom of roast). Tent loosely with aluminum foil and let rest for 20 minutes.

5. Slice lamb with grain into 3 equal pieces. Turn each piece and slice against grain into ¼-inch-thick slices. Serve.

Making Butterflied Leg of Lamb

1. PREPARE LAMB Using sharp knife, trim fat and connective tissue. Pound roast to even 1-inch thickness, then cut slits, spaced ½ inch apart, in fat cap in crosshatch pattern.

2. BLOOM AROMATICS AND SPICES Combine oil, aromatics, and spices in rimmed baking sheet and bake until softened and fragrant.

3. ROAST AND BROIL Place roast directly on top of aromatics and spices and roast until it registers 120 degrees. Broil lamb until surface is well browned and charred in spots and lamb registers 125 degrees.

4. CARVE AND SERVE Slice lamb with grain into 3 equal pieces. Turn each piece and slice against grain into ¼-inch-thick slices.

Roast Butterflied Leg of Lamb with Coriander, Rosemary, and Red Pepper

Omit cumin and mustard seeds. Toss 6 sprigs fresh rosemary and ½ teaspoon red pepper flakes with oil mixture in step 2.

Roast Butterflied Leg of Lamb with Coriander, Fennel, and Black Pepper

Substitute 1 tablespoon fennel seeds for cumin seeds and 1 tablespoon black peppercorns for mustard seeds.

Braised Lamb Shoulder Chops with Tomatoes and Red Wine

SERVES 4

WHY THIS RECIPE WORKS When buying lamb, many people turn to the tried-and-true—and expensive—rib or loin chop. The oddly shaped, much less expensive shoulder chop rarely gets a second look, which is unfortunate because it is less exacting to cook and a few chops make for an easy weeknight supper. Their assertive flavor and somewhat chewy texture are particularly well suited to braising; we wanted a recipe for braised shoulder chops that would yield tender meat and a rich, flavorful sauce. Because shoulder chops aren't a tough cut of meat, we found that they don't need to cook for a long time to become tender. A relatively quick stovetop braise of just 15 to 20 minutes was all it took for these chops to cook. The robust flavor of shoulder chops stands up well to an equally bold sauce. After sautéing some onion and garlic, we deglazed the pan with red wine. Tomatoes balanced out the acidity of the wine, and parsley added a hit of freshness.

We find lamb shoulder chops to be very flavorful, quick-cooking, and economical—perfect for a stovetop braise.

4 (8- to 12-ounce) lamb shoulder chops (round bone or blade), about ¾ inch thick, trimmed
   Salt and pepper
2 tablespoons extra-virgin olive oil
1 small onion, chopped fine
2 small garlic cloves, minced
⅓ cup dry red wine
1 cup canned whole peeled tomatoes, chopped
2 tablespoons minced fresh parsley

1. Pat chops dry with paper towels and season with salt and pepper. Heat 1 tablespoon oil in 12-inch skillet over medium-high heat until just smoking. Brown chops, in batches if necessary, 4 to 5 minutes per side; transfer to plate. Pour off fat from skillet.

2. Heat remaining 1 tablespoon oil in now-empty skillet over medium heat until shimmering. Add onion and cook until softened, about 5 minutes. Stir in garlic and cook until fragrant, about 30 seconds. Stir in wine, scraping up any browned bits. Bring to simmer and cook until reduced by half, 2 to 3 minutes. Stir in tomatoes.

3. Nestle chops into skillet along with any accumulated juices and return to simmer. Reduce heat to low, cover, and simmer gently until chops are tender and fork slips easily in and out of meat, 15 to 20 minutes. Transfer chops to serving platter, tent loosely with aluminum foil, and let rest while finishing sauce.

4. Stir parsley into sauce and simmer until sauce thickens, 2 to 3 minutes. Season with salt and pepper to taste. Spoon sauce over chops and serve.

VARIATION

Braised Lamb Shoulder Chops with Figs and North African Spices

Soak ⅓ cup dried figs in ⅓ cup warm water for 30 minutes. Drain, reserving liquid, and cut figs into quarters. Add 1 teaspoon ground coriander, ½ teaspoon ground cumin, ½ teaspoon cinnamon, and ⅛ teaspoon cayenne pepper to skillet with garlic. Omit red wine and replace with ⅓ cup fig soaking water. Add 2 tablespoons honey with tomatoes. Stir figs in with parsley.

Braised Lamb Shanks with Bell Peppers and Harissa
SERVES 4

WHY THIS RECIPE WORKS Intensely flavorful lamb shanks are ideal for braising; long, slow, moist cooking breaks down the collagen-rich connective tissue and fats that add flavor and body to the braising liquid and produces fall-apart tender meat. We found that braising our shanks in the oven—and turning them once halfway through cooking—provided more even heat than braising on the stovetop, and browning the shanks over high heat before braising added complex, roasted flavors. What gives this dish its unique character is the combination of slow-cooked bell peppers and the Tunisian condiment *harissa*—a potent blend of ground chilis, garlic, and spices. Chicken broth served as a perfect mild medium in which to meld the rich flavors of the lamb, the sweetness of the peppers, and the aromas of the harissa. To keep our sauce clean and light, we made sure to trim our shanks of all visible fat before cooking, and we strained and defatted the cooking liquid after braising. To add richness and flavor to the sauce, we blended the braised bell peppers into the cooking liquid, and we finished the sauce with fresh mint. We prefer to use our Harissa (page 316), but you can substitute store-bought harissa if you wish, though spiciness can vary greatly by brand. Serve with Simple Couscous (page 161).

4 (10- to 12-ounce) lamb shanks, trimmed
  Salt and pepper
1 tablespoon extra-virgin olive oil
1 onion, chopped fine
4 bell peppers (red, orange, and/or yellow), stemmed, seeded, and cut into 1-inch pieces
¼ cup harissa
2 tablespoons tomato paste
4 garlic cloves, minced
2½ cups chicken broth
2 bay leaves
1 tablespoon red wine vinegar
2 tablespoons minced fresh mint

1. Adjust oven rack to lower-middle position and heat oven to 350 degrees. Pat shanks dry with paper towels and season with salt and pepper. Heat oil in Dutch oven over medium-high heat until just smoking. Brown shanks on all sides, 8 to 10 minutes; transfer to bowl.

2. Add onion, peppers, and ½ teaspoon salt to fat left in pot and cook over medium heat until softened, about 5 minutes. Stir in 3 tablespoons harissa, tomato paste, and garlic and cook until

Browning lamb shanks on the stovetop before cooking them in the oven adds more complex flavor to this braise.

fragrant, about 30 seconds. Stir in broth and bay leaves, scraping up any browned bits, and bring to simmer.

3. Nestle shanks into pot and return to simmer. Cover, transfer pot to oven, and cook until lamb is tender and fork slips easily in and out of meat and peppers begin to break down, 2 to 2½ hours, turning shanks halfway through cooking. Transfer shanks to bowl, tent loosely with aluminum foil, and let rest while finishing sauce.

4. Strain braising liquid through fine-mesh strainer into fat separator; discard bay leaves and transfer solids to blender. Let braising liquid settle for 5 minutes, then pour defatted liquid into blender with solids and process until smooth, about 1 minute.

5. Transfer sauce to now-empty pot and stir in vinegar and remaining 1 tablespoon harissa. Return shanks and any accumulated juices to pot, bring to gentle simmer over medium heat, and cook, spooning sauce over shanks occasionally, until heated through, about 5 minutes. Season with salt and pepper to taste. Transfer shanks to serving platter, spoon 1 cup sauce over top, and sprinkle with mint. Serve, passing remaining sauce separately.

CHAPTER 10

Eggs

▪ FAST (less than 45 minutes start to finish)   ▪ VEGETARIAN
Photos (clockwise from top left): Potato, Swiss Chard, and Lamb Hash with Poached Eggs; Baked Eggs with Tomatoes, Feta, and Croutons; Israeli Eggplant and Egg Sandwiches; Scrambled Eggs with Piperade

Jarred piquillo peppers and fresh yellow bell peppers create a complex and flavorful sauce for this Tunisian egg dish.

Shakshuka

SERVES 4 **VEG**

WHY THIS RECIPE WORKS *Shakshuka* is a Tunisian dish featuring eggs poached in a spiced tomato, onion, and pepper sauce. The key to great shakshuka is balancing the piquancy, acidity, richness, and sweetness of its ingredients. Choosing the right pepper to star in this dish made all the difference. We compared the results when using fresh red bell peppers, roasted red bell peppers, and piquillo peppers, which are sweet roasted chiles. The fresh red bell peppers tasted flat and lackluster. We liked the roasted red bell peppers just fine, but the piquillo peppers were our favorite, boasting spicy-sweet and vibrant flavors. These small red peppers from Spain, sold in jars or cans, have a subtle hint of smokiness from being roasted over a wood fire. We added yellow bell peppers to the mix for a clean, fresh flavor and a contrast to the deep red sauce. We finished our shakshuka with a sprinkling of bright cilantro and salty, creamy feta cheese. Jarred roasted red peppers can be substituted for the piquillo peppers. You will need a 12-inch nonstick skillet with a tight-fitting lid for this recipe. Serve with pitas or crusty bread to mop up the sauce.

3 tablespoons extra-virgin olive oil
2 onions, chopped fine
2 yellow bell peppers, stemmed, seeded, and cut into ¼-inch pieces
4 garlic cloves, minced
2 teaspoons tomato paste
Salt and pepper
1 teaspoon ground cumin
1 teaspoon ground turmeric
⅛ teaspoon cayenne pepper
1½ cups jarred piquillo peppers, chopped coarse
1 (14.5-ounce) can diced tomatoes
¼ cup water
2 bay leaves
⅓ cup chopped fresh cilantro
4 large eggs
2 ounces feta cheese, crumbled (½ cup)

1. Heat oil in 12-inch nonstick skillet over medium-high heat until shimmering. Add onions and bell peppers and cook until softened and lightly browned, 8 to 10 minutes. Add garlic, tomato paste, 1½ teaspoons salt, cumin, turmeric, ¼ teaspoon pepper, and cayenne. Cook, stirring frequently, until tomato paste begins to darken, about 3 minutes.

2. Stir in piquillo peppers, tomatoes and their juice, water, and bay leaves. Bring to simmer and cook, stirring occasionally, until sauce is slightly thickened, 10 to 15 minutes.

Poaching Eggs in Sauce, Ratatouille, or Hash

To give eggs better flavor and streamline our recipes, we often poach eggs directly in the skillet with a sauce or hash rather than poaching them separately in water. Here's how to ensure that the whites cook through before the yolks set.

1. Off heat, make 4 shallow indentations (about 2 inches wide) in surface of sauce or hash using back of spoon.

2. Crack 1 egg into each indentation and season eggs with salt and pepper. Cover and cook over medium-low heat until egg whites are just set and yolks are still runny, 5 to 10 minutes.

3. Off heat, discard bay leaves and stir in ¼ cup cilantro. Transfer 2 cups sauce to blender and process until smooth, about 60 seconds. Return puree to skillet and bring sauce to simmer over medium-low heat.

4. Off heat, make 4 shallow indentations (about 2 inches wide) in surface of sauce using back of spoon. Crack 1 egg into each indentation and season eggs with salt and pepper. Cover and cook over medium-low heat until egg whites are just set and yolks are still runny, 4 to 6 minutes. Sprinkle with feta and remaining cilantro and serve immediately.

NOTES FROM THE TEST KITCHEN
Storing Eggs

In the test kitchen, we've tasted two- and three-month-old eggs and found them perfectly palatable. However, at four months, the white was very loose and the yolk had off-flavors, though it was still edible. Our advice is to use your discretion; if eggs smell odd or are discolored, pitch them. Older eggs also lack the structure-lending properties of fresh eggs, so beware when baking.

IN THE REFRIGERATOR

Eggs often suffer more from improper storage than from age. If your refrigerator has an egg tray in the door, don't use it—eggs should be stored on a shelf, where the temperature is below 40 degrees (the average refrigerator door temperature in our kitchen is closer to 45 degrees). Eggs are best stored in their cardboard or plastic carton, which protects them from absorbing flavors from other foods. The carton also helps maintain humidity, which slows down the evaporation of the eggs' moisture.

IN THE FREEZER

Extra whites can be frozen for later use, but we have found that their rising properties are compromised. Frozen whites are best in recipes that call for small amounts (like an egg wash) or that don't depend on whipping (like a scramble). Yolks can't be frozen as is, but adding sugar syrup (microwave 2 parts sugar to 1 part water, stirring occasionally, until sugar is dissolved) to the yolks allows them to be frozen. Stir a scant ¼ teaspoon of sugar syrup per yolk into the yolks before freezing. Defrosted yolks treated this way will behave just like fresh yolks in custards and other recipes.

Ratatouille with Poached Eggs
SERVES 4 **FAST** **VEG**

WHY THIS RECIPE WORKS Ratatouille is a classic French dish that takes summer vegetables to new heights. This flavorful stew also makes a great base for poached eggs as a healthy breakfast or dinner. After a couple of tries, we learned that it was crucial to brown the vegetables to develop and deepen their flavor, or else the dish would taste bland and soggy. Since zucchini and eggplant have very different cooking times, it was important to brown the zucchini first, then remove it from the pan before cooking the eggplant. Poaching the eggs right in the ratatouille worked like a charm and made this an easy one-pan meal. You will need a 12-inch nonstick skillet with a tight-fitting lid for this recipe. Leaving the skin on the eggplant helps keep the pieces intact during cooking. Serve with Garlic Toasts (page 56), if desired.

¼ cup extra-virgin olive oil
1 pound zucchini, cut into ¾-inch pieces
1 pound eggplant, cut into ¾-inch pieces
  Salt and pepper
1 onion, chopped fine
4 garlic cloves, minced
1 pound plum tomatoes, cored and cut into ½-inch pieces
½ cup chicken or vegetable broth
4 large eggs
¼ cup chopped fresh basil
1 ounce Parmesan cheese, grated (½ cup)

1. Heat 1 tablespoon oil in 12-inch nonstick skillet over medium-high heat until just smoking. Add zucchini and cook until well browned, about 5 minutes; transfer to bowl.

2. Add eggplant, 2 tablespoons oil, and ¼ teaspoon salt to now-empty skillet and cook over medium-high heat until eggplant is browned, 5 to 7 minutes. Stir in onion and remaining 1 tablespoon oil and cook until onion is softened, about 5 minutes. Stir in garlic and cook until fragrant, about 30 seconds. Stir in tomatoes and broth and simmer until vegetables are softened, 3 to 5 minutes. Stir in zucchini and any accumulated juice and season with salt and pepper to taste.

3. Off heat, make 4 shallow indentations (about 2 inches wide) in surface of ratatouille using back of spoon. Crack 1 egg into each indentation and season with salt and pepper. Cover and cook over medium-low heat until egg whites are just set and yolks are still runny, 4 to 6 minutes. Sprinkle with basil and Parmesan and serve immediately.

Potato, Swiss Chard, and Lamb Hash with Poached Eggs

SERVES 4

WHY THIS RECIPE WORKS We set out to create a simple breakfast hash inspired by bold Moroccan flavors. We decided on russet potatoes as the base of our hash, since tasters liked their fluffy interiors and crisp exteriors. To make the potatoes cook faster, we microwaved them before cooking them in a skillet. Ground lamb made a deeply savory counterpoint to the potatoes, and its rendered fat provided richness; some aromatics and warm Moroccan spices like cumin, coriander, and paprika offered balanced flavor. Tasters also liked the addition of Swiss chard for its slightly bitter, vegetal flavor; we started cooking the stems before adding the leaves so the stems would fully soften by the time the leaves were wilted. Because we were combining ingredients that cook at different rates, we cooked each element separately before mixing them together. Once we added the mixture to the skillet, we packed it down to ensure good contact with the hot pan, which encouraged deep browning and a crisp, crunchy exterior on our hash. Flipping the hash in portions was easier than flipping the whole thing at once. Finally, we cooked the eggs right in the hash by making divots with a spoon. You will need a 12-inch nonstick skillet with a tight-fitting lid for this recipe. If the potatoes aren't getting brown in step 4, turn up the heat.

1½ pounds russet potatoes, peeled and cut into
    ½-inch pieces
2 tablespoons extra-virgin olive oil
    Salt and pepper
1½ pounds Swiss chard, stems sliced ¼ inch thick,
    leaves sliced into ½-inch-wide strips
8 ounces ground lamb
1 onion, chopped fine
3 garlic cloves, minced
2 teaspoons paprika
1 teaspoon ground cumin
1 teaspoon ground coriander
¼ teaspoon cayenne pepper
4 large eggs
1 tablespoon minced fresh chives

1. Toss potatoes with 1 tablespoon oil, ½ teaspoon salt, and ¼ teaspoon pepper in bowl. Cover and microwave until potatoes are translucent around edges, 7 to 9 minutes, stirring halfway through microwaving; drain well.

2. Heat remaining 1 tablespoon oil in 12-inch nonstick skillet over medium-high heat until shimmering. Add chard stems and

Sautéing a small amount of lamb and using the fat to bloom spices and aromatics gives our Moroccan hash deep flavor.

¼ teaspoon salt and cook until softened and lightly browned, 5 to 7 minutes. Stir in chard leaves, 1 handful at a time, and cook until mostly wilted, about 4 minutes; transfer to bowl with potatoes.

3. Cook lamb in now-empty skillet over medium-high heat, breaking up meat with wooden spoon, until beginning to brown, about 5 minutes. Stir in onion and cook until softened and lightly browned, 5 to 7 minutes. Stir in garlic, paprika, cumin, coriander, and cayenne and cook until fragrant, about 30 seconds.

4. Stir in chard-potato mixture. Using back of spatula, gently pack chard-potato mixture into skillet and cook, without stirring, for 2 minutes. Flip hash, 1 portion at a time, and lightly repack into skillet. Repeat flipping process every few minutes until potatoes are well browned, 6 to 8 minutes.

5. Off heat, make 4 shallow indentations (about 2 inches wide) in surface of hash using back of spoon, pushing hash up into center and around edges of skillet (bottom of skillet should be exposed in each divot). Crack 1 egg into each indentation and season with salt and pepper. Cover and cook over medium-low heat until whites are just set and yolks are still runny, 4 to 6 minutes. Sprinkle with chives and serve immediately.

Fried Eggs with Potato and Parmesan Pancake
SERVES 8 VEG

WHY THIS RECIPE WORKS Potatoes are an ultraversatile Mediterranean ingredient; they're used throughout the region in a wide variety of recipes. We wanted to use potatoes to make a hearty pancake that could be served with a fried egg for either brunch or supper. We quickly found that producing a golden-brown crust for our potato pancake wasn't much of a problem, but the inside always came out gluey and half-cooked. To fix this, we first eliminated moisture by wringing the raw grated potatoes in a dish towel. Covering the potatoes to start, then uncovering them to finish cooking, created a surprisingly light texture. Our final breakthrough came when we removed excess starch by rinsing the raw potatoes in cold water, then tossed them with 1½ teaspoons of cornstarch to provide just enough starch to hold the cake together. A bit of Parmesan cheese enhanced the pancake's flavor and gave it a distinctly Mediterranean identity. You will need a 12-inch nonstick skillet with a tight-fitting lid for this recipe. For the best texture, shred the potatoes on the large shredding disk of a food processor. If using a box grater, cut the potatoes lengthwise so you are left with long shreds. Be sure to squeeze the potatoes as dry as possible.

2½ pounds Yukon Gold potatoes, peeled and shredded
1½ teaspoons cornstarch
   Salt and pepper
¼ cup plus 2 teaspoons extra-virgin olive oil
8 large eggs
1 ounce Parmesan cheese, grated (½ cup)
1 tablespoon minced fresh chives

1. Place potatoes in large bowl and fill bowl with cold water. Using hands, swirl to remove excess starch, then drain, leaving potatoes in colander.

2. Wipe bowl dry. Place one-third of potatoes in center of clean dish towel. Gather towel ends together and twist tightly to squeeze out moisture. Transfer potatoes to now-empty bowl and repeat process with remaining potatoes in 2 batches.

3. Sprinkle cornstarch, 1 teaspoon salt, and pinch pepper over potatoes. Using hands or fork, toss ingredients together until well combined.

4. Heat 2 tablespoons oil in 12-inch nonstick skillet over medium heat until shimmering. Add potato mixture and spread into even layer. Cover and cook for 6 minutes. Uncover and, using spatula, gently press potatoes down to form round cake. Cook, occasionally pressing on potatoes to shape into uniform round cake, until bottom is deep golden brown, 8 to 10 minutes.

5. Shake skillet to loosen pancake and slide onto large plate. Add 2 tablespoons oil to skillet and swirl to coat. Invert potato pancake onto second plate and slide potato pancake, browned side up, back into skillet. Cook, occasionally pressing down on pancake, until bottom is well browned, 8 to 10 minutes. Transfer pancake to cutting board and set aside while preparing eggs.

6. Crack eggs into 2 small bowls (4 eggs per bowl) and season with salt and pepper. Wipe skillet clean with paper towels. Heat remaining 2 teaspoons oil in now-empty skillet over medium heat until shimmering. Working quickly, pour 1 bowl of eggs in 1 side of skillet and second bowl of eggs in other side. Cover and cook for 2 minutes.

7. Remove skillet from heat and let sit, covered, about 2 minutes for runny yolks (white around edge of yolk will be barely opaque), about 3 minutes for soft but set yolks, and about 4 minutes for medium-set yolks. Slide eggs onto individual plates. Sprinkle pancake with Parmesan and chives, cut into wedges, and serve with eggs.

Frying Eight Eggs at Once

1. Crack eggs into small bowls (4 eggs per bowl) and season with salt and pepper.

2. Working quickly, pour 1 bowl of eggs in 1 side of skillet and second bowl of eggs in other side.

3. Cover and cook for 2 minutes. Remove skillet from heat and let sit, covered, until eggs achieve desired doneness.

We salt and then broil slices of eggplant to give them the best texture and flavor in our open-faced Israeli sandwiches.

Israeli Eggplant and Egg Sandwiches
SERVES 4 VEG

WHY THIS RECIPE WORKS *Sabich*, a soft pita stuffed with creamy fried eggplant, hard-cooked eggs, savory hummus, and crunchy pickles, is a popular Israeli street food. To create an appealing version that could be made at home, we started with the eggplant. Although it's traditionally fried, a few tests revealed that tasters preferred the flavor and texture of broiled eggplant. Salting the eggplant for 30 minutes before broiling helped to eliminate excess moisture and encourage deep, flavorful browning. Chopped dill pickles offered great briny flavor, and cherry tomatoes, red onion, and parsley provided bright, fresh notes. Sabich is often eaten as a sandwich, but we decided to lay the pitas flat and pile everything on top to create a beautiful presentation and make the dish easier to eat. Cutting our hard-cooked eggs into thin slices (as opposed to wedges) worked best, since the flat slices could easily be layered with the other ingredients. Finishing our open-faced sandwiches with a drizzle of our tangy Tahini-Yogurt Sauce and spicy *zhoug*, an Israeli hot sauce made with cilantro and parsley, brought all the elements together. We prefer to use our homemade Pita Bread (page 344) and Classic Hummus (page 16), but you can use store-bought varieties. If you can't find Aleppo pepper, you can substitute ¼ teaspoon paprika and ¼ teaspoon finely chopped red pepper flakes.

1 pound eggplant, sliced into ½-inch-thick rounds
  Salt and pepper
¼ cup extra-virgin olive oil
8 ounces cherry tomatoes, quartered
½ cup finely chopped dill pickles
¼ cup finely chopped red onion
¼ cup fresh parsley leaves
1 tablespoon lemon juice
1 garlic clove, minced
4 (8-inch) pita breads
1 cup hummus
6 hard-cooked large eggs, sliced thin (page 188)
½ cup Tahini-Yogurt Sauce (page 233)
½ cup Green Zhoug (page 316)
1 teaspoon ground dried Aleppo pepper

1. Spread eggplant on baking sheet lined with paper towels, sprinkle both sides with 2 teaspoons salt, and let sit for 30 minutes.

2. Adjust oven rack 4 inches from broiler element and heat broiler. Thoroughly pat eggplant dry with paper towels, arrange on aluminum foil–lined rimmed baking sheet in single layer, and lightly brush both sides with 2 tablespoons oil. Broil eggplant until spotty brown, about 5 minutes per side.

3. Combine tomatoes, pickles, onion, parsley, lemon juice, garlic, and remaining 2 tablespoons oil in bowl and season with salt and pepper to taste. Lay each pita on individual plate, spread with ¼ cup hummus, and top evenly with eggplant, tomato salad, and eggs. Drizzle with Tahini-Yogurt Sauce and Green Zhoug and sprinkle with Aleppo. Serve immediately.

Scrambled Eggs with Prosciutto and Asparagus
SERVES 6 to 8 FAST

WHY THIS RECIPE WORKS Fluffy, light, and creamy scrambled eggs are a perfect neutral backdrop for any number of Mediterranean ingredients. Cooking our eggs in olive oil gave them rich flavor and ensured that they remained tender throughout cooking. Adding a small amount of water to the eggs before whisking created the fluffiest texture since the water turned to steam during cooking. We decided on fresh asparagus, meaty prosciutto, and nutty Parmesan as our flavorful additions. We cooked the asparagus first to cook it through and achieve some light browning; using the same pan to cook the asparagus and the eggs kept our recipe streamlined. Once the eggs were done, we folded in the cooked asparagus, prosciutto, and Parmesan to warm them through without risking excess browning. If you don't have prosciutto, you can substitute any thinly sliced deli ham.

> 3 tablespoons extra-virgin olive oil
> 8 ounces asparagus, trimmed and cut on bias into ¼-inch lengths
> 12 large eggs
> 2 tablespoons water
> ½ teaspoon salt
> ¼ teaspoon pepper
> 2 ounces thinly sliced prosciutto, chopped coarse
> 1 ounce Parmesan cheese, grated (½ cup)

1. Heat 1 tablespoon oil in 12-inch nonstick skillet over medium heat until shimmering. Add asparagus and cook until crisp-tender and lightly browned, 2 to 4 minutes; transfer to bowl and cover to keep warm.

2. Beat eggs, water, salt, and pepper together with fork in bowl until thoroughly combined and mixture is pure yellow; do not overbeat.

3. Wipe skillet clean with paper towels. Heat remaining 2 tablespoons oil in now-empty skillet over medium heat until shimmering. Add egg mixture and, using heat-resistant rubber spatula, constantly and firmly scrape along bottom and sides of skillet until eggs begin to clump and spatula leaves trail on bottom of skillet, 1½ to 2 minutes.

4. Reduce heat to low and gently but constantly fold eggs until clumped and slightly wet, 30 to 60 seconds. Off heat, gently fold in asparagus, prosciutto, and Parmesan. Serve immediately.

Scrambling Eggs

1. Add egg mixture to skillet. Using heat-resistant rubber spatula, constantly and firmly scrape along bottom and sides of skillet until eggs begin to clump and spatula leaves trail.

2. Reduce heat to low and gently but constantly fold eggs until clumped and slightly wet, 30 to 60 seconds.

Buying Eggs

There are numerous—and often confusing—options when buying eggs at the supermarket. And when eggs are the focal point of a dish, their quality makes a big difference. Here's what we've learned in the test kitchen about buying eggs.

COLOR

The shell's hue depends on the breed of the chicken. The run-of-the-mill leghorn chicken produces the typical white egg. Brown-feathered birds, such as Rhode Island Reds, produce ecru- to coffee-colored eggs. Despite marketing hype extolling the virtues of nonwhite eggs, our tests proved that shell color has no effect on flavor.

FARM-FRESH AND ORGANIC

In our taste tests, farm-fresh eggs were standouts. The large yolks were bright orange and sat very high above the comparatively small whites, and the flavor of these eggs was exceptionally rich and complex. Organic eggs followed in second place, with eggs from hens raised on a vegetarian diet in third, and the standard supermarket eggs last. Differences were easily detected in egg-based dishes like a scramble or a frittata, but not in baked goods.

EGGS AND OMEGA-3S

Several companies are marketing eggs with a high level of omega-3 fatty acids, the healthful unsaturated fats also found in some fish. In our taste test, we found that more omega-3s translated into a richer egg flavor. Why? Commercially raised chickens usually peck on corn and soy, but chickens on an omega-3-enriched diet have supplements of greens, flaxseeds, and algae, which also add flavor, complexity, and color to their eggs. Read labels carefully and look for brands that guarantee at least 200 milligrams of omega-3s per egg.

HOW OLD ARE MY EGGS?

Egg cartons are marked with both a sell-by date and a pack date. The pack date is the day the eggs were packed, which is generally within a week of when they were laid but may be as much as 30 days later. The sell-by date is within 30 days of the pack date, which is the legal limit set by the U.S. Department of Agriculture (USDA). In short, a carton of eggs may be up to two months old by the end of the sell-by date. But according to the USDA, eggs are still fit for consumption for an additional three to five weeks past the sell-by date.

Steaming and then browning mushrooms and potatoes delivers tender, flavorful vegetables for our scramble.

Scrambled Eggs with Potatoes and Harissa

SERVES 6 to 8 **FAST** **VEG**

WHY THIS RECIPE WORKS For a spicy take on scrambled eggs, we looked to North Africa for inspiration and decided to include hearty red potatoes and mushrooms and piquant harissa, a spice paste that is used throughout the region. To ensure that the mushrooms and potatoes were cooked through, we added them to the pan with some water and covered them so they would steam and tenderize. We then uncovered the pan to evaporate the liquid and brown the vegetables. Separately, we scrambled our eggs into large, airy curds, removing them from the heat just before they were done to ensure they didn't overcook. A bit of harissa, drizzled on the finished eggs, gave the dish bold flavor. We prefer to use our homemade Harissa (page 316), but you can substitute store-bought harissa if you wish, though spiciness can vary greatly by brand.

3 tablespoons extra-virgin olive oil
8 ounces red potatoes, unpeeled, cut into ½-inch pieces
8 ounces cremini mushrooms, trimmed and halved if small or quartered if large

½ onion, chopped fine
½ cup plus 2 tablespoons water
  Salt and pepper
1 garlic clove, minced
12 large eggs
2 tablespoons harissa, plus extra for serving
2 tablespoons chopped fresh cilantro

1. Heat 1 tablespoon oil in 12-inch nonstick skillet over medium heat until shimmering. Add potatoes, mushrooms, onion, ½ cup water, and ¼ teaspoon salt. Cover and cook, stirring occasionally, until vegetables are softened, 8 to 10 minutes. Uncover and continue to cook, stirring occasionally, until liquid is evaporated and potatoes are golden brown, 3 to 5 minutes. Stir in garlic and cook until fragrant, about 30 seconds; transfer to bowl and cover to keep warm.

2. Beat eggs, ¾ teaspoon salt, ¼ teaspoon pepper, and remaining 2 tablespoons water together with fork in bowl until thoroughly combined and mixture is pure yellow; do not overbeat.

3. Wipe skillet clean with paper towels. Heat remaining 2 tablespoons oil in now-empty skillet over medium heat until shimmering. Add egg mixture and, using heat-resistant rubber spatula, constantly and firmly scrape along bottom and sides of skillet until eggs begin to clump and spatula leaves trail on bottom of skillet, 1½ to 2 minutes.

4. Reduce heat to low and gently but constantly fold eggs until clumped and slightly wet, 30 to 60 seconds. Off heat, gently fold in potato mixture. Drizzle with harissa and sprinkle with cilantro. Serve immediately, passing extra harissa separately.

Scrambled Eggs with Piperade

SERVES 6 to 8 **VEG**

WHY THIS RECIPE WORKS The pepper and tomato sauté known as *piperade* is a classic Spanish accompaniment to scrambled eggs. Piperade delivers richness, acidity, and tempered heat from a combination of fresh peppers, tomatoes, fragrant spices like paprika, and subtly spicy, fruity dried peppers. Since we had already perfected our scrambled egg technique, we focused our attention on achieving a great piperade. Tasters liked a combination of red bell peppers and Italian Cubanelle peppers for their sweetness and delicate fresh flavor. By using canned peeled tomatoes, we avoided chewy bits of tomato skin; draining the tomatoes of most of their juice kept the dish from being watery. Onion, garlic, bay leaf, and thyme offered aromatic complexity; a bit of sherry vinegar brought the flavors into focus. While in many piperade recipes the eggs are scrambled with the vegetable mixture, we found that the liquid from the produce caused the eggs to cook up stringy and wet rather than fluffy and creamy. We opted to cook the eggs separately and then plate the two elements alongside one another to preserve the clean yellow color of the eggs. We prefer to make this dish with Cubanelle peppers, which are chartreuse in color and look similar to banana peppers; if you can't find them, you can substitute green bell peppers.

5 tablespoons extra-virgin olive oil
1 large onion, chopped
1 bay leaf
Salt and pepper
4 garlic cloves, minced
2 teaspoons paprika
1 teaspoon minced fresh thyme or ¼ teaspoon dried
¾ teaspoon red pepper flakes
3 red bell peppers, stemmed, seeded, and cut into ½-inch-wide strips
3 Cubanelle peppers, stemmed, seeded, and cut into ½-inch-wide strips
1 (14-ounce) can whole peeled tomatoes, drained with ¼ cup juice reserved, chopped coarse
3 tablespoons minced fresh parsley
2 teaspoons sherry vinegar
12 large eggs
2 tablespoons water

1. Heat 3 tablespoons oil in 12-inch nonstick skillet over medium heat until shimmering. Add onion, bay leaf, and ½ teaspoon salt and cook until onion is softened and lightly browned, 5 to 7 minutes. Stir in garlic, paprika, thyme, and pepper flakes and cook until fragrant, about 1 minute. Add bell peppers, Cubanelle peppers, and 1 teaspoon salt, cover, and cook, stirring occasionally, until peppers begin to soften, about 10 minutes.

2. Reduce heat to medium-low. Add tomatoes and reserved juice and cook, uncovered, stirring occasionally, until mixture appears dry and peppers are tender but not mushy, 10 to 12 minutes. Off heat, discard bay leaf. Stir in 2 tablespoons parsley and vinegar and season with salt and pepper to taste; transfer to bowl and cover to keep warm.

3. Beat eggs, water, ½ teaspoon salt, and ¼ teaspoon pepper together with fork in bowl until thoroughly combined and mixture is pure yellow; do not overbeat.

4. Wipe skillet clean with paper towels. Heat remaining 2 tablespoons oil in now-empty skillet over medium heat until shimmering. Add egg mixture and, using heat-resistant rubber spatula, constantly and firmly scrape along bottom and sides of skillet until eggs begin to clump and spatula leaves trail on bottom of skillet, 1½ to 2 minutes.

5. Reduce heat to low and gently but constantly fold eggs until clumped and slightly wet, 30 to 60 seconds. Off heat, sprinkle with remaining 1 tablespoon parsley and serve immediately with pepper mixture.

Using less starchy Yukon Gold potatoes in our classic Spanish tortilla allows us to use much less oil to cook them.

Spanish Tortilla with Roasted Red Peppers and Peas

SERVES 6 VEG

WHY THIS RECIPE WORKS Spanish tortilla is a tapas bar favorite, boasting meltingly tender potatoes in a dense, creamy omelet. But the typical recipe calls for simmering the potatoes in up to 4 cups of extra-virgin olive oil. Using so much oil for a single and somewhat humble meal seemed excessive. We were able to cut the oil to a mere 6 tablespoons by substituting firmer, less starchy Yukon Gold potatoes for the standard russets. Traditional recipes call for flipping the tortilla with the help of a single plate, but when we tried this, the result was an egg-splattered floor. Sliding the omelet onto the plate, and then using a second plate to flip it, made a once-messy task foolproof. And while the tortilla was perfectly good plain, we liked it even better with roasted red peppers and peas; a dollop of our garlicky aïoli took it over the top. This dish can be served warm or at room temperature alongside olives and pickles as an appetizer or served with a salad as a light entrée. You will need a 10-inch nonstick skillet with a tight-fitting lid for this recipe. Serve with Garlic Aïoli (page 233).

1½ pounds Yukon Gold potatoes, peeled, quartered, and sliced ⅛ inch thick

1 small onion, halved and sliced thin

6 tablespoons plus 1 teaspoon extra-virgin olive oil
Salt and pepper

8 large eggs

½ cup jarred roasted red peppers, rinsed, patted dry, and cut into ½-inch pieces

½ cup frozen peas, thawed

1. Toss potatoes and onion with ¼ cup oil, ½ teaspoon salt, and ¼ teaspoon pepper in large bowl. Heat 2 tablespoons oil in 10-inch nonstick skillet over medium-high heat until shimmering. Add potato mixture to skillet and reduce heat to medium-low; set bowl aside without washing. Cover potatoes and cook, stirring every 5 minutes, until tender, about 25 minutes.

2. Beat eggs and ½ teaspoon salt together with fork in reserved bowl until thoroughly combined and mixture is pure yellow; do not overbeat. Gently fold in potato mixture, red peppers, and peas, making sure to scrape all of potato mixture out of skillet.

3. Heat remaining 1 teaspoon oil in now-empty skillet over medium-high heat until just smoking. Add egg mixture and cook, shaking skillet and folding mixture constantly for 15 seconds. Smooth top of egg mixture, reduce heat to medium, cover, and cook, gently shaking skillet every 30 seconds, until bottom is golden brown and top is lightly set, about 2 minutes.

4. Off heat, run heat-resistant rubber spatula around edge of skillet and shake skillet gently to loosen tortilla; it should slide around freely in skillet. Slide tortilla onto large plate, then invert onto second large plate and slide back into skillet browned side up. Tuck edges of tortilla into skillet with rubber spatula. Continue to cook over medium heat, gently shaking skillet every 30 seconds, until second side is golden brown, about 2 minutes. Slide tortilla onto cutting board and let cool slightly. Slice and serve hot, warm, or at room temperature.

Making Spanish Tortilla

1. COOK POTATOES Cook potatoes and onion in covered skillet, stirring every 5 minutes, until tender, about 25 minutes.

2. COMBINE EGGS AND VEGETABLES Beat together eggs and salt; fold in vegetables. Add egg mixture to skillet and cook, folding constantly for 15 seconds. Cover and continue to cook.

3. FLIP TORTILLA Loosen tortilla with rubber spatula and slide it onto large plate. Place second plate face down over tortilla and invert so that tortilla is browned side up.

4. FINISH Slide tortilla back into skillet, browned side up, then tuck edges into skillet with rubber spatula. Continue to cook until second side is golden brown. Slide onto cutting board, let cool slightly, and slice.

Egyptian Eggah with Ground Beef and Spinach
SERVES 4 to 6 `FAST`

WHY THIS RECIPE WORKS *Eggah*, the Arabic answer to Spanish tortilla, often features boldly spiced fillings in a hearty egg base. We started by choosing traditional Egyptian fillings of ground beef, spinach, and leeks. Using 90 percent lean ground beef ensured that our eggah didn't turn out greasy, and precooking the spinach in the microwave eliminated any excess moisture that could leave the dish soggy. A mixture of cumin, cinnamon, and cilantro enhanced the North African flavor profile. We precooked our filling and let it cool slightly before adding it to the beaten eggs. To cook our eggah, we borrowed a technique from our tortilla recipe (left), in which we cook the egg mixture in a hot skillet and then flip it halfway through using two plates. Eggah can be served hot, warm, or at room temperature. You will need a 10-inch nonstick skillet with a tight-fitting lid for this recipe.

8 ounces (8 cups) baby spinach

6 tablespoons water

4 teaspoons extra-virgin olive oil

1 pound leeks, whites and light green parts only, halved lengthwise, sliced thin, and washed thoroughly

8 ounces 90 percent lean ground beef

1 garlic clove, minced

1 teaspoon ground cumin

¼ teaspoon ground cinnamon

Precooking the filling before adding it to the beaten eggs ensures that our Egyptian omelet is evenly cooked.

Salt and pepper
8 large eggs
¼ cup minced fresh cilantro

1. Place spinach and ¼ cup water in large bowl, cover, and microwave until spinach is wilted and decreased in volume by about half, about 5 minutes. Remove bowl from microwave and keep covered for 1 minute. Transfer spinach to colander and gently press to release liquid. Transfer spinach to cutting board and chop coarse. Return to colander and press again.

2. Heat 1 teaspoon oil in 10-inch nonstick skillet over medium heat until shimmering. Add leeks and cook until softened, about 5 minutes. Add ground beef and cook, breaking up meat with wooden spoon, until beginning to brown, 5 to 7 minutes. Stir in garlic, cumin, cinnamon, ½ teaspoon salt, and ¼ teaspoon pepper and cook until fragrant, about 30 seconds. Stir in spinach until heated through, about 1 minute; transfer to bowl and let cool slightly.

3. Beat eggs, remaining 2 tablespoons water, ½ teaspoon salt, and ¼ teaspoon pepper together with fork in large bowl until thoroughly combined and mixture is pure yellow; do not overbeat. Gently fold in spinach mixture and cilantro, making sure to scrape all of spinach mixture out of skillet.

4. Heat remaining 1 tablespoon oil in now-empty skillet over medium-high heat until just smoking. Add egg mixture and cook, shaking skillet and folding mixture constantly for 15 seconds. Smooth top of egg mixture, reduce heat to medium, cover, and cook, gently shaking skillet every 30 seconds, until bottom is golden brown and top is lightly set, about 3 minutes.

5. Off heat, run heat-resistant rubber spatula around edge of skillet and shake skillet gently to loosen eggah; it should slide around freely in skillet. Slide eggah onto large plate, then invert onto second large plate and slide back into skillet browned side up. Tuck edges of eggah into skillet with rubber spatula. Continue to cook over medium heat, gently shaking skillet every 30 seconds, until second side is golden brown, about 2 minutes. Slide eggah onto cutting board and let cool slightly. Slice and serve hot, warm, or at room temperature.

Broccoli and Feta Frittata
SERVES 6 **FAST** **VEG**

WHY THIS RECIPE WORKS Hearty and simple, a frittata can make a great breakfast, lunch, or dinner. We found that the key to achieving the best texture was to use a combination stovetop-oven method. Stirring the eggs as they began to set on the stovetop was crucial to prevent the bottom of the frittata from overcooking; transferring the skillet to the oven allowed the eggs to gently cook through in the even heat. A small amount of milk helped the eggs stay tender without making them so delicate that they couldn't support the filling. As for our flavorful additions, we settled on several Mediterranean combinations: hearty broccoli with tangy feta and a bit of lemon zest; grassy asparagus with earthy goat cheese and fresh mint; and cremini mushrooms with nutty sherry vinegar and Pecorino. You will need a 12-inch oven-safe nonstick skillet for this recipe. These frittatas can be served hot, warm, or at room temperature.

12 large eggs
⅓ cup whole milk
    Salt
1 tablespoon extra-virgin olive oil
12 ounces broccoli florets, cut into ½-inch pieces (3½ to 4 cups)
    Pinch red pepper flakes
3 tablespoons water
½ teaspoon grated lemon zest plus ½ teaspoon juice
4 ounces feta cheese, crumbled into ½-inch pieces (1 cup)

1. Adjust oven rack to middle position and heat oven to 350 degrees. Beat eggs, milk, and ½ teaspoon salt together with

fork in bowl until thoroughly combined and mixture is pure yellow; do not overbeat.

2. Heat oil in 12-inch nonstick skillet over medium-high heat until shimmering. Add broccoli, pepper flakes, and ¼ teaspoon salt and cook, stirring frequently, until broccoli is crisp-tender and spotty brown, 7 to 9 minutes. Add water and lemon zest and juice and continue to cook, stirring constantly, until broccoli is just tender and no water remains in skillet, about 1 minute.

3. Add feta and egg mixture and, using heat-resistant rubber spatula, constantly and firmly scrape along bottom and sides of skillet until large curds form and spatula begins to leave trail on bottom of skillet but eggs are still very wet, about 30 seconds. Smooth curds into even layer and let cook without stirring for 30 seconds. Transfer skillet to oven and bake until frittata is slightly puffy and surface bounces back when lightly pressed, 6 to 9 minutes. Using rubber spatula, loosen frittata from skillet and transfer to cutting board. Let sit for 5 minutes before slicing and serving.

VARIATIONS

Asparagus and Goat Cheese Frittata `FAST` `VEG`
This recipe works best with thin or standard-size asparagus spears.
Omit broccoli, pepper flakes, and water. Add 1 pound asparagus, trimmed and cut into ¼-inch lengths, lemon zest and juice, ¼ teaspoon salt, and ¼ teaspoon pepper to oil in step 2; cook, stirring frequently, until asparagus is crisp-tender, 3 to 4 minutes. Continue with step 3, substituting 1 cup crumbled goat cheese for feta and adding 2 tablespoons chopped fresh mint with goat cheese and egg mixture.

Mushroom and Pecorino Frittata `FAST` `VEG`
Substitute 1 pound cremini mushrooms, stemmed and cut into ½-inch pieces, for broccoli and ¼ teaspoon pepper for red pepper flakes. Reduce water to 2 tablespoons and substitute 2 minced scallion whites, 1½ teaspoons minced fresh thyme, and 1 tablespoon sherry vinegar for lemon juice and zest. Substitute ¾ cup shredded Pecorino Romano for feta and add 2 thinly sliced scallion greens with Pecorino and egg mixture.

Removing a Frittata from the Pan

Run spatula around skillet edge to loosen frittata, then carefully slide it out onto serving platter or cutting board.

Baked Eggs with Tomatoes, Feta, and Croutons
SERVES 6 `VEG`

WHY THIS RECIPE WORKS The classic Greek dish called *avga feta domata* consists of eggs baked in a bed of savory tomato sauce and croutons and topped with tangy feta cheese. For our version, we opted to use fresh cherry tomatoes and roast them to make our sauce. Tossing the tomatoes with a mixture of oil, garlic, oregano, tomato paste, and a bit of sugar and salt enhanced the tomato flavor and encouraged deep caramelization. To prevent our croutons from becoming a mushy, pasty mess, we baked pieces of crusty bread (coated with a judicious amount of olive oil) in the oven while the tomatoes roasted. Folding the croutons and tomatoes together after this initial stint in the oven helped ensure perfectly chewy croutons with slightly crunchy centers. By baking the eggs in wide, shallow divots in the tomato-crouton mixture, we exposed more of the egg whites' surface area to the heat, allowing the whites to cook through before the yolks completely solidified. Letting the dish rest, covered, for just a few minutes before serving gave the eggs time to gently finish cooking. When it came to the cheese, tasters disliked the texture of baked feta, finding it rubbery and bland, so we simply sprinkled the feta on top just before serving. If you want your yolks fully cooked, bake until the whites are fully set before the resting period.

3 slices French or Italian bread, cut into ½-inch pieces (4 cups)
¼ cup extra-virgin olive oil
Salt and pepper
6 garlic cloves, sliced thin
5 teaspoons minced fresh oregano
2 teaspoons tomato paste
1 teaspoon sugar
2 pounds cherry tomatoes
6 large eggs
2 ounces feta cheese, crumbled (½ cup)

1. Adjust oven racks to upper-middle and lower-middle positions and heat oven to 450 degrees. Toss bread with 1 tablespoon oil in large bowl and season with salt and pepper. Spread bread into even layer in greased 13 by 9-inch baking dish; set aside.

2. Whisk garlic, 1 tablespoon oil, 1 tablespoon oregano, tomato paste, 1½ teaspoons salt, sugar, and ¼ teaspoon pepper together in large bowl. Add tomatoes and toss to combine. Transfer tomato mixture to parchment paper–lined rimmed baking sheet and push tomatoes toward center of sheet. Scrape any remaining garlic and tomato paste from bowl into center of tomatoes.

3. Bake bread on upper rack and tomatoes on lower rack, stirring occasionally, until bread is golden and tomatoes begin to soften, about 10 minutes. Remove croutons from oven and let cool in dish. Continue to bake tomatoes until blistered and browned, about 10 minutes.

4. Add tomatoes and 1 tablespoon oil to croutons, gently fold to combine, and smooth into even layer. Make 6 shallow indentations (about 2 inches wide) in surface of bread-tomato mixture using back of spoon. Crack 1 egg into each indentation and season eggs with salt and pepper.

5. Bake until whites are just beginning to set but still have some movement when dish is shaken, 10 to 12 minutes. Transfer dish to wire rack, tent loosely with aluminum foil, and let sit for 5 minutes. Sprinkle with feta and remaining 2 teaspoons oregano and drizzle with remaining 1 tablespoon oil. Serve immediately.

Greek-Style Zucchini and Egg Casserole
SERVES 6 to 8 `FAST` `VEG`

WHY THIS RECIPE WORKS Traditional Greek *sfougato* is an appealing, vegetable-centric baked egg dish with a texture somewhere between a light-as-air soufflé and a hearty frittata. Rather than consisting mostly of egg with a smattering of fillings, as a frittata would be, sfougato tends to be the opposite, with fewer eggs and a generous amount of zucchini, feta, and sometimes a small amount of ground beef. For our recipe, we opted to leave out the meat and focus on the clean zucchini flavor. To ensure that the casserole was pleasantly light and not dense, we mixed some milk into the eggs to keep them tender. We prevented the zucchini from releasing too much moisture and making our casserole soggy by grating it, salting it, and then wringing it dry in a clean dish towel. A brief sauté finished the job, and we took advantage of the hot pan to tame the harsh rawness of the garlic and scallions. Slightly sweet dill and zesty oregano, common additions to many recipes, complemented the bright, briny feta and the vegetal zucchini. This dish would pair nicely with a salad as a light lunch or brunch or with roasted potatoes and sausage for a heartier meal. Use the large holes of a box grater to shred the zucchini.

4 zucchini, shredded
Salt and pepper
1 tablespoon extra-virgin olive oil
8 scallions, sliced thin
2 garlic cloves, minced
6 large eggs
¼ cup whole milk
4 ounces feta cheese, crumbled (1 cup)
¼ cup minced fresh dill
1 tablespoon chopped fresh oregano

To rid the large amount of zucchini in our Greek egg casserole of its moisture, we grate, salt, and then sauté it.

1. Adjust oven rack to middle position and heat oven to 375 degrees. Toss zucchini with 1 teaspoon salt and let drain in fine-mesh strainer for 10 minutes. Wrap zucchini in clean dish towel, squeeze out excess liquid, and set aside.

2. Heat oil in 12-inch nonstick skillet over medium heat until shimmering. Add scallions and garlic and cook until scallions are softened, about 2 minutes. Stir in zucchini, cover, and cook until zucchini has released its liquid, 4 to 6 minutes. Uncover and continue to cook until zucchini is dry, about 1 minute; let cool slightly.

3. Beat eggs, milk, and ½ teaspoon pepper together with fork in bowl until thoroughly combined and mixture is pure yellow; do not overbeat. Stir in zucchini mixture, feta, dill, and oregano until combined. Transfer mixture to greased 13 by 9-inch baking dish and bake until eggs are just set and edges are beginning to brown, 20 to 25 minutes. Serve warm or at room temperature.

CHAPTER 11

Breads, Flatbreads, Pizzas, and More

▪ FAST (less than 45 minutes start to finish) ▢ VEGETARIAN
Photos (clockwise from top left): Socca with Swiss Chard, Pistachios, and Apricots; Pissaladière; Thin-Crust Pizza with Prosciutto and Arugula; Chicken B'stilla

A well-hydrated dough and a preheated baking stone ensure that our pita has a hollow interior perfect for stuffing.

Pita Bread

MAKES eight 8-inch pitas   VEG

WHY THIS RECIPE WORKS Pita breads vary dramatically depending on the region of the world where they're made. The thin, wheaty versions, often called Arabic bread, hail from all over the Middle East. We're partial to Greek-style pita, which has a pillowy interior ideal for sopping up sauces and dips, and a structure strong enough to support savory sandwich ingredients like Falafel (page 181) or Grilled Chicken Souvlaki (page 300). To create a light crumb with substantial chew we turned to bread flour, but even though this pita was light, it was also tough. Increasing the amount of olive oil in the dough from 1 tablespoon to a generous ¼ cup tenderized the crumb nicely. While traditional Greek pita doesn't always have a pocket meant for stuffing (it's often held like a taco and wrapped around sandwich fixings), we felt that our pita was lacking without it. The tricks to getting the dough to puff up during baking and create this open pocket were a well-hydrated dough and a hot oven: We preheated a baking stone in a 500-degree oven; as soon as the dough hit the hot stone, the top and bottom exteriors began to set. Meanwhile, all that water in the dough turned to a cloud of steam inside, creating pressure outward. The exterior maintained its shape without stretching, and the steam inflated the dough into a balloon, creating the perfect pocket. Our favorite baking stone from Old Stone Oven measures 16½ by 14½ inches. If you have a smaller baking stone, you may need to bake the pitas individually. Pitas can be stored in a zipper-lock bag at room temperature for up to five days.

3⅔ cups (20⅛ ounces) bread flour
2½ teaspoons instant or rapid-rise yeast
2 teaspoons salt
1⅓ cups water, room temperature
¼ cup extra-virgin olive oil
2½ teaspoons sugar

1. Whisk flour, yeast, and salt together in bowl of stand mixer. Whisk water, oil, and sugar together in 4-cup liquid measuring cup until sugar has dissolved.

2. Using dough hook on low speed, slowly add water mixture to flour mixture and mix until cohesive dough starts to form and no dry flour remains, about 2 minutes, scraping down sides of bowl as needed. Increase speed to medium-low and knead until dough is smooth and elastic and clears sides of bowl, about 8 minutes.

3. Transfer dough to lightly floured counter and knead by hand to form smooth, round ball, about 30 seconds. Place dough seam side down in lightly greased large bowl or container, cover tightly with plastic wrap, and let rise until doubled in size, 1 to 1½ hours.

4. Press down on dough to deflate. Transfer dough to lightly floured counter and divide into quarters, then cut each quarter into halves (about 4 ounces each); cover loosely with greased plastic.

5. Working with 1 piece of dough at a time (keep remaining pieces covered), form into rough ball by stretching dough around your thumbs and pinching edges together so that top is smooth.

6. Generously coat 1 dough ball with flour and place on well-floured counter. Press and roll into 8-inch round of even thickness and cover loosely with greased plastic. (If dough resists stretching, let it relax for 10 to 20 minutes before trying to stretch it again.) Repeat with remaining balls. Let dough rounds rest for 20 minutes.

7. One hour before baking, adjust oven rack to lower-middle position, place baking stone on rack, and heat oven to 500 degrees. Gently transfer 2 dough rounds to well-floured pizza peel. Slide rounds onto stone and bake until single air pocket is just beginning to form, about 1 minute.

8. Working quickly, flip pitas using metal spatula and continue to bake until light golden brown, 1 to 2 minutes. Transfer pitas to plate and cover with dish towel. Repeat with remaining dough rounds in 3 batches, allowing oven to reheat for 5 minutes after each batch. Let pitas cool for 10 minutes before serving.

Shaping and Baking Pita

1. Form dough into rough ball by stretching it around your thumbs and pinching edges together so that top is smooth.

2. Press and roll balls into 8-inch rounds of even thickness and cover loosely with greased plastic; let rounds rest for 20 minutes.

3. Transfer 2 dough rounds to well-floured pizza peel. Slide rounds onto stone and bake until single air pocket is just beginning to form.

4. Flip pitas and continue to bake until light golden brown; transfer to plate. Repeat with remaining dough rounds in 3 batches.

Socca

MAKES five 6-inch flatbreads, serving 4 to 6   FAST   VEG

WHY THIS RECIPE WORKS *Socca* is a savory flatbread made with chickpea flour that is popular in southern France. The loose, pancakelike batter comes together in less than a minute—simply whisk together chickpea flour, water, olive oil, salt, and pepper. Traditionally the batter is poured into a cast-iron skillet and baked in a wood-burning oven to make a large socca with a blistered top and a smoky flavor. But in a home oven this technique produced socca that was dry and limp. So we ditched the oven for the more direct heat of the stovetop, which gave us crisp, golden-brown socca. But flipping the skillet-size socca wasn't as easy as we'd hoped. We solved this problem by making several smaller flatbreads instead. As a bonus, the smaller flatbreads had a higher ratio of crunchy crust to tender interior. To complement our savory flatbreads, we came up with a couple of flavorful toppings. Chickpea flour is also sold as garbanzo bean flour or ceci flour and is available in most well-stocked supermarkets. Serve with Tzatziki (page 19) or Muhammara (page 22), if desired.

1½ cups (6¾ ounces) chickpea flour
½ teaspoon salt
½ teaspoon pepper
½ teaspoon ground turmeric
1½ cups water
6 tablespoons plus 1 teaspoon extra-virgin olive oil

1. Adjust oven rack to middle position and heat oven to 200 degrees. Set wire rack in rimmed baking sheet and place in oven. Whisk chickpea flour, salt, pepper, and turmeric together in bowl. Slowly whisk in water and 3 tablespoons oil until combined and smooth.

2. Heat 2 teaspoons oil in 8-inch nonstick skillet over medium-high heat until shimmering. Add ½ cup batter to skillet, tilting skillet to coat bottom evenly. Reduce heat to medium and cook until crisp at edges and golden brown on bottom, 3 to 5 minutes. Flip socca and continue to cook until second side is browned, 2 to 3 minutes. Transfer to wire rack in oven and repeat with remaining oil and batter. Slice and serve.

VARIATIONS

Socca with Swiss Chard, Pistachios, and Apricots
FAST   VEG

Heat 1 tablespoon extra-virgin olive oil in 12-inch nonstick skillet over medium heat until shimmering. Add 1 finely chopped onion and cook until softened, about 5 minutes. Stir in 2 minced garlic cloves, ¾ teaspoon cumin, ¼ teaspoon salt, and ⅛ teaspoon allspice and cook until fragrant, about 30 seconds. Stir in 12 ounces Swiss chard, stemmed and chopped, and 3 tablespoons finely chopped dried apricots and cook until chard is wilted, 4 to 6 minutes. Off heat, stir in 2 tablespoons finely chopped toasted pistachios and 1 teaspoon white wine vinegar. Season with salt and pepper to taste. Top each cooked socca with ⅓ cup chard mixture before slicing and serving.

Socca with Caramelized Onions and Rosemary   VEG
Substitute 1½ teaspoons minced fresh rosemary for turmeric in socca batter. Heat 1 tablespoon extra-virgin olive oil in 12-inch nonstick skillet over high heat until shimmering. Add 3 onions, halved and sliced thin, ½ teaspoon light brown sugar, and ¼ teaspoon salt and stir to coat. Cook, stirring occasionally, until onions begin to soften and release some moisture, about 5 minutes. Reduce heat to medium and continue to cook, stirring often, until onions are well caramelized, 30 to 35 minutes. (If onions are sizzling or scorching, reduce heat. If onions are not browning after 15 to 20 minutes, increase heat.) Off heat, stir in 1 teaspoon sherry vinegar and season with salt and pepper to taste. Top each cooked socca with 1 tablespoon grated Parmesan and scant ¼ cup onion mixture before slicing and serving.

To ensure crisp and sturdy lavash, we brush them with olive oil and bake them before adding hearty toppings.

Lavash with Tomatoes, Spinach, and Green Olives

MAKES two 12 by 9-inch flatbreads, serving 4 to 6

FAST **VEG**

WHY THIS RECIPE WORKS The Middle Eastern flatbread known as lavash has a crisp, crackerlike texture that makes a great base for a quick and easy vegetarian dinner. Store-bought lavash tasted great and kept the recipe streamlined, and to make sure the flatbreads were crisp enough to support the toppings, we brushed them with oil and toasted them quickly in the oven. A combination of thawed frozen spinach, fresh tomato, and briny green olives made for a simple yet flavorful topping. Two types of cheese, mildly nutty fontina and full-flavored Parmesan, gave our lavash more complex flavor; sprinkling the Parmesan on top and allowing it to brown slightly in the hot oven offered an appealing finish. For another flavor variation, we used mellow cauliflower, fennel, and fragrant coriander.

10 ounces frozen spinach, thawed and squeezed dry
4 ounces fontina cheese, shredded (1 cup)
1 tomato, cored and cut into ½-inch pieces
½ cup pitted large brine-cured green olives, chopped
3 garlic cloves, minced
¼ teaspoon red pepper flakes
¼ teaspoon salt
¼ teaspoon pepper
2 (12 by 9-inch) lavash breads
2 tablespoons extra-virgin olive oil
1 ounce Parmesan cheese, grated (½ cup)

1. Adjust oven racks to upper-middle and lower-middle positions and heat oven to 475 degrees. Combine spinach, fontina, tomato, olives, garlic, pepper flakes, salt, and pepper in bowl. Brush both sides of lavash with oil, lay on 2 baking sheets, and bake until golden brown, about 4 minutes, flipping lavash halfway through baking.

2. Spread spinach mixture evenly on each lavash and sprinkle with Parmesan. Bake until cheese is melted and spotty brown, 6 to 8 minutes, switching and rotating sheets halfway through baking. Slice and serve.

VARIATION

Lavash with Cauliflower, Fennel, and Coriander

FAST **VEG**

Omit spinach, tomato, and olives. Heat 2 tablespoons extra-virgin olive oil in 12-inch skillet over medium heat until shimmering. Add 2 cups chopped cauliflower florets, 1 chopped fennel bulb, 3 tablespoons water, 1 teaspoon ground coriander, and ½ teaspoon salt. Cover and cook, stirring occasionally, until vegetables are tender, 6 to 8 minutes; let cool slightly. Substitute 1 cup shredded whole-milk mozzarella cheese for fontina and combine with cauliflower mixture, garlic, and spices before topping lavash. Substitute ½ cup crumbled goat cheese for Parmesan. Sprinkle with 1 thinly sliced scallion before serving.

Pissaladière

MAKES two 14 by 8-inch tarts, serving 4 to 6

WHY THIS RECIPE WORKS *Pissaladière* is a pizzalike tart from Provence that is prized for its contrast of salty black olives and anchovies against a backdrop of sweet caramelized onions and earthy thyme. Supporting this rustic flavor combination is a wheaty crust with a texture that is part chewy pizza and part crisp cracker. The tart is easy enough to prepare, but each ingredient must be handled carefully. We made the dough in a food processor and kneaded it just enough so that it had the structure to stand up to the heavy toppings. To keep our crust thin and prevent it from bubbling, we poked it all over with the tines of a fork. Starting the onions covered and then uncovering them to finish left them perfectly browned and caramelized and prevented them from burning. We stirred in a bit of water when the onions finished caramelizing to keep them from clumping when we spread them on the crust. To protect the black olives and fresh thyme from burning in the oven, we spread them on the dough first and then covered them with the onions. Finally, we chopped the anchovies to keep them from overpowering the other flavors, but some fish-loving tasters opted to add more whole fillets on top. Some baking stones can crack under the intense heat of the broiler; be sure to check the manufacturer's website.

DOUGH

- 3 cups (16½ ounces) bread flour
- 2 teaspoons sugar
- ½ teaspoon instant or rapid-rise yeast
- 1⅓ cups ice water
- 1 tablespoon extra-virgin olive oil
- 1½ teaspoons salt

TOPPINGS

- ¼ cup extra-virgin olive oil
- 2 pounds onions, halved and sliced ¼ inch thick
- 1 teaspoon packed brown sugar
- ½ teaspoon salt
- 1 tablespoon water
- ½ cup pitted niçoise olives, chopped coarse
- 8 anchovy fillets, rinsed, patted dry, and chopped coarse, plus 12 fillets for garnish (optional)
- 2 teaspoons minced fresh thyme
- 1 teaspoon fennel seeds
- ½ teaspoon pepper
- 2 tablespoons minced fresh parsley

1. FOR THE DOUGH Pulse flour, sugar, and yeast in food processor until combined, about 5 pulses. With processor running, slowly add ice water and process until dough is just combined and no dry flour remains, about 10 seconds. Let dough rest for 10 minutes.

2. Add oil and salt to dough and process until dough forms satiny, sticky ball that clears sides of bowl, 30 to 60 seconds. Transfer dough to lightly floured counter and knead by hand to form smooth, round ball, about 30 seconds. Place dough seam side down in lightly greased large bowl or container, cover tightly with plastic wrap, and refrigerate for at least 24 hours or up to 3 days.

3. FOR THE TOPPINGS Heat 2 tablespoons oil in 12-inch nonstick skillet over medium heat until shimmering. Stir in onions, sugar, and salt. Cover and cook, stirring occasionally, until onions are softened and have released their juice, about

10 minutes. Remove lid and continue to cook, stirring often, until onions are golden brown, 10 to 15 minutes. Transfer onions to bowl, stir in water, and let cool completely before using.

4. One hour before baking, adjust oven rack 4 inches from broiler element, set baking stone on rack, and heat oven to 500 degrees. Press down on dough to deflate. Transfer dough to clean counter, divide in half, and cover loosely with greased plastic. Pat 1 piece of dough (keep remaining piece covered) into 4-inch round. Working around circumference of dough, fold edges toward center until ball forms.

5. Flip ball seam side down and, using your cupped hands, drag in small circles on counter until dough feels taut and round and all seams are secured on underside. (If dough sticks to your hands, lightly dust top of dough with flour.) Repeat with remaining piece of dough. Space dough balls 3 inches apart, cover loosely with greased plastic, and let rest for 1 hour.

6. Heat broiler for 10 minutes. Meanwhile, generously coat 1 dough ball with flour and place on well-floured counter. Press and roll into 14 by 8-inch oval. Transfer oval to well-floured pizza peel and reshape as needed. (If dough resists stretching, let it relax for 10 to 20 minutes before trying to stretch it again.) Using fork, poke entire surface of oval 10 to 15 times.

7. Brush dough oval with 1 tablespoon oil, then sprinkle evenly with ¼ cup olives, half of chopped anchovies, 1 teaspoon thyme, ½ teaspoon fennel seeds, and ¼ teaspoon pepper, leaving ½-inch border around edge. Arrange half of onions on top, followed by 6 whole anchovies, if using.

8. Slide flatbread carefully onto baking stone and return oven to 500 degrees. Bake until bottom crust is evenly browned and edges are crisp, 13 to 15 minutes, rotating flatbread halfway through baking. Transfer flatbread to wire rack and let cool for 5 minutes. Sprinkle with 1 tablespoon parsley, slice, and serve. Heat broiler for 10 minutes. Repeat with remaining dough, oil, and toppings, returning oven to 500 degrees when flatbread is placed on stone.

NOTES FROM THE TEST KITCHEN

A Stand-In Baking Stone and Peel

A baking stone is a terrific investment if you enjoy making breads, flatbreads, and pizza, and a peel makes the process easier. But you can make do with rimless or inverted baking sheets for both the stone and the peel. To improvise a baking stone, preheat a baking sheet for 30 minutes. For an improvised peel, cover a rimless or an inverted rimmed baking sheet with parchment paper, shape and top the pizza on the parchment, and slide parchment and pizza directly onto the preheated stone.

A spiced onion jam contrasts nicely with earthy mushrooms in our vegetarian take on this Palestinian flatbread.

Mushroom Musakhan

MAKES two 15 by 8-inch flatbreads, serving 4 to 6 VEG

WHY THIS RECIPE WORKS *Musakhan* is a popular Palestinian dish featuring a flatbread topped with roasted chicken, caramelized onions, pine nuts, and tart sumac. We wanted to create a mushroom version that still had the distinctive flavor of the original dish. Sautéed portobello mushrooms made a perfect topping; tasters loved their robust flavor and juicy flesh. Next we made a warm-spiced caramelized onion jam. The traditional base, *taboon* bread, is a thick, crisp flatbread that is traditionally cooked in a clay oven. For a version we could make at home, we made a dough with whole-wheat flour and bread flour for good flavor and bite. To ensure crisp edges, we cooked the flatbreads on a preheated baking stone, and we superheated the oven by briefly turning on the broiler before baking the musakhan. Some baking stones can crack under the intense heat of the broiler; be sure to check the manufacturer's website. Serve with yogurt.

DOUGH

1½ cups (8¼ ounces) whole-wheat flour
1 cup (5½ ounces) bread flour
2 teaspoons honey
¾ teaspoon instant or rapid-rise yeast
1¼ cups ice water
2 tablespoons extra-virgin olive oil
1¾ teaspoons salt

TOPPINGS

½ cup extra-virgin olive oil
2 tablespoons minced fresh oregano or 2 teaspoons dried
4 garlic cloves, minced
1½ tablespoons ground sumac
¼ teaspoon ground allspice
⅛ teaspoon ground cardamom
2 pounds onions, halved and sliced ¼ inch thick
2 teaspoons packed light brown sugar
Salt and pepper
¼ cup pine nuts
2 pounds portobello mushroom caps, gills removed, caps halved and sliced ½ inch thick
2 tablespoons minced fresh chives

1. FOR THE DOUGH Pulse whole-wheat flour, bread flour, honey, and yeast in food processor until combined, about 5 pulses. With processor running, slowly add ice water and process until dough is just combined and no dry flour remains, about 10 seconds. Let dough rest for 10 minutes.

2. Add oil and salt to dough and process until dough forms satiny, sticky ball that clears sides of bowl, 30 to 60 seconds. Transfer dough to lightly oiled counter and knead by hand to form smooth, round ball, about 30 seconds. Place dough seam side down in lightly greased large bowl or container, cover tightly with plastic wrap, and refrigerate for at least 18 hours or up to 2 days.

3. FOR THE TOPPINGS Combine 1 tablespoon oil, oregano, garlic, sumac, allspice, and cardamom in bowl. Heat 2 tablespoons oil in 12-inch nonstick skillet over high heat until shimmering. Add onions, sugar, and ½ teaspoon salt and stir to coat. Cook, stirring occasionally, until onions begin to soften and release some moisture, about 5 minutes. Reduce heat to medium and continue to cook, stirring often, until onions are well caramelized, 35 to 40 minutes. (If onions are sizzling or scorching, reduce heat. If onions are not browning after 15 to 20 minutes, increase heat.) Push onions to sides of skillet. Add oregano-garlic mixture to center and cook, mashing mixture into skillet, until fragrant, about 30 seconds. Stir oregano-garlic mixture into onions.

4. Transfer onion mixture to food processor and pulse to jamlike consistency, about 5 pulses. Transfer to bowl, stir in pine nuts, and season with salt and pepper to taste; let cool completely before using.

5. Wipe skillet clean with paper towels. Heat 2 tablespoons oil in now-empty skillet over medium-high heat until shimmering. Add half of mushrooms and ½ teaspoon salt and cook, stirring occasionally, until evenly browned, 8 to 10 minutes; transfer to separate bowl. Repeat with 2 tablespoons oil, remaining mushrooms, and ½ teaspoon salt; transfer to bowl and let cool completely before using.

6. One hour before baking, adjust oven rack 4 inches from broiler element, set baking stone on rack, and heat oven to 500 degrees. Press down on dough to deflate. Transfer dough to clean counter, divide in half, and cover loosely with greased plastic. Pat 1 piece of dough (keep remaining piece covered) into 4-inch round. Working around circumference of dough, fold edges toward center until ball forms.

7. Flip ball seam side down and, using your cupped hands, drag in small circles on counter until dough feels taut and round and all seams are secured on underside. (If dough sticks to your hands, lightly dust top of dough with flour.) Repeat with remaining piece of dough. Space dough balls 3 inches apart, cover loosely with greased plastic, and let rest for 1 hour.

8. Heat broiler for 10 minutes. Meanwhile, generously coat 1 dough ball with flour and place on well-floured counter. Press and roll into 12 by 8-inch oval. Transfer oval to well-floured pizza peel and stretch into 15 by 8-inch oval. (If dough resists stretching, let it relax for 10 to 20 minutes before trying to stretch it again.) Using fork, poke entire surface of oval 10 to 15 times.

9. Spread half of onion mixture evenly on dough, edge to edge, and arrange half of mushrooms on top. Slide flatbread carefully onto baking stone and return oven to 500 degrees. Bake until bottom crust is evenly browned and edges are crisp, about 10 minutes, rotating flatbread halfway through baking. Transfer flatbread to wire rack and let cool for 5 minutes. Drizzle with 1½ teaspoons oil and sprinkle with 1 tablespoon chives. Slice and serve.

10. Heat broiler for 10 minutes. Repeat with remaining dough and toppings, returning oven to 500 degrees when flatbread is placed on stone.

Lahmacun

MAKES four 9-inch flatbreads, serving 4 to 6

WHY THIS RECIPE WORKS *Lahmacun* is a meat pie traditionally found in Armenian and Turkish cuisines; it makes a unique appetizer when served with a dollop of Greek yogurt, pickled vegetables, and fresh herbs. The base is very thin and delightfully doughy, with a crisp, spottily charred edge; the topping features ground lamb, warm spices, hot pepper paste, and aromatics. To achieve the perfect harmony of doughy middle and crisp edges while simultaneously cooking the meat topping, we tested several cooking methods, including cooking on the stove in a cast-iron

Quick-cooking ground lamb and hot pepper paste top this savory Middle Eastern flatbread.

skillet, baking in a hot oven on a baking stone, and simply baking on sheets in a moderate oven. The last method proved best: Baked this way, the flatbreads remained soft while the lamb cooked most of the way through. To crisp the edges and finish cooking the topping, we ran the flatbreads under the broiler. It is important to use ice water in the dough to prevent it from overheating in the food processor. We recommend King Arthur brand bread flour. You can find Turkish hot pepper paste in the international foods section of your supermarket or at Middle Eastern markets; if you can't, increase the tomato paste to 3 tablespoons, the smoked hot paprika to 1 teaspoon, and the salt in the topping to ¾ teaspoon. If you cannot fit two flatbreads on a single baking sheet, bake and broil the flatbreads in batches.

DOUGH

1¾ cups (9⅔ ounces) bread flour
1 teaspoon sugar
¾ teaspoon instant or rapid-rise yeast
¾ cup ice water
2 tablespoons extra-virgin olive oil
1 teaspoon salt

TOPPING

- 3 tablespoons Turkish hot pepper paste
- 1 tablespoon tomato paste
- 1 garlic clove, minced
- ¾ teaspoon smoked hot paprika
- ¾ teaspoon ground allspice
- ½ teaspoon salt
- 1 cup coarsely chopped red bell pepper
- ⅔ cup coarsely chopped onion
- 4 ounces ground lamb
- ¼ cup chopped fresh parsley

1. FOR THE DOUGH Pulse flour, sugar, and yeast in food processor until combined, about 5 pulses. With processor running, slowly add ice water and process until dough is just combined and no dry flour remains, about 10 seconds. Let dough rest for 10 minutes.

2. Add oil and salt to dough and process until dough forms satiny, sticky ball that clears sides of bowl, 30 to 60 seconds. Transfer dough to lightly floured counter and knead by hand to form smooth, round ball, about 30 seconds. Place dough seam side down in lightly greased large bowl or container, cover tightly with plastic wrap, and refrigerate for at least 24 hours or up to 3 days.

3. Press down on dough to deflate. Transfer dough to lightly floured counter, divide into quarters, and cover loosely with greased plastic. Working with 1 piece of dough at a time (keep remaining pieces covered), form into rough ball by stretching dough around your thumbs and pinching edges together so that top is smooth. Space balls 3 inches apart, cover loosely with greased plastic, and let rest for 1 hour.

4. FOR THE TOPPING Process pepper paste, tomato paste, garlic, paprika, allspice, and salt in clean, dry workbowl until well combined, about 20 seconds, scraping down sides of bowl as needed. Add bell pepper and onion and pulse until finely ground, about 10 pulses. Add lamb and parsley and pulse until well combined, about 8 pulses.

5. Adjust oven racks to upper-middle and lower-middle positions and heat oven to 350 degrees. Grease 2 rimmed baking sheets. Generously coat 1 dough ball with flour and place on well-floured counter. Press and roll into 9-inch round. Arrange round on prepared sheet, with edges fitted snugly into 1 corner of sheet, and reshape as needed. (If dough resists stretching, let it relax for 10 to 20 minutes before trying to stretch it again.) Repeat with remaining dough balls, arranging 2 rounds on each sheet in opposite corners.

6. Using back of spoon, spread one-quarter of topping in thin layer on surface of each dough round, leaving ¼-inch border around edge.

7. Bake until edges of flatbreads are set but still pale, 10 to 12 minutes, switching and rotating sheets halfway through baking. Remove flatbreads from oven and heat broiler.

8. Return 1 sheet to upper rack and broil until edges of flatbreads are crisp and spotty brown and filling is set, 2 to 4 minutes. Transfer flatbreads to wire rack with spatula and let cool for 5 minutes before serving. Repeat broiling with remaining flatbreads.

Za'atar Bread

MAKES one flatbread, serving 6 to 8 VEG

WHY THIS RECIPE WORKS Inspired by *mana'eesh*, a round Arabic flatbread covered with a thick coating of *za'atar* and olive oil, we set out to develop a recipe for a finger-licking-good snack bread, great for dipping in yogurt sauces or eating on its own. Za'atar, used frequently in the eastern Mediterranean, is a blend of wild thyme, ground sumac (a tart, fruity spice), and sesame seeds. To showcase this delicious blend, we started by kneading together a simple dough from all-purpose flour, salt, yeast, water, sugar, and olive oil and stretching it across a baking sheet. The result was a spongy, cakey bread with a dense, cottony crumb—not what we were looking for. Swapping out the all-purpose flour for higher-protein bread flour helped us develop chew. And we let the dough rise for 24 hours in the refrigerator, which made for uniformly sized air bubbles and created more flavor. Coating the bottom of the pan with a generous amount of olive oil before baking essentially fried the bottom of the flatbread as it baked, and shifting the oven rack to the lower-middle position for baking created a crisp, golden base. It is important to use ice water in the dough to prevent it from overheating in the food processor. We recommend King Arthur brand bread flour. We prefer to use our homemade Za'atar (page 316), but you can substitute store-bought za'atar if you wish, though flavor can vary by brand.

- 3½ cups (19¼ ounces) bread flour
- 2½ teaspoons instant or rapid-rise yeast
- 2½ teaspoons sugar
- 1⅓ cups ice water
- ½ cup plus 2 tablespoons extra-virgin olive oil
- 2 teaspoons salt
- ⅓ cup za'atar
  Coarse sea salt

1. Pulse flour, yeast, and sugar in food processor until combined, about 5 pulses. With processor running, slowly add ice water and process until dough is just combined and no dry flour remains, about 10 seconds. Let dough rest for 10 minutes.

2. Add 2 tablespoons oil and salt to dough and process until dough forms satiny, sticky ball that clears sides of bowl, 30 to 60 seconds. Transfer dough to lightly floured counter and knead by hand to form smooth, round ball, about 30 seconds. Place

We let the dough for our *za'atar*-topped flatbread rise in the fridge to develop the best flavor and most even texture.

dough seam side down in lightly greased large bowl or container, cover tightly with plastic wrap, and refrigerate for at least 24 hours or up to 3 days.

3. Remove dough from refrigerator and let sit at room temperature for 1 hour. Coat rimmed baking sheet with 2 tablespoons oil. Gently press down on dough to deflate any large gas pockets. Transfer dough to prepared sheet and, using your fingertips, press out to uniform thickness, taking care not to tear dough. (Dough may not fit snugly into corners.) Cover loosely with greased plastic and let dough rest for 1 hour.

4. Adjust oven rack to lower-middle position and heat oven to 375 degrees. Using your fingertips, gently press dough into corners of sheet and dimple entire surface.

5. Combine remaining 6 tablespoons oil and za'atar in bowl. Using back of spoon, spread oil mixture in even layer on entire surface of dough to edge.

6. Bake until bottom crust is evenly browned and edges are crisp, 20 to 25 minutes, rotating sheet halfway through baking. Let bread cool in sheet for 10 minutes, then transfer to cutting board with spatula. Sprinkle with sea salt, slice, and serve warm.

Red Pepper Coques

MAKES 4 coques, serving 6 to 8 `VEG`

WHY THIS RECIPE WORKS *Coques* are thin and crunchy Catalan flatbreads served in many tapas bars. Some are sweet, featuring a topping of candied fruit and nuts, but we set our sights on an intensely savory version topped with bold Spanish flavors. To get the perfect crust for our coques, we started with our Thin-Crust Pizza dough (page 354) since it produced a thin, flavorful crust that was appropriate for this dish. But to set our crust apart from pizza and get an extra-crisp base, we increased the amount of oil in the dough from 1 to 3 tablespoons and brushed each coca with more oil before baking. Parbaking the dough before topping it helped prevent a soggy crust and created a sturdy base. For a deeply flavorful topping, we started with onions and roasted red peppers. Garlic, red pepper flakes, and sherry vinegar brought depth, heat, and rounded acidity. We cooked the topping before spreading it on the parbaked dough to intensify the flavors. It is important to use ice water in the dough to prevent it from overheating in the food processor. We recommend King Arthur brand bread flour. If you cannot fit two coques on a single baking sheet, bake them in two batches.

DOUGH

  3 cups (16½ ounces) bread flour
  2 teaspoons sugar
  ½ teaspoon instant or rapid-rise yeast
 1⅓ cups ice water
  3 tablespoons extra-virgin olive oil
 1½ teaspoons salt

TOPPING

  ½ cup extra-virgin olive oil
  2 large onions, halved and sliced thin
  2 cups jarred roasted red peppers, patted dry and sliced thin
  3 tablespoons sugar
  3 garlic cloves, minced
 1½ teaspoons salt
  ¼ teaspoon red pepper flakes
  2 bay leaves
  3 tablespoons sherry vinegar
  ¼ cup pine nuts (optional)
  1 tablespoon minced fresh parsley

1. FOR THE DOUGH Pulse flour, sugar, and yeast in food processor until combined, about 5 pulses. With processor running, slowly add ice water and process until dough is just combined and no dry flour remains, about 10 seconds. Let dough rest for 10 minutes.

2. Add oil and salt to dough and process until dough forms satiny, sticky ball that clears sides of bowl, 30 to 60 seconds. Transfer

Parcooking the dough and the topping separately creates a crisp, ultraflavorful Spanish flatbread.

6. Adjust oven racks to upper-middle and lower-middle positions and heat oven to 500 degrees. Coat 2 rimmed baking sheets with 2 tablespoons oil each. Generously coat 1 dough ball with flour and place on well-floured counter. Press and roll into 14 by 5-inch oval. Arrange oval on prepared sheet, with long edge fitted snugly against 1 long side of sheet, and reshape as needed. (If dough resists stretching, let it relax for 10 to 20 minutes before trying to stretch it again.) Repeat with remaining dough balls, arranging 2 ovals on each sheet, spaced ½ inch apart. Using fork, poke surface of dough 10 to 15 times.

7. Brush dough ovals with remaining 1 tablespoon oil and bake until puffed, 6 to 8 minutes, switching and rotating sheets halfway through baking.

8. Scatter onion mixture evenly over flatbreads, from edge to edge, then sprinkle with pine nuts, if using. Bake until topping is heated through and edges of flatbreads are deep golden brown and crisp, about 15 minutes, switching and rotating sheets halfway through baking. Let flatbreads cool on sheets for 10 minutes, then transfer to cutting board using metal spatula. Sprinkle with parsley, slice, and serve.

Rosemary Focaccia

MAKES two 9-inch round loaves, serving 6 to 8   VEG

WHY THIS RECIPE WORKS We wanted to create a recipe for a light, airy focaccia with a pleasantly crisp crust. Traditional Italian recipes start with a sponge, which is made with water, yeast, and flour. The sponge helped develop structure, depth of flavor, and a hint of tang in the loaf. Once we had incorporated the sponge into our dough, we used a series of gentle folds to help develop the gluten structure even further while also incorporating air for a tender interior crumb. Olive oil is a key ingredient in focaccia, but we found that if we added it straight to the dough, it could turn the bread dense and cakelike. Instead, we baked the bread in round cake pans, where a couple of tablespoons of oil coating the exterior could be contained. Before baking, we poked the dough surface 25 to 30 times to pop large air bubbles and allow any extra gas to escape. Then we sprinkled the dough with a healthy dose of chopped fresh rosemary. Out of the oven, our focaccia boasted a crackly, crisp bottom, a deeply browned top, and an interior that was open and airy. It is important to use fresh, not dried, rosemary. Be sure to reduce the temperature immediately after putting the loaves in the oven.

dough to lightly floured counter and knead by hand to form smooth, round ball, about 30 seconds. Place dough seam side down in lightly greased large bowl or container, cover tightly with plastic wrap, and refrigerate for at least 24 hours or up to 3 days.

3. **FOR THE TOPPING** Heat 3 tablespoons oil in 12-inch non-stick skillet over medium heat until shimmering. Stir in onions, red peppers, sugar, garlic, salt, pepper flakes, and bay leaves. Cover and cook, stirring occasionally, until onions are softened and have released their juice, about 10 minutes. Remove lid and continue to cook, stirring often, until onions are golden brown, 10 to 15 minutes. Off heat, discard bay leaves. Transfer onion mixture to bowl, stir in vinegar, and let cool completely before using.

4. Press down on dough to deflate. Transfer dough to clean counter, divide into quarters, and cover loosely with greased plastic. Working with 1 piece of dough at a time (keep remaining pieces covered), form into rough ball by stretching dough around your thumbs and pinching edges together so that top is smooth.

5. Place ball seam side down on counter and, using your cupped hands, drag in small circles until dough feels taut and round. Space dough balls 3 inches apart, cover loosely with greased plastic, and let rest for 1 hour.

SPONGE

½ cup (2½ ounces) all-purpose flour

⅓ cup water, room temperature

¼ teaspoon instant or rapid-rise yeast

For focaccia that is rich but light, we bake it in olive oil–coated cake pans and poke the dough with a fork before baking.

DOUGH

2½ cups (12½ ounces) all-purpose flour

1¼ cups water, room temperature

1 teaspoon instant or rapid-rise yeast

Kosher salt

¼ cup extra-virgin olive oil

2 tablespoons chopped fresh rosemary

1. FOR THE SPONGE Stir all ingredients together in large bowl with wooden spoon until well combined. Cover tightly with plastic wrap and let sit at room temperature until sponge has risen and begins to collapse, about 6 hours (sponge can sit at room temperature for up to 24 hours).

2. FOR THE DOUGH Stir flour, water, and yeast into sponge with wooden spoon until well combined. Cover bowl tightly with plastic and let dough rest for 15 minutes.

3. Stir 2 teaspoons salt into dough with wooden spoon until thoroughly incorporated, about 1 minute. Cover bowl tightly with plastic and let dough rest for 30 minutes.

4. Using greased bowl scraper (or rubber spatula), fold dough over itself by gently lifting and folding edge of dough toward middle. Turn bowl 45 degrees and fold dough again; repeat turning bowl and folding dough 6 more times (total of 8 folds). Cover tightly with plastic and let rise for 30 minutes. Repeat folding and rising. Fold dough again, then cover bowl tightly with plastic and let dough rise until nearly doubled in size, 30 minutes to 1 hour.

5. One hour before baking, adjust oven rack to upper-middle position, place baking stone on rack, and heat oven to 500 degrees. Coat two 9-inch round cake pans with 2 tablespoons oil each. Sprinkle each pan with ½ teaspoon salt. Transfer dough to lightly floured counter and dust top with flour. Divide dough in half and cover loosely with greased plastic. Working with 1 piece of dough at a time (keep remaining piece covered), shape into 5-inch round by gently tucking under edges.

6. Place dough rounds seam side up in prepared pans, coat bottoms and sides with oil, then flip rounds over. Cover loosely with greased plastic and let dough rest for 5 minutes.

7. Using your fingertips, gently press each dough round into corners of pan, taking care not to tear dough. (If dough resists stretching, let it relax for 5 to 10 minutes before trying to stretch it again.) Using fork, poke surface of dough 25 to 30 times, popping any large bubbles. Sprinkle 1 tablespoon rosemary evenly over top of each loaf, cover loosely with greased plastic, and let dough rest until slightly bubbly, about 10 minutes.

8. Place pans on baking stone and reduce oven temperature to 450 degrees. Bake until tops are golden brown, 25 to 30 minutes, rotating pans halfway through baking. Let loaves cool in pans for 5 minutes. Remove loaves from pans and transfer to wire rack. Brush tops with any oil remaining in pans and let cool for 30 minutes. Serve warm or at room temperature.

Folding Dough

1. Using greased bowl scraper (or rubber spatula), fold dough over itself by gently lifting and folding edge of dough toward middle.

2. Turn bowl 45 degrees and fold dough again; repeat turning bowl and folding dough 6 more times (total of 8 folds).

Putting the baking stone near the top of the oven helps our classic pizza develop good browning.

Thin-Crust Pizza

MAKES two 13-inch pizzas, serving 4 to 6 **VEG**

WHY THIS RECIPE WORKS Our ideal pizza recipe is inspired by classic Italian versions of this famed flatbread: a thin, crisp, and spottily charred crust with a tender yet chewy interior, topped with a handful of simple but flavor-packed ingredients. High-protein bread flour resulted in a chewy, nicely tanned pizza crust, and the right proportions of flour, water, and yeast gave us dough that would stretch and would retain moisture as it baked. We kneaded the dough quickly in a food processor, then let it proof in the refrigerator for at least a day to develop its flavors. After we shaped and topped the pizza (either with our simple homemade tomato sauce and cheese or one of our other flavorful toppings), it went onto a blazing-hot baking stone to cook. Placing the stone near the top of the oven allowed the top as well as the bottom of the pizza to brown. Some baking stones can crack under the intense heat of the broiler; be sure to check the manufacturer's website. It is important to use ice water in the dough to prevent it from overheating in the food processor. We recommend King Arthur brand bread flour. Shape the second dough ball while the first pizza bakes, but don't top the pizza until right before you bake it.

If you add more toppings, keep them light or they may weigh down the thin crust. The sauce will yield more than is needed in the recipe; extra sauce can be refrigerated for up to 1 week or frozen for up to 1 month.

DOUGH

- 3 cups (16½ ounces) bread flour
- 2 teaspoons sugar
- ½ teaspoon instant or rapid-rise yeast
- 1⅓ cups ice water
- 1 tablespoon extra-virgin olive oil
- 1½ teaspoons salt

SAUCE AND TOPPINGS

- 1 (28-ounce) can whole peeled tomatoes, drained with juice reserved
- 1 tablespoon extra-virgin olive oil
- 2 garlic cloves, minced
- 1 teaspoon red wine vinegar
- 1 teaspoon dried oregano
- ½ teaspoon salt
- ¼ teaspoon pepper
- 1 ounce Parmesan cheese, grated fine (½ cup)
- 8 ounces whole-milk mozzarella cheese, shredded (2 cups)

1. FOR THE DOUGH Pulse flour, sugar, and yeast in food processor until combined, about 5 pulses. With processor running, slowly add ice water and process until dough is just combined and no dry flour remains, about 10 seconds. Let dough rest for 10 minutes.

2. Add oil and salt to dough and process until dough forms satiny, sticky ball that clears sides of bowl, 30 to 60 seconds. Transfer dough to lightly oiled counter and knead by hand to form smooth, round ball, about 30 seconds. Place dough seam side down in lightly greased large bowl or container, cover tightly with plastic wrap, and refrigerate for at least 24 hours or up to 3 days.

3. FOR THE SAUCE AND TOPPINGS Process tomatoes, oil, garlic, vinegar, oregano, salt, and pepper in clean, dry workbowl until smooth, about 30 seconds. Transfer mixture to 2-cup liquid measuring cup and add reserved tomato juice until sauce measures 2 cups. Reserve 1 cup sauce; set aside remaining sauce for another use.

4. One hour before baking, adjust oven rack 4 inches from broiler element, set baking stone on rack, and heat oven to 500 degrees. Press down on dough to deflate. Transfer dough to clean counter, divide in half, and cover loosely with greased plastic. Pat 1 piece of dough (keep remaining piece covered) into 4-inch round. Working around circumference of dough, fold edges toward center until ball forms.

5. Flip ball seam side down and, using your cupped hands, drag in small circles on counter until dough feels taut and round and all seams are secured on underside. (If dough sticks to your hands, lightly dust top of dough with flour.) Repeat with remaining piece of dough. Space dough balls 3 inches apart, cover loosely with greased plastic, and let rest for 1 hour.

6. Heat broiler for 10 minutes. Meanwhile, coat 1 dough ball generously with flour and place on well-floured counter. Using your fingertips, gently flatten into 8-inch round, leaving 1 inch of outer edge slightly thicker than center. Using your hands, gently stretch dough into 12-inch round, working along edge and giving disk quarter turns.

7. Transfer dough to well-floured pizza peel and stretch into 13-inch round. Using back of spoon or ladle, spread ½ cup tomato sauce in even layer on surface of dough, leaving ¼-inch border around edge. Sprinkle ¼ cup Parmesan evenly over sauce, followed by 1 cup mozzarella.

8. Slide pizza carefully onto baking stone and return oven to 500 degrees. Bake until crust is well browned and cheese is bubbly and partially browned, 8 to 10 minutes, rotating pizza halfway through baking. Transfer pizza to wire rack and let cool for 5 minutes before slicing and serving. Heat broiler for 10 minutes. Repeat with remaining dough, sauce, and toppings, returning oven to 500 degrees when pizza is placed on stone.

Making Thin-Crust Pizza

1. MAKE DOUGH Process flour, sugar, and yeast, then slowly add ice water. Let dough rest for 10 minutes. Add oil and salt and process until dough forms sticky ball.

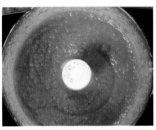

2. PREPARE SAUCE Process drained tomatoes with oil, garlic, vinegar, oregano, salt, and pepper until smooth. Transfer to liquid measuring cup and add reserved juice until sauce measures 2 cups.

3. SHAPE PIZZA Coat 1 dough ball with flour. Gently flatten to 8-inch round, leaving outer edge slightly thicker than center. Using your hands, gently stretch dough into 12-inch round.

4. TOP PIZZA Transfer dough to well-floured pizza peel and stretch into 13-inch round. Spread sauce evenly on dough. Sprinkle ¼ cup Parmesan and 1 cup mozzarella over sauce.

TOPPINGS FOR THIN-CRUST PIZZA

MUSHROOM AND FENNEL PIZZA TOPPING

If desired, mince the fennel fronds and sprinkle them over the pizza before serving.

Toss 4 ounces cremini mushrooms, trimmed and sliced thin, and ½ fennel bulb, cored and sliced thin, with 1 tablespoon extra-virgin olive oil in bowl and season with salt and pepper. Microwave until vegetables are softened and release liquid, 2 to 3 minutes. Drain vegetables, then toss with 2 teaspoons minced fresh thyme. Sprinkle evenly over pizza before baking. Drizzle white truffle oil, if desired, lightly over pizza before serving. (Makes enough topping for 1 pizza.)

OLIVE, CAPER, AND SPICY GARLIC PIZZA TOPPING

Be sure to rinse the capers and anchovies, if using, or the pizza will be very salty.

Combine ⅓ cup pitted kalamata olives, halved, 2 tablespoons capers, rinsed and patted dry, 2 anchovy fillets, rinsed, patted dry, and chopped coarse (optional), 1 small minced garlic clove, 1 teaspoon extra-virgin olive oil, and ⅛ teaspoon red pepper flakes in bowl. Sprinkle evenly over pizza before baking. Sprinkle ¼ cup fresh parsley leaves over pizza before serving. (Makes enough topping for 1 pizza.)

PROSCIUTTO AND ARUGULA PIZZA TOPPING

This topping is added to the fully baked pizza before serving. Don't dress the arugula too far in advance or it will turn soggy.

Toss 1 cup baby arugula with 2 teaspoons extra-virgin olive oil in bowl and season with salt and pepper to taste. Sprinkle 2 ounces thinly sliced prosciutto, cut into 1-inch strips, and dressed arugula over pizza before serving. Makes enough topping for 1 pizza.)

Whole-Wheat Pizza with Feta, Figs, and Honey

MAKES two 13-inch pizzas, serving 4 to 6 VEG

WHY THIS RECIPE WORKS We thought that a nutty, flavorful whole-wheat pizza crust would be a perfect backdrop for bold-flavored Mediterranean toppings. But using whole-wheat flour alone would give us a dense crust, so we incorporated just enough structure-building white bread flour. Increasing the amount of water in the dough made it easier to stretch and gave the crust better chew. But because our dough was so wet, simply preheating the pizza stone in a 500-degree oven wasn't enough; we found we needed to heat the stone under the broiler's high heat so that the crust would brown before the toppings overcooked. After perfecting our thin, crisp, earthy-tasting crust, we realized that the sweet-tart flavors of traditional sauce and cheese clashed with it. Instead, we topped our crust with garlic-infused olive oil, sweet fresh figs, verdant basil, and briny feta cheese. A drizzle of honey completed our unique Mediterranean flavor profile. We also developed two other topping combinations that would complement the whole-wheat crust. It is important to use ice water in the dough to prevent it from overheating in the food processor. We recommend King Arthur brand bread flour. Shape the second dough ball while the first pizza bakes, but don't top the pizza until right before you bake it. Some baking stones can crack under the intense heat of the broiler; be sure to check the manufacturer's website.

DOUGH

- 1½ cups (8¼ ounces) whole-wheat flour
- 1 cup (5½ ounces) bread flour
- 2 teaspoons honey
- ¾ teaspoon instant or rapid-rise yeast
- 1¼ cups ice water
- 2 tablespoons extra-virgin olive oil
- 1¾ teaspoons salt

GARLIC OIL AND TOPPINGS

- 2 tablespoons extra-virgin olive oil
- 2 garlic cloves, minced
- ½ teaspoon pepper
- ½ teaspoon dried thyme
- ⅛ teaspoon salt
- 1 cup fresh basil leaves
- 4 ounces feta cheese, crumbled (1 cup)
- 8 ounces fresh figs, stemmed and quartered lengthwise (1½ cups)
- 2 tablespoons honey

1. FOR THE DOUGH Pulse whole-wheat flour, bread flour, honey, and yeast in food processor until combined, about 5 pulses. With processor running, slowly add ice water and process until dough

A combination of whole-wheat flour and bread flour in our hearty pizza crust offers the best balance of flavor and chew.

is just combined and no dry flour remains, about 10 seconds. Let dough rest for 10 minutes.

2. Add oil and salt to dough and process until dough forms satiny, sticky ball that clears sides of bowl, 45 to 60 seconds. Transfer dough to lightly oiled counter and knead by hand to form smooth, round ball, about 30 seconds. Place dough seam side down in lightly greased large bowl or container, cover tightly with plastic wrap, and refrigerate for at least 18 hours or up to 2 days.

3. FOR THE GARLIC OIL AND TOPPINGS Heat oil in 8-inch skillet over medium-low heat until shimmering. Add garlic, pepper, thyme, and salt and cook, stirring constantly, until fragrant, about 30 seconds. Transfer to bowl and let cool completely before using.

4. One hour before baking, adjust oven rack 4 inches from broiler element, set baking stone on rack, and heat oven to 500 degrees. Press down on dough to deflate. Transfer dough to clean counter, divide in half, and cover loosely with greased plastic. Pat 1 piece of dough (keep remaining piece covered) into 4-inch round. Working around circumference of dough, fold edges toward center until ball forms.

5. Flip dough ball seam side down and, using your cupped hands, drag in small circles on counter until dough feels taut and round and all seams are secured on underside. (If dough sticks to your hands, lightly dust top of dough with flour.) Repeat with remaining piece of dough. Space dough balls 3 inches apart, cover loosely with greased plastic, and let rest for 1 hour.

6. Heat broiler for 10 minutes. Meanwhile, generously coat 1 dough ball with flour and place on well-floured counter. Using your fingertips, gently flatten into 8-inch round, leaving 1 inch of outer edge slightly thicker than center. Using your hands, gently stretch dough into 12-inch round, working along edge and giving disk quarter turns.

7. Transfer dough to well-floured pizza peel and stretch into 13-inch round. Using back of spoon, spread half of garlic oil in even layer on surface of dough, leaving ¼-inch border around edge. Layer ½ cup basil leaves over garlic oil. Sprinkle with ½ cup feta, followed by ¾ cup figs.

8. Slide pizza carefully onto baking stone and return oven to 500 degrees. Bake until crust is well browned and cheese is partially browned, 8 to 10 minutes, rotating pizza halfway through baking. Transfer pizza to wire rack and drizzle 1 tablespoon honey over surface. Let cool for 5 minutes before slicing and serving. Heat broiler for 10 minutes. Repeat with remaining dough, garlic oil, and toppings, returning oven to 500 degrees when pizza is placed on stone.

VARIATIONS

Whole-Wheat Pizza with Artichokes, Ricotta, and Parmesan VEG

While we prefer the flavor and texture of jarred whole baby artichokes, you can substitute 8 ounces of frozen artichoke hearts, thawed and patted dry, for the jarred.

For topping, omit honey and basil. Increase oil to 3 tablespoons, substitute ½ teaspoon dried oregano for thyme, and add ⅛ teaspoon red pepper flakes to skillet along with garlic in step 3. Toss 1¼ cups jarred whole baby artichokes packed in water, quartered, rinsed, and patted dry, with 1 tablespoon garlic oil and 1 tablespoon lemon juice. Combine ½ cup whole-milk ricotta, ¼ teaspoon lemon zest, ⅛ teaspoon salt, and pinch pepper in bowl. Substitute ¼ cup grated Parmesan for feta and artichokes for figs. After baking, dollop half of ricotta mixture evenly on surface of each pizza and let cool for 5 minutes.

Whole-Wheat Pizza with Pesto and Goat Cheese VEG

For topping, omit figs and honey. Increase basil leaves to 2 cups and process with 7 tablespoons extra-virgin olive oil, ¼ cup pine nuts, 3 minced garlic cloves, and ½ teaspoon salt in food processor until smooth, scraping down sides of bowl as needed, about 1 minute. Stir in ¼ cup finely grated Parmesan or Pecorino Romano cheese and season with salt and pepper to taste. Substitute pesto for garlic oil and basil leaves and ½ cup crumbled goat cheese for feta.

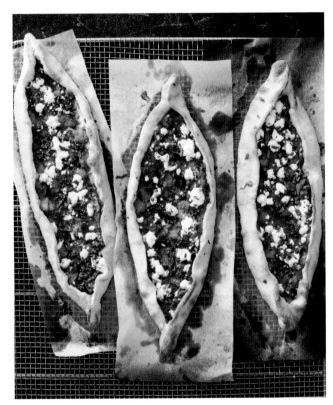

Shaping our canoe-shaped Turkish flatbreads on parchment paper makes them easy to transfer to a baking stone.

Turkish Pide with Eggplant and Tomatoes
MAKES 6 pide, serving 6 to 8 VEG

WHY THIS RECIPE WORKS *Pide* is a Turkish flatbread that can be easily identified by its signature canoe shape. Like Italian pizza, pide varies from region to region and even from family to family, so the first task in developing our recipe was to identify what we liked. First, we focused on the dough. We tested a few traditional recipes and found that tasters preferred a cold-fermented dough with a crisp outer crust and chewy, irregular interior. Next, we turned to toppings. Tasters loved the classic Turkish combination of eggplant, red bell pepper, and tomatoes. We found that salting the eggplant was unnecessary since sautéing the veggies eliminated any excess moisture. Pulsing canned whole tomatoes in the food processor gave our topping the best texture. We accented the vegetables with smoky paprika and spicy red pepper flakes, a healthy amount of mint, and some briny, creamy feta. Shaping the pide on individual parchment sheets made transferring the little boats to our preheated baking stone easy and efficient. It is important to use ice water in the dough to prevent it from overheating in the food processor. We recommend King Arthur brand bread flour. Press and roll the remaining 3 dough balls into ovals while the first set of pide bake, but don't top and shape the pide until right before baking.

DOUGH

3 cups (16½ ounces) bread flour
2 teaspoons sugar
½ teaspoon instant or rapid-rise yeast
1⅓ cups ice water
1 tablespoon extra-virgin olive oil
1½ teaspoons salt

TOPPINGS

1 (28-ounce) can whole peeled tomatoes
5 tablespoons extra-virgin olive oil
1 pound eggplant, cut into ½-inch pieces
½ red bell pepper, chopped
    Salt and pepper
3 garlic cloves, minced
¼ teaspoon red pepper flakes
½ teaspoon smoked paprika
6 tablespoons minced fresh mint
6 ounces feta cheese, crumbled (1½ cups)

1. FOR THE DOUGH Pulse flour, sugar, and yeast in food processor until combined, about 5 pulses. With processor running, slowly add ice water and process until dough is just combined and no dry flour remains, about 10 seconds. Let dough rest for 10 minutes.

2. Add oil and salt to dough and process until dough forms satiny, sticky ball that clears sides of bowl, 30 to 60 seconds. Transfer dough to lightly oiled counter and knead by hand to form smooth, round ball, about 30 seconds. Place dough seam side down in lightly greased large bowl or container, cover tightly with plastic wrap, and refrigerate for at least 24 hours or up to 3 days.

3. FOR THE TOPPINGS Pulse tomatoes and their juice in food processor until coarsely ground, about 12 pulses. Heat 2 tablespoons oil in 12-inch nonstick skillet over medium-high heat until shimmering. Add eggplant, bell pepper, and ½ teaspoon salt and cook, stirring occasionally, until softened and beginning to brown, 5 to 7 minutes. Stir in garlic, pepper flakes, and paprika and cook until fragrant, about 30 seconds.

4. Add tomatoes, bring to simmer, and cook, stirring occasionally, until mixture is very thick and measures 3½ cups, about 10 minutes. Off heat, stir in ¼ cup mint and season with salt and pepper to taste; let cool completely before using.

5. One hour before baking, adjust oven rack 4 inches from broiler element, set baking stone on rack, and heat oven to 500 degrees. Press down on dough to deflate. Transfer dough to clean counter and divide in half, then cut each half into thirds (about 4¾ ounces each); cover loosely with greased plastic. Working with 1 piece of dough at a time (keep remaining pieces covered), form into rough ball by stretching dough around your thumbs and pinching edges together so that top is smooth. Space balls 3 inches apart, cover loosely with greased plastic, and let rest for 1 hour.

6. Cut six 16 by 6-inch pieces of parchment paper. Generously coat 1 dough ball with flour and place on well-floured counter. Press and roll into 14 by 5½-inch oval. Arrange oval on parchment rectangle and reshape as needed. (If dough resists stretching, let it relax for 10 to 20 minutes before trying to stretch it again.) Repeat with 2 more dough balls and parchment rectangles.

7. Brush dough ovals with oil, then top each with ½ cup eggplant mixture and ¼ cup feta, leaving ¾-inch border around edges. Fold long edges of dough over filling to form canoe shape and pinch ends together to seal. Brush outer edges of dough with oil and transfer pide (still on parchment rectangles) to pizza peel.

8. Slide each parchment rectangle with pide onto baking stone, spacing pide at least 1 inch apart. Bake until crust is golden brown and edges are crisp, 10 to 15 minutes. Transfer pide to wire rack, discard parchment, and let cool for 5 minutes. Sprinkle with 1 tablespoon mint, slice, and serve. Repeat with remaining 3 dough balls, 3 parchment rectangles, oil, and toppings.

Shaping Turkish Pide

1. Press and roll 1 dough ball into 14 by 5½-inch oval on well-floured counter. Arrange oval on parchment rectangle and reshape as needed.

2. Brush oval with oil, then top with ½ cup eggplant mixture and ¼ cup feta, leaving ¾-inch border around edges.

3. Fold long edges of dough over filling to form canoe shape and pinch ends together to seal. Brush outer edges of dough with oil.

Store-bought phyllo dough makes an easy and crisp casing for our savory Greek-inspired hand pies.

Fennel, Olive, and Goat Cheese Hand Pies

MAKES 15 triangles, serving 6 to 8 VEG

WHY THIS RECIPE WORKS Phyllo dough, a paper-thin dough used in sweet and savory pastries throughout the eastern Mediterranean, makes a perfect crisp parcel for hand pies. We found that not only was store-bought phyllo easy to use, it was also sturdy enough to support the filling. As for the filling, tasters liked a Greek-inspired combination of goat cheese, kalamata olives, and fennel, which we brightened up with lemon zest and juice. Phyllo dough is also available in larger 18 by 14-inch sheets; if using, cut them in half to make 14 by 9-inch sheets. Do not thaw the phyllo in the microwave; let it sit in the refrigerator overnight or on the counter for 4 to 5 hours. While working with the phyllo, cover the sheets with plastic wrap, then a damp dish towel to prevent drying.

FILLING
1 tablespoon extra-virgin olive oil
1 large fennel bulb, stalks discarded, bulb halved, cored, and sliced thin
3 garlic cloves, minced
½ cup dry white wine

6 ounces goat cheese, crumbled (1½ cups)
¼ cup pitted kalamata olives, chopped fine
2 tablespoons chopped fresh oregano
2 teaspoons grated lemon zest plus 1 tablespoon juice
Salt and pepper

PIES
10 (14 by 9-inch) phyllo sheets, thawed
¼ cup extra-virgin olive oil

1. FOR THE FILLING Heat oil in 12-inch skillet over medium heat until shimmering. Add fennel and cook until softened and lightly browned, 8 to 10 minutes. Stir in garlic and cook until fragrant, about 30 seconds. Stir in wine, cover, and cook for 5 minutes. Uncover and continue to cook until liquid has evaporated and fennel is very tender, 3 to 5 minutes.

2. Transfer fennel mixture to medium bowl and let cool to room temperature, about 15 minutes. Gently stir in goat cheese, olives, oregano, and lemon zest and juice until combined. Season with salt and pepper to taste.

3. FOR THE PIES Adjust oven rack to lower-middle position and heat oven to 375 degrees. Place 1 phyllo sheet on counter with long side parallel to counter edge, brush lightly with oil, then top with second phyllo sheet. Cut phyllo vertically into three 9 by 4⅔-inch strips. Place generous 1 tablespoon filling on bottom left-hand corner of each strip. Fold up phyllo to form right-angle triangle, gently pressing on filling as needed to create even layer. Continue folding up and over, as if folding a flag, to end of strip. Brush triangle with oil and place seam side down in parchment paper–lined rimmed baking sheet. Repeat with remaining phyllo sheets and filling to make 15 triangles.

4. Bake triangles until golden brown, 10 to 15 minutes, rotating sheet halfway through baking. Let triangles cool on sheet for 5 minutes. Serve.

Assembling Hand Pies

1. After cutting phyllo sheets into 3 strips, place 1 tablespoon filling on bottom left-hand corner of each strip.

2. Fold phyllo over filling to form right-angle triangle. Continue to fold up and over until you reach end of strip.

Mushroom Tart

MAKES one 9-inch tart, serving 4 to 6   VEG

WHY THIS RECIPE WORKS A simple, Italian-inspired vegetable tart makes a perfect light meal or company-worthy appetizer, so we set our sights on developing a recipe with a flavorful and fool-proof crust, a creamy base, and a topping of hearty mushrooms. We started with the crust. Because we wanted to use only olive oil and no butter in our crust, getting it to be tender and flaky (without being brittle) was a challenge. In the end, it came down to finding the correct ratio of olive oil to water. A 2:1 ratio proved best, creating a rich crust with deep savory flavor and a sliceable texture. For the filling, we needed to ensure that the mushrooms didn't leach moisture into the tart, so we cooked them until they had released their moisture and were dry enough to build flavorful browning. Aromatic thyme and garlic rounded out the mushrooms' earthy flavor. A trio of cheeses—Parmesan, ricotta, and mozzarella—made a nicely balanced base layer under the mushrooms. We also developed two simple variations: one with fresh, sweet tomatoes and another with thin slices of zucchini. We prefer the light flavor of part-skim ricotta here, but whole-milk ricotta can be substituted; do not use fat-free ricotta.

CRUST

1¾ cups (8¾ ounces) all-purpose flour
1 tablespoon sugar
¾ teaspoon salt
⅔ cup extra-virgin olive oil
⅓ cup water

FILLING

2 tablespoons extra-virgin olive oil
1 pound white mushrooms, trimmed and sliced thin
   Salt and pepper
2 teaspoons minced fresh thyme
1 garlic clove, minced
1 ounce Parmesan cheese, grated (½ cup)
4 ounces (½ cup) part-skim ricotta cheese
1 ounce mozzarella cheese, shredded (¼ cup)

1. FOR THE CRUST Adjust oven rack to lowest position and heat oven to 350 degrees. Whisk flour, sugar, and salt together in bowl. Stir in oil and water with wooden spoon until large clumps of dough form and no dry flour remains.

2. Sprinkle walnut-size clumps of dough evenly into bottom of 9-inch tart pan with removable bottom. Working outward from center, press dough into even layer, sealing any cracks. Working around edge, press dough firmly into corners with fingers. Go around edge once more, pressing dough up sides and into fluted ridges. Use thumb to level off top edge. Use excess dough to patch any holes.

3. Place pan on wire rack set in rimmed baking sheet and bake until crust is light golden brown and firm to touch, about 50 minutes, rotating pan halfway through baking. Let tart shell cool completely on sheet before filling.

4. FOR THE FILLING Heat 1 tablespoon oil in 12-inch non-stick skillet over medium-high heat until shimmering. Add mushrooms and ½ teaspoon salt and cook until dry and lightly browned, about 15 minutes. Stir in thyme and garlic and cook until fragrant, about 1 minute.

5. Combine Parmesan, ricotta, mozzarella, and remaining 1 tablespoon oil in bowl and season with salt and pepper to taste. Spread ricotta mixture evenly on bottom of tart shell, then spoon mushroom mixture on top. Bake tart on sheet until heated through and beginning to bubble around edges, 20 to 25 minutes, rotating sheet halfway through baking.

6. Let tart cool on sheet for at least 10 minutes or up to 2 hours. Remove outer metal ring of tart pan, slide thin metal spatula between tart and pan bottom, and carefully slide tart onto serving platter. Sprinkle with basil and cut into wedges. Serve.

Shaping a Press-In Tart Shell

1. Sprinkle walnut-size clumps of dough evenly into tart pan.

2. Working outward from center, press dough into even layer, sealing any cracks. Working around edge, press dough firmly into corners with your fingers.

3. Go around edge once more, pressing dough up sides and into fluted ridges. Use your thumb to level off top edge.

Tomato Tart `VEG`

Omit mushroom mixture in step 5. Spread 3 plum tomatoes, cored and sliced ¼ inch thick, on several layers of paper towels and sprinkle with ½ teaspoon salt. Let tomatoes drain for 30 minutes, then blot dry with paper towels. Combine 2 tablespoons oil and 1 minced garlic clove in small bowl. After spreading ricotta mixture in tart shell, shingle tomatoes attractively on top in concentric circles. Drizzle with garlic-oil mixture and bake as directed.

Zucchini Tart `VEG`

Omit mushroom mixture in step 5. Spread 1 large zucchini, sliced into ¼-inch-thick rounds, on several layers of paper towels and sprinkle with ½ teaspoon salt. Let zucchini drain for 30 minutes, then blot dry with paper towels. Combine 2 tablespoons oil and 1 minced garlic clove in small bowl. After spreading ricotta mixture in tart shell, shingle zucchini attractively on top in concentric circles. Drizzle with garlic-oil mixture and bake as directed.

Spanakopita

SERVES 10 to 12 `VEG`

WHY THIS RECIPE WORKS The roots of *spanakopita*, a savory spinach and feta pie with trademark layers of flaky, crisp phyllo, run deep in Greek culture, yet most versions are nothing more than soggy layers of phyllo with a sparse, bland filling. We wanted a casserole-style pie with a perfect balance of zesty spinach filling and shatteringly crisp phyllo crust—and we didn't want to spend all day in the kitchen. Using store-bought phyllo was an easy timesaver. Among the various spinach options—baby, frozen, mature curly-leaf—tasters favored the bold flavor of fresh curly-leaf spinach that had been microwaved, coarsely chopped, then squeezed of excess moisture. Crumbling the feta into fine pieces ensured a salty tang in every bite, and the addition of Greek yogurt buffered the assertiveness of the feta. We found that Pecorino Romano (a good stand-in for a traditional Greek hard sheep's-milk cheese) added complexity to the filling and, when sprinkled between the sheets of phyllo, helped the flaky layers hold together. Using a baking sheet rather than a baking dish allowed excess moisture to evaporate easily, ensuring a crisp crust. If you can't find curly-leaf spinach, you can substitute flat-leaf spinach; do not substitute baby spinach. Full-fat sour cream can be substituted for the whole-milk Greek yogurt. Phyllo dough is also available in larger 18 by 14-inch sheets; if using, cut them in half to make 14 by 9-inch sheets. Do not thaw the phyllo in the microwave; let it sit in the refrigerator overnight or on the counter for 4 to 5 hours. While working with the phyllo, cover the sheets with plastic wrap, then a damp kitchen towel to prevent drying.

To prevent our traditional spanakopita from becoming soggy, we microwave and wring out fresh curly-leaf spinach.

FILLING

- 20 ounces curly-leaf spinach, stemmed
- ¼ cup water
- 8 ounces feta cheese, crumbled (2 cups)
- ¾ cup whole-milk Greek yogurt
- 4 scallions, sliced thin
- 2 large eggs, lightly beaten
- ¼ cup minced fresh mint
- 2 tablespoons minced fresh dill
- 3 garlic cloves, minced
- 1 teaspoon grated lemon zest plus 1 tablespoon juice
- 1 teaspoon ground nutmeg
- ½ teaspoon pepper
- ¼ teaspoon salt
- ⅛ teaspoon cayenne pepper

PHYLLO LAYERS

- 7 tablespoons extra-virgin olive oil
- 8 ounces (14 by 9-inch) phyllo, thawed
- 1½ ounces Pecorino Romano cheese, grated (¾ cup)
- 2 teaspoons sesame seeds (optional)

1. FOR THE FILLING Place spinach and water in bowl. Cover and microwave until spinach is wilted and volume is halved, about 5 minutes. Remove bowl from microwave and keep covered for 1 minute. Transfer spinach to colander and gently press to release liquid. Transfer spinach to cutting board and chop coarse. Return to colander and press again. Stir spinach and remaining ingredients in bowl until thoroughly combined.

2. FOR THE PHYLLO LAYERS Adjust oven rack to lower-middle position and heat oven to 425 degrees. Line rimmed baking sheet with parchment paper. Using pastry brush, lightly brush 14 by 9-inch rectangle in center of parchment with oil to cover area same size as phyllo. Lay 1 phyllo sheet on oiled parchment and brush thoroughly with oil. Repeat with 9 more phyllo sheets, brushing each with oil (you should have total of 10 layers of phyllo).

3. Spread spinach mixture evenly on phyllo, leaving ¼-inch border on all sides. Cover spinach with 6 more phyllo sheets, brushing each with oil and sprinkling each with about 2 tablespoons Pecorino. Lay 2 more phyllo sheets on top, brushing each with oil (these layers should not be sprinkled with Pecorino).

4. Working from center outward, use palms of your hands to compress layers and press out any air pockets. Using sharp knife, score spanakopita through top 3 layers of phyllo into 24 equal pieces. Sprinkle with sesame seeds (if using). Bake until phyllo is golden and crisp, 20 to 25 minutes. Let spanakopita cool on sheet for at least 10 minutes or up to 2 hours. Slide spanakopita, still on parchment, to cutting board. Cut into squares and serve.

Working with Phyllo Dough

Phyllo dough, tissue-thin layers of pastry dough, is available in two sizes: full-size sheets that are 18 by 14 inches (about 20 per box) and half-size sheets that are 14 by 9 inches (about 40 per box). The smaller sheets are more common, so we use those in our recipes. If you buy the large sheets, simply cut them in half. Here are some other pointers that make working with this delicate dough easier:

THAW THE PHYLLO DOUGH COMPLETELY BEFORE USING Frozen phyllo must be thawed before using. This is best achieved by placing the phyllo in the refrigerator for at least 12 hours.

KEEP THE PHYLLO COVERED WHEN USING Phyllo dries out very quickly. As soon as the phyllo is removed from its plastic sleeve, unfold the dough and carefully flatten it with your hands. Cover with plastic wrap, then a damp dish towel.

THROW OUT BADLY TORN SHEETS OF DOUGH Usually each box has one or two badly torn sheets of phyllo that can't be salvaged. But if the sheets have just small cuts or tears, you can still work with them—put them in the middle of the pastry, where imperfections will go unnoticed. If all of the sheets have the exact same tear, alternate the orientation of each sheet when assembling the pastry.

DON'T REFREEZE LEFTOVER DOUGH Leftover sheets cannot be refrozen, but they can be rerolled, wrapped in plastic wrap, and stored in the refrigerator for up to five days.

Assembling Spanakopita

1. Lay 1 phyllo sheet on oiled parchment and brush thoroughly with oil. Repeat with 9 more phyllo sheets, brushing each with oil to form bottom crust.

2. Spread spinach mixture on bottom crust, leaving ¼-inch border on all sides.

3. Layer 8 more phyllo sheets on top of spinach mixture. Working from center outward, use palms of your hands to compress layers and press out any air pockets.

4. Using sharp knife, score spanakopita through top 3 layers of phyllo into 24 equal pieces. Sprinkle with sesame seeds (if using).

Pumpkin Borek

SERVES 10 to 12 **VEG**

WHY THIS RECIPE WORKS *Borek* is a savory filled pastry found throughout the eastern Mediterranean. It's traditionally made by layering sheets of thin dough with a variety of appealing fillings that can include meat, vegetables, and cheese. Borek can take the shape of rounds, casseroles, rolled cigars, and even hand pies. After testing several different recipes, we decided to make a Turkish-style casserole filled with winter squash and cheese. Boreks are traditionally made using *yufka* dough, which is thicker and doughier than phyllo but thinner than a flour tortilla. Because yufka dough is not widely available, we turned to phyllo to be our stand-in. Although we typically brush each layer of phyllo with oil to help crisp the sheets into individual flaky layers, we instead painted small stacks of phyllo with a mixture of egg and milk for this recipe. This saturated the thin layers and glued them together, forming a noodle-like dough that mimicked the chew and thickness of traditional yufka. Pumpkin is used frequently in Turkish cooking, and canned pumpkin puree made an ultrasimple and flavorful base for our filling. We seasoned the puree with white wine, garlic, and ginger and created a second filling layer with rich cottage cheese, salty halloumi, and fresh mint. Tasters couldn't get enough of the finished borek with its sweet, savory, chewy layers that came together into a presentation-worthy dish. Phyllo dough is also available in larger 18 by 14-inch sheets; if using, cut them in half to make 14 by 9-inch sheets. Do not thaw the phyllo in the microwave; let it sit in the refrigerator overnight or on the counter for 4 to 5 hours. While working with the phyllo, cover the sheets with plastic wrap, then a damp dish towel to prevent drying.

FILLING

- 1 tablespoon extra-virgin olive oil
- 1 large onion, chopped
- 1½ teaspoons salt
- 3 garlic cloves, minced
- 1 teaspoon grated fresh ginger
- ½ teaspoon pepper
- 1½ cups dry white wine
- 3 (15-ounce) cans unsweetened pumpkin puree
- 5 large eggs
- 12 ounces halloumi cheese, grated (3 cups)
- 8 ounces (1 cup) cottage cheese
- ½ cup chopped fresh mint

LAYERS

- ⅓ cup whole milk
- 1 large egg
- 2 pounds (14 by 9-inch) phyllo, thawed

Sheets of phyllo re-create the texture of the traditional dough typically used in this savory Mediterranean pastry.

1. FOR THE FILLING Heat oil in 10-inch skillet over medium-high heat until shimmering. Add onion and salt and cook until softened, about 5 minutes. Stir in garlic, ginger, and pepper and cook until fragrant, about 30 seconds. Stir in wine, bring to simmer, and cook, stirring occasionally, until onion is very tender and mixture has reduced slightly and measures 1¼ cups, 15 to 20 minutes.

2. Transfer onion mixture to food processor and let cool slightly. Add pumpkin and eggs and process until mixture is thoroughly combined and smooth, about 3 minutes, scraping down sides of bowl as needed. Combine halloumi, cottage cheese, and mint in separate bowl.

3. FOR THE LAYERS Adjust oven rack to middle position and heat oven to 400 degrees. Whisk milk and egg together in bowl until combined. Trim 50 phyllo sheets to 12½ by 8½ inches.

4. Spread 1 cup pumpkin filling on bottom of greased 13 by 9-inch baking dish. Lay 5 phyllo sheets in dish, brush with egg mixture, then top with 5 more phyllo sheets.

5. Brush phyllo with egg mixture, then spread 2⅓ cups pumpkin filling evenly on top. Lay 5 more phyllo sheets in dish, brush with egg mixture, then top with 5 more phyllo sheets.

6. Brush phyllo with egg mixture, then spread half of cheese mixture evenly on top. Lay 5 more phyllo sheets in dish, brush with egg mixture, then top with 5 more phyllo sheets.

7. Working from center outward, use palms of your hands to gently compress layers and press out any air pockets. Repeat layering in steps 5 and 6, then brush top with egg mixture.

8. Trim 10 phyllo sheets to 13 by 9 inches. Spread remaining pumpkin filling evenly on phyllo layers. Lay 5 large phyllo sheets in dish, brush with egg mixture, then top with 5 more large phyllo sheets. Gently compress layers and wipe away excess filling that may have leaked out along sides of dish. Brush top with egg mixture and bake until borek registers 165 degrees and top is puffed and golden brown, 40 to 45 minutes. Let cool for 30 minutes before serving.

Making Pumpkin Borek

1. MAKE PUMPKIN AND CHEESE FILLINGS Process onion-wine mixture with pumpkin and eggs until mixture is thoroughly combined and smooth. Combine halloumi, cottage cheese, and mint in separate bowl.

2. START LAYERING Spread 1 cup pumpkin filling on bottom of greased 13 by 9-inch baking dish, then build layers of phyllo, egg mixture, pumpkin filling, and cheese filling.

3. MAKE FINAL LAYER Spread remaining pumpkin filling evenly on phyllo layers and top with remaining 10 phyllo sheets. Gently compress layers and wipe away excess filling that may have leaked out along sides of dish.

4. BAKE Brush top with egg mixture and bake until borek registers 165 degrees and top is puffed and golden brown, 40 to 45 minutes. Let cool for 30 minutes before serving.

Spiced chicken and a layer of almonds, cinnamon, and sugar give our Moroccan pie its trademark sweet-savory contrast.

Chicken B'stilla
SERVES 10 to 12

WHY THIS RECIPE WORKS *B'stilla* is an impressive Moroccan tart whose savory filling is customarily made with pigeon and richly flavored with almonds and cinnamon sugar. The most cherished qualities of this dish are its many contrasts: crisp yet juicy, sweet yet savory, succulent yet wholesome. For a version that could be made in an American kitchen, we started by swapping the pigeon for chicken thighs, which we cooked gently in a spiced broth to ensure that they were moist and flavorful. We also used the rich cooking liquid as the base of the traditional custardlike component of the pie. Although b'stilla is usually made with layers of a paper-thin dough called *warqa*, we found that readily available phyllo worked perfectly. We decided to assemble the pie in the same skillet we had used to cook the chicken, since this created a wide, thin pie that was easy to serve. We lined the pan with phyllo, poured in the chicken-egg mixture, and topped it with more phyllo as well as a traditional mixture of slivered almonds tossed with cinnamon and sugar. The pie tasted great, but the nut topping was too dry and loose. Instead, we encased the almond mixture in phyllo to make the base of the pie; that way, it could soak up the rich juices from the chicken above it. A customary sprinkling of cinnamon sugar on the baked pie drove home the sweet-savory contrasts. Phyllo dough is also available in larger 18 by 14-inch sheets; if using, cut them in half to make 14 by 9-inch sheets. Do not thaw the phyllo in the microwave; let it sit in the refrigerator overnight or on the counter for 4 to 5 hours. While working with the phyllo, cover the sheets with plastic wrap, then a damp dish towel to prevent drying.

½ cup extra-virgin olive oil
1 onion, chopped fine
¾ teaspoon salt
1 tablespoon grated fresh ginger
½ teaspoon pepper
½ teaspoon ground turmeric
½ teaspoon paprika
1½ cups water
2 pounds boneless, skinless chicken thighs, trimmed
6 large eggs
½ cup minced fresh cilantro
1 pound (14 by 9-inch) phyllo, thawed
1½ cups slivered almonds, toasted and chopped
¼ cup confectioners' sugar
1 tablespoon ground cinnamon

1. Heat 1 tablespoon oil in 12-inch nonstick skillet over medium heat until shimmering. Add onion and salt and cook until softened, about 5 minutes. Stir in ginger, pepper, turmeric, and paprika and cook until fragrant, about 30 seconds. Add water and chicken and bring to simmer. Reduce heat to low, cover, and cook until chicken registers 175 degrees, 15 to 20 minutes. Transfer chicken to cutting board, let cool slightly, then shred into bite-size pieces using 2 forks; transfer to large bowl.

2. Whisk eggs together in small bowl. Bring cooking liquid to boil over high heat and cook until reduced to about 1 cup, about 10 minutes. Reduce heat to low. Whisking constantly, slowly pour eggs into broth and cook until mixture resembles loose scrambled eggs, 6 to 8 minutes; transfer to bowl with chicken. Stir in cilantro until combined. Wipe skillet clean with paper towels and let cool completely.

3. Adjust oven rack to middle position and heat oven to 375 degrees. Brush 1 phyllo sheet with oil and arrange in bottom of cooled skillet with short side against side of pan. Some phyllo will overhang edge of skillet; leave in place. Turn skillet 30 degrees. Brush second phyllo sheet with oil and arrange in skillet, leaving any overhanging phyllo in place. Repeat turning and layering with 10 more phyllo sheets in pinwheel pattern, brushing each with oil, to cover entire circumference of skillet (you should have total of 12 layers of phyllo).

4. Combine almonds, 3 tablespoons sugar, and 2 teaspoons cinnamon and sprinkle over phyllo in skillet. Lay 2 phyllo sheets evenly across top of almond mixture and brush top with oil. Rotate skillet 90 degrees and lay 2 more phyllo sheets evenly across top; do not brush with oil. Spoon chicken mixture into skillet and spread into even layer.

5. Stack 5 phyllo sheets on counter and brush top with oil. Fold phyllo in half crosswise and brush top with oil. Lay phyllo stack on center of chicken mixture.

6. Fold overhanging phyllo over filling and phyllo stack, pleating phyllo every 2 to 3 inches, and press to seal. Brush top with oil and bake until phyllo is crisp and golden, 35 to 40 minutes.

7. Combine remaining 1 tablespoon sugar and remaining 1 teaspoon cinnamon in small bowl. Let b'stilla cool in skillet for 15 minutes. Using rubber spatula, carefully slide b'stilla out onto cutting board. Dust top with cinnamon sugar, slice, and serve.

Assembling Chicken B'stilla

1. Brush 1 phyllo sheet with oil and arrange in bottom of skillet with short side against side of pan. Continue layering 11 more phyllo sheets in skillet in pinwheel pattern.

2. Sprinkle almond mixture over phyllo in skillet, then lay 2 phyllo sheets across top and brush with oil. Rotate skillet 90 degrees and lay 2 more phyllo sheets across top.

3. Spoon chicken mixture into skillet and spread into even layer. Stack 5 phyllo sheets and brush with oil. Fold in half, brush top with oil, and lay on chicken mixture.

4. Fold overhanging phyllo over filling and phyllo stack, pleating phyllo every 2 to 3 inches, and press to seal. Brush top with oil before baking.

■ FAST (less than 45 minutes start to finish)

Photos (clockwise from top left): Olive Oil–Yogurt Cake; Melon, Plums, and Cherries with Mint and Vanilla; Greek Sesame-Honey Bars; Turkish Stuffed Apricots with Rose Water and Pistachios

A syrup made from water, sugar, and honey turns fresh apricot wedges into a traditional Greek sweet.

Apricot Spoon Sweets

MAKES 4 cups

WHY THIS RECIPE WORKS The serving of "spoon sweets" in Greece and parts of the Middle East is a long-standing ritual. A special jar of fruit with a spoon hanging from its neck appears whenever visitors arrive. Each visitor takes a spoonful of the sweet fruit straight from the jar. We wanted a recipe for this welcoming treat using apricots. While traditionally an all-honey syrup is used to preserve the fruit, we found it to be far too sweet. We settled on a syrup made of water, sugar, and honey that we boiled until it was thick enough to coat the apricots when serving. Once the syrup was reduced, we added the apricots and lemon juice and simmered them briefly to achieve the perfect texture for the fruit. The acidity of the lemon juice balanced the sweetness of the syrup and also helped to prevent the apricots from oxidizing, or turning brown. Select apricots that yield slightly when pressed.

1½ cups sugar
 1 cup honey
 ¾ cup water
1½ pounds ripe but firm apricots, pitted and cut into
     ½-inch wedges
 2 tablespoons lemon juice

1. Bring sugar, honey, and water to boil in Dutch oven over high heat and cook, stirring occasionally, until syrup measures 2 cups, about 10 minutes.

2. Add apricots and lemon juice and return to boil. Reduce heat to medium-low and simmer, stirring occasionally, until apricots soften and release their juice, about 5 minutes. Remove pot from heat and let cool completely.

3. Transfer apricots and syrup to airtight container and refrigerate for 24 hours before serving. (Fruit can be refrigerated for up to 1 week.)

Dried Fruit Compote

SERVES 6

WHY THIS RECIPE WORKS We set out to create a delicately spiced, naturally sweet compote of succulent figs, supple apricots, and tangy cherries that could provide a polished finish to a slice of Olive Oil–Yogurt Cake (page 386) or a bowl of Greek Lemon Rice Pudding (page 388), but that was robust enough to hold its own as an elegant, understated dessert with a dollop of yogurt or crème fraîche. We started with whole (rather than sliced or chopped) dried fruits and simmered them in a light syrup composed mostly of water with just a few tablespoons of honey. A couple of cinnamon sticks and some ground coriander added a uniquely woodsy-floral aroma. We simmered the dried figs and apricots together before adding the cherries toward the end of cooking to ensure that each component was cooked to perfection. As the mixture cooked, the fruit became plump and tender, breaking down just enough to create a lush, flavorful sauce. Use large Turkish or Calimyrna figs in this recipe; Black Mission figs are too small and dense. This compote can be served warm, at room temperature, or chilled.

 4 cups water
 3 tablespoons honey
 2 (2-inch) strips lemon zest plus 1 tablespoon juice
 2 cinnamon sticks
1¼ teaspoons ground coriander
 2 cups (12 ounces) dried Turkish or Calimyrna
     figs, stemmed
 ¾ cup dried apricots
 ½ cup dried cherries

1. Bring water, honey, lemon zest and juice, cinnamon sticks, and coriander to boil in large saucepan over medium-high heat and cook, stirring occasionally, until honey has dissolved, about 2 minutes.

2. Stir in figs and apricots and return to boil. Reduce heat to medium-low and simmer, stirring occasionally, until fruit is plump and tender, about 30 minutes.

3. Stir in cherries and cook until cherries are plump and tender, figs are just beginning to break apart, and liquid is thickened and syrupy, 15 to 20 minutes. Off heat, discard lemon zest and cinnamon sticks and let mixture cool slightly. Serve warm, at room temperature, or chilled.

Turkish Stuffed Apricots with Rose Water and Pistachios
SERVES 6

WHY THIS RECIPE WORKS Stuffed apricots are an iconic Turkish dessert. The authentic version calls for rehydrating dried apricots before candying them in a sugar syrup, filling them with a cream made from water buffalo milk, and topping them with pistachios. We found that by tweaking the sugar concentration of the syrup, we could simultaneously cook, candy, and rehydrate our apricots. This not only streamlined our recipe but also tempered any excessive sweetness. Bay leaves and cardamom pods steeped in our syrup contributed aromatic depth to the fruit. Thick Greek yogurt made a perfect substitute for the hard-to-find water buffalo cream; we added a bit of rose water to the yogurt to enhance the floral qualities of the apricots. Chopped toasted pistachios made for a traditional finish, and their crunch contrasted beautifully with the rich yogurt and tender fruit. Rose water can be found in Middle Eastern markets as well as in the international food aisle of many supermarkets; if you cannot find it, simply omit it. Look for whole dried apricots that are roughly 1½ inches in diameter.

½ cup plain Greek yogurt
¼ cup sugar
½ teaspoon rose water
½ teaspoon grated lemon zest plus 1 tablespoon juice
    Salt
2 cups water
4 green cardamom pods, cracked
2 bay leaves
24 whole dried apricots
¼ cup shelled pistachios, toasted and chopped fine

1. Combine yogurt, 1 teaspoon sugar, rose water, lemon zest, and pinch salt in small bowl. Refrigerate filling until ready to use.

We simmer dried apricots in a bay- and cardamom-scented sugar syrup to rehydrate them and infuse them with flavor.

2. Bring water, cardamom pods, bay leaves, lemon juice, and remaining sugar to simmer in small saucepan over medium-low heat and cook, stirring occasionally, until sugar has dissolved, about 2 minutes. Stir in apricots, return to simmer, and cook,

Stuffing Apricots

1. Transfer filling to small zipper-lock bag and snip off 1 corner to create ½-inch opening. Pipe filling evenly into opening of each apricot.

2. Dip exposed filling into pistachios; transfer to platter and drizzle with spiced syrup before serving.

stirring occasionally, until plump and tender, 25 to 30 minutes. Using slotted spoon, transfer apricots to plate and let cool to room temperature.

3. Discard cardamom pods and bay leaves. Bring syrup to boil over high heat and cook, stirring occasionally, until thickened and measures about 3 tablespoons, 4 to 6 minutes; let cool to room temperature.

4. Place pistachios in shallow dish. Place filling in small zipper-lock bag and snip off 1 corner to create ½-inch opening. Pipe filling evenly into opening of each apricot and dip exposed filling into pistachios; transfer to serving platter. Drizzle apricots with syrup and serve.

Honey-Glazed Peaches with Hazelnuts
SERVES 6 FAST

WHY THIS RECIPE WORKS We wanted a warm, summery dessert that would put fragrant peaches in the spotlight, with just enough added sweetness to amplify the fruit's complex flavors. To achieve nicely tender peaches and a flavorful glaze, we tried tossing the halved and pitted peaches with sugar and baking them until the sugar caramelized. However, the peaches turned to mush by the time we achieved any browning. We found our solution in the direct, intense heat of the broiler. We tossed the peaches with a little sugar, salt, and lemon juice for balance; this seasoned the fruit and extracted some juice that began the glazing process. After broiling them briefly, we brushed them with a mixture of honey and fruity extra-virgin olive oil and then returned them to the broiler until they were beautifully glazed. Reducing the accumulated juice until it was syrupy intensified the peach flavor and made

For intensely flavorful glazed peaches, we broil the fruit and then reduce the accumulated juice to make a thick syrup.

for an attractive, shiny glaze. Toasted hazelnuts added a contrasting crunch to the dessert. Select peaches that yield slightly when pressed. These peaches are best served warm with Greek yogurt.

Peeling Peaches

If your peaches are firm, you should be able to peel them with a sharp vegetable peeler. If they are too soft to withstand the pressure of a peeler, you'll need to blanch them in a pot of simmering water for 30 seconds and then shock them in a bowl of ice water before peeling.

1. Score small X at base of each peach with paring knife.

2. Lower peaches into boiling water and simmer until skins loosen, 30 to 60 seconds.

3. Immediately transfer peaches to ice water and let cool for 1 minute.

4. Using paring knife, remove strips of loosened peel, starting at X on base of each peach.

2 tablespoons lemon juice

1 tablespoon sugar

¼ teaspoon salt

6 ripe but firm peaches, peeled, halved, and pitted

⅓ cup water

¼ cup honey

1 tablespoon extra-virgin olive oil

¼ cup hazelnuts, toasted, skinned, and chopped coarse

1. Adjust oven rack 6 inches from broiler element and heat broiler. Combine lemon juice, sugar, and salt in large bowl. Add peaches and toss to combine, making sure to coat all sides with sugar mixture.

2. Arrange peaches cut side up in 12-inch broilersafe skillet and spoon any remaining sugar mixture into peach cavities. Pour water around peaches in skillet. Broil until peaches are just beginning to brown, 11 to 15 minutes.

3. Combine honey and oil in bowl and microwave until warm, about 20 seconds, then stir to combine. Using potholders, remove skillet from oven. Being careful of hot skillet handle, brush half of honey mixture on peaches. Return peaches to oven and continue to broil until spotty brown, 5 to 7 minutes.

4. Carefully remove skillet from oven, brush peaches with remaining honey mixture, and transfer to serving platter, leaving juice behind. Bring accumulated juice in skillet to simmer over medium heat and cook, whisking frequently to combine, until syrupy, about 1 minute. Pour syrup over peaches and sprinkle with hazelnuts. Serve.

Warm Figs with Goat Cheese and Honey

SERVES 4 to 6 FAST

WHY THIS RECIPE WORKS A piece of barely enhanced fresh fruit is a common ending to many Mediterranean meals, and figs are a perfect candidate: Their sweet, juicy flesh and delicate flavor need little adornment. We started by choosing the ripest, plumpest figs we could find. Halving them and topping them with a bit of tangy goat cheese offset their sweetness nicely. A brief stint in a hot oven was enough to warm the figs and cheese through, and topping each one with a walnut half, toasted to bring out its flavor, offered pleasant crunchy contrast. Finally, a drizzle of honey (tasters preferred milder-flavored options like clover) brought all the elements together with a hit of floral sweetness.

We make an ultrasimple fruit dessert by pairing fresh figs with tangy goat cheese and toasted walnuts.

1½ ounces goat cheese

8 fresh figs, halved lengthwise

16 walnut halves, toasted

3 tablespoons honey

1. Adjust oven rack to middle position and heat oven to 500 degrees. Spoon heaping ½ teaspoon goat cheese onto each fig half and arrange in parchment paper–lined rimmed baking sheet. Bake figs until heated through, about 4 minutes; transfer to serving platter.

2. Place 1 walnut half on top of each fig half and drizzle with honey. Serve.

Peaches and Cherries Poached in Spiced Red Wine

SERVES 6 FAST

WHY THIS RECIPE WORKS Poached fruit makes an elegant Mediterranean-style dessert; poaching allows the shape and texture of the fruit to remain intact while improving its tenderness and enhancing rather than masking its flavor. Sweet cherries and floral peaches made a perfect pair when poached in a red wine syrup. We found that a 2:1 ratio of wine to sugar was necessary to achieve a glossy syrup that would nicely coat the fruit. Boiling the delicate fruit directly in the syrup caused it to break down too much; instead, we boiled the syrup first to dissolve the sugar, then allowed the fruit to cook gently by pouring the hot syrup over it. Slicing the peaches thin ensured that they would cook at the same rate as the cherries. To infuse the fruit with flavor as it cooled in the wine syrup, we added half a cinnamon stick (a whole one was overpowering) and a couple of whole cloves to the mix. Select peaches that yield slightly when pressed. Serve this compote as is, with a bit of the poaching syrup, or with Greek yogurt or crème fraîche.

1 pound fresh sweet cherries, pitted and halved
1 pound ripe but firm peaches, peeled, halved, pitted, and sliced ¼ inch thick
½ cinnamon stick
2 whole cloves
2 cups dry red wine
1 cup sugar

Combine cherries, peaches, cinnamon stick, and cloves in large bowl. Bring red wine and sugar to boil in small saucepan over high heat and cook, stirring occasionally, until sugar has dissolved, about 5 minutes. Pour syrup over fruit, cover, and let cool to room temperature. Discard cinnamon stick and cloves. Serve.

Halving and Pitting Peaches

Cut peach in half, pole to pole, using crease in peach skin as guide. Grasp both halves of fruit and twist apart. Halves will come apart cleanly so pit can be easily removed.

A combination stovetop and oven-roasting method produces pears with deeply browned exteriors and great depth of flavor.

Roasted Pears with Dried Apricots and Pistachios

SERVES 4 to 6

WHY THIS RECIPE WORKS Pears, roasted until perfectly tender and bronzed and dressed up with a few simple embellishments, make an ideal after-dinner treat. Since pears contain a lot of liquid, we knew we needed to drive off some moisture before we could achieve any browning. To do this, we started cooking the pears on the stovetop to jump-start their cooking. Transferring the skillet to the oven for the remainder of the cooking time ensured even and consistent browning and fork-tender flesh. With our pear treatment settled, we decided to make the most of the flavorful browned bits left in the pan by making a quick pan sauce. White wine, lemon juice, and cardamom offered an aromatic Mediterranean flavor profile. A small amount of sugar and some dried apricots brought balanced sweetness. For textural contrast, we sprinkled on a handful of toasted pistachios just before serving. Select pears that yield slightly when pressed. We prefer Bosc pears in this recipe, but Comice and Bartlett pears also work. Use a medium-bodied dry white wine such as Sauvignon Blanc or Chardonnay here. The fruit can be served as is or with plain Greek yogurt.

2 tablespoons extra-virgin olive oil

4 ripe but firm Bosc or Bartlett pears (6 to 7 ounces each), peeled, halved, and cored

1¼ cups dry white wine

½ cup dried apricots, quartered

⅓ cup sugar

¼ teaspoon ground cardamom

⅛ teaspoon salt

1 teaspoon lemon juice

⅓ cup shelled pistachios, toasted and chopped

1. Adjust oven rack to middle position and heat oven to 450 degrees. Heat oil in 12-inch ovensafe skillet over medium-high heat until shimmering. Place pears cut side down in skillet and cook, without moving them, until just beginning to brown, 3 to 5 minutes.

2. Transfer skillet to oven and roast pears for 15 minutes. Being careful of hot skillet handle, flip pears and continue to roast until toothpick slips easily in and out of pears, 10 to 15 minutes.

3. Using potholders, remove skillet from oven and carefully transfer pears to serving platter. Add wine, apricots, sugar, cardamom, and salt to now-empty skillet and bring to simmer over medium-high heat. Cook, whisking to scrape up any browned bits, until sauce is reduced and has consistency of maple syrup, 7 to 10 minutes. Off heat, stir in lemon juice. Pour sauce over pears and sprinkle with pistachios. Serve.

VARIATIONS

Roasted Apples with Dried Figs and Walnuts

Use a medium-bodied dry red wine such as Pinot Noir here.

Substitute 4 Gala apples for pears, 1¼ cups dry red wine for white wine, ½ cup dried figs for apricots, ¾ teaspoon pepper for cardamom, and ⅓ cup walnuts for pistachios.

Coring Pears

1. Peel pear and cut in half through core.

2. Use melon baller to cut around central core using circular motion. Draw melon baller to top of pear, then remove blossom end.

Roasted Plums with Dried Cherries and Almonds

Substitute 4 unpeeled plums for pears, ½ cup dried cherries for apricots, ¼ teaspoon ground cinnamon for cardamom, and ⅓ cup sliced almonds for pistachios. Reduce oven roasting time in step 2 to 5 minutes per side.

White Wine–Poached Pears with Lemon and Herbs
SERVES 6 to 8

WHY THIS RECIPE WORKS Poached pears are a classic French dessert that is surprisingly simple to make at home. We wanted a recipe for meltingly tender pears that we could serve chilled, using the poaching liquid as an aromatic sauce. We discovered that not all varieties of pears worked equally well; Bartlett and Bosc won tasters over with their honeyed sweetness and clean appearance. Cutting the pears in half ensured that they cooked evenly from base to stem end. We tested poaching the fruit in water, fruit juice, and wine and found that white wine offered a nuanced flavor that tasters loved, especially when enhanced with bright, fresh additions like lemon, mint, and thyme. To poach six pears at once, we found it was necessary to use a full bottle of wine and turn the pears several times as they cooked. We then removed them from the pot and reduced the cooking liquid to a syrupy consistency before pouring it back over the fruit. Letting the pears cool in the syrup prevented them from drying out; it also allowed them to absorb some of the syrup, giving them a candied translucency and making them plump, sweet, and pleasantly spiced. Select pears that yield slightly when pressed. Use a medium-bodied dry white wine such as Sauvignon Blanc or Chardonnay here. The fruit can be served as is or with crème fraîche.

1 vanilla bean

1 (750-ml) bottle dry white wine

¾ cup sugar

6 (2-inch) strips lemon zest

5 sprigs fresh mint

3 sprigs fresh thyme

½ cinnamon stick

⅛ teaspoon salt

6 ripe but firm Bosc or Bartlett pears (8 ounces each), peeled, halved, and cored

1. Cut vanilla bean in half lengthwise. Using tip of paring knife, scrape out seeds. Bring wine, sugar, lemon zest, mint sprigs, thyme sprigs, cinnamon stick, salt, and vanilla seeds and pod to boil in large saucepan over high heat and cook, stirring occasionally, until sugar has dissolved, about 5 minutes.

2. Add pears and return to boil. Reduce heat to medium-low, cover, and simmer until pears are tender and toothpick slips easily in and out of pears, 10 to 20 minutes, gently turning pears over every 5 minutes.

3. Using slotted spoon, transfer pears to shallow casserole dish. Bring syrup to simmer over medium heat and cook, stirring occasionally, until slightly thickened and measures 1¼ to 1½ cups, about 15 minutes. Strain syrup through fine-mesh strainer over pears; discard solids. Let pears cool to room temperature, then cover and refrigerate until well chilled, at least 2 hours or up to 3 days. Serve.

Melon, Plums, and Cherries with Mint and Vanilla
SERVES 4 to 6   FAST

WHY THIS RECIPE WORKS A fresh fruit salad is great at any Mediterranean breakfast, for dessert, or even as a mid-afternoon snack. We were after a salad with balanced fruit flavor and sweetness. A combination of cantaloupe, plums, and cherries not only offered a range of complementary flavors but also looked beautiful. A small amount of sugar encouraged the fruit to release its juices, creating a more cohesive salad. We balanced the sweetness with fresh lime juice, but tasters wanted more complexity. Mashing the sugar with fresh mint before stirring it into the fruit worked perfectly and ensured even distribution of flavor throughout the salad. Since our fruit salad had come together so easily, we decided to apply the same techniques to a combination of peaches and berries, using fresh basil in place of the mint and a small amount of pepper to bring the flavors to life. Blueberries can be substituted for the cherries.

  4 teaspoons sugar
  1 tablespoon minced fresh mint
  3 cups cantaloupe, cut into ½-inch pieces
  2 plums, halved, pitted, and cut into ½-inch pieces
  8 ounces fresh sweet cherries, pitted and halved
  ¼ teaspoon vanilla extract
  1 tablespoon lime juice, plus extra for seasoning

Combine sugar and mint in large bowl. Using rubber spatula, press mixture into side of bowl until sugar becomes damp, about 30 seconds. Add cantaloupe, plums, cherries, and vanilla and gently toss to combine. Let sit at room temperature, stirring occasionally, until fruit releases its juices, 15 to 30 minutes. Stir in lime juice and season with extra lime juice to taste. Serve.

Mashing sugar with fresh mint before stirring it into the fruit gives our salad balanced, complex flavor.

VARIATION
Peaches, Blackberries, and Strawberries with Basil and Pepper
SERVES 4 to 6   FAST
Nectarines can be substituted for the peaches.

  4 teaspoons sugar
  2 tablespoons chopped fresh basil
  ½ teaspoon pepper
  3 peaches, halved, pitted, and cut into ½-inch pieces
 10 ounces (2 cups) blackberries
 10 ounces strawberries, hulled and quartered (2 cups)
  1 tablespoon lime juice, plus extra for seasoning

Combine sugar, basil, and pepper in large bowl. Using rubber spatula, press mixture into side of bowl until sugar becomes damp, about 30 seconds. Add peaches, blackberries, and strawberries and gently toss to combine. Let sit at room temperature, stirring occasionally, until fruit releases its juices, 15 to 30 minutes. Stir in lime juice and season with extra lime juice to taste. Serve.

Strawberries with Balsamic Vinegar
SERVES 6 FAST

WHY THIS RECIPE WORKS Strawberries with balsamic vinegar may sound a bit trendy, but this Italian combination actually dates back hundreds of years. We wanted to pay homage to this tradition and create our own dessert in which the vinegar enhanced, not overwhelmed, the flavor of bright summer berries. But high-end aged balsamic vinegars can cost a pretty penny, so we opted instead to use an inexpensive vinegar and employ a few tricks to coax more flavor from it. First, we simmered the vinegar with sugar to approximate the syrupy texture of an aged vinegar. Next we tried to enhance the flavor with honey or vanilla, but these flavors were overpowering; a squirt of fresh lemon juice brought just the right amount of brightness. We tossed the berries with light brown sugar—rather than the traditional granulated sugar—and a pinch of pepper for the most complex flavor. Once we mixed the sliced berries and sugar together, it took about 15 minutes for the sugar to dissolve and the berries to release their juice; if the strawberries sat any longer than this, they continued to soften and became quite mushy. If you don't have light brown sugar on hand, sprinkle the berries with an equal amount of granulated white sugar. Serve the berries and syrup as is or with lightly sweetened mascarpone cheese.

⅓ cup balsamic vinegar
2 teaspoons granulated sugar
½ teaspoon lemon juice
2 pounds strawberries, hulled and sliced lengthwise ¼ inch thick (5 cups)
¼ cup packed light brown sugar
Pinch pepper

1. Bring vinegar, granulated sugar, and lemon juice to simmer in small saucepan over medium heat and cook, stirring occasionally, until thickened and measures about 3 tablespoons, about 3 minutes. Transfer syrup to small bowl and let cool completely.
2. Gently toss strawberries with brown sugar and pepper in large bowl. Let sit at room temperature, stirring occasionally, until strawberries begin to release their juice, 10 to 15 minutes. Pour syrup over strawberries and gently toss to combine. Serve.

Nectarines and Berries in Prosecco
SERVES 6 to 8 FAST

WHY THIS RECIPE WORKS For a celebratory yet light Mediterranean-inspired dessert, we wanted to combine fresh fruit with sparkling wine. After some enjoyable experimentation,

To make a composed and cohesive combination, we macerate fruit with sugar before pouring sparkling wine on top.

we settled on nectarines and berries as our fruit and prosecco for the wine. But simply pouring prosecco over lightly sugared fruit resulted in disappointingly disparate flavors. Instead, we tossed the fruit with sugar and allowed the mixture to macerate. The nectarines and berries softened and released some of their juices, which, when combined with the chilled wine, contributed to a more cohesive flavor profile. Orange liqueur added some depth as well as some nice citrus notes. Our harmonious blend of fruit and fizz made a refreshing ending to a summer meal. Peaches or plums can be substituted for the nectarines. While we prefer to use prosecco here, any young, fruity sparkling wine will work.

10 ounces (2 cups) blackberries or raspberries
10 ounces strawberries, hulled and quartered (2 cups)
1 pound nectarines, pitted and cut into ¼-inch wedges
¼ cup sugar, plus extra as needed
1 tablespoon orange liqueur, such as Grand Marnier or triple sec
1 tablespoon chopped fresh mint
¼ teaspoon grated lemon zest
1 cup chilled prosecco

Gently toss blackberries, strawberries, nectarines, sugar, orange liqueur, mint, and lemon zest together in large bowl. Let sit at room temperature, stirring occasionally, until fruit begins to release its juices, 10 to 15 minutes. Just before serving, pour prosecco over fruit and season with extra sugar to taste. Serve.

Individual Fresh Berry Gratins
SERVES 4

WHY THIS RECIPE WORKS *Zabaglione* is a traditional Italian custard flavored with wine and often accompanied by fresh berries. To turn this simple combination into a full-flavored dessert worthy of serving to guests, we turned it into a gratin. We macerated the berries with a little bit of sugar to encourage them to release their flavorful juices. For the custard, we whisked together egg yolks, sugar, and wine over a pot of barely simmering water; keeping the heat low and using a glass bowl rather than a metal one guarded against overcooking. Tasters preferred the flavor of light, crisp white wine to the more traditional Marsala, but the decreased sugar made our custard runny. To make up for the loss of structure without making the custard achingly sweet, we folded in some whipped cream. Dividing the berries and custard among individual ramekins made for a pretty presentation and easier serving. Running the gratins briefly under the broiler produced warm, succulent berries and a golden-brown crust on the zabaglione. You will need four shallow 6-ounce broilersafe gratin dishes, but a broilersafe pie plate or gratin dish can be used instead. When making the zabaglione, make sure to cook the egg mixture in a glass bowl over water that is barely simmering; glass conducts heat more evenly and gently than metal. Although we prefer to make this recipe with a mixture of blackberries, blueberries, raspberries, and strawberries, you can use 3 cups of just one type of berry. Do not use frozen berries for this recipe. To prevent scorching, pay close attention to the gratins when broiling. Use a medium-bodied dry white wine such as Sauvignon Blanc or Chardonnay in this recipe.

BERRY MIXTURE
- 11 ounces (2¼ cups) blackberries, blueberries, and/or raspberries
- 4 ounces strawberries, hulled and halved lengthwise if small or quartered if large (¾ cup)
- 2 teaspoons granulated sugar
  Pinch salt

ZABAGLIONE
- 3 large egg yolks
- 3 tablespoons granulated sugar
- 3 tablespoons dry white wine

For perfect Italian *zabaglione*, we use dry white wine instead of sweet and fold in whipped cream for structure.

- 2 teaspoons packed light brown sugar
- 3 tablespoons heavy cream, chilled

1. FOR THE BERRY MIXTURE Line rimmed baking sheet with aluminum foil. Toss berries, strawberries, sugar, and salt together in bowl. Divide berry mixture evenly among 4 shallow 6-ounce gratin dishes set in prepared sheet; set aside.

2. FOR THE ZABAGLIONE Whisk egg yolks, 2 tablespoons plus 1 teaspoon granulated sugar, and wine together in medium bowl until sugar has dissolved, about 1 minute. Set bowl over saucepan of barely simmering water and cook, whisking constantly, until mixture is frothy. Continue to cook, whisking constantly, until mixture is slightly thickened, creamy, and glossy, 5 to 10 minutes (mixture will form loose mounds when dripped from whisk). Remove bowl from saucepan and whisk constantly for 30 seconds to cool slightly. Transfer bowl to refrigerator and chill until egg mixture is completely cool, about 10 minutes.

3. Meanwhile, adjust oven rack 6 inches from broiler element and heat broiler. Combine brown sugar and remaining 2 teaspoons granulated sugar in bowl.

4. Whisk heavy cream in large bowl until it holds soft peaks, 30 to 90 seconds. Using rubber spatula, gently fold whipped cream into cooled egg mixture. Spoon zabaglione over berries and sprinkle sugar mixture evenly on top. Let sit at room temperature for 10 minutes, until sugar dissolves.

5. Broil gratins until sugar is bubbly and caramelized, 1 to 4 minutes. Serve immediately.

NOTES FROM THE TEST KITCHEN

Washing and Storing Berries

Washing berries before you use them is always a safe practice, and we think that the best way to wash them is to place the berries in a colander and rinse them gently under running water for at least 30 seconds. As for drying berries, we've tested a variety of methods and have found that a salad spinner lined with a buffering layer of paper towels is the best approach.

It's particularly important to store berries carefully, because they are prone to growing mold and rotting quickly. If the berries aren't going to be used immediately, we recommend cleaning them with a mild vinegar solution (3 cups of water mixed with 1 cup of distilled white vinegar), which will destroy the bacteria, then drying them and storing them in a paper towel–lined airtight container.

Cooking honey to the proper temperature guarantees the best flavor and texture in these Greek sesame treats.

Greek Sesame-Honey Bars

MAKES 32 bars

WHY THIS RECIPE WORKS The delectable treats known as *pasteli* can be found in shops, kiosks, and households all over Greece. The most authentic pasteli are made with just two ingredients—toasted sesame seeds and honey—though versions made with other seeds and nuts are also common. We wanted to develop an easy, traditional recipe that would yield crisp, flavorful bars with just a bit of chew. We started by toasting the sesame seeds in a moderately hot oven, stirring them often to ensure that they toasted evenly. (We found that freshly toasted seeds had a much more complex flavor than store-bought pretoasted seeds.) As the seeds cooled, we cooked the honey on the stovetop to a temperature between 300 and 310 degrees—any lower and the bars remained unappealingly chewy and sticky, but any higher and the honey tasted harsh and bitter. Adding a bit of salt to the honey-sesame mixture underscored the flavors nicely. We let the mixture cool slightly in a foil-lined baking pan, which made it easy to lift the bars out and slice them. We were careful not to let them cool for too long or they became difficult to cut. These bars are best made with an assertive honey, such as a spicy clover honey.

1¾ cups sesame seeds
¾ cup honey
¼ teaspoon salt

1. Adjust oven rack to middle position and heat oven to 350 degrees. Make foil sling for 8-inch square baking pan by folding 2 long sheets of aluminum foil so each is 8 inches wide. Lay sheets of foil in pan perpendicular to each other, with extra foil hanging over edges of pan. Push foil into corners and up sides of pan, smoothing foil flush to pan, then grease foil.

2. Spread sesame seeds in even layer in rimmed baking sheet and toast, stirring often, until golden, 10 to 12 minutes; immediately transfer to bowl.

3. Heat honey in large saucepan over medium-high heat until bubbling. Reduce heat to medium-low and cook, gently swirling pan occasionally, until honey is deep amber and registers 300 to 310 degrees, 4 to 5 minutes. Off heat, stir in sesame seeds and salt until thoroughly combined.

4. Working quickly, carefully pour honey–sesame seed mixture into prepared pan and push into corners with greased rubber spatula. Let sit until cool enough to touch but still malleable, about 5 minutes. Using lightly greased fingers, gently press mixture into even layer. Let cool until firm, about 20 minutes. (Do not let bars sit for longer than 20 minutes or they will be too hard to cut.)

5. Using foil overhang, lift bars out of pan and transfer to cutting board; discard foil. Cut into thirty-two 2 by 1-inch bars and transfer to wire rack. Let bars cool completely, about 1 hour, then transfer to airtight container. Let sit at room temperature until fully crisp, about 8 hours. Serve. (Bars can be stored at room temperature for up to 1 month.)

Making a Foil Sling

To make bars easy to remove from pan, make foil sling by laying two 8-inch-wide sheets of foil in pan perpendicular to each other. Push foil into corners and up sides of pan, letting excess foil hang over edges.

Shopping for Honey

Honey is used throughout the Mediterranean in both sweet and savory applications. When shopping for honey, there are several important things to know. There are two distinct categories of honey: traditional, which is pressure filtered to remove pollen and create a clear appearance, and raw, which is only lightly filtered and retains much of its pollen. Although both traditional and raw honeys can vary greatly in flavor, we generally prefer raw honey, which is much more nuanced and balanced in flavor than traditional honey. But traditional versus raw is only one piece of the puzzle: The bees' diet also affects the flavor of the honey. While bees that feed mostly on clover produce a mild-flavored honey, bees with a more varied diet produce a more complexly flavored honey. Our favorite product, Nature Nate's 100% Pure Raw and Unfiltered Honey, sources its honey from bees that feed on a blend of wildflowers, clover, Chinese tallow, and vetch; it is slightly bitter and floral, with a deep, balanced sweetness. We also recommend staying away from very strongly flavored honeys, such as buckwheat honey, when baking. The flavor of the honey you use will come through in baked goods, and our tasters weren't fond of the distinct, strong flavor of buckwheat, which took away from the other flavors in recipes.

For biscotti that are crisp but not too hard, we use whole eggs as the only source of fat in our recipe.

Lemon-Anise Biscotti
MAKES about 48 biscotti

WHY THIS RECIPE WORKS A Sicilian specialty, biscotti should be crunchy (but not tooth-cracking) and full of flavor—perfect with an afternoon cup of coffee. After testing recipes that used whole eggs, egg yolks, and egg whites, we discovered that whole eggs created the best crisp texture. Although some recipes called for an additional fat such as butter or oil, we found that these only muddled the flavors of the cookies. We opted to include lemon zest for subtle citrus notes and anise seeds for their delicate licorice flavor. Because biscotti are baked twice—once in loaves, then again after the loaves are sliced—using a full tablespoon of zest and anise seeds was necessary so that the flavors would come through even after the long stay in the oven.

  2 cups (10 ounces) all-purpose flour
  1 teaspoon baking powder
  ¼ teaspoon salt
  1 cup (7 ounces) sugar
  2 large eggs

1 tablespoon grated lemon zest
1 tablespoon anise seeds
¼ teaspoon vanilla extract

1. Adjust oven rack to middle position and heat oven to 350 degrees. Using ruler and pencil, draw two 13 by 2-inch rectangles, spaced 3 inches apart, on piece of parchment paper. Grease baking sheet and place parchment on it, marked side down.

2. Whisk flour, baking powder, and salt together in small bowl. In large bowl, whisk sugar and eggs together until pale yellow. Whisk in lemon zest, anise seeds, and vanilla until combined. Using rubber spatula, stir in flour mixture until just combined.

3. Divide dough in half. Using floured hands, form each half into 13 by 2-inch rectangle, using lines on parchment as guide. Using rubber spatula lightly coated with vegetable oil spray, smooth tops and sides of loaves. Bake until loaves are golden and just beginning to crack on top, about 35 minutes, rotating sheet halfway through baking.

4. Let loaves cool on sheet for 10 minutes, then transfer to cutting board. Reduce oven temperature to 325 degrees. Using serrated knife, slice each loaf on slight bias into ½-inch-thick slices.

5. Arrange cookies cut side down on sheet about ½ inch apart and bake until crisp and golden brown on both sides, about 15 minutes, flipping cookies halfway through baking. Let cool completely on wire rack before serving. (Biscotti can be stored at room temperature for up to 1 month.)

VARIATIONS
Honey-Lavender Biscotti
MAKES about 48 biscotti
Dried lavender blossoms can be found in spice and herbal stores. If you can't find the lavender blossoms, this recipe makes very good honey biscotti.

2¼ cups (11¼ ounces) all-purpose flour
1 teaspoon baking powder
½ teaspoon baking soda
¼ teaspoon salt
⅔ cup (4⅔ ounces) sugar
3 large eggs
3 tablespoons honey
2 tablespoons grated orange zest
1 tablespoon dried lavender (optional)
½ teaspoon vanilla extract

1. Adjust oven rack to middle position and heat oven to 350 degrees. Using ruler and pencil, draw two 13 by 2-inch rectangles, spaced 3 inches apart, on piece of parchment paper. Grease baking sheet and place parchment on it, marked side down.

2. Whisk flour, baking powder, baking soda, and salt together in small bowl. In large bowl, whisk sugar and eggs together until pale yellow. Whisk in honey, orange zest, lavender, if using, and vanilla until combined. Using rubber spatula, stir in flour mixture until just combined.

3. Divide dough in half. Using floured hands, form each half into 13 by 2-inch rectangle, using lines on parchment as guide. Using rubber spatula lightly coated with vegetable oil spray, smooth tops and sides of loaves. Bake until loaves are golden and just beginning to crack on top, about 35 minutes, rotating sheet halfway through baking.

4. Let loaves cool on sheet for 10 minutes, then transfer to cutting board. Reduce oven temperature to 325 degrees. Using serrated knife, slice each loaf on slight bias into ½-inch-thick slices.

Making Biscotti

1. MAKE STENCIL Draw two 13 by 2-inch rectangles, spaced 3 inches apart, on piece of parchment paper. Place parchment marked side down on greased baking sheet.

2. SHAPE DOUGH After preparing dough, divide in half and with floured hands form each half into loaf on parchment-lined sheet, using lines as guide.

3. SLICE COOKIES Transfer partially baked loaves to cutting board. Using serrated knife, slice each loaf on slight bias into ½-inch-thick slices.

4. BAKE AGAIN Space slices, with 1 cut side down, about ½ inch apart on baking sheet. Bake until crisp and golden brown on both sides, about 15 minutes, flipping cookies halfway through baking.

5. Arrange cookies cut side down on sheet about ½ inch apart and bake until crisp and golden brown on both sides, about 15 minutes, flipping cookies halfway through baking. Let cool completely on wire rack before serving. (Biscotti can be stored at room temperature for up to 1 month.)

Spiced Biscotti

MAKES about 48 biscotti

If desired, substitute 3 whole eggs for the 2 eggs and 2 egg yolks in this recipe.

2¼ cups (11¼ ounces) all-purpose flour
  1 teaspoon baking powder
  ½ teaspoon baking soda
  ½ teaspoon ground cloves
  ½ teaspoon ground cinnamon
  ¼ teaspoon ground ginger
  ¼ teaspoon salt
  ¼ teaspoon ground white pepper
  1 cup (7 ounces) sugar
  2 large eggs plus 2 large yolks
  ½ teaspoon vanilla extract

1. Adjust oven rack to middle position and heat oven to 350 degrees. Using ruler and pencil, draw two 13 by 2-inch rectangles, spaced 3 inches apart, on piece of parchment paper. Grease baking sheet and place parchment on it, marked side down.

2. Whisk flour, baking powder, baking soda, cloves, cinnamon, ginger, salt, and pepper together in small bowl. In large bowl, whisk sugar and eggs and egg yolks together until pale yellow. Whisk in vanilla until combined. Using rubber spatula, stir in flour mixture until just combined.

3. Divide dough in half. Using floured hands, form each half into 13 by 2-inch rectangle, using lines on parchment as guide. Using rubber spatula lightly coated with vegetable oil spray, smooth tops and sides of loaves. Bake until loaves are golden and just beginning to crack on top, about 35 minutes, rotating sheet halfway through baking.

4. Let loaves cool on sheet for 10 minutes, then transfer to cutting board. Reduce oven temperature to 325 degrees. Using serrated knife, slice each loaf on slight bias into ½-inch-thick slices.

5. Arrange cookies cut side down on sheet about ½ inch apart and bake until crisp and golden brown on both sides, about 15 minutes, flipping cookies halfway through baking. Let cool completely on wire rack before serving. (Biscotti can be stored at room temperature for up to 1 month.)

These traditional Italian cookies get their richness and flavor from slivered almonds, pine nuts, and sugar.

Pignoli

MAKES about 18 cookies

WHY THIS RECIPE WORKS With an appealingly light texture from egg whites (no yolks) and a nutty flavor profile, the classic southern Italian cookies known as *pignoli* require only a few ingredients and are simple to make. For the base, most recipes we found relied on almond paste, but we achieved a deeper, richer almond flavor and more controlled sweetness by simply processing slivered almonds with granulated sugar. Some recipes include lemon or orange zest, but we found that these additions were more a distraction than an asset. Our base was a little sticky, but it was still easy enough to roll into balls, then coat in pine nuts for the traditional finish to this after-dinner cookie. There was no need to toast the pine nuts ahead of time since they toasted as the cookies baked.

1⅔ cups slivered almonds
1⅓ cups (9⅓ ounces) sugar
  2 large egg whites
  1 cup pine nuts

1. Adjust oven racks to upper-middle and lower-middle positions and heat oven to 375 degrees. Line 2 baking sheets with parchment paper.

2. Process almonds and sugar in food processor until finely ground, about 30 seconds. Scrape down sides of bowl and add egg whites. Continue to process until smooth (dough will be wet), about 30 seconds; transfer mixture to bowl. Place pine nuts in shallow dish.

3. Working with 1 scant tablespoon dough at a time, roll into balls, roll in pine nuts to coat, and space 2 inches apart on prepared sheets.

4. Bake cookies until light golden brown, 13 to 15 minutes, switching and rotating sheets halfway through baking. Let cookies cool on sheets for 5 minutes, then transfer to wire rack. Let cookies cool to room temperature before serving. (Cookies can be stored in airtight container at room temperature for up to 4 days.)

Fig Phyllo Cookies
MAKES about 24 cookies

WHY THIS RECIPE WORKS For a delicate, pleasantly chewy cookie that would make a good light dessert or afternoon snack and would be equally welcome on any holiday table, we turned to Sicilian *cuccidati* for inspiration. Cuccidati are fig cookies traditionally made with buttery pastry dough and glazed with sugar; for a lighter version, we opted for phyllo instead of pastry dough and swapped the glaze for an aromatic syrup. To make the filling, we simmered dried figs in a spiced syrup until they were plump and tender, then pureed them in a food processor with toasted walnuts and sherry to create a thick, flavorful paste. For the dough, we found that layering just three sheets of phyllo gave us the thickness and flakiness we were after. We brushed each layer with fruity olive oil and then dusted them with confectioners' sugar to help the sheets adhere to one another. To shape our cookies, we piped the fig puree onto the dough and rolled it to make a thin log that could be sliced into pieces. After baking, we brushed the rolls with an orange-scented syrup to keep them moist and give them a festive, polished finish. We prefer Turkish or Calimyrna figs in this recipe, but Black Mission figs work as well. Phyllo dough is also available in larger 18 by 14-inch sheets; if using, cut them in half to make 14 by 9-inch sheets. Do not thaw the phyllo in the microwave; let it sit in the refrigerator overnight or on the counter for 4 to 5 hours. While working with the phyllo, cover the sheets with plastic wrap, then a damp dish towel to prevent drying.

We roll confectioners' sugar–coated phyllo around a jammy fig filling for attractive cookies that hold their shape.

SUGAR SYRUP
¼ cup granulated sugar
2 tablespoons water
2 tablespoons honey
2 (2-inch) strips orange zest plus 2 tablespoons juice

FIG FILLING
1½ cups (9 ounces) dried figs, stemmed and halved
¾ cup water
½ cup granulated sugar
1 teaspoon orange zest
½ teaspoon anise seeds
½ cup walnuts, toasted and chopped coarse
1 tablespoon dry sherry

PASTRY
6 (14 by 9-inch) phyllo sheets, thawed
¼ cup extra-virgin olive oil
2 tablespoons confectioners' sugar

1. FOR THE SUGAR SYRUP Bring all ingredients to boil in small saucepan over medium-high heat and cook, stirring occasionally, until sugar has dissolved, about 2 minutes. Reduce heat to medium-low and simmer until syrup is thickened and slightly reduced, about 3 minutes. Discard zest and transfer syrup to bowl; set aside.

2. FOR THE FIG FILLING Bring figs, water, sugar, orange zest, and anise seeds to simmer in now-empty saucepan over medium heat and cook until thickened and syrupy, about 5 minutes. Let mixture cool to room temperature, about 1 hour.

3. Process fig mixture in food processor until paste forms, about 15 seconds. Scrape down sides of bowl, add walnuts and sherry, and pulse until walnuts are finely chopped, about 10 pulses. Transfer fig-walnut mixture to zipper-lock bag and snip off 1 corner to create 1-inch opening.

4. FOR THE PASTRY Adjust oven rack to middle position and heat oven to 375 degrees. Line rimmed baking sheet with parchment paper. Place 1 phyllo sheet on counter with long side parallel to counter edge, brush lightly with oil, then dust with 1 teaspoon sugar. Repeat with 2 more phyllo sheets, brushing each with oil and dusting with 1 teaspoon sugar (you should have total of 3 layers of phyllo).

5. Pipe half of filling along bottom edge of phyllo, leaving 1½-inch border along edge. Fold bottom edge of phyllo over filling, then continue rolling phyllo away from you into firm cylinder. With cylinder seam side down, use serrated knife to cut cylinder into 12 equal pieces. Arrange cookies on prepared sheet, spaced 1½ inches apart. Repeat with remaining 3 phyllo sheets, oil, and filling and arrange on sheet.

6. Bake cookies until light golden brown, 15 to 20 minutes, rotating sheet halfway through baking. Drizzle warm cookies with syrup and let cool for 5 minutes. Transfer cookies to wire rack and let cool completely before serving. (Cookies can be stored at room temperature for up to 4 days.)

Baklava

MAKES 32 to 40 pieces

WHY THIS RECIPE WORKS We wanted our classic baklava recipe to produce a crisp, flaky pastry that was light yet rich, filled with fragrant nuts and spices, and sweetened just assertively enough to pair with a Turkish coffee. To achieve this goal, we sprinkled store-bought phyllo dough with three separate layers of nuts (tasters liked a combination of almonds and walnuts) flavored with cinnamon and cloves. We brushed the phyllo layers with just enough olive oil to make them crisp and flaky, but not so much that the result was greasy. We found that cutting the baklava through rather than just scoring it before baking helped it absorb the sugar syrup. Finally, allowing the baklava to sit overnight before serving

Slicing baklava all the way through before baking allows the pastry to soak up more of the flavorful sugar syrup.

dramatically improved its flavor. A straight-sided traditional (not nonstick) metal baking pan works best for making baklava. If you don't have this type of pan, a glass baking dish will work. Phyllo dough is also available in larger 18 by 14-inch sheets; if using, cut them in half to make 14 by 9-inch sheets. Do not thaw the phyllo in the microwave; let it sit in the refrigerator overnight or on the counter for 4 to 5 hours. While working with the phyllo, cover the sheets with plastic wrap, then a damp dish towel to prevent drying. Use the nicest, most intact phyllo sheets for the bottom and top layers; use sheets with tears or ones that are smaller than the size of the pan in the middle layers, where their imperfections will go unnoticed.

SUGAR SYRUP
1¼ cups (8¾ ounces) sugar
¾ cup water
⅓ cup honey
3 (2-inch) strips lemon zest plus 1 tablespoon juice
1 cinnamon stick
5 whole cloves
⅛ teaspoon salt

NUT FILLING

1¾ cups slivered almonds

1 cup walnuts

2 tablespoons sugar

1¼ teaspoons ground cinnamon

¼ teaspoon ground cloves

⅛ teaspoon salt

PASTRY

5 tablespoons extra-virgin olive oil

1 pound (14 by 9-inch) phyllo, thawed

1. FOR THE SUGAR SYRUP Bring all ingredients to boil in small saucepan over medium-high heat and cook, stirring occasionally, until sugar has dissolved, about 5 minutes. Transfer syrup to 2-cup liquid measuring cup and let cool to room temperature. Discard spices and zest; set aside.

2. FOR THE NUT FILLING Pulse almonds in food processor until very finely chopped, about 20 pulses; transfer to medium bowl. Pulse walnuts in food processor until very finely chopped, about 15 pulses; transfer to bowl with almonds and toss to combine. Measure out 1 tablespoon nuts and set aside for garnish. Add sugar, cinnamon, cloves, and salt to nut mixture and toss well to combine.

3. FOR THE PASTRY Adjust oven rack to lower-middle position and heat oven to 300 degrees. Lay 1 phyllo sheet in bottom of greased 13 by 9-inch baking pan and brush thoroughly with oil. Repeat with 7 more phyllo sheets, brushing each with oil (you should have total of 8 layers of phyllo).

4. Sprinkle 1 cup nut filling evenly over phyllo. Cover nut filling with 6 more phyllo sheets, brushing each with oil, then sprinkle with 1 cup nut filling. Repeat with 6 phyllo sheets, oil, and remaining 1 cup nut filling.

5. Cover nut filling with 8 more phyllo sheets, brushing each layer, except final layer, with oil. Working from center outward, use palms of your hands to compress layers and press out any air pockets. Spoon remaining oil (about 2 tablespoons) on top layer and brush to cover surface.

6. Using serrated knife with pointed tip, cut baklava into diamonds. Bake baklava until golden and crisp, about 1½ hours, rotating pan halfway through baking.

7. Immediately pour all but 2 tablespoons cooled syrup over cut lines (syrup will sizzle when it hits hot pan). Drizzle remaining 2 tablespoons syrup over surface. Garnish center of each piece with pinch reserved ground nuts. Let baklava cool completely in pan, about 3 hours, then cover with aluminum foil and let sit at room temperature for about 8 hours before serving.

NOTES FROM THE TEST KITCHEN

Storing Nuts

Since nuts are high in oil, they can become rancid fairly quickly if not properly stored. In the test kitchen, we store all nuts in the freezer in sealed freezer-safe zipper-lock bags. Frozen nuts will keep for months, and there's no need to defrost them before chopping or toasting. If you use toasted nuts often, you can toast them in large batches and, when the nuts are cool, transfer them to a zipper-lock bag, then freeze them. Do not use pretoasted frozen nuts for recipes in which a crisp texture is desired, such as salads.

Making Baklava

1. MAKE BASE Place 8 phyllo sheets in greased baking pan, brushing each sheet with oil.

2. START LAYERING Spread 1 cup nut filling over bottom stack of phyllo. Place 6 phyllo sheets over nut layer, brushing each sheet with oil. Repeat with another 1 cup nut filling and 6 more sheets of phyllo.

3. FINISH ASSEMBLING Spread remaining 1 cup nut filling over phyllo. Finish with 8 more sheets of oiled phyllo. Using your hands, compress layers to remove air pockets, working from center outward.

4. BAKE AND DRIZZLE WITH SYRUP Cut baklava into diamonds using serrated knife, then bake. Pour syrup over cut lines of baked baklava. Garnish each piece with chopped nuts.

We use the food processor to grind the almonds and make the batter for our classic almond cake.

Almond Cake
SERVES 12

WHY THIS RECIPE WORKS Almond cake is a popular dessert in countries like Spain and Italy, and it's easy to understand why: This single-layer cake is so rich in flavor that it requires no frosting, and it's remarkably simple to make. We wanted our recipe to produce an almond cake with plenty of nutty flavor and a light, open crumb. We found that using finely ground almonds and a bit of almond extract gave us a cake with a cleaner and more pronounced almond flavor than that of a cake made with store-bought almond paste. To avoid the overly dense gluten structure that can result from using too much all-purpose flour, we relied on the protein structure of eggs to create a tender, delicate crumb. We used a food processor to assemble our batter in stages. We started by grinding toasted blanched almonds along with our dry ingredients and set the mixture aside. Then, in the same processor bowl,

we processed our eggs and sugar for just 30 seconds to create a light, fluffy mixture. (When we processed the egg mixture for too long, we incorporated too much air, which resulted in a domed cake.) Finally, we streamed in our olive oil and pulsed in the almond mixture before transferring the batter to a cake pan. For added elegance and a decorative finish we sprinkled the cake with sliced almonds and a mixture of lemon zest and sugar before baking. If you can't find blanched sliced almonds, grind slivered almonds for the batter and use unblanched sliced almonds for the topping.

1½ cups plus ⅓ cup blanched sliced almonds, toasted
¾ cup (3¾ ounces) all-purpose flour
¾ teaspoon salt
¼ teaspoon baking powder
⅛ teaspoon baking soda
4 large eggs
1¼ cups (8¾ ounces) plus 2 tablespoons sugar
1 tablespoon plus ½ teaspoon grated lemon zest (2 lemons)
¾ teaspoon almond extract
½ cup extra-virgin olive oil

1. Adjust oven rack to middle position and heat oven to 300 degrees. Grease 9-inch round cake pan and line with parchment paper. Pulse 1½ cups almonds, flour, salt, baking powder, and baking soda in food processor until almonds are finely ground, 10 to 15 pulses; transfer to bowl.

2. Process eggs, 1¼ cups sugar, 1 tablespoon lemon zest, and almond extract in now-empty processor until pale yellow and frothy, about 30 seconds. With processor running, slowly add oil in steady stream until incorporated, about 10 seconds. Add almond mixture and pulse to combine, 4 to 5 pulses.

3. Transfer batter to prepared pan and smooth into even layer. Using your fingers, combine remaining 2 tablespoons sugar and remaining ½ teaspoon lemon zest in small bowl until fragrant, 5 to 10 seconds. Sprinkle top of cake evenly with remaining ⅓ cup almonds followed by sugar-zest mixture.

4. Bake until center of cake is set and bounces back when gently pressed and toothpick inserted in center comes out clean, 55 to 65 minutes, rotating pan after 40 minutes.

5. Let cake cool in pan on wire rack for 15 minutes. Run paring knife around sides of pan. Remove cake from pan, discarding parchment, and let cool completely on rack, about 2 hours. Serve.

Toasted polenta delivers deep corn flavor to this rustic upside-down cake featuring sweet, caramelized oranges.

Orange Polenta Cake

SERVES 12

WHY THIS RECIPE WORKS A rustic polenta cake infused with bright citrus flavor and topped with beautiful glazed orange slices makes for a perfect Italian-inspired dessert. We wanted ours to have great corn flavor and a moist, tender crumb. First, we needed to figure out how to incorporate the polenta. Uncooked polenta left our cake with hard bits throughout. Although some recipes call for cooking a batch of polenta and stirring it into the batter, this was a bit labor intensive for what we hoped would be a simple recipe. We found our answer in instant polenta, which required only hydrating to become tender; tasters preferred the richness of polenta hydrated with milk rather than water. Toasting the polenta brought out more depth of flavor. To make an easy yet elegant topping for our cake, we sprinkled some sugar and cornstarch in the bottom of the cake pan and arranged thinly sliced oranges over it. We poured the cake batter directly on top of the oranges, which caramelized beautifully during baking. A bit of orange zest in the cake batter reinforced the fresh citrus flavor. Do not substitute regular or premade polenta for the instant polenta. Be sure to break up any large clumps of the polenta with your fingers before

adding it to the batter or the cake will have bits of hard polenta throughout. If using a dark-colored cake pan, start checking the cake for doneness 5 to 10 minutes earlier. Serve this cake as is or with lightly sweetened whipped cream.

1½ cups (8¼ ounces) instant polenta
1½ cups whole milk
2 oranges plus 2 teaspoons grated orange zest
⅓ cup (2⅓ ounces) packed brown sugar
2 teaspoons cornstarch
   Salt
1 cup (5 ounces) all-purpose flour
1 teaspoon baking powder
½ teaspoon baking soda
3 large eggs
1 cup (7 ounces) granulated sugar
6 tablespoons extra-virgin olive oil
2 teaspoons vanilla extract

1. Adjust oven rack to middle position and heat oven to 350 degrees. Spread polenta in rimmed baking sheet and toast in oven until fragrant, about 10 minutes; transfer to large bowl. Stir in milk and orange zest and let sit until liquid is fully absorbed, about 10 minutes. Using your hands, break polenta into fine crumbs; set aside.

2. Grease 9-inch round cake pan, line with parchment paper, then grease parchment. Combine brown sugar, cornstarch, and ⅛ teaspoon salt in small bowl and sprinkle evenly in bottom of prepared pan. Cut away peel and pith from oranges, then slice crosswise into ⅛-inch-thick slices. Arrange orange slices in single layer over sugar mixture (some slices may overlap slightly).

3. Whisk flour, baking powder, baking soda, and ½ teaspoon salt together in bowl. Using stand mixer fitted with paddle attachment, beat eggs and granulated sugar together on medium speed until pale and tripled in volume, 6 to 8 minutes. Reduce speed to low, slowly add oil and vanilla, and beat until combined. Add polenta crumbs and beat until combined. Add flour mixture in 3 additions until combined, scraping down sides of bowl as needed. Give batter final stir by hand.

4. Pour batter over oranges in pan and spread into even layer. Bake until cake is golden brown and toothpick inserted into center comes out clean, 50 to 60 minutes, rotating pan halfway through baking.

5. Let cake cool in pan on wire rack for 15 minutes. Run paring knife around sides of pan. Place wire rack over pan and, holding rack tightly, invert cake onto rack and let sit until cake releases itself from pan, about 1 minute. Place rack on baking sheet to catch drips. Remove pan; gently scrape off any orange slices stuck in pan and arrange on top of cake. Let cake cool completely, about 2 hours. Serve.

Olive Oil–Yogurt Cake

SERVES 12

WHY THIS RECIPE WORKS Popular throughout Spain and France, this simple cake exists in many forms—with or without citrus; glazed, drenched in syrup, dusted with confectioners' sugar, or unadorned; baked in a cake pan, baking dish, loaf pan, or Bundt pan—but the basic recipe is the same: Extra-virgin olive oil and yogurt are combined with eggs, sugar, flour, and leavener (usually baking powder and sometimes baking soda) to create a moist, delicate cake with a slightly coarse crumb and a subtly tangy, mildly fruity aroma. We tested our way through numerous versions and found we preferred our cake without citrus in the batter to enable the subtle aroma of the olive oil to shine through. We tested a range of yogurt types and found that the most traditional—plain whole-milk yogurt—yielded the best results; the crusts and crumbs of cakes made with Greek yogurt were too thick and dense, and cakes made with low-fat yogurts were too dry and crumbly. We preferred the graceful form of the Bundt pan and found that an easy-to-make lemon glaze (with a touch of tangy yogurt) was enough to transform this modest everyday cake into an elegant dessert. Serve with Nectarines and Berries in Prosecco (page 375) or Dried Fruit Compote (page 368), or simply enjoy with tea or coffee. For the best flavor, be sure to use high-quality extra-virgin olive oil here.

CAKE

  3 cups (15 ounces) all-purpose flour
  1 tablespoon baking powder
  1 teaspoon salt
1¼ cups (8¾ ounces) granulated sugar
  4 large eggs
1¼ cups extra-virgin olive oil
  1 cup plain whole-milk yogurt

LEMON GLAZE

2–3 tablespoons lemon juice
  1 tablespoon plain whole-milk yogurt
  2 cups (8 ounces) confectioners' sugar

1. FOR THE CAKE Adjust oven rack to lower-middle position and heat oven to 350 degrees. Grease 12-cup nonstick Bundt pan. Whisk flour, baking powder, and salt together in bowl. In separate large bowl, whisk sugar and eggs together until sugar is mostly dissolved and mixture is pale and frothy, about 1 minute. Whisk in oil and yogurt until combined. Using rubber spatula, stir in flour mixture until combined and no dry flour remains.

2. Pour batter into prepared pan, smooth top, and gently tap pan on counter to settle batter. Bake until cake is golden brown and wooden skewer inserted into center comes out clean, 40 to 45 minutes, rotating pan halfway through baking.

Whole-milk yogurt gives this traditional cake tang and richness, and extra-virgin olive oil offers subtle, fruity notes.

3. FOR THE LEMON GLAZE Whisk 2 tablespoons lemon juice, yogurt, and confectioners' sugar together in bowl until smooth, adding more lemon juice gradually as needed until glaze is thick but still pourable (mixture should leave faint trail across bottom of mixing bowl when drizzled from whisk). Let cake cool in pan for 10 minutes, then gently turn cake out onto wire rack. Drizzle half of glaze over warm cake and let cool for 1 hour. Drizzle remaining glaze over cake and let cool completely, about 2 hours. Serve.

Lemon Yogurt Mousse with Blueberry Sauce

SERVES 6

WHY THIS RECIPE WORKS A creamy, refreshing, and slightly tangy chilled lemon mousse is a perfect way to highlight the ubiquitous Mediterranean citrus fruit. Greek yogurt, with its thick texture and tangy flavor, made a good base for our mousse. Unflavored gelatin and whipped egg whites held the mousse together without weighing it down. A combination of lemon zest and juice gave us well-rounded, bold citrus flavor. Vibrant berry sauces complemented the bright citrus flavor of the mousse. You will need six

4-ounce ramekins for this recipe. You can substitute 1 cup of frozen blueberries for the fresh berries. Do not substitute low-fat or nonfat Greek yogurt in this recipe.

BLUEBERRY SAUCE

 4 ounces (¾ cup) blueberries
 2 tablespoons sugar
 2 tablespoons water
  Pinch salt

MOUSSE

 ¾ teaspoon unflavored gelatin
 3 tablespoons water
 ½ cup whole Greek yogurt
 ¼ cup heavy cream
 1½ teaspoons grated lemon zest plus 3 tablespoons juice
 1 teaspoon vanilla extract
 ⅛ teaspoon salt
 3 large egg whites
 ¼ teaspoon cream of tartar
 6 tablespoons (2⅔ ounces) sugar

1. FOR THE BLUEBERRY SAUCE Bring blueberries, sugar, water, and salt to simmer in medium saucepan over medium heat. Cook, stirring occasionally, until sugar has dissolved and fruit is heated through, 2 to 4 minutes.

2. Transfer mixture to blender and process until smooth, about 20 seconds. Strain puree through fine-mesh strainer, pressing on solids to extract as much puree as possible (you should have about ½ cup). Spoon sauce evenly into six 4-ounce ramekins and refrigerate until chilled, about 20 minutes.

Two Ways to Separate Eggs

A. WITH SHELL Using broken shell halves, gently transfer egg white from one shell to another, leaving yolk behind.

B. BY HAND Cup your hand over small bowl, transfer egg into your palm, and slowly unclench your fingers to allow white to slide through.

3. FOR THE MOUSSE Sprinkle gelatin over water in bowl and let sit until gelatin softens, about 5 minutes. In separate bowl, whisk yogurt, heavy cream, lemon zest and juice, vanilla, and salt together until smooth.

4. Whisk egg whites, cream of tartar, and sugar together in bowl of stand mixer. Set bowl over saucepan of barely simmering water and cook, whisking constantly, until mixture has tripled in volume and registers about 160 degrees, 5 to 10 minutes.

5. Off heat, quickly whisk in hydrated gelatin until dissolved. Transfer bowl to stand mixer fitted with whisk attachment and whip on medium-high speed until stiff, shiny peaks form, 4 to 6 minutes. Add yogurt mixture and continue to whip until just combined, 30 to 60 seconds.

6. Divide mousse evenly among chilled ramekins, cover tightly with plastic wrap, and refrigerate until chilled and set, 6 to 8 hours. Serve chilled.

VARIATIONS

Lemon Yogurt Mousse with Raspberry Sauce

Substitute 1 cup fresh or frozen raspberries for blueberries.

Lemon Yogurt Mousse with Strawberry Sauce

Substitute 1 cup halved fresh or frozen strawberries for blueberries and reduce amount of water to 2 teaspoons.

Semolina Pudding with Almonds and Dates
SERVES 6 to 8

WHY THIS RECIPE WORKS Sweetened milk puddings are popular throughout the Middle East and can be flavored with a variety of aromatic ingredients like rose water, orange blossom water, and more. We decided to infuse ours with cardamom and saffron for a unique and exotic flavor profile. Traditional semolina flour, which is made from durum wheat, thickened the pudding nicely and gave it a pleasantly coarse texture; toasting the semolina added more depth of flavor. Almonds brought a nutty crunch, and dates offered a contrasting honeyed sweetness. Traditional recipes often call for chilling the pudding, but we liked it warm so the texture was creamy rather than firm.

 1 tablespoon extra-virgin olive oil
 ¾ cup fine semolina flour
 4½ cups whole milk, plus extra as needed
 ½ cup sugar
 ½ teaspoon ground cardamom
 ⅛ teaspoon saffron threads, crumbled
 ⅛ teaspoon salt
 ½ cup slivered almonds, toasted and chopped
 3 ounces pitted dates, sliced thin (½ cup)

1. Heat oil in 12-inch skillet over medium heat until shimmering. Add semolina and cook, stirring occasionally, until fragrant, 3 to 5 minutes; transfer to bowl.

2. Bring milk, sugar, cardamom, saffron, and salt to simmer in large saucepan over medium heat. Whisking constantly, slowly add semolina, 1 tablespoon at a time, and cook until mixture thickens slightly and begins to bubble, about 3 minutes. Remove saucepan from heat, cover, and let pudding rest for 30 minutes.

3. Stir pudding to loosen and adjust consistency with extra warm milk as needed. Sprinkle individual portions with almonds and dates before serving.

Greek Lemon Rice Pudding
SERVES 8

WHY THIS RECIPE WORKS Traditional Greek rice pudding should have a thick, velvety-smooth texture and taste of little more than sweet milk and vanilla with a hint of lemony brightness. Since the pudding has a short ingredient list, we found that balance was key. For the most appealing rice flavor and satisfyingly rich consistency, we cooked short-grain white rice (its starchy texture produced a silkier pudding than long-grain rice) in water, then added whole milk to make the pudding. Bay leaves, a traditional addition to this type of pudding, offered a balanced floral note. Adding the lemon zest off the heat ensured that the lemony flavor wasn't dulled by cooking. We adjusted the texture of the pudding just before serving so that it would be nicely thick and creamy but not heavy.

 2 cups water
 1 cup Arborio rice
 ½ teaspoon salt
 1 vanilla bean
 4½ cups whole milk, plus extra as needed
 ½ cup sugar
 ½ cinnamon stick
 2 bay leaves
 2 teaspoons grated lemon zest

1. Bring water to boil in large saucepan over medium-high heat. Stir in rice and salt. Reduce heat to low, cover, and simmer gently until water is almost fully absorbed, 15 to 20 minutes.

2. Cut vanilla bean in half lengthwise. Using tip of paring knife, scrape out seeds. Stir vanilla bean and seeds, milk, sugar, cinnamon stick, and bay leaves into rice. Increase heat to medium-high and bring to simmer. Cook, uncovered, stirring often, until rice is soft and pudding has thickened to consistency of yogurt, 35 to 45 minutes.

We found that using short-grain Arborio rice gives Greek pudding a silky-smooth texture.

3. Off heat, discard bay leaves, cinnamon stick, and vanilla bean. Stir in lemon zest. Transfer pudding to large bowl and let cool completely, about 2 hours. Stir pudding to loosen and adjust consistency with extra milk as needed. Serve at room temperature or chilled.

Raspberry Sorbet
MAKES 1 quart, serving 8

WHY THIS RECIPE WORKS Fruit sorbets technically are ices, as in Italian ice. To make a light, refreshing raspberry sorbet that was beautifully creamy and smooth, we had to overcome the jagged, unpleasant ice crystals that often develop on homemade sorbets and avoid the tendency toward crumbly, dull results. Finding the right balance of water and sugar was key; corn syrup helped to create a smooth texture without oversweetening. Freezing a small amount of the base separately, then adding it back into the rest helped superchill the mix, making it freeze faster and more smoothly. We also added some additional pectin to bump up the raspberries' natural pectin, which helped keep the whole thing from turning into a puddle too quickly at room temperature.

If using a canister-style ice cream machine, be sure to freeze the empty canister for at least 24 hours and preferably 48 hours before churning. For self-refrigerating machines, prechill the canister by running the machine for 5 to 10 minutes before pouring in the sorbet mixture. If using frozen berries, thaw them before proceeding. For fruit pectin we recommend both Sure-Jell for Less or No Sugar Needed Recipes and Ball RealFruit Low or No-Sugar Needed Pectin.

  1 cup water
  1 teaspoon low- or no-sugar-needed fruit pectin
  ⅛ teaspoon salt
  1¼ pounds (4 cups) fresh or frozen raspberries
  ½ cup (3½ ounces) plus 2 tablespoons sugar
  ¼ cup light corn syrup

1. Heat water, pectin, and salt in medium saucepan over medium-high heat, stirring occasionally, until pectin has fully dissolved, about 5 minutes. Remove saucepan from heat and let mixture cool slightly, about 10 minutes.

2. Process raspberries, sugar, corn syrup, and cooled water mixture in blender or food processor until smooth, about 30 seconds. Strain mixture through fine-mesh strainer, pressing on solids to extract as much liquid as possible. Transfer 1 cup mixture to small bowl and place remaining mixture in large bowl. Cover both bowls with plastic wrap. Place large bowl in refrigerator and small bowl in freezer and chill for at least 4 hours or up to 24 hours. (Small bowl of base will freeze solid.)

3. Remove mixtures from refrigerator and freezer. Scrape frozen base from small bowl into large bowl of base. Stir occasionally until frozen base has fully dissolved. Transfer mixture to ice cream machine and churn until mixture has consistency of thick milkshake and color lightens, 15 to 25 minutes.

Superchilling Raspberry Sorbet

1. Transfer 1 cup berry puree to small bowl. Cover bowls; freeze small bowl and refrigerate large bowl for at least 4 hours or up to 1 day.

2. Scrape frozen base into large bowl. Stir until completely combined. Transfer to ice cream maker and churn until color lightens.

4. Transfer sorbet to airtight container, pressing firmly to remove any air pockets, and freeze until firm, at least 2 hours or up to 5 days. Let sorbet sit at room temperature for 5 minutes before serving.

Lemon Ice
MAKES 1 quart, serving 8

WHY THIS RECIPE WORKS We wanted a refreshing Italian lemon ice that struck a perfect sweet-tart balance and hit lots of high notes—without so much as a trace of bitterness. A cup of sugar gave our lemon ice the ideal amount of sweetness; less sugar left it with a pronounced bitterness, and more sugar made our ice taste like frozen lemonade. Spring water had a cleaner, less metallic flavor than tap water. We opted to add a bit of vodka to ensure a soft, creamy, slightly slushy texture and a pinch of salt to boost the flavor. To achieve an ice with a fluffy, coarse-grained texture and crystalline crunch, we froze the mixture in ice cube trays and then pulsed the cubes in the food processor. The addition of vodka yields the best texture, but it can be omitted if desired.

  2¼ cups water, preferably spring water
  1 cup lemon juice (6 lemons)
  1 cup (7 ounces) sugar
  2 tablespoons vodka (optional)
  ⅛ teaspoon salt

1. Whisk all ingredients together in bowl until sugar has dissolved. Pour mixture into 2 ice cube trays and freeze until solid, at least 3 hours or up to 5 days.

2. Place medium bowl in freezer. Pulse half of ice cubes in food processor until creamy and no large lumps remain, about 18 pulses. Transfer mixture to chilled bowl and return to freezer. Repeat pulsing remaining ice cubes; transfer to bowl. Serve immediately.

VARIATIONS
Minted Lemon Ice
Bring 1 cup water, sugar, and salt to simmer in small saucepan over medium-high heat, stirring occasionally. Off heat, stir in ½ cup torn fresh mint leaves and let steep for 5 minutes. Strain mixture through fine-mesh strainer into medium bowl. Stir in remaining 1¼ cups water, lemon juice, and vodka and let cool to room temperature, about 15 minutes. Freeze and pulse ice cubes as directed.

Orange Ice
Reduce lemon juice to 2 tablespoons and sugar to ¾ cup. Add ¾ cup orange juice (2 oranges) to mixture in step 1.

NUTRITIONAL INFORMATION FOR OUR RECIPES

When developing our recipes for this book, we consulted Oldways to come up with guiding nutritional principles to make sure our recipes would fit into a healthy Mediterranean diet. Although there are no hard-and-fast rules when it comes to nutritional numbers, we tried our best to make sure that every recipe contained reasonable amounts of calories and fat and, most importantly, a limited amount of saturated fat.

Analyzing recipes for their nutritional values is a tricky business, and we did our best to be as realistic and accurate as possible throughout this book. We were absolutely strict about measuring when cooking and never resorted to guessing or estimating. We also didn't play games when analyzing the recipes in the nutritional program to make the numbers look better. To calculate

the nutritional values of our recipes per serving, we used The Food Processor SQL by ESHA Research. When using this program, we entered all the ingredients, using weights for important ingredients such as meat, cheese, and most vegetables. We also used all of our preferred brands in these analyses. When the recipe called for seasoning with an unspecified amount of salt and pepper (often raw meat), we added ½ teaspoon of salt and ¼ teaspoon of pepper to the analysis. We did not, however, include additional salt or pepper when the food was "seasoned to taste" at the end of cooking.

Note: Unless otherwise indicated, information applies to a single serving. If there is a range in the serving size in the recipe, we used the highest number of servings to calculate the nutritional values.

	Cal	Fat (g)	Sat Fat (g)	Chol (mg)	Carb (g)	Protein (g)	Fiber (g)	Sodium (mg)
Meze, Antipasti, Tapas, and Other Small Plates								
Classic Hummus (per ¼ cup)	130	10	1.5	0	8	3	2	230
Hummus with Smoked Paprika (per ¼ cup)	140	11	1.5	0	8	4	2	230
Roasted Red Pepper Hummus (per ¼ cup)	140	11	1.5	0	8	4	2	250
Artichoke-Lemon Hummus (per ¼ cup)	140	10	1.5	0	9	4	2	280
Roasted Garlic Hummus (per ¼ cup)	140	10	1.5	0	11	4	2	230
Garlic and Rosemary White Bean Dip (per ¼ cup)	150	11	1.5	0	9	4	3	260
Caper and Tarragon White Bean Dip (per ¼ cup)	150	11	1.5	0	9	4	3	270
Sun-Dried Tomato and Feta White Bean Dip (per ¼ cup)	200	15	4	15	11	6	3	360
Tzatziki (per 2 tablespoons)	20	1.5	1	0	1	1	0	40
Beet Tzatziki (per 2 tablespoons)	45	3.5	1.5	5	2	1	0	85
Caponata (per ¼ cup)	90	4.5	0.5	0	12	2	3	150
Creamy Turkish Nut Dip (per 2 tablespoons)	180	17	2	0	5	4	2	170
Baba Ghanoush (per ¼ cup)	80	6	1	0	8	2	3	220
Muhammara (per ¼ cup)	170	14	2	0	9	3	1	370
Provençal-Style Anchovy Dip (per 3 tablespoons)	160	15	1.5	5	5	5	2	210
Skordalia (per ¼ cup)	140	10	1.5	0	11	2	1	180
Olive Oil–Sea Salt Pita Chips	210	14	2	0	17	3	1	300
Rosemary-Parmesan Pita Chips	240	16	3	5	17	6	1	360
Lavash Crackers	200	8	1	15	26	5	2	340
Quick Toasted Almonds (per ¼ cup)	220	20	1.5	0	8	8	4	290
Rosemary Almonds (per ¼ cup)	220	20	1.5	0	8	8	5	290
Orange-Fennel Almonds (per ¼ cup)	220	20	1.5	0	8	8	5	290
Spiced Almonds (per ¼ cup)	220	20	1.5	0	8	8	5	290
Lemon-Garlic Almonds (per ¼ cup)	220	20	1.5	0	8	8	5	290
Marinated Green and Black Olives (per ¼ cup)	170	18	2	0	3	0	1	510
Marinated Olives with Baby Mozzarella (per ¼ cup)	230	22	6	20	2	5	0	410
Marinated Green Olives with Feta (per ¼ cup)	230	22	6	25	3	4	0	650
Marinated Cauliflower and Chickpeas with Saffron	110	7	1	0	9	3	2	600
Marinated Artichokes	140	14	2	0	3	1	1	20
Giardiniera	30	0	0	0	7	1	1	880
Yogurt Cheese (per ¼ cup)	70	4	2.5	15	6	4	0	55
Lemon-Dill Yogurt Cheese (per ¼ cup)	80	4	2.5	15	6	4	0	130
Honey-Walnut Yogurt Cheese (per ¼ cup)	130	8	3	15	11	5	0	130

	Cal	Fat (g)	Sat Fat (g)	Chol (mg)	Carb (g)	Protein (g)	Fiber (g)	Sodium (mg)
Spicy Whipped Feta with Roasted Red Peppers (per 3 tablespoons)	130	12	4.5	20	2	3	0	260
Broiled Feta with Olive Oil and Parsley	120	10	6	35	2	5	0	350
Pan-Fried Halloumi	140	11	6	20	2	6	0	300
Pan-Fried Halloumi with Garlic-Parsley Sauce	170	15	6	20	2	6	0	300
Toasted Bread for Bruschetta	150	5	0.5	0	23	4	1	270
Bruschetta with Arugula Pesto and Goat Cheese	240	14	2.5	5	24	6	1	420
Bruschetta with Ricotta, Tomatoes, and Basil	220	10	3	15	26	7	2	530
Bruschetta with Black Olive Pesto, Ricotta, and Basil	230	12	3.5	15	25	7	1	330
Bruschetta with Artichoke Hearts and Parmesan	210	10	2	5	25	7	2	520
Prosciutto-Wrapped Stuffed Dates	240	12	2	15	29	8	3	570
Prosciutto-Wrapped Stuffed Dates with Pistachios and Balsamic Vinegar	220	9	1.5	15	31	9	3	560
Stuffed Grape Leaves	110	4	0.5	0	17	2	1	180
Stuffed Grape Leaves with Currants and Pine Nuts	150	7	0.5	0	21	3	2	180
Sizzling Garlic Shrimp	160	14	2	55	3	6	1	320
Mussels Escabèche	160	9	1.5	30	6	14	0	400
Chili-Marinated Calamari with Oranges	260	15	2	265	11	19	2	810
Stuffed Sardines	170	11	1.5	20	10	10	1	200

Soups								
Classic Gazpacho	60	0	0	0	11	2	3	810
Classic Croutons	60	4	0.5	0	6	1	0	65
Garlic Croutons	60	4	0.5	0	6	1	0	65
White Gazpacho	390	32	4	0	20	9	5	250
Chilled Cucumber and Yogurt Soup	150	9	7	15	9	8	2	620
Classic Chicken Broth	20	0	0	0	0	4	0	276
Vegetable Broth Base	9	0	0	0	0	1	0	288
Provençal Vegetable Soup	270	17	3	5	24	8	5	800
Roasted Eggplant and Tomato Soup	230	15	2	0	21	3	6	920
Roasted Red Pepper Soup with Smoked Paprika and Cilantro Yogurt	140	6	2	10	18	4	4	670
Turkish Tomato, Bulgur, and Red Pepper Soup	140	4	0.5	0	20	3	4	820
Artichoke Soup à la Barigoule	210	11	3.5	10	19	7	3	890
Risi e Bisi	320	10	2.5	10	39	15	5	860
French Lentil Soup	220	6	2	10	27	12	7	720
French Lentil Soup with Spinach	230	6	2	10	28	13	8	750
French Lentil Soup with Fragrant Spices	220	6	2	10	27	12	7	720
Spanish-Style Lentil and Chorizo Soup	690	43	13	75	42	34	11	1440
Red Lentil Soup with North African Spices	290	11	1.5	0	36	13	6	800
Moroccan-Style Chickpea Soup	230	8	1	0	33	6	6	980
Sicilian Chickpea and Escarole Soup	250	8	1.5	5	48	15	22	1040
Garlic Toasts	150	6	0.5	0	19	3	1	240
Greek White Bean Soup	320	6	1	0	51	16	27	870
Pasta e Fagioli with Orange and Fennel	240	7	2.5	10	32	13	5	930
Spiced Fava Bean Soup	180	8	1	0	20	7	5	870
Avgolemono	100	2.5	1	95	11	7	0	970
Avgolemono with Chicken	150	3.5	1	125	11	17	0	990
Avgolemono with Saffron	100	2.5	1	95	11	7	0	970
Spicy Moroccan-Style Chicken and Lentil Soup	280	10	1.5	50	22	27	6	970
Spicy Moroccan-Style Lamb and Lentil Soup	310	13	3	35	25	24	6	850
Lamb and Mint Sharba	250	7	2.5	35	26	21	3	800
Spanish-Style Meatball Soup with Saffron	270	14	3.5	25	12	22	2	830
Spanish-Style Meatball Soup with Saffron and Kale	290	14	4	25	15	23	3	840

	Cal	Fat (g)	Sat Fat (g)	Chol (mg)	Carb (g)	Protein (g)	Fiber (g)	Sodium (mg)
Picada (per tablespoon)	35	2.5	0	0	2	1	0	35
Provençal Fish Soup	230	9	2.5	65	5	26	2	920
Shellfish Soup with Leeks and Turmeric	220	7	1	150	17	18	2	840
Salads								
Basic Green Salad	20	1.5	0	0	1	1	1	0
Tricolor Salad with Balsamic Vinaigrette	80	7	1	0	3	1	1	60
Green Salad with Marcona Almonds and Manchego Cheese	190	17	4	5	2	4	1	200
Arugula Salad with Fennel and Shaved Parmesan	130	11	2	5	5	3	2	180
Green Salad with Artichokes and Olives	110	9	2	5	5	3	1	270
Arugula Salad with Figs, Prosciutto, Walnuts, and Parmesan	270	20	3.5	15	15	10	3	530
Arugula Salad with Pear, Almonds, Goat Cheese, and Apricots	250	13	3.5	5	30	6	5	180
Asparagus and Arugula Salad with Cannellini Beans	170	12	1.5	0	13	5	4	330
Asparagus, Red Pepper, and Spinach Salad with Goat Cheese	180	16	4.5	10	5	6	2	300
Citrus Salad with Radicchio, Dates, and Smoked Almonds	260	13	1.5	0	36	4	8	270
Citrus Salad with Arugula, Golden Raisins, and Walnuts	260	15	1.5	0	32	4	7	220
Bitter Greens Salad with Olives and Feta	130	10	3	10	6	3	3	490
Kale Salad with Sweet Potatoes and Pomegranate Vinaigrette	190	12	1.5	0	20	3	4	270
Mâche Salad with Cucumber and Mint	120	11	1.5	0	5	2	2	100
Salade Niçoise	420	25	4.5	125	26	23	5	1070
Warm Spinach Salad with Feta and Pistachios	130	10	2.5	5	6	3	2	105
Seared Tuna Salad with Olive Dressing	310	15	2	40	12	29	3	540
Classic Vinaigrette (per tablespoon)	100	11	1.5	0	0	0	0	90
Lemon Vinaigrette (per tablespoon)	100	11	1.5	0	0	0	0	90
Balsamic-Mustard Vinaigrette (per tablespoon)	110	11	1.5	0	1	0	0	140
Walnut Vinaigrette (per tablespoon)	100	11	1	0	0	0	0	90
Herb Vinaigrette (per tablespoon)	100	11	1.5	0	0	0	0	90
Tahini-Lemon Dressing (per tablespoon)	90	9	1.5	0	1	1	0	150
Asparagus Salad with Oranges, Feta, and Hazelnuts	390	33	7	20	17	11	7	490
Roasted Beet Salad with Blood Oranges and Almonds	260	12	3	15	31	7	8	570
Roasted Beet and Carrot Salad with Cumin and Pistachios	210	13	2	0	19	4	6	310
Fava Bean and Radish Salad	140	10	1.5	0	10	4	3	230
Green Bean Salad with Cilantro Sauce	190	16	2	0	9	3	3	230
Green Bean and Potato Salad with Cilantro Sauce	210	16	2	0	14	3	3	310
Brussels Sprout Salad with Pecorino and Pine Nuts	190	16	3	5	9	6	3	400
Moroccan-Style Carrot Salad	120	7	1	0	13	1	3	240
Moroccan-Style Carrot Salad with Harissa and Feta	180	14	3.5	10	14	3	3	400
North African Cauliflower Salad with Chermoula	190	11	1.5	0	22	4	5	160
Mediterranean Chopped Salad	270	19	6	25	18	9	5	920
Sesame-Lemon Cucumber Salad	100	8	1	0	6	1	1	290
Yogurt-Mint Cucumber Salad	130	8	1.5	5	11	4	2	340
Algerian-Style Fennel, Orange, and Olive Salad	160	10	1.5	0	17	2	5	180
Algerian-Style Fennel, Orange, and Radish Salad	160	10	1.5	0	17	2	5	240
Fennel and Apple Salad with Smoked Mackerel	220	17	3	20	11	7	3	490
Country-Style Greek Salad	190	15	4	15	10	4	2	430
Shaved Mushroom and Celery Salad	150	12	2.5	5	5	6	1	300
Panzanella Salad with White Beans and Arugula	360	16	3	5	42	13	5	760
Fattoush	340	25	3.5	0	25	5	4	320

	Cal	Fat (g)	Sat Fat (g)	Chol (mg)	Carb (g)	Protein (g)	Fiber (g)	Sodium (mg)
French Potato Salad with Dijon and Fines Herbes	190	10	1.5	0	25	3	3	260
French Potato Salad with Fennel, Tomatoes, and Olives	210	10	1.5	0	27	3	4	310
French Potato Salad with Radishes, Cornichons, and Capers	200	10	1.5	0	25	3	3	460
Roasted Winter Squash Salad with Za'atar and Parsley	240	13	2	0	32	5	5	300
Tomato Salad with Feta and Cumin-Yogurt Dressing	110	7	3.5	15	9	5	3	340
Tomato Salad with Tuna, Capers, and Black Olives	160	11	1.5	10	9	8	3	450
Cherry Tomato Salad with Feta and Olives	130	10	3.5	15	8	4	2	320
Cherry Tomato Salad with Basil and Fresh Mozzarella	180	13	6	25	6	8	2	210
Tomato and Burrata Salad with Pangrattato and Basil	290	24	7	25	15	9	2	330
Grilled Vegetable and Halloumi Salad	270	20	8	30	15	9	2	410
Zucchini Ribbon Salad with Shaved Parmesan	230	20	5	15	3	10	1	390

Rice and Grains

	Cal	Fat (g)	Sat Fat (g)	Chol (mg)	Carb (g)	Protein (g)	Fiber (g)	Sodium (mg)
Basmati Rice Pilaf with Currants and Toasted Almonds	220	5	0	0	41	4	2	100
Basmati Rice Pilaf with Peas, Scallions, and Lemon	190	3	0	0	37	4	2	100
Spiced Basmati Rice with Cauliflower and Pomegranate	180	6	1	0	28	4	3	200
Herbed Basmati Rice and Pasta Pilaf	280	8	1	0	47	5	1	830
Herbed Basmati Rice and Pasta Pilaf with Golden Raisins and Almonds	380	12	1.5	0	59	7	3	830
Herbed Basmati Rice and Pasta Pilaf with Pomegranate and Walnuts	350	14	1.5	0	50	6	2	830
Herbed Basmati Rice and Pasta Pilaf with Yogurt	290	8	1.5	0	47	5	1	830
Spiced Baked Rice with Roasted Sweet Potatoes and Fennel	360	16	2	0	48	5	5	590
Baked Brown Rice with Roasted Red Peppers and Onions	220	4.5	0.5	0	41	4	2	610
Baked Brown Rice with Peas, Feta, and Mint	260	7	2.5	10	41	7	3	630
Brown Rice with Tomatoes and Chickpeas	260	6	0.5	0	46	8	6	630
Rice Salad with Oranges, Olives, and Almonds	260	9	1	0	41	5	3	590
Brown Rice Salad with Asparagus, Goat Cheese, and Lemon	310	14	3	5	40	8	4	920
Stovetop White Rice	250	2.5	0	0	49	4	1	390
Foolproof Baked Brown Rice	280	4.5	0.5	0	53	5	2	300
Seafood Risotto	450	14	2	70	56	21	3	1120
Paniscia	420	15	4	25	51	17	9	900
Spanish-Style Brothy Rice with Clams and Salsa Verde	480	14	2	45	47	28	2	1010
Indoor Paella	650	25	7	185	59	45	4	1660
Indoor Paella in a Paella Pan	660	25	7	185	59	45	4	1680
Grilled Paella	680	26	6	165	63	46	3	1900
Vegetable Paella	470	16	2	0	71	10	8	1360
Vegetable Paella in a Paella Pan	490	16	2	0	74	10	12	1240
Creamy Parmesan Polenta	170	8	2	5	20	6	2	770
Sautéed Cherry Tomato and Fresh Mozzarella Polenta Topping	130	10	3	10	5	4	1	45
Broccoli Rabe, Sun-Dried Tomato, and Pine Nut Polenta Topping	130	11	1.5	0	6	4	3	320
Herbed Barley Pilaf	250	8	1	0	41	5	8	200
Barley with Roasted Carrots, Snow Peas, and Lemon-Yogurt Sauce	460	24	3.5	5	55	12	13	490
Barley with Lentils, Mushrooms, and Tahini-Yogurt Sauce	440	15	2.5	0	63	16	15	670
Egyptian Barley Salad	280	10	2.5	10	41	7	7	320
Barley Risotto	320	8	2	5	45	9	9	680
Barley Risotto with Mushrooms and Red Wine	330	9	2	5	46	11	9	680

	Cal	Fat (g)	Sat Fat (g)	Chol (mg)	Carb (g)	Protein (g)	Fiber (g)	Sodium (mg)
Bulgur Salad with Carrots and Almonds	300	17	2	0	35	7	7	330
Bulgur Salad with Grapes and Feta	310	16	3	10	36	8	6	290
Bulgur Pilaf with Cremini Mushrooms	220	8	1	0	33	6	5	450
Bulgur with Chickpeas, Spinach, and Za'atar	200	8	1	0	28	5	5	410
Bulgur with Herbed Lamb and Roasted Red Peppers	320	15	6	40	33	14	5	670
Tabbouleh	190	14	2	0	14	3	3	210
Spiced Tabbouleh	190	15	2	0	14	3	3	210
Warm Farro with Lemon and Herbs	240	9	1	0	39	6	5	200
Warm Farro with Mushrooms and Thyme	250	9	1	0	39	7	4	200
Warm Farro with Fennel and Parmesan	270	10	1.5	5	41	9	6	300
Farro Salad with Asparagus, Snap Peas, and Tomatoes	280	11	2.5	10	41	9	6	400
Farro Salad with Cucumber, Yogurt, and Mint	260	9	1.5	0	40	7	5	200
Parmesan Farrotto	310	14	2.5	5	38	11	4	850
Farrotto with Pancetta, Asparagus, and Peas	360	16	4	20	41	15	6	1070
Freekeh Salad with Butternut Squash, Walnuts, and Raisins	410	20	2.5	0	52	9	10	300
Freekeh Pilaf with Dates and Cauliflower	360	13	2	0	53	10	12	340
Warm Wheat Berries with Zucchini, Red Pepper, and Oregano	230	5	0.5	0	39	7	7	300
Wheat Berry Salad with Orange and Carrots	240	5	0.5	0	42	7	8	310
Wheat Berry Salad with Figs, Pine Nuts, and Goat Cheese	320	13	2.5	5	44	9	7	260

Pasta and Couscous

	Cal	Fat (g)	Sat Fat (g)	Chol (mg)	Carb (g)	Protein (g)	Fiber (g)	Sodium (mg)
Penne with Roasted Cherry Tomato Sauce	390	11	1.5	0	64	11	5	400
Penne with Roasted Cherry Tomatoes, Olives, Capers, and Pine Nuts	430	16	1.5	0	64	12	5	570
Penne with Roasted Cherry Tomatoes, Arugula, and Goat Cheese	440	15	4	10	64	15	5	490
Penne and Fresh Tomato Sauce with Fennel and Orange	410	11	1.5	0	68	12	7	320
Penne and Fresh Tomato Sauce with Spinach and Feta	430	13	4	15	66	15	6	490
Farfalle with Zucchini, Tomatoes, and Pine Nuts	450	18	2	0	64	13	5	400
Farfalle with Zucchini, Tomatoes, Olives, and Feta	480	18	4.5	15	65	15	5	620
Spaghetti al Limone	480	23	4	5	56	14	3	560
Tagliatelle with Artichokes and Parmesan	520	18	3	5	68	17	3	800
Parmesan Bread Crumbs (per tablespoon)	60	4.5	1	0	3	1	0	65
Lemon-Chili Bread Crumbs (per tablespoon)	50	4	0.5	0	3	1	0	35
Orecchiette with Broccoli Rabe and White Beans	460	14	2.5	5	66	19	7	610
Orecchiette with Broccoli Rabe and Sausage	430	12	3.5	20	59	22	5	700
Whole-Wheat Spaghetti with Greens, Beans, and Pancetta	490	15	6	30	66	26	15	1210
Whole-Wheat Spaghetti with Greens, Beans, Tomatoes, and Garlic Chips	440	13	2.5	5	63	20	14	1090
Whole-Wheat Spaghetti with Lentils, Pancetta, and Escarole	510	17	3.5	15	68	21	15	770
Spanish-Style Toasted Pasta with Shrimp	460	15	2	160	50	27	4	1520
Spaghetti with Mussels, Lemon, and White Wine	370	5	0.5	20	59	18	3	410
Spaghetti with Clams and Roasted Tomatoes	670	12	1.5	90	79	56	6	2040
Linguine ai Frutti di Mare	580	15	2.5	145	71	32	4	800
Rigatoni with Warm-Spiced Beef Ragu	420	8	2.5	25	63	20	4	560
Rigatoni with Minted Lamb Ragu	430	7	2.5	45	64	24	5	600
Orzo Salad with Arugula and Sun-Dried Tomatoes	320	17	2.5	5	34	9	2	440
Orzo Salad with Pecorino, Radicchio, and Chickpeas	290	12	2	5	37	9	3	460
Orzo Salad with Radishes, Capers, and Anchovies	290	15	2.5	5	31	9	2	540
Toasted Orzo with Fennel, Orange, and Olives	300	7	1.5	5	47	11	3	510
Orzo with Shrimp, Feta, and Lemon	540	13	4	175	70	33	3	1460

	Cal	Fat (g)	Sat Fat (g)	Chol (mg)	Carb (g)	Protein (g)	Fiber (g)	Sodium (mg)
Orzo with Greek Sausage and Spiced Yogurt	270	7	2.5	15	37	12	2	380
Baked Orzo with Eggplant and Tomatoes	380	13	4	15	53	14	5	800
No-Cook Fresh Tomato Sauce (per ⅔ cup)	120	10	1.5	0	7	2	2	10
Quick Tomato Sauce (per ⅔ cup)	120	7	1	0	13	3	3	380
Classic Marinara Sauce (per ⅔ cup)	120	7	1	0	10	2	2	350
Classic Basil Pesto (per 2 tablespoons)	210	22	3	5	2	3	1	85
Roasted Red Pepper Pesto (per 2 tablespoons)	100	10	1.5	0	2	1	1	45
Tomato and Almond Pesto (per 2 tablespoons)	90	8	1.5	0	2	2	1	55
Green Olive and Orange Pesto (per 2 tablespoons)	140	13	2	5	2	3	1	150
Simple Couscous	260	5	0.5	0	45	7	3	520
Simple Couscous with Dates and Pistachios	410	15	2	0	59	11	5	520
Simple Couscous with Carrots, Raisins, and Pine Nuts	390	13	1.5	0	59	9	5	540
Spiced Vegetable Couscous	350	15	2	0	45	9	6	760
Moroccan-Style Couscous with Chickpeas	340	10	1.5	0	50	10	6	730
Couscous with Turkish Sausage and Preserved Lemon	410	13	3	15	61	11	5	720
Couscous with Lamb, Chickpeas, and Orange	420	11	2.5	30	56	21	6	560
Simple Pearl Couscous	250	2.5	0	0	48	8	3	200
Simple Pearl Couscous with Tomatoes, Olives, and Ricotta Salata	450	21	4	15	53	13	4	570
Simple Pearl Couscous with Radishes and Watercress	440	20	4.5	10	52	14	4	370
Simple Pearl Couscous with Peas, Feta, and Pickled Shallots	450	17	4	15	61	14	6	240
Hearty Pearl Couscous with Eggplant, Spinach, and Beans	370	12	1.5	0	54	12	8	790

Beans								
French Lentils with Carrots and Parsley	160	5	0.5	0	23	7	6	220
French Lentils with Swiss Chard	160	5	0.5	0	22	8	6	320
Lentils with Spinach and Garlic Chips	160	5	0.5	0	22	8	6	230
Mujaddara	460	14	2.5	5	70	14	9	810
Crispy Onions (per ¼ cup)	90	5	0.5	0	13	1	2	100
Koshari	410	12	1.5	0	64	13	9	1250
Spiced Lentil Salad with Winter Squash	260	13	2	0	29	8	7	220
Lentil Salad with Olives, Mint, and Feta	240	14	2.5	5	21	8	5	280
Lentil Salad with Hazelnuts and Goat Cheese	260	16	2.5	0	21	9	5	260
Lentil Salad with Carrots and Cilantro	220	12	1.5	0	22	7	6	220
Lentil Salad with Spinach, Walnuts, and Parmesan	270	17	2.5	5	22	11	6	310
Chickpeas with Garlic and Parsley	170	11	1.5	0	16	4	3	430
Chickpeas with Bell Peppers, Scallions, and Basil	180	11	1.5	0	17	4	4	430
Chickpeas with Smoked Paprika and Cilantro	170	10	1.5	0	16	4	3	430
Chickpeas with Saffron, Mint, and Yogurt	210	11	1.5	0	23	5	4	440
Chickpeas with Spinach, Chorizo, and Smoked Paprika	270	14	3	10	25	12	8	650
Stewed Chickpeas with Eggplant and Tomatoes	250	11	1.5	0	31	7	8	700
Spicy Chickpeas with Turnips	210	7	0.5	0	31	8	7	640
Chickpea Salad with Carrots, Arugula, and Olives	180	11	1.5	0	17	4	4	570
Chickpea Salad with Fennel and Arugula	170	11	1.5	0	16	4	4	520
Chickpea Salad with Roasted Red Peppers and Feta	200	13	3	10	15	6	3	670
Chickpea Cakes	320	20	3	65	26	9	4	360
Falafel	80	5	0.5	0	10	3	5	110
Pink Pickled Turnips (per ¼ cup)	20	0	0	0	5	0	1	580
Black-Eyed Peas with Walnuts and Pomegranate	250	15	2	0	24	7	5	440
Cranberry Beans with Warm Spices	290	8	1	0	40	14	15	400
Cranberry Beans with Fennel, Grapes, and Pine Nuts	240	11	1	0	33	7	6	160
Mashed Fava Beans with Cumin and Garlic	180	7	1	0	22	10	6	650

	Cal	Fat (g)	Sat Fat (g)	Chol (mg)	Carb (g)	Protein (g)	Fiber (g)	Sodium (mg)
Mashed Fava Beans with Cucumbers, Olives, and Feta	200	8	2	5	22	10	6	720
Spicy Mashed Fava Beans with Yogurt	190	7	1	0	23	10	6	650
Mashed Fava Beans with Sautéed Escarole and Parmesan	260	13	2.5	5	27	10	7	780
Gigante Beans with Spinach and Feta	290	16	5	20	28	12	8	760
Turkish Pinto Bean Salad with Tomatoes, Eggs, and Parsley	350	18	3	70	35	14	9	760
Easy-Peel Hard-Cooked Eggs	70	5	1.5	185	0	6	0	70
Moroccan Braised White Beans with Lamb	290	6	1.5	15	40	17	15	400
Sicilian White Beans and Escarole	140	4	0.5	0	22	7	8	690
White Bean Salad	130	7	1	0	13	5	4	260
White Bean Salad with Tomatoes and Olives	130	7	1	0	12	5	4	280
White Bean Salad with Sautéed Squid and Pepperoncini	340	15	2.5	175	28	21	7	980
Hearty Tuscan Bean Stew	440	10	2.5	15	64	23	24	1150
North African Vegetable and Bean Stew	220	11	1.5	0	27	6	6	1060

Vegetables								
Roasted Artichokes with Lemon Vinaigrette	400	28	4	0	35	11	17	1170
Braised Artichokes with Tomatoes and Thyme	170	5	0.5	0	27	9	12	710
Artichoke, Pepper, and Chickpea Tagine	350	14	3	5	48	10	7	1160
Pan-Roasted Asparagus with Cherry Tomatoes and Kalamata Olives	100	6	1	0	8	5	4	85
Pan-Roasted Asparagus with Toasted Garlic and Parmesan	80	5	1	0	6	5	3	40
Roasted Asparagus	80	6	1	0	6	4	3	190
Roasted Asparagus with Mint-Orange Gremolata	90	6	1	0	6	4	3	190
Roasted Asparagus with Tarragon-Lemon Gremolata	90	6	1	0	6	4	3	190
Braised Asparagus, Peas, and Radishes with Tarragon	140	9	1.5	0	11	5	4	390
Stuffed Bell Peppers with Spiced Beef, Currants, and Feta	420	18	6	60	43	22	7	680
Stuffed Bell Peppers with Spiced Lamb, Currants, and Feta	480	26	10	65	43	20	7	690
Broccoli Rabe with Garlic and Red Pepper Flakes	90	8	1	0	4	3	3	180
Broccoli Rabe with Sun-Dried Tomatoes and Pine Nuts	150	13	1.5	0	6	5	3	200
Broccoli Rabe with Red Bell Pepper, Olives, and Feta	130	10	2.5	10	6	5	3	290
Sautéed Cabbage with Parsley and Lemon	80	4.5	0.5	0	8	1	3	320
Sautéed Cabbage with Fennel and Garlic	110	8	1.5	0	9	3	4	380
Spicy Roasted Carrots with Cilantro	100	5	0.5	0	14	1	3	270
Slow-Cooked Whole Carrots	70	2.5	0	0	11	1	3	270
Slow-Cooked Whole Carrots with Green Olive and Raisin Relish	160	9	1	0	19	1	4	530
Slow-Cooked Whole Carrots with Pine Nut Relish	130	8	0.5	0	14	2	4	370
Slow-Cooked Whole Carrots with Onion-Balsamic Relish	140	10	1.5	0	14	1	4	370
Skillet-Roasted Cauliflower	160	12	2	0	10	3	3	480
Skillet-Roasted Cauliflower with Capers and Pine Nuts	160	14	2	0	9	4	3	430
Skillet-Roasted Spiced Cauliflower with Pistachios	160	12	2	0	10	4	4	460
Braised Cauliflower with Garlic and White Wine	120	8	1.5	0	9	3	3	170
Braised Cauliflower with Capers and Anchovies	130	8	1.5	0	9	4	3	250
Braised Cauliflower with Sumac and Mint	120	9	1.5	0	9	4	3	190
Cauliflower Cakes	300	22	7	60	19	12	5	800
Roasted Celery Root with Yogurt and Sesame Seeds	140	8	1.5	0	16	3	3	410
Marinated Eggplant with Capers and Mint	120	10	1.5	0	7	1	3	130
Broiled Eggplant with Basil	90	7	1	0	7	1	3	280
Grilled Eggplant with Yogurt Sauce	180	15	2.5	5	11	3	4	110
Stuffed Eggplant with Bulgur	310	15	4	15	39	11	12	680

	Cal	Fat (g)	Sat Fat (g)	Chol (mg)	Carb (g)	Protein (g)	Fiber (g)	Sodium (mg)
Braised Fennel with Radicchio and Parmesan	150	9	1	0	13	3	4	270
Fava Beans with Artichokes, Asparagus, and Peas	160	3	0	0	25	11	10	790
Roasted Green Beans with Pecorino and Pine Nuts	150	12	2	0	9	3	3	190
Roasted Green Beans with Almonds and Mint	130	11	1.5	0	9	2	3	170
Braised Green Beans with Potatoes and Basil	230	12	1.5	0	28	4	6	1080
Garlicky Braised Kale	190	12	1.5	0	18	8	6	340
Roasted Mushrooms with Parmesan and Pine Nuts	230	16	2.5	5	16	10	4	290
Roasted Mushrooms with Harissa and Mint	190	13	2	0	16	7	4	340
Roasted Mushrooms with Roasted Garlic and Smoked Paprika	170	11	1.5	0	16	7	4	310
Grilled Portobello Mushrooms and Shallots with Rosemary-Dijon Vinaigrette	180	14	2	0	10	3	2	130
Greek-Style Garlic-Lemon Potatoes	160	7	1	0	21	3	2	200
Greek-Style Garlic-Lemon Potatoes with Olives and Feta	190	9	2.5	10	22	4	2	300
Roasted Root Vegetables with Lemon-Caper Sauce	210	8	1	0	32	6	7	410
Roasted Radicchio, Fennel, and Parsnips with Lemon-Basil Sauce	210	7	1	0	33	4	7	350
Grilled Radicchio with Garlic and Rosemary-Infused Oil	160	14	2	0	7	2	1	30
Sautéed Spinach with Yogurt and Dukkah	180	14	2.5	5	10	6	4	240
Sautéed Swiss Chard with Garlic	100	7	1	0	7	3	3	440
Sautéed Swiss Chard with Pancetta and Caramelized Shallots	170	11	2.5	10	11	7	3	710
Sautéed Swiss Chard with Currants and Pine Nuts	160	12	1.5	0	12	4	3	440
Roasted Winter Squash with Tahini and Feta	230	12	2	5	30	5	5	250
Roasted Tomatoes	300	28	4	0	10	2	3	160
Sautéed Cherry Tomatoes	50	2.5	0	0	6	1	1	105
Sautéed Cherry Tomatoes with Capers and Anchovies	80	4	0.5	0	10	2	2	330
Stuffed Tomatoes with Couscous, Olives, and Orange	350	17	5	10	40	11	6	840
Stuffed Tomatoes with Couscous, Capers, and Pine Nuts	350	17	4	10	41	10	6	830
Stuffed Tomatoes with Couscous, Currants, and Pistachios	350	16	4	15	44	10	6	850
Sautéed Zucchini Ribbons	70	6	1	0	5	2	1	110
Sautéed Zucchini Ribbons with Mint and Pistachios	90	7	1	0	5	2	2	110
Grilled Zucchini and Red Onion with Lemon-Basil Dressing	150	14	2	0	5	1	1	500
Zucchini and Feta Fritters	230	20	5	80	7	6	1	400
Stuffed Zucchini with Spiced Lamb, Dried Apricots, and Pine Nuts	500	32	8	40	39	16	7	450
Greek Stewed Zucchini	100	6	1	0	10	3	2	420
Summer Vegetable Gratin	190	13	2.5	5	13	6	3	520
Grilled Vegetable Kebabs with Grilled Lemon Dressing	130	10	1.5	0	9	3	3	230
Mechouia	170	12	1.5	0	14	3	5	210
Ratatouille	230	16	2	0	20	4	7	700
Ciambotta	270	15	2	0	31	5	6	780
Tahini Sauce (per 2 tablespoons)	70	6	1	0	3	2	1	120
Tahini-Yogurt Sauce (per 2 tablespoons)	80	6	1.5	0	3	3	0	230
Yogurt-Herb Sauce (per 2 tablespoons)	80	4	2.5	15	7	5	0	60
Lemon-Yogurt Sauce (per 2 tablespoons)	20	1	0.5	5	2	1	0	15
Cucumber-Yogurt Sauce (per ¼ cup)	40	3.5	0.5	0	1	2	0	10
Garlic Aïoli (per tablespoon)	100	12	2	20	0	0	0	60
Seafood								
Broiled Bluefish with Preserved Lemon and Zhoug	330	25	4	70	2	23	0	520
Broiled Grape Leaf–Wrapped Grouper	390	30	4.5	40	6	24	1	1080
Lemon-Herb Hake Fillets with Garlic Potatoes	360	15	2	50	32	24	2	360

	Cal	Fat (g)	Sat Fat (g)	Chol (mg)	Carb (g)	Protein (g)	Fiber (g)	Sodium (mg)
Hake in Saffron Broth with Chorizo and Potatoes	280	13	3.5	70	10	27	1	750
Provençal Braised Hake	230	8	1	50	12	22	4	770
Pan-Roasted Halibut with Chermoula	200	12	2	55	1	21	0	270
Braised Halibut with Leeks and Mustard	340	16	2.5	55	17	23	2	570
Braised Halibut with Carrots and Coriander	220	11	1.5	35	12	15	3	300
Braised Halibut with Fennel and Tarragon	220	11	1.5	35	11	16	4	400
Baked Stuffed Mackerel with Red Pepper and Preserved Lemon	360	28	5	80	6	22	1	850
Grilled Whole Mackerel with Lemon and Marjoram	280	21	4.5	80	1	21	0	730
Grilled Whole Mackerel with Orange and Fennel	280	21	4.5	80	1	21	0	730
Grilled Whole Mackerel with Lime and Coriander	280	21	4.5	80	1	21	0	730
Pan-Roasted Monkfish with Oregano–Black Olive Relish	230	16	2.5	30	2	17	0	370
Grilled Whole Sardines	110	7	1.5	30	1	11	0	105
Pan-Roasted Sea Bass	140	6	1	45	1	21	0	370
Pan-Roasted Sea Bass with Green Olive, Almond, and Orange Relish	380	29	3.5	45	7	24	2	560
Pan-Roasted Sea Bass with Roasted Red Pepper, Hazelnut, and Thyme Relish	370	29	3.5	45	5	23	2	410
Pan-Roasted Sea Bass with Wild Mushrooms	300	17	2.5	45	11	26	2	390
Grilled Sea Bass with Citrus and Black Olive Salad	240	10	1.5	45	16	22	5	350
Grilled Whole Sea Bass with Salmoriglio Sauce	330	27	4	45	1	21	0	380
Poached Snapper with Crispy Artichokes and Sherry-Tomato Vinaigrette	400	30	4.5	40	7	25	1	610
Whole Roasted Snapper with Citrus Vinaigrette	300	23	3.5	40	3	23	1	960
Sautéed Sole	230	16	2.5	50	5	15	0	630
Sautéed Sole with Fresh Tomato Relish	280	20	3	50	9	16	1	630
Sautéed Sole with Grapefruit and Basil Relish	320	19	3	50	22	16	6	630
Swordfish en Cocotte with Shallots, Cucumber, and Mint	360	25	4.5	75	8	24	3	540
Grilled Swordfish Skewers with Tomato-Scallion Caponata	310	18	3	75	13	24	4	600
Grilled Swordfish with Italian Salsa Verde	370	29	5	75	2	24	1	540
Grilled Swordfish with Eggplant, Tomato, and Chickpea Salad	310	20	3	50	15	18	5	560
Grilled Tuna Steaks with Romesco	310	16	2.5	45	9	29	1	840
Bouillabaisse	260	9	1.5	80	11	27	2	880
Sicilian Fish Stew	330	16	3	75	17	25	3	970
Monkfish Tagine	180	10	1.5	30	9	18	2	270
Greek-Style Shrimp with Tomatoes and Feta	290	16	6	130	14	17	3	1200
Shrimp with White Beans	370	19	2.5	105	29	21	8	1150
Garlicky Roasted Shrimp with Parsley and Anise	170	11	1.5	145	2	16	0	840
Grilled Marinated Shrimp Skewers	130	8	1	105	2	12	0	680
Seared Scallops with Orange-Lime Dressing	210	15	2	25	5	14	0	440
Grilled Scallop and Zucchini Skewers with Basil Vinaigrette	270	20	3	25	9	15	1	940
Oven-Steamed Mussels	360	14	2.5	85	13	36	0	960
Oven-Steamed Mussels with Leeks and Pernod	410	18	4.5	100	17	37	1	970
Clams Steamed in White Wine	390	10	1.5	90	16	45	1	1820
Clams with Pearl Couscous, Chorizo, and Leeks	720	17	4.5	90	71	61	5	2330
Spanish Shellfish Stew	460	19	3	95	21	35	2	1440
Spanish Shellfish Stew with Lobster	410	18	2.5	90	18	28	2	1000
Calamari Stew with Garlic and Tomatoes	330	13	2	350	23	27	3	930
Stuffed Squid	370	15	2	265	30	23	4	870
Grilled Squid with Lemon and Garlic	260	19	3	265	4	18	0	340

	Cal	Fat (g)	Sat Fat (g)	Chol (mg)	Carb (g)	Protein (g)	Fiber (g)	Sodium (mg)
Red Wine–Braised Octopus	480	8	1.5	220	14	71	0	1070
Spanish Grilled Octopus Salad with Orange and Bell Pepper	440	21	3	145	14	46	2	970
Greek Grilled Octopus Salad with Celery and Fennel	430	21	3	145	13	46	2	990
Poultry and Meat								
Sautéed Chicken Cutlets with Romesco Sauce	320	20	2.5	85	7	27	1	770
Sautéed Chicken Cutlets with Sun-Dried Tomato Sauce	350	23	3	85	9	28	2	690
Sautéed Chicken Cutlets with Olive-Orange Sauce	330	20	3	85	10	28	2	740
Sautéed Chicken Breasts with Cherry Tomatoes, Zucchini, and Yellow Squash	330	17	2.5	85	17	30	4	460
Pan-Seared Chicken Breasts with Chickpea Salad	460	26	3.5	85	24	32	6	950
Chicken in Turkish Walnut Sauce	630	47	5	85	19	38	5	1090
Spanish-Style Braised Chicken and Almonds	210	10	2	125	5	21	1	450
Braised Chicken with Mushrooms and Tomatoes	180	5	1	80	7	18	1	350
Roasted Chicken Thighs with Moroccan Pistachio and Currant Sauce	370	29	7	120	6	21	1	320
Roasted Chicken Thighs with Fennel, Olive, and Orange Sauce	380	31	7	120	3	21	1	450
Za'atar-Rubbed Butterflied Chicken	610	43	10	165	0	52	0	530
Grilled Chicken alla Diavola	640	45	10	165	4	52	1	1030
Grilled Chicken Kebabs with Tomato-Feta Salad	300	17	5	100	6	29	1	430
Grilled Chicken Souvlaki	460	19	3.5	85	39	32	2	620
Chicken Bouillabaisse	480	22	6	115	21	43	3	730
Rouille (per tablespoon)	140	14	1.5	10	3	1	0	40
Chicken Tagine with Chickpeas and Apricots	310	8	1.5	110	22	37	3	430
Pomegranate-Glazed Roasted Quail	610	38	10	195	15	50	0	500
Pomegranate Molasses (per tablespoon)	60	0	0	0	14	0	0	10
Kibbeh	170	13	3.5	20	9	7	2	170
Grilled Beef Kebabs with Lemon and Rosemary Marinade	310	16	3	55	14	28	3	940
Grilled Beef Kebabs with North African Marinade	320	16	3	55	14	28	3	950
Flank Steak Peperonata	370	24	6	75	11	26	3	730
Grilled Flank Steak with Grilled Vegetables and Salsa Verde	370	24	6	80	11	27	4	370
Italian Salsa Verde (per tablespoon)	70	7	1	0	1	1	1	80
Braised Oxtails with White Beans, Tomatoes, and Aleppo Pepper	510	27	10	170	16	52	4	990
Pomegranate-Braised Beef Short Ribs with Prunes and Sesame	330	14	5	55	32	19	2	230
Grilled Spiced Pork Skewers with Onion and Caper Relish	360	24	4	85	13	23	2	640
Greek-Style Braised Pork with Leeks	370	21	6	70	14	23	2	520
Spice-Rubbed Pork Tenderloin with Fennel, Tomatoes, Artichokes, and Olives	260	10	2	75	15	28	5	680
Braised Greek Sausages with Peppers	280	15	4.5	35	14	21	3	900
Sausage and White Beans with Mustard Greens	290	14	3.5	25	20	19	6	1010
Lamb Meatballs with Leeks and Yogurt Sauce	490	39	18	140	10	27	1	690
Grilled Lamb Kofte	480	40	14	85	9	26	2	780
Grilled Greek-Style Lamb Pita Sandwiches	660	37	17	100	50	32	3	1070
Grilled Lamb Shish Kebabs	390	27	10	100	9	27	2	450
Grilled Marinated Lamb Shoulder Chops with Asparagus	350	25	5	65	6	25	2	600
Roast Butterflied Leg of Lamb with Coriander, Cumin, and Mustard Seeds	370	27	12	105	0	29	0	450
Roast Butterflied Leg of Lamb with Coriander, Rosemary, and Red Pepper	370	27	12	105	0	29	0	450

	Cal	Fat (g)	Sat Fat (g)	Chol (mg)	Carb (g)	Protein (g)	Fiber (g)	Sodium (mg)
Roast Butterflied Leg of Lamb with Coriander, Fennel, and Black Pepper	370	27	12	105	1	29	1	450
Braised Lamb Shoulder Chops with Tomatoes and Red Wine	610	46	20	135	6	36	1	550
Braised Lamb Shoulder Chops with Figs and North African Spices	660	46	20	135	23	37	3	550
Braised Lamb Shanks with Bell Peppers and Harissa	490	33	10	100	16	31	5	1220
Lamb Tagine with Olives and Lemon	530	40	17	115	8	32	1	660
Green Zhoug (per tablespoon)	100	11	1.5	0	1	0	0	75
Harissa (per tablespoon)	110	11	1.5	0	2	1	1	150
Ras el Hanout (per tablespoon)	20	1	0	0	3	1	1	0
Za'atar (per tablespoon)	20	1.5	0	0	2	1	1	5
Dukkah (per 2 tablespoons)	60	4	0	0	5	3	2	240
Herbes de Provence (per tablespoon)	10	0	0	0	2	0	1	0

Eggs								
Shakshuka	300	19	5	200	20	11	3	1380
Ratatouille with Poached Eggs	310	22	4.5	190	19	14	6	430
Potato, Swiss Chard, and Lamb Hash with Poached Eggs	470	24	8	225	42	23	6	780
Fried Eggs with Potato and Parmesan Pancake	280	14	3	190	26	11	2	430
Israeli Eggplant and Egg Sandwiches	640	36	7	280	58	27	13	2120
Scrambled Eggs with Prosciutto and Asparagus	190	14	4	285	2	14	1	510
Scrambled Eggs with Potatoes and Harissa	210	15	3.5	280	8	11	1	440
Scrambled Eggs with Piperade	220	16	3.5	280	7	11	2	760
Spanish Tortilla with Roasted Red Peppers and Peas	340	21	4	250	24	12	2	550
Egyptian Eggah with Ground Beef and Spinach	220	13	4	275	7	17	2	540
Broccoli and Feta Frittata	240	17	7	390	5	17	1	530
Asparagus and Goat Cheese Frittata	270	21	9	395	4	18	2	520
Mushroom and Pecorino Frittata	270	20	9	400	5	18	1	490
Baked Eggs with Tomatoes, Feta, and Croutons	260	17	4.5	195	16	11	2	840
Greek-Style Zucchini and Egg Casserole	140	9	4	155	6	9	1	490

Breads, Flatbreads, Pizzas, and More								
Pita Bread	330	7	1	0	54	10	2	580
Socca	240	17	2	0	18	6	5	170
Socca with Swiss Chard, Pistachios, and Apricots	70	3.5	0.5	0	7	2	2	220
Socca with Caramelized Onions and Rosemary	320	21	3.5	5	24	10	6	390
Lavash with Tomatoes, Spinach, and Green Olives	250	14	5	25	18	11	2	580
Lavash with Cauliflower, Fennel, and Coriander	260	16	5	20	20	9	3	420
Pissaladière	420	13	2	5	61	11	4	900
Mushroom Musakhan	590	29	4	0	73	15	10	900
Lahmacun	250	9	2.5	15	30	9	2	950
Za'atar Bread	430	18	2.5	0	53	10	3	590
Red Pepper Coques	460	22	3	0	54	9	2	980
Rosemary Focaccia	250	7	1	0	39	6	2	420
Thin-Crust Pizza	490	14	7	30	65	20	3	1210
Thin-Crust Pizza with Mushroom and Fennel Topping	520	17	7	30	67	21	4	1320
Thin-Crust Pizza with Olive, Caper, and Spicy Garlic Topping	510	16	7	30	65	21	3	1350
Thin-Crust Pizza with Prosciutto and Arugula Topping	530	17	7	40	65	23	3	1460
Whole-Wheat Pizza with Feta, Figs, and Honey	420	15	4.5	15	64	12	6	900
Whole-Wheat Pizza with Artichokes, Ricotta, and Parmesan	410	16	4	15	52	14	6	1000
Whole-Wheat Pizza with Pesto and Goat Cheese	500	29	5	5	51	13	5	960

	Cal	Fat (g)	Sat Fat (g)	Chol (mg)	Carb (g)	Protein (g)	Fiber (g)	Sodium (mg)
Turkish Pide with Eggplant and Tomatoes	230	15	5	25	16	7	3	480
Fennel, Olive, and Goat Cheese Hand Pies	200	14	4.5	10	11	5	1	200
Mushroom Tart	370	25	5	10	27	8	1	450
Tomato Tart	380	27	5	10	26	7	1	450
Zucchini Tart	380	27	5	10	26	7	1	450
Spanakopita	240	17	7	55	14	9	2	420
Pumpkin Borek	430	17	8	120	47	18	5	1020
Chicken B'stilla	420	24	4	165	27	24	3	440
Fruit and Sweets								
Apricot Spoon Sweets	160	0	0	0	40	0	0	0
Dried Fruit Compote	250	0.5	0	0	61	3	8	10
Turkish Stuffed Apricots with Rose Water and Pistachios	160	4.5	2	5	28	3	3	40
Honey-Glazed Peaches with Hazelnuts	170	6	0.5	0	31	2	3	100
Warm Figs with Goat Cheese and Honey	150	7	1.5	5	22	3	2	35
Peaches and Cherries Poached in Spiced Red Wine	270	0	0	0	55	2	3	0
Roasted Pears with Dried Apricots and Pistachios	290	8	1	0	44	2	6	50
Roasted Apples with Dried Figs and Walnuts	260	9	1	0	38	2	5	55
Roasted Plums with Dried Cherries and Almonds	220	7	1	0	29	2	2	55
White Wine–Poached Pears with Lemon and Herbs	230	0	0	0	42	1	4	45
Melon, Plums, and Cherries with Mint and Vanilla	70	0	0	0	18	1	2	15
Peaches, Blackberries, and Strawberries with Basil and Pepper	80	0.5	0	0	20	2	5	0
Strawberries with Balsamic Vinegar	100	0	0	0	25	1	3	5
Nectarines and Berries in Prosecco	110	0	0	0	20	1	3	0
Individual Fresh Berry Gratins	190	8	4	150	26	3	4	40
Greek Sesame-Honey Bars	70	4	0.5	0	8	1	1	20
Lemon-Anise Biscotti	40	0	0	10	9	1	0	25
Honey-Lavender Biscotti	40	0	0	10	9	1	0	40
Spiced Biscotti	45	0	0	15	9	1	0	35
Pignoli	170	10	1	0	18	4	2	5
Fig Phyllo Cookies	110	4	0.5	0	17	1	1	25
Baklava	140	7	1	0	18	2	1	85
Almond Cake	310	18	2.5	60	32	6	2	190
Orange Polenta Cake	310	9	2	50	52	5	3	240
Olive Oil–Yogurt Cake	520	26	4	65	67	7	1	340
Lemon Yogurt Mousse with Blueberry Sauce	150	6	4	15	21	4	1	110
Lemon Yogurt Mousse with Raspberry Sauce	150	6	4	15	21	4	2	110
Lemon Yogurt Mousse with Strawberry Sauce	150	6	4	15	21	4	1	110
Semolina Pudding with Almonds and Dates	270	10	3	15	40	8	2	95
Greek Lemon Rice Pudding	220	4.5	2.5	15	39	6	1	210
Raspberry Sorbet	130	0	0	0	33	1	5	50
Lemon Ice	110	0	0	0	27	0	0	40
Minted Lemon Ice	110	0	0	0	27	0	0	40
Orange Ice	90	0	0	0	21	0	0	40

CONVERSIONS AND EQUIVALENTS

Some say cooking is a science and an art. We would say that geography has a hand in it, too. Flour milled in the United Kingdom and elsewhere will feel and taste different from flour milled in the United States. So we cannot promise that the loaf of bread you bake in Canada or England will taste the same as a loaf baked in the States, but we can offer guidelines for converting weights and measures. We also recommend that you rely on your instincts when making our recipes. Refer to the visual cues provided. If the bread dough hasn't "come together in a ball," as described, you may need to add more flour—even if the recipe doesn't tell you to. You be the judge.

The recipes in this book were developed using standard U.S. measures following U.S. government guidelines. The charts below offer equivalents for U.S., metric, and imperial (U.K.) measures. All conversions are approximate and have been rounded up or down to the nearest whole number.

EXAMPLE:

1 teaspoon = 4.9292 milliliters, rounded up to 5 milliliters
1 ounce = 28.3495 grams, rounded down to 28 grams

VOLUME CONVERSIONS	
U.S.	**METRIC**
1 teaspoon	5 milliliters
2 teaspoons	10 milliliters
1 tablespoon	15 milliliters
2 tablespoons	30 milliliters
¼ cup	59 milliliters
⅓ cup	79 milliliters
½ cup	118 milliliters
¾ cup	177 milliliters
1 cup	237 milliliters
1¼ cups	296 milliliters
1½ cups	355 milliliters
2 cups (1 pint)	473 milliliters
2½ cups	591 milliliters
3 cups	710 milliliters
4 cups (1 quart)	0.946 liter
1.06 quarts	1 liter
4 quarts (1 gallon)	3.8 liters

WEIGHT CONVERSIONS	
OUNCES	**GRAMS**
½	14
¾	21
1	28
1½	43
2	57
2½	71
3	85
3½	99
4	113
4½	128
5	142
6	170
7	198
8	227
9	255
10	283
12	340
16 (1 pound)	454

CONVERSIONS FOR INGREDIENTS COMMONLY USED IN BAKING

Baking is an exacting science. Because measuring by weight is far more accurate than measuring by volume, and thus more likely to achieve reliable results, in our recipes we provide ounce measures in addition to cup measures for many ingredients. Refer to the chart below to convert these measures into grams.

INGREDIENT	OUNCES	GRAMS
1 cup all-purpose flour*	5	142
1 cup whole-wheat flour	5½	156
1 cup granulated (white) sugar	7	198
1 cup packed brown sugar (light or dark)	7	198
1 cup confectioners' sugar	4	113

* U.S. all-purpose flour, the most frequently used flour in this book, does not contain leaveners, as some European flours do. These leavened flours are called self-rising or self-raising. If you are using self-rising flour, take this into consideration before adding leavening to a recipe.

OVEN TEMPERATURES

FAHRENHEIT	CELSIUS	GAS MARK
225	105	¼
250	120	½
275	135	1
300	150	2
325	165	3
350	180	4
375	190	5
400	200	6
425	220	7
450	230	8
475	245	9

CONVERTING FAHRENHEIT TO CELSIUS

We include doneness temperatures in many of the recipes in this book. We recommend an instant-read thermometer for the job. Refer to the above table to convert Fahrenheit degrees to Celsius. Or, for temperatures not represented in the chart, use this simple formula:

Subtract 32 degrees from the Fahrenheit reading, then divide the result by 1.8 to find the Celsius reading.

EXAMPLE:
"Roast chicken until thighs register 175 degrees."
To convert:
175°F – 32 = 143°
143° ÷ 1.8 = 79.44°C, rounded down to 79°C

Index

Note: Page references in *italics* indicate recipe photographs.
■ FAST (less than 45 minutes start to finish)   ■ VEGETARIAN

A

Aïoli, Garlic ■ ■, 233
Algerian-Style Fennel, Orange, and
    Olive Salad ■ ■, 88
Algerian-Style Fennel, Orange, and
    Radish Salad ■ ■, 88
Almond(s)
  Baklava, *382*, 382–83
  and Blood Oranges, Roasted Beet Salad
    with ■, 82
  Bulgur Salad with Grapes and Feta ■, 125
  Cake, 384, *384*
  and Carrots, Bulgur Salad with ■, *124*,
    124–25
  and Chicken, Spanish-Style Braised,
    295, *295*
  Chicken B'stilla, *364*, 364–65
  Couscous with Lamb, Chickpeas, and
    Orange, 164, *164*
  and Dates, Semolina Pudding with, 387–88
  and Dried Cherries, Roasted Plums
    with, 373
  and Golden Raisins, Herbed Basmati Rice
    and Pasta Pilaf with ■, 104
  Green Olive, and Orange Relish, Pan-Roasted
    Sea Bass with ■, 255
  Green Olive and Orange Pesto ■ ■, 149
  Grilled Tuna Steaks with Romesco ■, *265*,
    265–66
  Lemon-Garlic ■ ■, 17
  Marcona, and Manchego Cheese, Green
    Salad with ■ ■, 68
  and Mint, Roasted Green Beans
    with ■ ■, 217
  Orange-Fennel ■ ■, 17
  Oranges, and Olives, Rice Salad with ■, 107
  Pear, Goat Cheese, and Apricots, Arugula
    Salad with ■ ■, 73–74
  Picada ■ ■, 63
  Pignoli, *380*, 380–81
  Provençal-Style Anchovy Dip, 22–23, *23*
  Quick Toasted ■ ■, 17
  Rosemary ■ ■, 17
  Smoked, Radicchio, and Dates, Citrus Salad
    with ■ ■, 75, *75*
  Spiced ■ ■, 17

Almond(s) *(cont.)*
  Toasted, and Currants, Basmati Rice Pilaf
    with ■, 102–3
  and Tomato Pesto ■ ■, 149
  White Gazpacho ■, 43, *43*
Anchovy(ies)
  about, 23
  Braised Artichokes with Tomatoes and
    Thyme, 197
  and Capers, Braised Cauliflower
    with ■, 209
  and Capers, Sautéed Cherry Tomatoes
    with ■, 229
  Dip, Provençal-Style, 22–23, *23*
  Italian Salsa Verde ■, 310
  Pissaladière, *342*, 346–47
  Radishes, and Capers, Orzo Salad with, 158
  Salade Niçoise, 78–79, *79*
  Stuffed Squid, 282–83
Anise-Lemon Biscotti, *378*, 378–79
Antipasti. *See* **Small Plates**
Apple(s)
  and Fennel Salad with Smoked Mackerel,
    89, *89*
  Roasted, with Dried Figs and Walnuts, 373
Apricot(s)
  and Chickpeas, Chicken Tagine with, *303*,
    303–4
  Dried, and Pistachios, Roasted Pears with,
    372, 372–73
  Dried, Spiced Lamb, and Pine Nuts, Stuffed
    Zucchini with, *234*, 234–35
  Dried Fruit Compote, 368–69
  Pear, Almonds, and Goat Cheese, Arugula
    Salad with ■ ■, 73–74
  Spoon Sweets, 368, *368*
  Swiss Chard, and Pistachios, Socca with ■ ■,
    342, 345
  Turkish Stuffed, with Rose Water and
    Pistachios, *369*, 369–70
Artichoke(s)
  Asparagus, and Peas, Fava Beans with ■,
    215, 215–16
  baby, preparing, 28
  Braised, with Tomatoes and Thyme, 197
  Crispy, and Sherry-Tomato Vinaigrette,
    Poached Snapper with, 258–59, *259*

Artichoke(s) *(cont.)*
  Fennel, Tomatoes, and Olives, Spice-Rubbed
    Pork Tenderloin with, 315, *315*
  fresh, selecting, 197
  Hearts and Parmesan, Bruschetta
    with ■ ■, 33
  -Lemon Hummus ■, 16
  Marinated ■, *28*, 28–29
  and Olives, Green Salad with ■ ■, 69, *69*
  and Parmesan, Tagliatelle with, *143*, 143–44
  Pepper, and Chickpea Tagine ■, 198, *198*
  processed, buying, 143
  Ricotta, and Parmesan, Whole-Wheat Pizza
    with ■, 357
  Roasted, with Lemon Vinaigrette ■, *196*,
    196–97
  Soup à la Barigoule, 50–51, *51*
  Vegetable Paella ■, *116*, 116–18
Arugula
  about, 70
  and Asparagus Salad with Cannellini
    Beans ■ ■, 74
  Carrots, and Olives, Chickpea Salad
    with ■ ■, *179*, 179
  and Fennel, Chickpea Salad
    with ■ ■, *168*, 180
  Golden Raisins, and Walnuts, Citrus Salad
    with ■ ■, 75
  Green Salad with Artichokes and
    Olives ■ ■, 69, *69*
  Pesto and Goat Cheese, Bruschetta
    with ■ ■, 33
  prewashed, buying, 68
  and Prosciutto Pizza Topping ■, *342*, 355
  Roasted Beet Salad with Blood Oranges
    and Almonds ■, 82
  Roasted Cherry Tomatoes, and Goat Cheese,
    Penne with ■, 139
  Salad with Fennel and Shaved
    Parmesan ■ ■, 69
  Salad with Figs, Prosciutto, Walnuts,
    and Parmesan ■, 73, *73*
  Salad with Pear, Almonds, Goat Cheese,
    and Apricots ■ ■, 73–74
  Seared Tuna Salad with Olive Dressing ■,
    80–81
  serving suggestions, 70